MY CLUELESS FIRST FRIEND

story and art by **TAKU KAWAMURA**

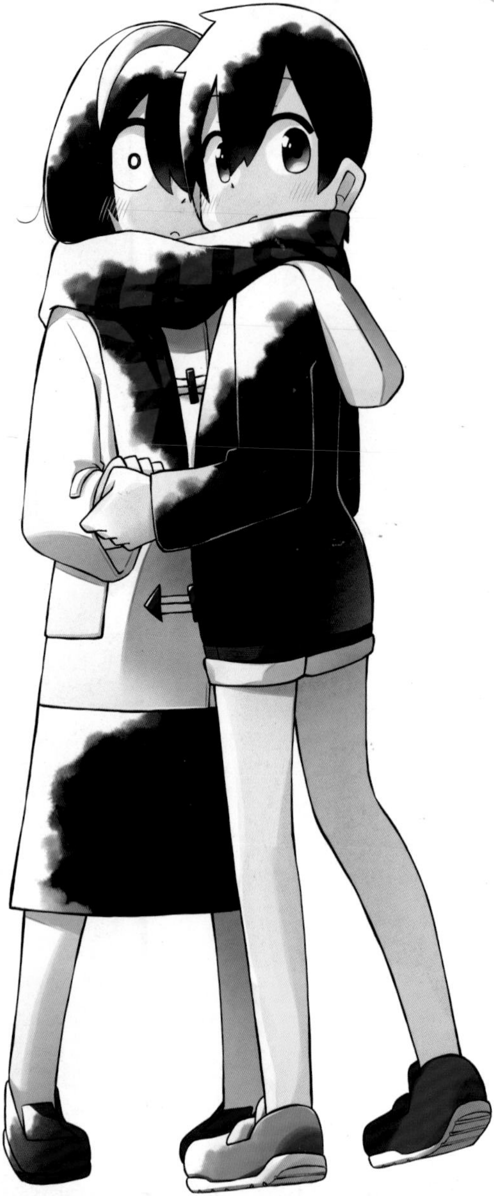

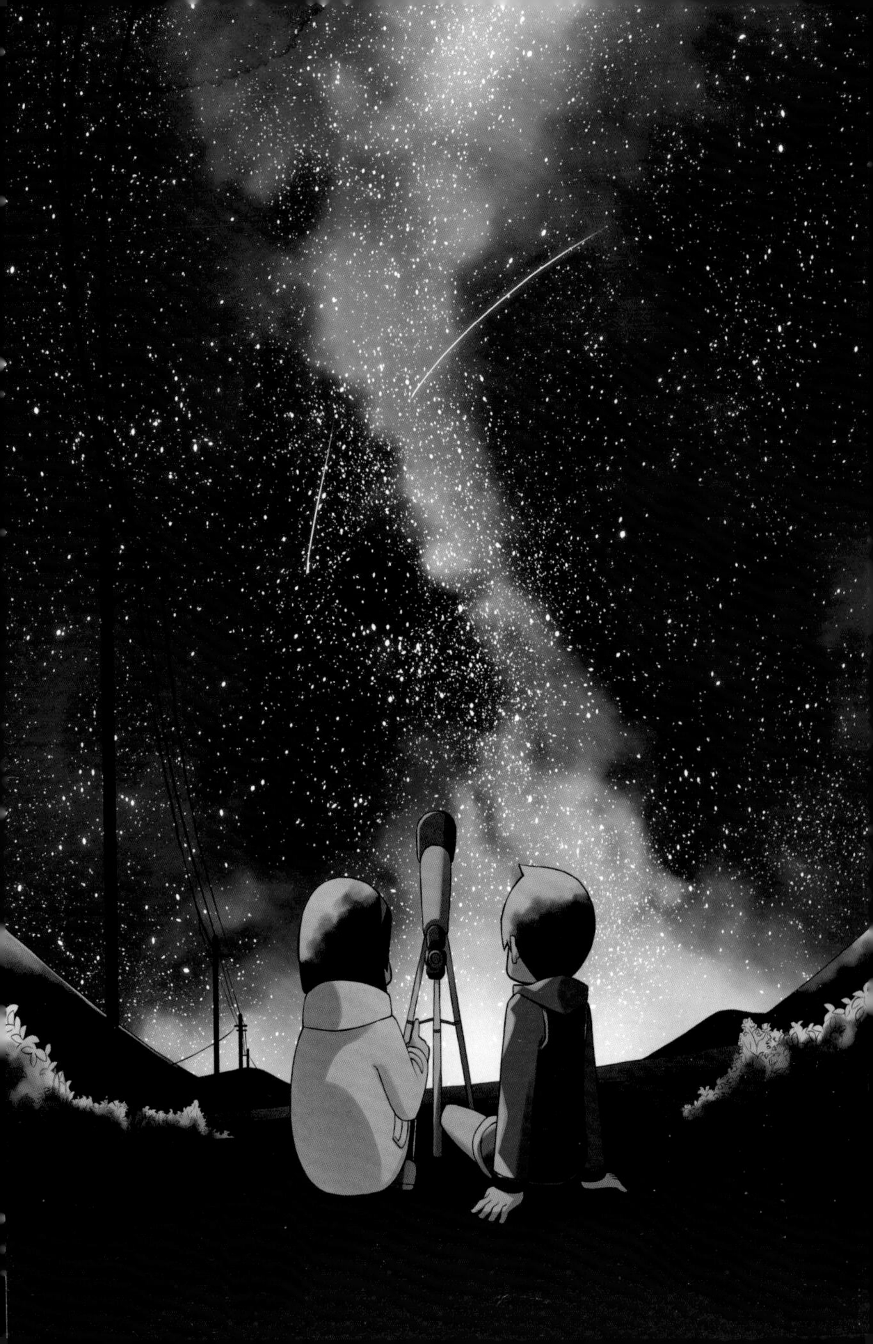

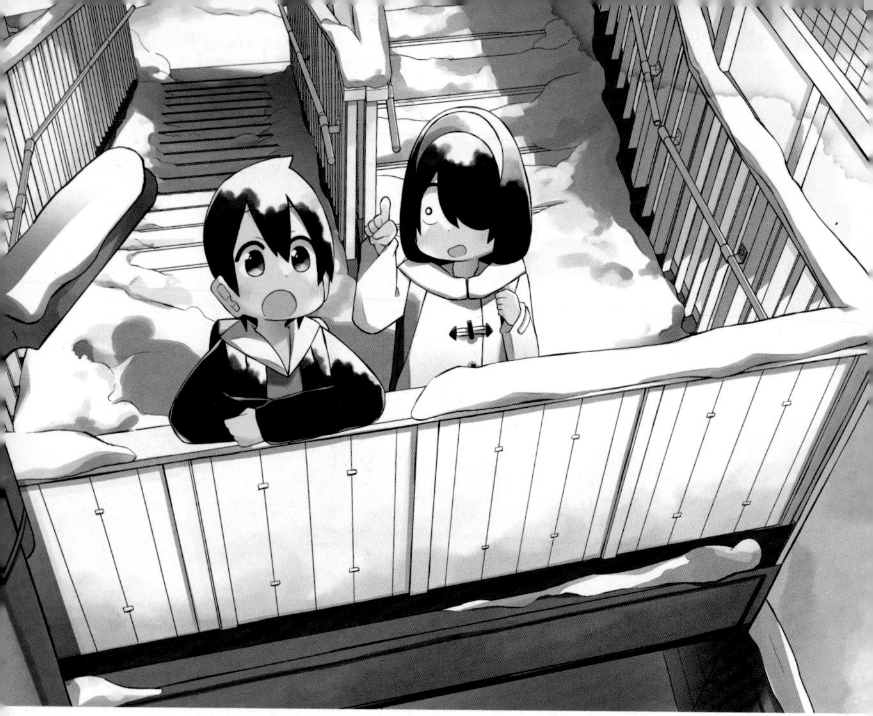

CONTENTS

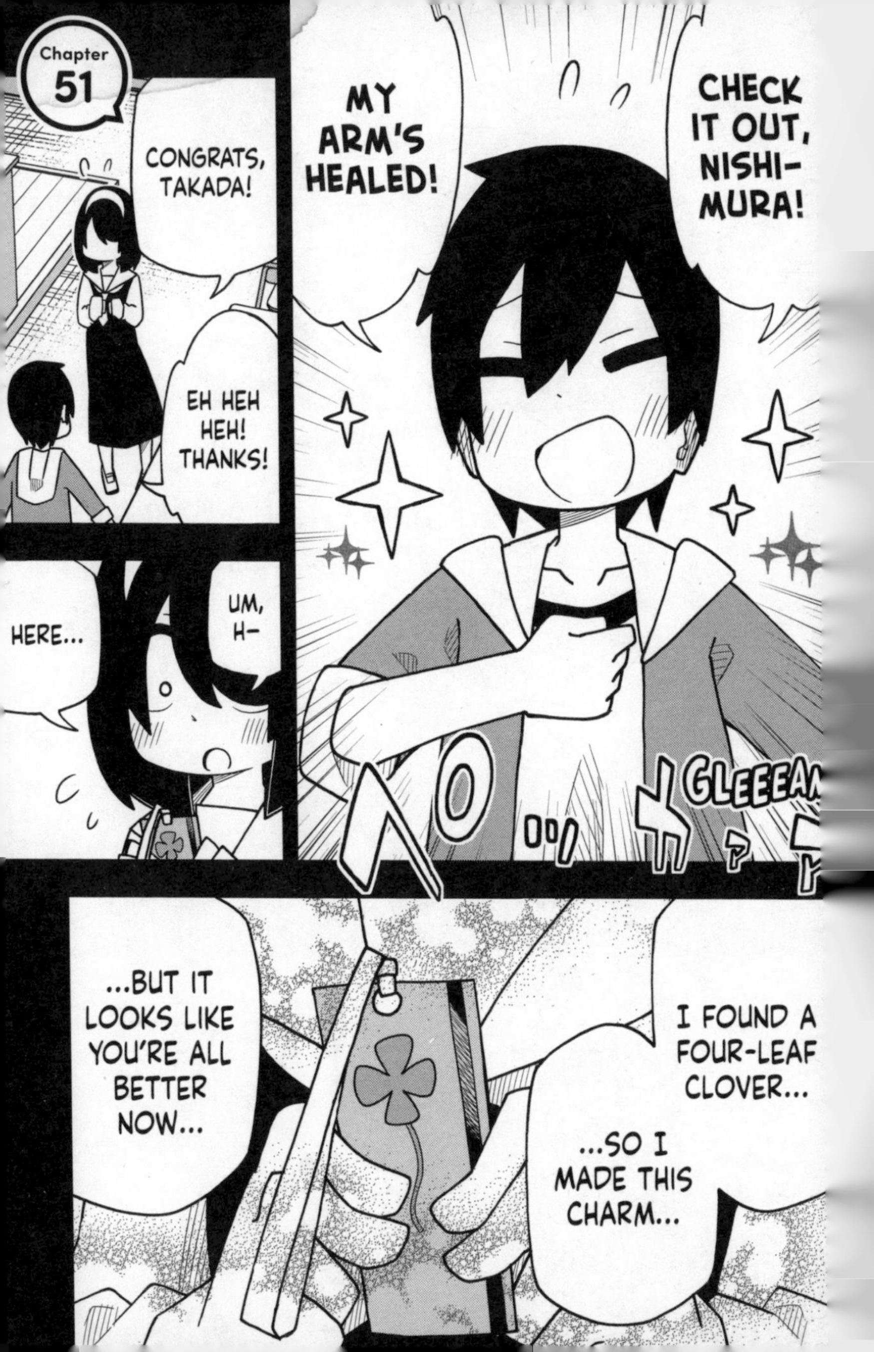

Chapter 51
CHECK IT OUT, NISHIMURA!
MY ARM'S HEALED!
GLEEEAM
CONGRATS, TAKADA!
EH HEH HEH! THANKS!
UM, H-
HERE...
I FOUND A FOUR-LEAF CLOVER...
...SO I MADE THIS CHARM...
...BUT IT LOOKS LIKE YOU'RE ALL BETTER NOW...

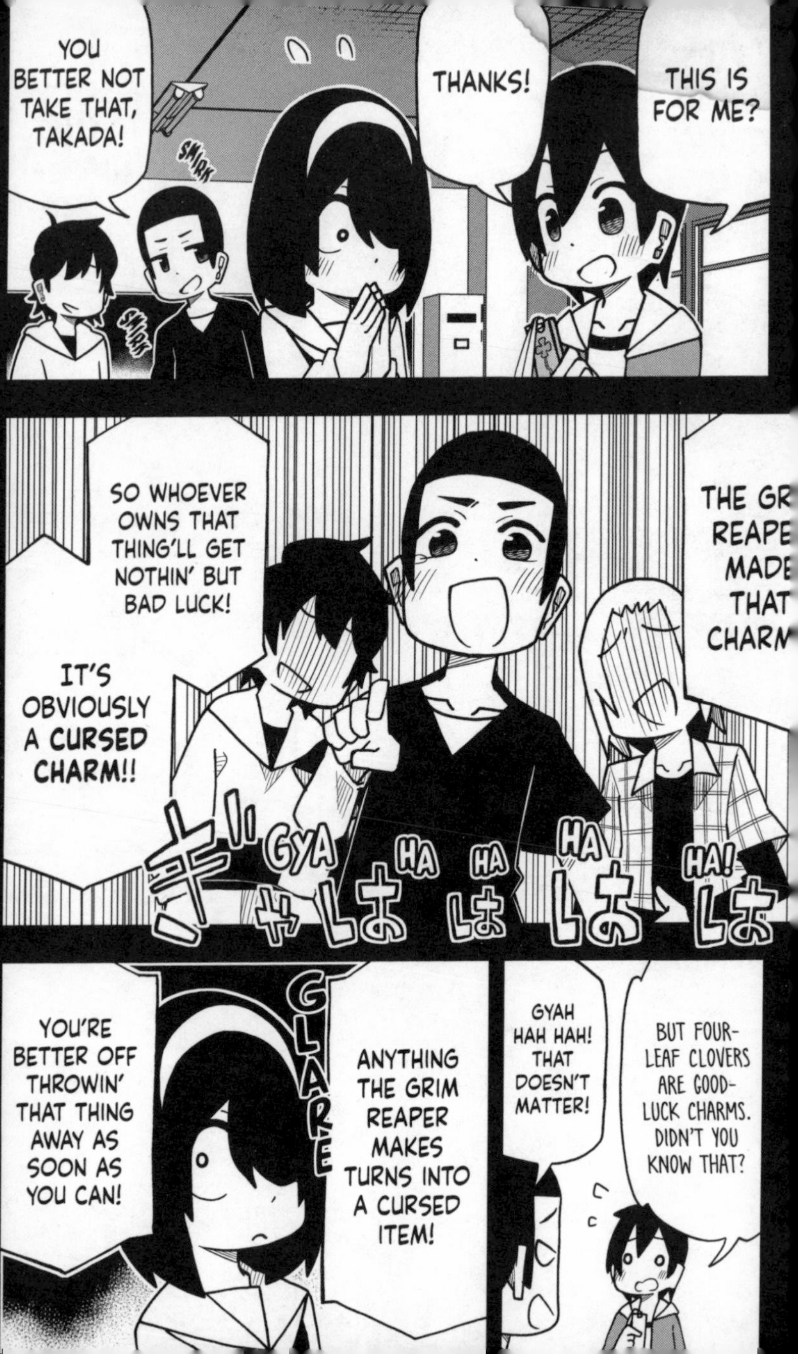
THIS IS FOR ME?
THANKS!
YOU BETTER NOT TAKE THAT, TAKADA!
SMIRK
SMIRK
THE GR REAPE MADE THAT CHARM
SO WHOEVER OWNS THAT THING'LL GET NOTHIN' BUT BAD LUCK!
IT'S OBVIOUSLY A **CURSED CHARM!!**
GYA HA HA HA HA!
ぎゃはははは
BUT FOUR-LEAF CLOVERS ARE GOOD-LUCK CHARMS. DIDN'T YOU KNOW THAT?
GYAH HAH HAH! THAT DOESN'T MATTER!
ANYTHING THE GRIM REAPER MAKES TURNS INTO A CURSED ITEM!
GLARE
YOU'RE BETTER OFF THROWIN' THAT THING AWAY AS SOON AS YOU CAN!

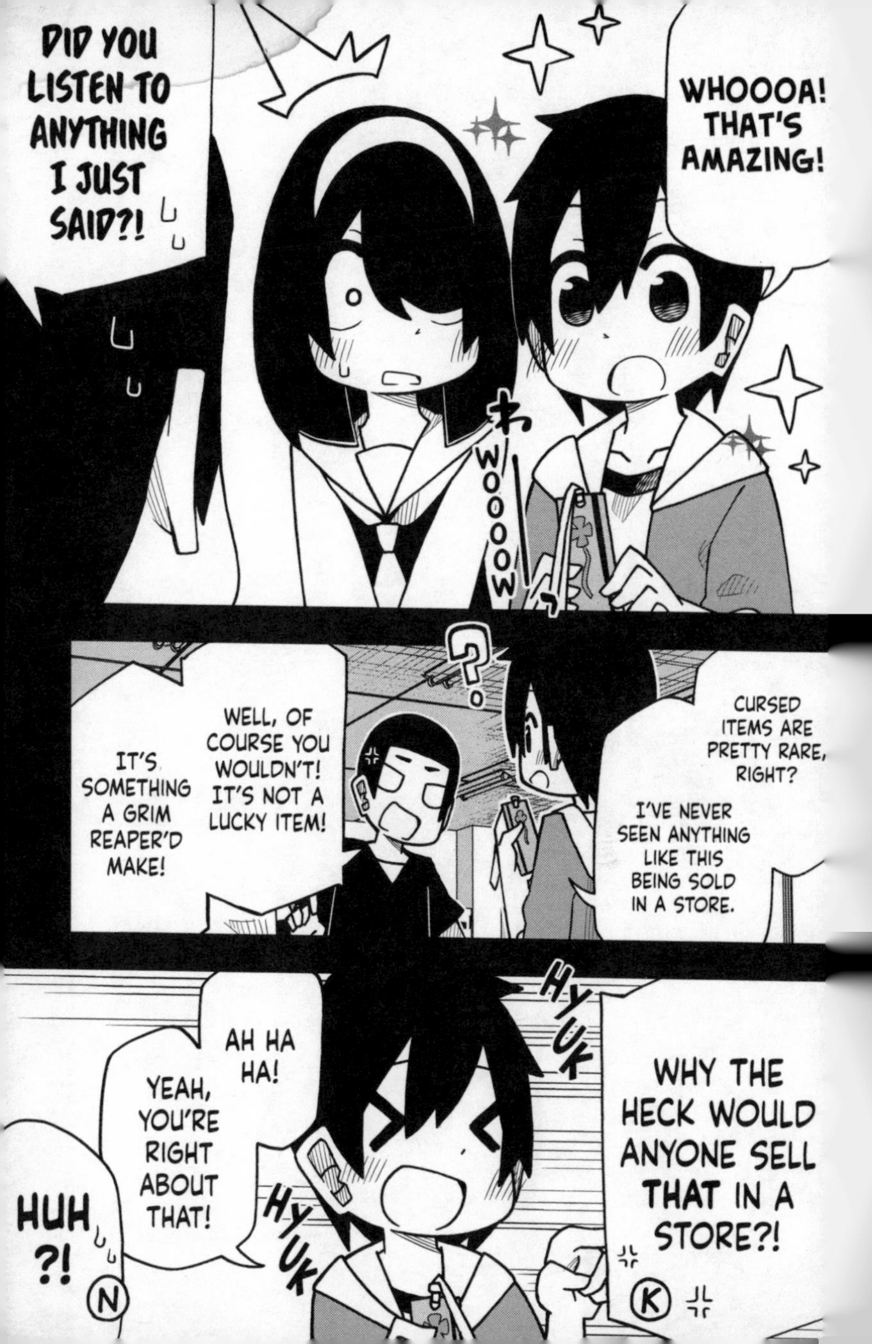
WHOOOA! THAT'S AMAZING!
WOOOOOW
DID YOU LISTEN TO ANYTHING I JUST SAID?!
CURSED ITEMS ARE PRETTY RARE, RIGHT?
I'VE NEVER SEEN ANYTHING LIKE THIS BEING SOLD IN A STORE.
WELL, OF COURSE YOU WOULDN'T! IT'S NOT A LUCKY ITEM!
IT'S SOMETHING A GRIM REAPER'D MAKE!
WHY THE HECK WOULD ANYONE SELL THAT IN A STORE?!
K
HYUK
HYUK
AH HA HA!
YEAH, YOU'RE RIGHT ABOUT THAT!
HUH?!
N

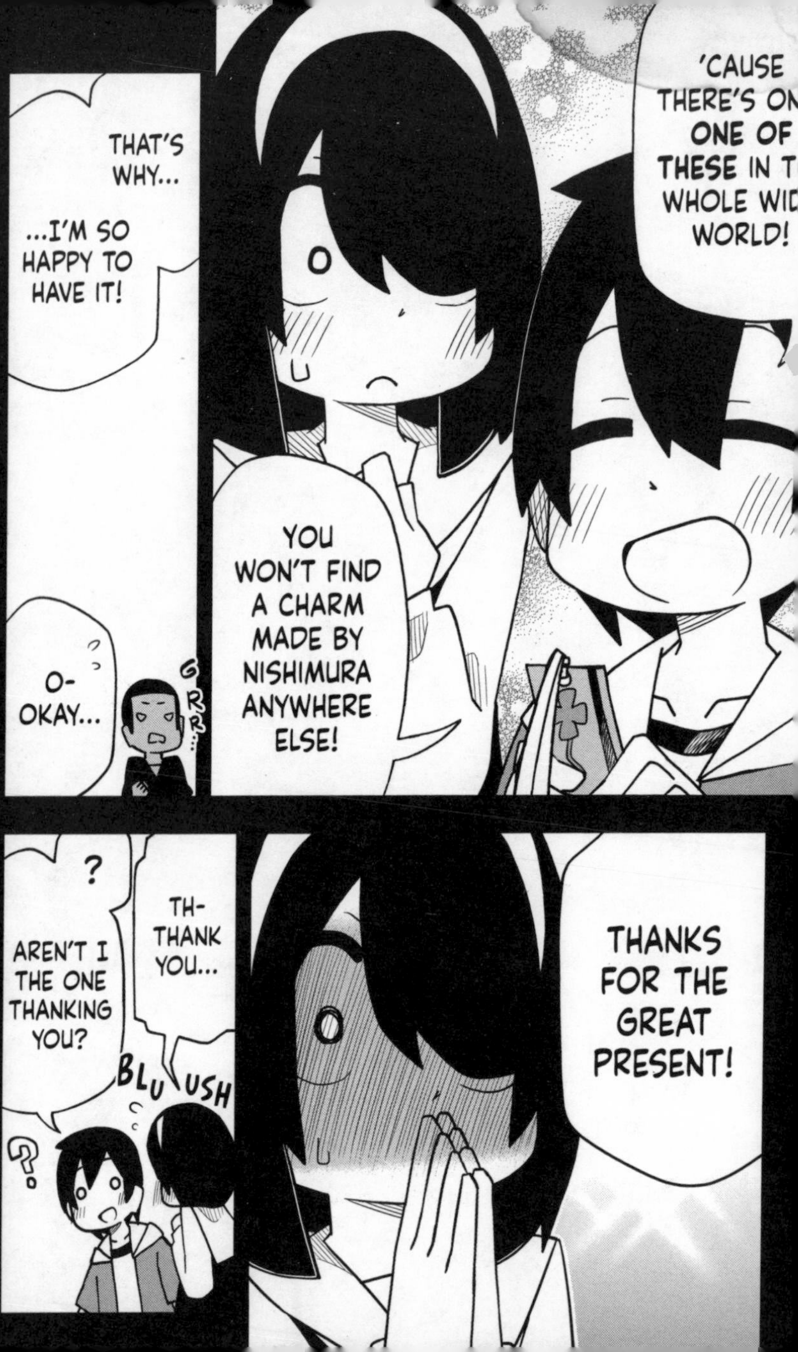
'CAUSE THERE'S ON ONE OF THESE IN T WHOLE WID WORLD!
YOU WON'T FIND A CHARM MADE BY NISHIMURA ANYWHERE ELSE!
THAT'S WHY...
...I'M SO HAPPY TO HAVE IT!
GRR...
O-OKAY...
THANKS FOR THE GREAT PRESENT!
TH-THANK YOU...
BLUSH
?
AREN'T I THE ONE THANKING YOU?
?

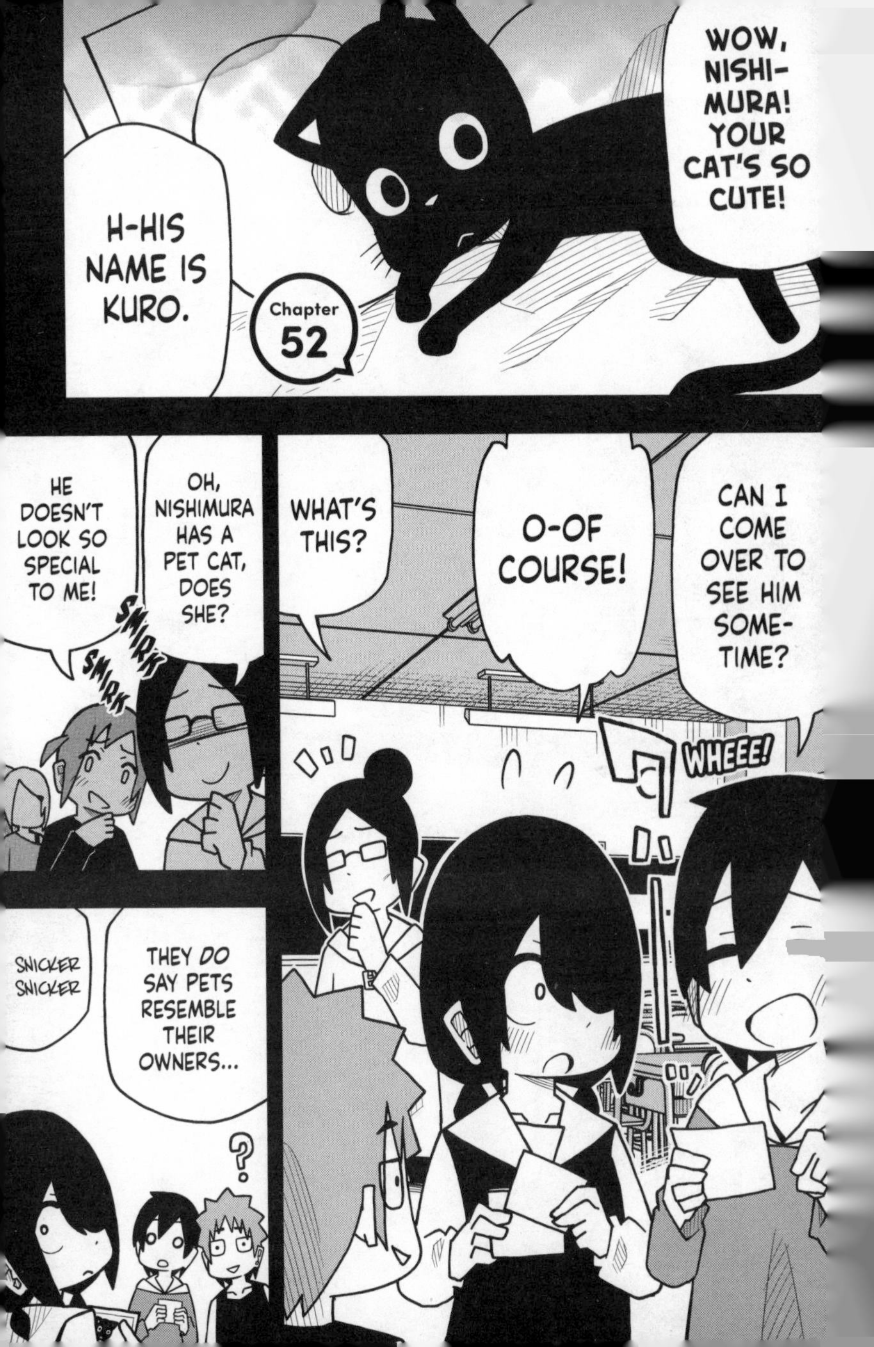
WOW, NISHIMURA! YOUR CAT'S SO CUTE!
H-HIS NAME IS KURO.
Chapter 52
CAN I COME OVER TO SEE HIM SOMETIME?
O-OF COURSE!
WHEEE!
WHAT'S THIS?
OH, NISHIMURA HAS A PET CAT, DOES SHE?
HE DOESN'T LOOK SO SPECIAL TO ME!
SMIRK
SMIRK
THEY *DO* SAY PETS RESEMBLE THEIR OWNERS...
SNICKER SNICKER
?

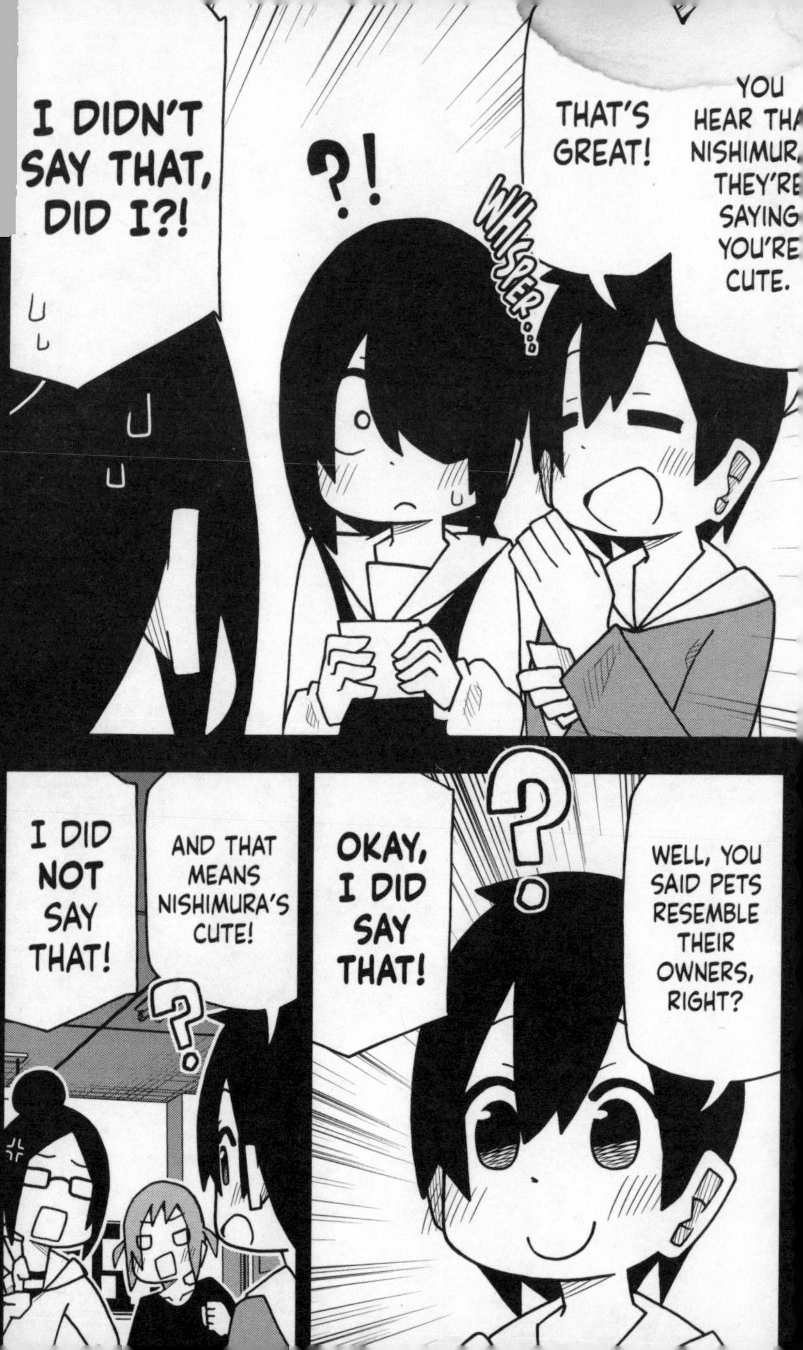

YOU HEAR THA NISHIMUR THEY'RE SAYING YOU'RE CUTE.
THAT'S GREAT!
WHISPER...
?!
I DIDN'T SAY THAT, DID I?!
WELL, YOU SAID PETS RESEMBLE THEIR OWNERS, RIGHT?
OKAY, I DID SAY THAT!
AND THAT MEANS NISHIMURA'S CUTE!
I DID NOT SAY THAT!

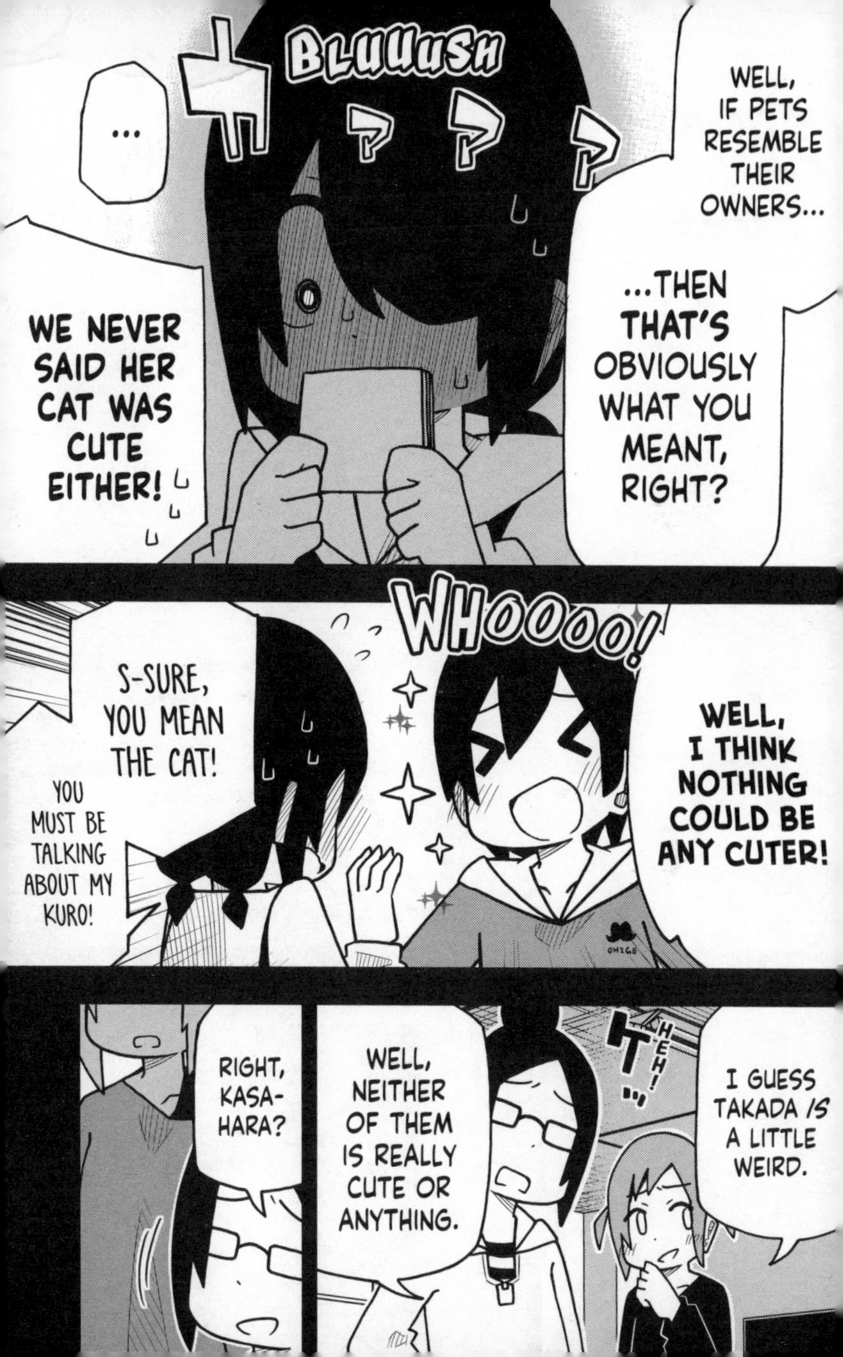
WELL, IF PETS RESEMBLE THEIR OWNERS...
...THEN THAT'S OBVIOUSLY WHAT YOU MEANT, RIGHT?
BLUUUSH
...
WE NEVER SAID HER CAT WAS CUTE EITHER!
WHOOOO!
WELL, I THINK NOTHING COULD BE ANY CUTER!
OHIGE
S-SURE, YOU MEAN THE CAT!
YOU MUST BE TALKING ABOUT MY KURO!
HEH!
I GUESS TAKADA *IS* A LITTLE WEIRD.
WELL, NEITHER OF THEM IS REALLY CUTE OR ANYTHING.
RIGHT, KASAHARA?

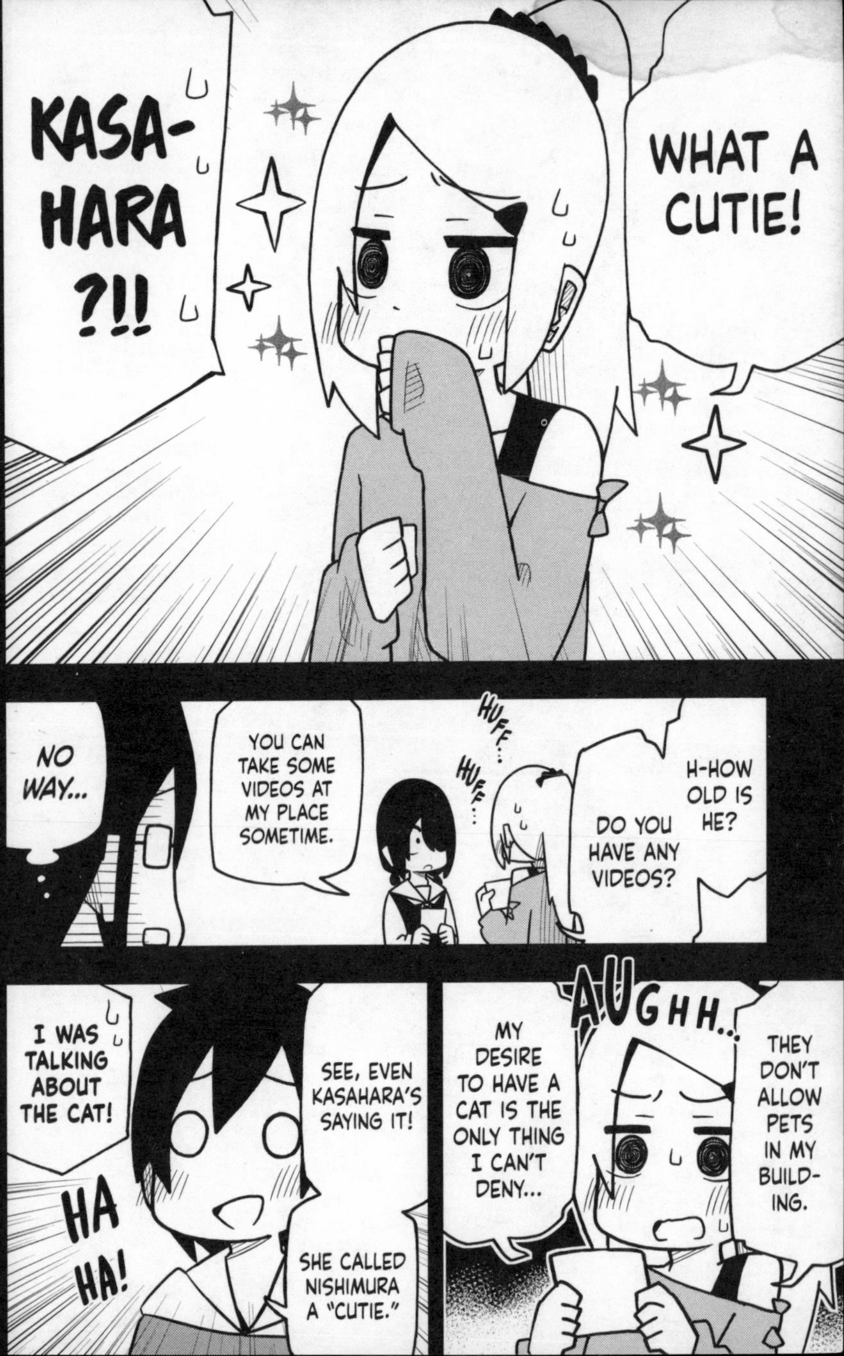

WHAT A CUTIE!
KASA-HARA ?!!
H-HOW OLD IS HE?
DO YOU HAVE ANY VIDEOS?
HUFF... HUFF...
YOU CAN TAKE SOME VIDEOS AT MY PLACE SOMETIME.
NO WAY...
THEY DON'T ALLOW PETS IN MY BUILD-ING.
AUGHH...
MY DESIRE TO HAVE A CAT IS THE ONLY THING I CAN'T DENY...
SEE, EVEN KASAHARA'S SAYING IT!
I WAS TALKING ABOUT THE CAT!
SHE CALLED NISHIMURA A "CUTIE."
HA HA!

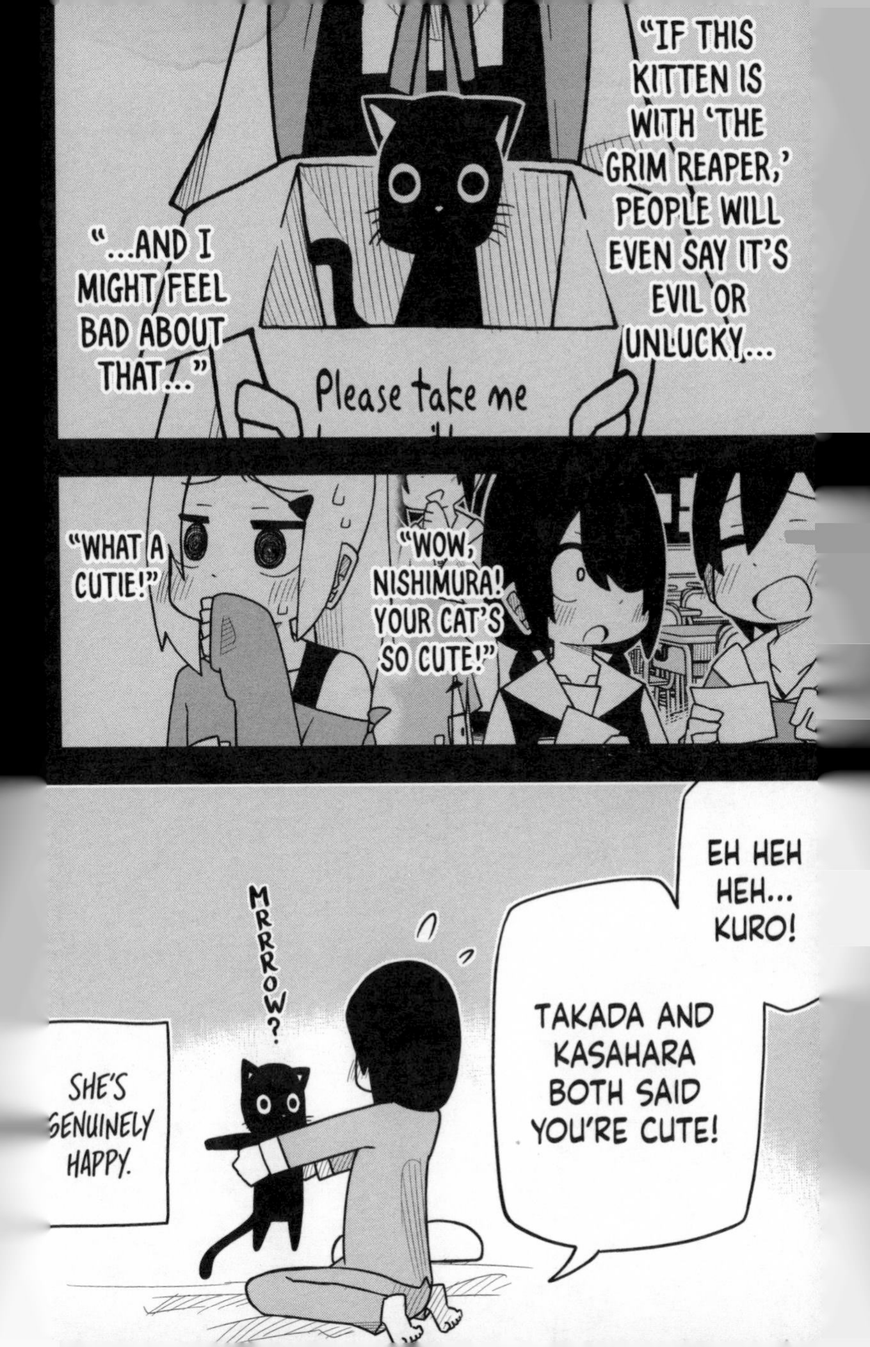
"IF THIS KITTEN IS WITH 'THE GRIM REAPER,' PEOPLE WILL EVEN SAY IT'S EVIL OR UNLUCKY...
"...AND I MIGHT FEEL BAD ABOUT THAT..."
Please take me
"WOW, NISHIMURA! YOUR CAT'S SO CUTE!"
"WHAT A CUTIE!"
EH HEH HEH... KURO!
TAKADA AND KASAHARA BOTH SAID YOU'RE CUTE!
MRRROW?
SHE'S GENUINELY HAPPY.

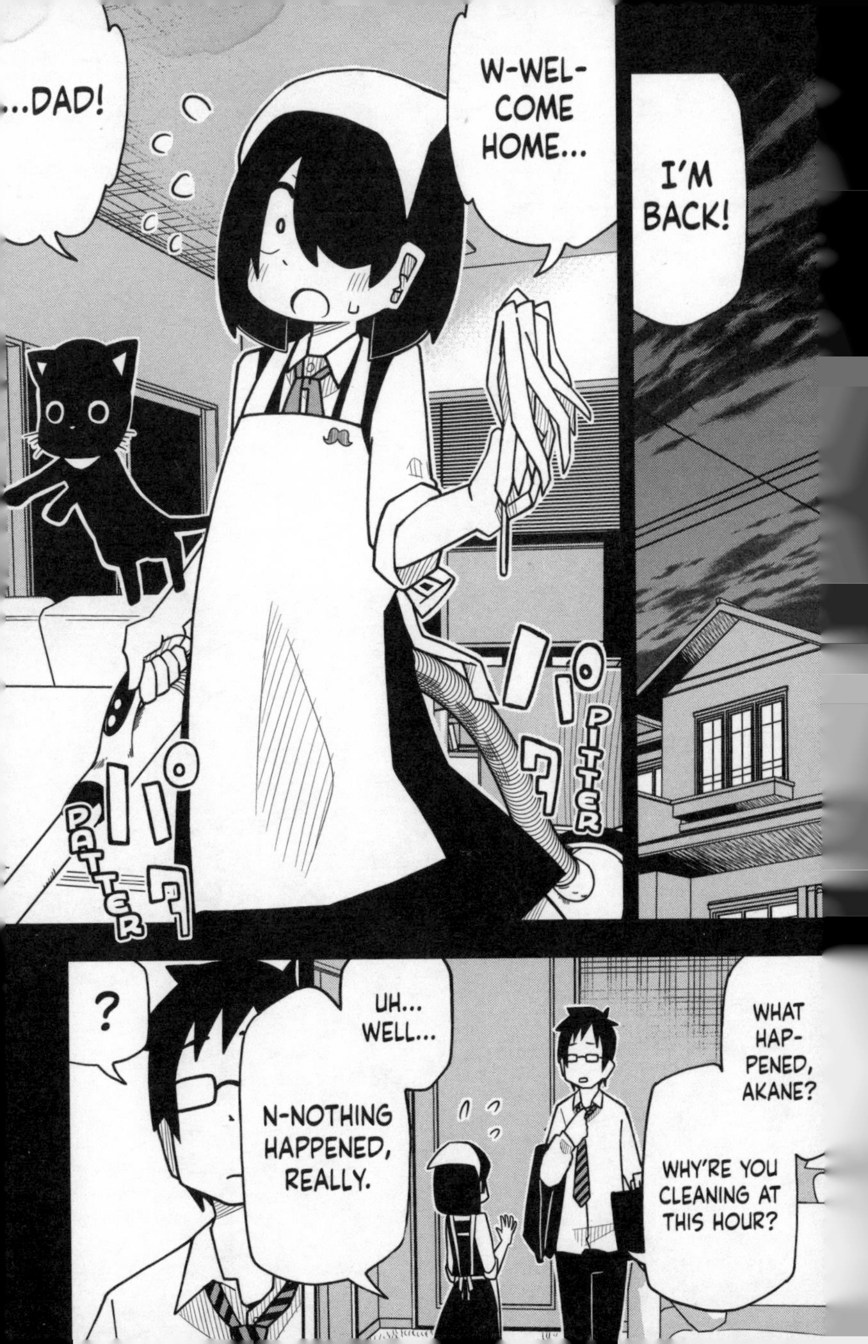
I'M BACK!
W-WEL-COME HOME...
...DAD!
PITTER
PATTER
WHAT HAP-PENED, AKANE?
WHY'RE YOU CLEANING AT THIS HOUR?
UH... WELL...
N-NOTHING HAPPENED, REALLY.
?

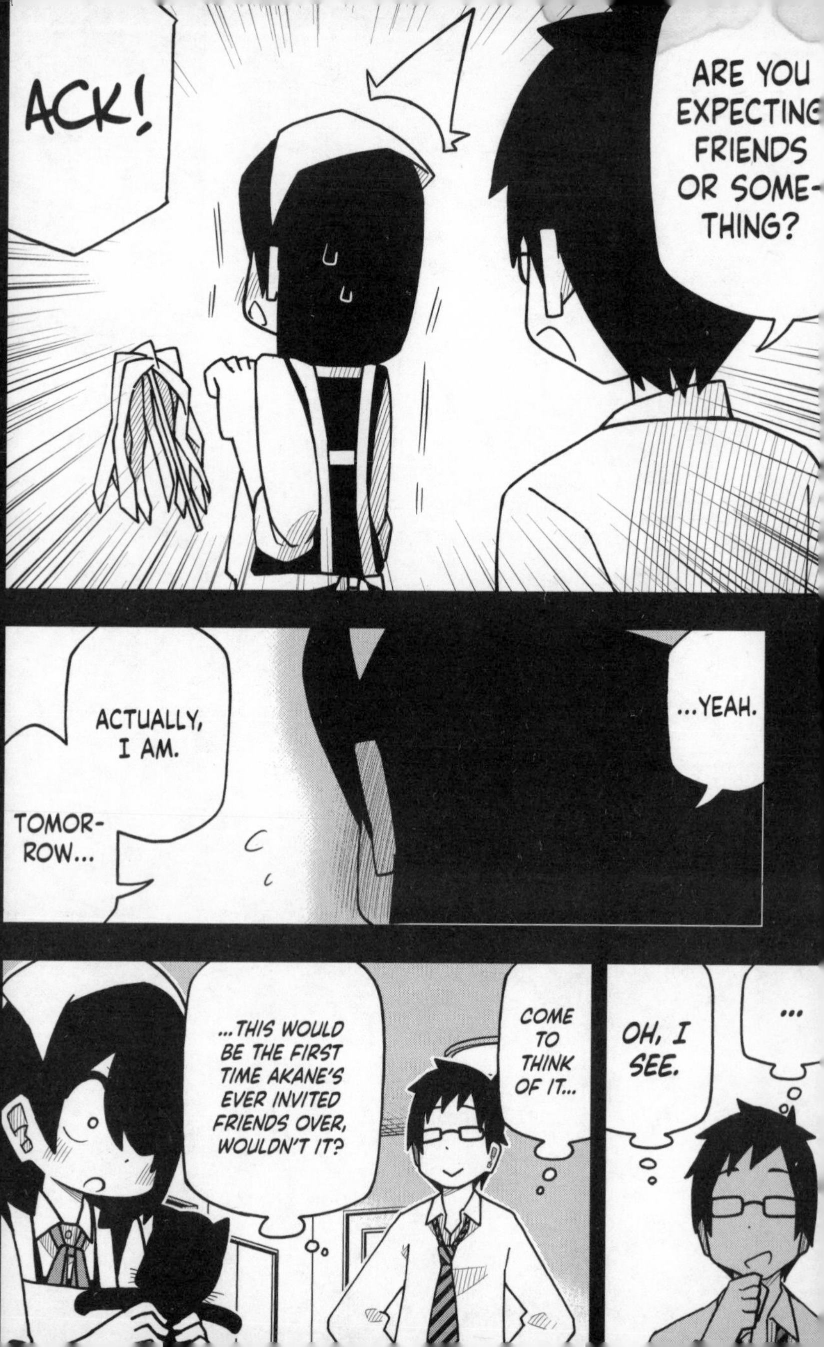
ARE YOU EXPECTING FRIENDS OR SOME-THING?
ACK!
...YEAH.
ACTUALLY, I AM.
TOMOR-ROW...
...
OH, I SEE.
COME TO THINK OF IT...
...THIS WOULD BE THE FIRST TIME AKANE'S EVER INVITED FRIENDS OVER, WOULDN'T IT?

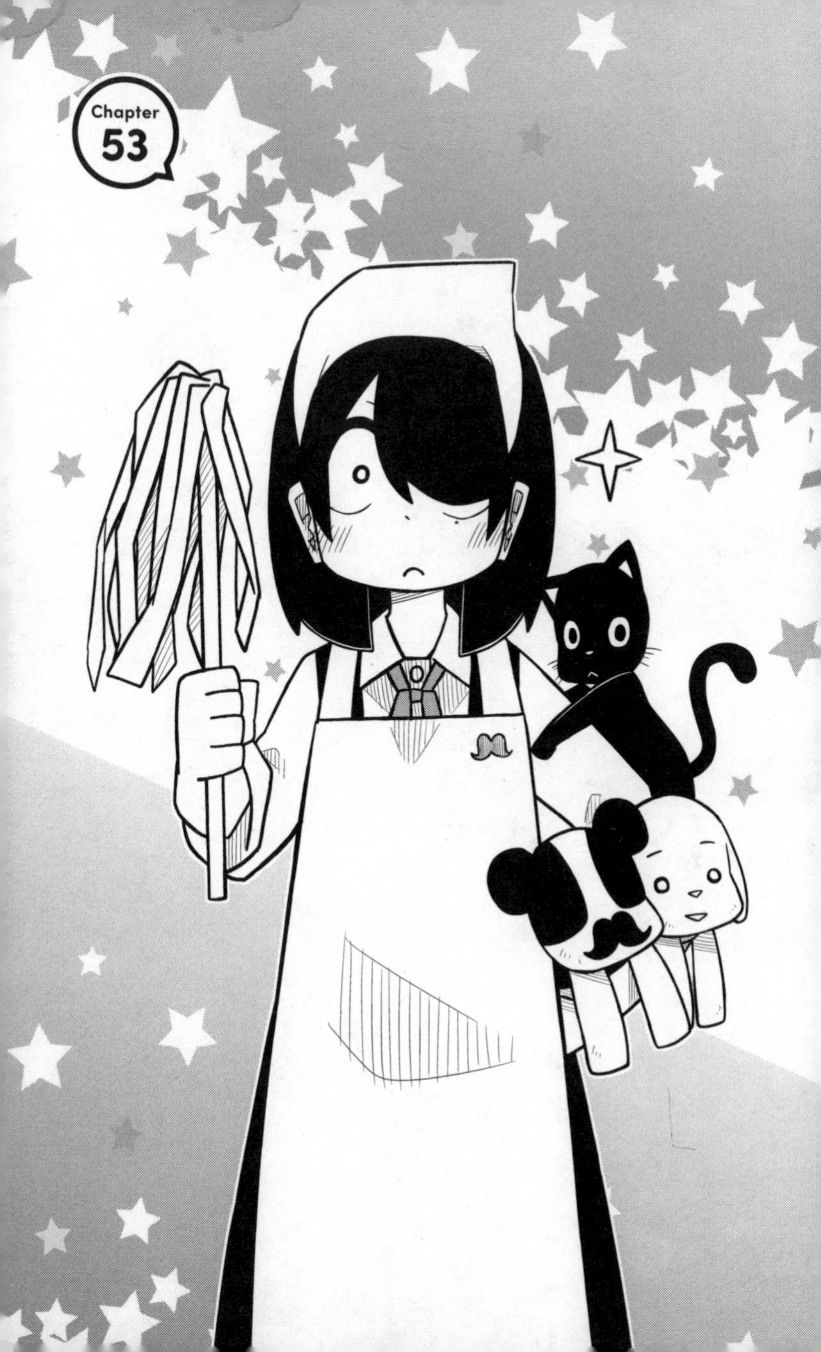
Chapter
53

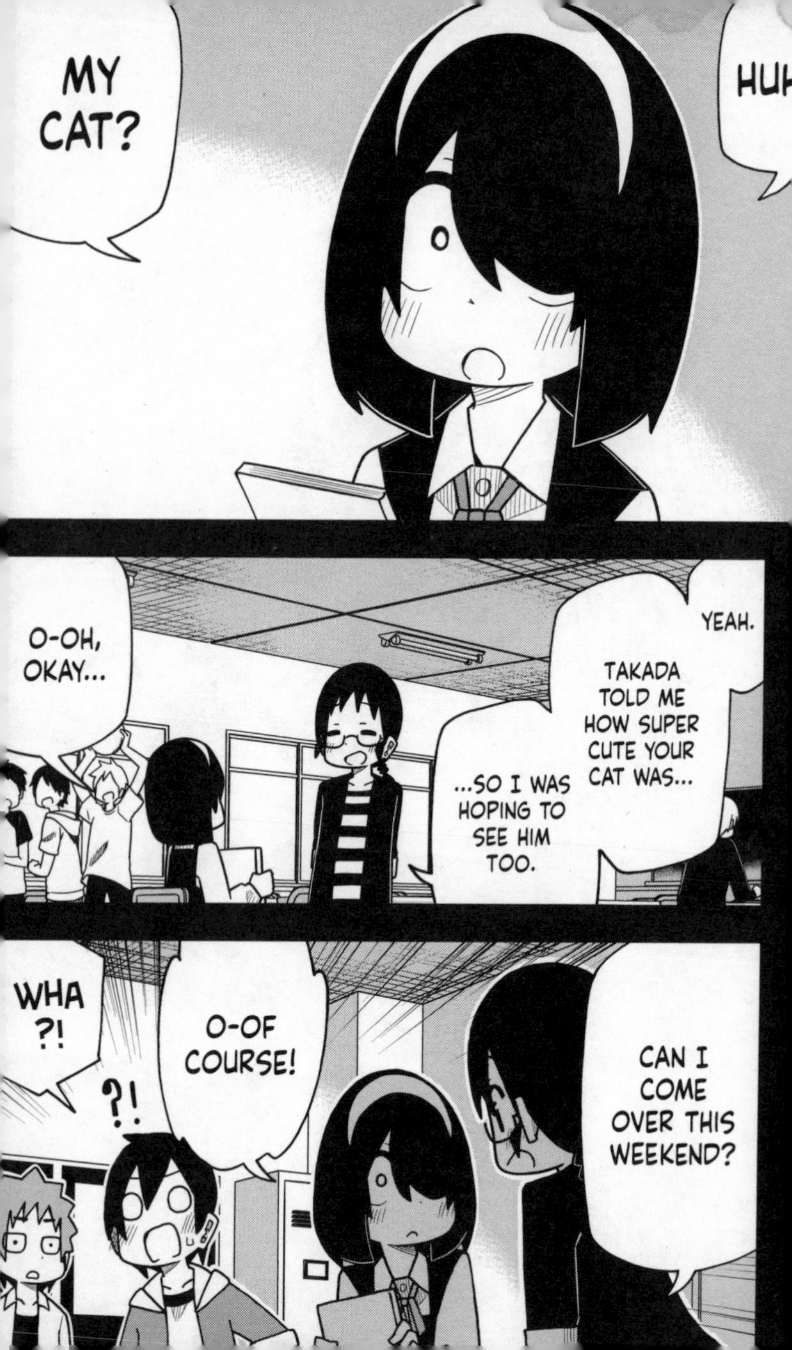

HU
MY CAT?
YEAH.
TAKADA TOLD ME HOW SUPER CUTE YOUR CAT WAS...
...SO I WAS HOPING TO SEE HIM TOO.
O-OH, OKAY...
CAN I COME OVER THIS WEEKEND?
O-OF COURSE!
?!
WHA ?!

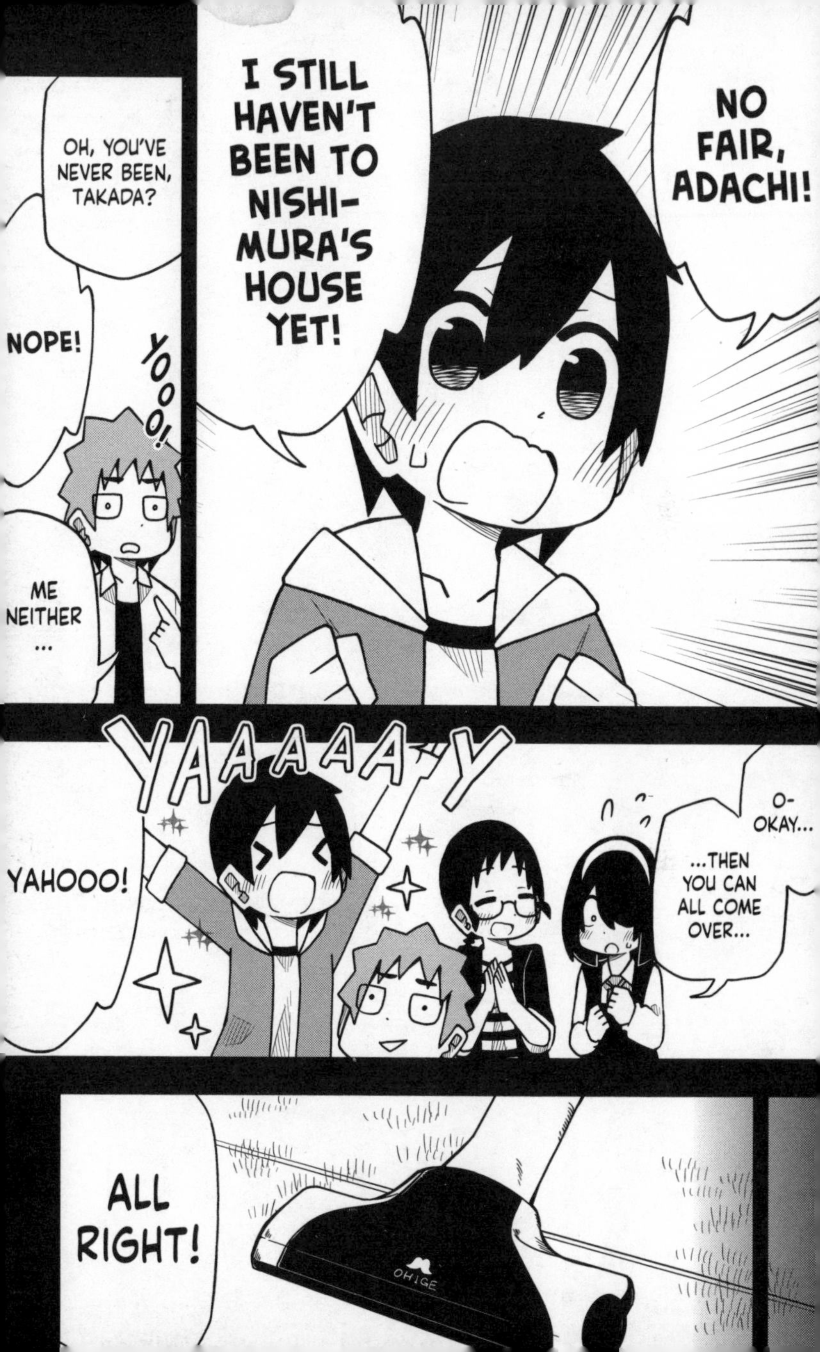
NO FAIR, ADACHI!
I STILL HAVEN'T BEEN TO NISHI-MURA'S HOUSE YET!
OH, YOU'VE NEVER BEEN, TAKADA?
NOPE!
YOOOO!
ME NEITHER ...
O-OKAY...
...THEN YOU CAN ALL COME OVER...
YAAAAAY
YAHOOO!
ALL RIGHT!
OHIGE

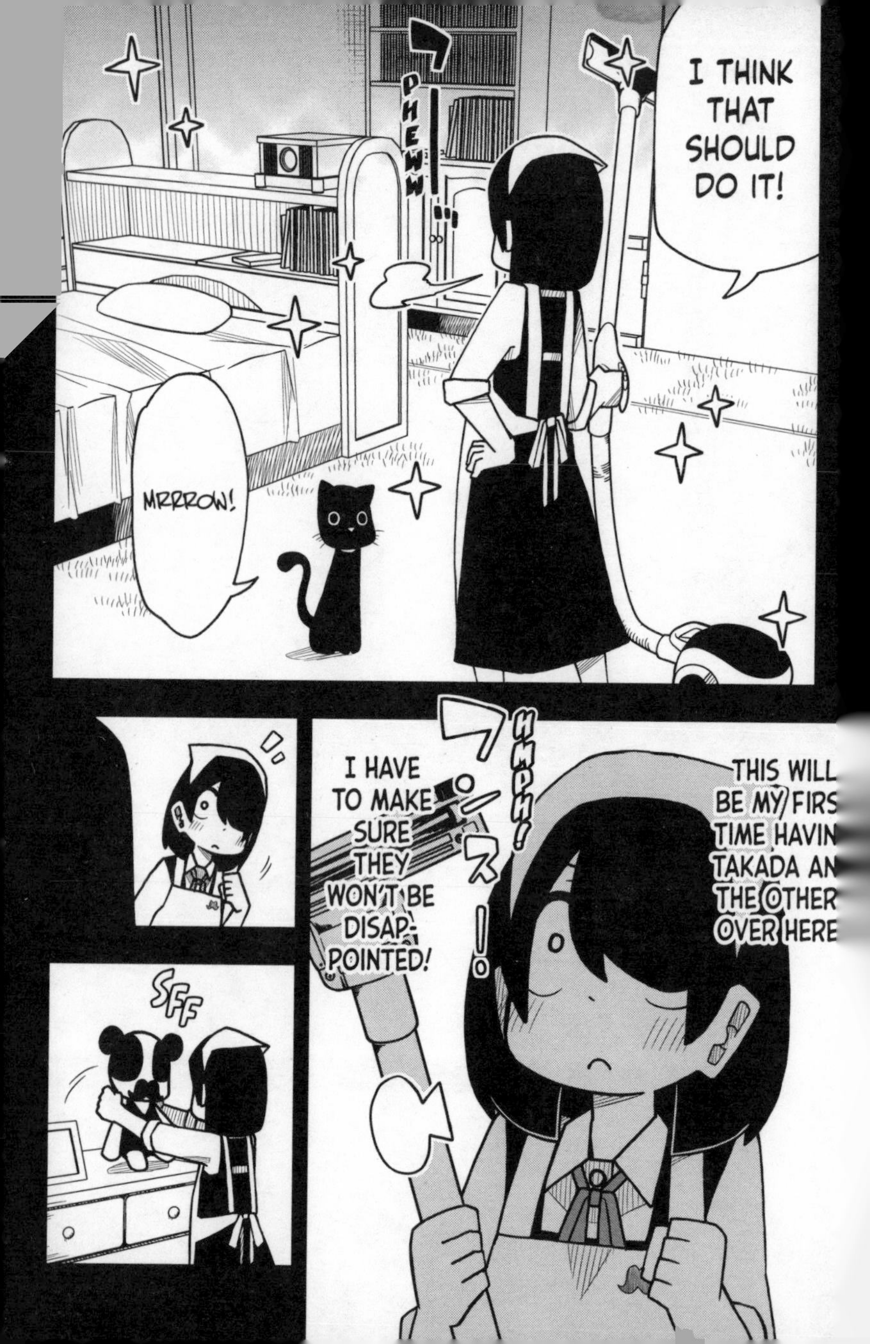
I THINK THAT SHOULD DO IT!
PHEWW
MRRROW!
THIS WILL BE MY FIRS TIME HAVIN TAKADA AN THE OTHER OVER HERE
HMPH!
I HAVE TO MAKE SURE THEY WON'T BE DISAP-POINTED!
SFF

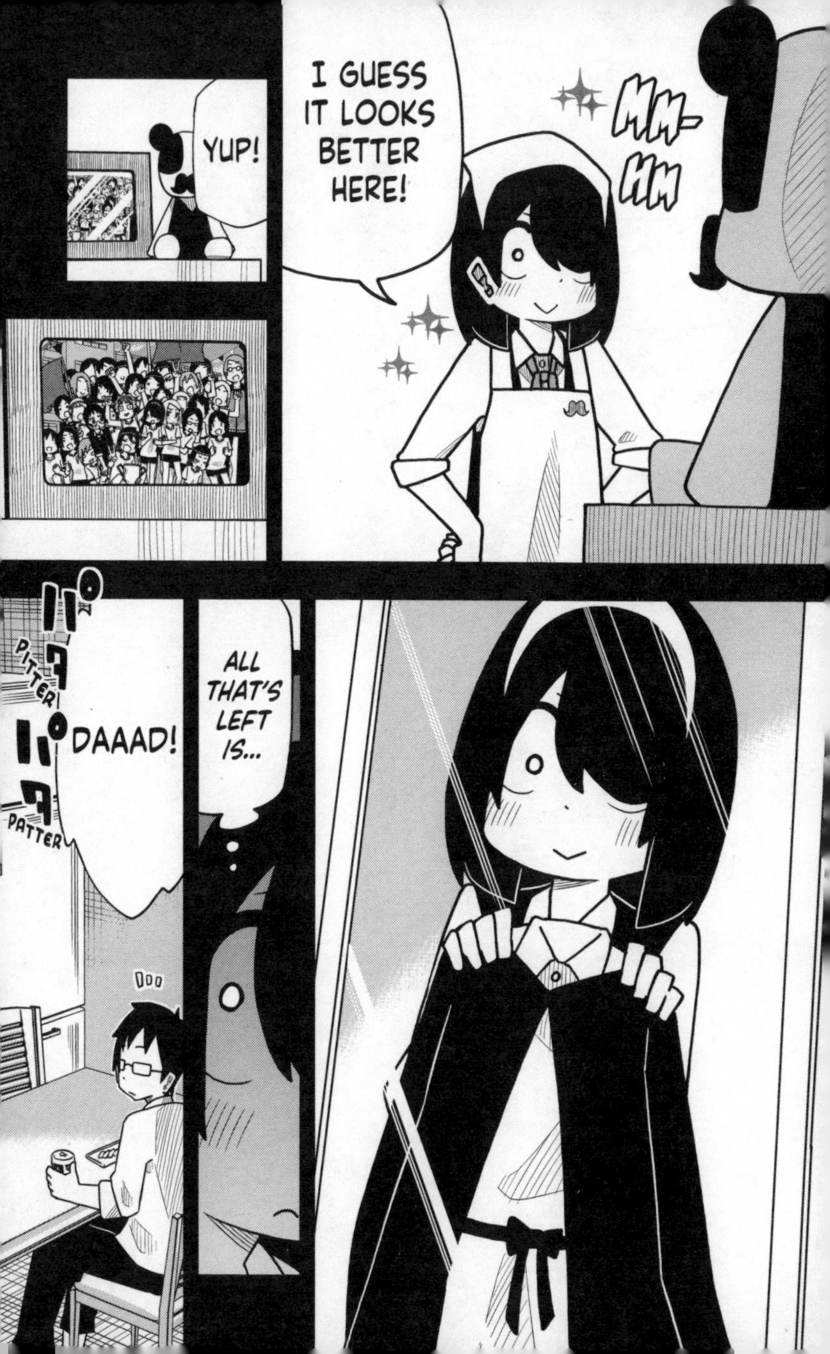
MM-HM
I GUESS IT LOOKS BETTER HERE!
YUP!
ALL THAT'S LEFT IS...
DAAAD!
PITTER PATTER

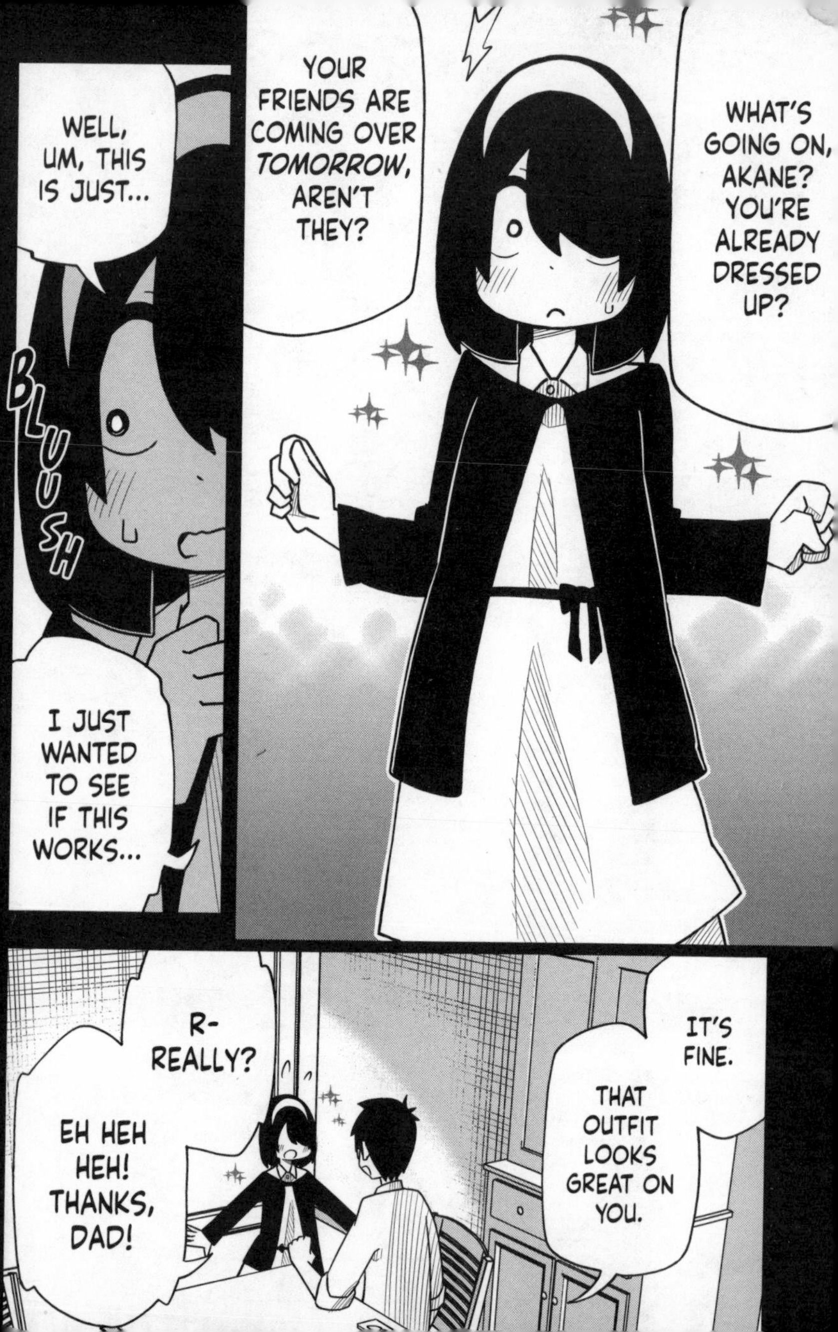
WHAT'S GOING ON, AKANE? YOU'RE ALREADY DRESSED UP?
YOUR FRIENDS ARE COMING OVER *TOMORROW*, AREN'T THEY?
WELL, UM, THIS IS JUST...
BLUUSH
I JUST WANTED TO SEE IF THIS WORKS...
IT'S FINE.
THAT OUTFIT LOOKS GREAT ON YOU.
R-REALLY?
EH HEH HEH! THANKS, DAD!

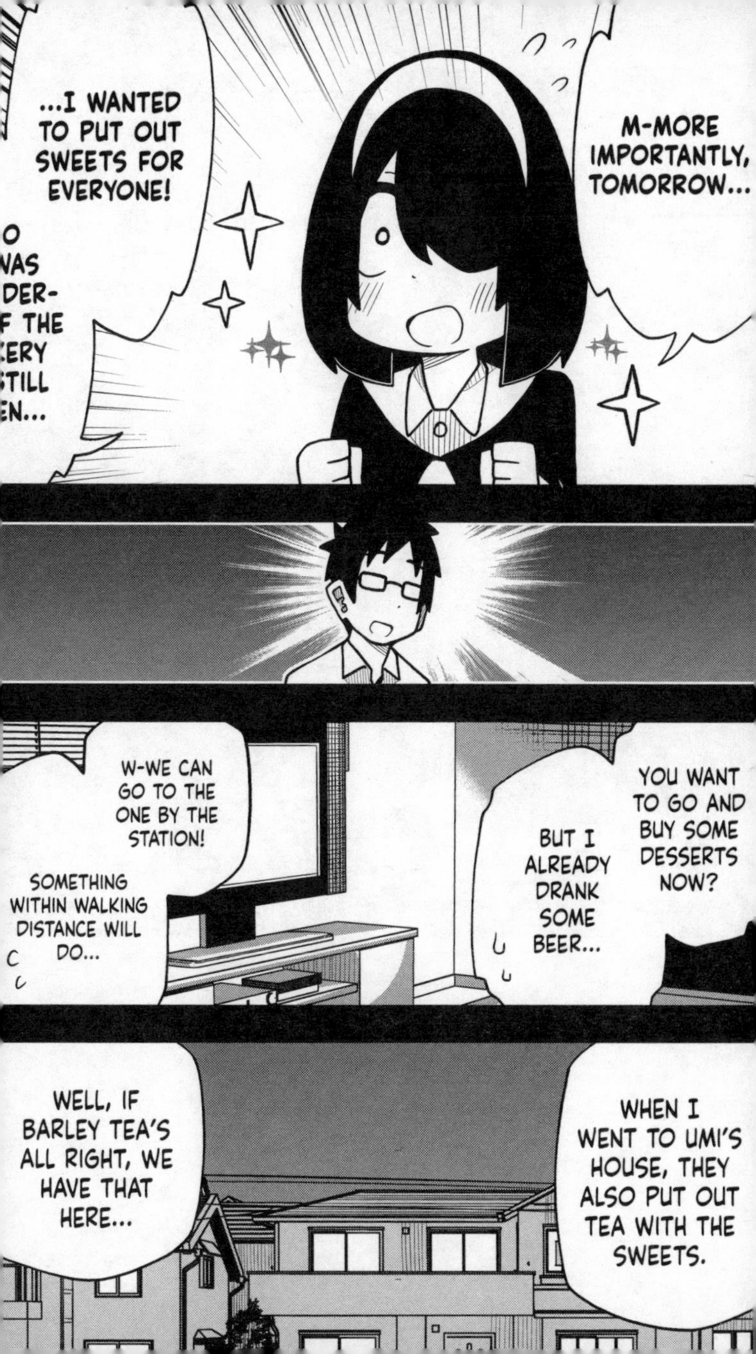
M-MORE IMPORTANTLY, TOMORROW...
...I WANTED TO PUT OUT SWEETS FOR EVERYONE!
YOU WANT TO GO AND BUY SOME DESSERTS NOW?
BUT I ALREADY DRANK SOME BEER...
W-WE CAN GO TO THE ONE BY THE STATION!
SOMETHING WITHIN WALKING DISTANCE WILL DO...
WHEN I WENT TO UMI'S HOUSE, THEY ALSO PUT OUT TEA WITH THE SWEETS.
WELL, IF BARLEY TEA'S ALL RIGHT, WE HAVE THAT HERE...

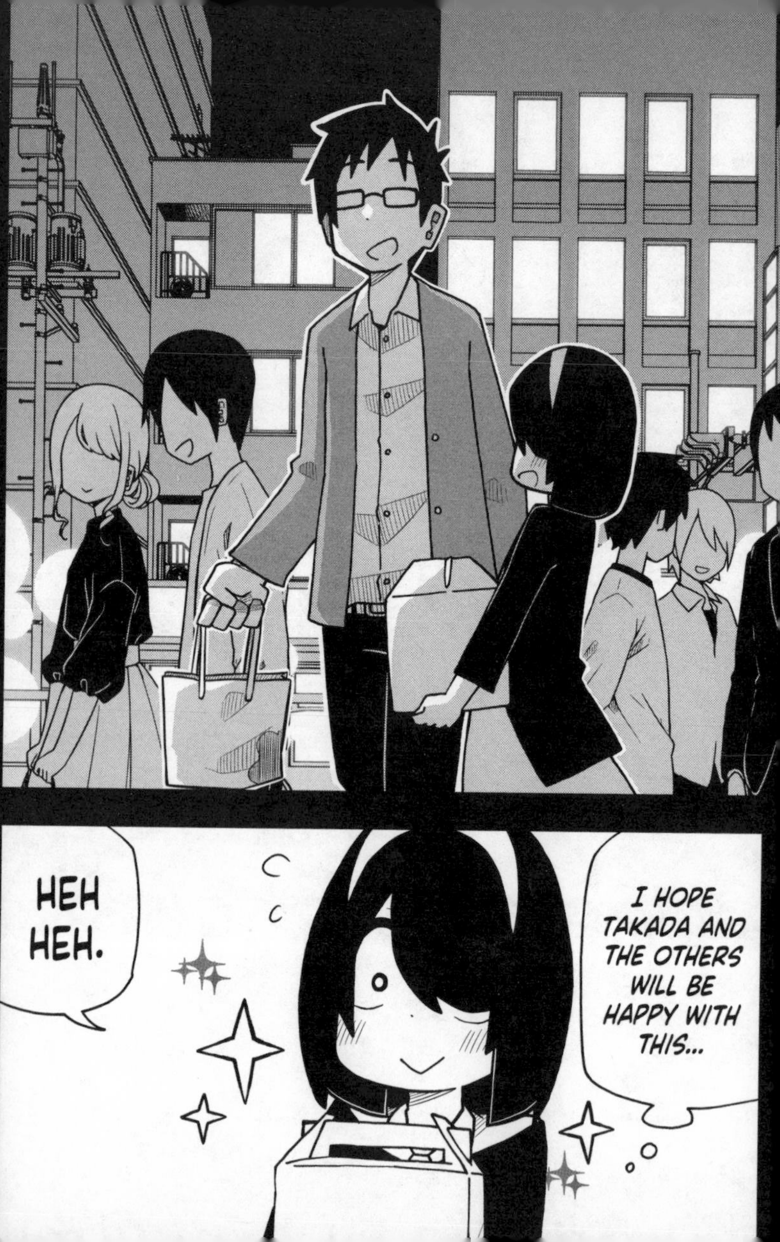
I HOPE TAKADA AND THE OTHERS WILL BE HAPPY WITH THIS...
HEH HEH.

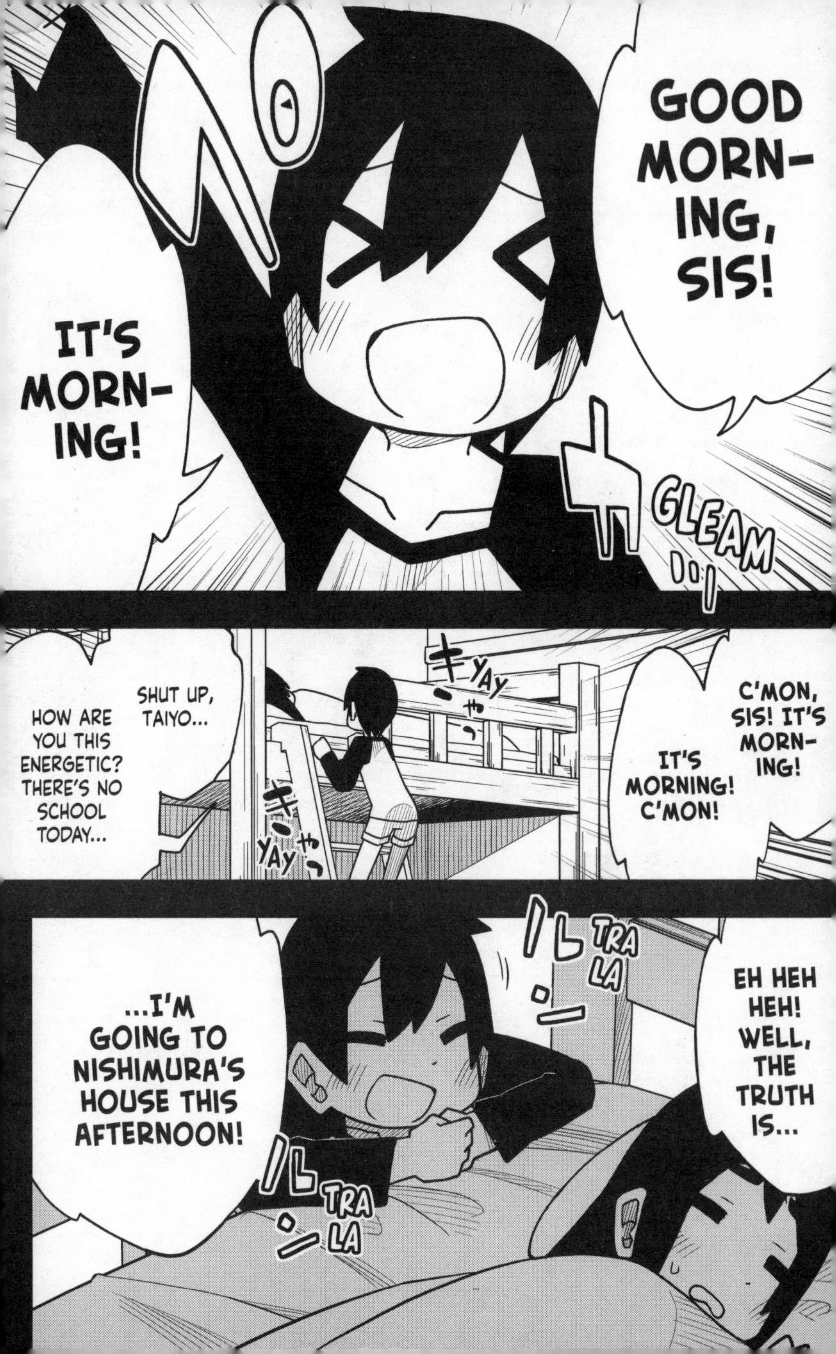
GOOD MORNING, SIS!
IT'S MORNING!
GLEAM
C'MON, SIS! IT'S MORNING!
IT'S MORNING! C'MON!
YAY
YAY
SHUT UP, TAIYO...
HOW ARE YOU THIS ENERGETIC? THERE'S NO SCHOOL TODAY...
EH HEH HEH! WELL, THE TRUTH IS...
TRA LA
...I'M GOING TO NISHIMURA'S HOUSE THIS AFTERNOON!
TRA LA

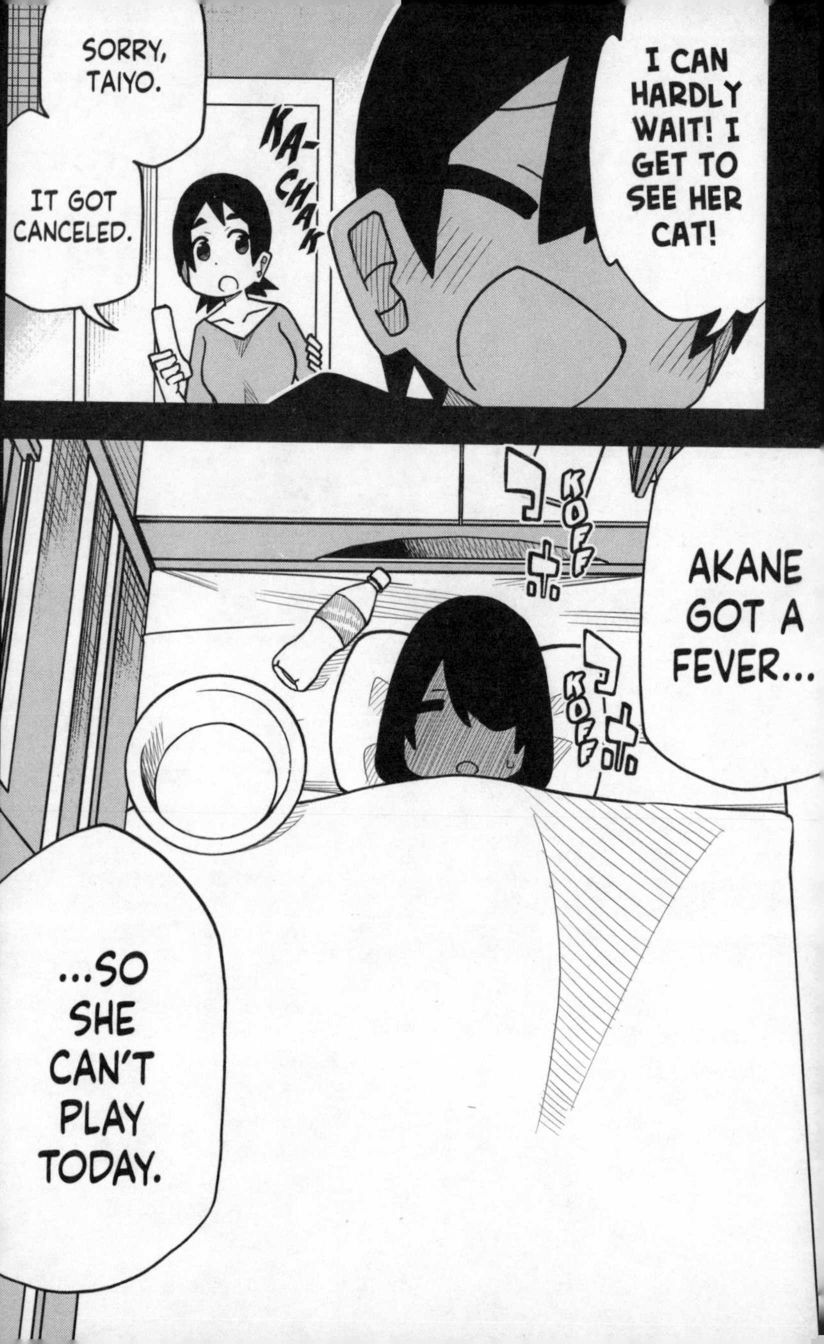
I CAN HARDLY WAIT! I GET TO SEE HER CAT!
KA-CHAK
SORRY, TAIYO.
IT GOT CANCELED.
AKANE GOT A FEVER...
KOFF
KOFF
...SO SHE CAN'T PLAY TODAY.

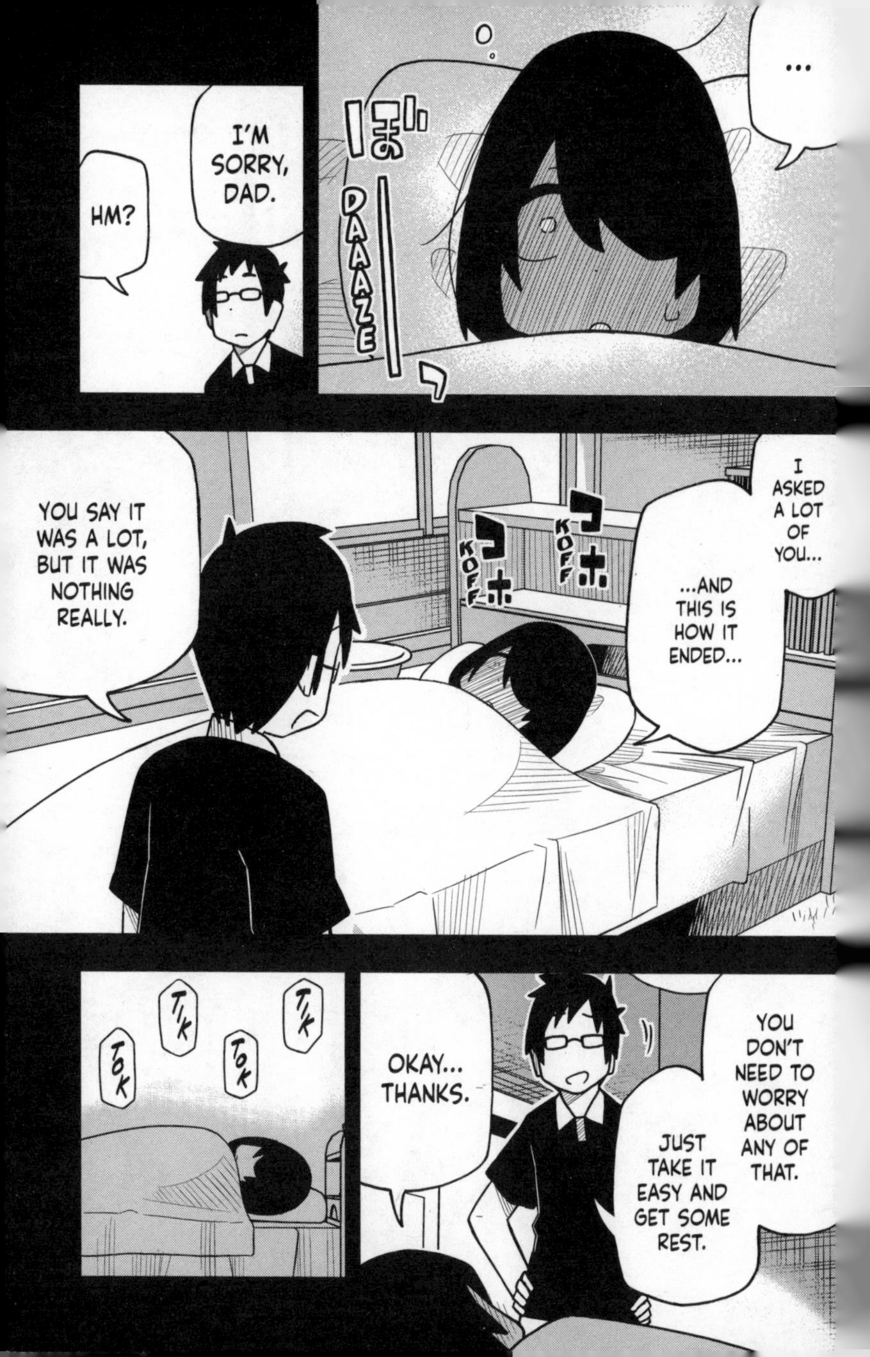
...
DAAAAZE
I'M SORRY, DAD.
HM?
I ASKED A LOT OF YOU...
...AND THIS IS HOW IT ENDED...
KOFF KOFF
YOU SAY IT WAS A LOT, BUT IT WAS NOTHING REALLY.
YOU DON'T NEED TO WORRY ABOUT ANY OF THAT.
JUST TAKE IT EASY AND GET SOME REST.
OKAY... THANKS.
TIK TOK
TIK TOK

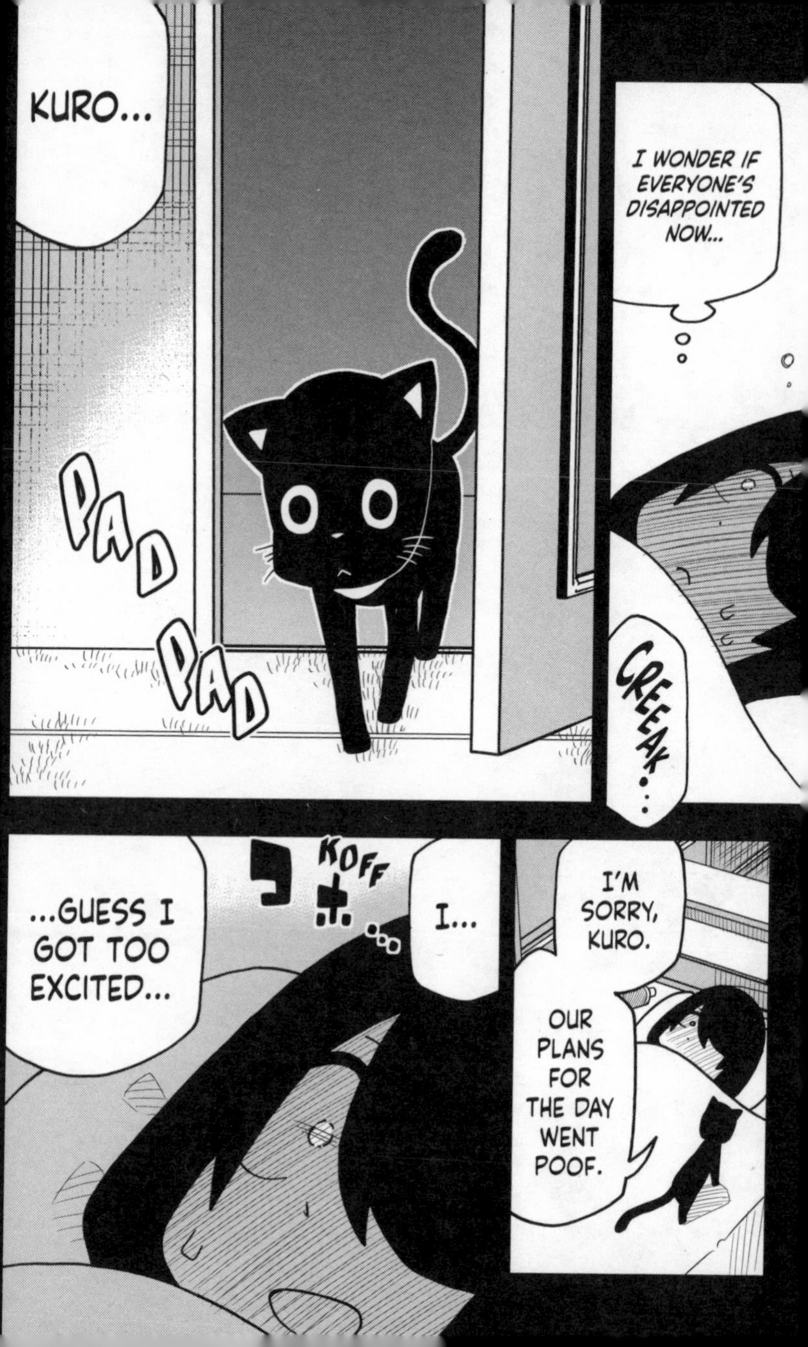
I WONDER IF EVERYONE'S DISAPPOINTED NOW...
CREEAK...
KURO...
PAD PAD
PAD PAD
I'M SORRY, KURO.
OUR PLANS FOR THE DAY WENT POOF.
I...
KOFF
...GUESS I GOT TOO EXCITED...

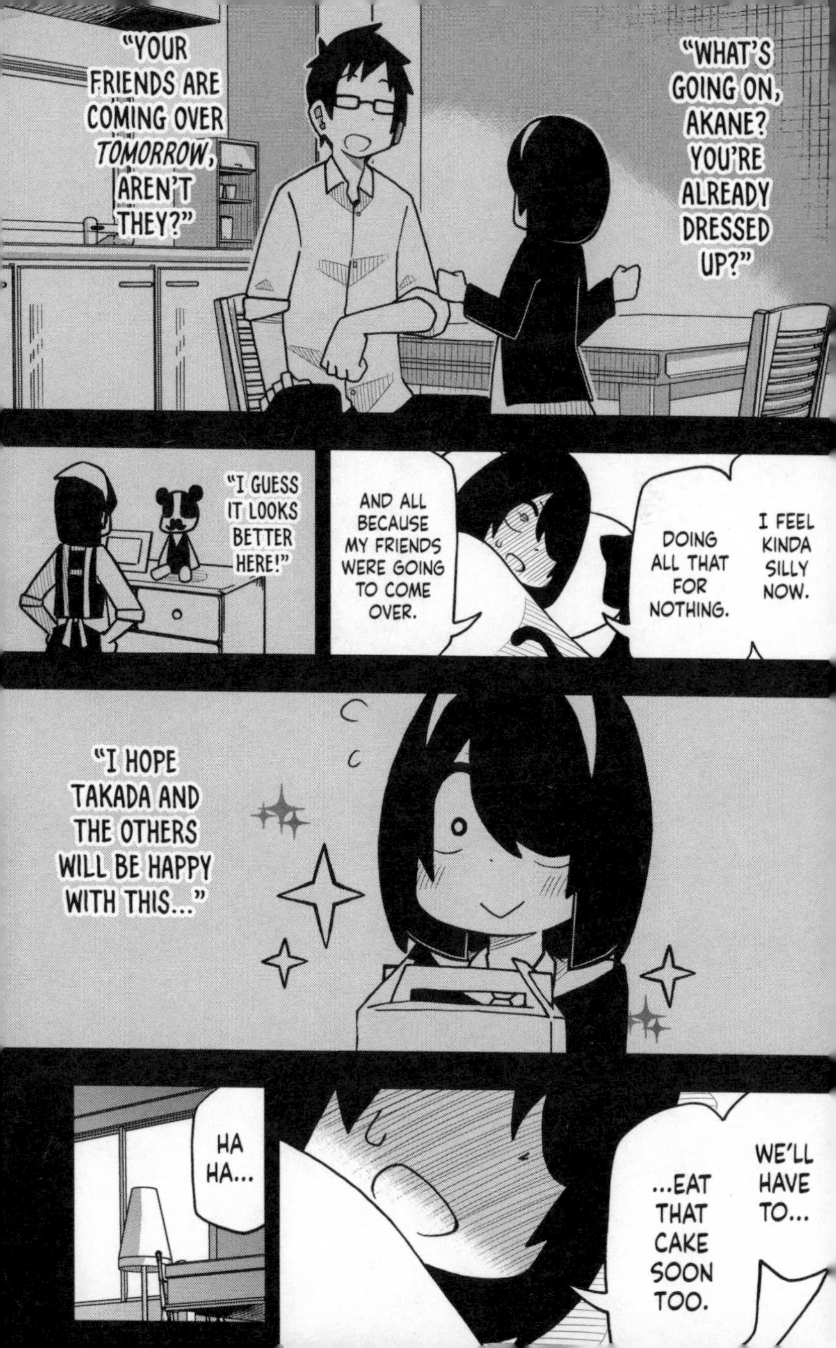
"WHAT'S GOING ON, AKANE? YOU'RE ALREADY DRESSED UP?"
"YOUR FRIENDS ARE COMING OVER *TOMORROW*, AREN'T THEY?"
I FEEL KINDA SILLY NOW.
DOING ALL THAT FOR NOTHING.
AND ALL BECAUSE MY FRIENDS WERE GOING TO COME OVER.
"I GUESS IT LOOKS BETTER HERE!"
"I HOPE TAKADA AND THE OTHERS WILL BE HAPPY WITH THIS..."
WE'LL HAVE TO...
...EAT THAT CAKE SOON TOO.
HA HA...

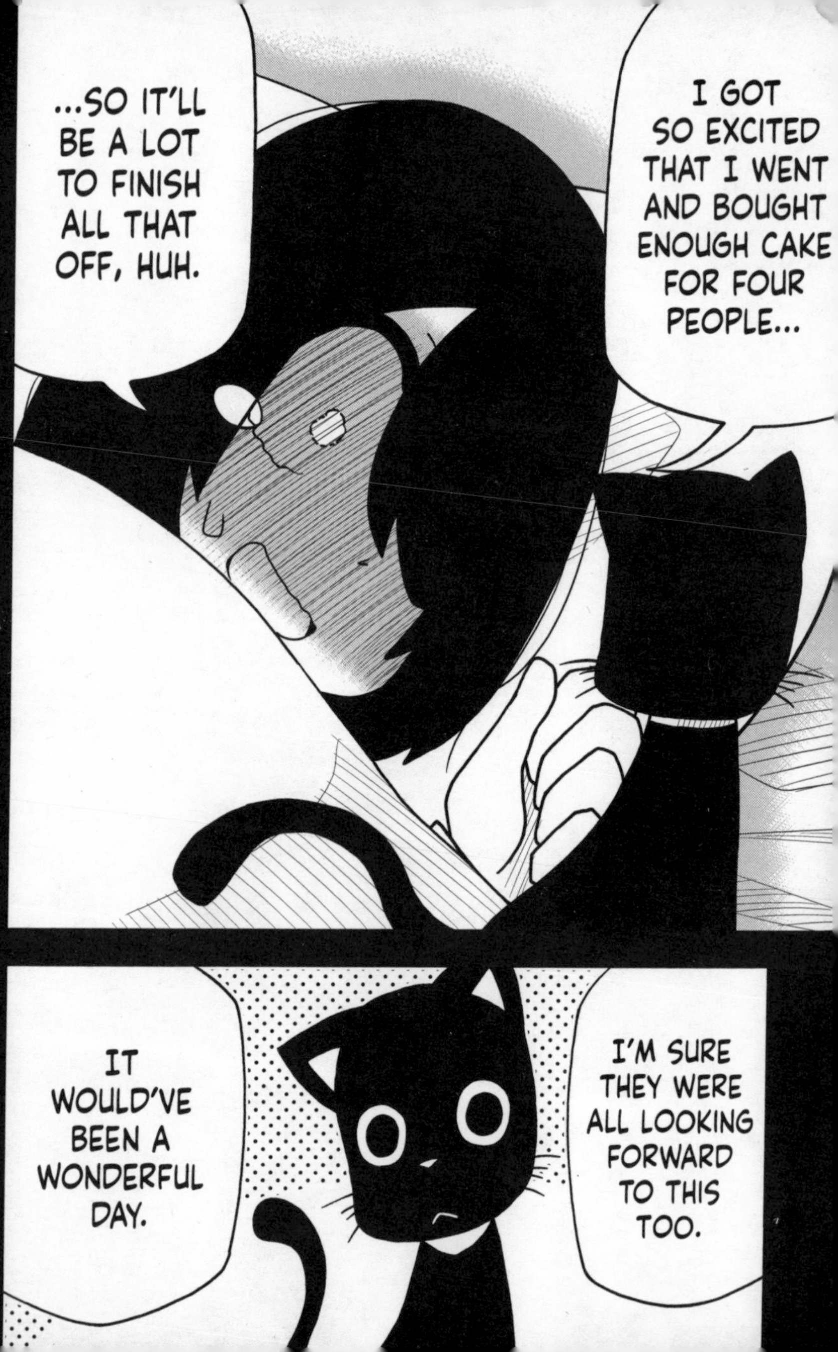
I GOT SO EXCITED THAT I WENT AND BOUGHT ENOUGH CAKE FOR FOUR PEOPLE...
...SO IT'LL BE A LOT TO FINISH ALL THAT OFF, HUH.
I'M SURE THEY WERE ALL LOOKING FORWARD TO THIS TOO.
IT WOULD'VE BEEN A WONDERFUL DAY.

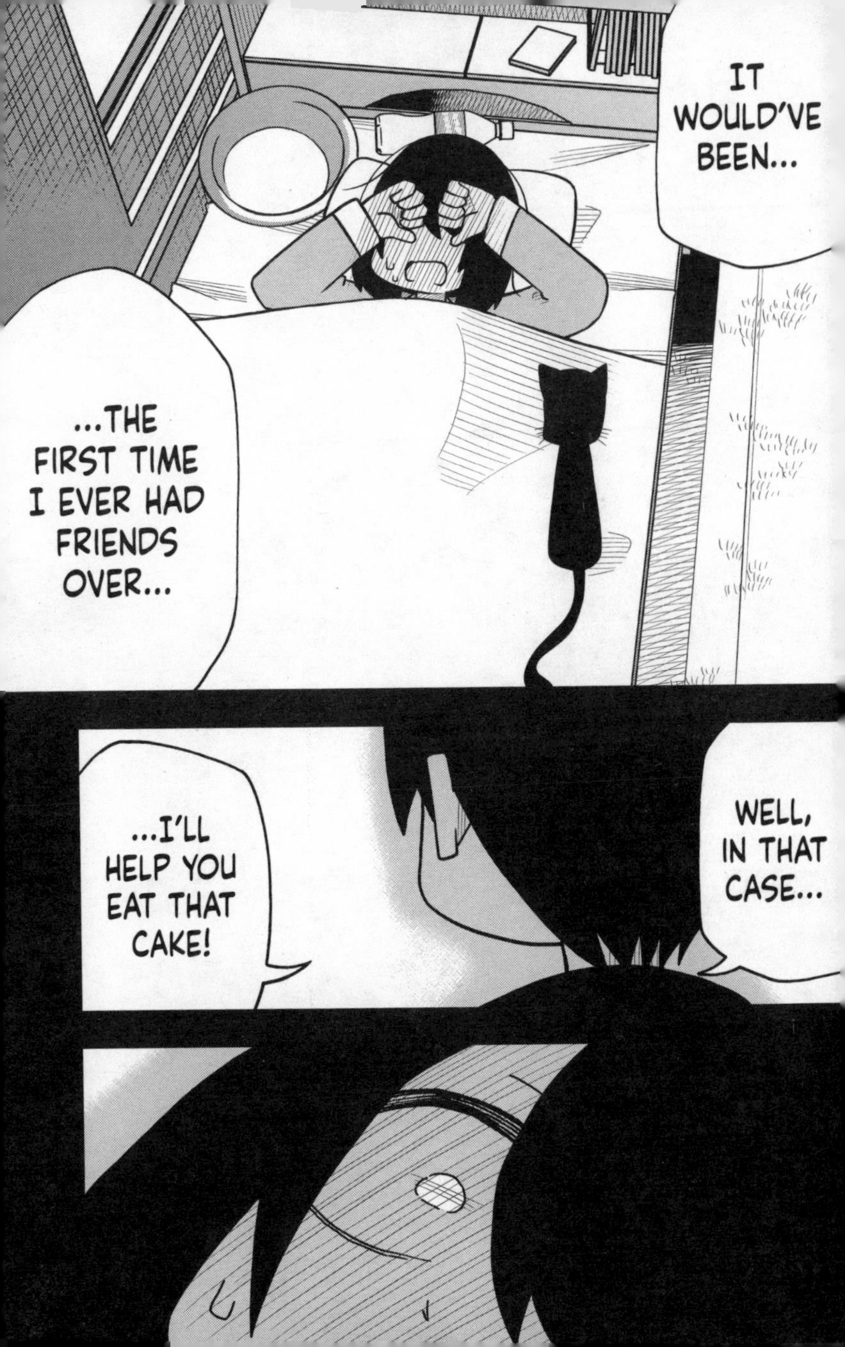
IT WOULD'VE BEEN...
...THE FIRST TIME I EVER HAD FRIENDS OVER...
WELL, IN THAT CASE...
...I'LL HELP YOU EAT THAT CAKE!

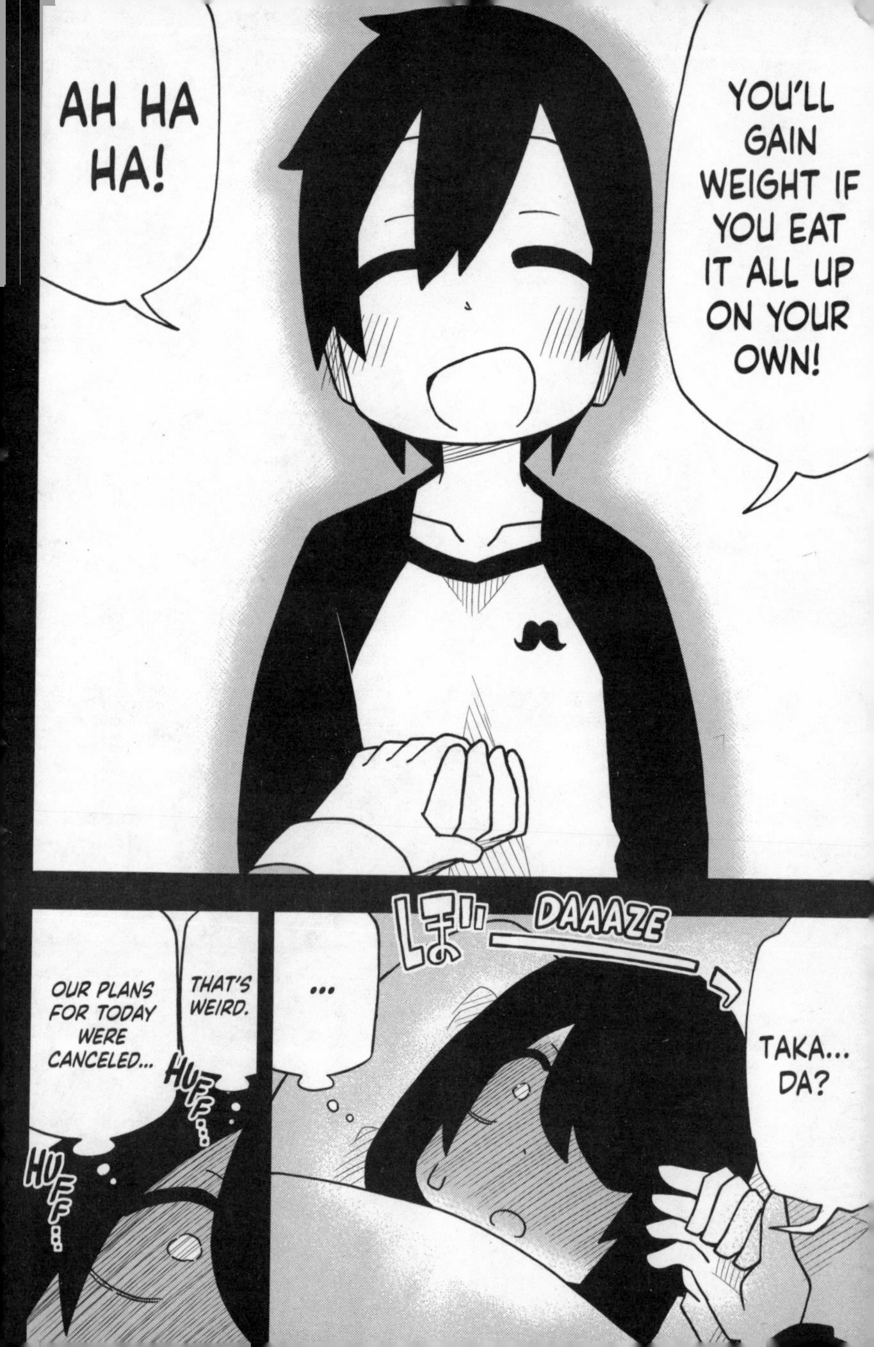
YOU'LL GAIN WEIGHT IF YOU EAT IT ALL UP ON YOUR OWN!
AH HA HA!
DAAAZE
TAKA... DA?
...
THAT'S WEIRD.
OUR PLANS FOR TODAY WERE CANCELED...
HUFF...
HUFF...

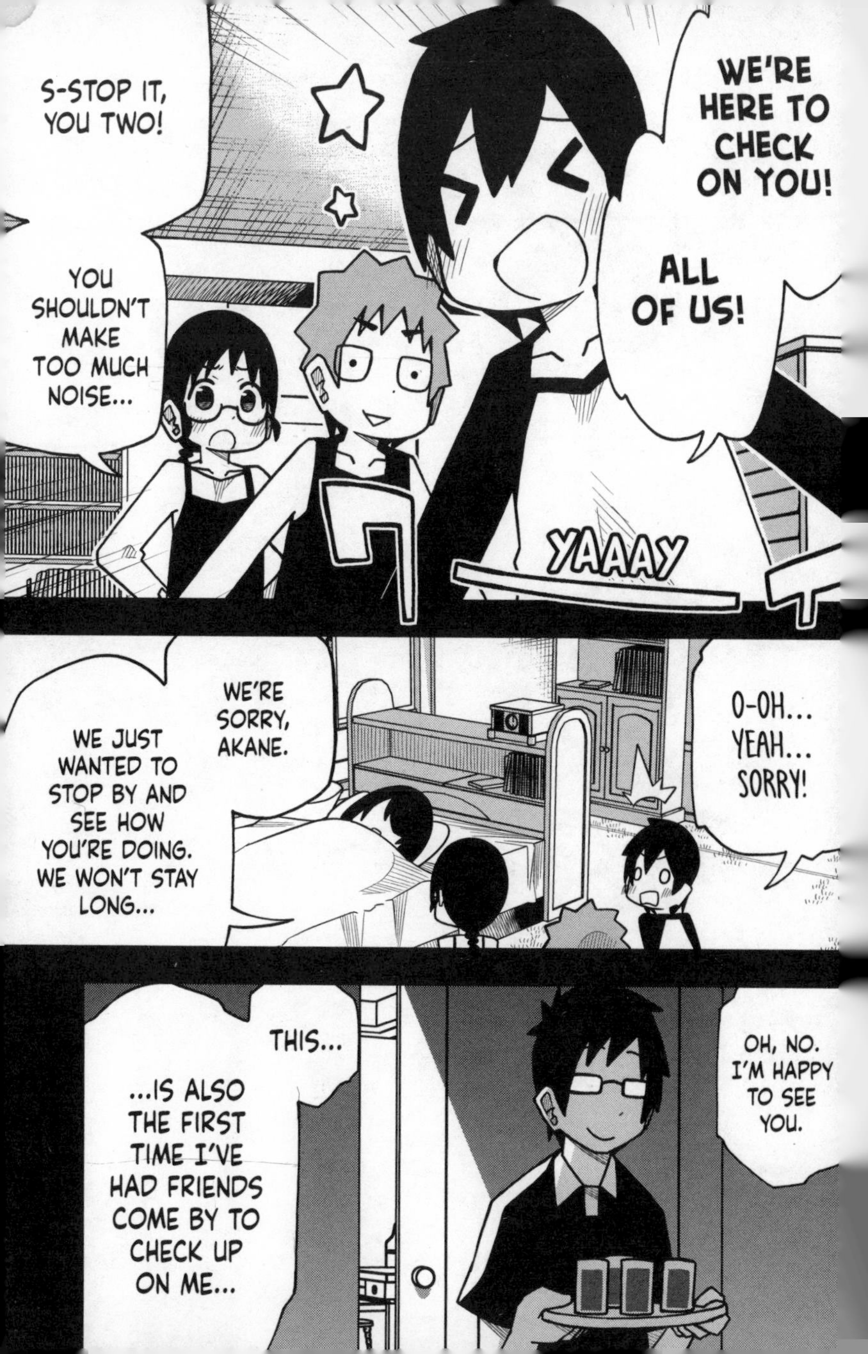
WE'RE HERE TO CHECK ON YOU!
ALL OF US!
YAAAY
S-STOP IT, YOU TWO!
YOU SHOULDN'T MAKE TOO MUCH NOISE...
O-OH... YEAH... SORRY!
WE'RE SORRY, AKANE.
WE JUST WANTED TO STOP BY AND SEE HOW YOU'RE DOING. WE WON'T STAY LONG...
OH, NO. I'M HAPPY TO SEE YOU.
THIS...
...IS ALSO THE FIRST TIME I'VE HAD FRIENDS COME BY TO CHECK UP ON ME...

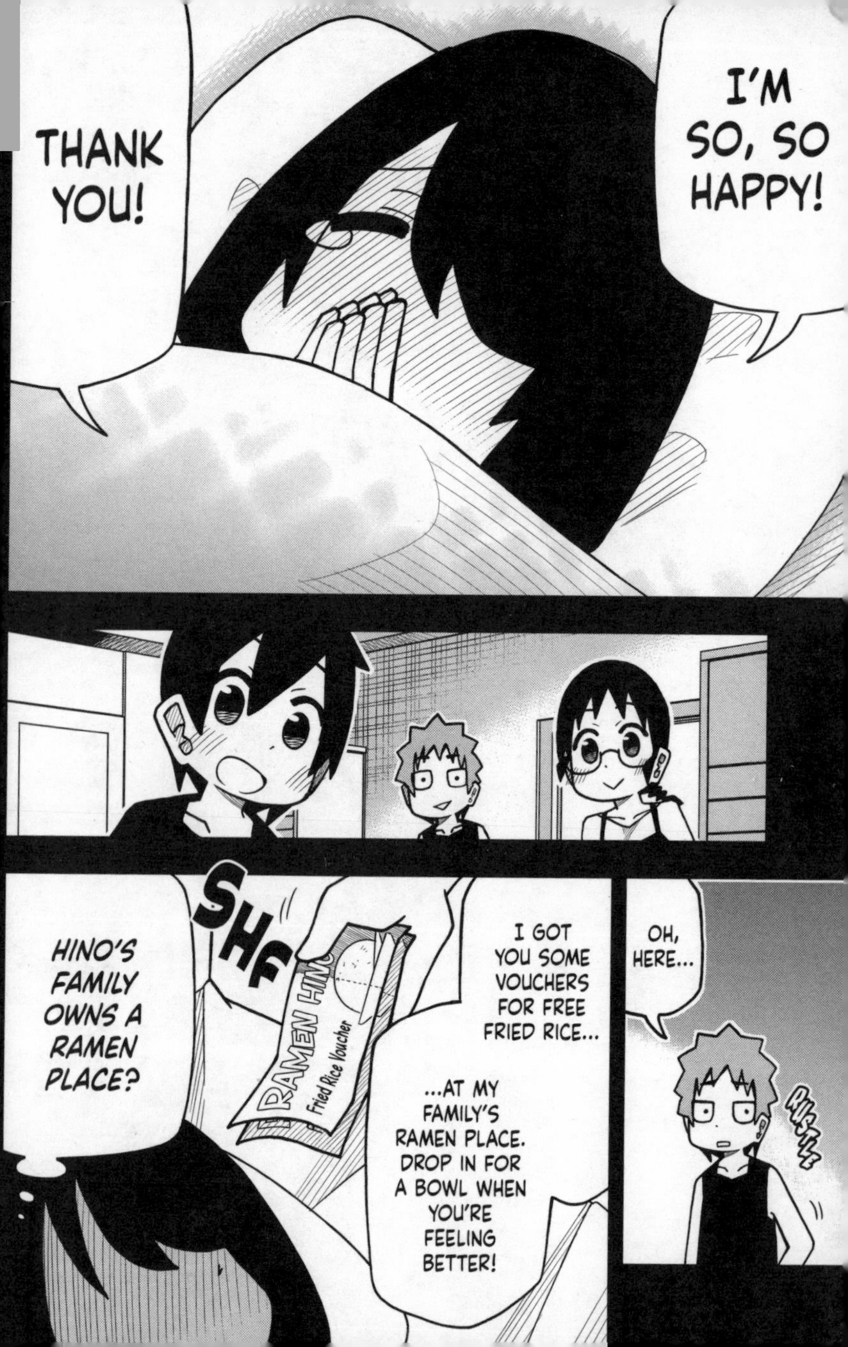
I'M SO, SO HAPPY!
THANK YOU!
OH, HERE...
RUSTLE
I GOT YOU SOME VOUCHERS FOR FREE FRIED RICE...
...AT MY FAMILY'S RAMEN PLACE. DROP IN FOR A BOWL WHEN YOU'RE FEELING BETTER!
SHF
RAMEN HIN
Fried Rice Voucher
HINO'S FAMILY OWNS A RAMEN PLACE?

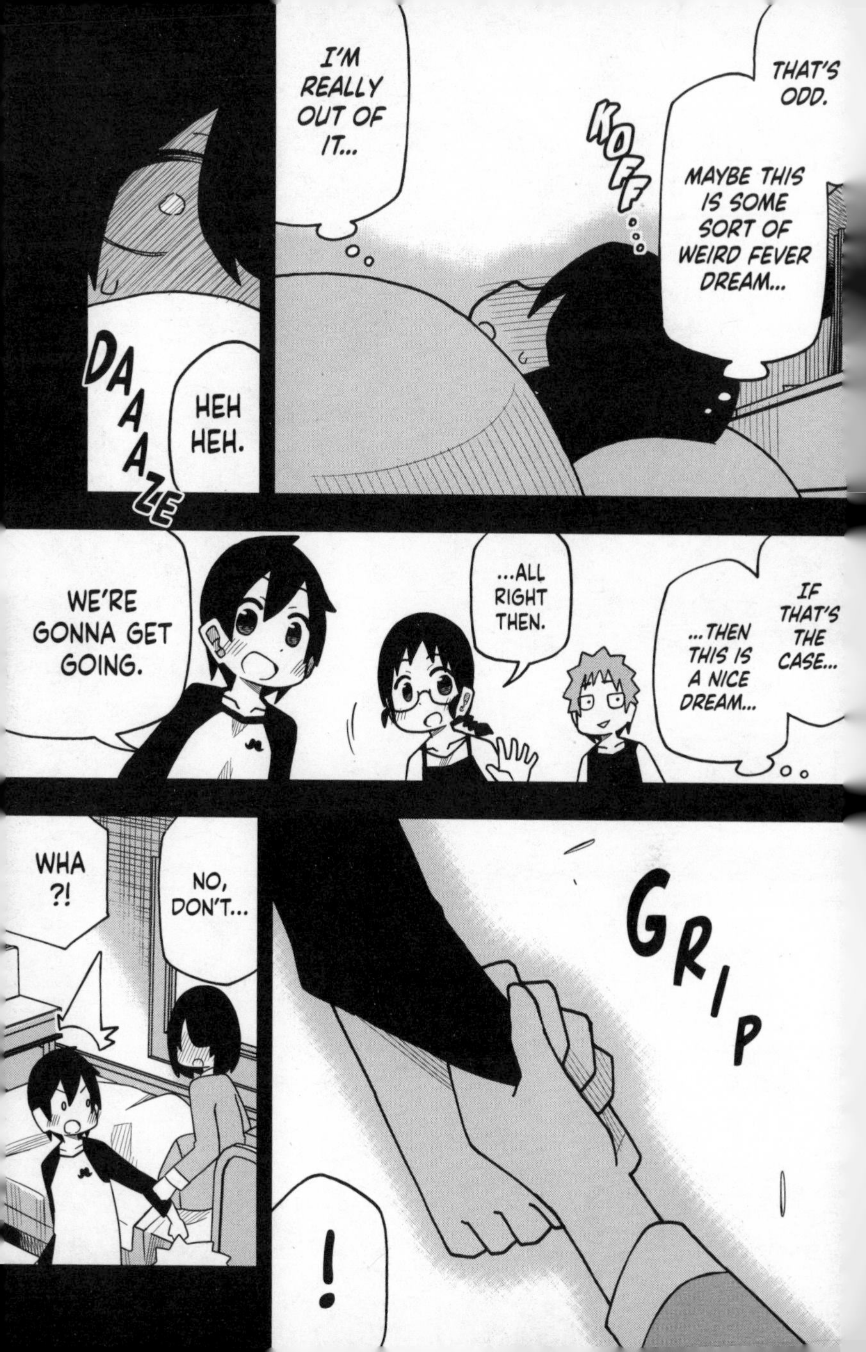
THAT'S ODD.
KOFF...
MAYBE THIS IS SOME SORT OF WEIRD FEVER DREAM...
I'M REALLY OUT OF IT...
HEH HEH.
DAAAAZE
IF THAT'S THE CASE...
...THEN THIS IS A NICE DREAM...
...ALL RIGHT THEN.
WE'RE GONNA GET GOING.
GRIP
!
NO, DON'T...
WHA ?!

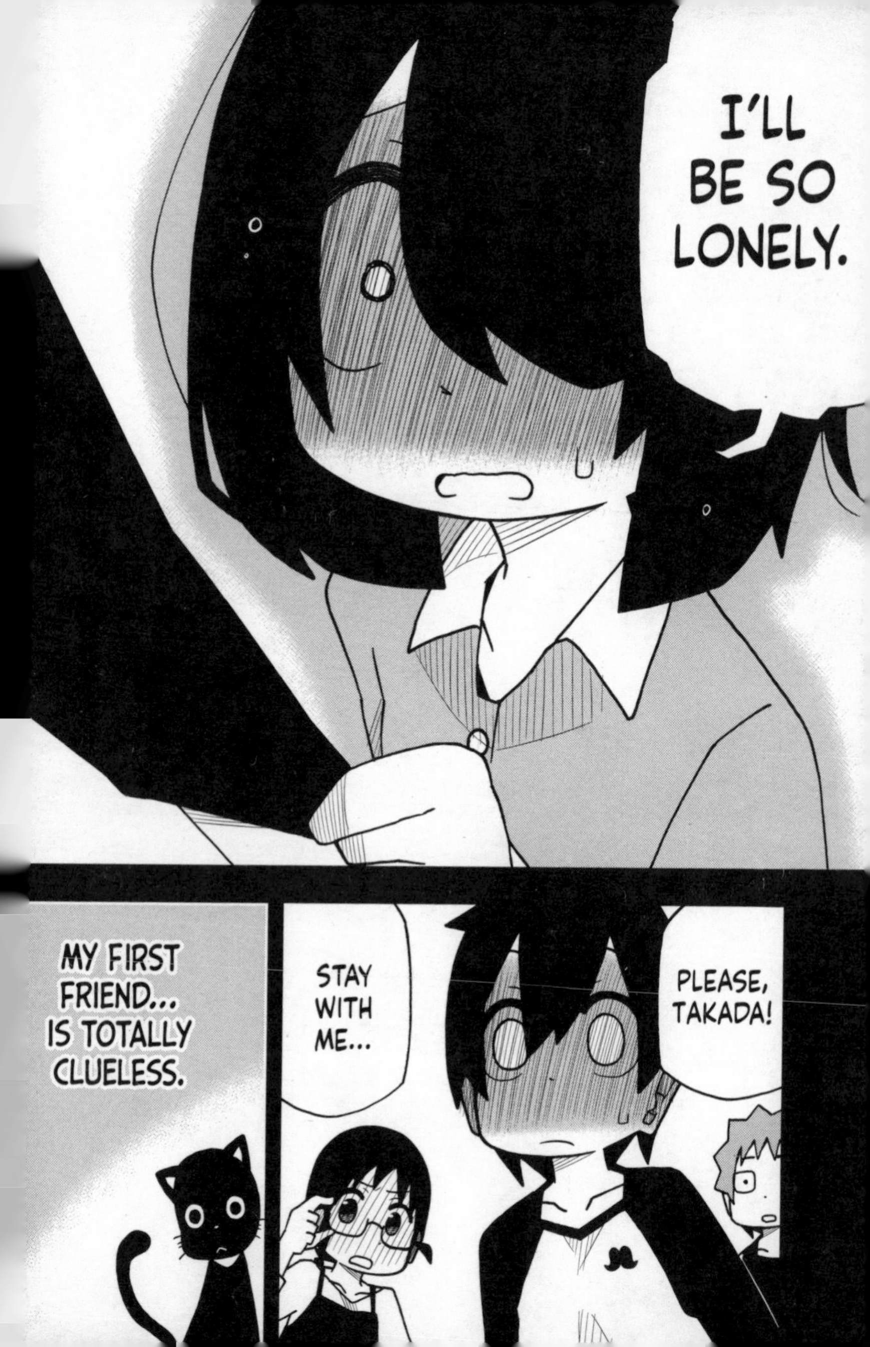
I'LL BE SO LONELY.
PLEASE, TAKADA!
STAY WITH ME...
MY FIRST FRIEND... IS TOTALLY CLUELESS.

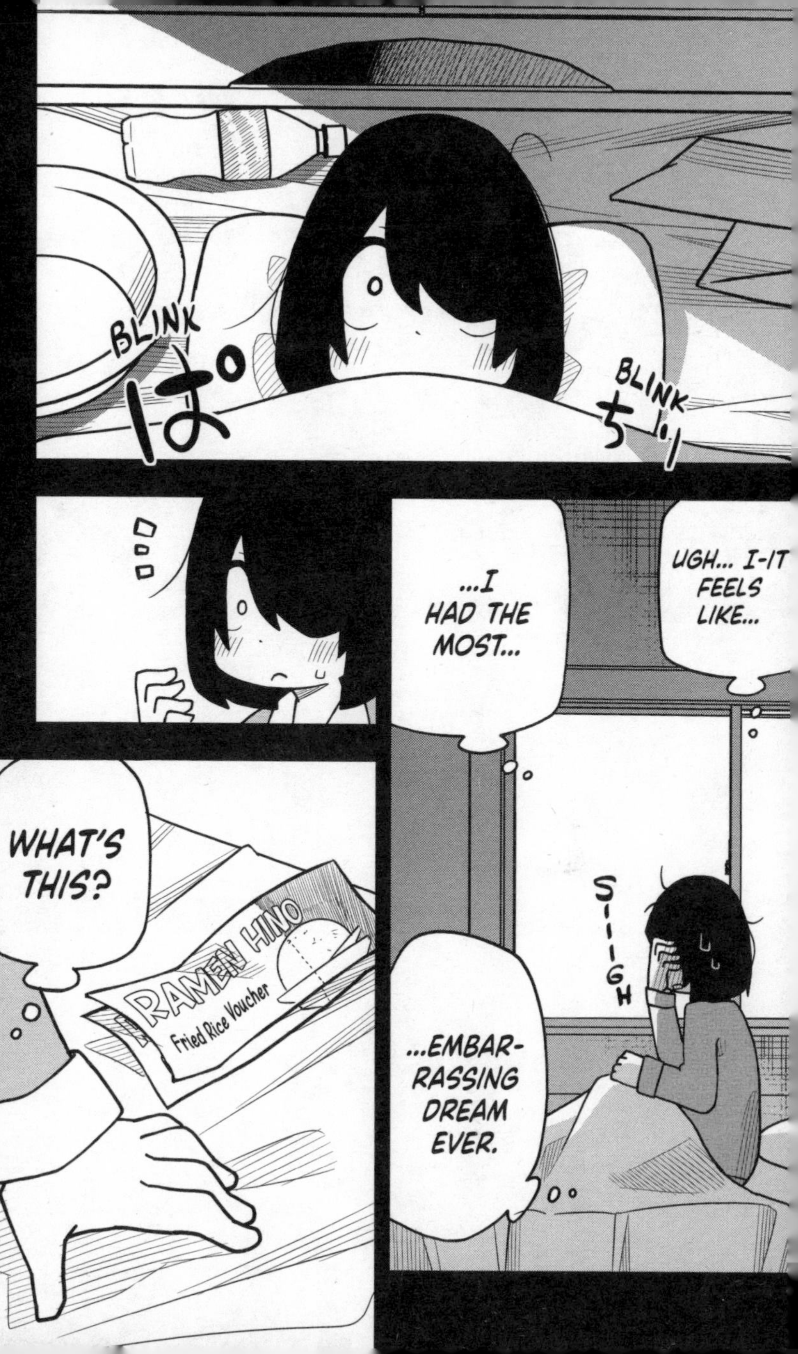
BLINK
BLINK
UGH... I-IT FEELS LIKE...
...I HAD THE MOST...
SIGH
...EMBARRASSING DREAM EVER.
...
WHAT'S THIS?
RAMEN HINO
Fried Rice Voucher

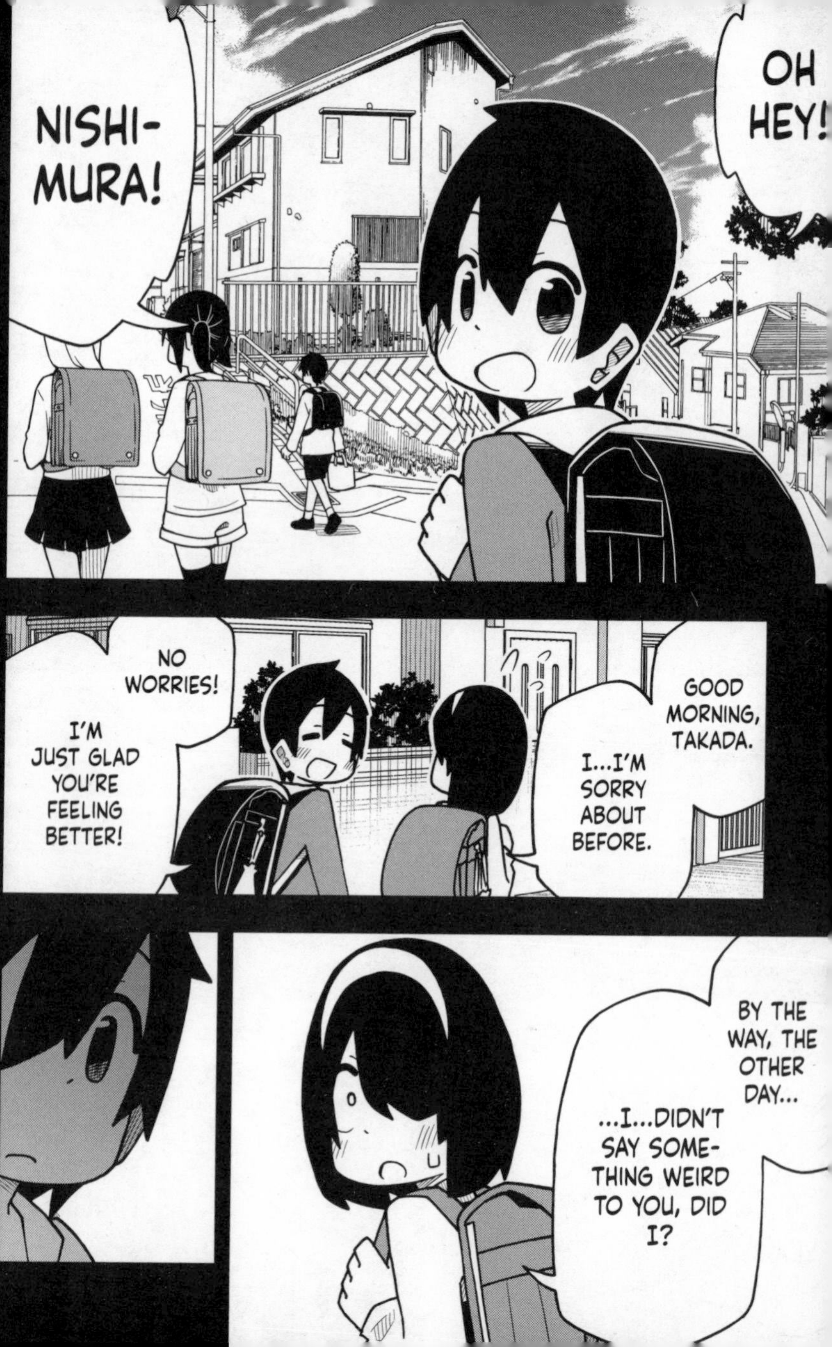
OH HEY!
NISHI-MURA!
GOOD MORNING, TAKADA.
I...I'M SORRY ABOUT BEFORE.
NO WORRIES!
I'M JUST GLAD YOU'RE FEELING BETTER!
BY THE WAY, THE OTHER DAY...
...I...DIDN'T SAY SOME-THING WEIRD TO YOU, DID I?

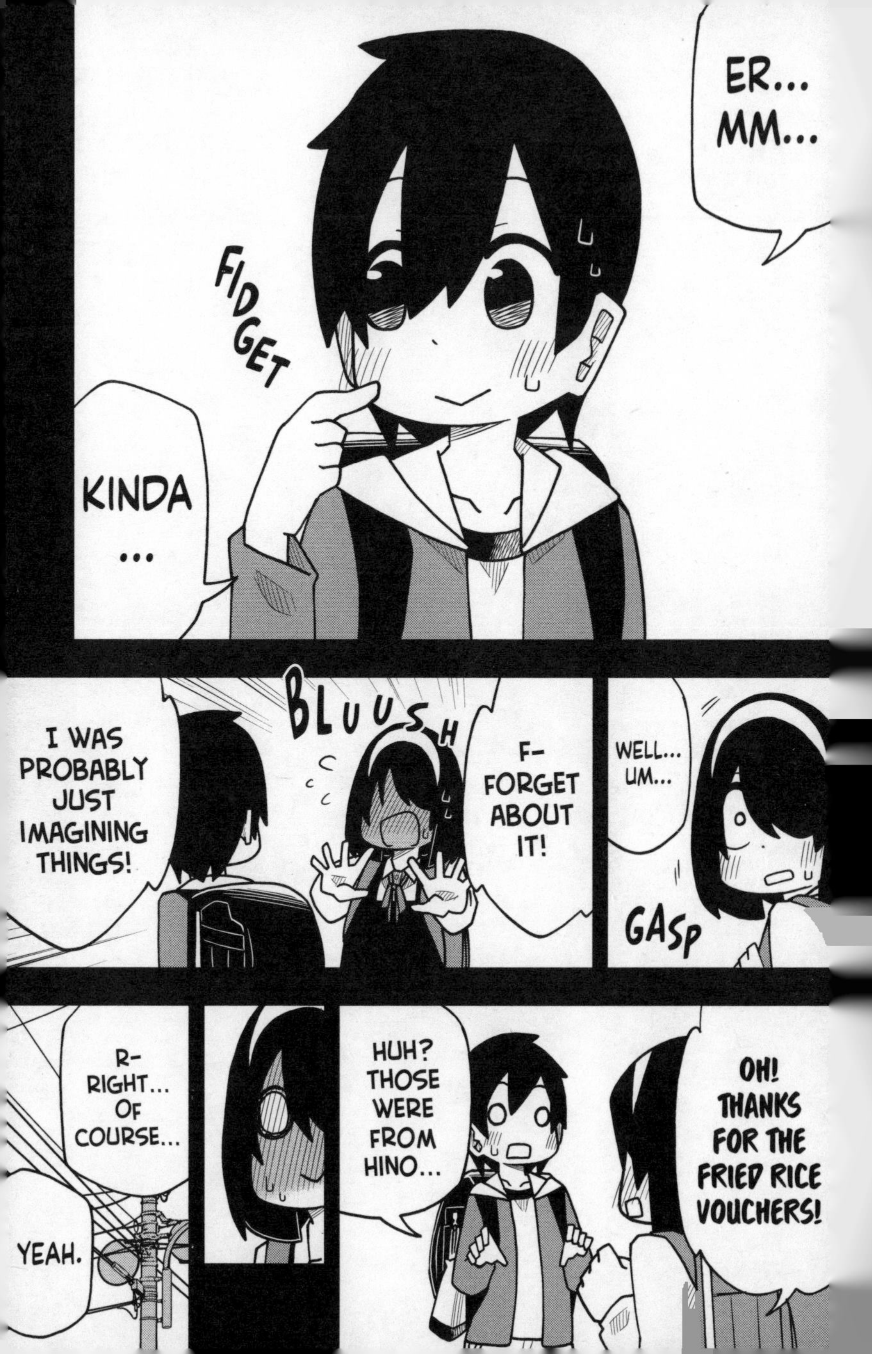
ER... MM...
FIDGET
KINDA ...
WELL... UM...
GASP
F- FORGET ABOUT IT!
BLUUSH
I WAS PROBABLY JUST IMAGINING THINGS!
OH! THANKS FOR THE FRIED RICE VOUCHERS!
HUH? THOSE WERE FROM HINO...
R- RIGHT... OF COURSE...
YEAH.

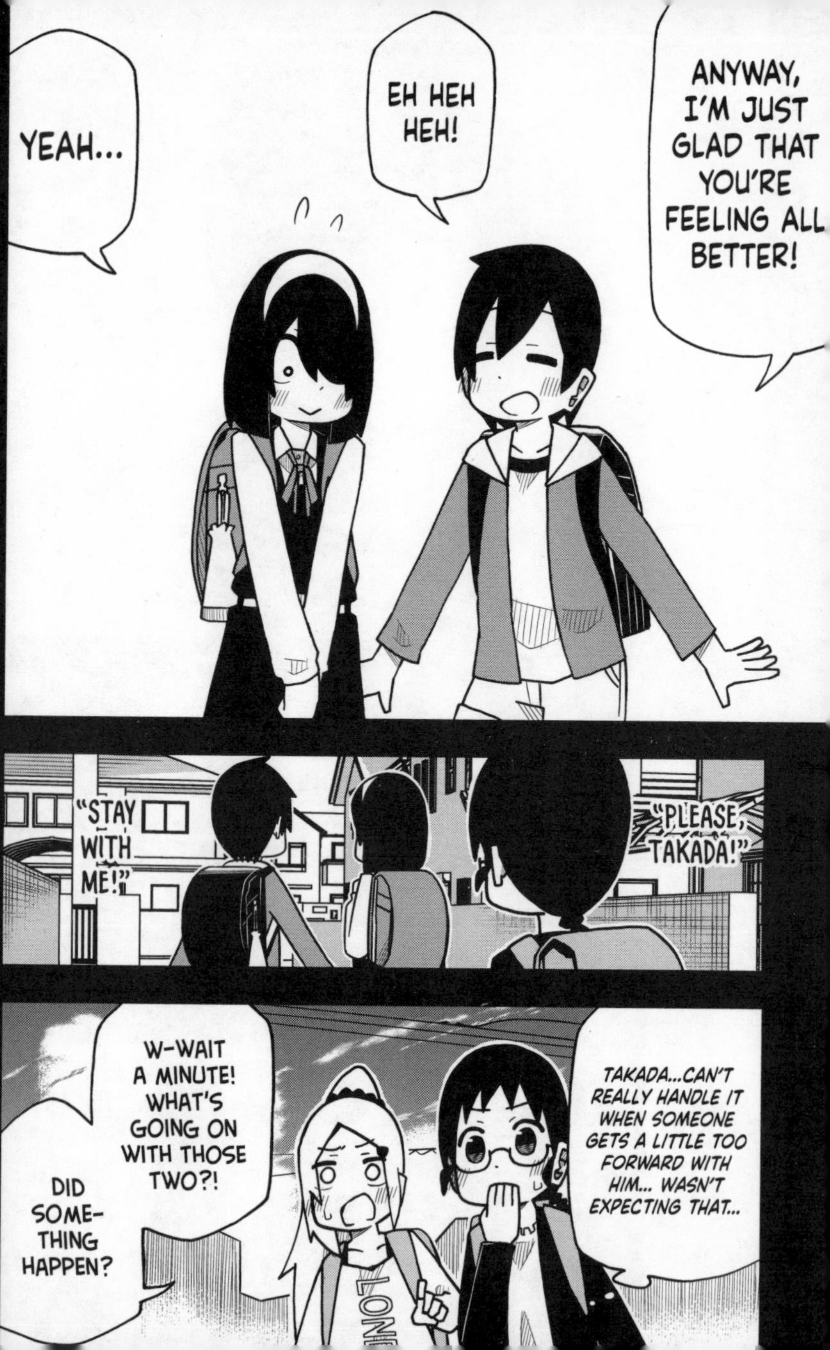
ANYWAY, I'M JUST GLAD THAT YOU'RE FEELING ALL BETTER!
EH HEH HEH!
YEAH...
"PLEASE, TAKADA!"
"STAY WITH ME!"
TAKADA...CAN'T REALLY HANDLE IT WHEN SOMEONE GETS A LITTLE TOO FORWARD WITH HIM... WASN'T EXPECTING THAT...
W-WAIT A MINUTE! WHAT'S GOING ON WITH THOSE TWO?!
DID SOME-THING HAPPEN?

MY CLUELESS
FIRST FRIEND

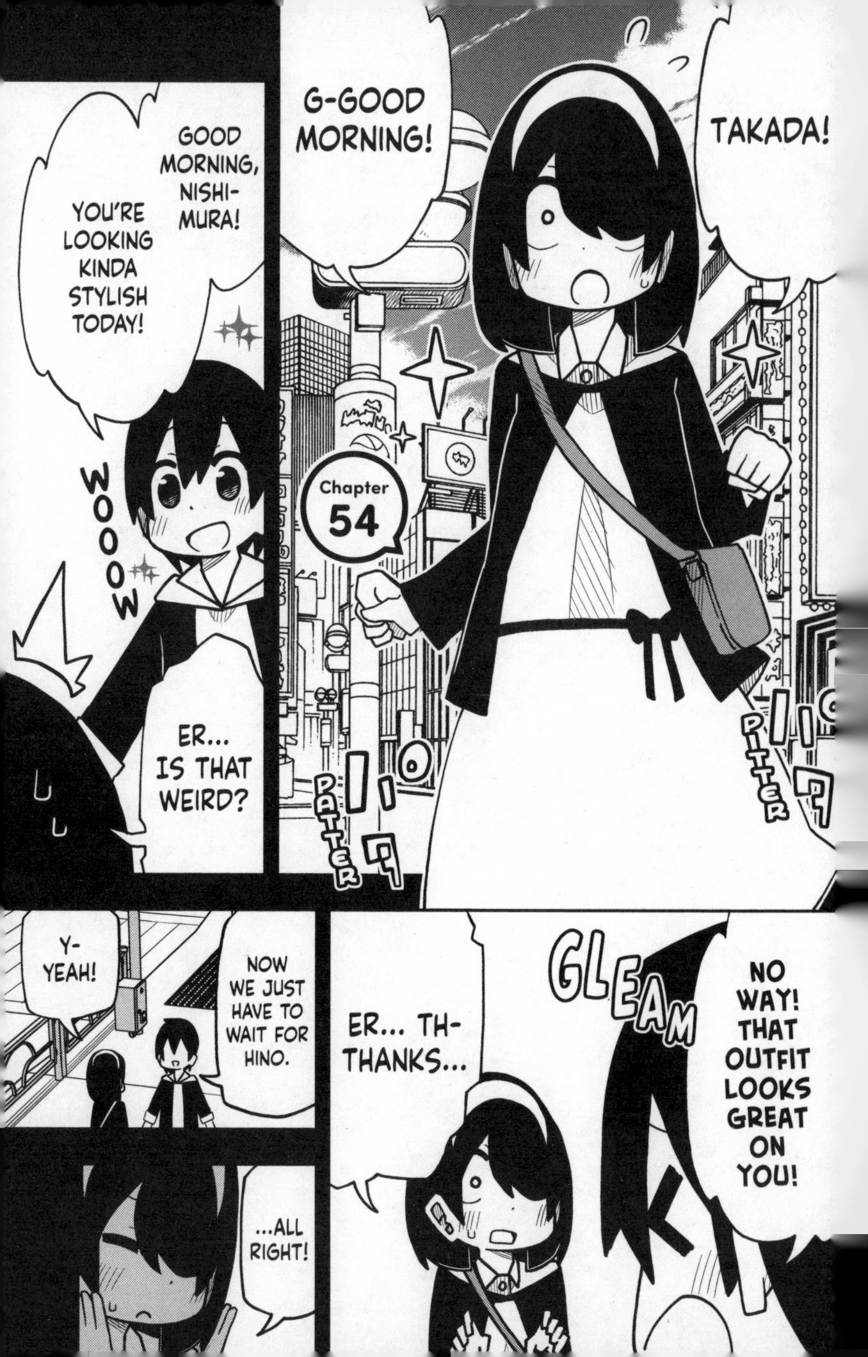
TAKADA!
G-GOOD MORNING!
Chapter 54
PITTER
PATTER
GOOD MORNING, NISHIMURA!
YOU'RE LOOKING KINDA STYLISH TODAY!
WOOOOW
ER... IS THAT WEIRD?
GLEAM
NO WAY! THAT OUTFIT LOOKS GREAT ON YOU!
ER... TH-THANKS...
NOW WE JUST HAVE TO WAIT FOR HINO.
Y-YEAH!
...ALL RIGHT!

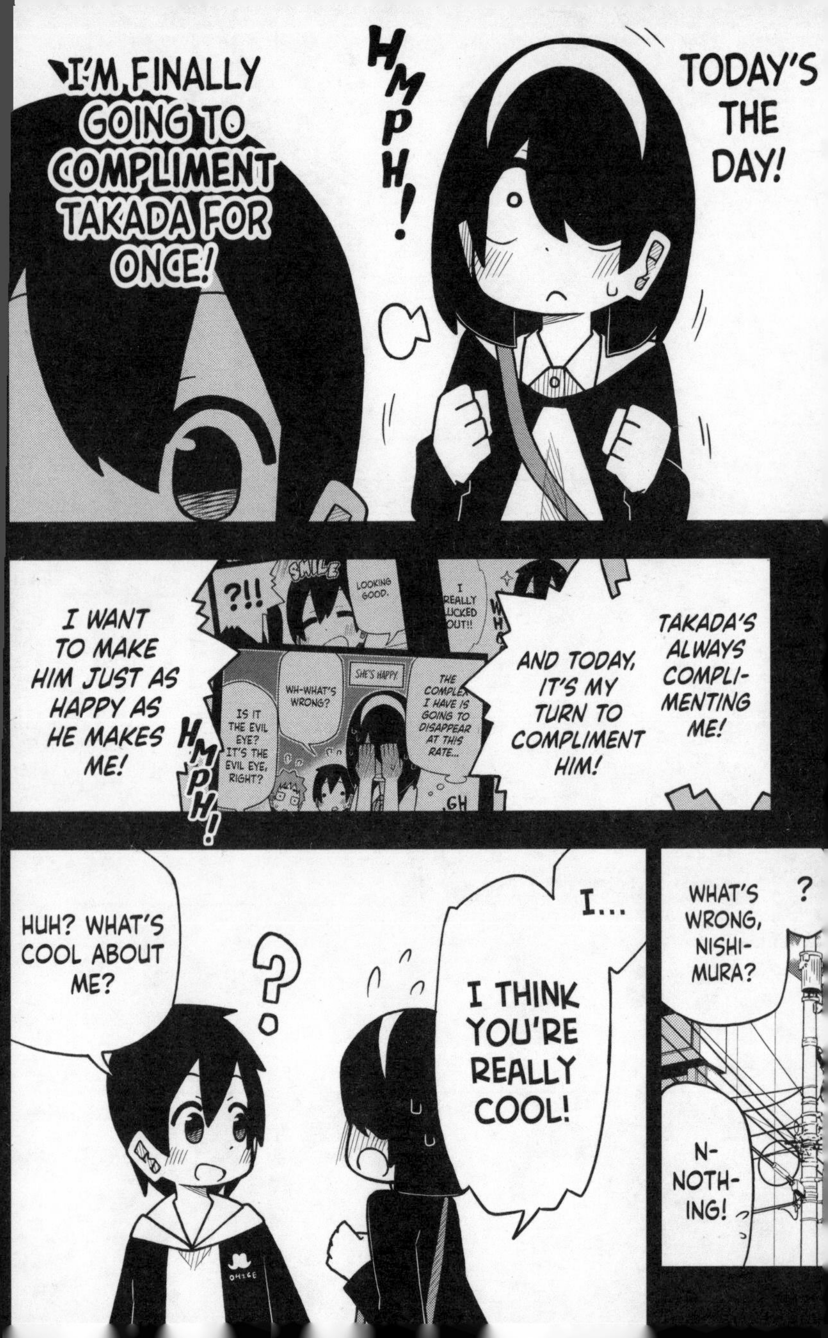
TODAY'S THE DAY!
HMPH!
I'M FINALLY GOING TO COMPLIMENT TAKADA FOR ONCE!
TAKADA'S ALWAYS COMPLIMENTING ME!
AND TODAY, IT'S MY TURN TO COMPLIMENT HIM!
LOOKING GOOD.
SMILE
?!!
SHE'S HAPPY
THE COMPLEX I HAVE IS GOING TO DISAPPEAR AT THIS RATE...
WH-WHAT'S WRONG?
IS IT THE EVIL EYE? IT'S THE EVIL EYE, RIGHT?
I WANT TO MAKE HIM JUST AS HAPPY AS HE MAKES ME!
HMPH!
WHAT'S WRONG, NISHIMURA?
?
N-NOTHING!
I...
I THINK YOU'RE REALLY COOL!
HUH? WHAT'S COOL ABOUT ME?
?

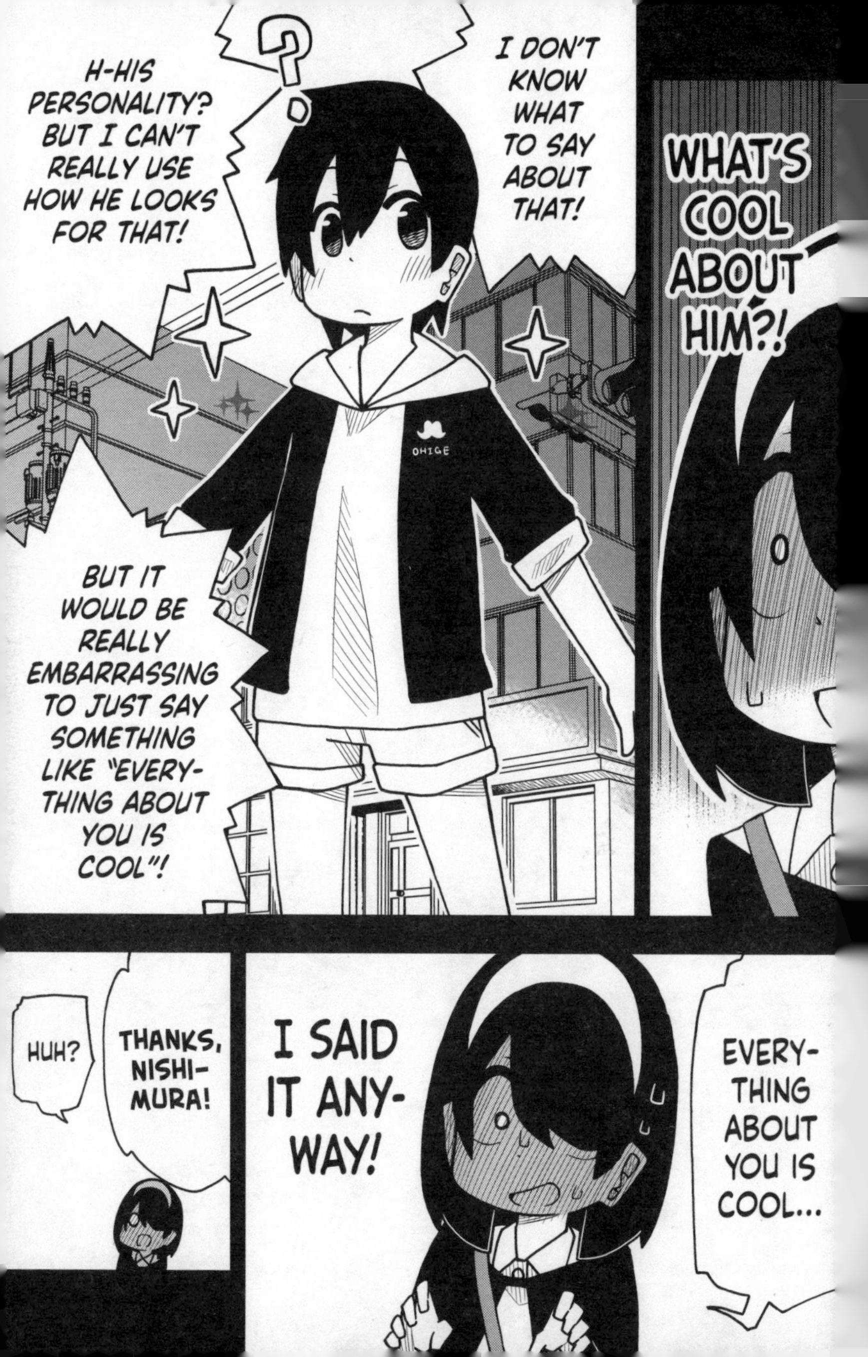
WHAT'S COOL ABOUT HIM?!
I DON'T KNOW WHAT TO SAY ABOUT THAT!
H-HIS PERSONALITY? BUT I CAN'T REALLY USE HOW HE LOOKS FOR THAT!
OHIGE
BUT IT WOULD BE REALLY EMBARRASSING TO JUST SAY SOMETHING LIKE "EVERY-THING ABOUT YOU IS COOL"!
EVERY-THING ABOUT YOU IS COOL...
I SAID IT ANY-WAY!
THANKS, NISHI-MURA!
HUH?

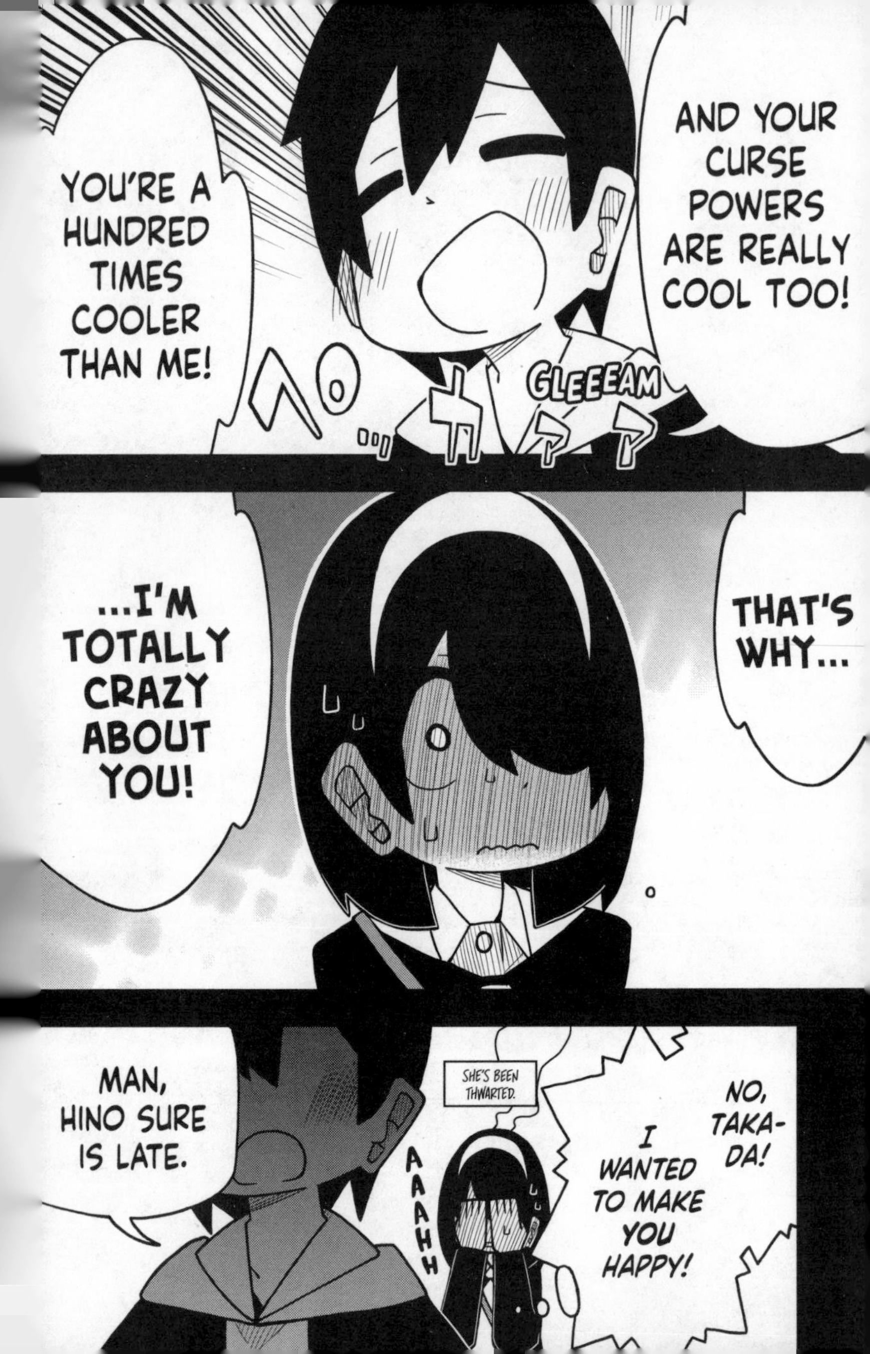
AND YOUR CURSE POWERS ARE REALLY COOL TOO!
GLEEEAM
YOU'RE A HUNDRED TIMES COOLER THAN ME!
THAT'S WHY...
...I'M TOTALLY CRAZY ABOUT YOU!
NO, TAKA-DA!
I WANTED TO MAKE YOU HAPPY!
SHE'S BEEN THWARTED.
AAAHH
MAN, HINO SURE IS LATE.

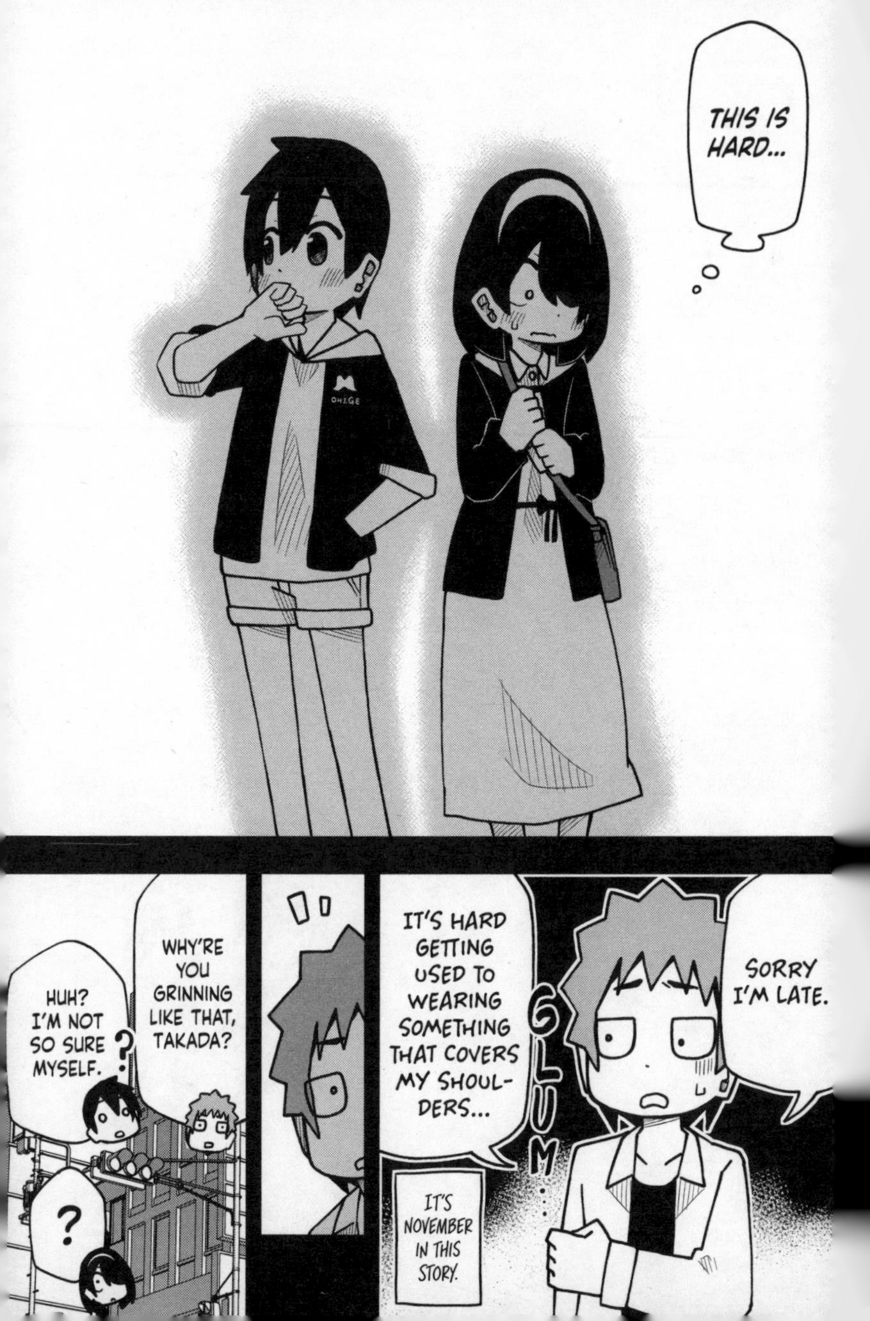
THIS IS HARD...
SORRY I'M LATE.
IT'S HARD GETTING USED TO WEARING SOMETHING THAT COVERS MY SHOUL-DERS...
GLUUM...
IT'S NOVEMBER IN THIS STORY.
WHY'RE YOU GRINNING LIKE THAT, TAKADA?
HUH? I'M NOT SO SURE MYSELF.
?
?

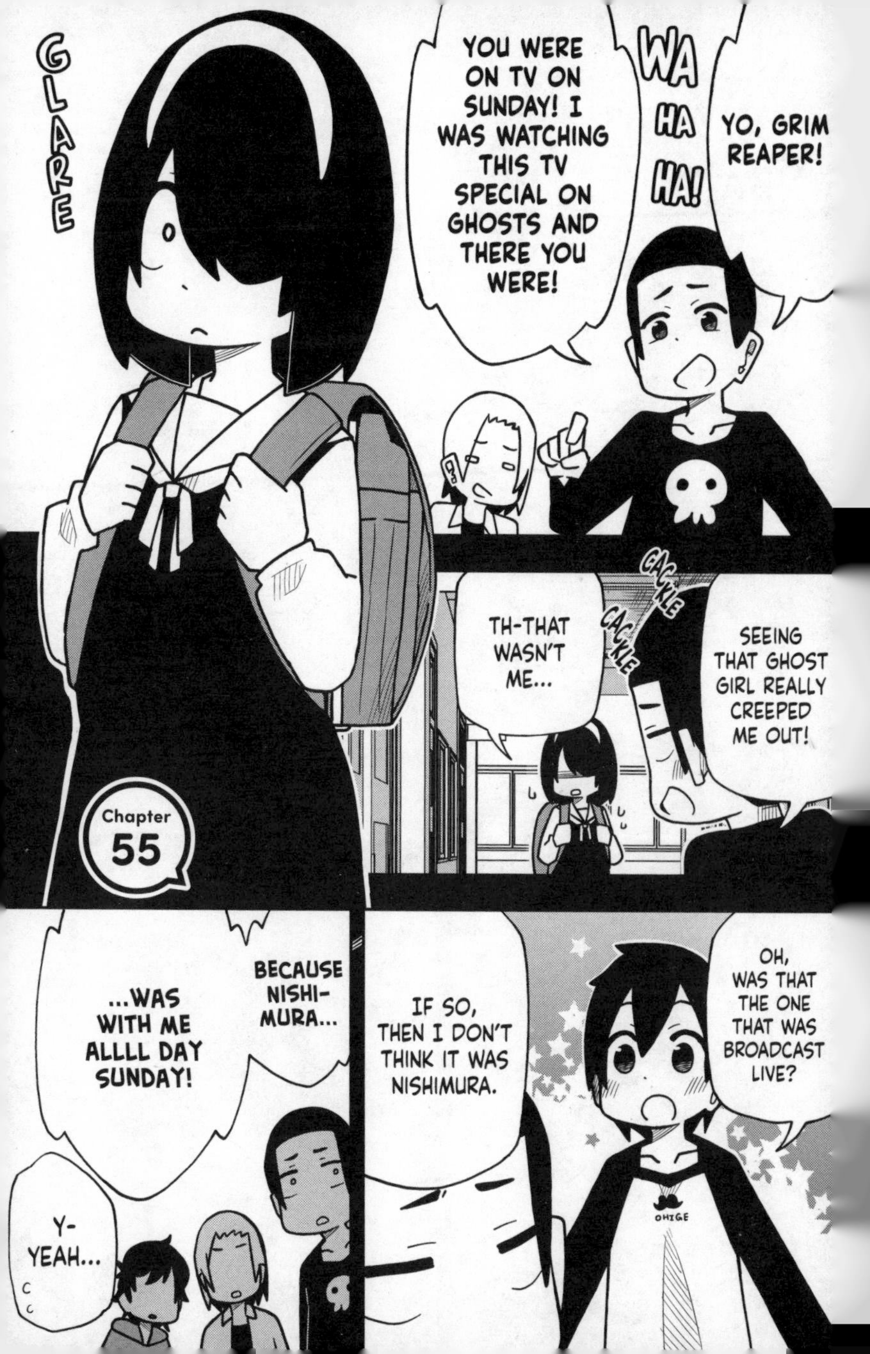
YO, GRIM REAPER!
WA HA HA!
YOU WERE ON TV ON SUNDAY! I WAS WATCHING THIS TV SPECIAL ON GHOSTS AND THERE YOU WERE!
SEEING THAT GHOST GIRL REALLY CREEPED ME OUT!
CACKLE CACKLE
TH-THAT WASN'T ME...
GLARE
Chapter 55
OH, WAS THAT THE ONE THAT WAS BROADCAST LIVE?
IF SO, THEN I DON'T THINK IT WAS NISHIMURA.
OHIGE
BECAUSE NISHI-MURA...
...WAS WITH ME ALLLL DAY SUNDAY!
Y-YEAH...

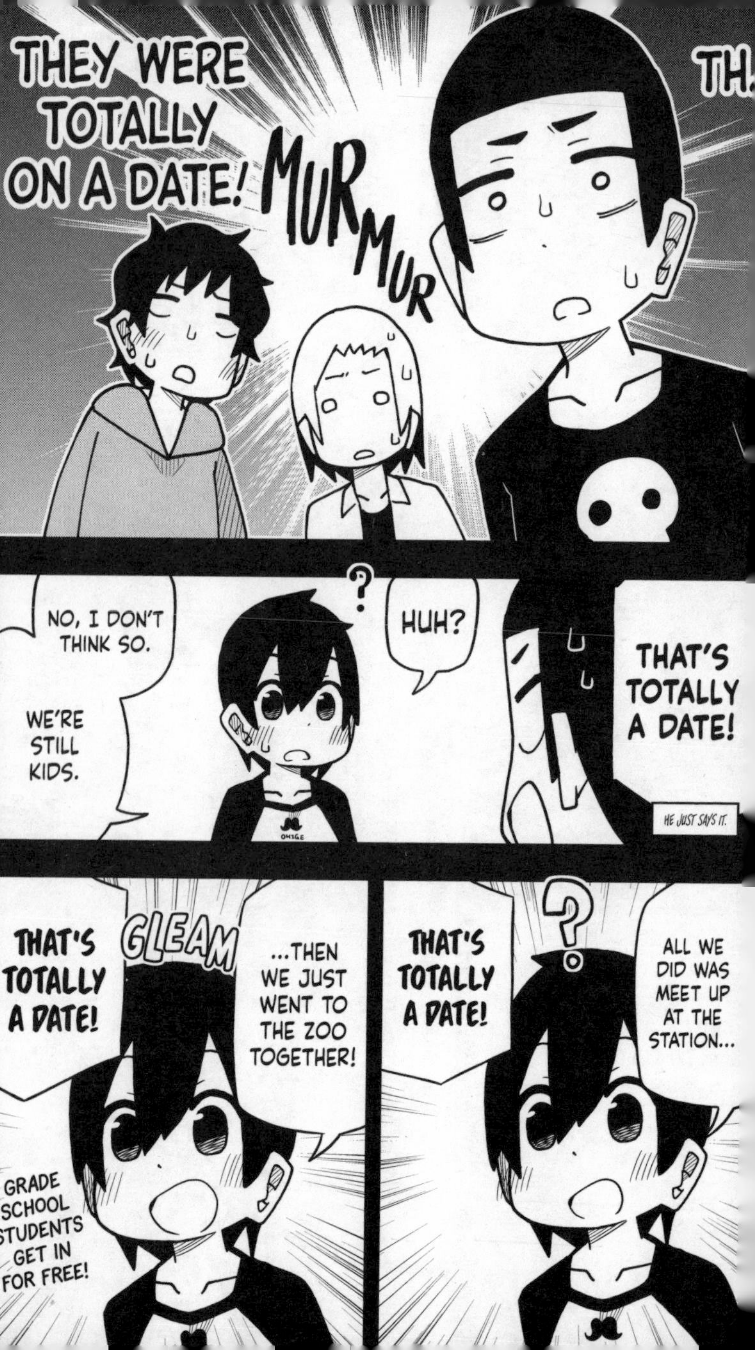
THEY WERE TOTALLY ON A DATE!
MURMUR
THAT'S TOTALLY A DATE!
HE JUST SAYS IT.
HUH?
NO, I DON'T THINK SO.
WE'RE STILL KIDS.
ALL WE DID WAS MEET UP AT THE STATION...
THAT'S TOTALLY A DATE!
...THEN WE JUST WENT TO THE ZOO TOGETHER!
GLEAM
THAT'S TOTALLY A DATE!
GRADE SCHOOL STUDENTS GET IN FOR FREE!

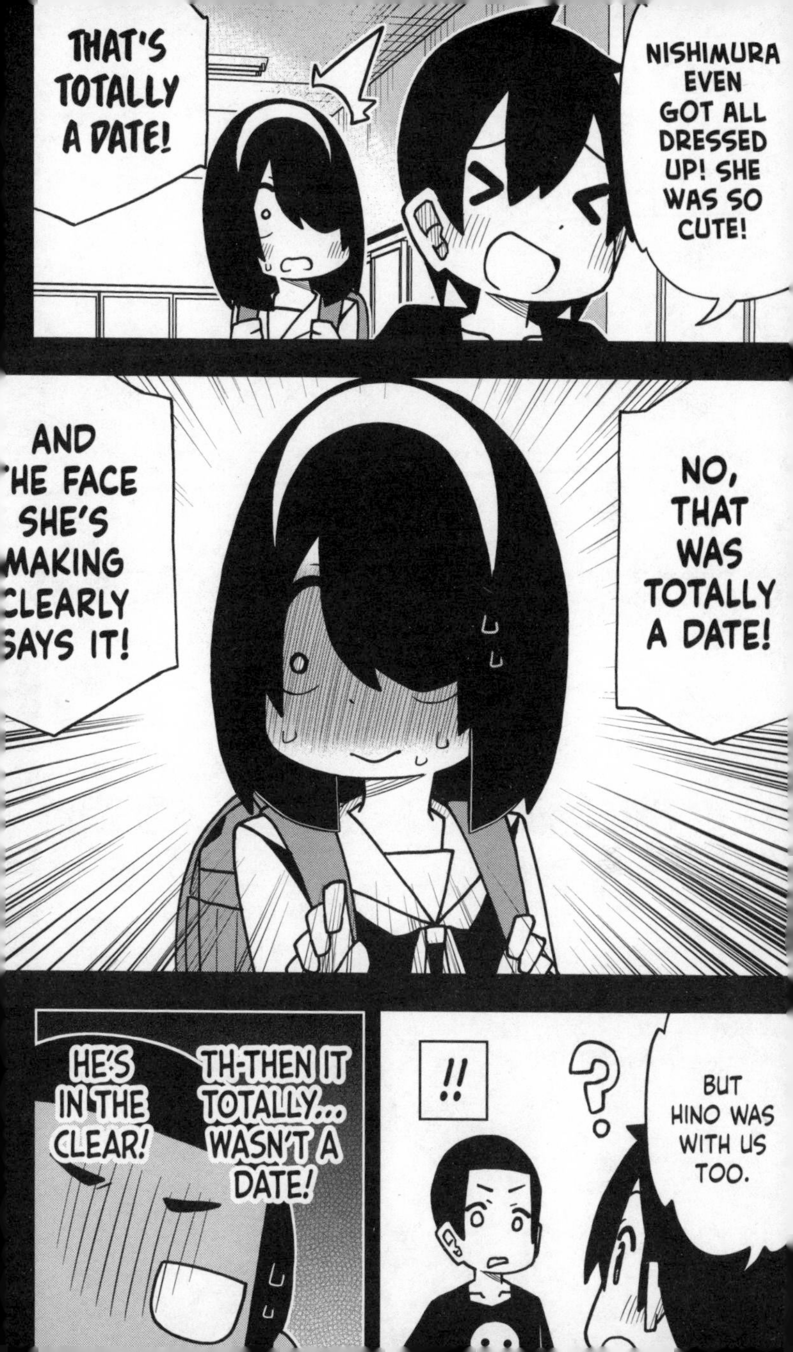
NISHIMURA EVEN GOT ALL DRESSED UP! SHE WAS SO CUTE!
THAT'S TOTALLY A DATE!
NO, THAT WAS TOTALLY A DATE!
AND THE FACE SHE'S MAKING CLEARLY SAYS IT!
BUT HINO WAS WITH US TOO.
?
!!
TH-THEN IT TOTALLY... WASN'T A DATE!
HE'S IN THE CLEAR!

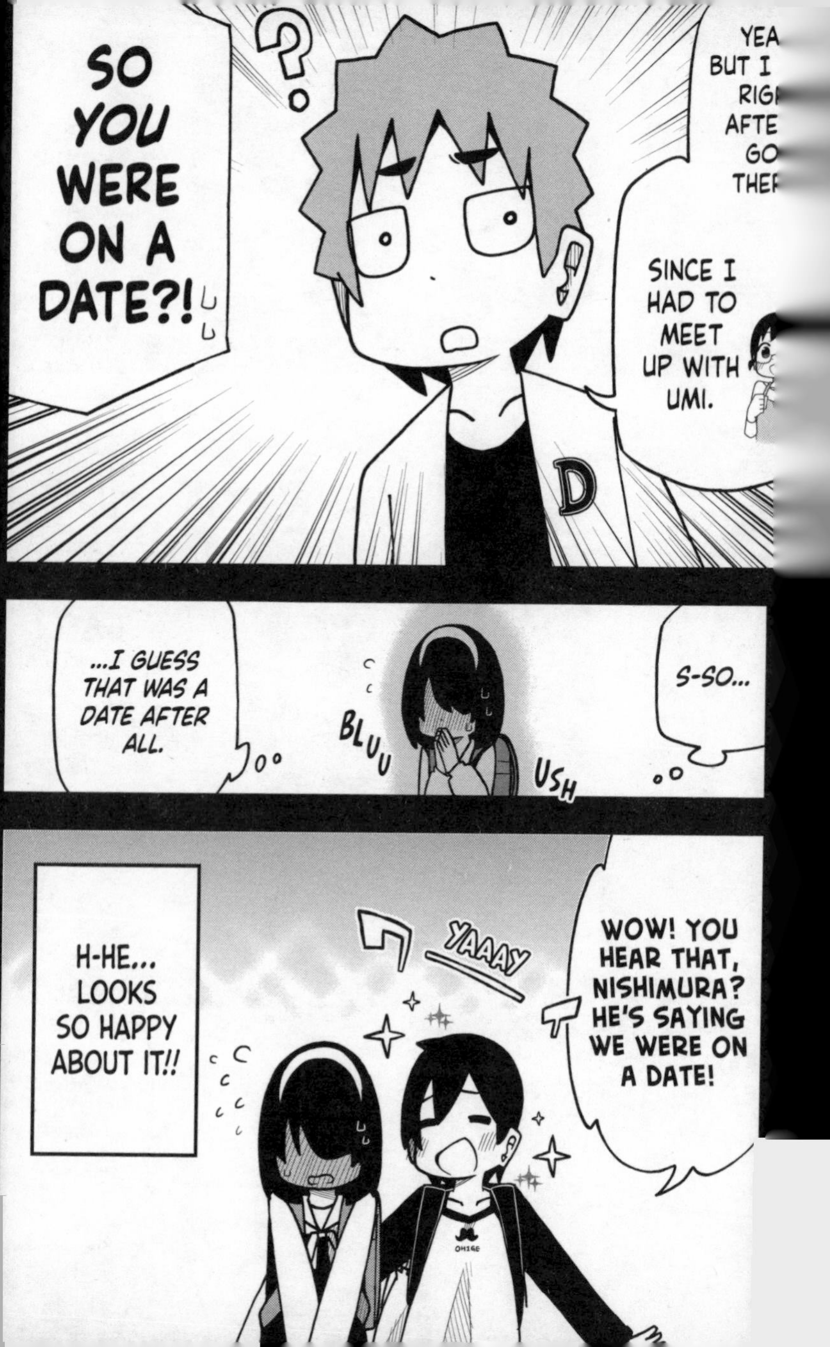
YEA BUT I RIG AFTE GO THER
SINCE I HAD TO MEET UP WITH UMI.
SO YOU WERE ON A DATE?!
S-SO...
BLUUSH
...I GUESS THAT WAS A DATE AFTER ALL.
WOW! YOU HEAR THAT, NISHIMURA? HE'S SAYING WE WERE ON A DATE!
YAAAY
H-HE... LOOKS SO HAPPY ABOUT IT!!
OHIGE

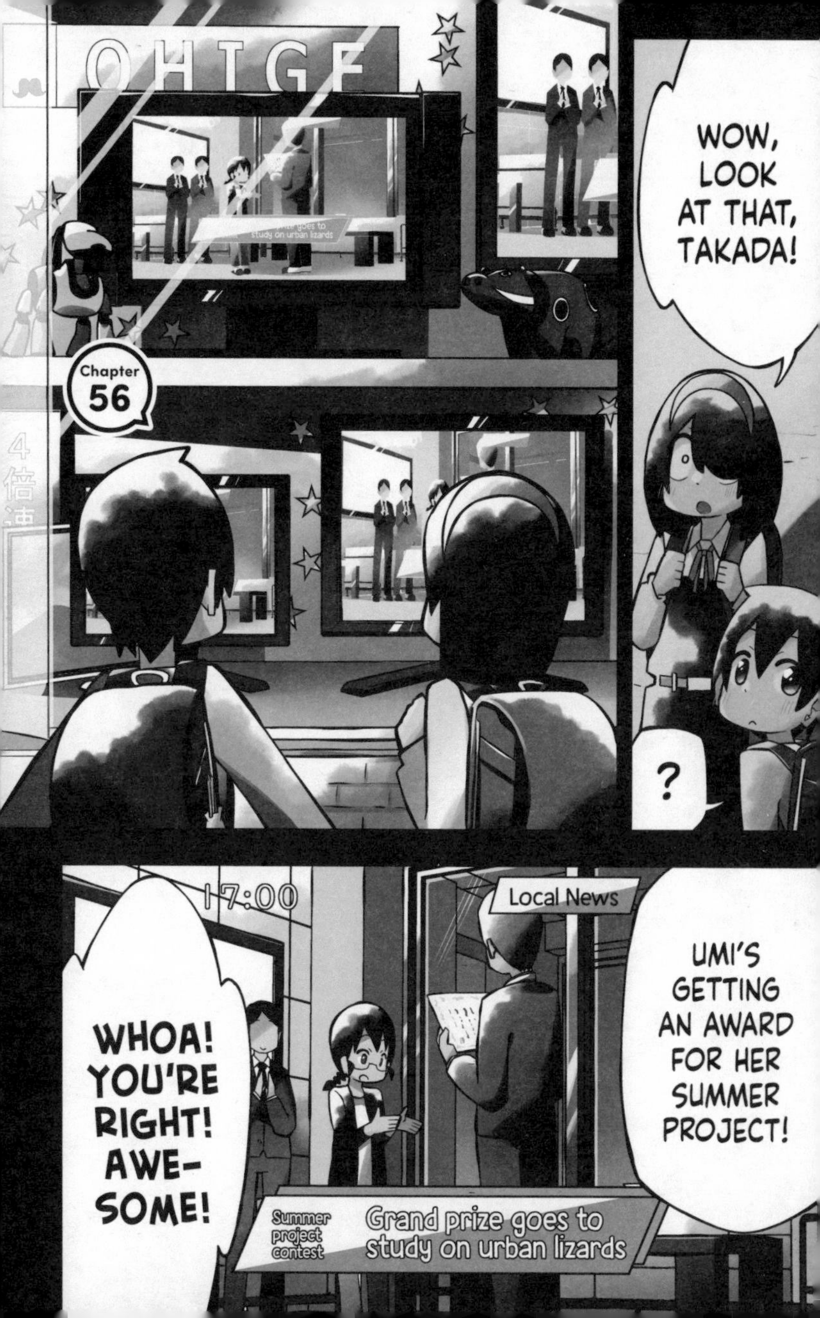
WOW, LOOK AT THAT, TAKADA!
?
OHTGE
Chapter 56
UMI'S GETTING AN AWARD FOR HER SUMMER PROJECT!
Local News
17:00
Summer project contest
Grand prize goes to study on urban lizards
WHOA! YOU'RE RIGHT! AWE-SOME!

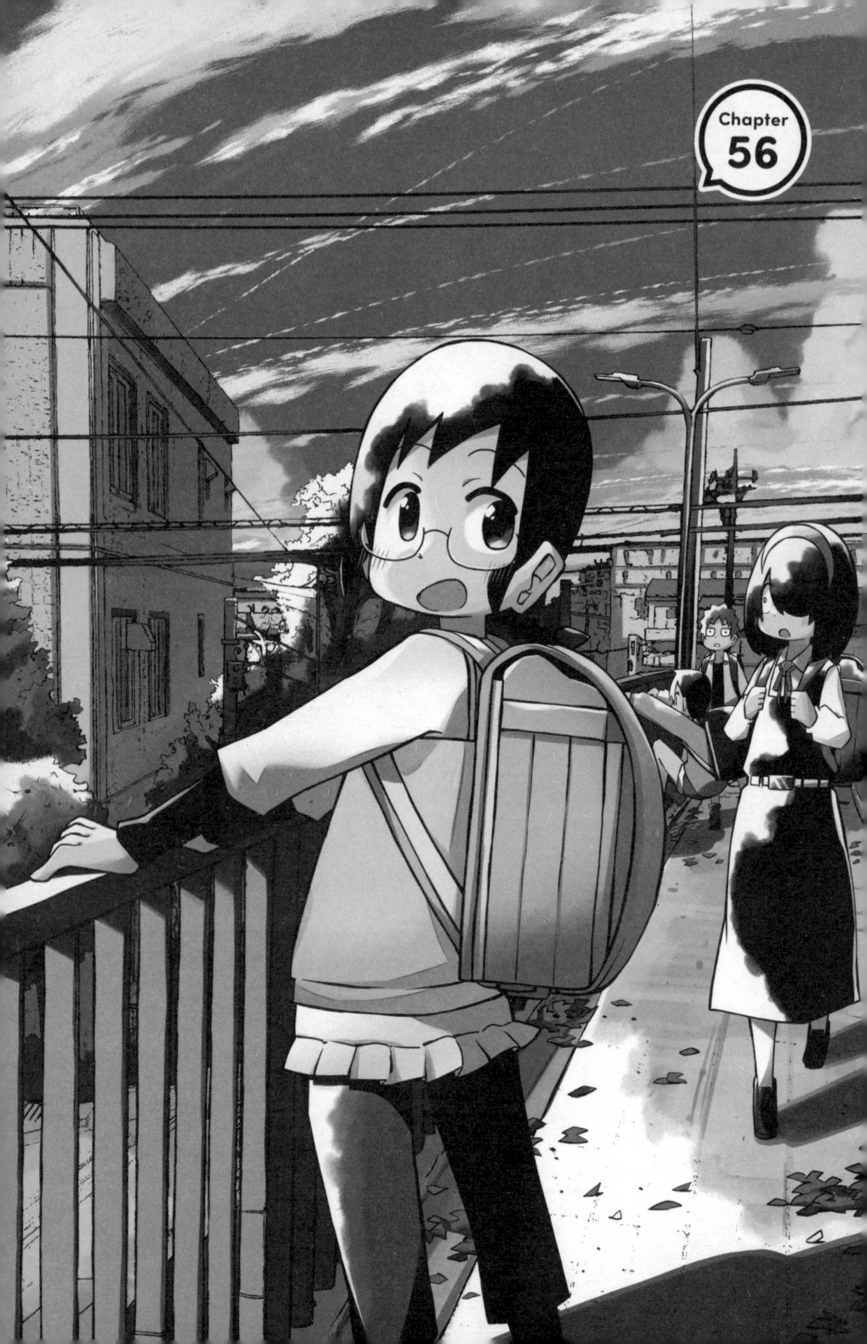
Chapter
56

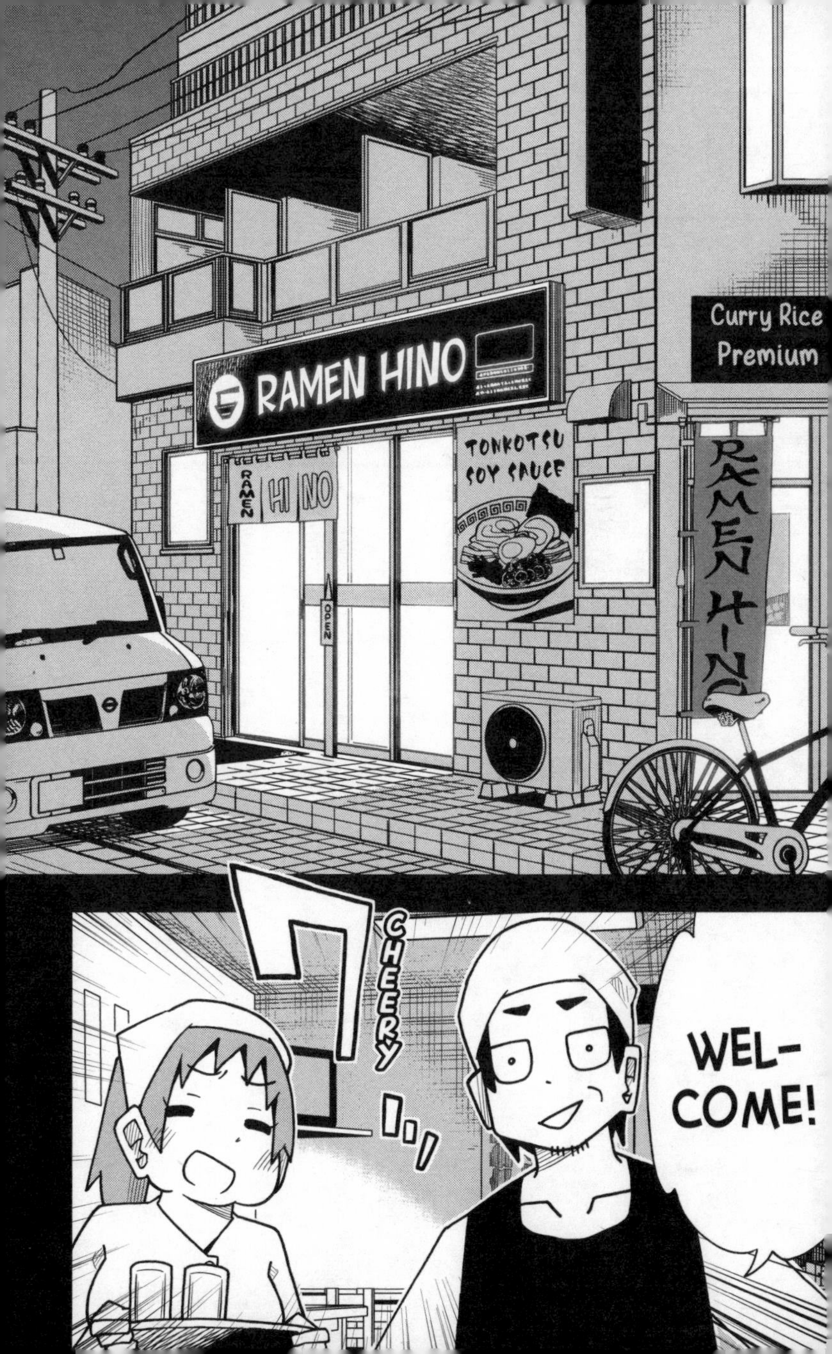
Curry Rice
Premium
RAMEN HINO
TONKOTSU
SOY SAUCE
RAMEN HINO
OPEN
RAMEN HINO
WEL-
COME!
CHEERY

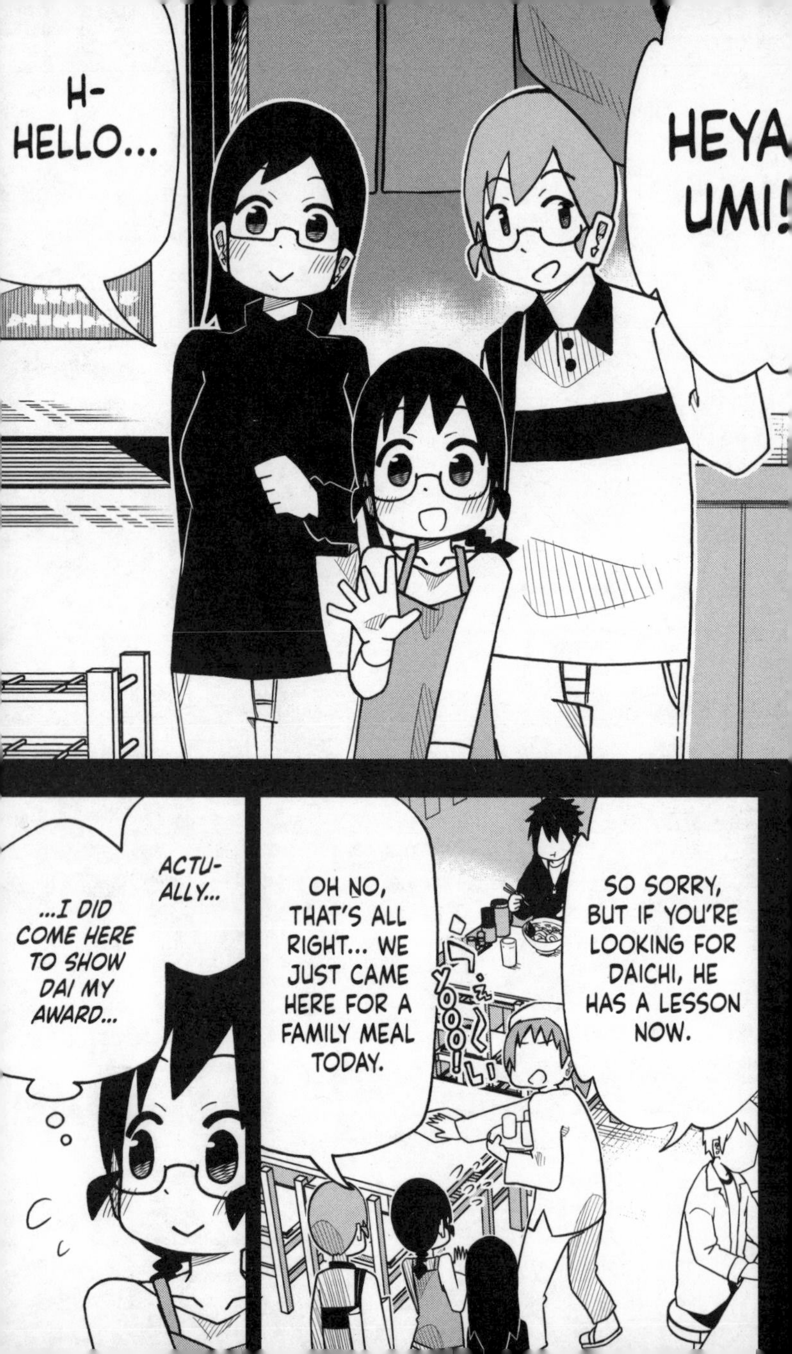
HEYA UMI!
H-HELLO...
SO SORRY, BUT IF YOU'RE LOOKING FOR DAICHI, HE HAS A LESSON NOW.
YOOOO!
OH NO, THAT'S ALL RIGHT... WE JUST CAME HERE FOR A FAMILY MEAL TODAY.
ACTU-ALLY...
...I DID COME HERE TO SHOW DAI MY AWARD...

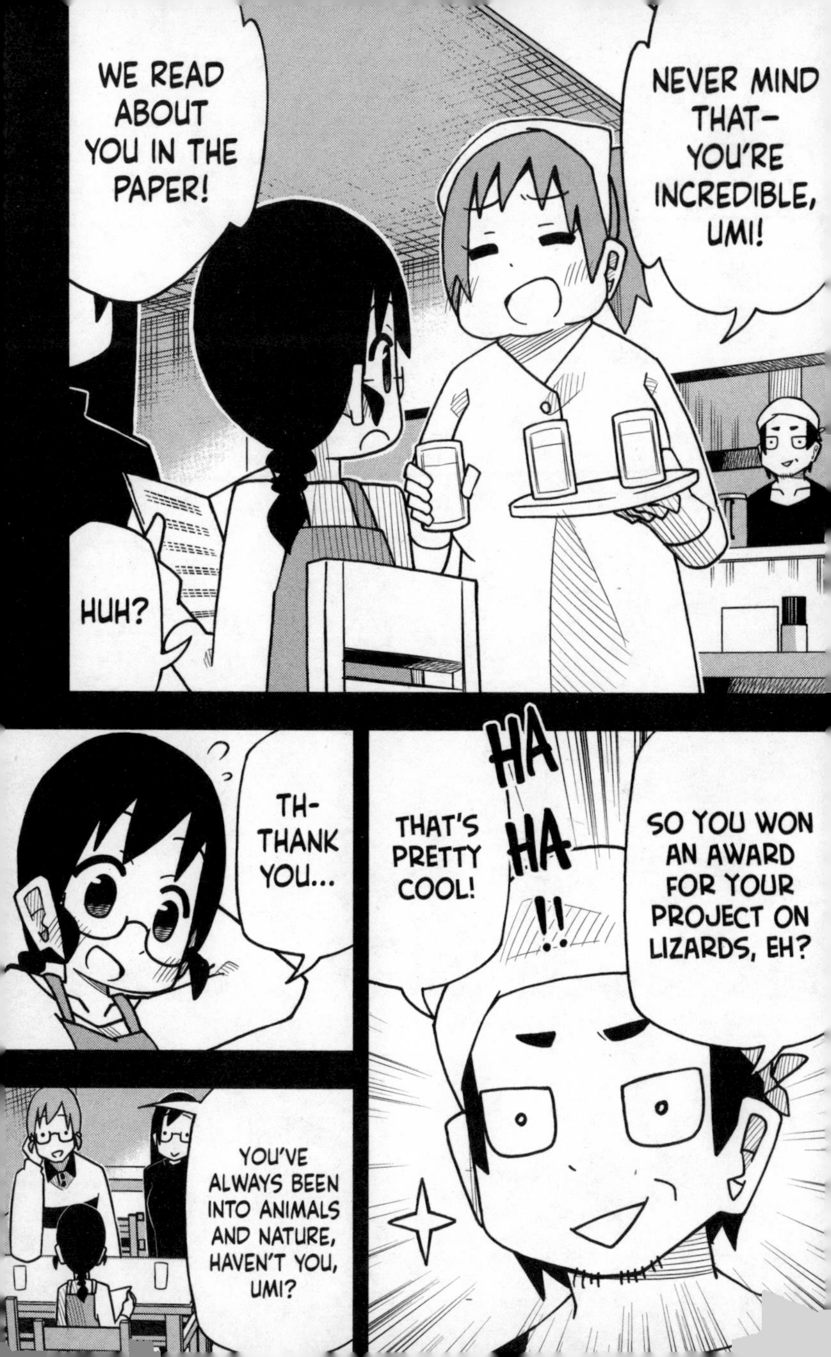
NEVER MIND THAT— YOU'RE INCREDIBLE, UMI!
WE READ ABOUT YOU IN THE PAPER!
HUH?
SO YOU WON AN AWARD FOR YOUR PROJECT ON LIZARDS, EH?
HA HA!!
THAT'S PRETTY COOL!
TH- THANK YOU...
YOU'VE ALWAYS BEEN INTO ANIMALS AND NATURE, HAVEN'T YOU, UMI?

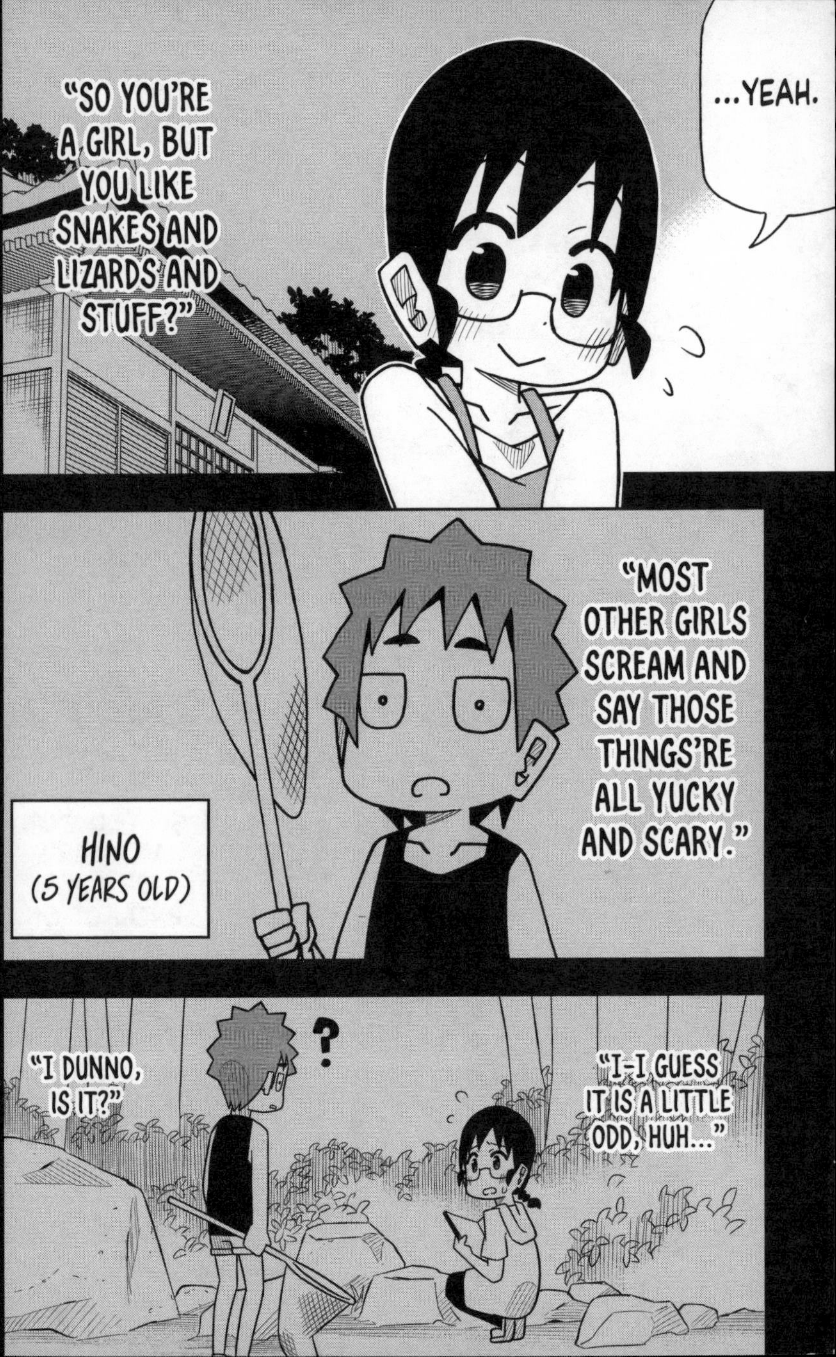
...YEAH.
"SO YOU'RE A GIRL, BUT YOU LIKE SNAKES AND LIZARDS AND STUFF?"
"MOST OTHER GIRLS SCREAM AND SAY THOSE THINGS'RE ALL YUCKY AND SCARY."
HINO (5 YEARS OLD)
"I-I GUESS IT IS A LITTLE ODD, HUH..."
?
"I DUNNO, IS IT?"

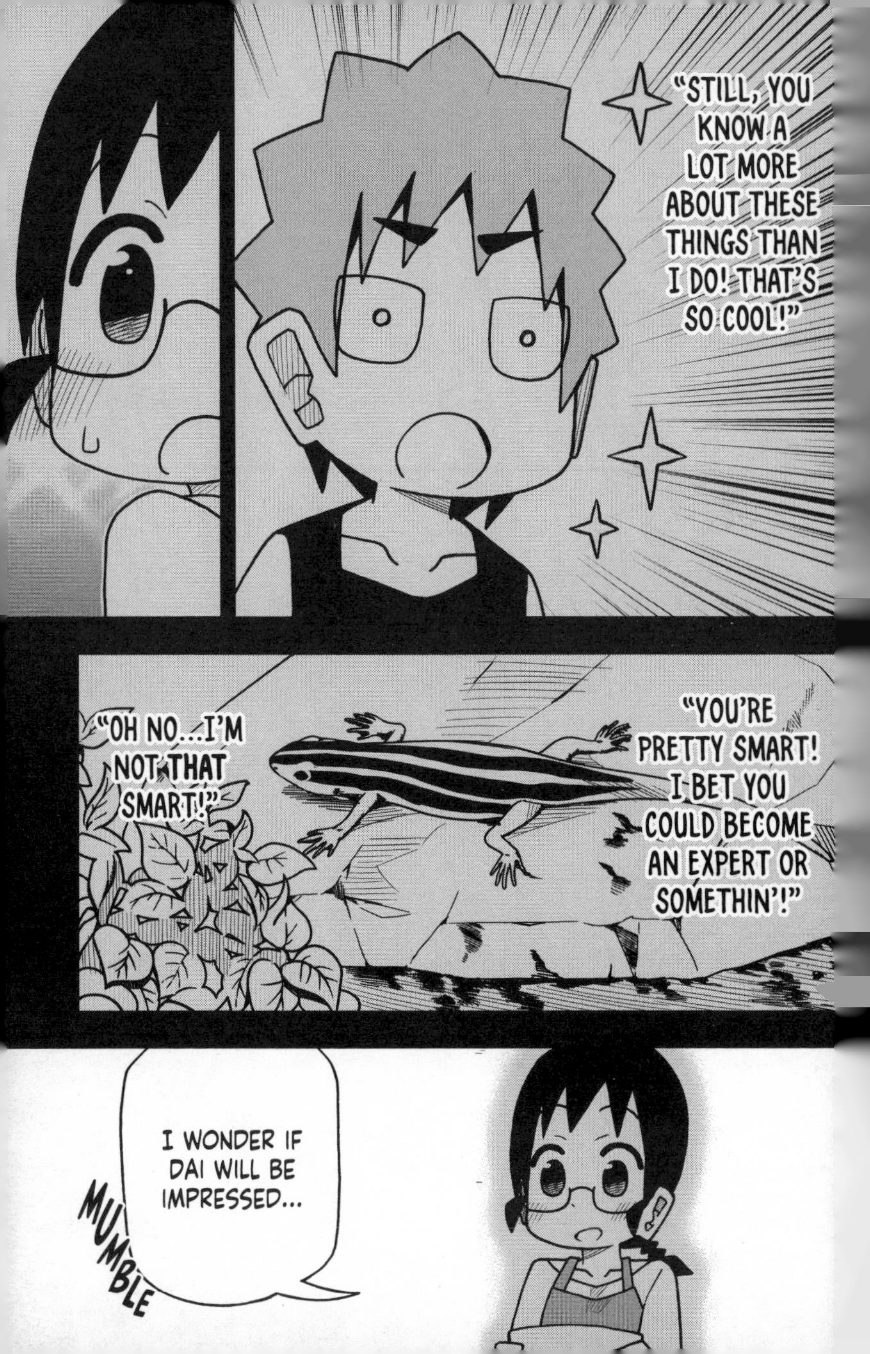
"STILL, YOU KNOW A LOT MORE ABOUT THESE THINGS THAN I DO! THAT'S SO COOL!"
"YOU'RE PRETTY SMART! I BET YOU COULD BECOME AN EXPERT OR SOMETHIN'!"
"OH NO...I'M NOT THAT SMART!"
I WONDER IF DAI WILL BE IMPRESSED...
MUMBLE

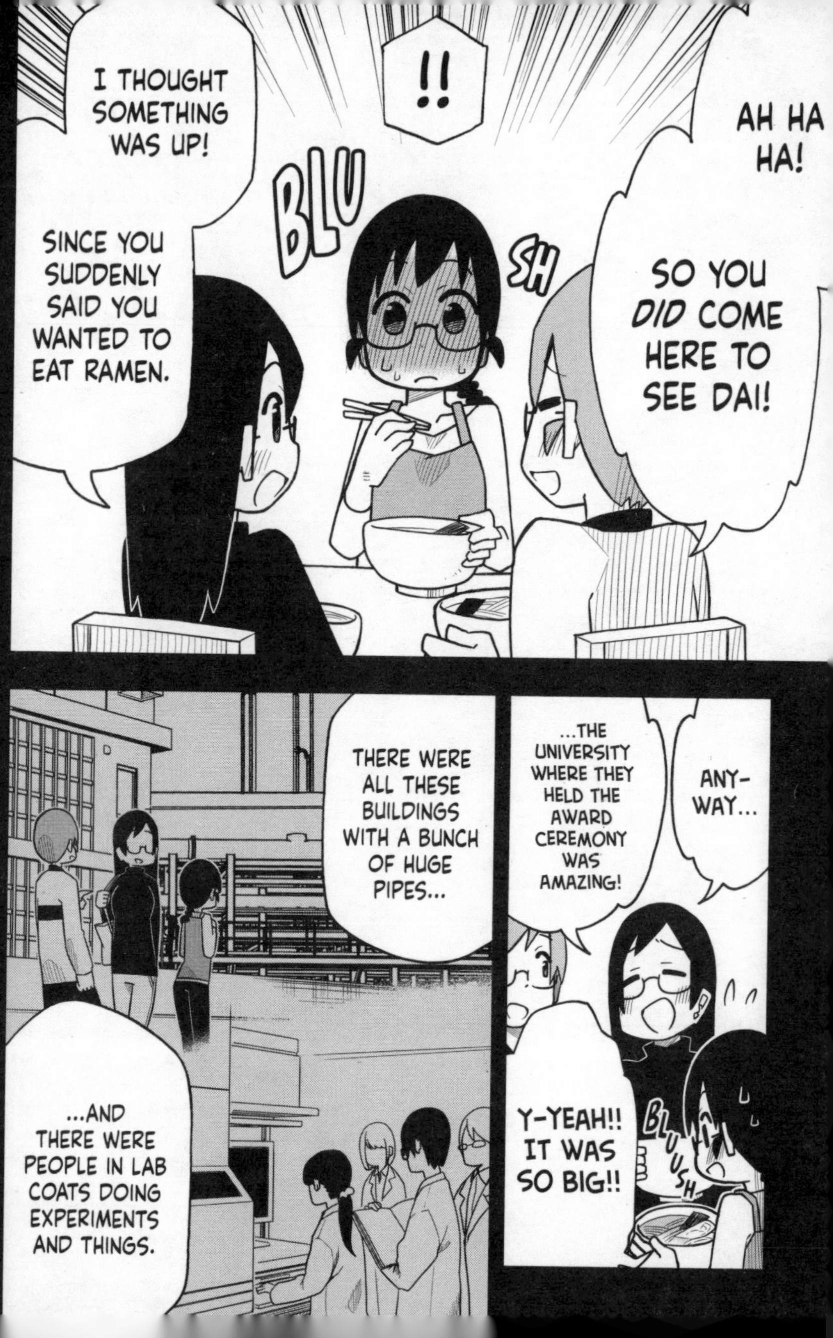
AH HA HA!
SO YOU *DID* COME HERE TO SEE DAI!
!!
BLU SH
I THOUGHT SOMETHING WAS UP!
SINCE YOU SUDDENLY SAID YOU WANTED TO EAT RAMEN.
ANY-WAY...
...THE UNIVERSITY WHERE THEY HELD THE AWARD CEREMONY WAS AMAZING!
BLUUSH
Y-YEAH!! IT WAS SO BIG!!
THERE WERE ALL THESE BUILDINGS WITH A BUNCH OF HUGE PIPES...
...AND THERE WERE PEOPLE IN LAB COATS DOING EXPERIMENTS AND THINGS.

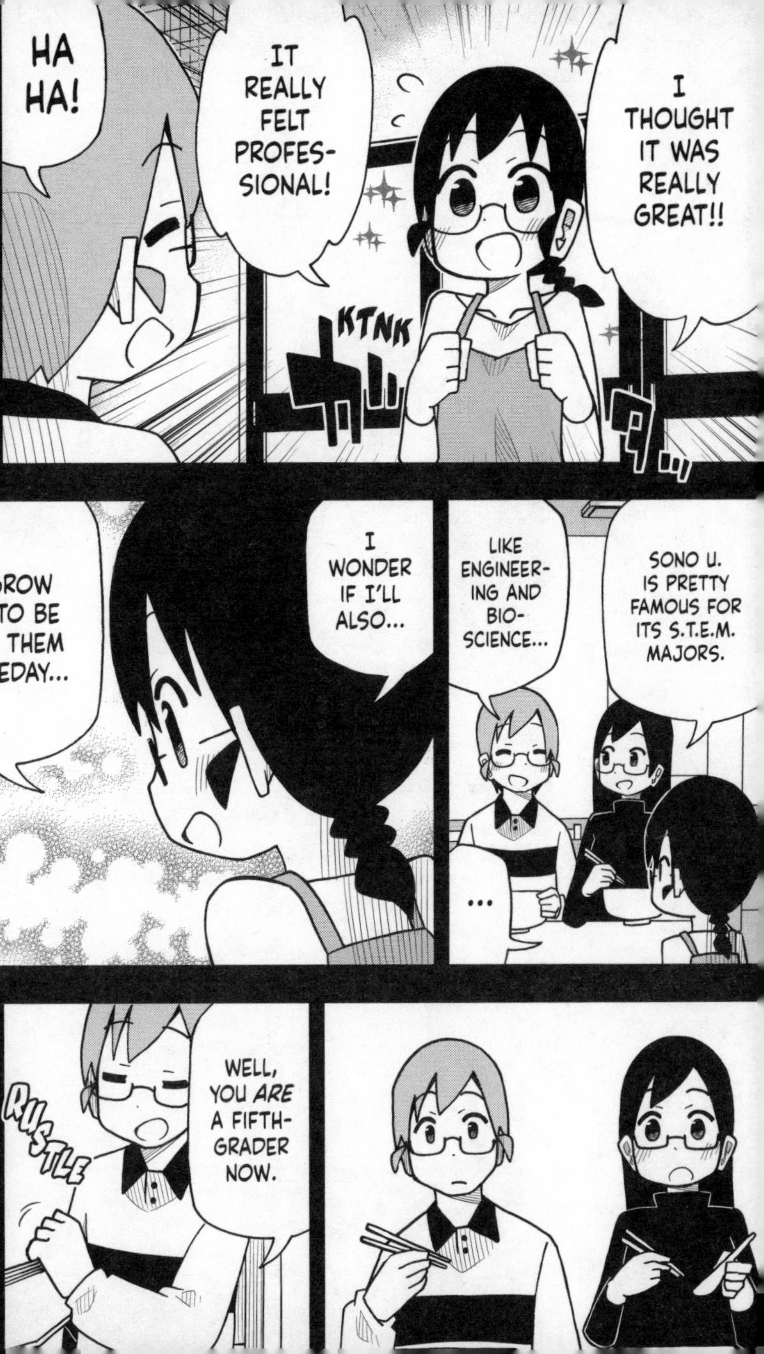

I THOUGHT IT WAS REALLY GREAT!!
IT REALLY FELT PROFES-SIONAL!
HA HA!
KTNK
SONO U. IS PRETTY FAMOUS FOR ITS S.T.E.M. MAJORS.
LIKE ENGINEER-ING AND BIO-SCIENCE...
...
I WONDER IF I'LL ALSO...
...GROW UP TO BE LIKE THEM SOMEDAY...
WELL, YOU *ARE* A FIFTH-GRADER NOW.
RUSTLE

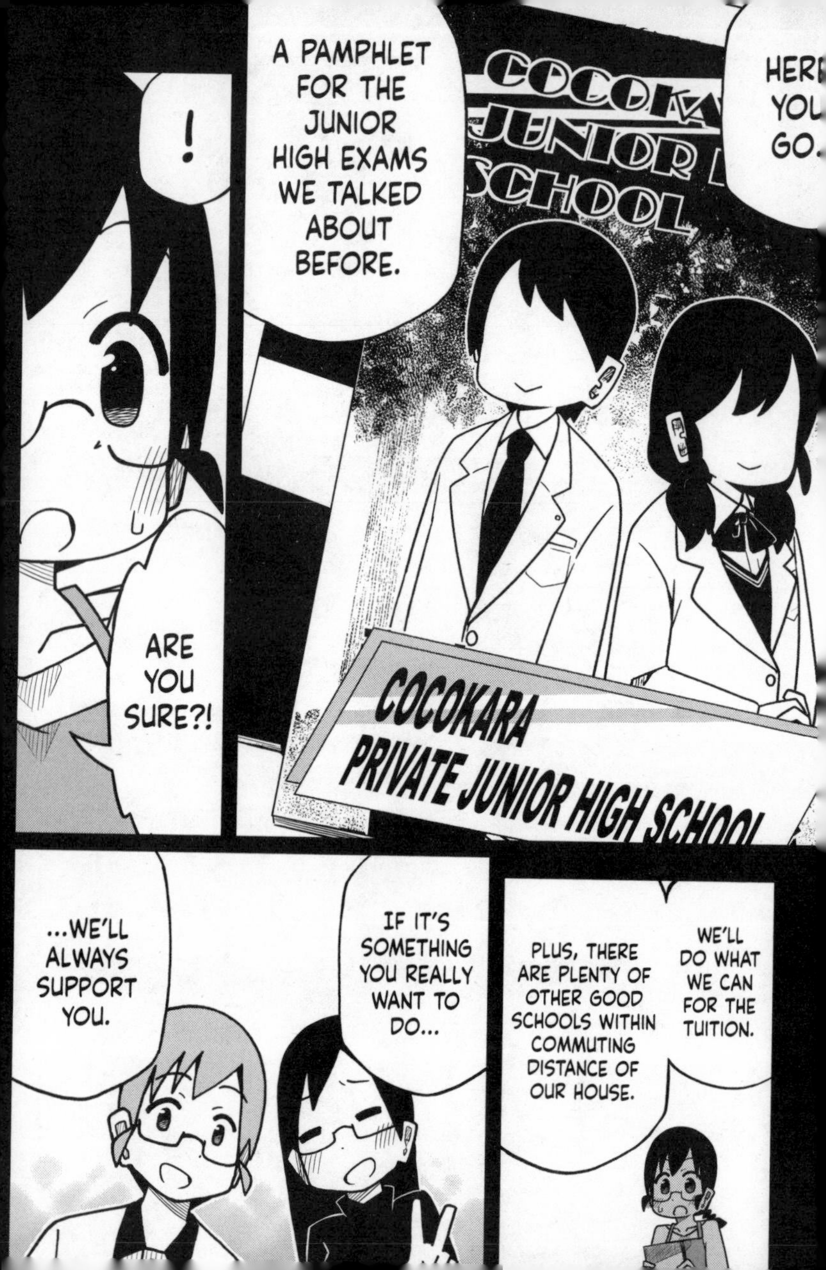
HERE YOU GO.
A PAMPHLET FOR THE JUNIOR HIGH EXAMS WE TALKED ABOUT BEFORE.
COCOKARA PRIVATE JUNIOR HIGH SCHOOL
!
ARE YOU SURE?!
WE'LL DO WHAT WE CAN FOR THE TUITION.
PLUS, THERE ARE PLENTY OF OTHER GOOD SCHOOLS WITHIN COMMUTING DISTANCE OF OUR HOUSE.
IF IT'S SOMETHING YOU REALLY WANT TO DO...
...WE'LL ALWAYS SUPPORT YOU.

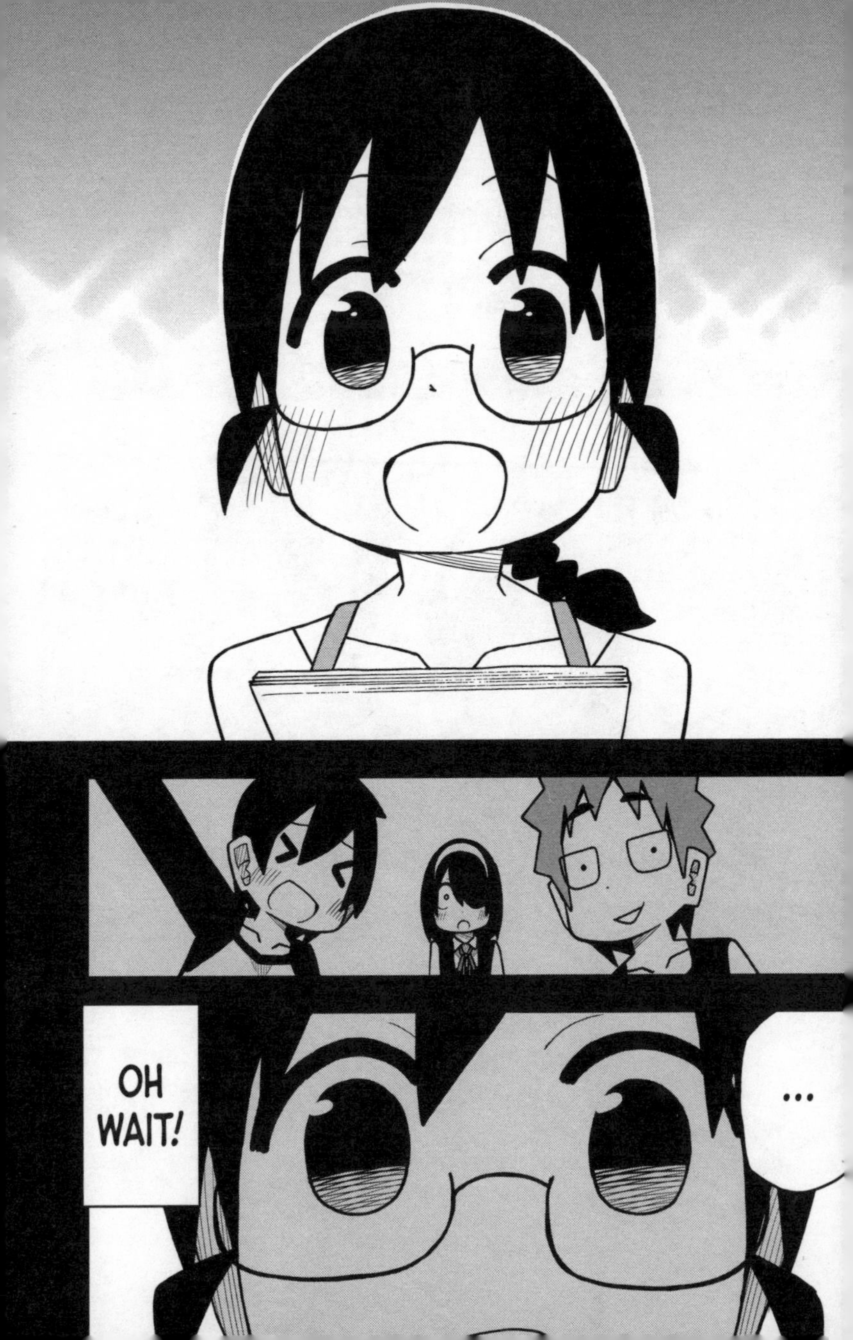
...
OH WAIT!

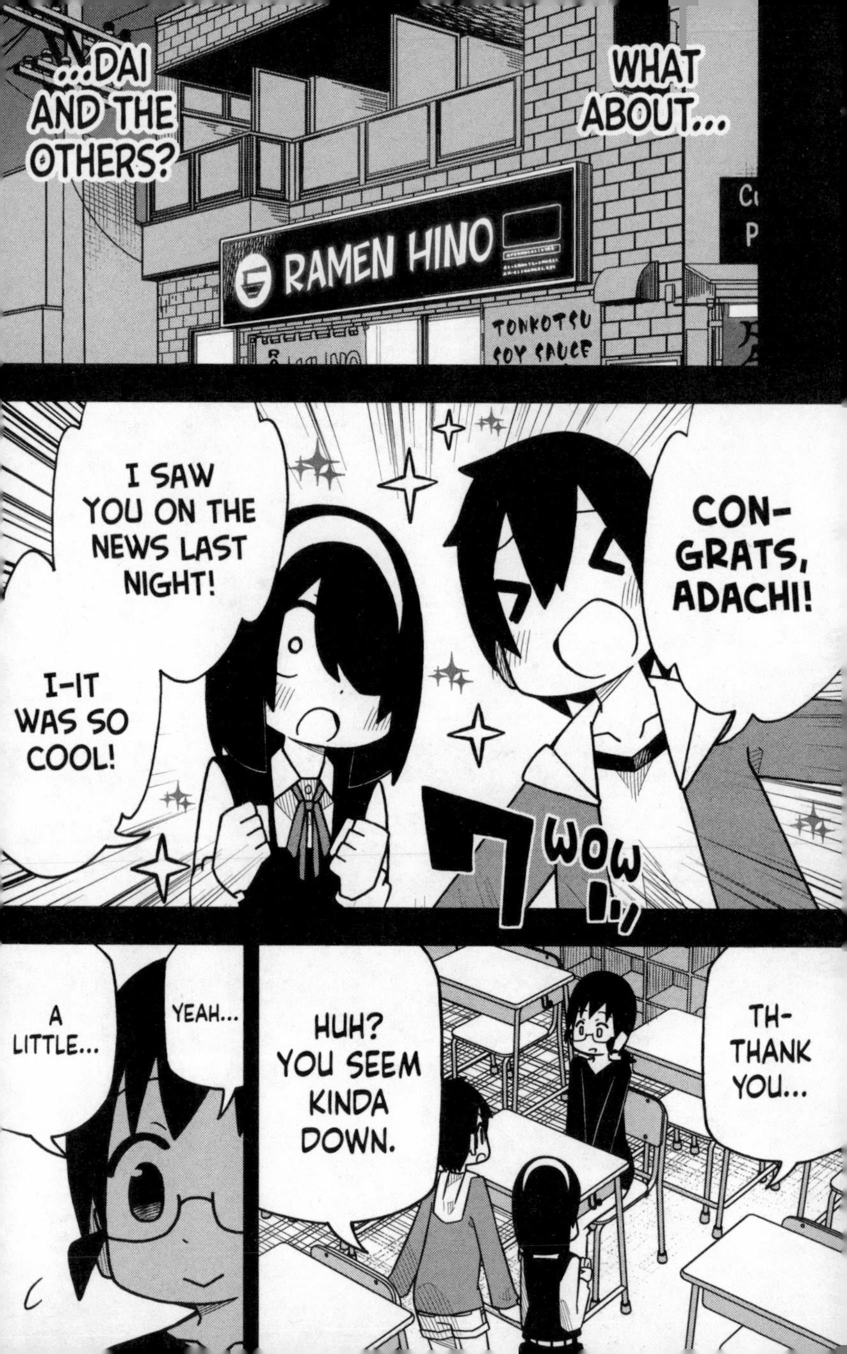
WHAT ABOUT...
...DAI AND THE OTHERS?
RAMEN HINO
TONKOTSU SOY SAUCE
CON-GRATS, ADACHI!
I SAW YOU ON THE NEWS LAST NIGHT!
I-IT WAS SO COOL!
WOW
TH-THANK YOU...
HUH? YOU SEEM KINDA DOWN.
YEAH...
A LITTLE...

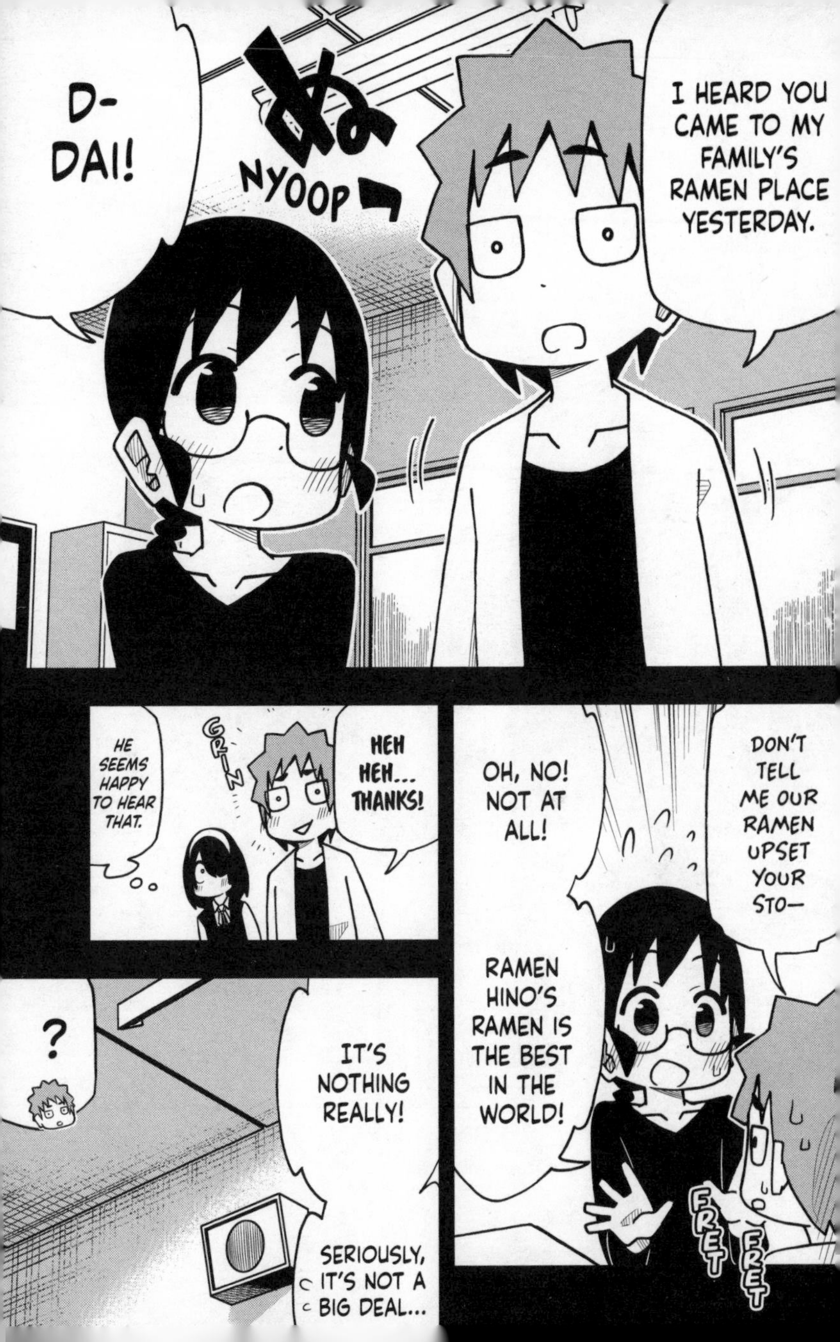
I HEARD YOU CAME TO MY FAMILY'S RAMEN PLACE YESTERDAY.
NYOOP
D-DAI!
DON'T TELL ME OUR RAMEN UPSET YOUR STO—
OH, NO! NOT AT ALL!
RAMEN HINO'S RAMEN IS THE BEST IN THE WORLD!
FRET FRET
HEH HEH... THANKS!
GRIN
HE SEEMS HAPPY TO HEAR THAT.
IT'S NOTHING REALLY!
SERIOUSLY, IT'S NOT A BIG DEAL...
?

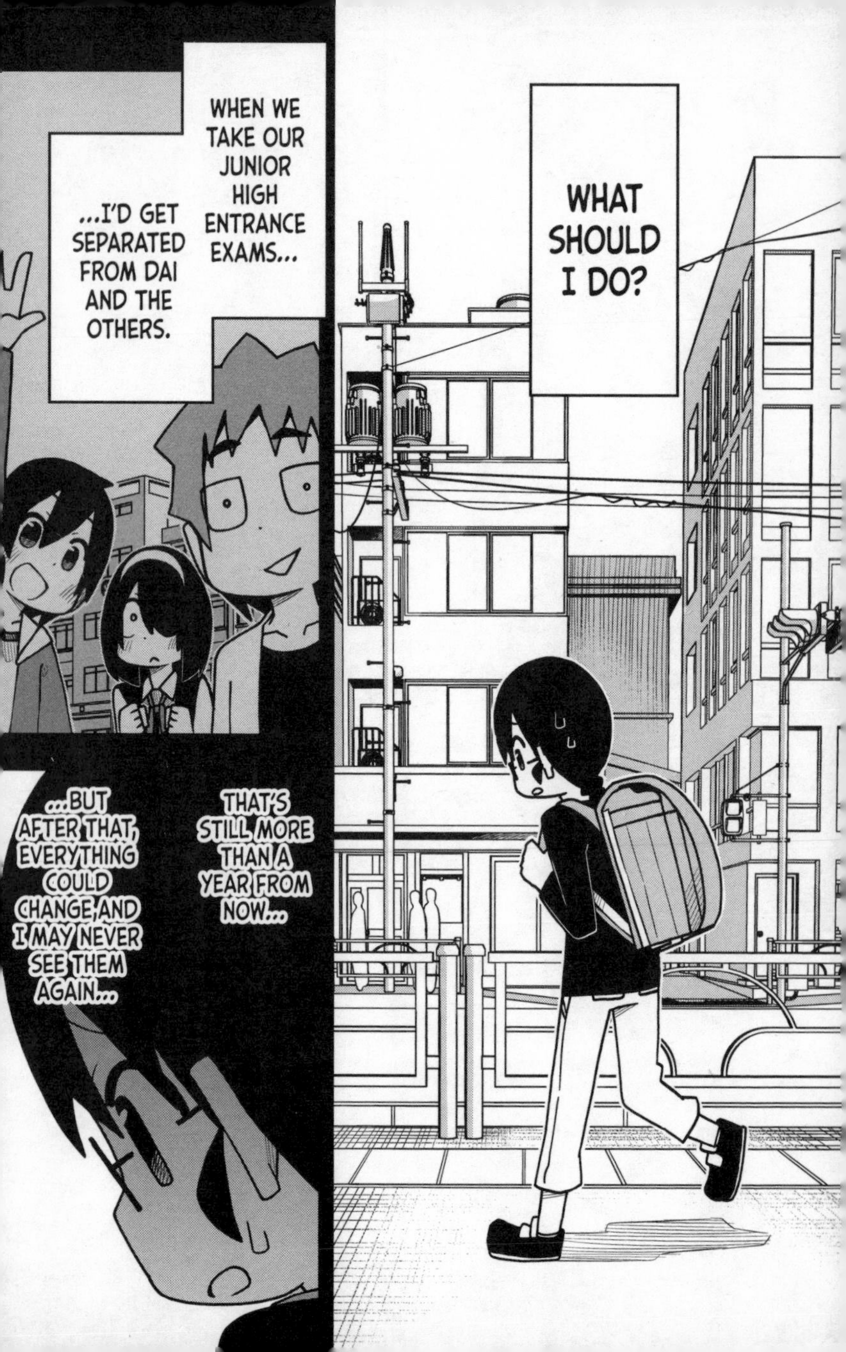
WHAT SHOULD I DO?
WHEN WE TAKE OUR JUNIOR HIGH ENTRANCE EXAMS...
...I'D GET SEPARATED FROM DAI AND THE OTHERS.
THAT'S STILL MORE THAN A YEAR FROM NOW...
...BUT AFTER THAT, EVERYTHING COULD CHANGE, AND I MAY NEVER SEE THEM AGAIN...

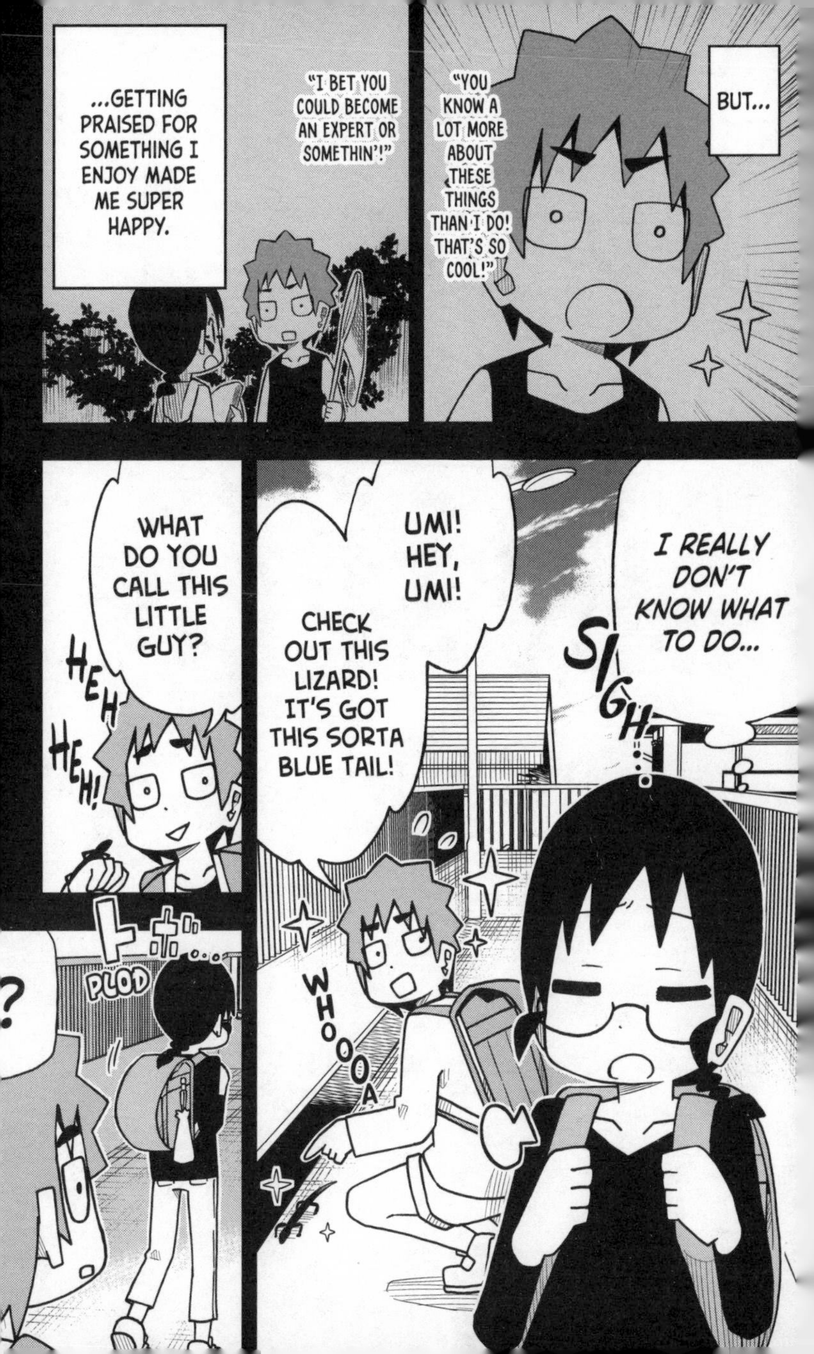
BUT...
"YOU KNOW A LOT MORE ABOUT THESE THINGS THAN I DO! THAT'S SO COOL!"
"I BET YOU COULD BECOME AN EXPERT OR SOMETHIN'!"
...GETTING PRAISED FOR SOMETHING I ENJOY MADE ME SUPER HAPPY.
I REALLY DON'T KNOW WHAT TO DO...
SIGH...
UMI! HEY, UMI!
CHECK OUT THIS LIZARD! IT'S GOT THIS SORTA BLUE TAIL!
WHOOOOA
WHAT DO YOU CALL THIS LITTLE GUY?
HEH HEH HEH!
PLOD
?

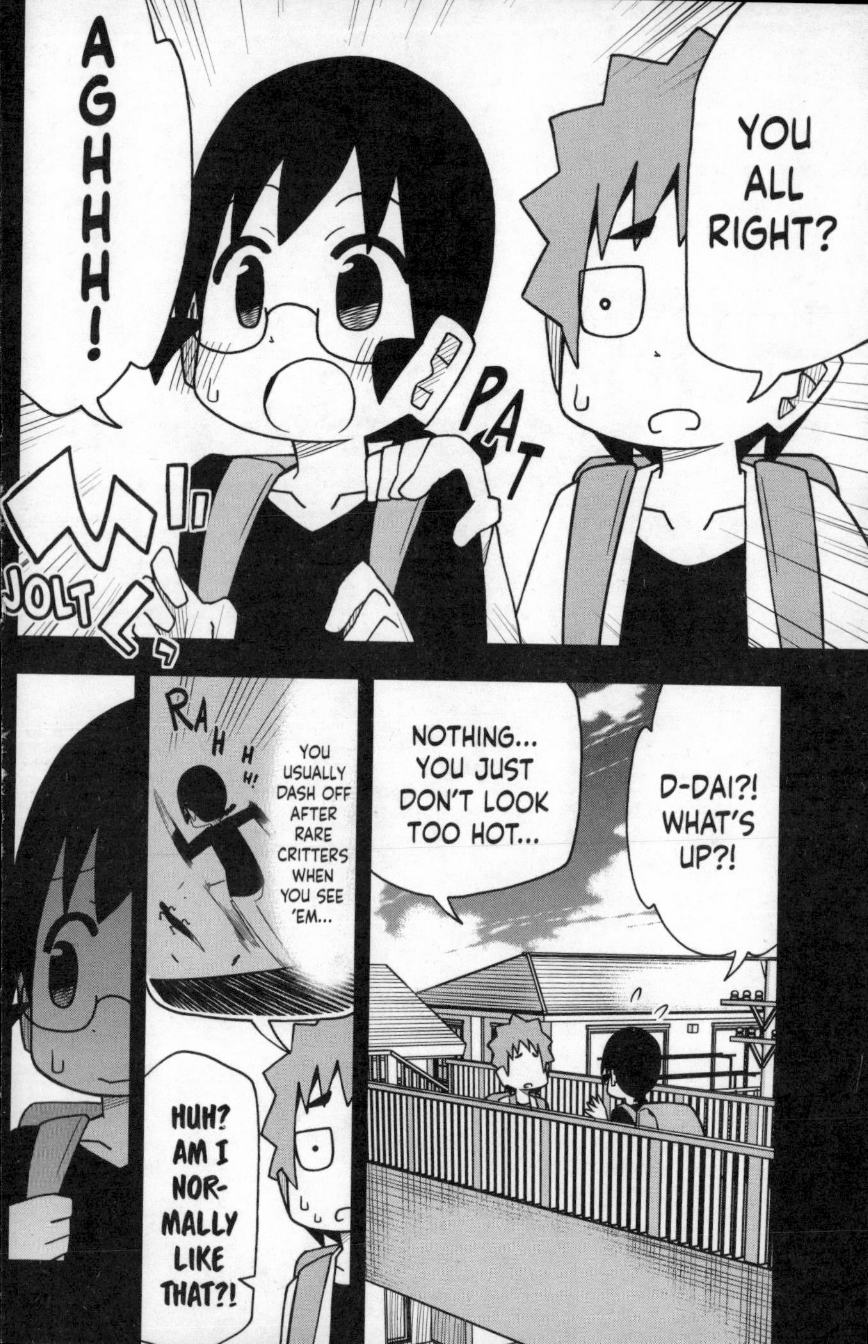
YOU ALL RIGHT?
PAT
AGHHH!
JOLT
D-DAI?! WHAT'S UP?!
NOTHING... YOU JUST DON'T LOOK TOO HOT...
YOU USUALLY DASH OFF AFTER RARE CRITTERS WHEN YOU SEE 'EM...
RAHHH!
HUH? AM I NOR-MALLY LIKE THAT?!

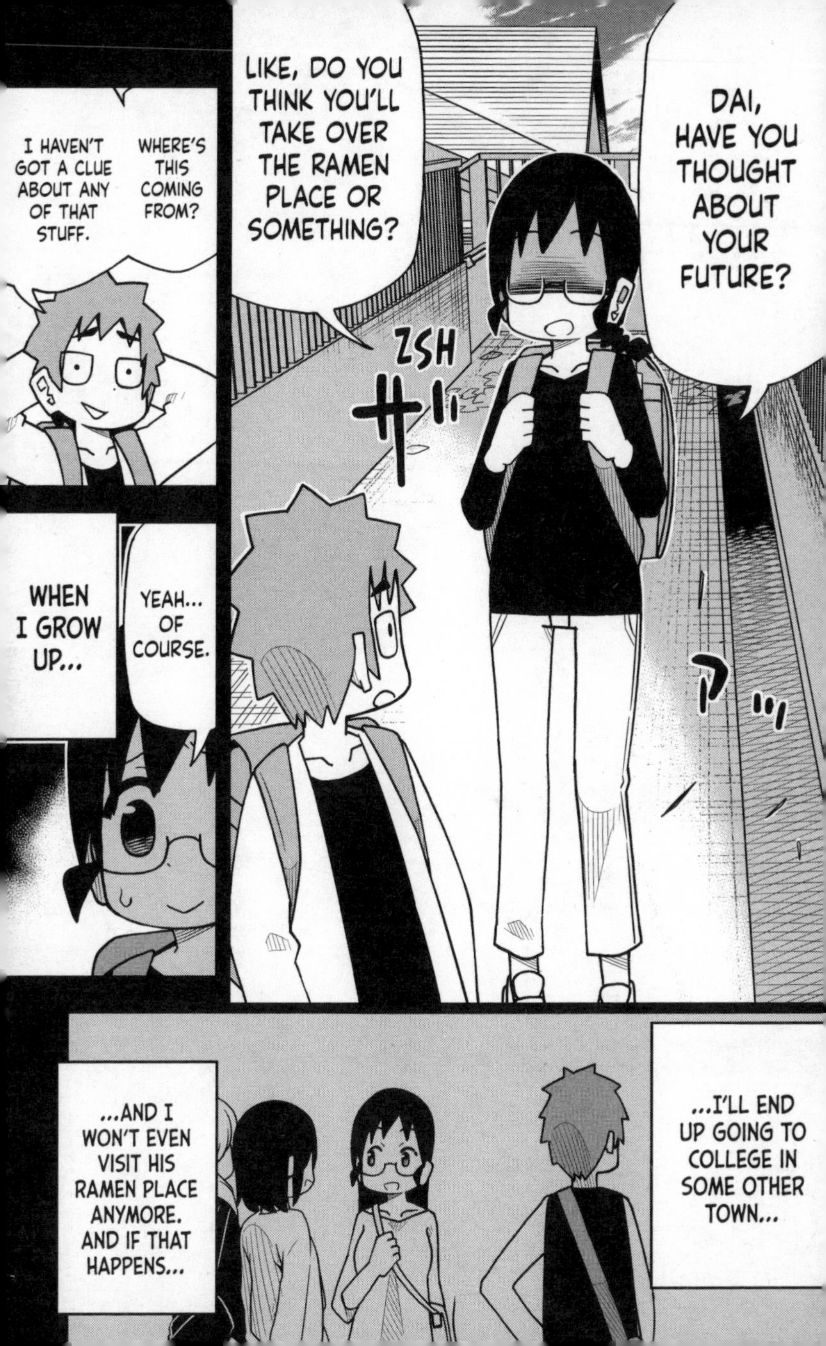
DAI, HAVE YOU THOUGHT ABOUT YOUR FUTURE?
LIKE, DO YOU THINK YOU'LL TAKE OVER THE RAMEN PLACE OR SOMETHING?
ZSH
WHERE'S THIS COMING FROM?
I HAVEN'T GOT A CLUE ABOUT ANY OF THAT STUFF.
YEAH... OF COURSE.
WHEN I GROW UP...
...I'LL END UP GOING TO COLLEGE IN SOME OTHER TOWN...
...AND I WON'T EVEN VISIT HIS RAMEN PLACE ANYMORE. AND IF THAT HAPPENS...

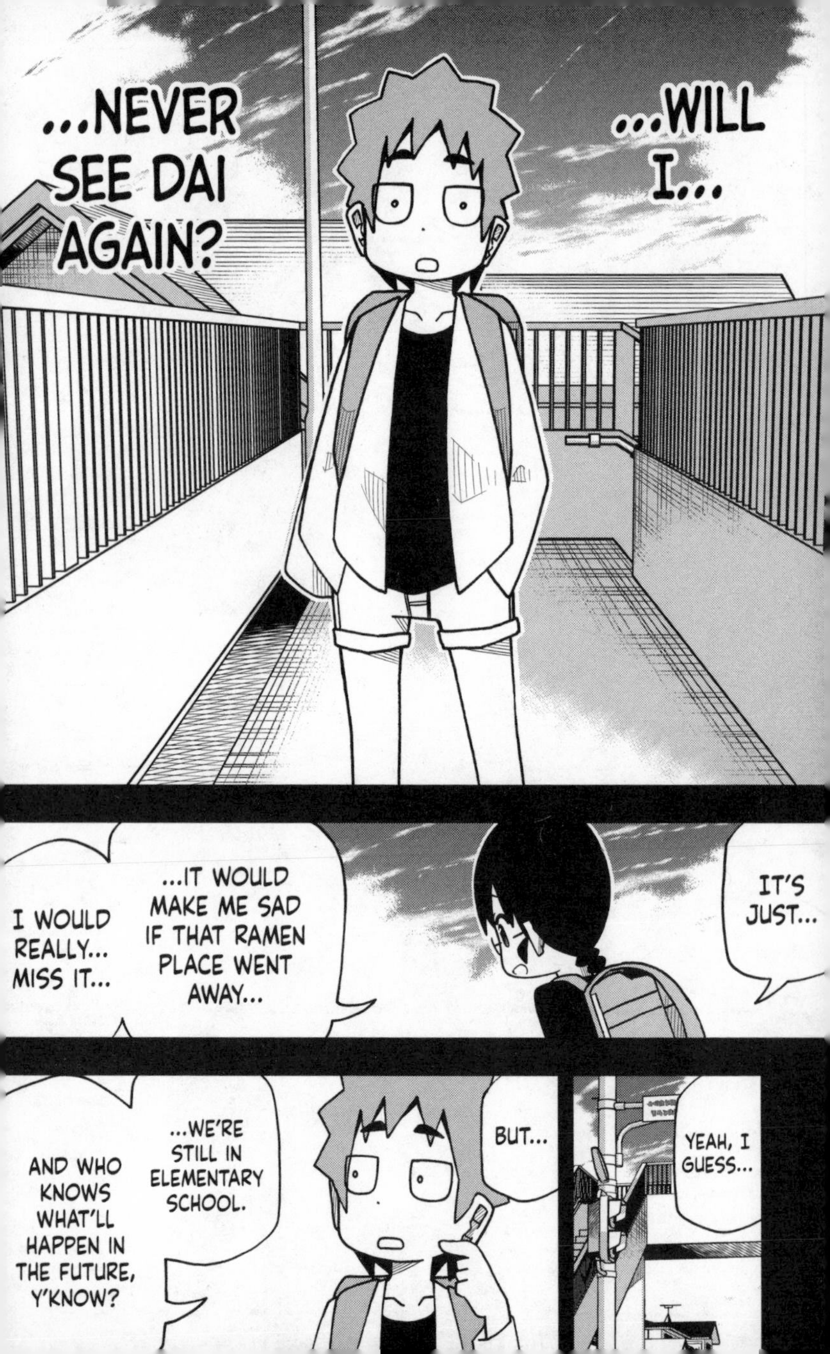
...WILL I...
...NEVER SEE DAI AGAIN?
IT'S JUST...
...IT WOULD MAKE ME SAD IF THAT RAMEN PLACE WENT AWAY...
I WOULD REALLY... MISS IT...
YEAH, I GUESS...
BUT...
...WE'RE STILL IN ELEMENTARY SCHOOL.
AND WHO KNOWS WHAT'LL HAPPEN IN THE FUTURE, Y'KNOW?

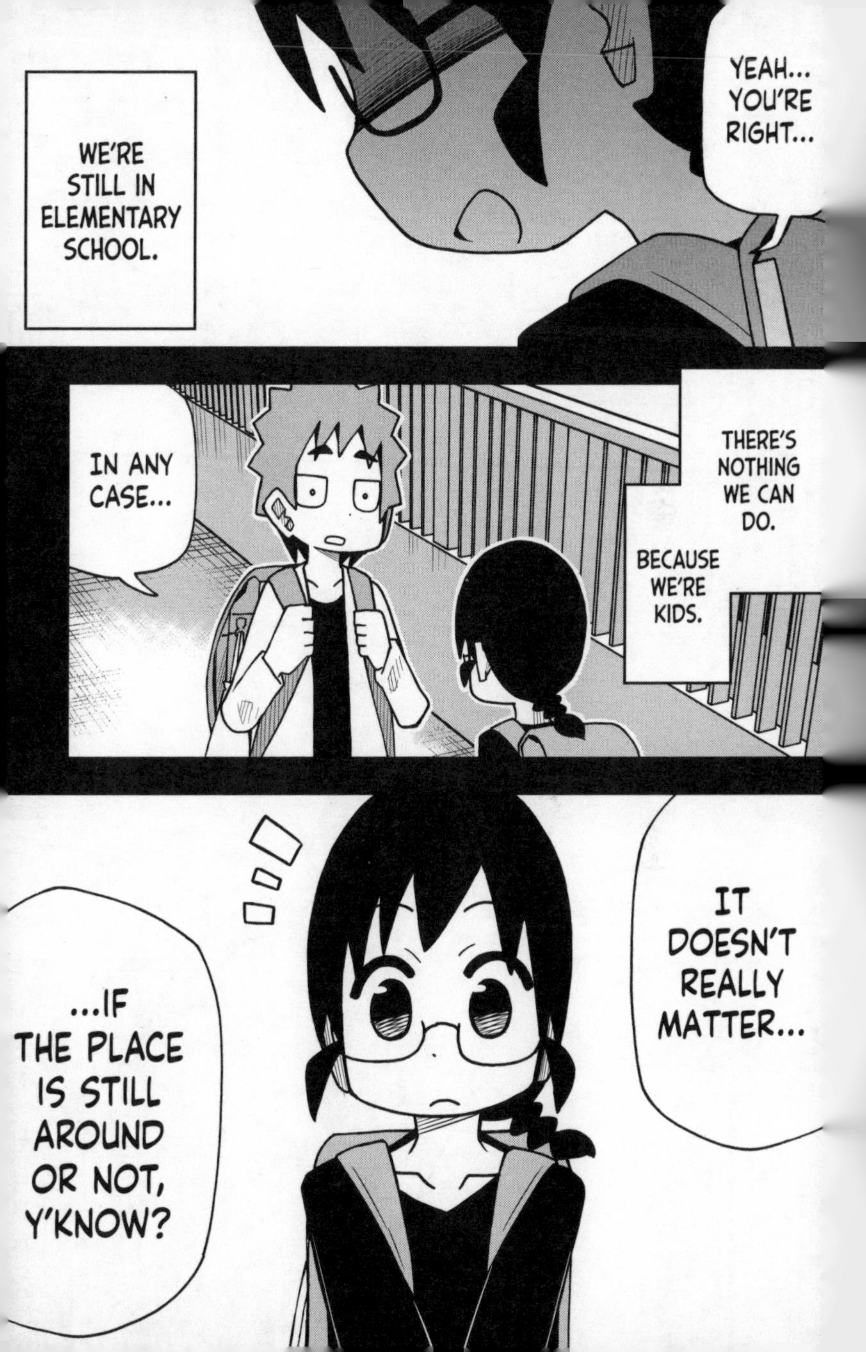
YEAH... YOU'RE RIGHT...
WE'RE STILL IN ELEMENTARY SCHOOL.
THERE'S NOTHING WE CAN DO.
BECAUSE WE'RE KIDS.
IN ANY CASE...
IT DOESN'T REALLY MATTER...
...IF THE PLACE IS STILL AROUND OR NOT, Y'KNOW?

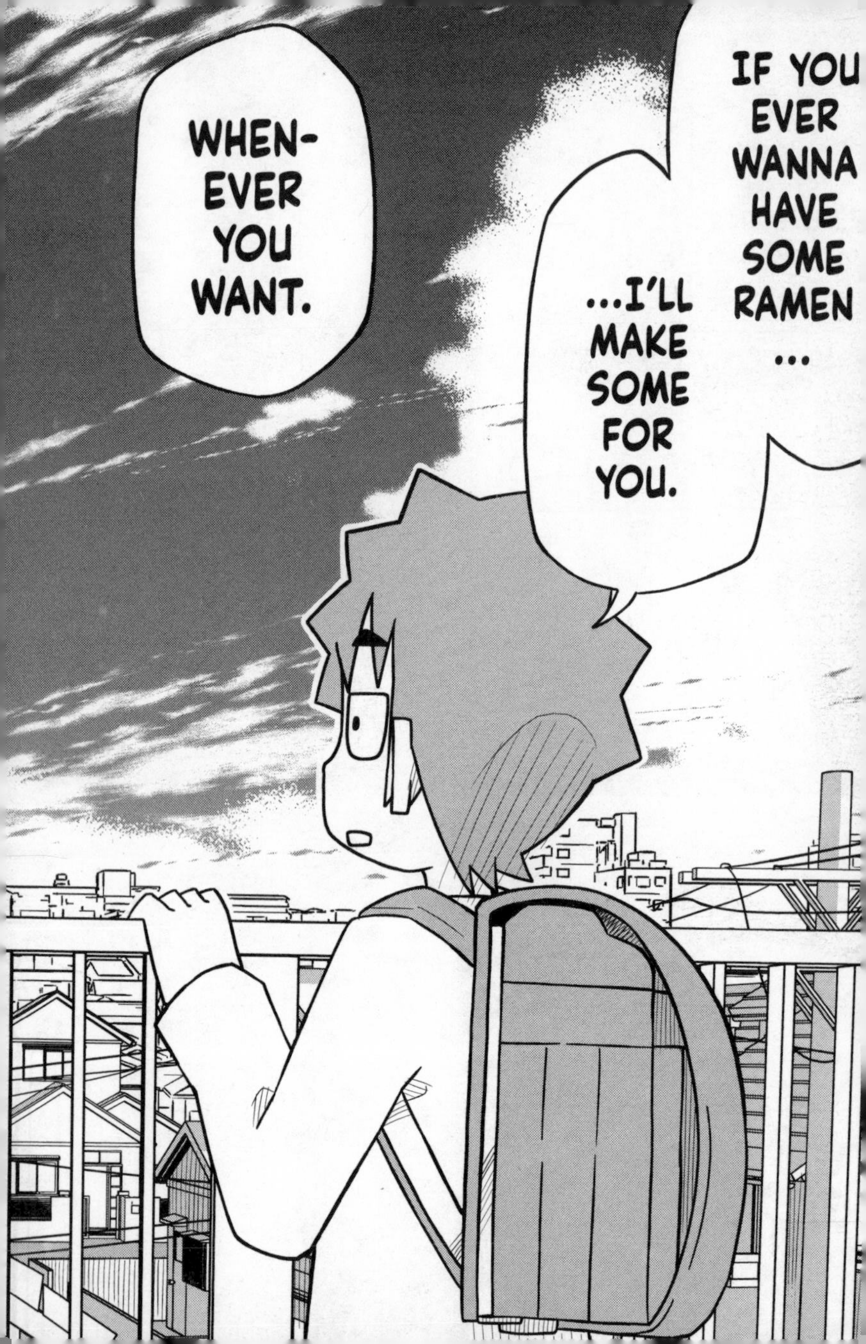
IF YOU EVER WANNA HAVE SOME RAMEN ...
...I'LL MAKE SOME FOR YOU.
WHEN-EVER YOU WANT.

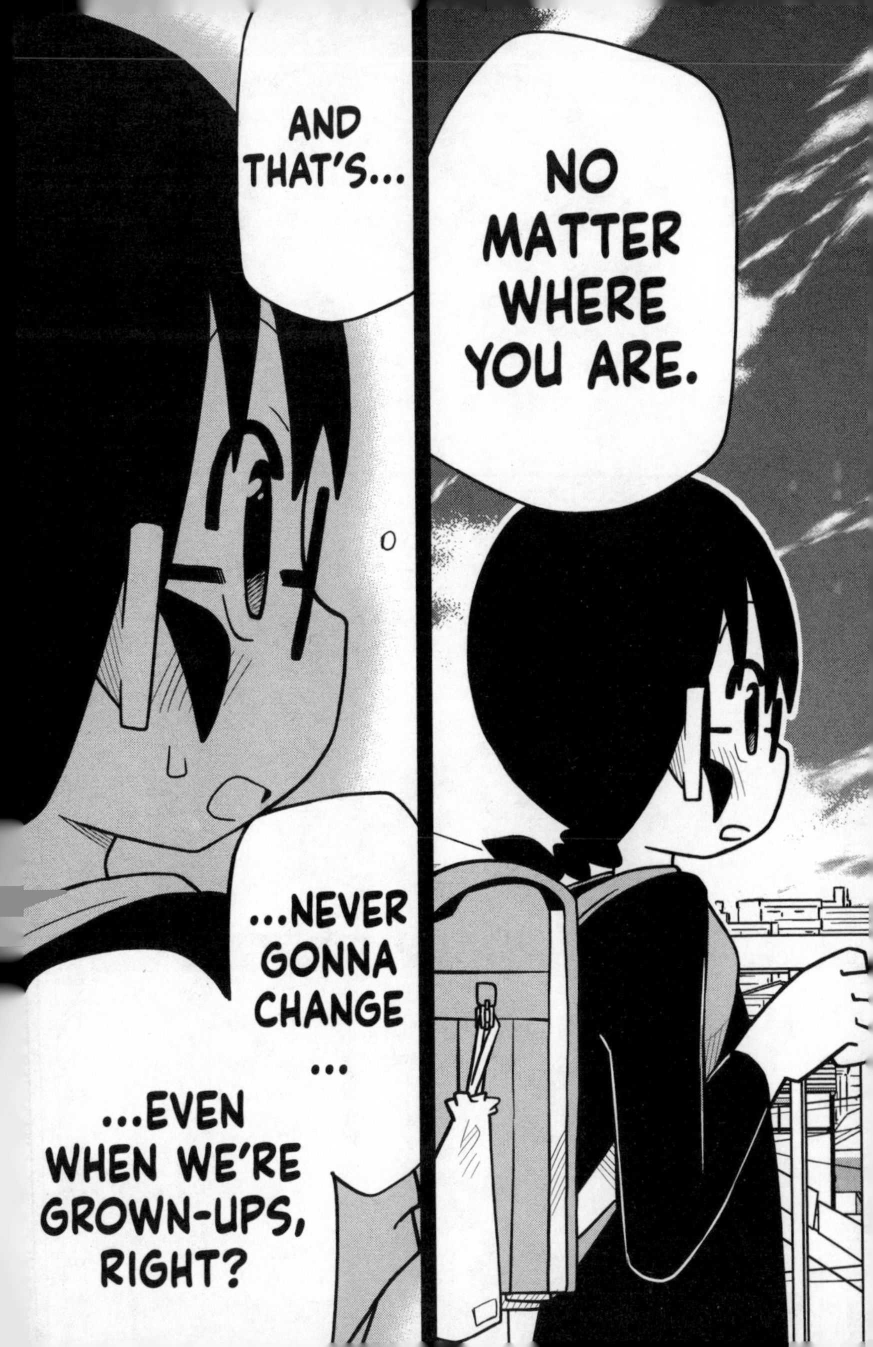
NO MATTER WHERE YOU ARE.
AND THAT'S...
...NEVER GONNA CHANGE ...
...EVEN WHEN WE'RE GROWN-UPS, RIGHT?

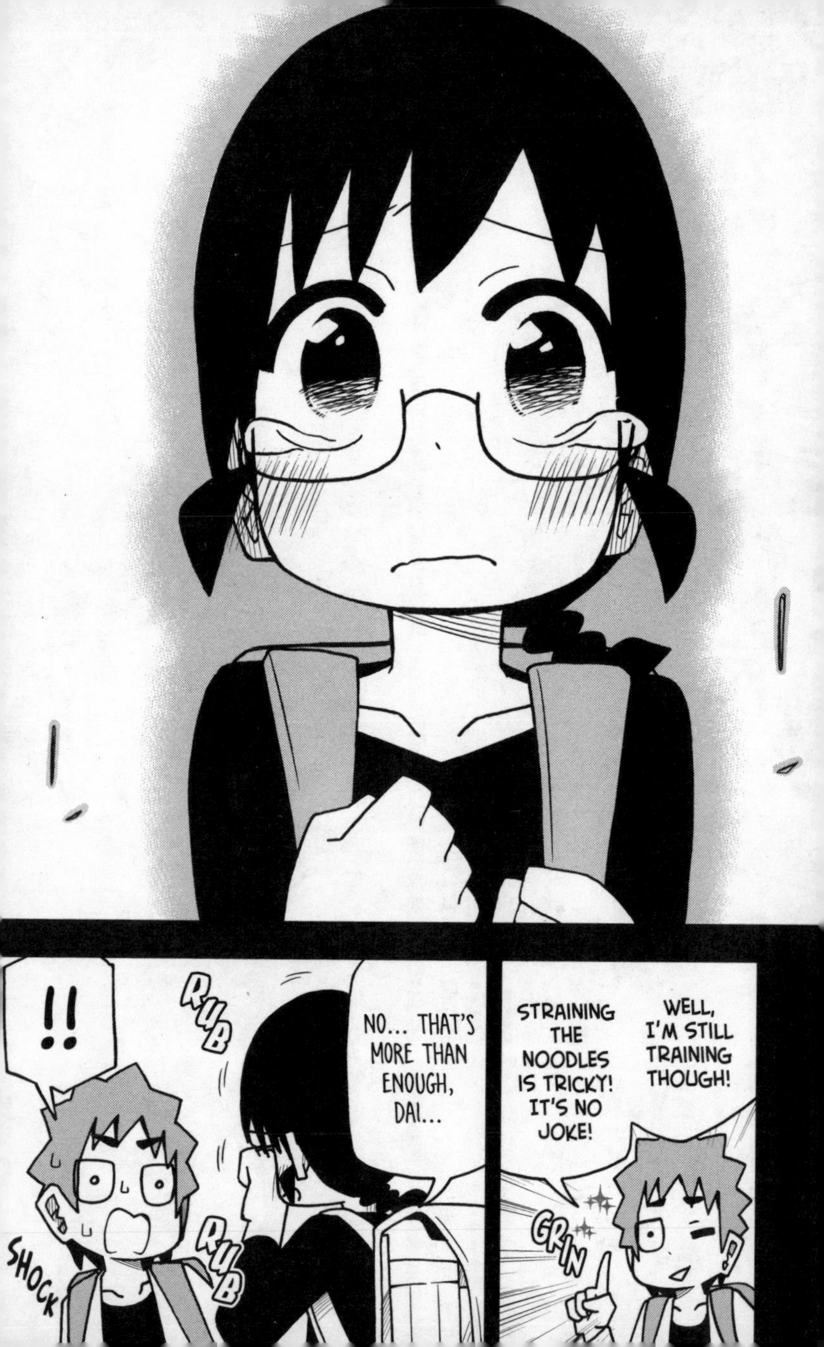
WELL, I'M STILL TRAINING THOUGH!
STRAINING THE NOODLES IS TRICKY! IT'S NO JOKE!
GRIN
NO... THAT'S MORE THAN ENOUGH, DAI...
RUB
RUB
!!
SHOCK

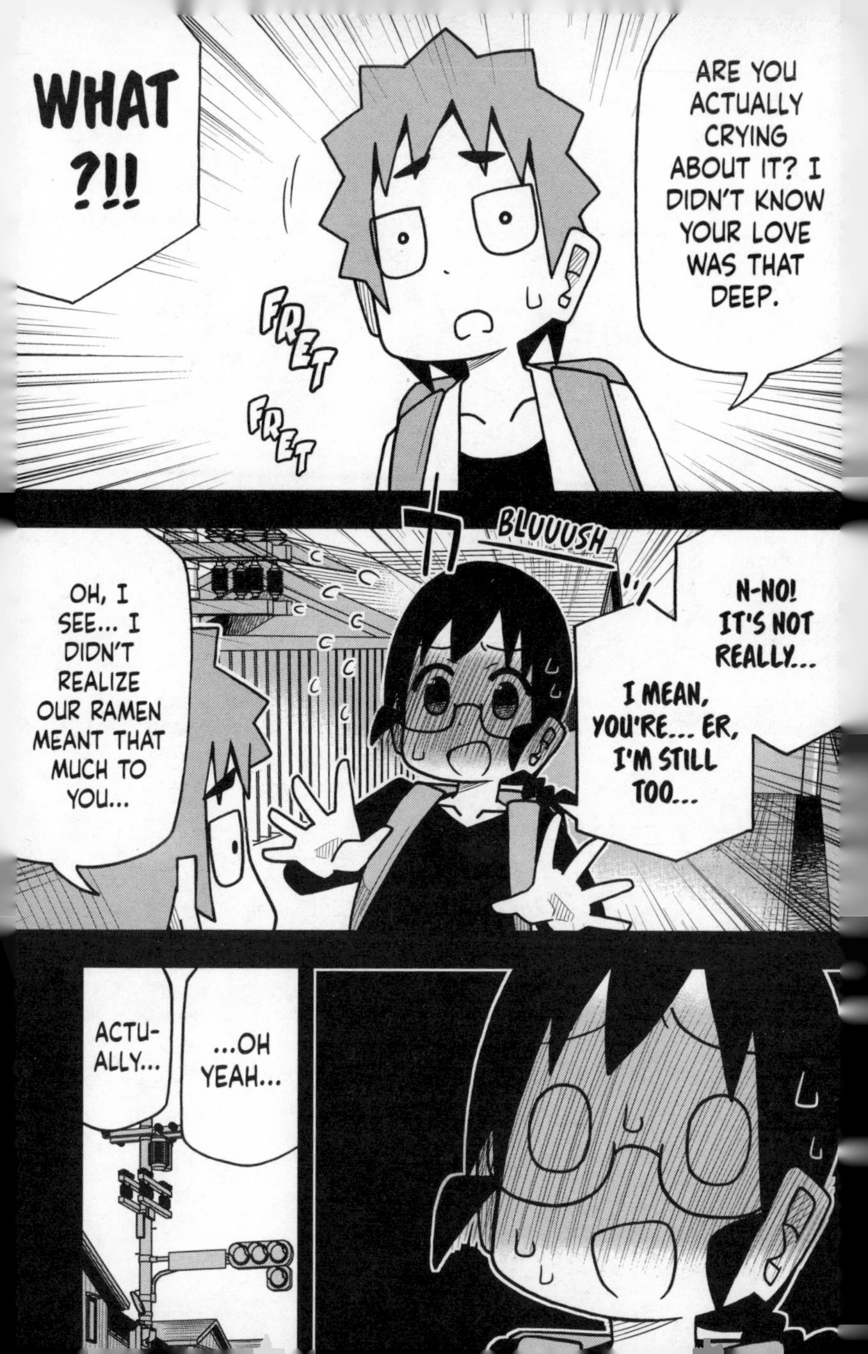
ARE YOU ACTUALLY CRYING ABOUT IT? I DIDN'T KNOW YOUR LOVE WAS THAT DEEP.
WHAT ?!!
FRET
FRET
BLUUUSH
N-NO! IT'S NOT REALLY...
I MEAN, YOU'RE... ER, I'M STILL TOO...
OH, I SEE... I DIDN'T REALIZE OUR RAMEN MEANT THAT MUCH TO YOU...
...OH YEAH...
ACTU-ALLY...

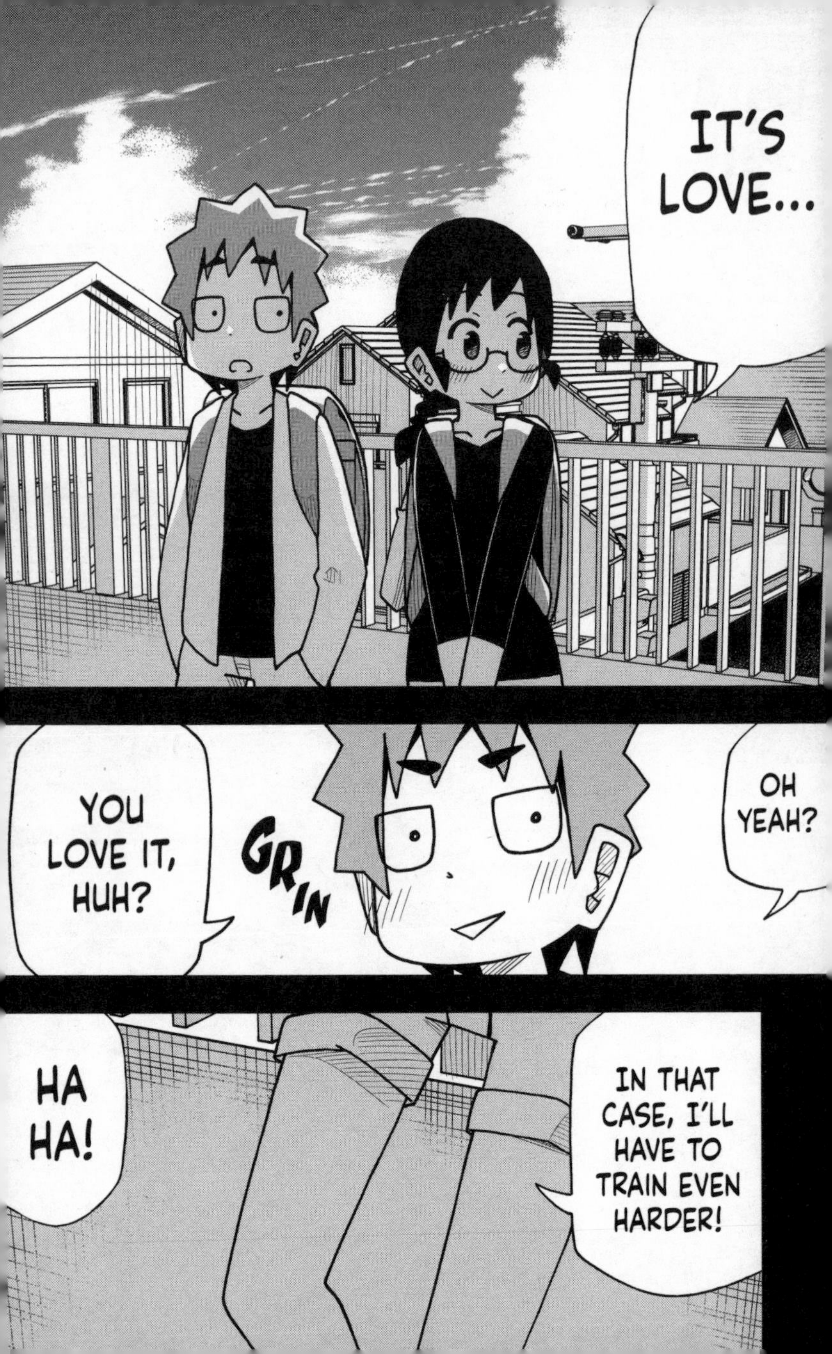
IT'S LOVE...
OH YEAH?
GRIN
YOU LOVE IT, HUH?
IN THAT CASE, I'LL HAVE TO TRAIN EVEN HARDER!
HA HA!

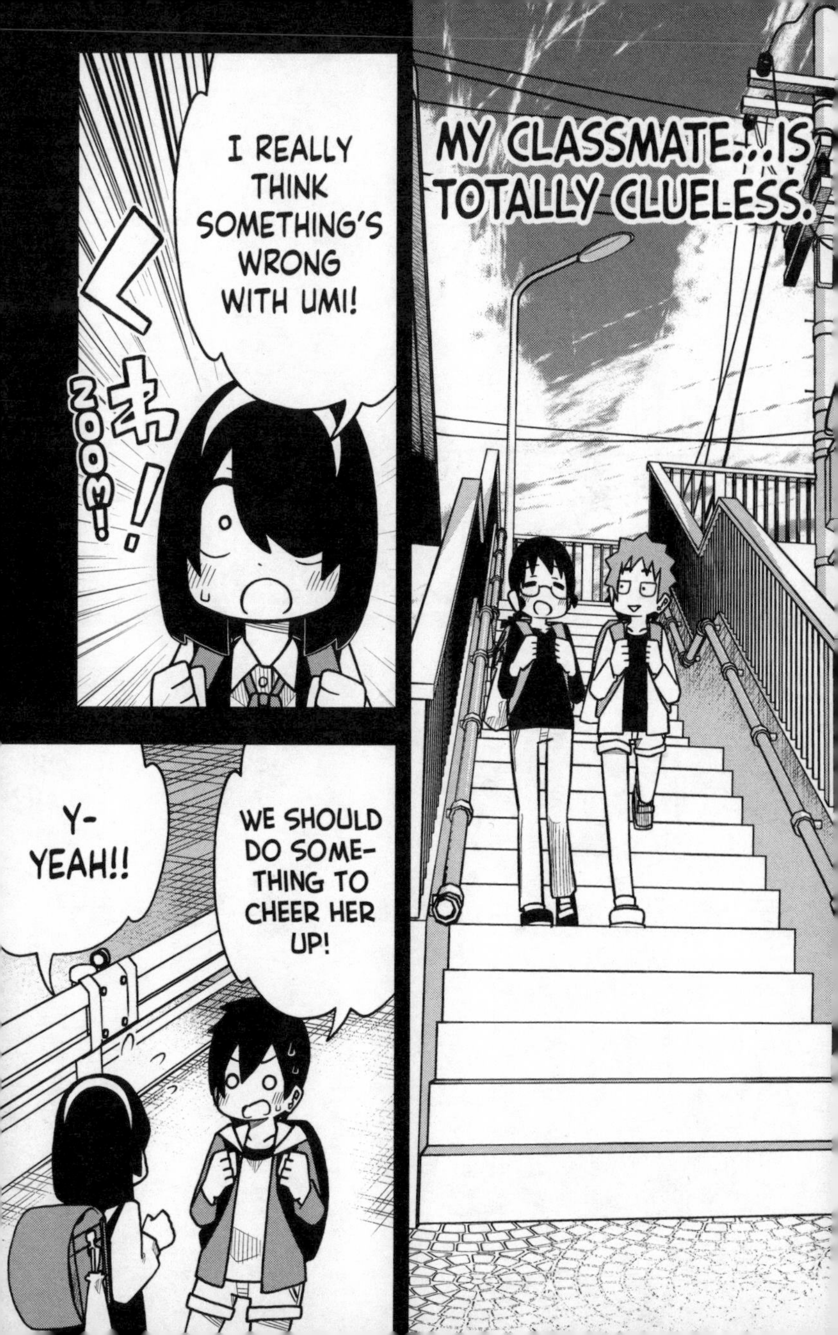
MY CLASSMATE... IS TOTALLY CLUELESS.
I REALLY THINK SOMETHING'S WRONG WITH UMI!
ZOOM!
WE SHOULD DO SOMETHING TO CHEER HER UP!
Y-YEAH!!

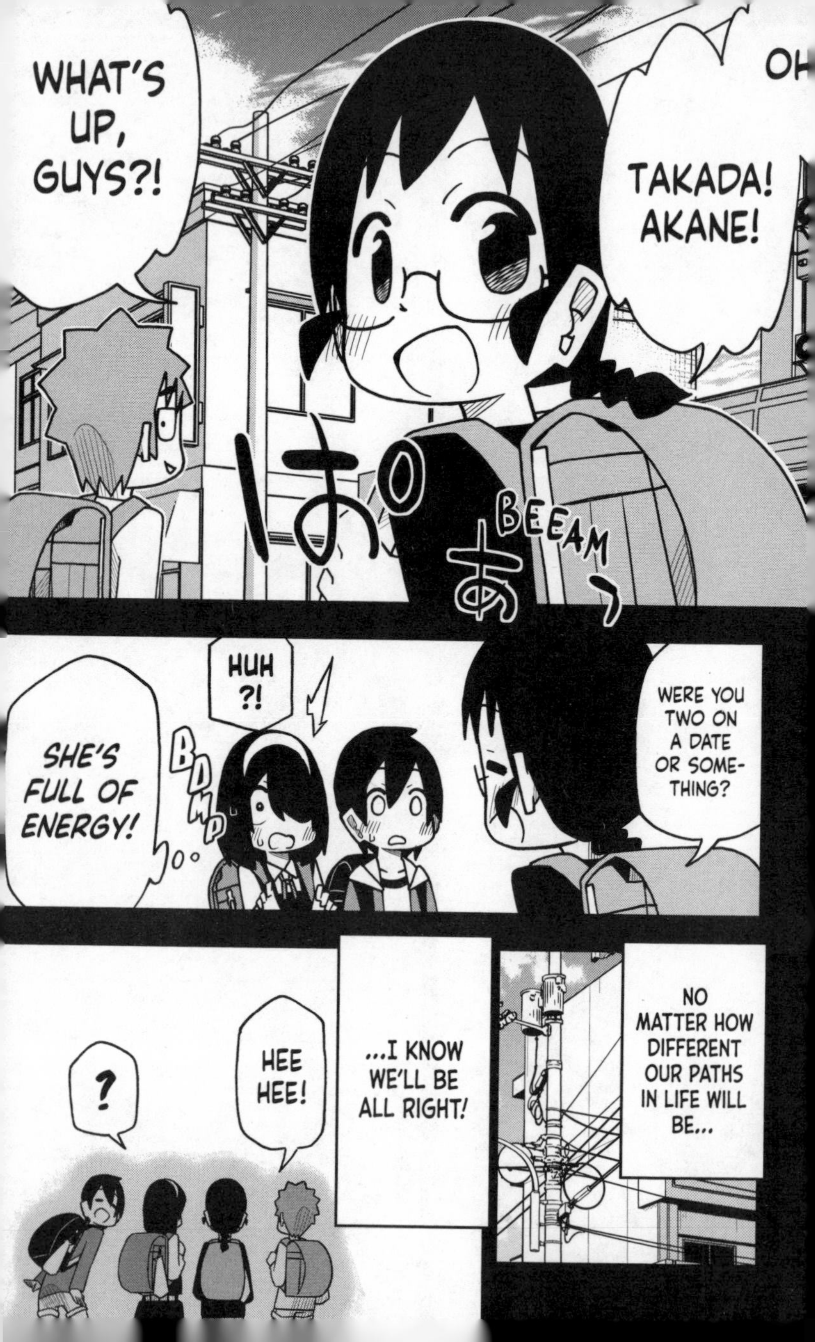
OH TAKADA! AKANE!
WHAT'S UP, GUYS?!
BEEAM
WERE YOU TWO ON A DATE OR SOME-THING?
HUH?!
BDMP
SHE'S FULL OF ENERGY!
NO MATTER HOW DIFFERENT OUR PATHS IN LIFE WILL BE...
...I KNOW WE'LL BE ALL RIGHT!
HEE HEE!
?

MY CLUELESS
FIRST FRIEND

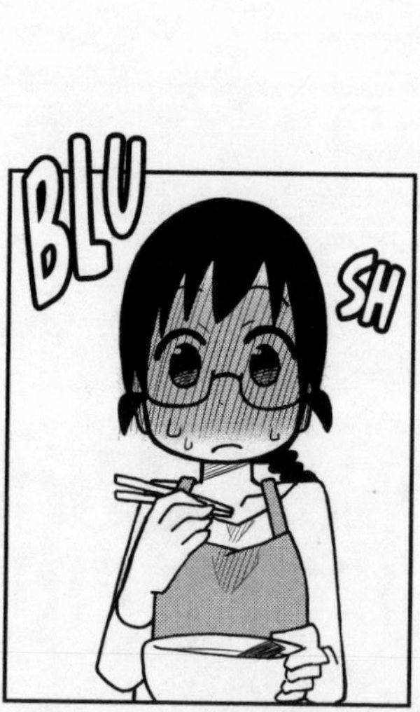
BLUSH

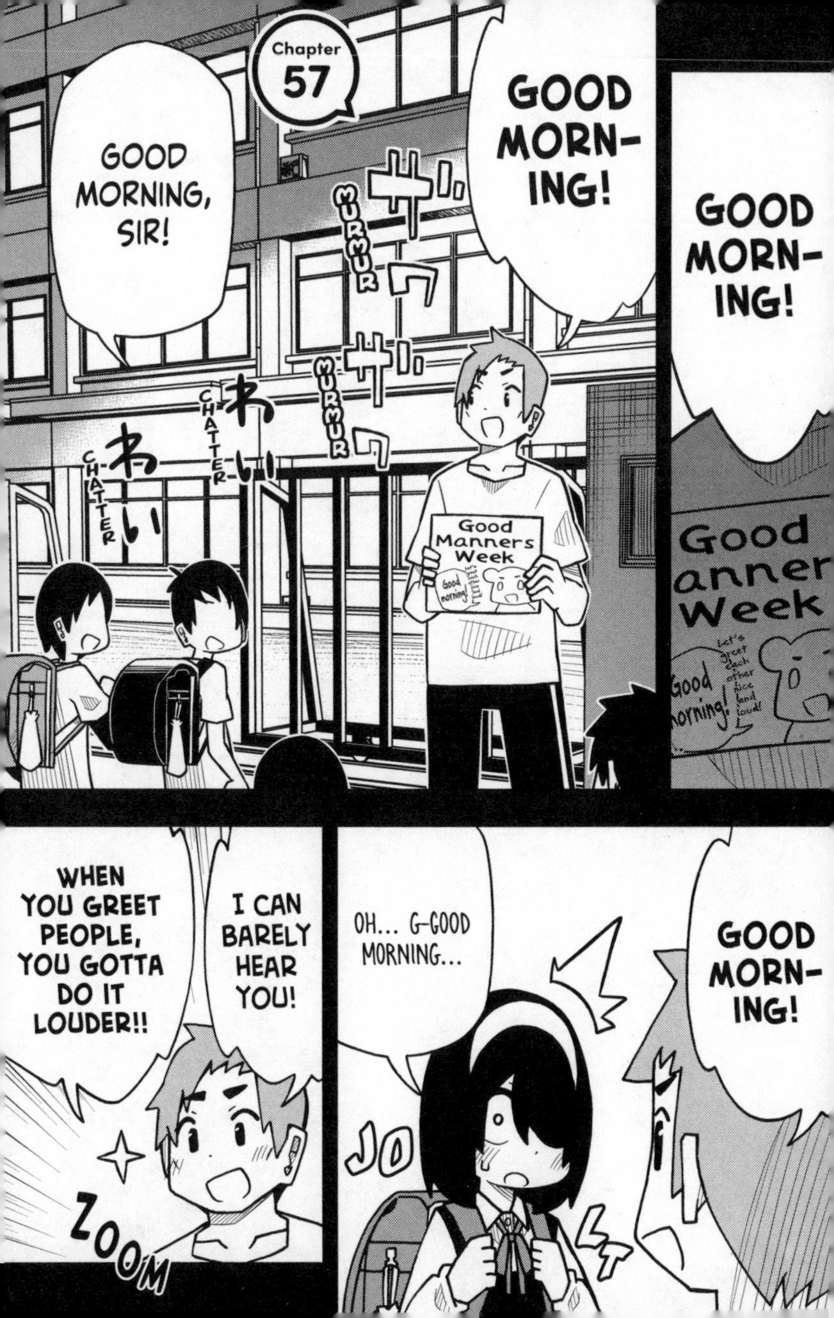
GOOD MORNING!
Good anner Week
Good morning!
Let's greet each other nice and loud!
Chapter 57
GOOD MORNING!
MURMUR
MURMUR
GOOD MORNING, SIR!
CHATTER
CHATTER
Good Manners Week
Good morning!
GOOD MORNING!
OH... G-GOOD MORNING...
JOLT
I CAN BARELY HEAR YOU!
WHEN YOU GREET PEOPLE, YOU GOTTA DO IT LOUDER!!
ZOOM

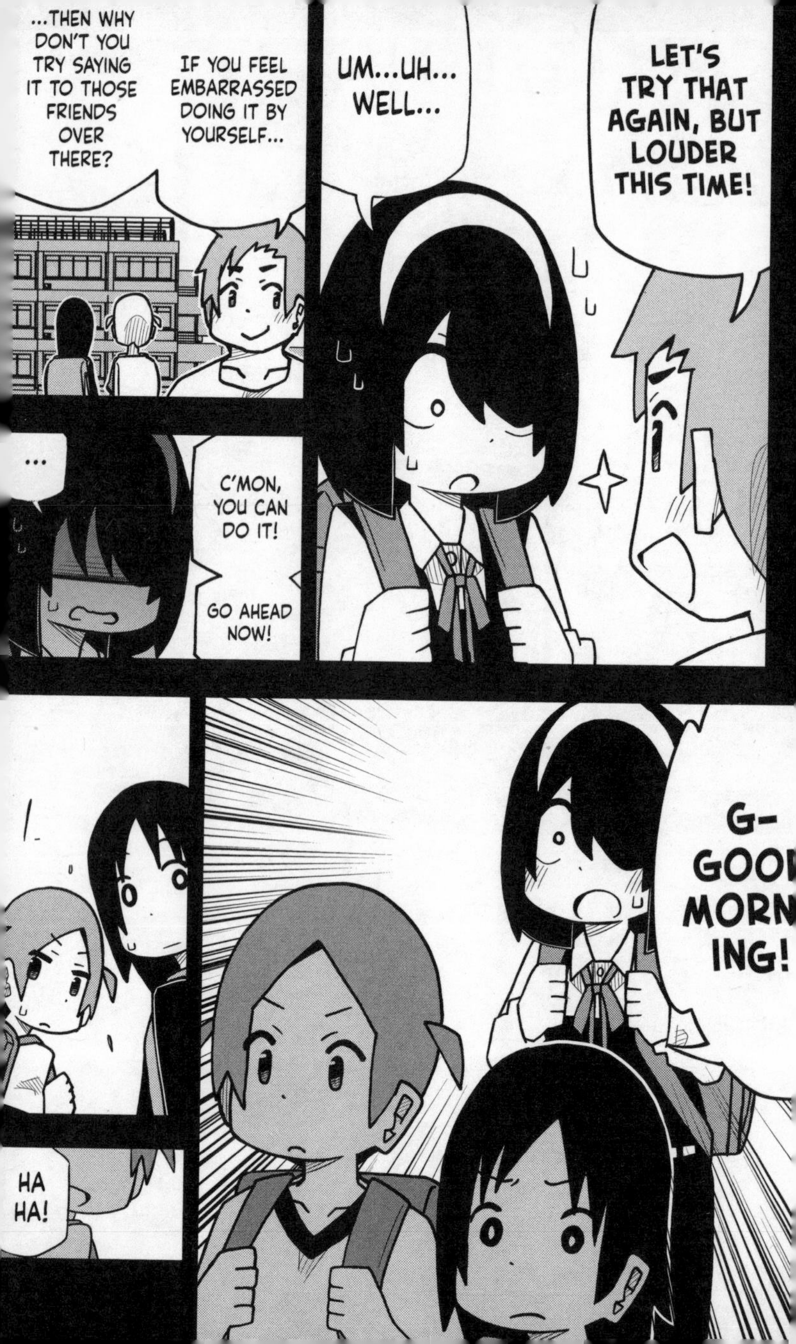
LET'S TRY THAT AGAIN, BUT LOUDER THIS TIME!
UM...UH... WELL...
IF YOU FEEL EMBARRASSED DOING IT BY YOURSELF...
...THEN WHY DON'T YOU TRY SAYING IT TO THOSE FRIENDS OVER THERE?
C'MON, YOU CAN DO IT!
GO AHEAD NOW!
...
G- GOO MORN ING!
!
HA HA!

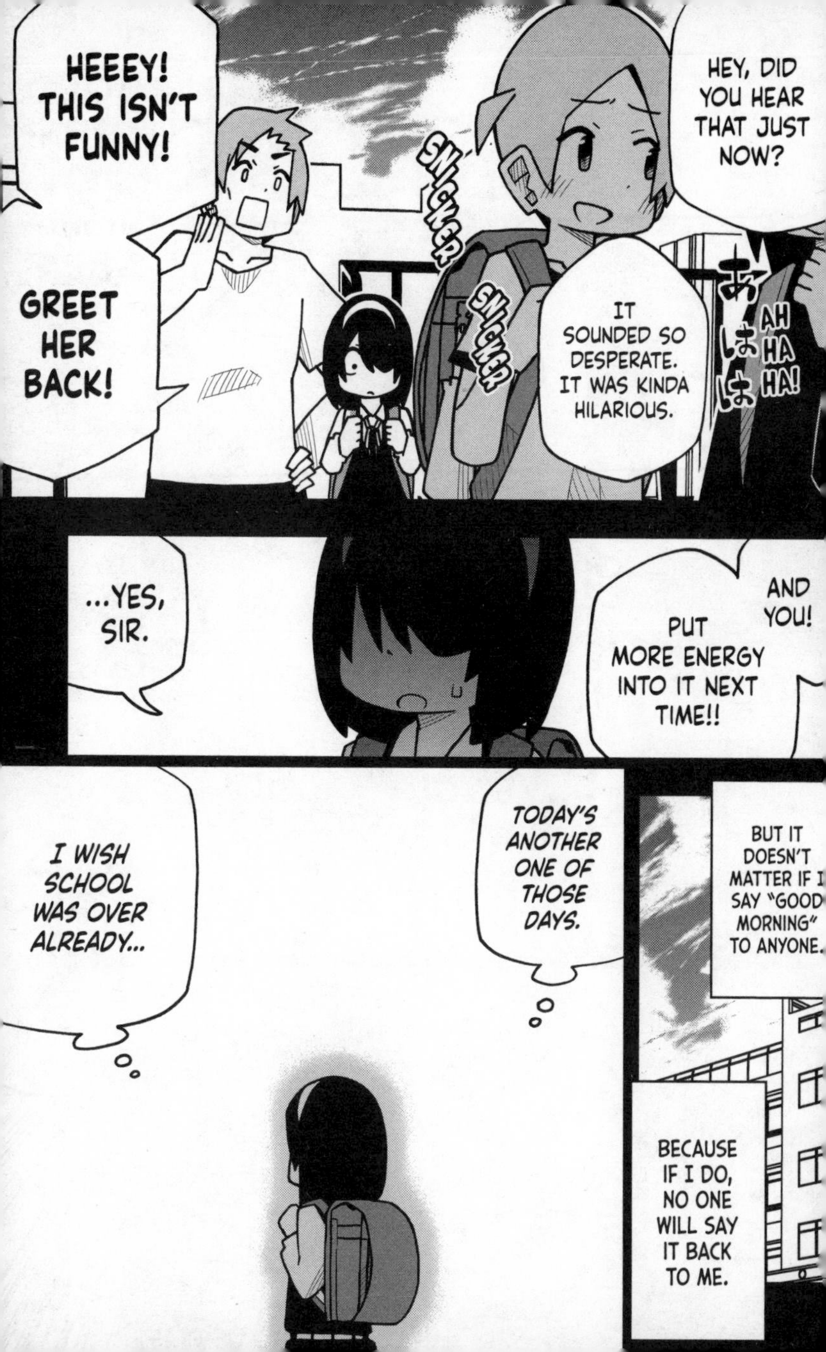
HEY, DID YOU HEAR THAT JUST NOW?
あはは
AH HA HA!
IT SOUNDED SO DESPERATE. IT WAS KINDA HILARIOUS.
SNICKER
SNICKER
HEEEY! THIS ISN'T FUNNY!
GREET HER BACK!
AND YOU!
PUT MORE ENERGY INTO IT NEXT TIME!!
...YES, SIR.
BUT IT DOESN'T MATTER IF I SAY "GOOD MORNING" TO ANYONE.
BECAUSE IF I DO, NO ONE WILL SAY IT BACK TO ME.
TODAY'S ANOTHER ONE OF THOSE DAYS.
I WISH SCHOOL WAS OVER ALREADY...

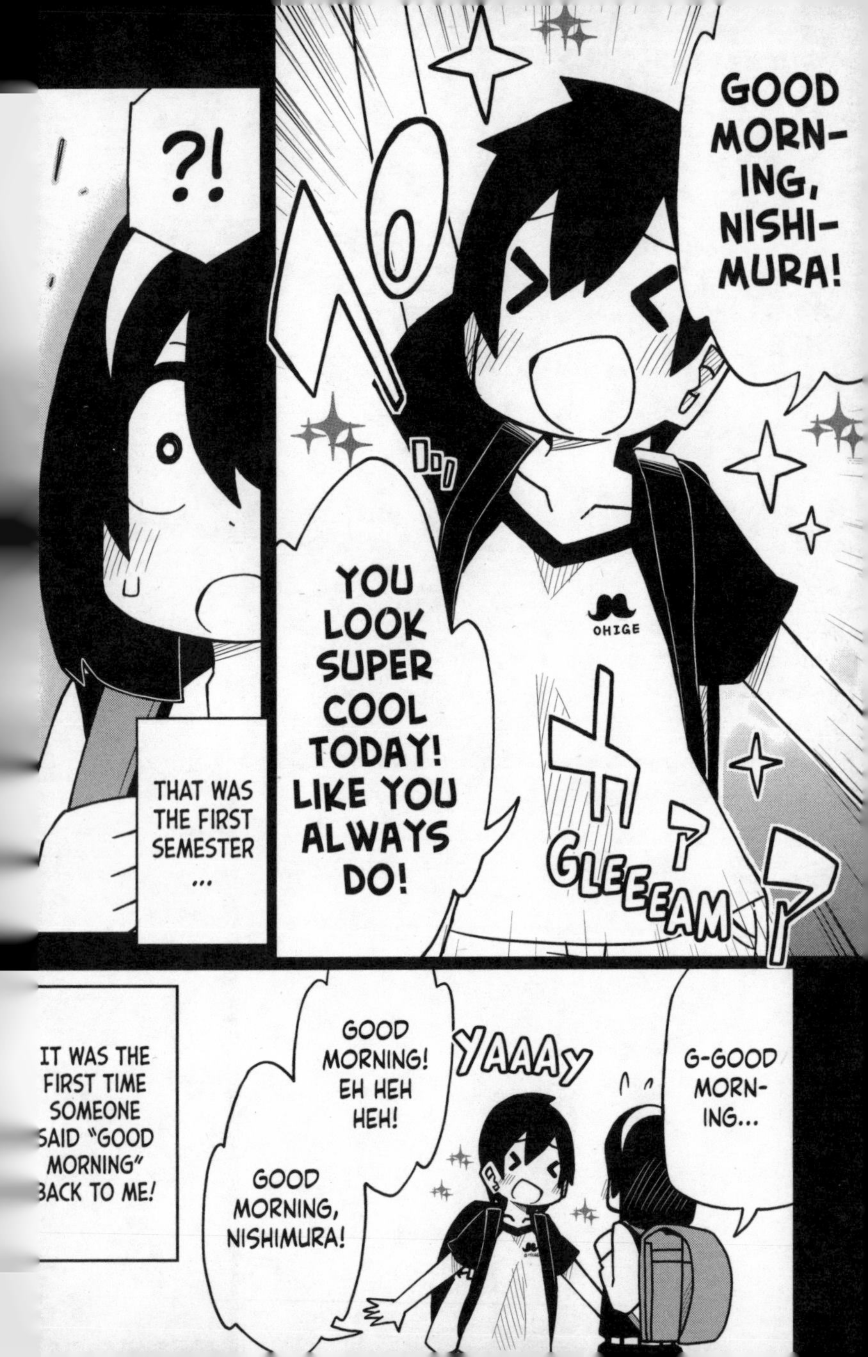
GOOD MORNING, NISHIMURA!
YOU LOOK SUPER COOL TODAY! LIKE YOU ALWAYS DO!
GLEEEAM
?!
THAT WAS THE FIRST SEMESTER ...
G-GOOD MORNING...
YAAAy
GOOD MORNING! EH HEH HEH!
GOOD MORNING, NISHIMURA!
IT WAS THE FIRST TIME SOMEONE SAID "GOOD MORNING" BACK TO ME!

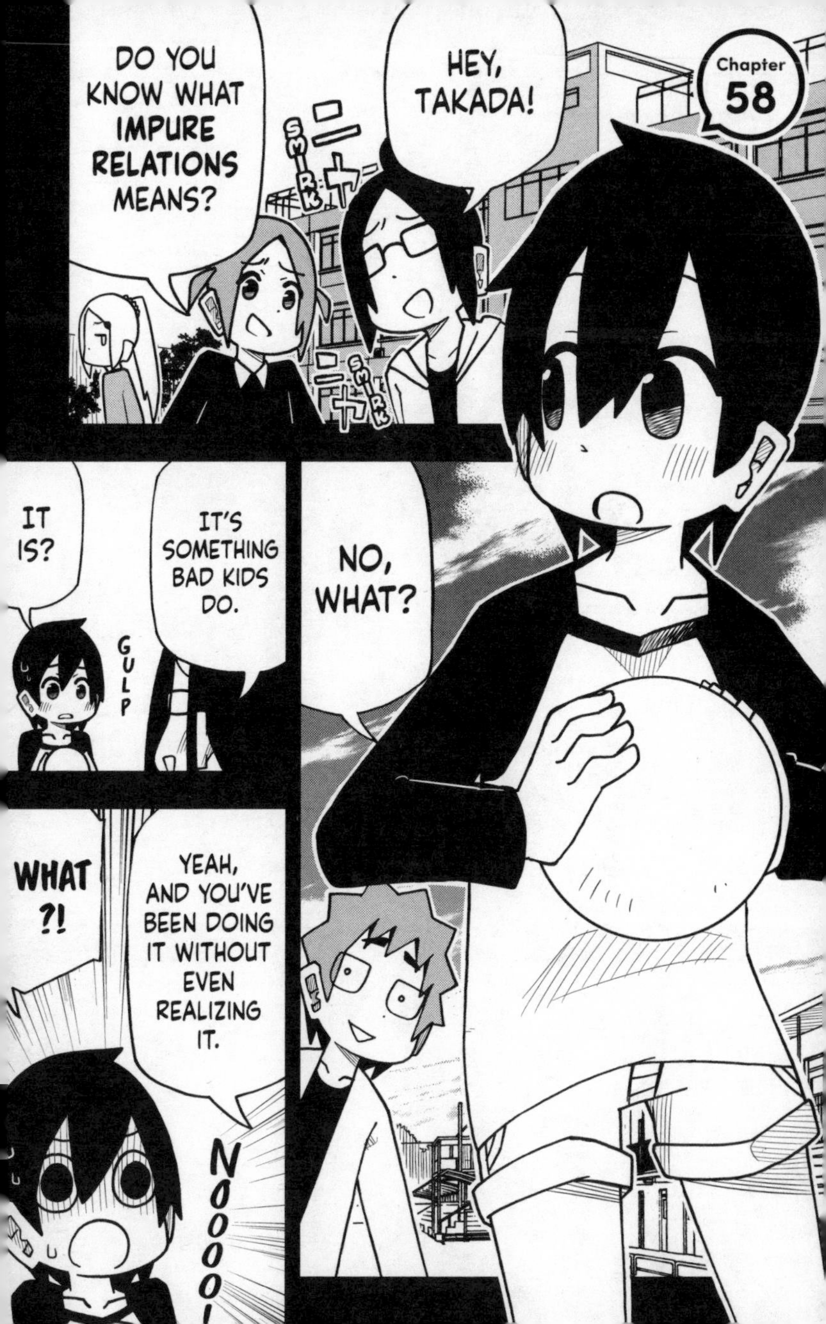
Chapter 58
HEY, TAKADA!
DO YOU KNOW WHAT IMPURE RELATIONS MEANS?
SMIRK
SMIRK
NO, WHAT?
IT'S SOMETHING BAD KIDS DO.
IT IS?
GULP
YEAH, AND YOU'VE BEEN DOING IT WITHOUT EVEN REALIZING IT.
WHAT?!
NOOOOO

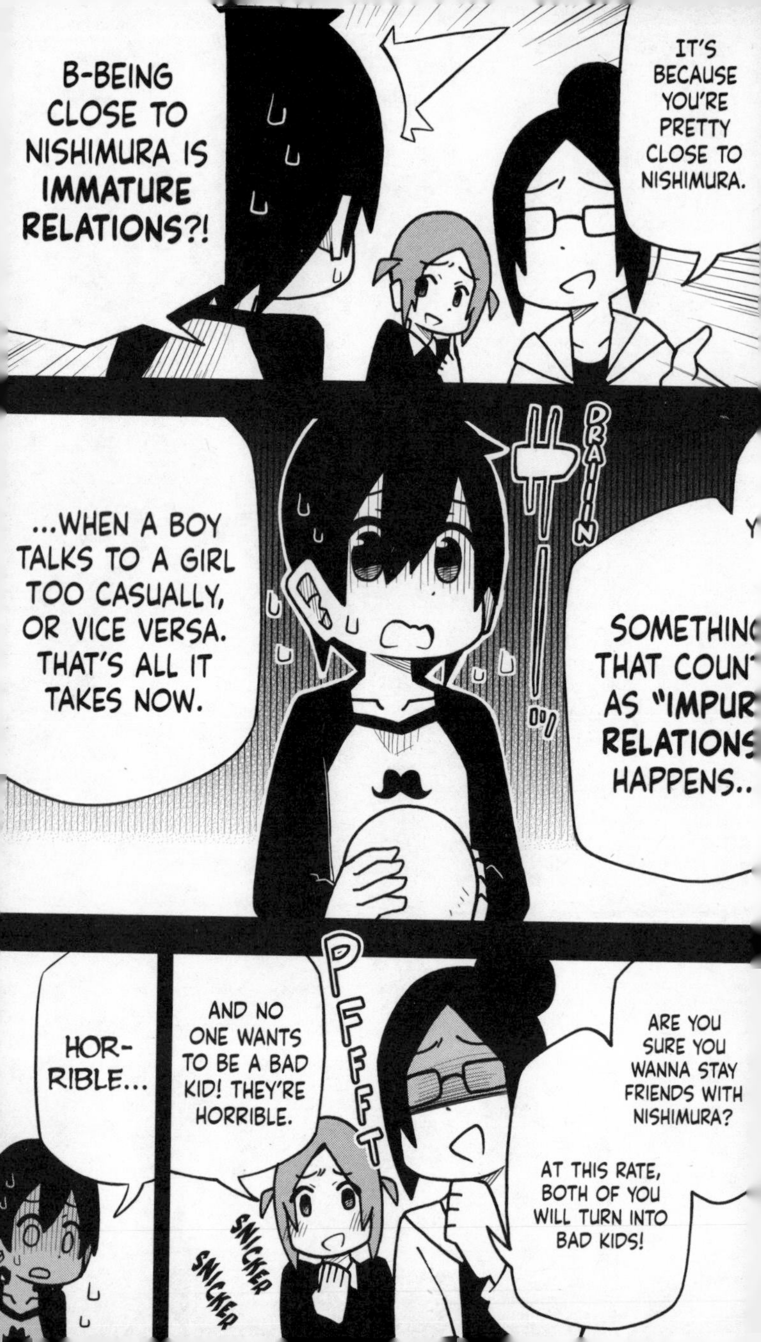
IT'S BECAUSE YOU'RE PRETTY CLOSE TO NISHIMURA.
B-BEING CLOSE TO NISHIMURA IS IMMATURE RELATIONS?!
Y
SOMETHIN THAT COUN AS "IMPUR RELATION HAPPENS..
DRAIIN
...WHEN A BOY TALKS TO A GIRL TOO CASUALLY, OR VICE VERSA. THAT'S ALL IT TAKES NOW.
ARE YOU SURE YOU WANNA STAY FRIENDS WITH NISHIMURA?
AT THIS RATE, BOTH OF YOU WILL TURN INTO BAD KIDS!
PFFFT
AND NO ONE WANTS TO BE A BAD KID! THEY'RE HORRIBLE.
SNICKER SNICKER
HOR-RIBLE...

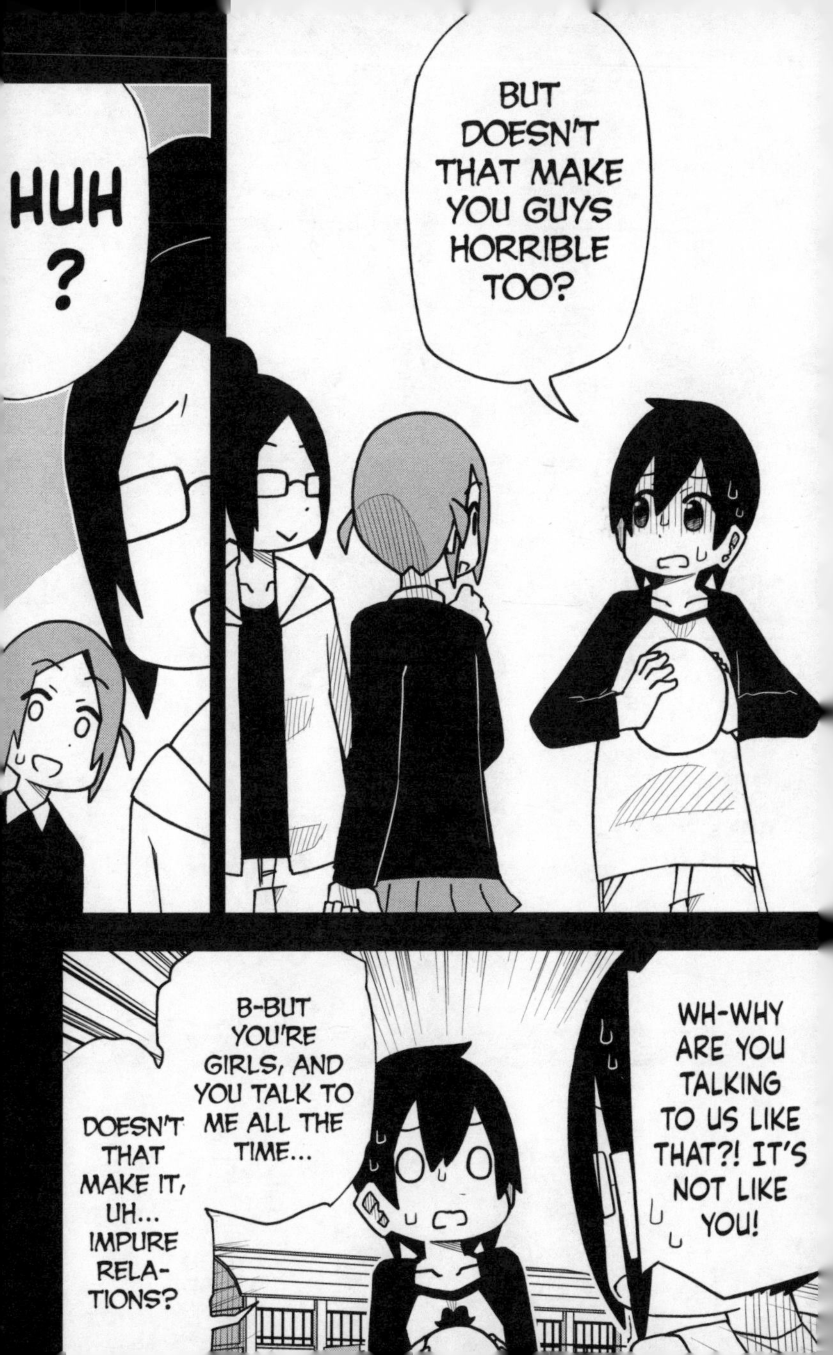
BUT DOESN'T THAT MAKE YOU GUYS HORRIBLE TOO?
HUH ?
WH-WHY ARE YOU TALKING TO US LIKE THAT?! IT'S NOT LIKE YOU!
B-BUT YOU'RE GIRLS, AND YOU TALK TO ME ALL THE TIME...
DOESN'T THAT MAKE IT, UH... IMPURE RELA-TIONS?

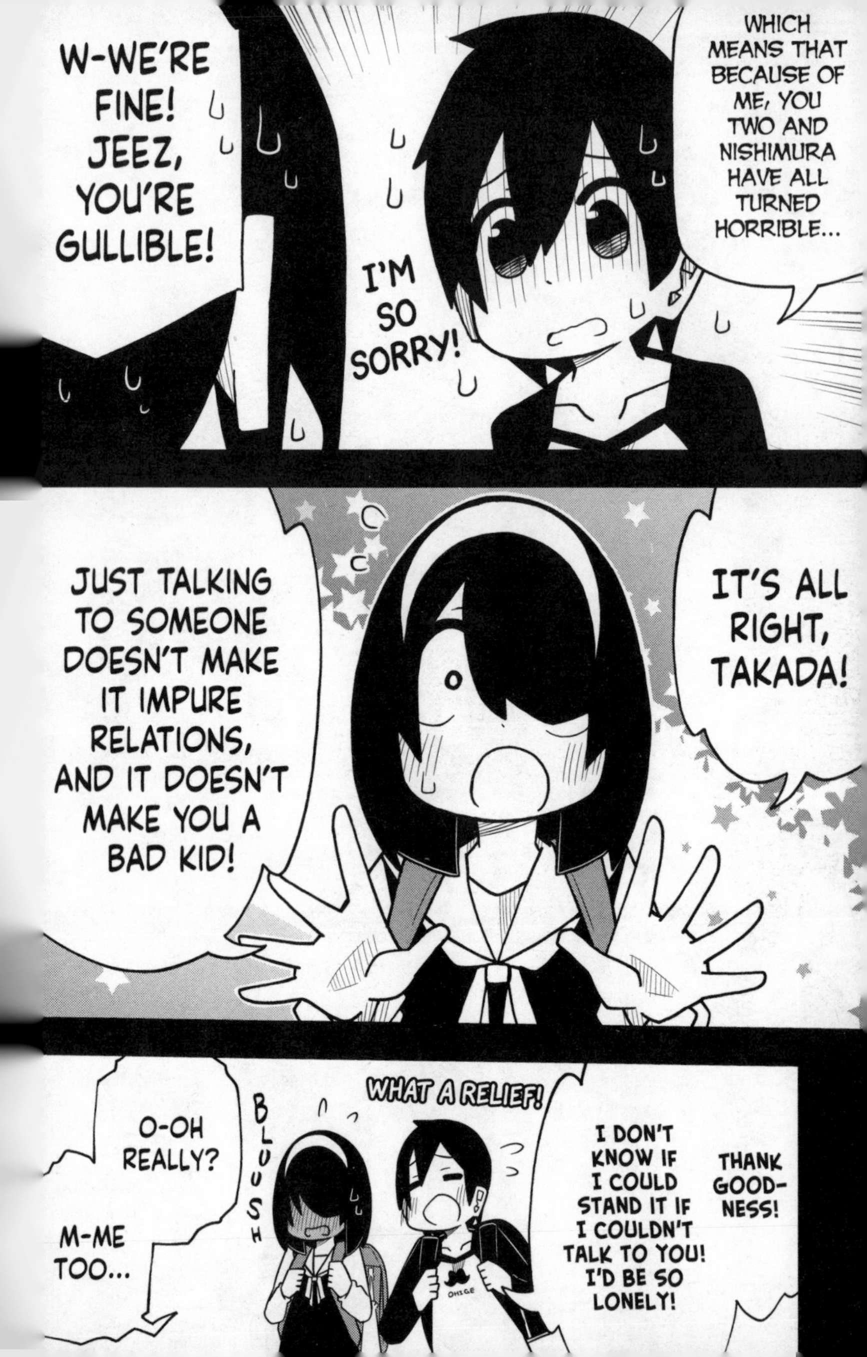
WHICH MEANS THAT BECAUSE OF ME, YOU TWO AND NISHIMURA HAVE ALL TURNED HORRIBLE...
I'M SO SORRY!
W-WE'RE FINE! JEEZ, YOU'RE GULLIBLE!
IT'S ALL RIGHT, TAKADA!
JUST TALKING TO SOMEONE DOESN'T MAKE IT IMPURE RELATIONS, AND IT DOESN'T MAKE YOU A BAD KID!
THANK GOODNESS!
I DON'T KNOW IF I COULD STAND IT IF I COULDN'T TALK TO YOU! I'D BE SO LONELY!
WHAT A RELIEF!
OHIGE
BLUUSH
O-OH REALLY?
M-ME TOO...

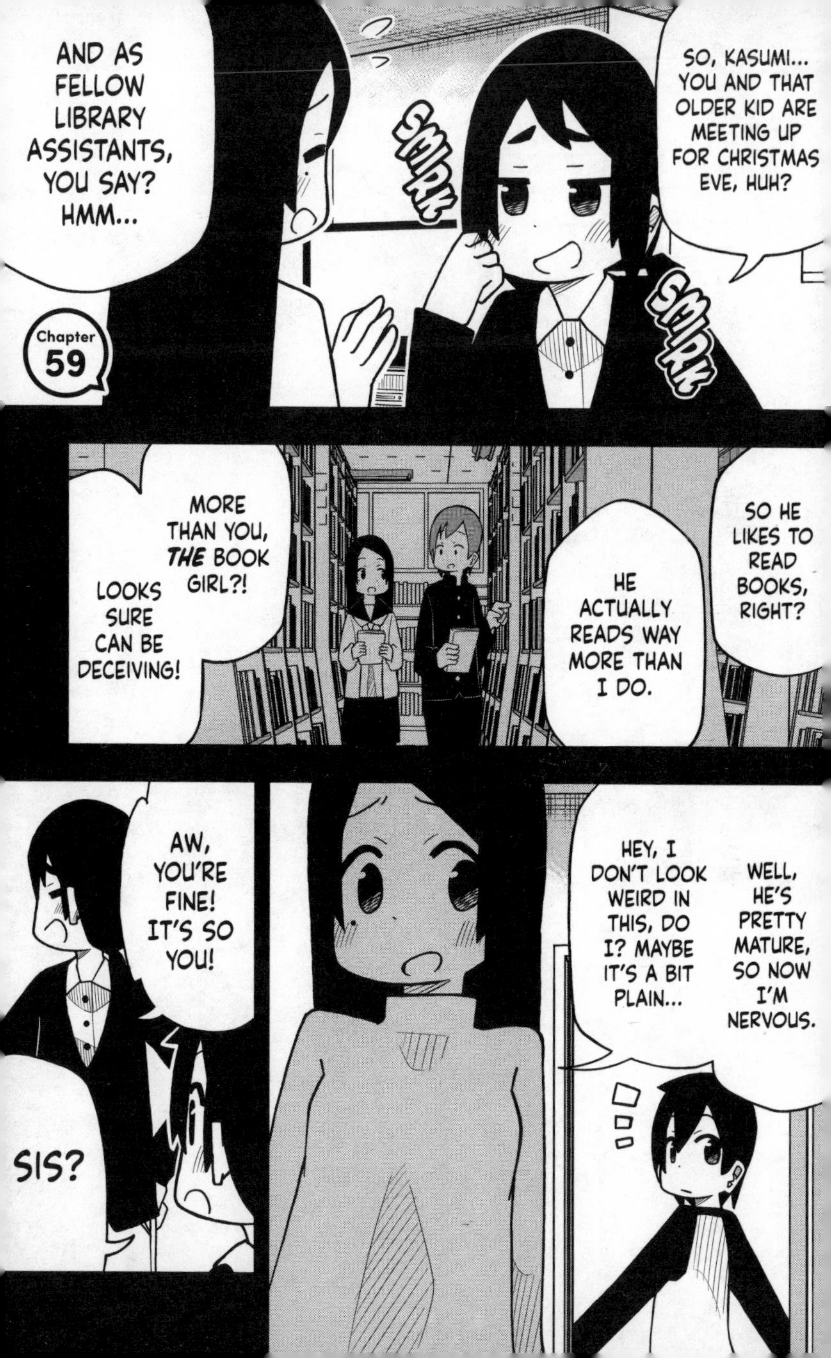
SO, KASUMI... YOU AND THAT OLDER KID ARE MEETING UP FOR CHRISTMAS EVE, HUH?
SMIRK
SMIRK
AND AS FELLOW LIBRARY ASSISTANTS, YOU SAY? HMM...
Chapter 59
SO HE LIKES TO READ BOOKS, RIGHT?
HE ACTUALLY READS WAY MORE THAN I DO.
MORE THAN YOU, *THE* BOOK GIRL?!
LOOKS SURE CAN BE DECEIVING!
WELL, HE'S PRETTY MATURE, SO NOW I'M NERVOUS.
HEY, I DON'T LOOK WEIRD IN THIS, DO I? MAYBE IT'S A BIT PLAIN...
AW, YOU'RE FINE! IT'S SO YOU!
SIS?

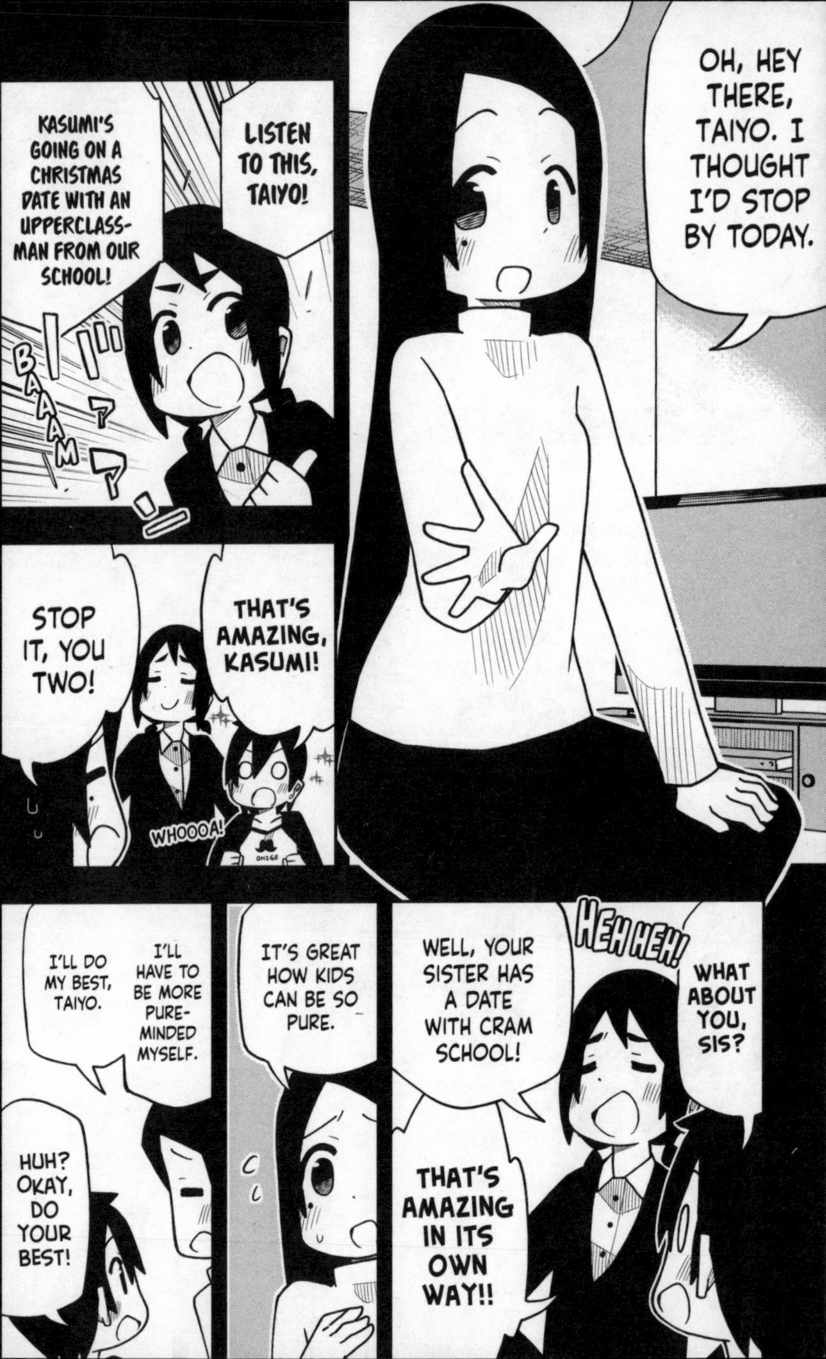
OH, HEY THERE, TAIYO. I THOUGHT I'D STOP BY TODAY.
LISTEN TO THIS, TAIYO!
KASUMI'S GOING ON A CHRISTMAS DATE WITH AN UPPERCLASSMAN FROM OUR SCHOOL!
BAAAAM
THAT'S AMAZING, KASUMI!
STOP IT, YOU TWO!
WHOOOA!
OHIGE
WHAT ABOUT YOU, SIS?
HEH HEH!
WELL, YOUR SISTER HAS A DATE WITH CRAM SCHOOL!
THAT'S AMAZING IN ITS OWN WAY!!
IT'S GREAT HOW KIDS CAN BE SO PURE.
I'LL HAVE TO BE MORE PURE-MINDED MYSELF.
I'LL DO MY BEST, TAIYO.
HUH? OKAY, DO YOUR BEST!

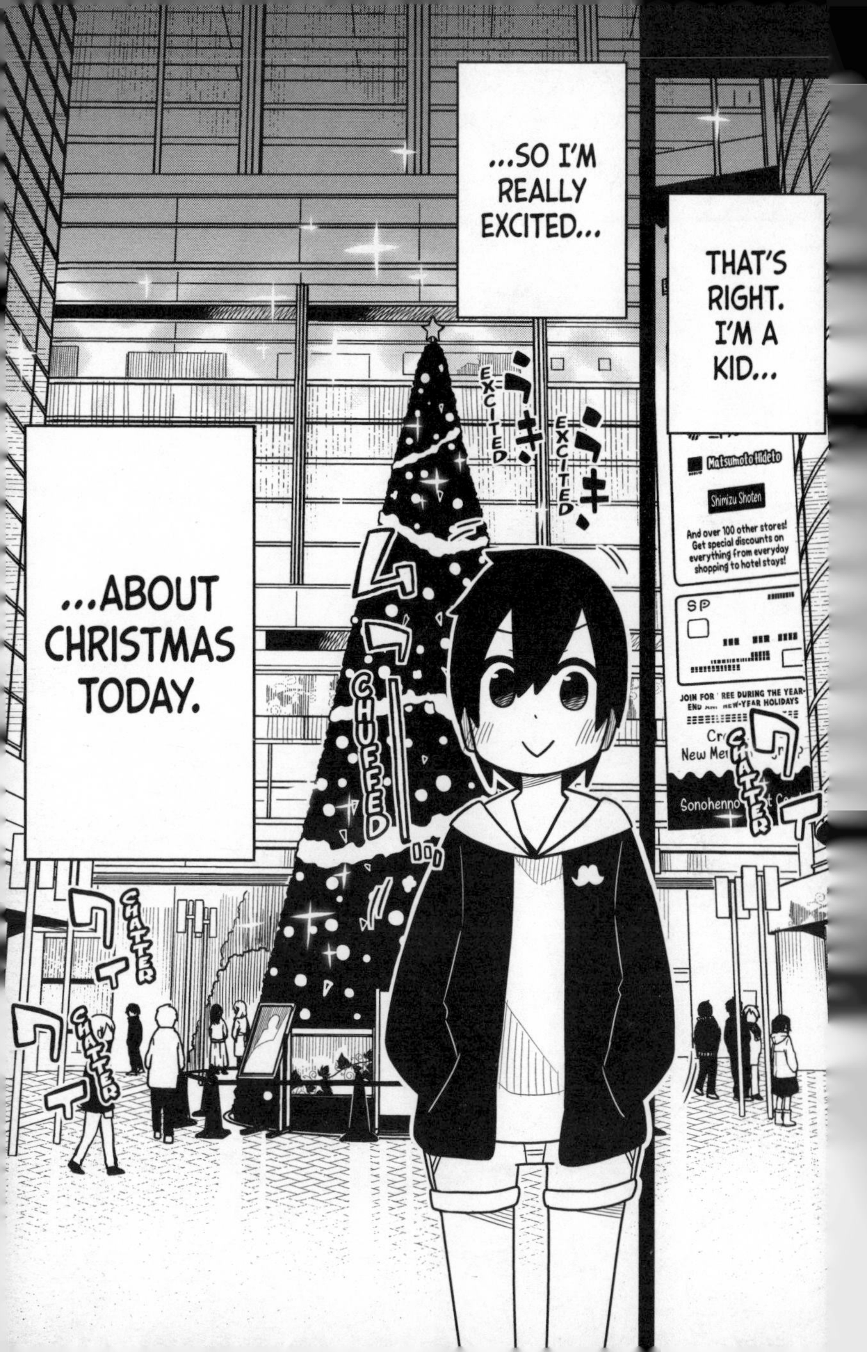
THAT'S RIGHT. I'M A KID...
...SO I'M REALLY EXCITED...
EXCITED
EXCITED
Matsumoto Hideto
Shimizu Shoten
And over 100 other stores! Get special discounts on everything from everyday shopping to hotel stays!
SP
CHATTER
CHUFFED
...ABOUT CHRISTMAS TODAY.
CHATTER
CHATTER

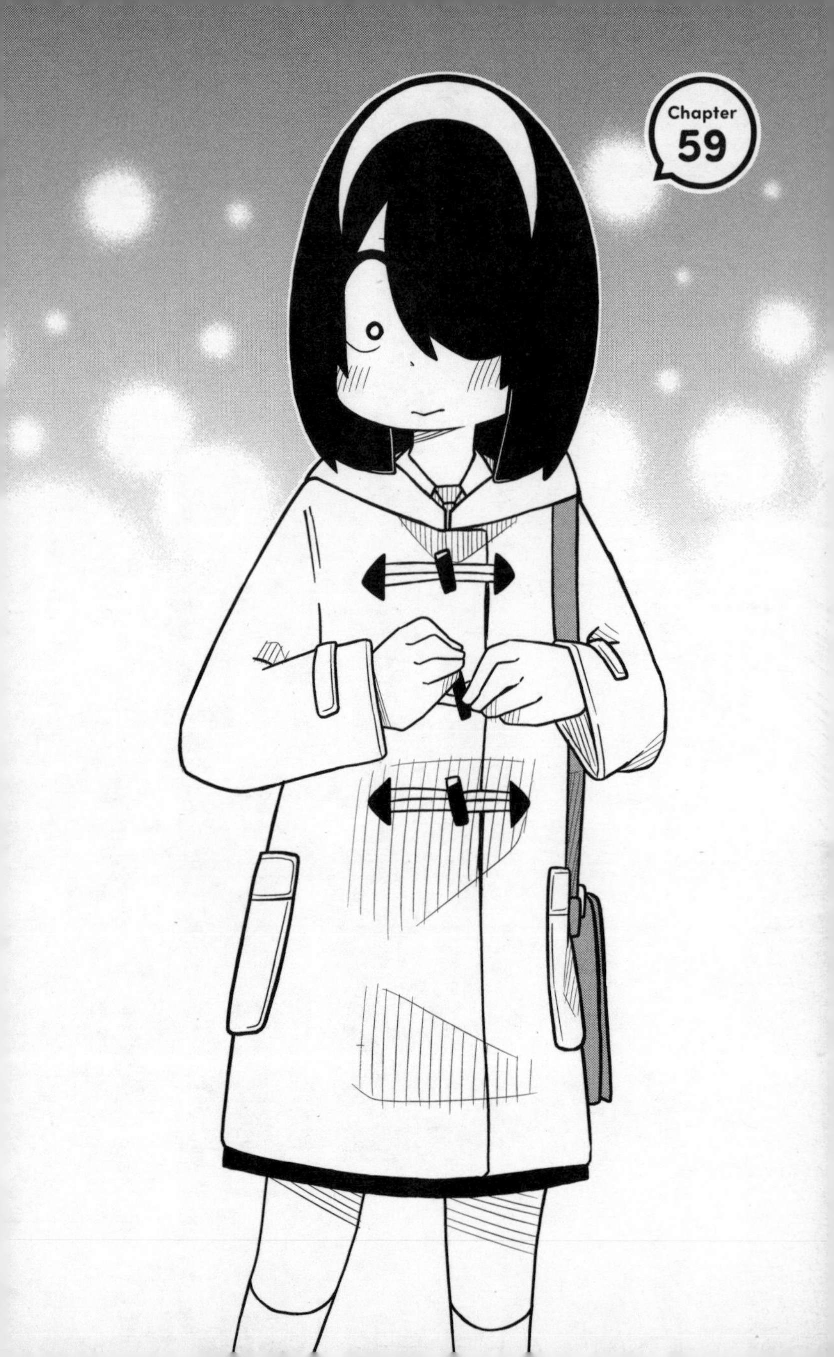
Chapter
59

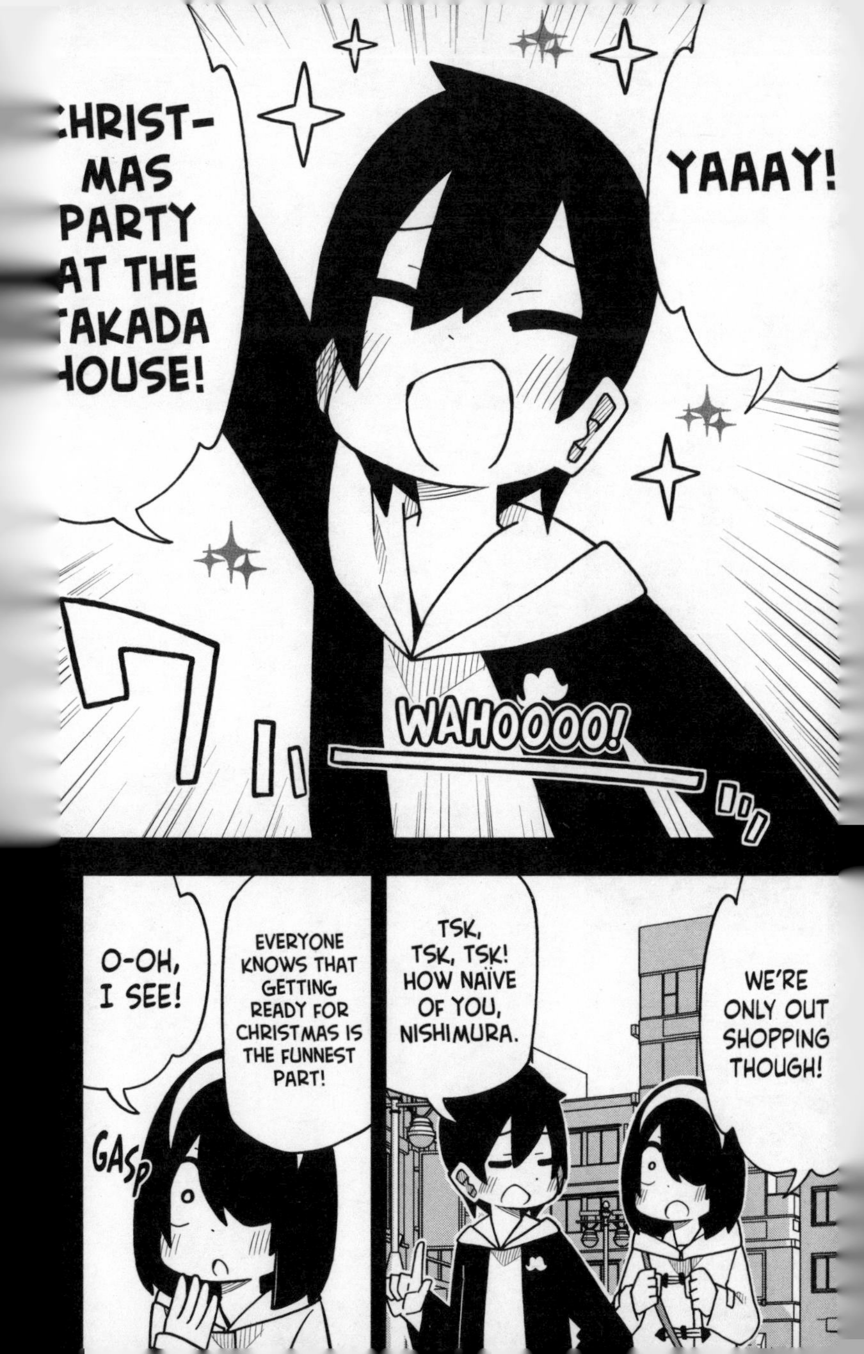
YAAAY!
CHRIST-MAS PARTY AT THE TAKADA HOUSE!
WAHOOOO!
WE'RE ONLY OUT SHOPPING THOUGH!
TSK, TSK, TSK! HOW NAÏVE OF YOU, NISHIMURA.
EVERYONE KNOWS THAT GETTING READY FOR CHRISTMAS IS THE FUNNEST PART!
O-OH, I SEE!
GASP

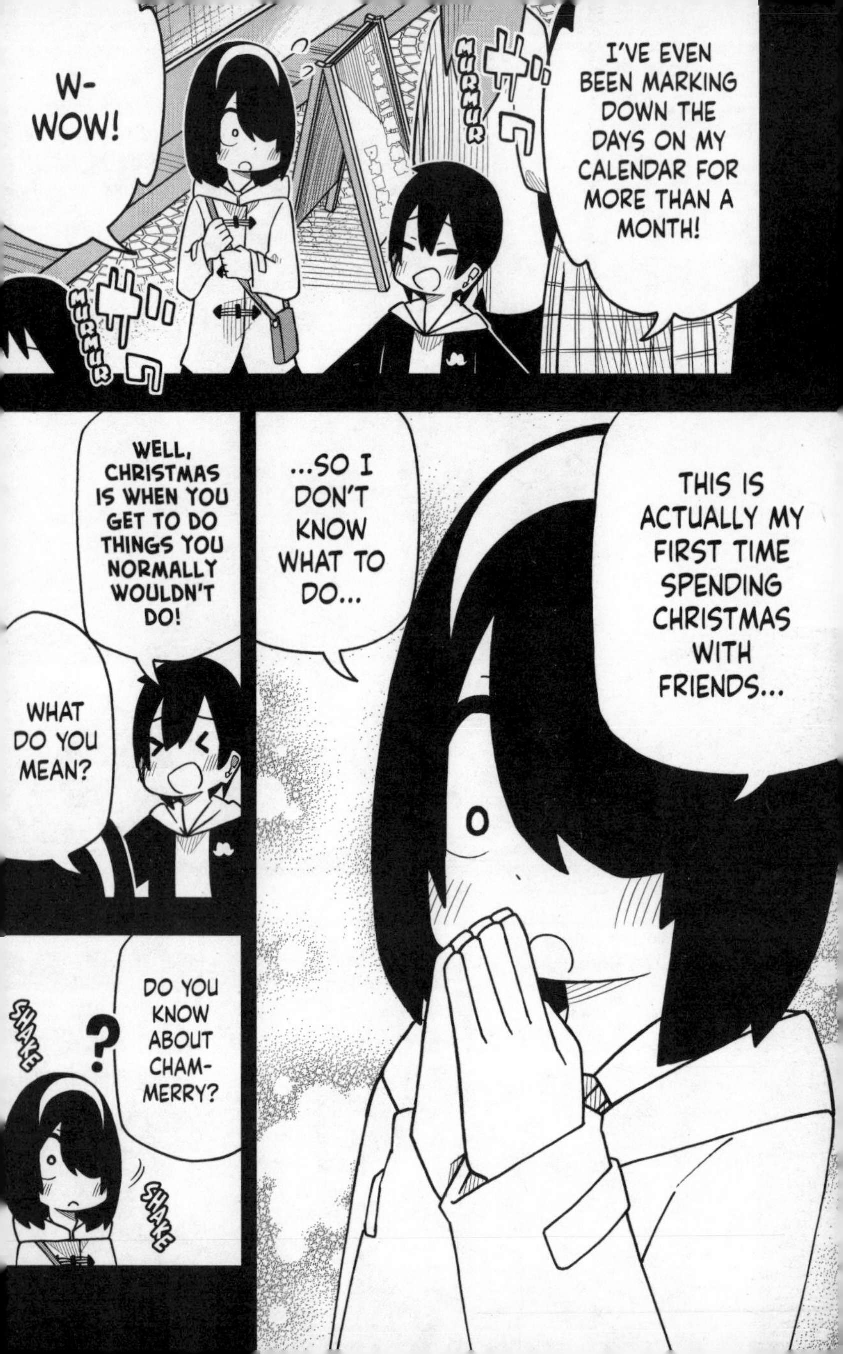
I'VE EVEN BEEN MARKING DOWN THE DAYS ON MY CALENDAR FOR MORE THAN A MONTH!
MURMUR
W-WOW!
MURMUR
THIS IS ACTUALLY MY FIRST TIME SPENDING CHRISTMAS WITH FRIENDS...
...SO I DON'T KNOW WHAT TO DO...
WELL, CHRISTMAS IS WHEN YOU GET TO DO THINGS YOU NORMALLY WOULDN'T DO!
WHAT DO YOU MEAN?
DO YOU KNOW ABOUT CHAM-MERRY?
?
SHAKE
SHAKE

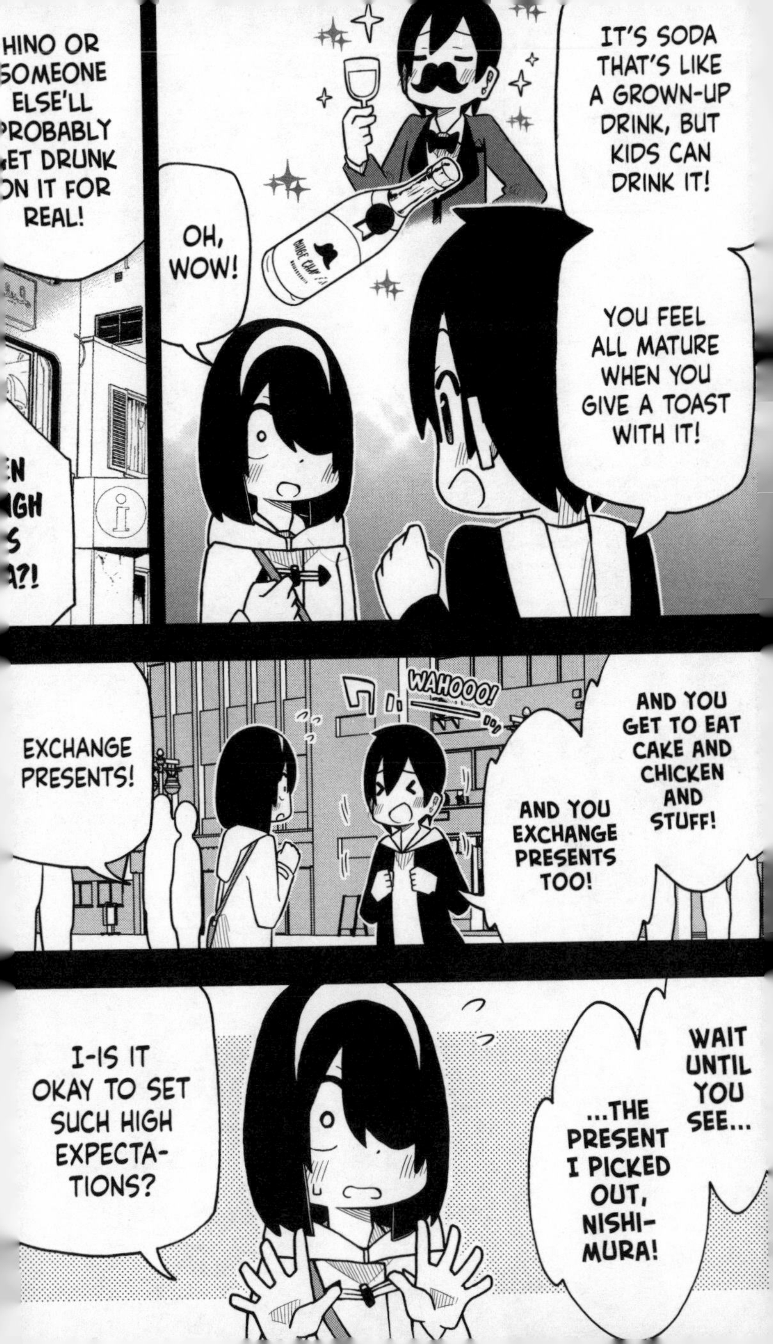
IT'S SODA THAT'S LIKE A GROWN-UP DRINK, BUT KIDS CAN DRINK IT!
OH, WOW!
YOU FEEL ALL MATURE WHEN YOU GIVE A TOAST WITH IT!
HINO OR SOMEONE ELSE'LL PROBABLY GET DRUNK ON IT FOR REAL!
WAHOOO!
AND YOU GET TO EAT CAKE AND CHICKEN AND STUFF!
AND YOU EXCHANGE PRESENTS TOO!
EXCHANGE PRESENTS!
WAIT UNTIL YOU SEE...
...THE PRESENT I PICKED OUT, NISHIMURA!
I-IS IT OKAY TO SET SUCH HIGH EXPECTA-TIONS?

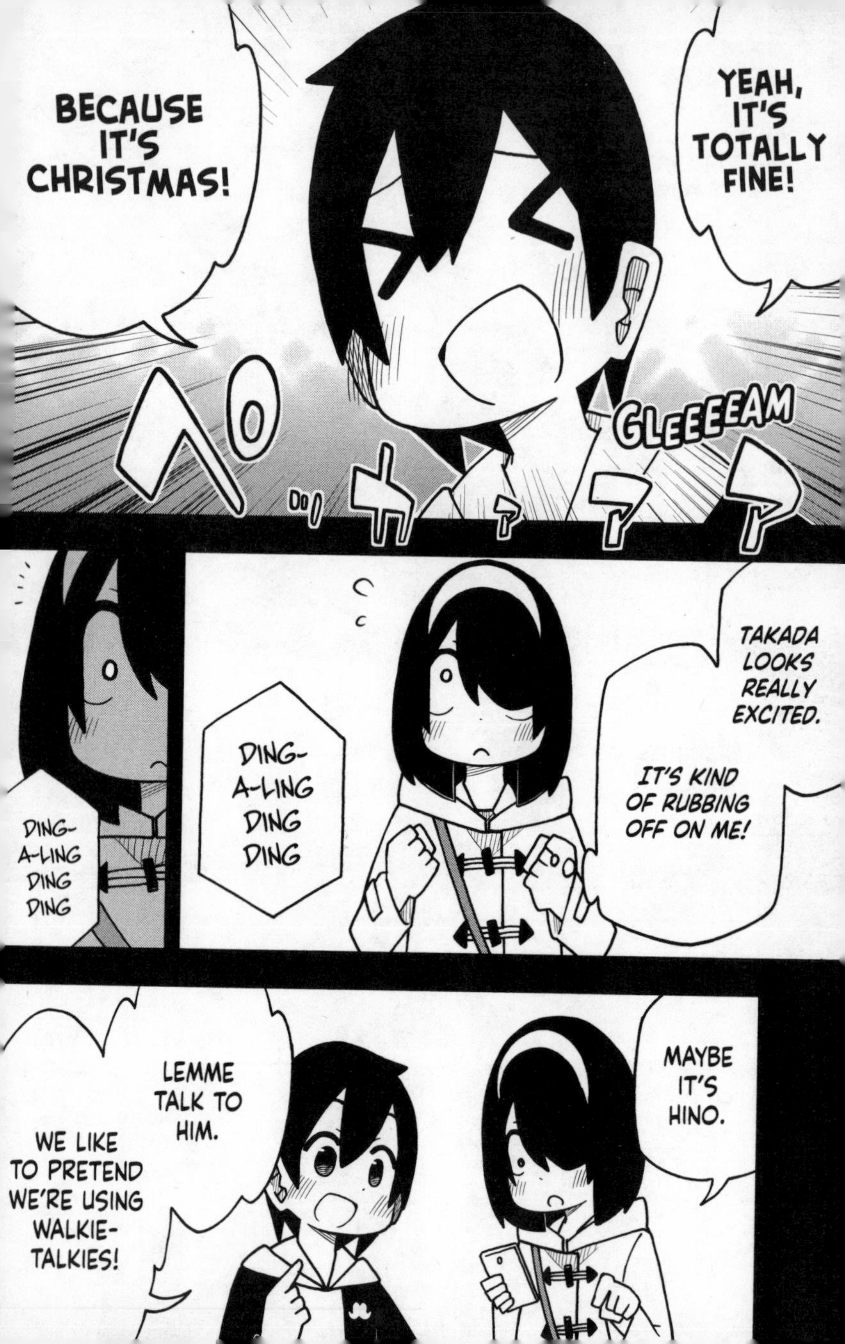
YEAH, IT'S TOTALLY FINE!
BECAUSE IT'S CHRISTMAS!
GLEEEEAM
TAKADA LOOKS REALLY EXCITED.
IT'S KIND OF RUBBING OFF ON ME!
DING-A-LING DING DING
DING-A-LING DING DING
MAYBE IT'S HINO.
LEMME TALK TO HIM.
WE LIKE TO PRETEND WE'RE USING WALKIE-TALKIES!

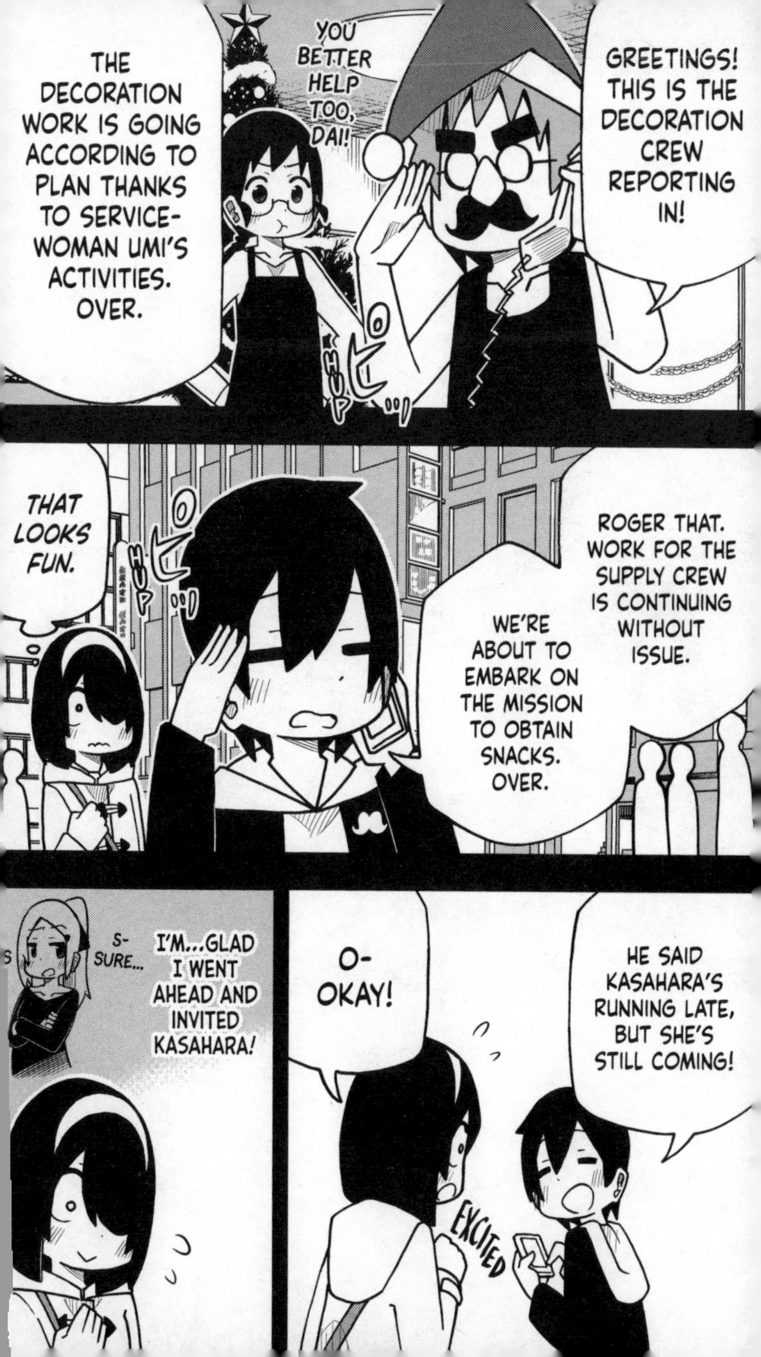
GREETINGS! THIS IS THE DECORATION CREW REPORTING IN!
YOU BETTER HELP TOO, DAI!
THE DECORATION WORK IS GOING ACCORDING TO PLAN THANKS TO SERVICE-WOMAN UMI'S ACTIVITIES. OVER.
HUP
ROGER THAT. WORK FOR THE SUPPLY CREW IS CONTINUING WITHOUT ISSUE.
WE'RE ABOUT TO EMBARK ON THE MISSION TO OBTAIN SNACKS. OVER.
HUP
THAT LOOKS FUN.
HE SAID KASAHARA'S RUNNING LATE, BUT SHE'S STILL COMING!
O- OKAY!
EXCITED
I'M...GLAD I WENT AHEAD AND INVITED KASAHARA!
S- SURE...

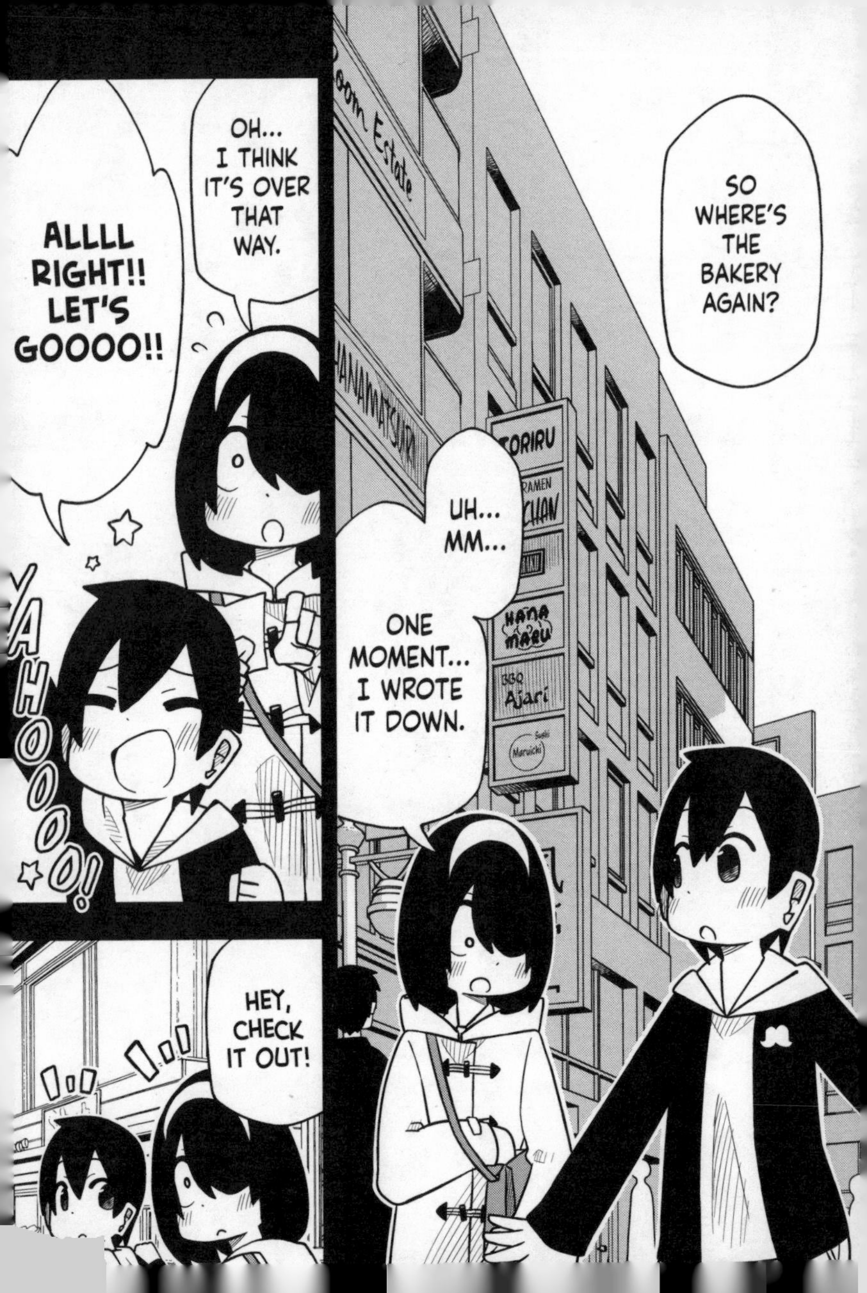
SO WHERE'S THE BAKERY AGAIN?
UH... MM...
ONE MOMENT... I WROTE IT DOWN.
TORIRU
HANA MARU
BBQ Ajari
Sushi Maruichi
OH... I THINK IT'S OVER THAT WAY.
ALLLL RIGHT!! LET'S GOOOO!!
YAHOOOOO!
HEY, CHECK IT OUT!

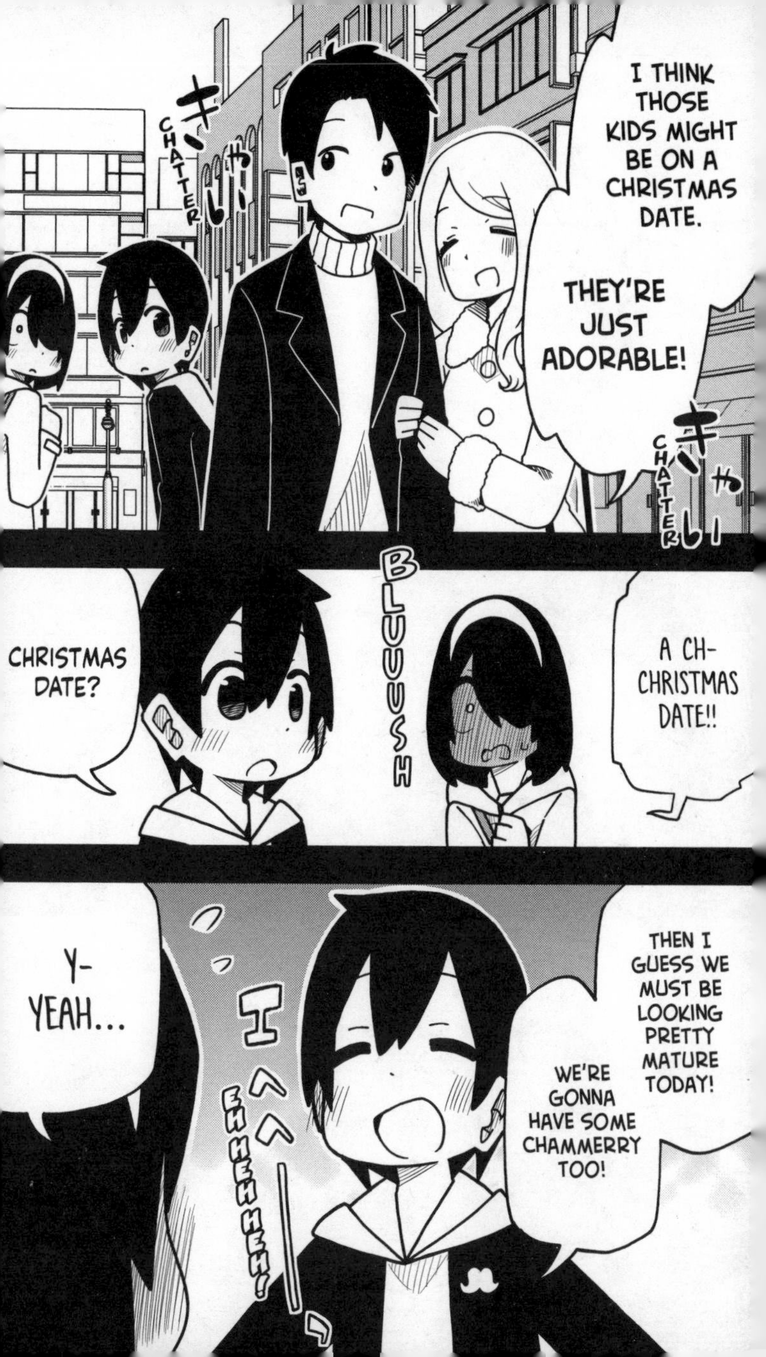
I THINK THOSE KIDS MIGHT BE ON A CHRISTMAS DATE.
THEY'RE JUST ADORABLE!
CHATTER
CHATTER
A CH- CHRISTMAS DATE!!
BLUUUSH
CHRISTMAS DATE?
THEN I GUESS WE MUST BE LOOKING PRETTY MATURE TODAY!
WE'RE GONNA HAVE SOME CHAMMERRY TOO!
EHHEHHEH!
Y-YEAH...

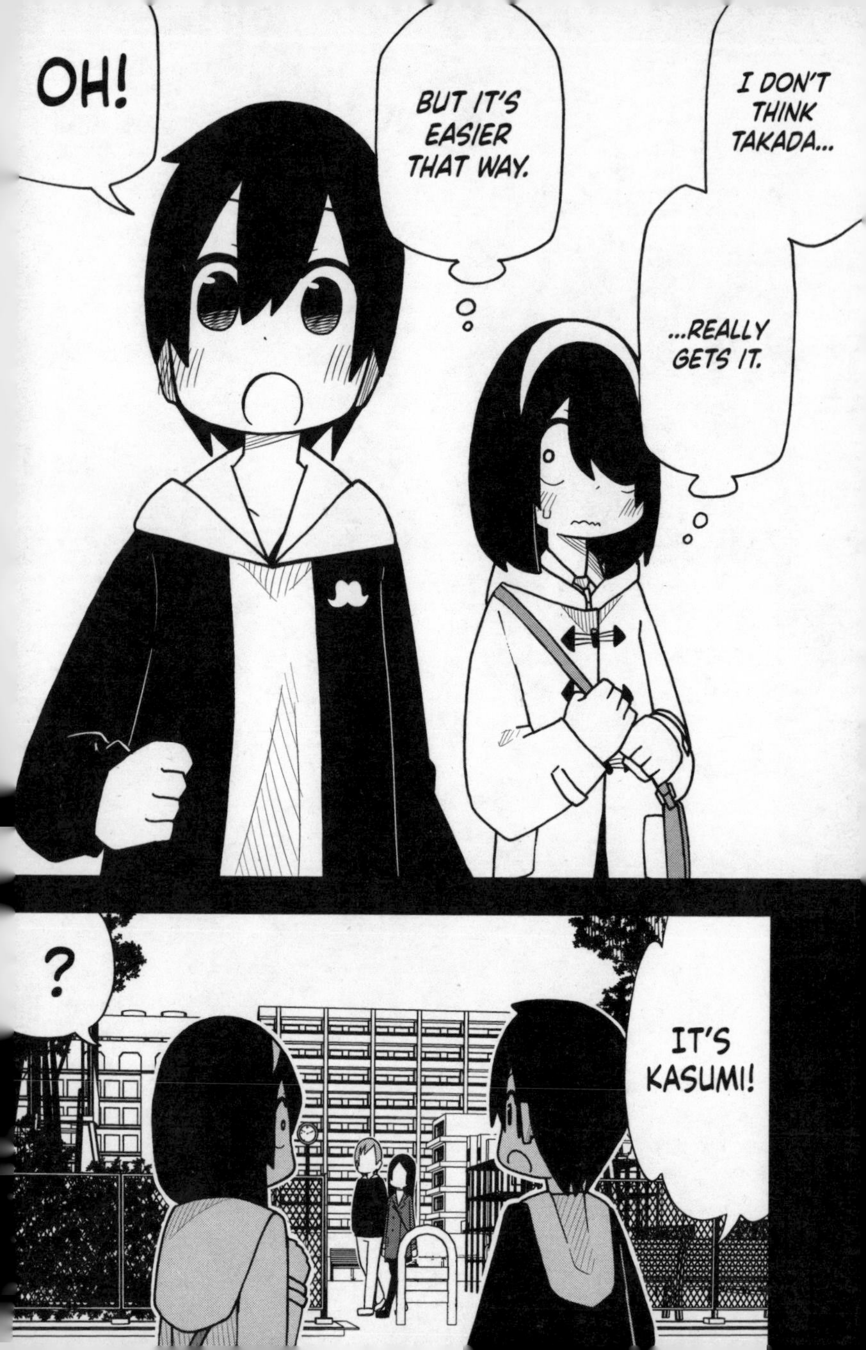
I DON'T THINK TAKADA...
...REALLY GETS IT.
BUT IT'S EASIER THAT WAY.
OH!
IT'S KASUMI!
?

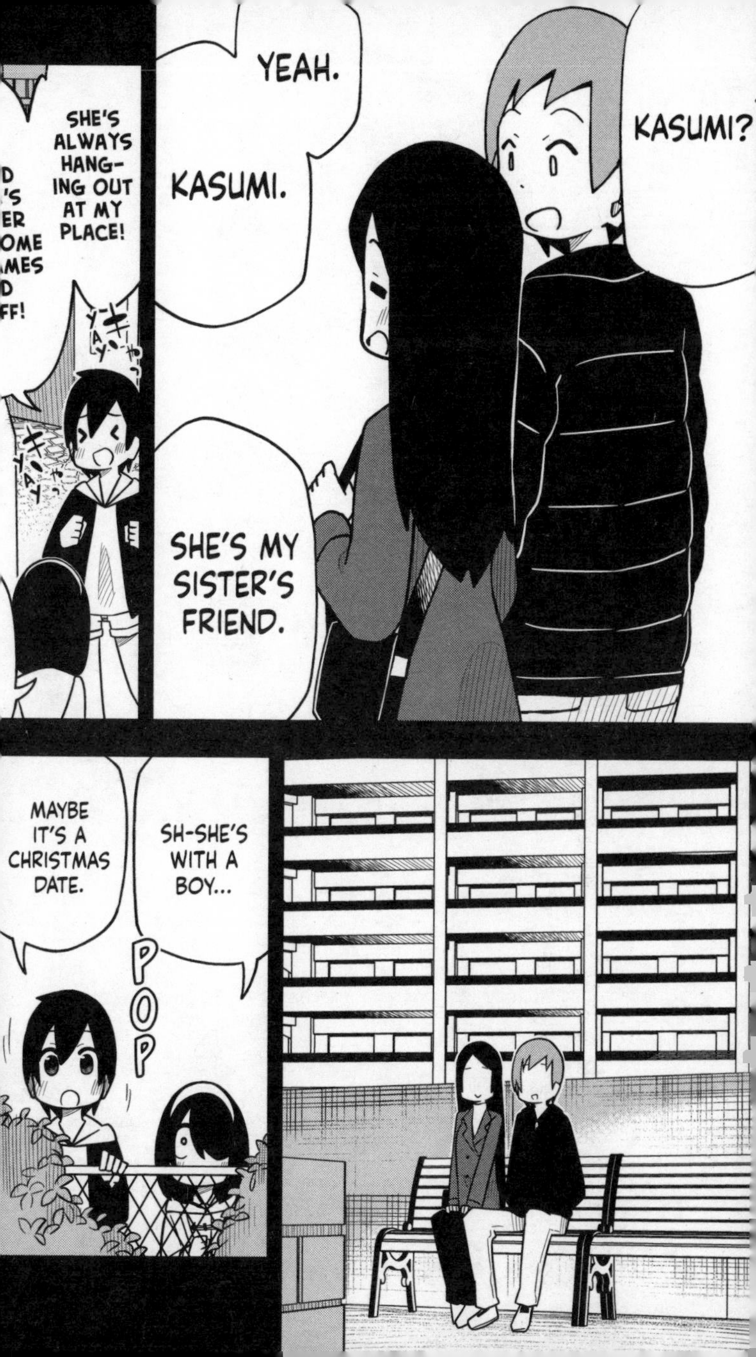

KASUMI?
YEAH.
KASUMI.
SHE'S MY SISTER'S FRIEND.
SHE'S ALWAYS HANGING OUT AT MY PLACE!
YAY
YAY
SH-SHE'S WITH A BOY...
MAYBE IT'S A CHRISTMAS DATE.
POP

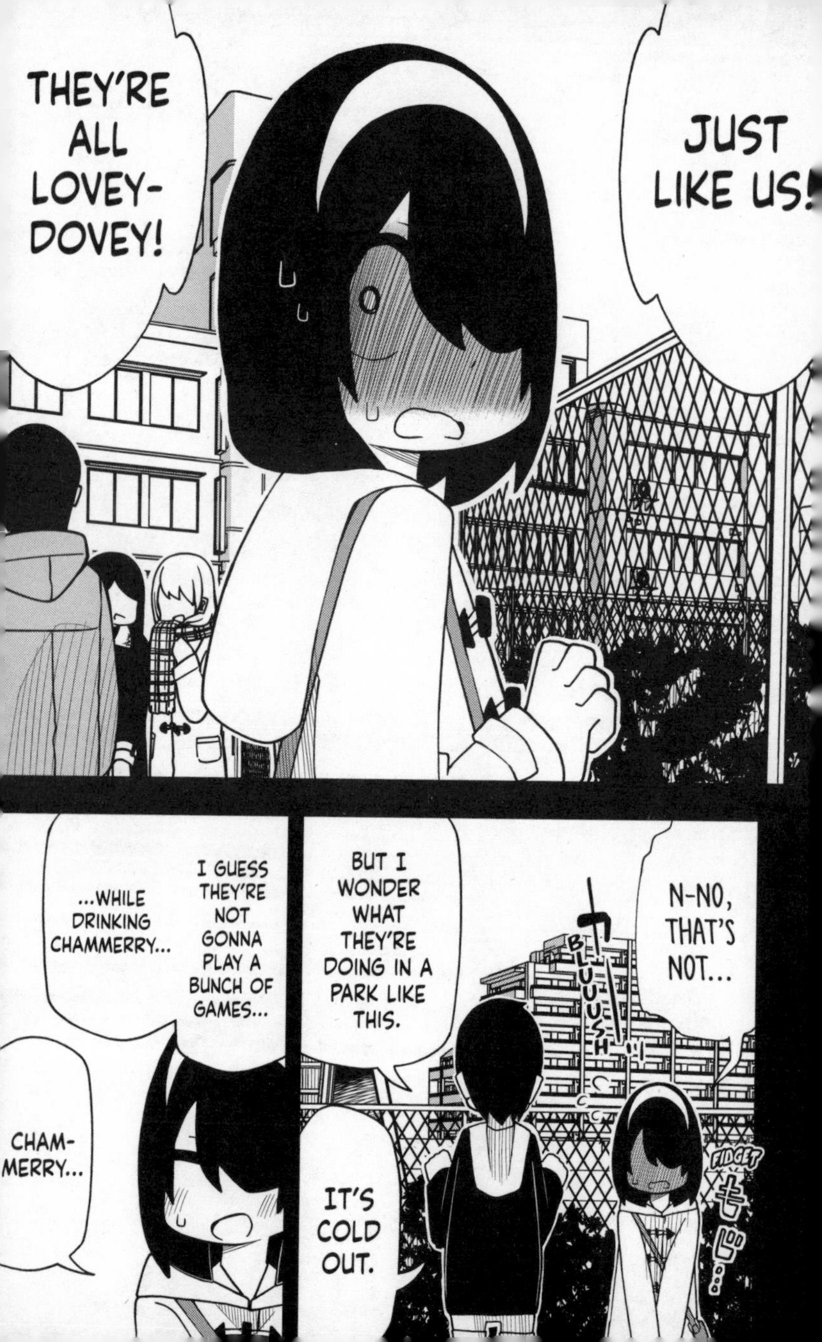
JUST LIKE US!
THEY'RE ALL LOVEY-DOVEY!
N-NO, THAT'S NOT...
BLUUUSH
BUT I WONDER WHAT THEY'RE DOING IN A PARK LIKE THIS.
FIDGET
IT'S COLD OUT.
I GUESS THEY'RE NOT GONNA PLAY A BUNCH OF GAMES...
...WHILE DRINKING CHAMMERRY...
CHAM-MERRY...

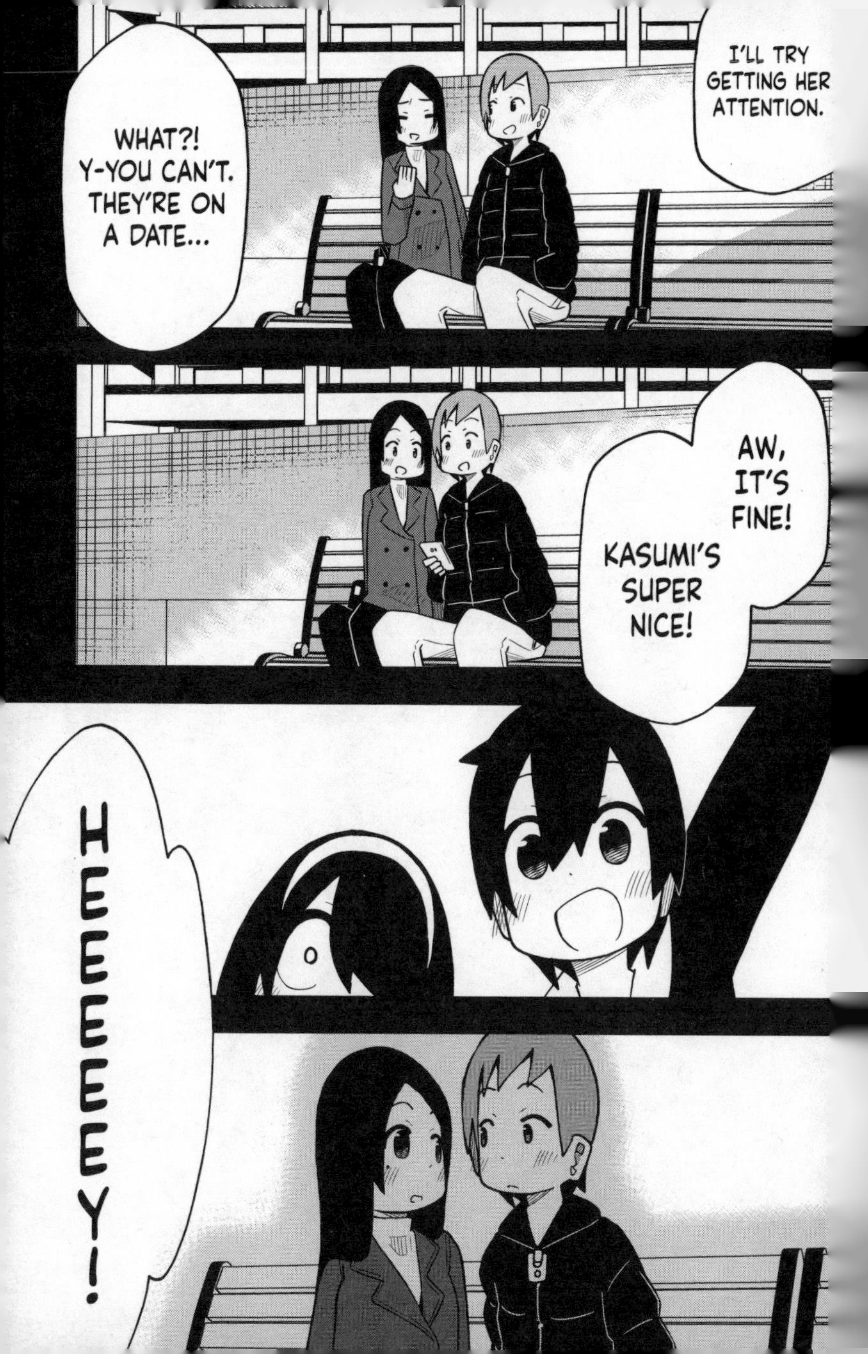
I'LL TRY GETTING HER ATTENTION.
WHAT?! Y-YOU CAN'T. THEY'RE ON A DATE...
AW, IT'S FINE!
KASUMI'S SUPER NICE!
HEEEEEY!

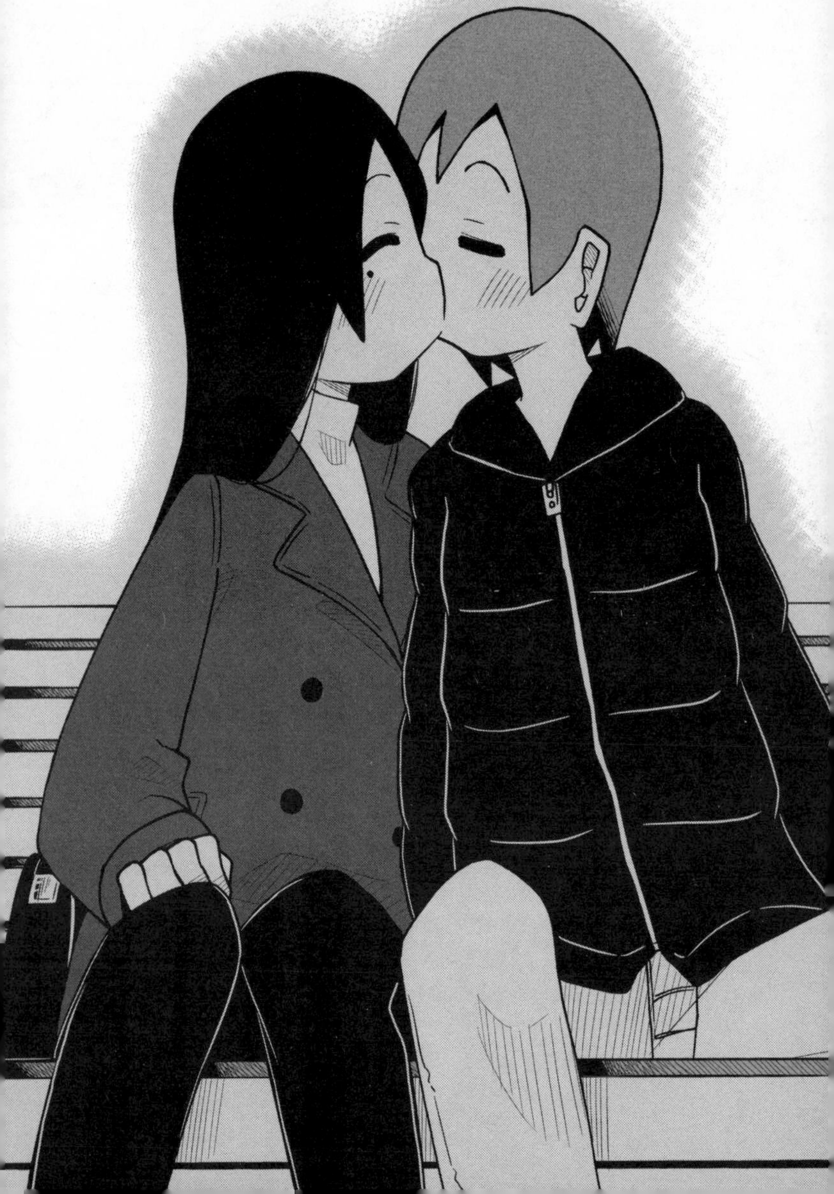

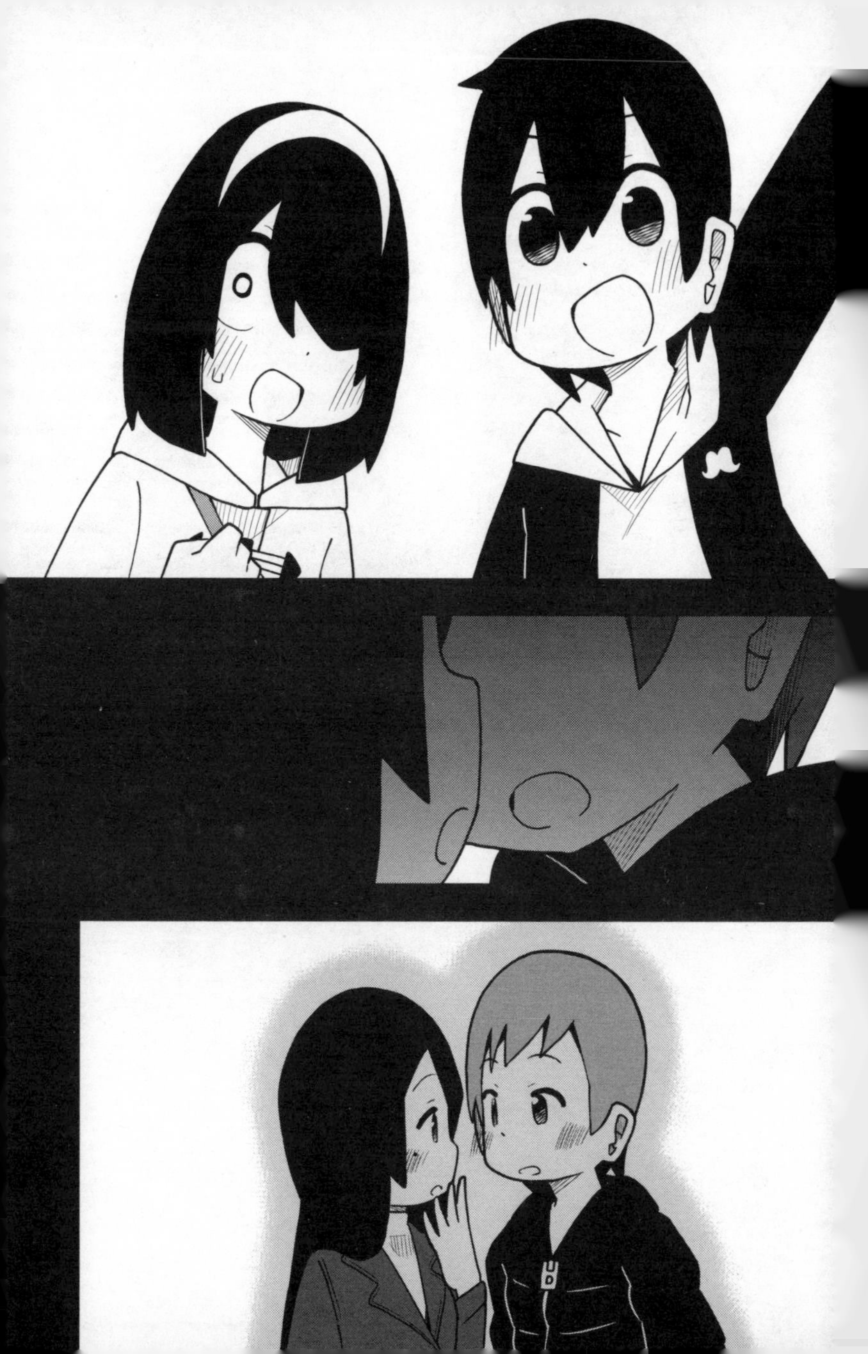

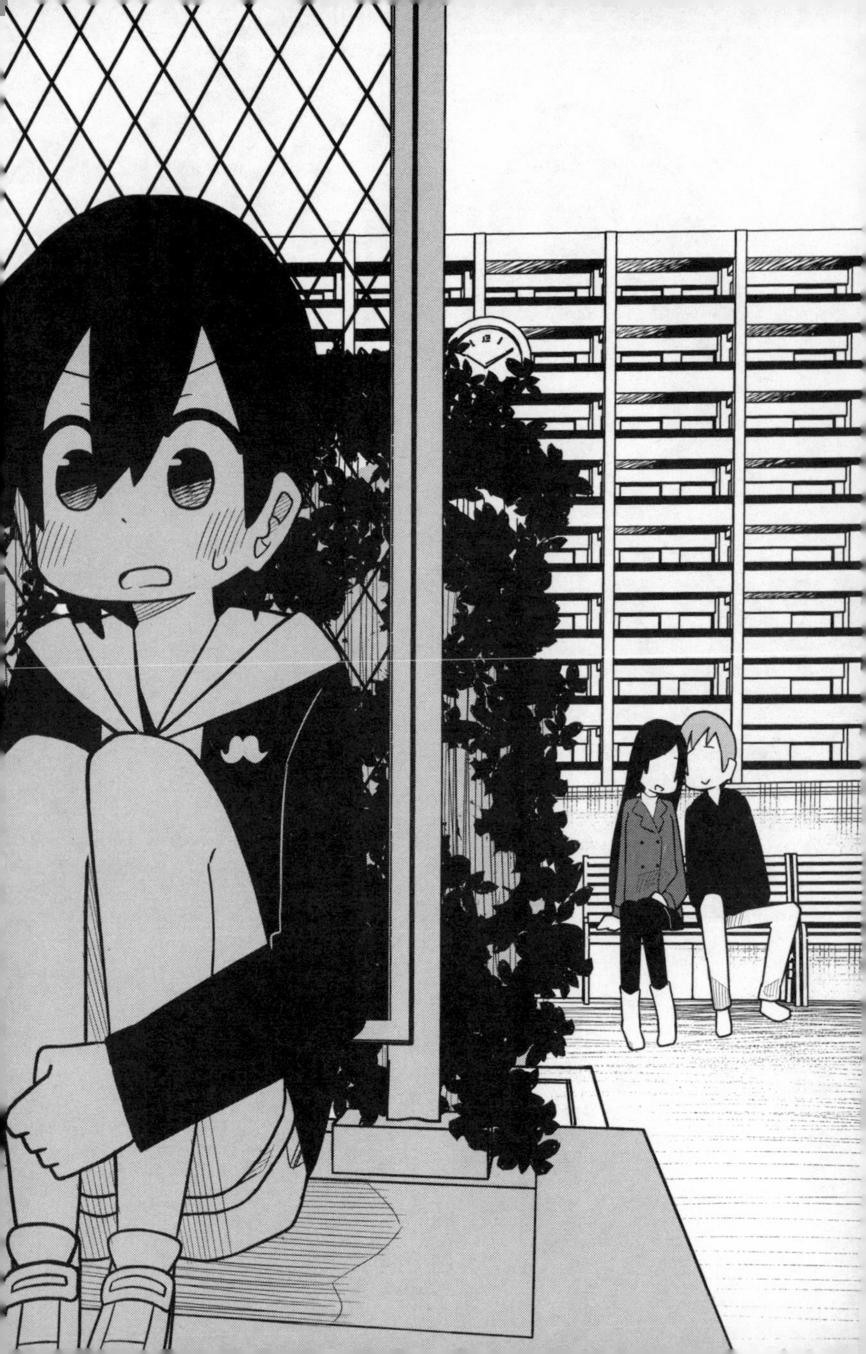

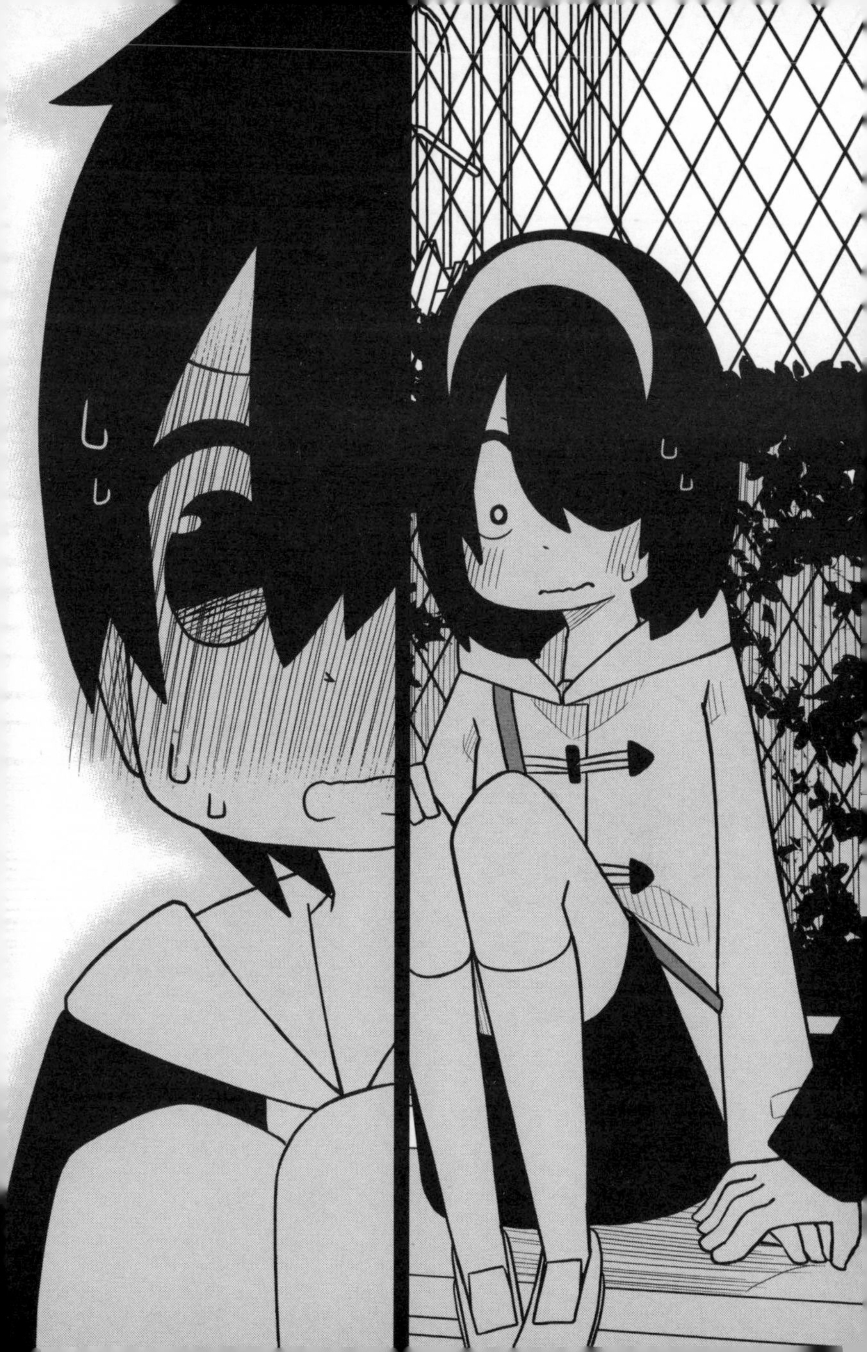

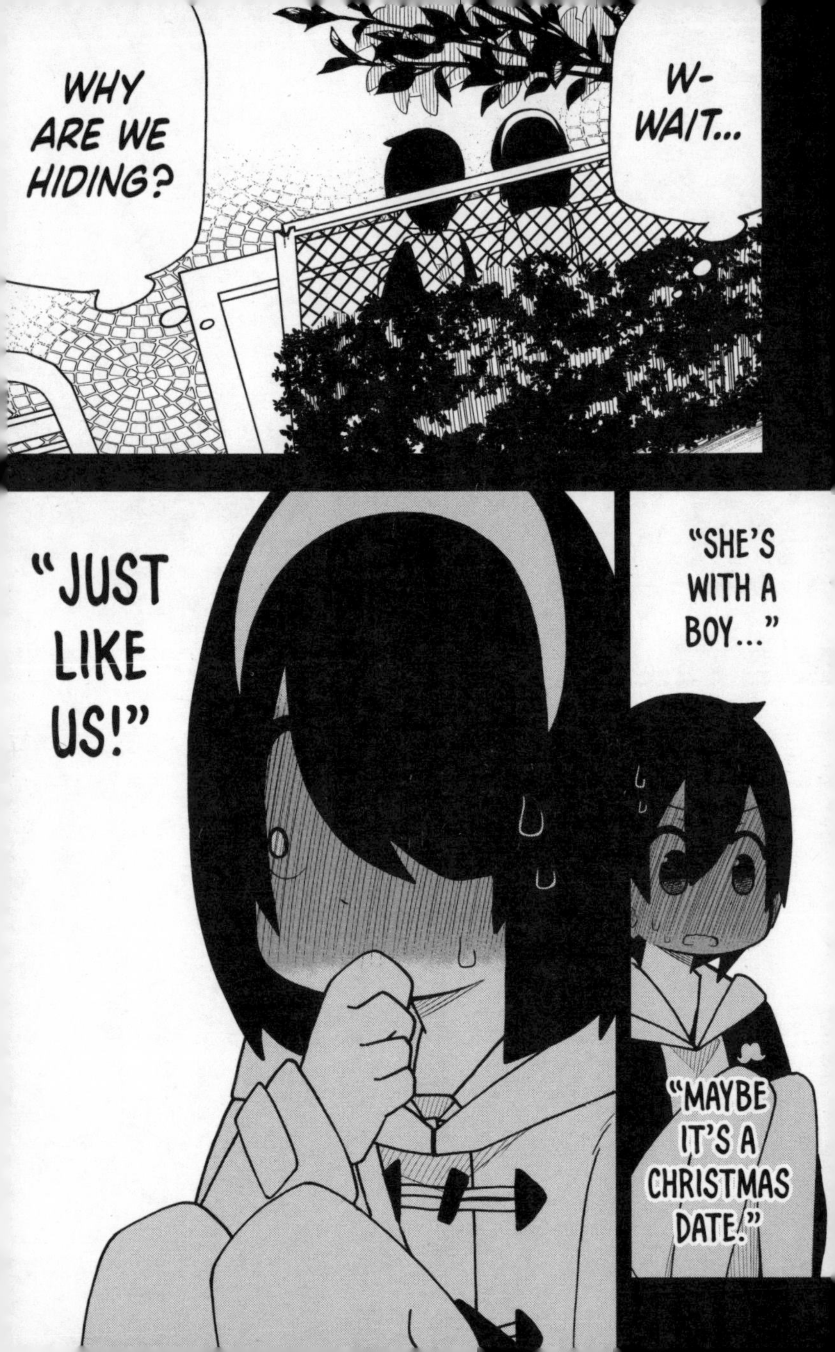
W-WAIT...
WHY ARE WE HIDING?
"SHE'S WITH A BOY..."
"MAYBE IT'S A CHRISTMAS DATE."
"JUST LIKE US!"

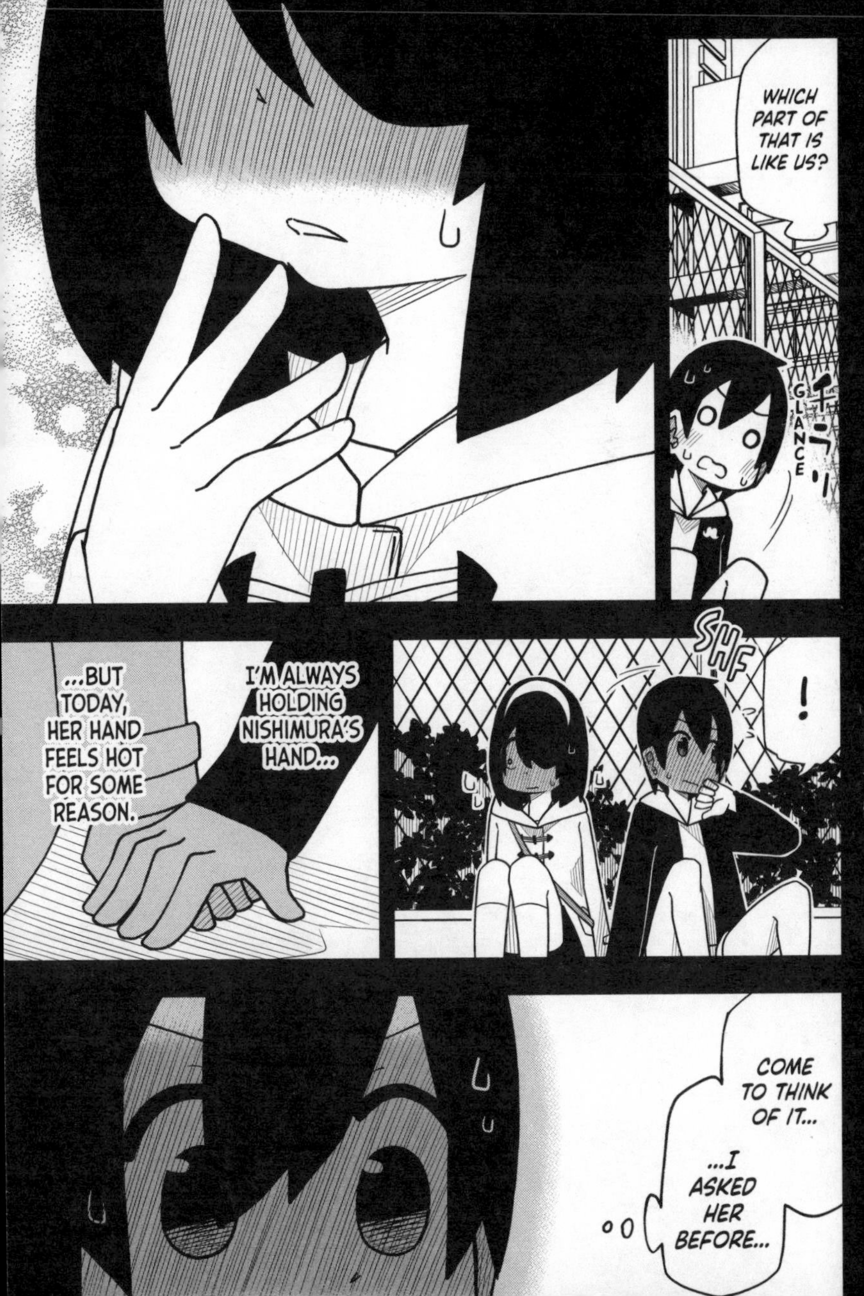
WHICH PART OF THAT IS LIKE US?
GLANCE
SHF
!
I'M ALWAYS HOLDING NISHIMURA'S HAND...
...BUT TODAY, HER HAND FEELS HOT FOR SOME REASON.
COME TO THINK OF IT...
...I ASKED HER BEFORE...

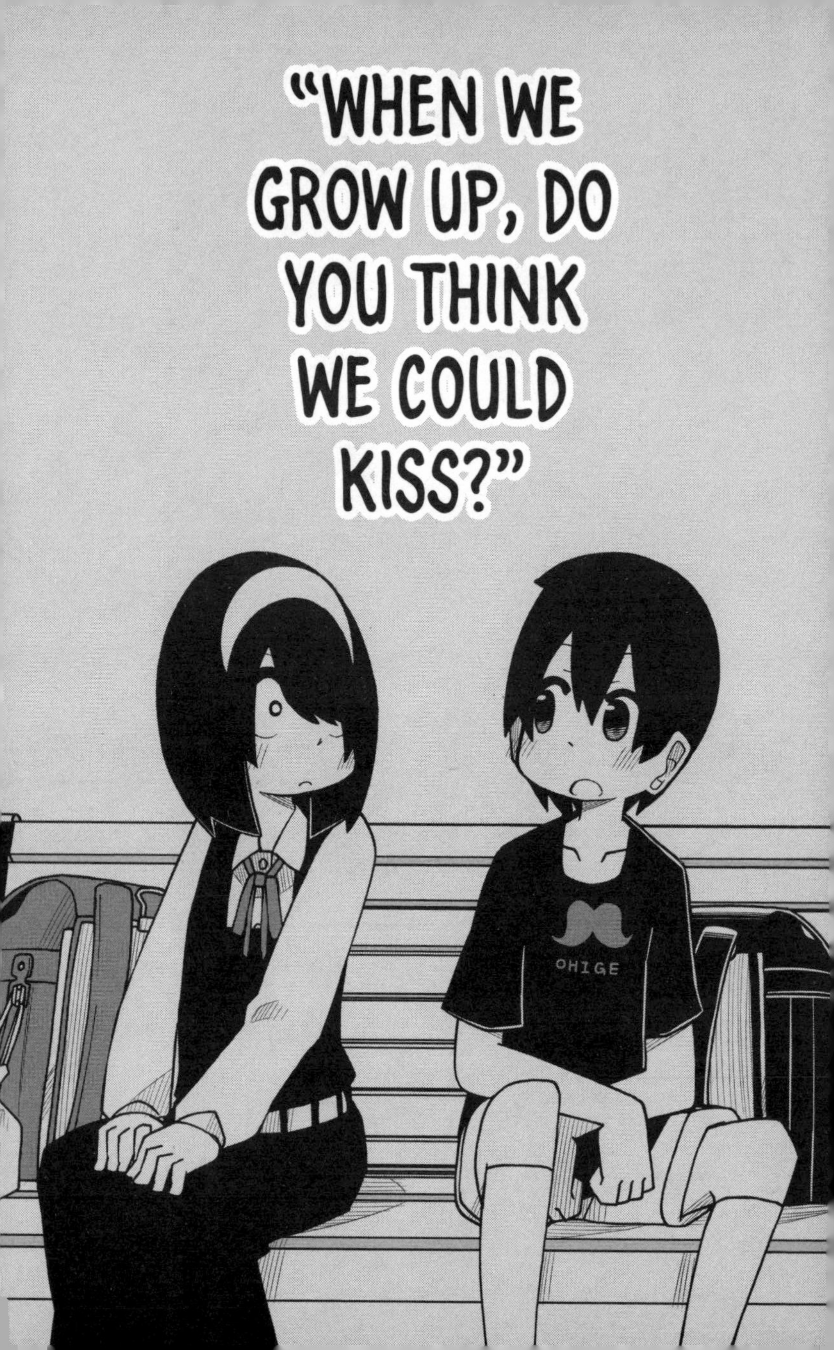
"WHEN WE GROW UP, DO YOU THINK WE COULD KISS?"
OHIGE

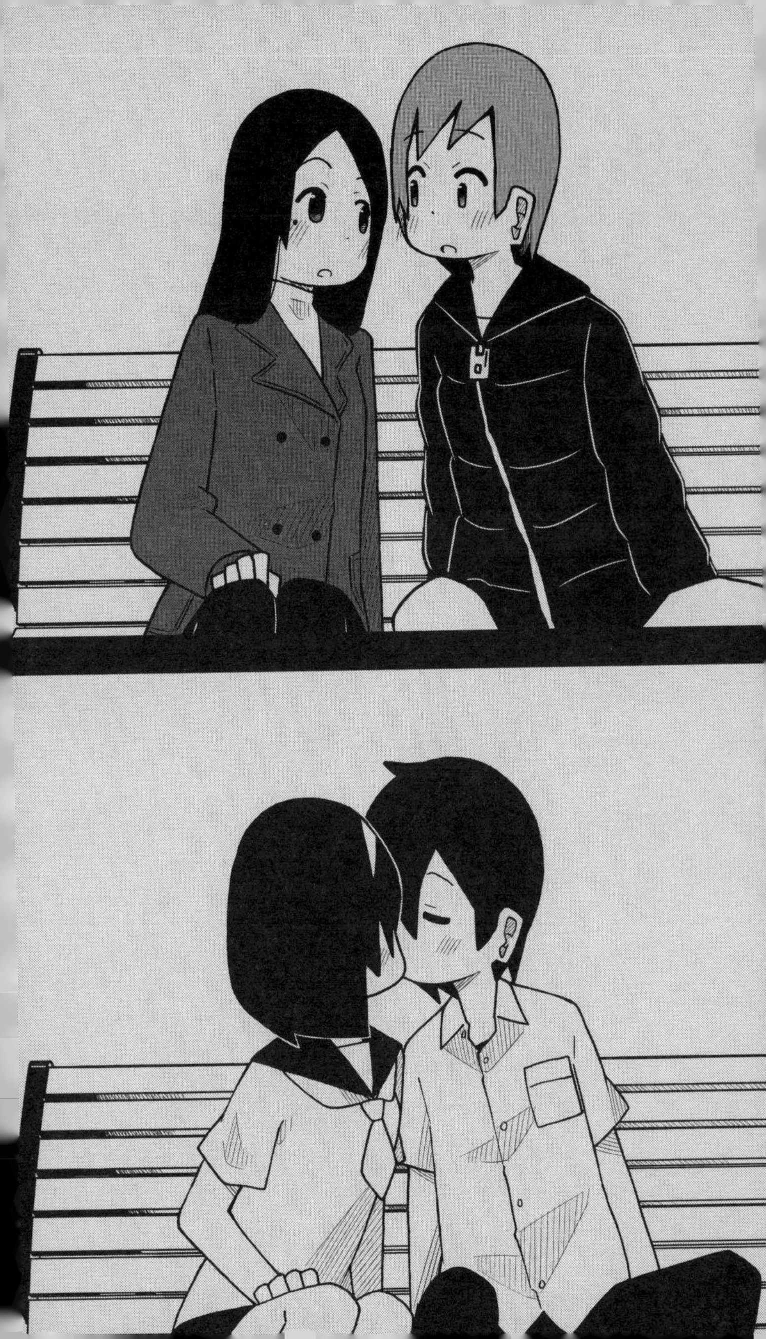

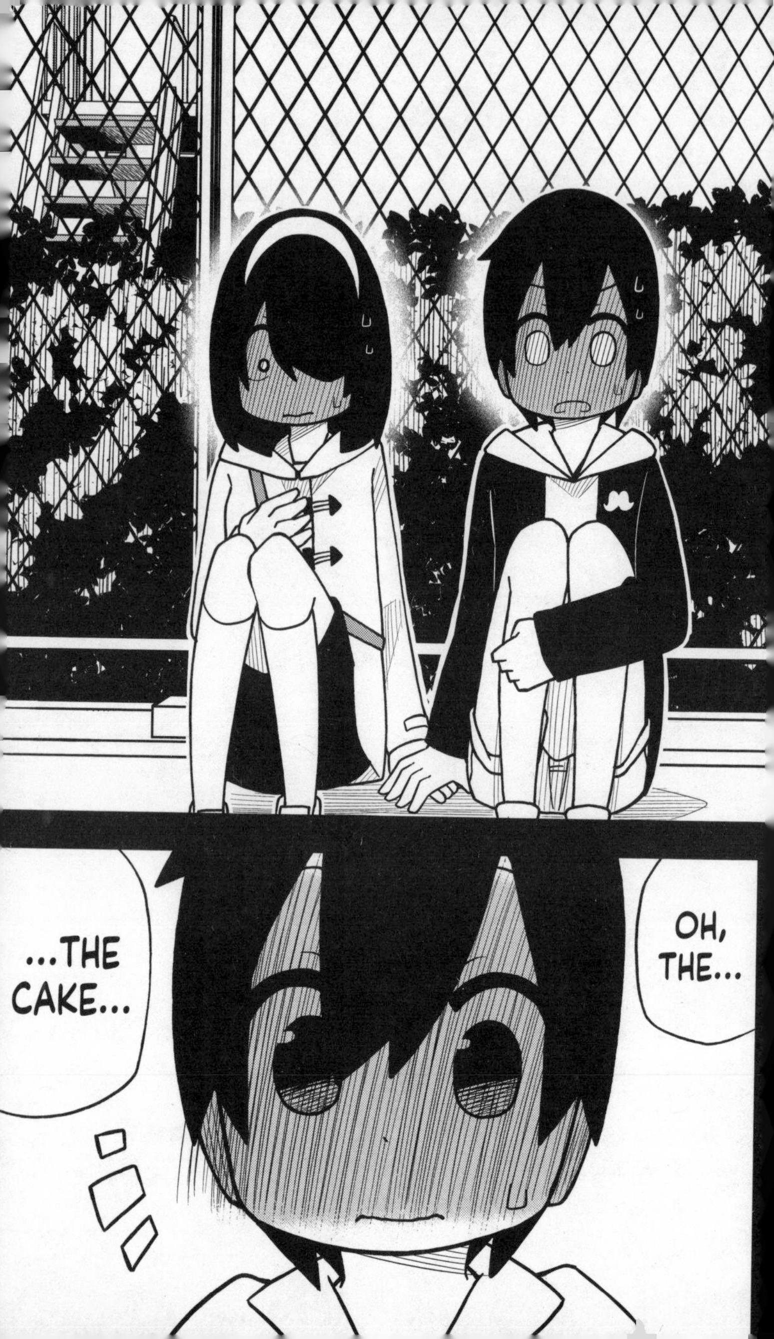
OH, THE...
...THE CAKE...

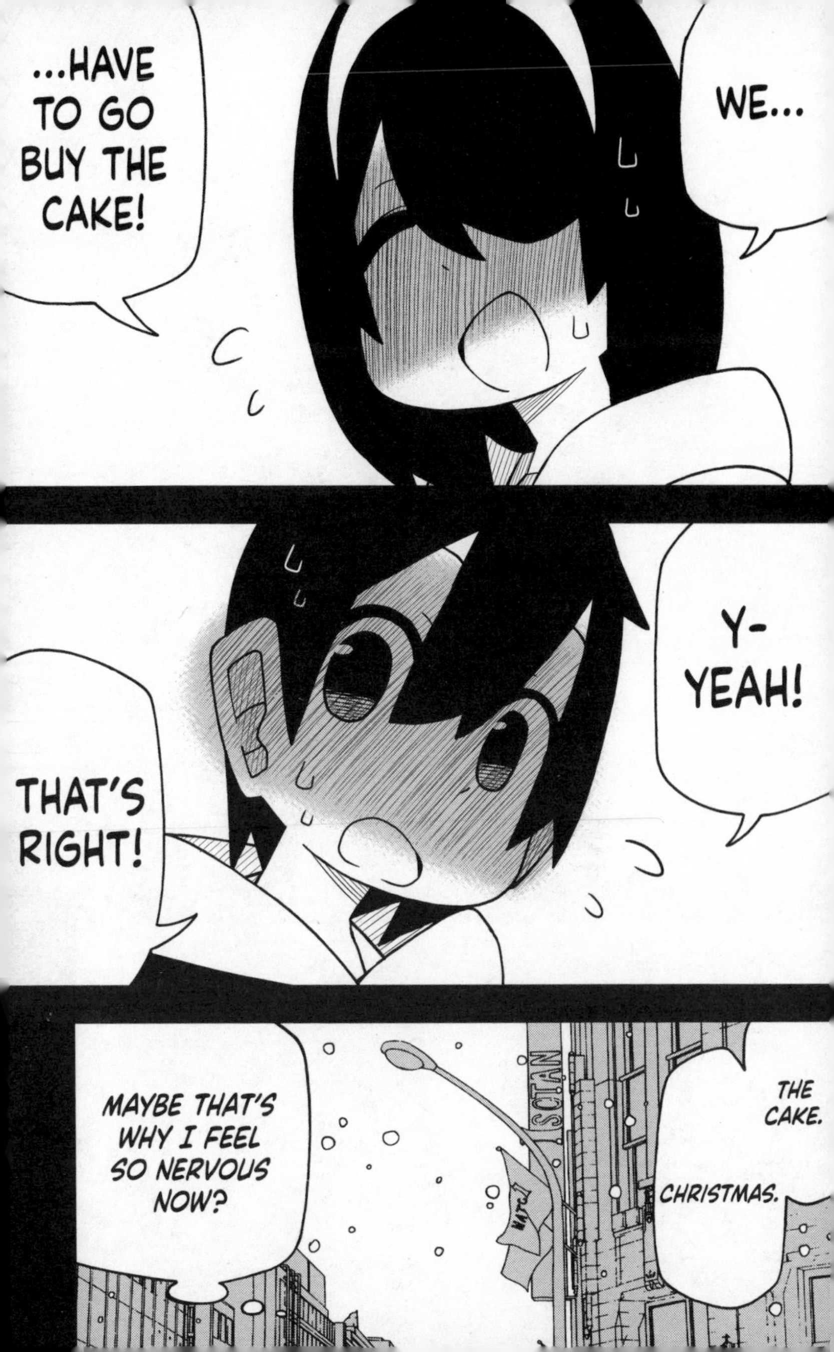
WE...
...HAVE TO GO BUY THE CAKE!
Y-YEAH!
THAT'S RIGHT!
THE CAKE.
CHRISTMAS.
MAYBE THAT'S WHY I FEEL SO NERVOUS NOW?

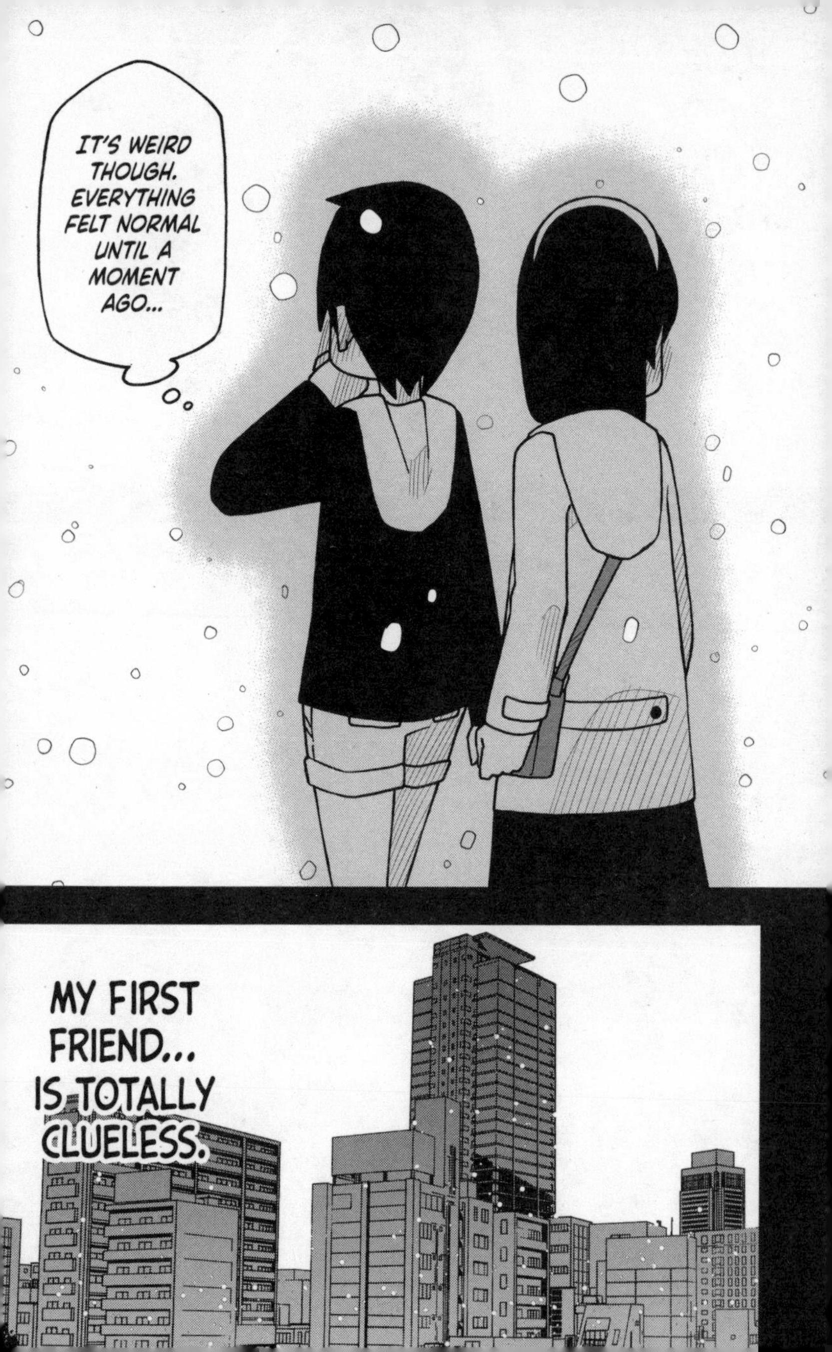
IT'S WEIRD THOUGH. EVERYTHING FELT NORMAL UNTIL A MOMENT AGO...
MY FIRST FRIEND... IS TOTALLY CLUELESS.

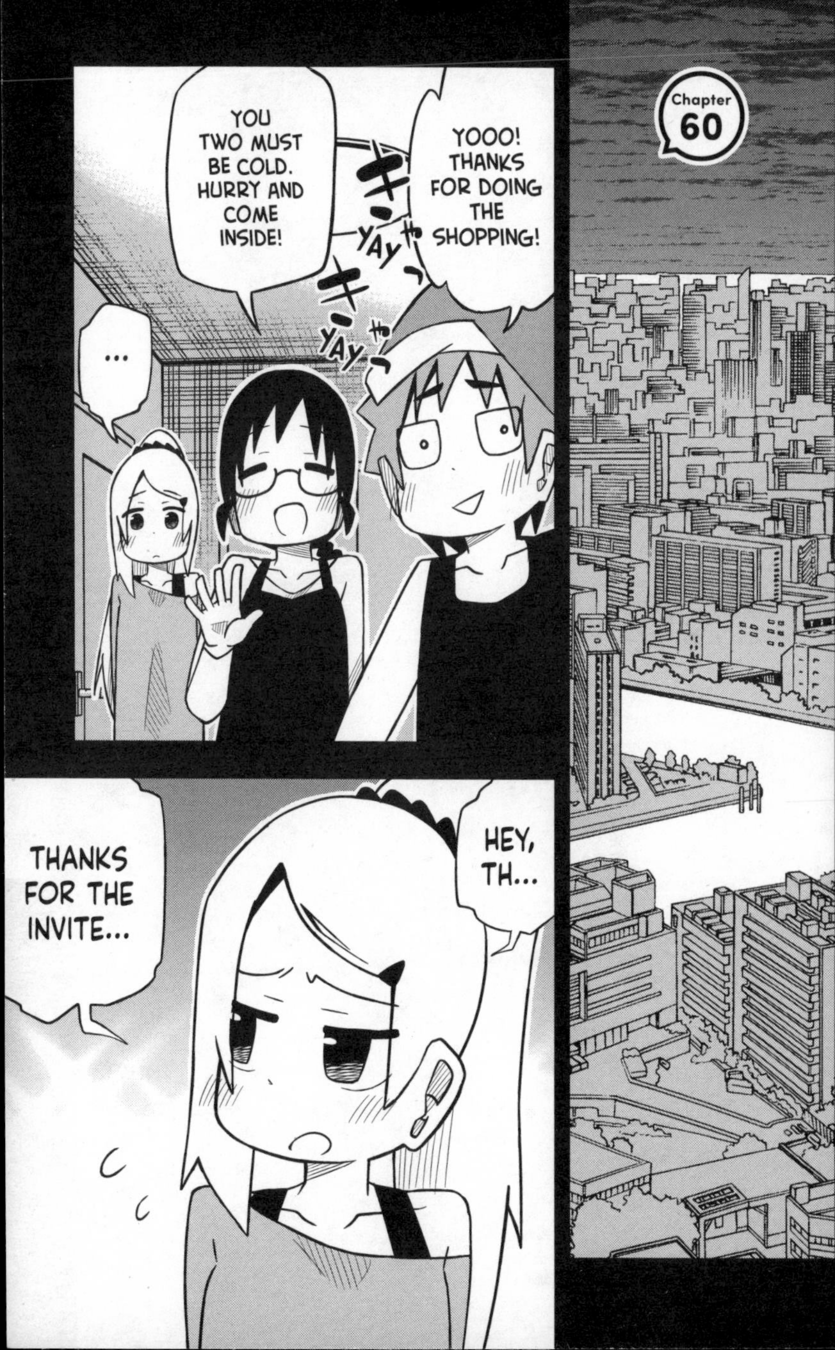
Chapter 60
YOOO! THANKS FOR DOING THE SHOPPING!
YOU TWO MUST BE COLD. HURRY AND COME INSIDE!
YAY
YAY
...
HEY, TH...
THANKS FOR THE INVITE...

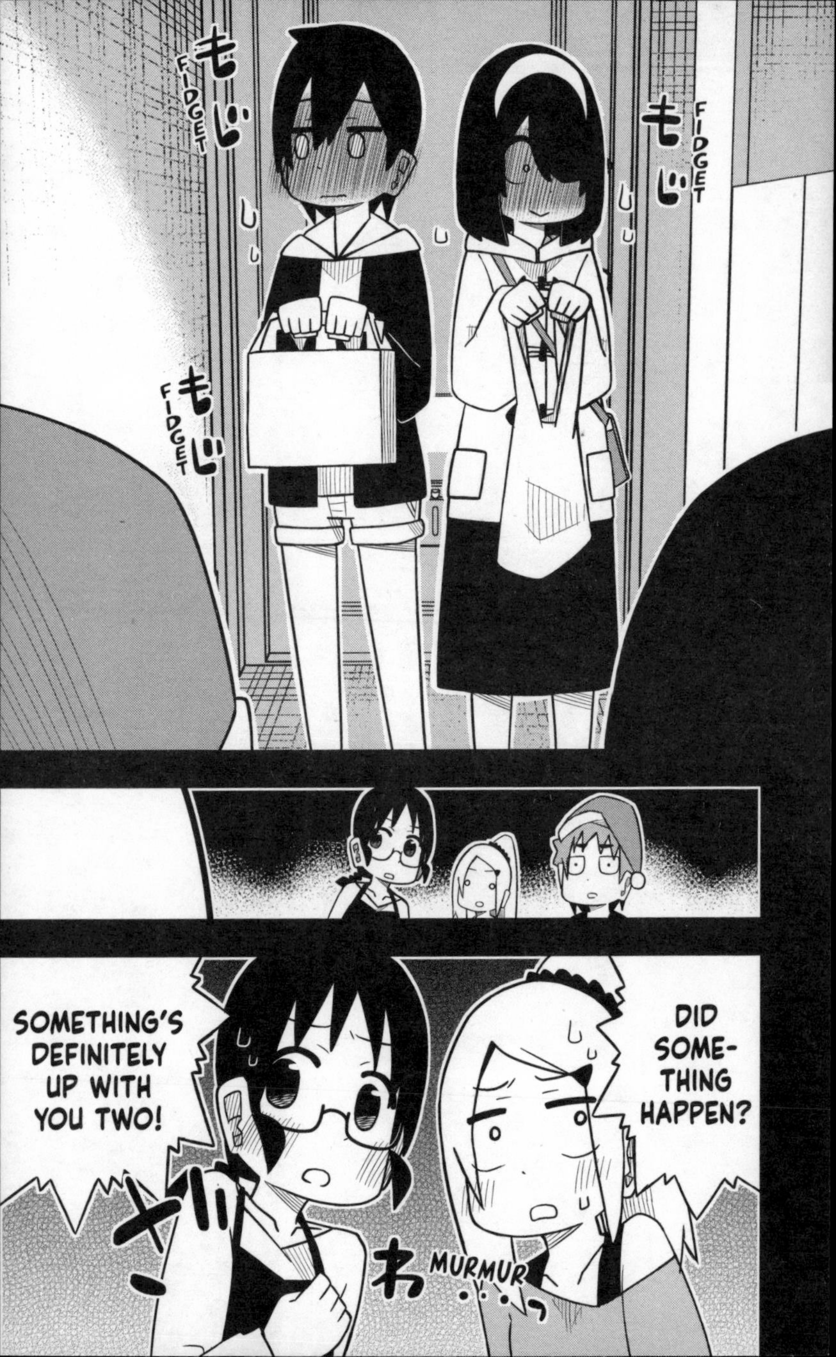
もじ
FIDGET
もじ
FIDGET
もじ
FIDGET
DID SOME-THING HAPPEN?
SOMETHING'S DEFINITELY UP WITH YOU TWO!
わ
MURMUR

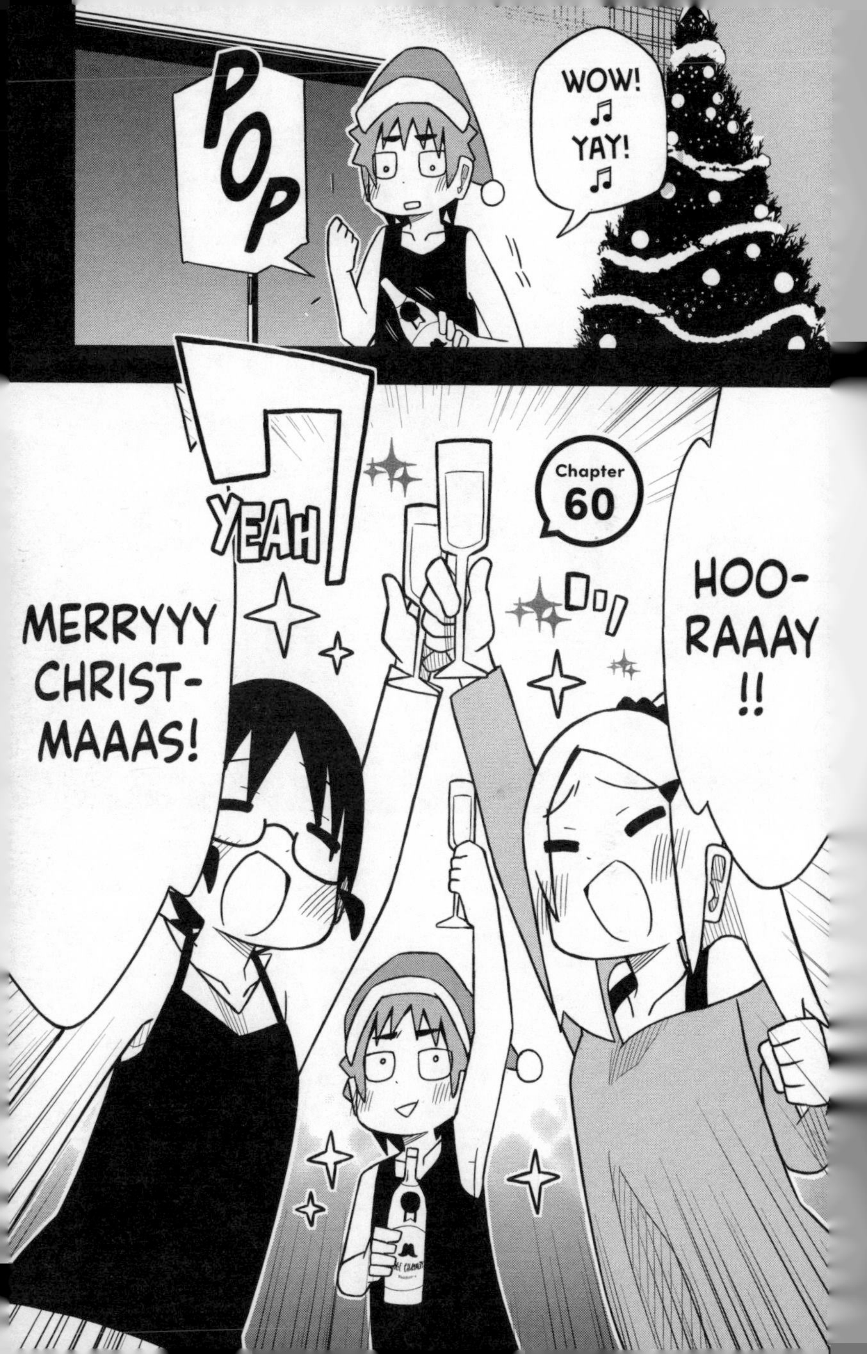
WOW! ♫ YAY! ♫
POP
HOO-RAAAY!!
Chapter 60
DOII
YEAH
MERRYYY CHRIST-MAAAS!

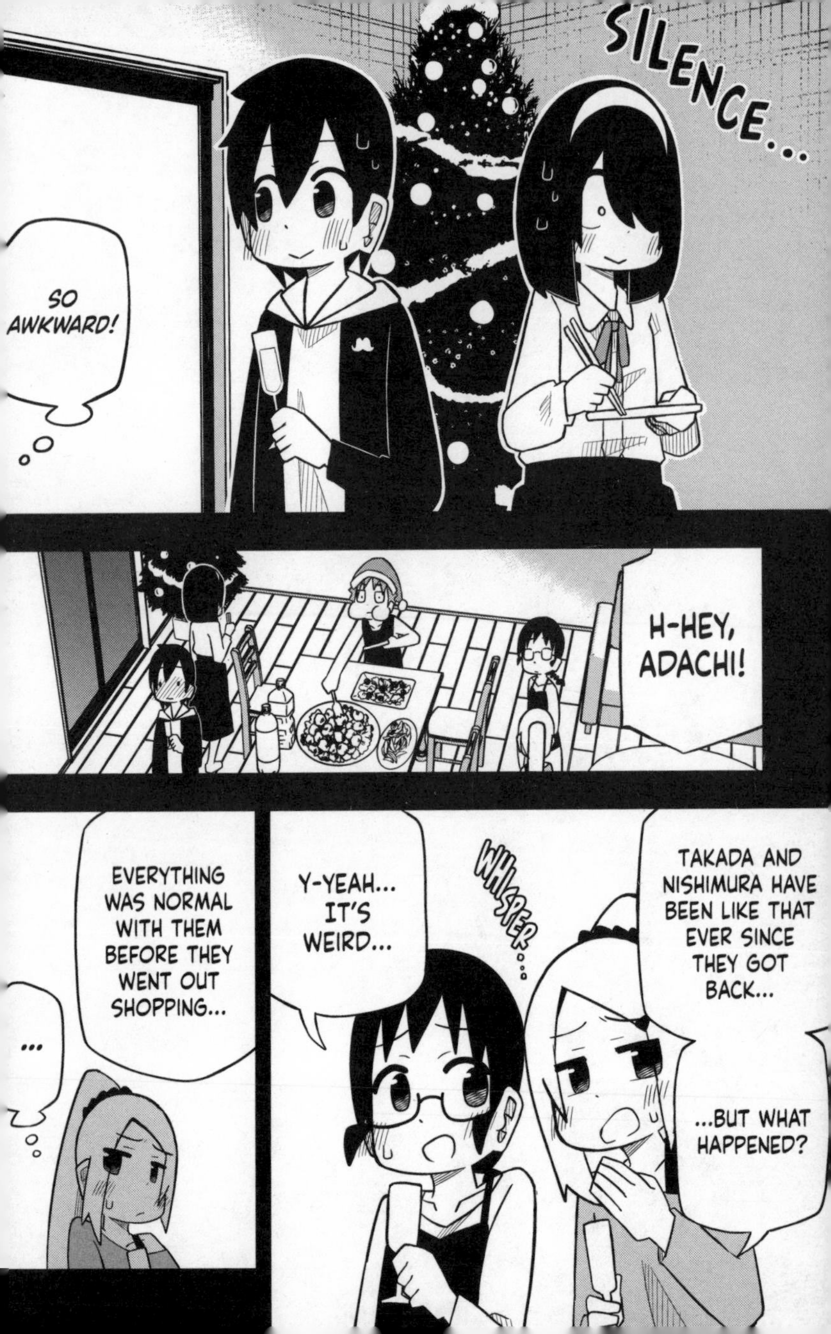
SILENCE...
SO AWKWARD!
H-HEY, ADACHI!
TAKADA AND NISHIMURA HAVE BEEN LIKE THAT EVER SINCE THEY GOT BACK...
WHISPER...
Y-YEAH... IT'S WEIRD...
...BUT WHAT HAPPENED?
EVERYTHING WAS NORMAL WITH THEM BEFORE THEY WENT OUT SHOPPING...
...

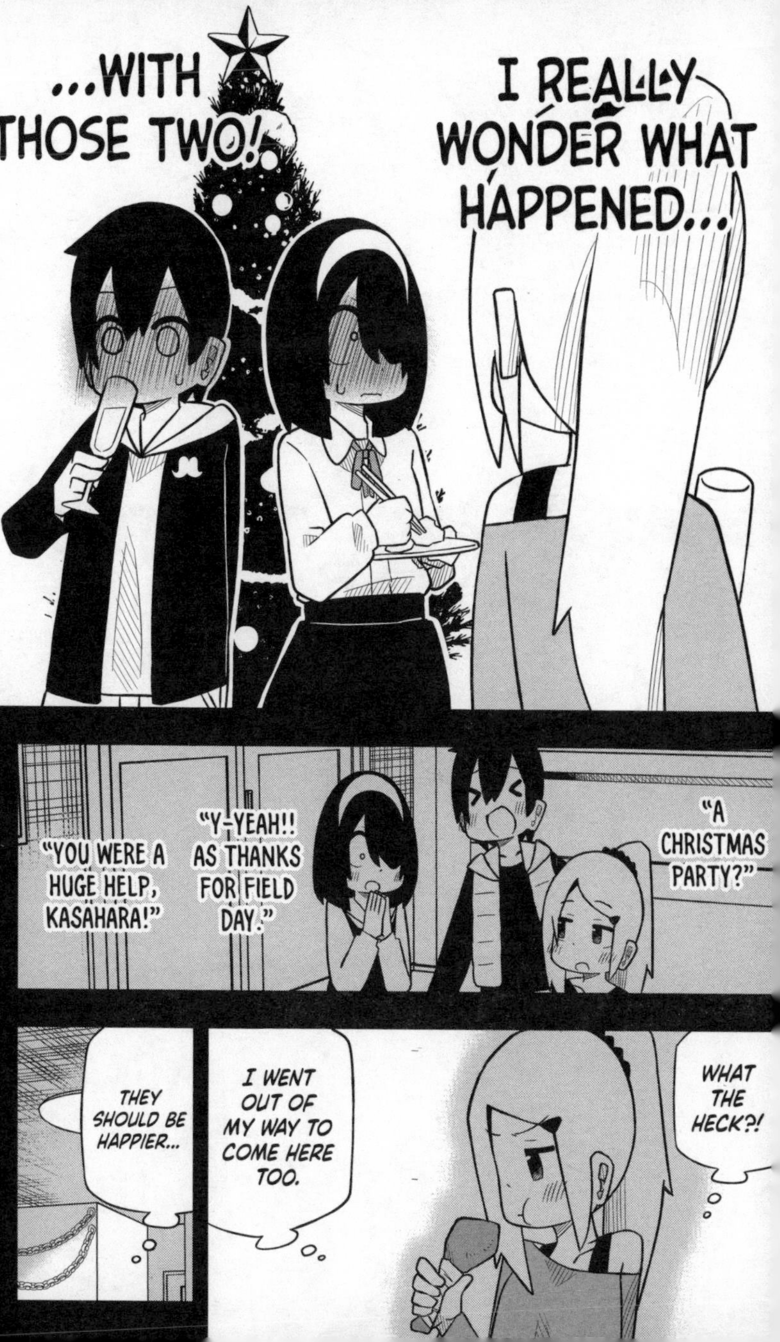
I REALLY WONDER WHAT HAPPENED...
...WITH THOSE TWO!
"A CHRISTMAS PARTY?"
"Y-YEAH!! AS THANKS FOR FIELD DAY."
"YOU WERE A HUGE HELP, KASAHARA!"
WHAT THE HECK?!
I WENT OUT OF MY WAY TO COME HERE TOO.
THEY SHOULD BE HAPPIER...

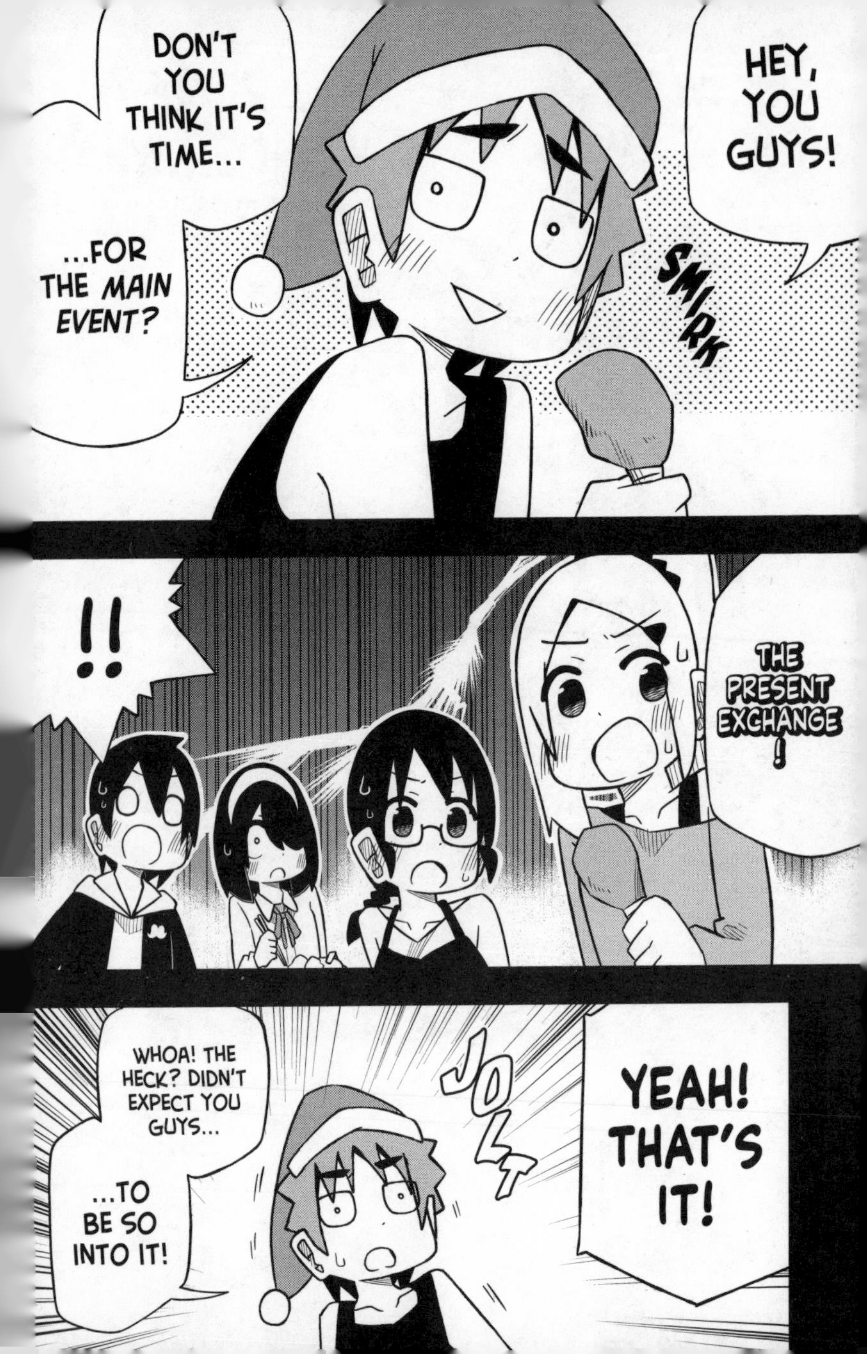
HEY, YOU GUYS!
SMIRK
DON'T YOU THINK IT'S TIME...
...FOR THE MAIN EVENT?
THE PRESENT EXCHANGE!
!!
YEAH! THAT'S IT!
JOLT
WHOA! THE HECK? DIDN'T EXPECT YOU GUYS...
...TO BE SO INTO IT!

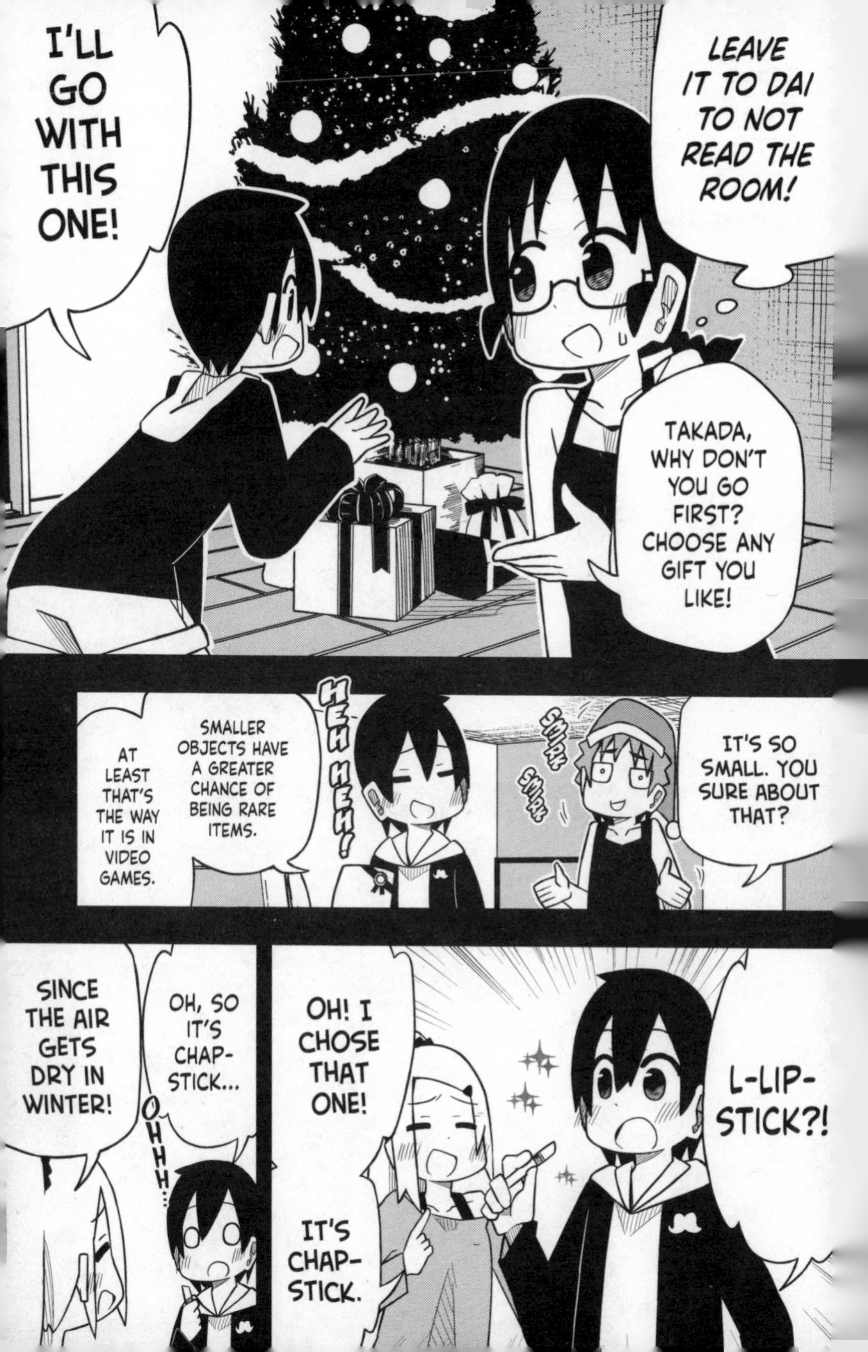
LEAVE IT TO DAI TO NOT READ THE ROOM!
TAKADA, WHY DON'T YOU GO FIRST? CHOOSE ANY GIFT YOU LIKE!
I'LL GO WITH THIS ONE!
IT'S SO SMALL. YOU SURE ABOUT THAT?
SMIRK
SMIRK
HEH HEH HEH!
SMALLER OBJECTS HAVE A GREATER CHANCE OF BEING RARE ITEMS.
AT LEAST THAT'S THE WAY IT IS IN VIDEO GAMES.
L-LIP-STICK?!
OH! I CHOSE THAT ONE!
IT'S CHAP-STICK.
OH, SO IT'S CHAP-STICK...
OHHH...
SINCE THE AIR GETS DRY IN WINTER!

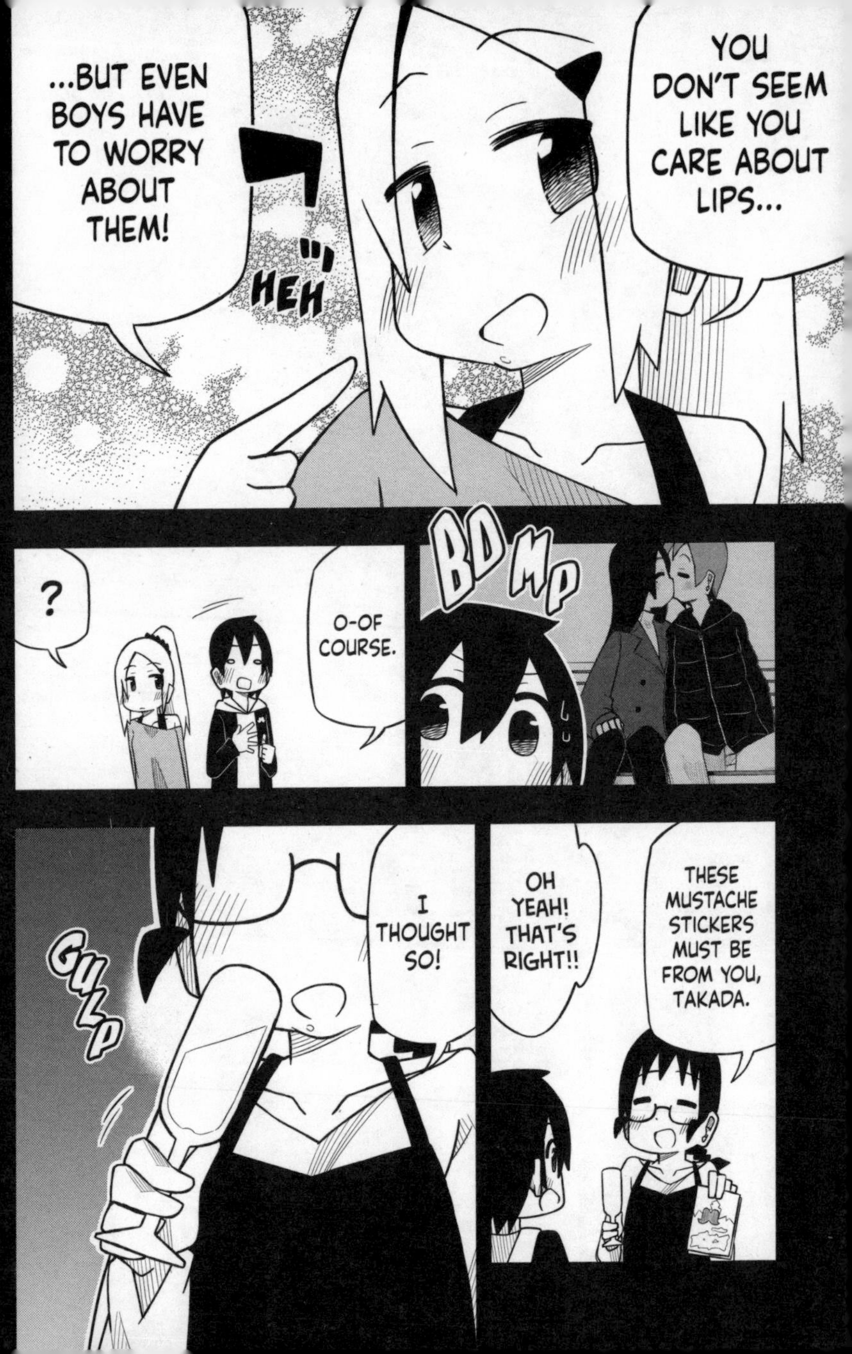
YOU DON'T SEEM LIKE YOU CARE ABOUT LIPS...
HEH
...BUT EVEN BOYS HAVE TO WORRY ABOUT THEM!
BDMP
O-OF COURSE.
?
THESE MUSTACHE STICKERS MUST BE FROM YOU, TAKADA.
OH YEAH! THAT'S RIGHT!!
I THOUGHT SO!
GULP

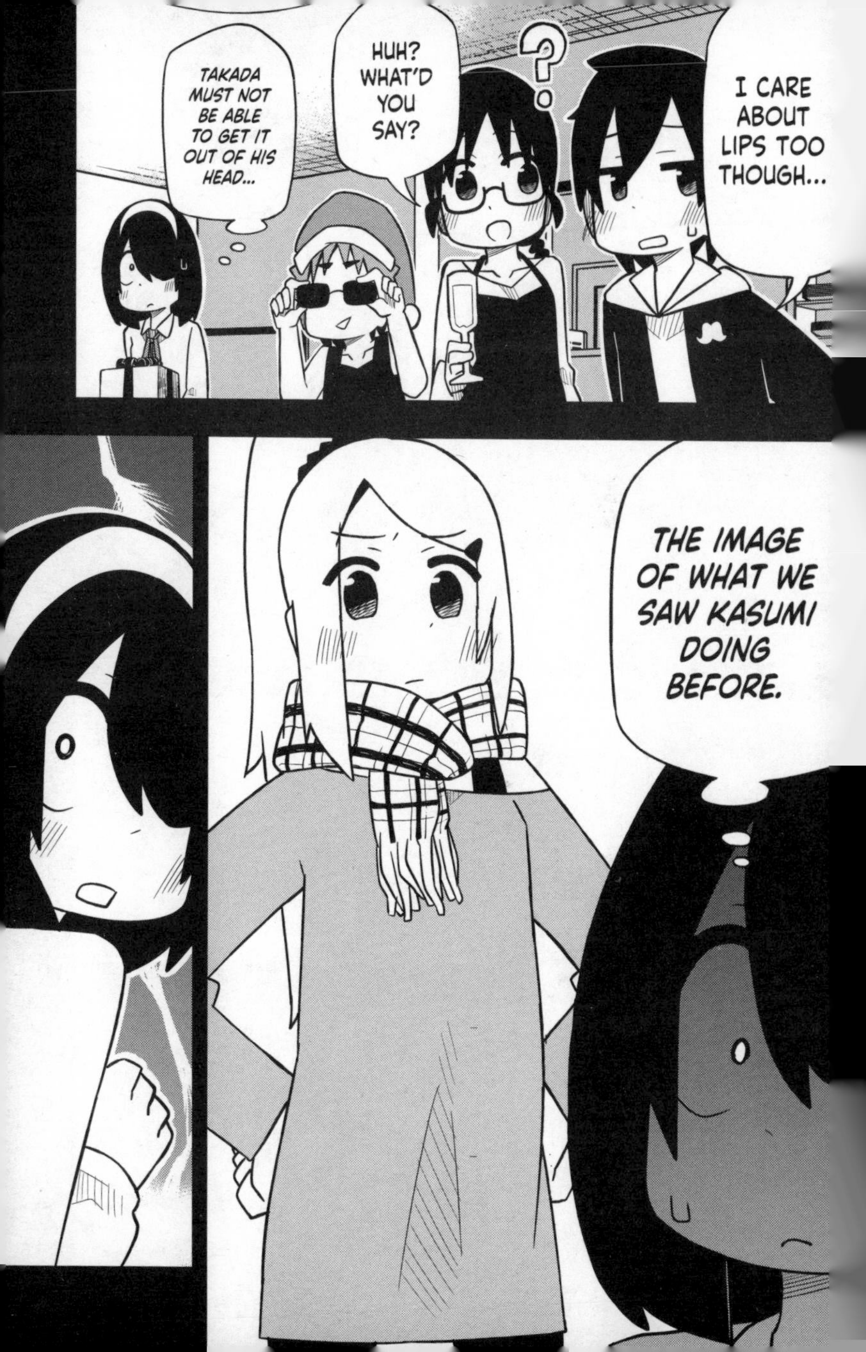
I CARE ABOUT LIPS TOO THOUGH...
HUH? WHAT'D YOU SAY?
TAKADA MUST NOT BE ABLE TO GET IT OUT OF HIS HEAD...
THE IMAGE OF WHAT WE SAW KASUMI DOING BEFORE.

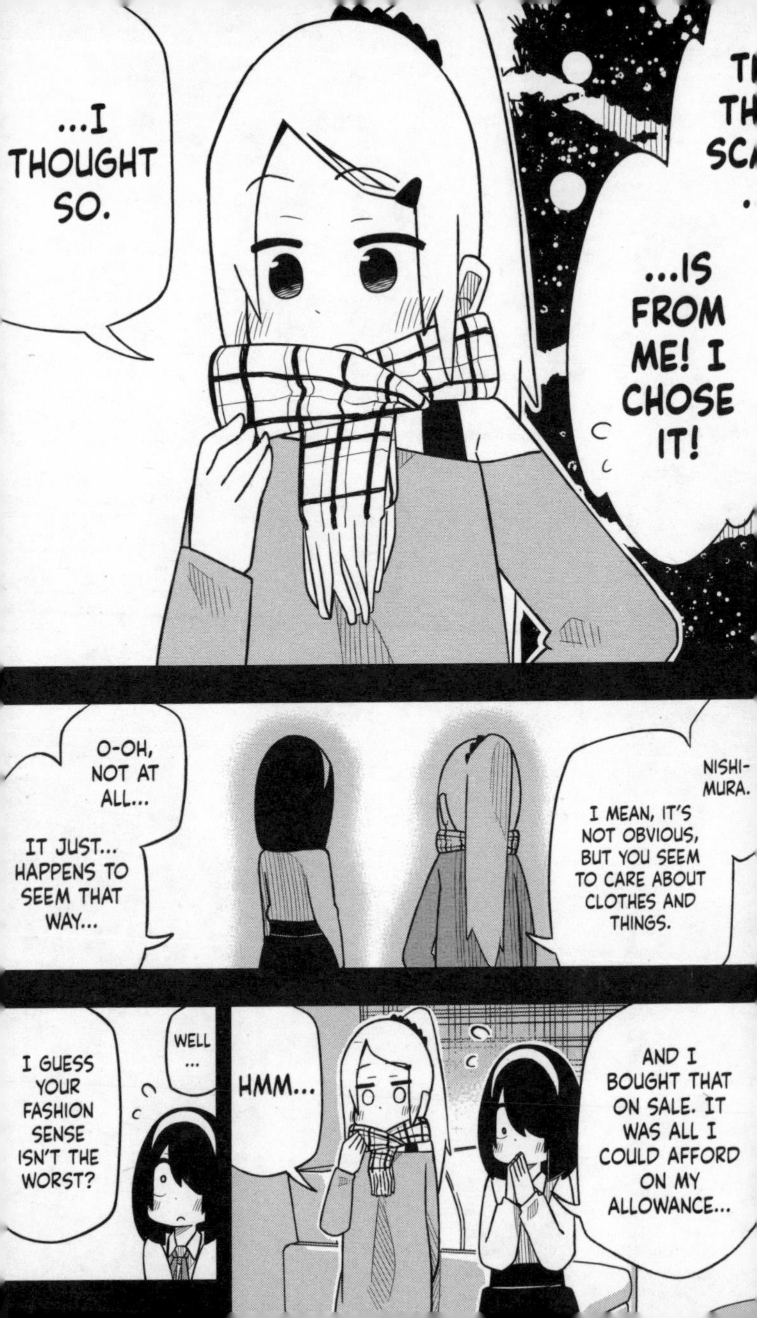
...IS FROM ME! I CHOSE IT!
...I THOUGHT SO.
NISHI-MURA.
I MEAN, IT'S NOT OBVIOUS, BUT YOU SEEM TO CARE ABOUT CLOTHES AND THINGS.
O-OH, NOT AT ALL...
IT JUST... HAPPENS TO SEEM THAT WAY...
AND I BOUGHT THAT ON SALE. IT WAS ALL I COULD AFFORD ON MY ALLOWANCE...
HMM...
WELL ...
I GUESS YOUR FASHION SENSE ISN'T THE WORST?

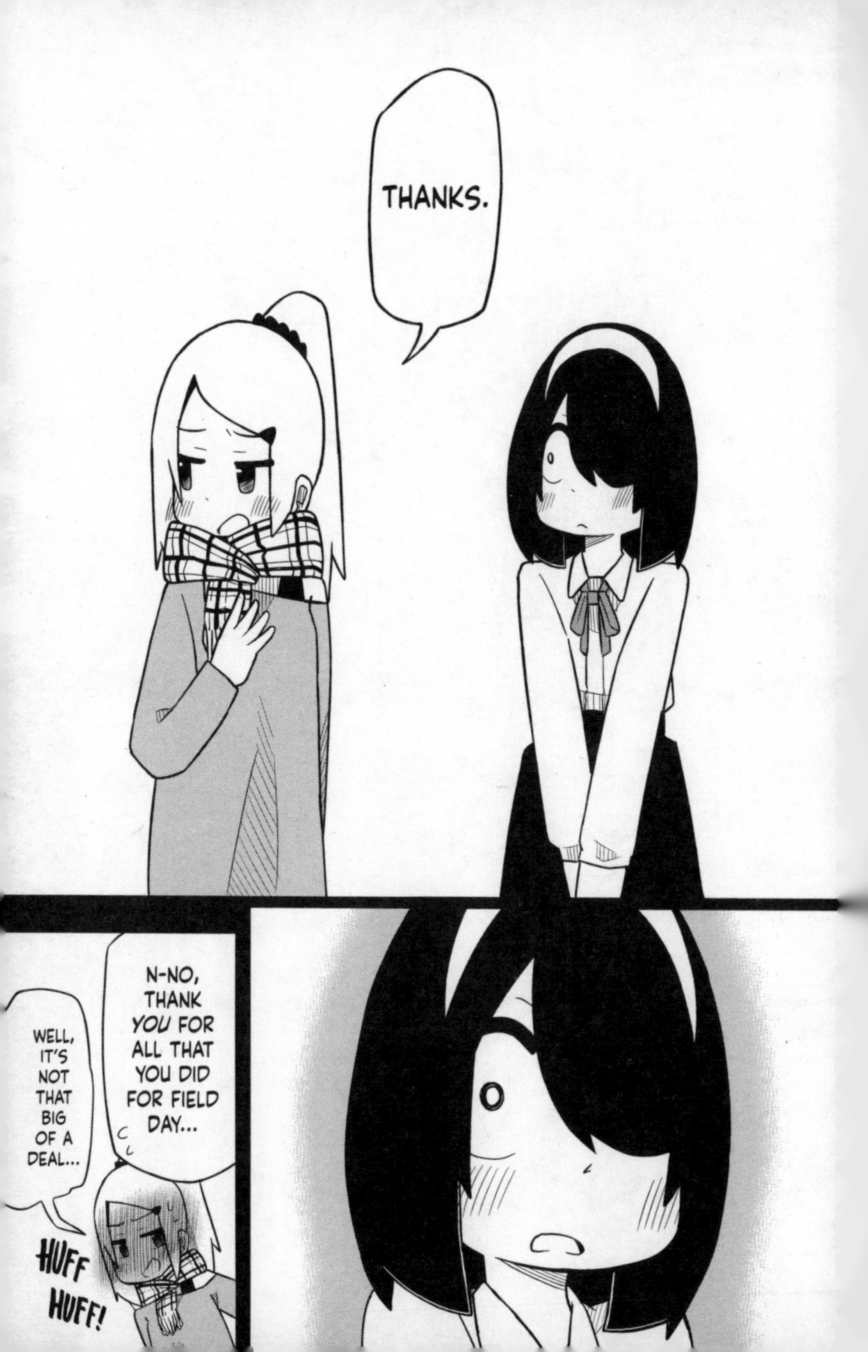
THANKS.
N-NO, THANK *YOU* FOR ALL THAT YOU DID FOR FIELD DAY...
WELL, IT'S NOT THAT BIG OF A DEAL...
HUFF HUFF!

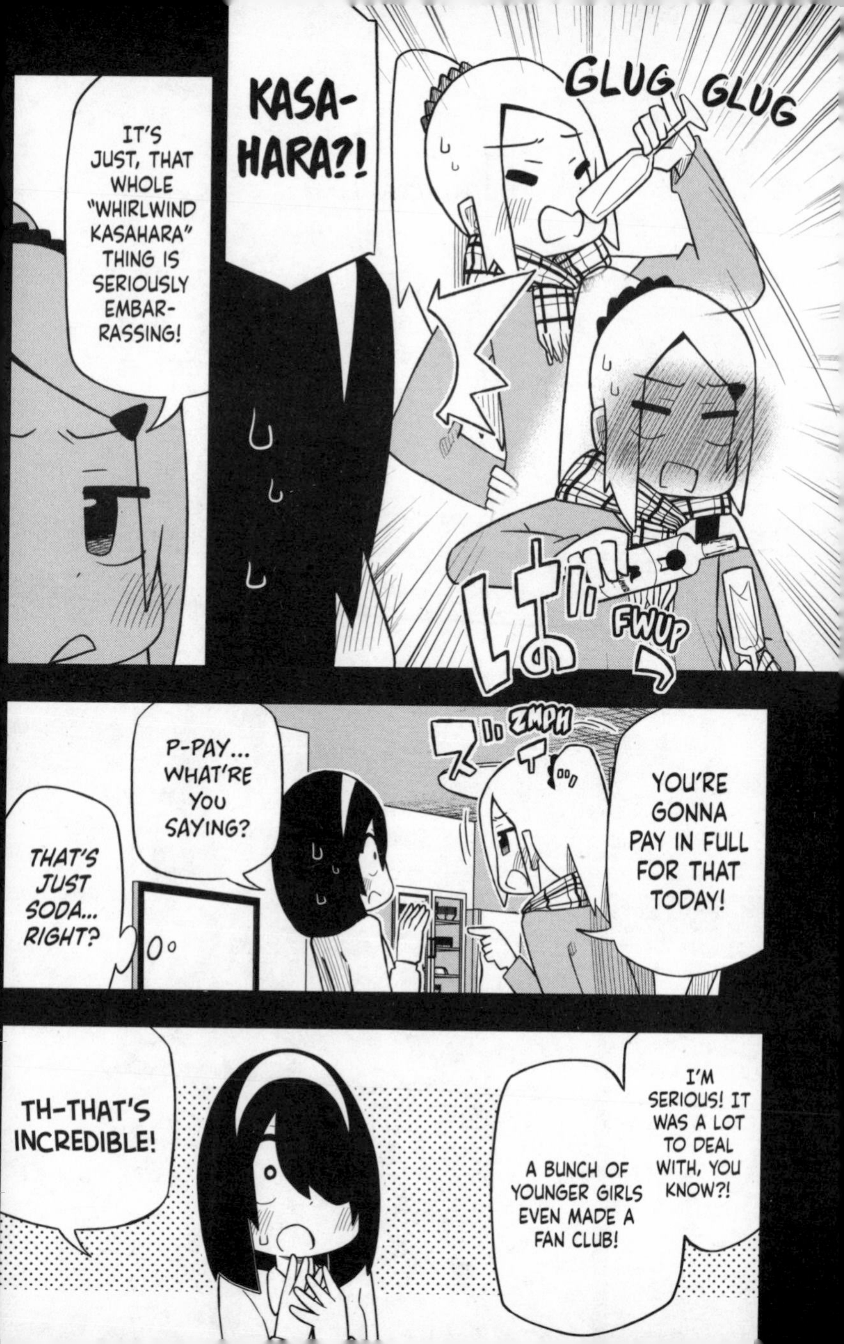
GLUG GLUG
KASA-HARA?!
FWUP
IT'S JUST, THAT WHOLE "WHIRLWIND KASAHARA" THING IS SERIOUSLY EMBAR-RASSING!
YOU'RE GONNA PAY IN FULL FOR THAT TODAY!
ZMPH
P-PAY... WHAT'RE YOU SAYING?
THAT'S JUST SODA... RIGHT?
I'M SERIOUS! IT WAS A LOT TO DEAL WITH, YOU KNOW?!
A BUNCH OF YOUNGER GIRLS EVEN MADE A FAN CLUB!
TH-THAT'S INCREDIBLE!

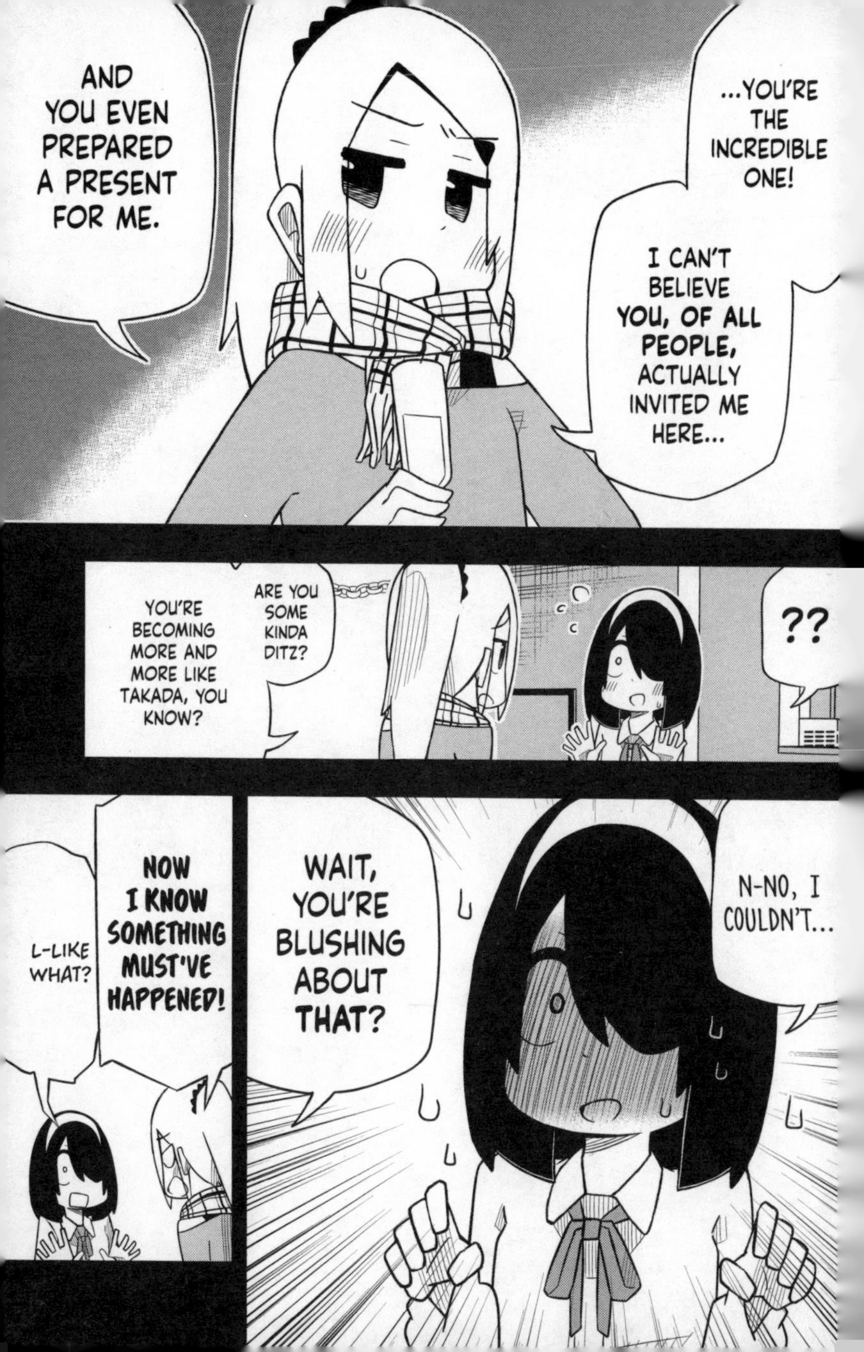
...YOU'RE THE INCREDIBLE ONE!
I CAN'T BELIEVE YOU, OF ALL PEOPLE, ACTUALLY INVITED ME HERE...
AND YOU EVEN PREPARED A PRESENT FOR ME.
??
ARE YOU SOME KINDA DITZ?
YOU'RE BECOMING MORE AND MORE LIKE TAKADA, YOU KNOW?
N-NO, I COULDN'T...
WAIT, YOU'RE BLUSHING ABOUT THAT?
NOW I KNOW SOMETHING MUST'VE HAPPENED!
L-LIKE WHAT?

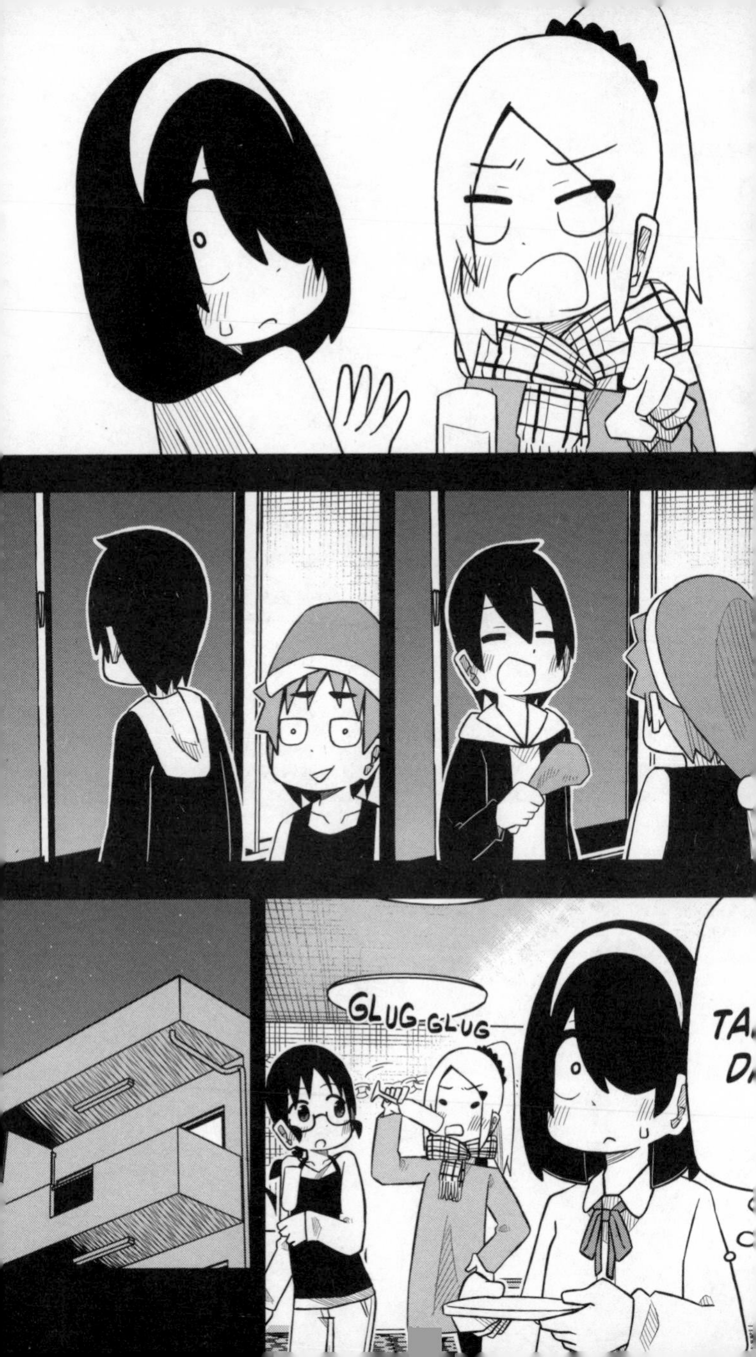
GLUG-GLUG

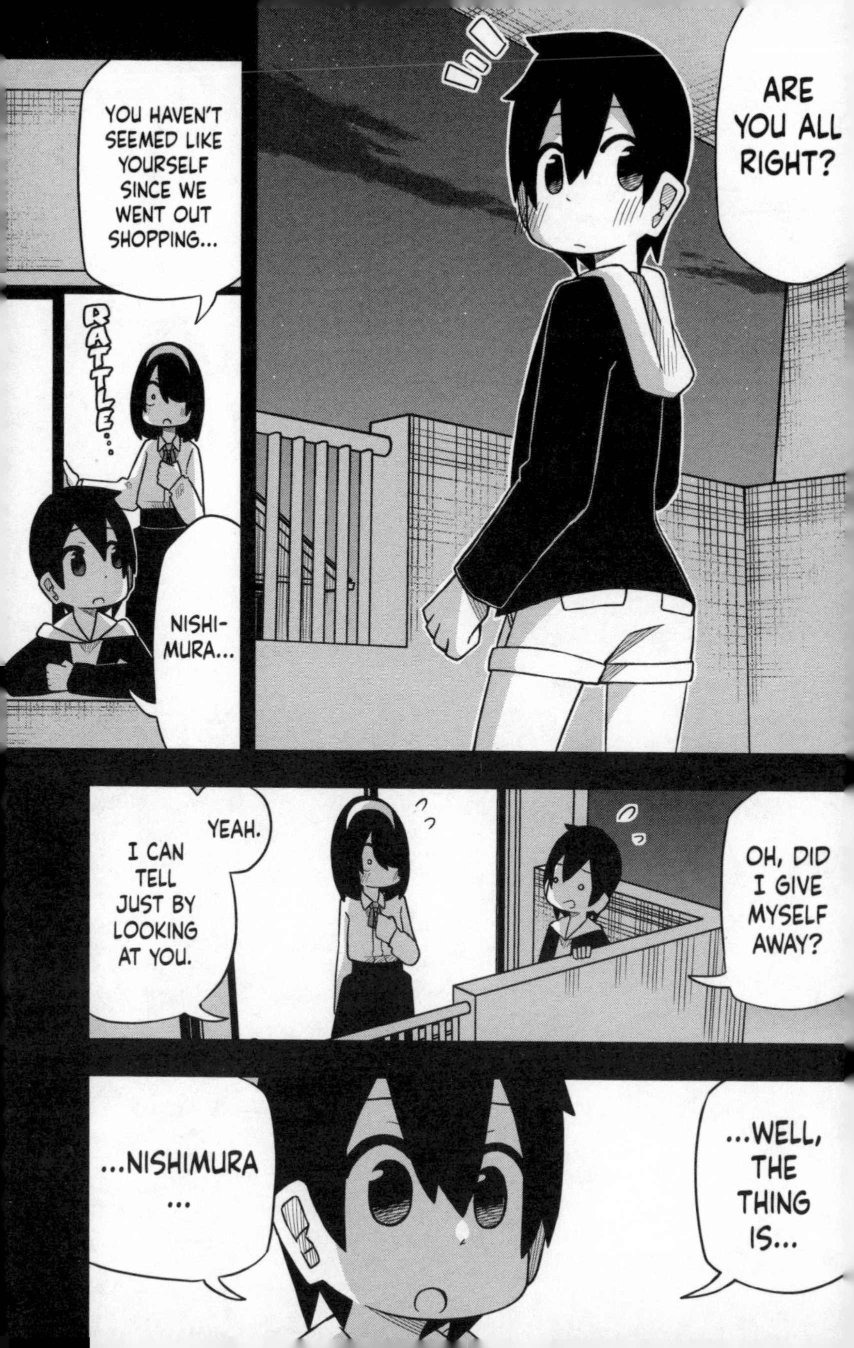
ARE YOU ALL RIGHT?
YOU HAVEN'T SEEMED LIKE YOURSELF SINCE WE WENT OUT SHOPPING...
RATTLE...
NISHI-MURA...
OH, DID I GIVE MYSELF AWAY?
YEAH. I CAN TELL JUST BY LOOKING AT YOU.
...WELL, THE THING IS...
...NISHIMURA ...

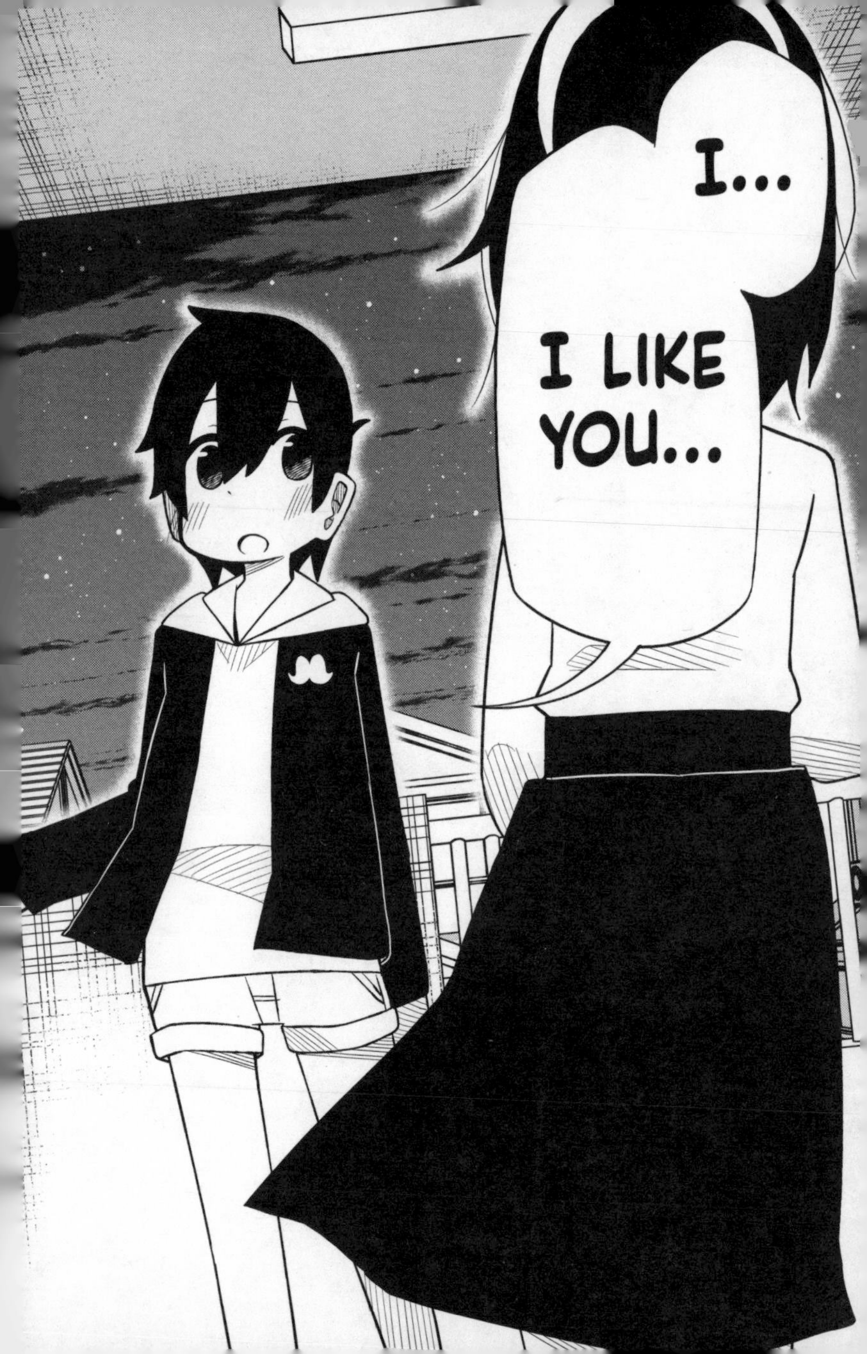
I...
I LIKE YOU...

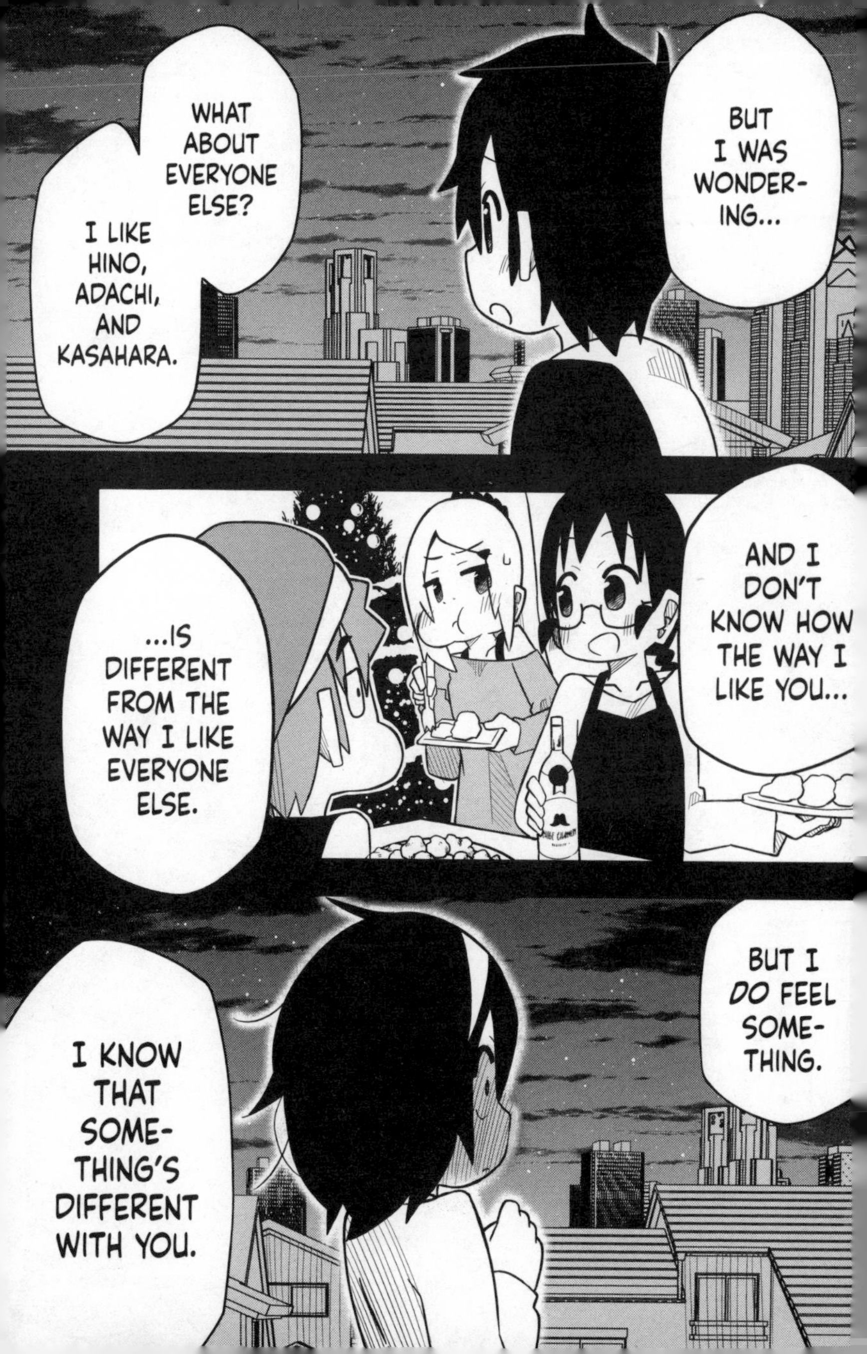
BUT I WAS WONDER-ING...
WHAT ABOUT EVERYONE ELSE?
I LIKE HINO, ADACHI, AND KASAHARA.
AND I DON'T KNOW HOW THE WAY I LIKE YOU...
...IS DIFFERENT FROM THE WAY I LIKE EVERYONE ELSE.
BUT I *DO* FEEL SOME-THING.
I KNOW THAT SOME-THING'S DIFFERENT WITH YOU.

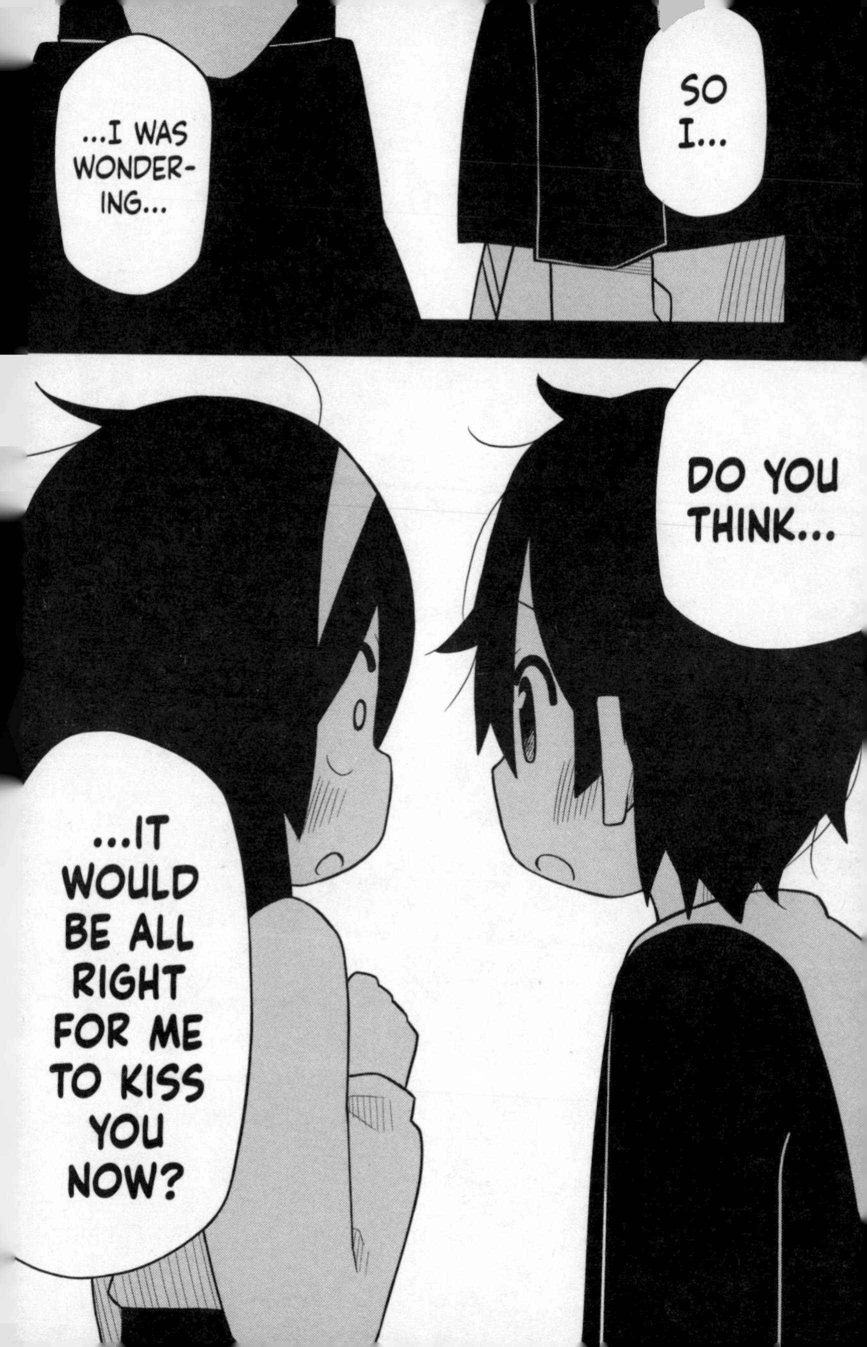
SO I...
...I WAS WONDER-ING...
DO YOU THINK...
...IT WOULD BE ALL RIGHT FOR ME TO KISS YOU NOW?

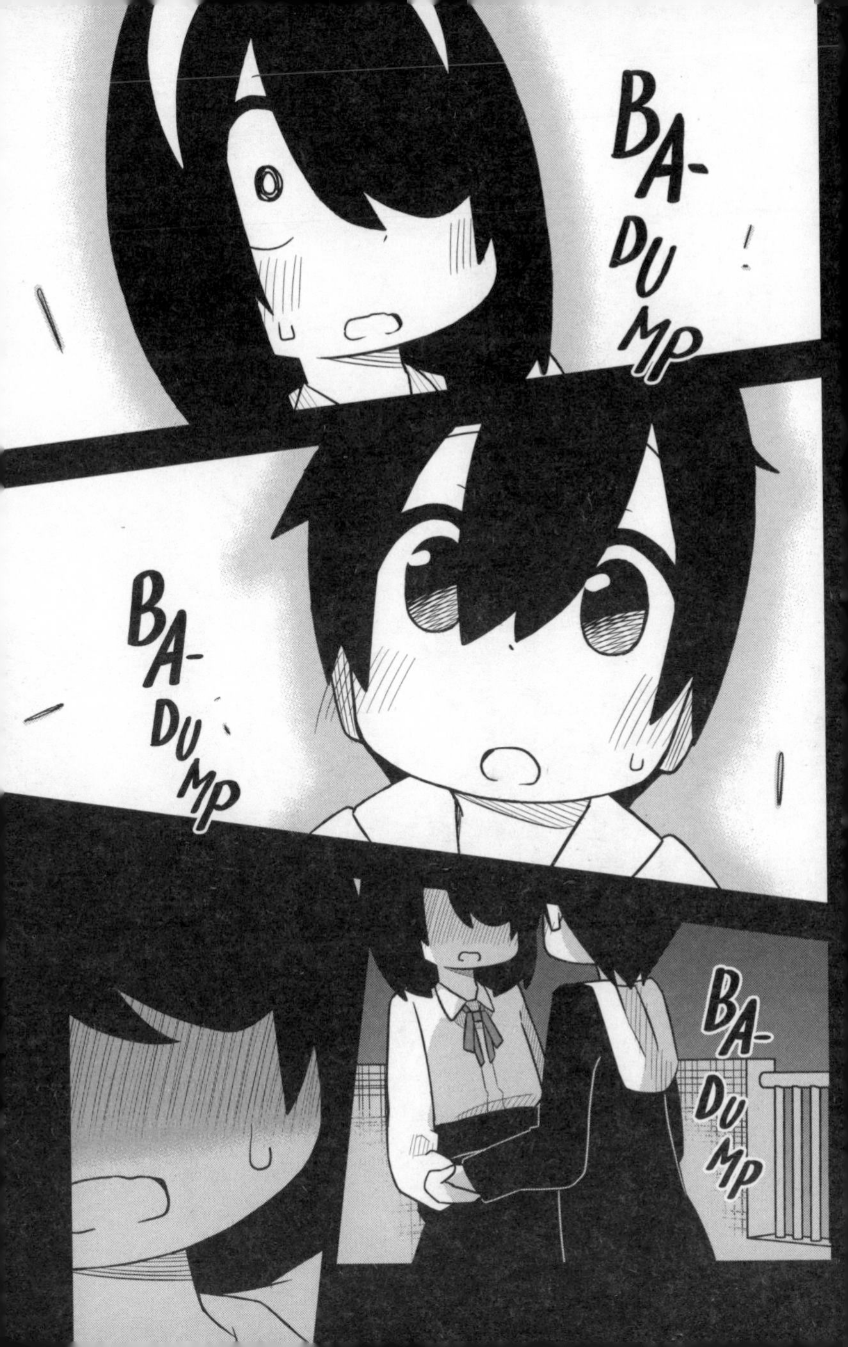
BA-DUMP
!
BA-DUMP
BA-DUMP

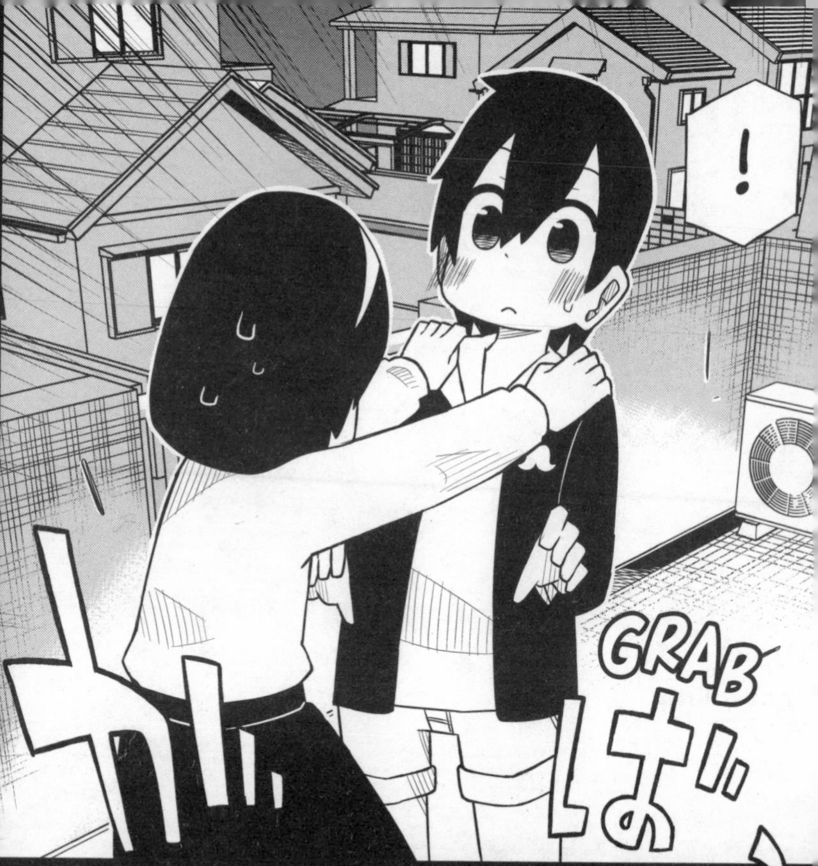
!
GRAB
はし

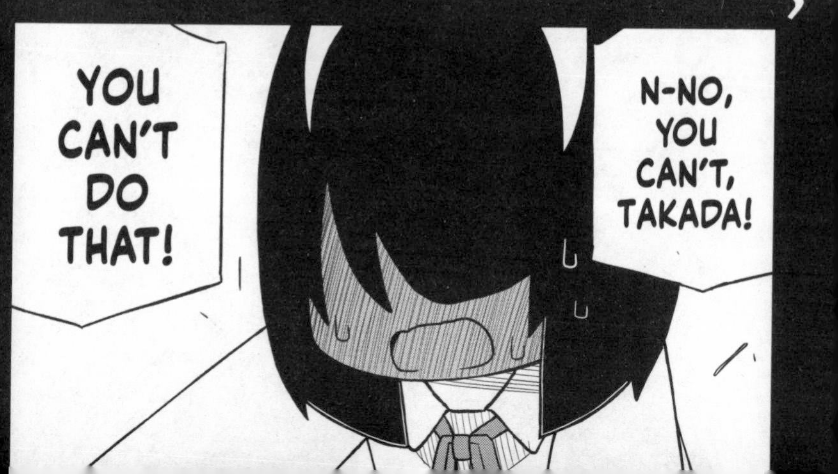
N-NO, YOU CAN'T, TAKADA!
YOU CAN'T DO THAT!

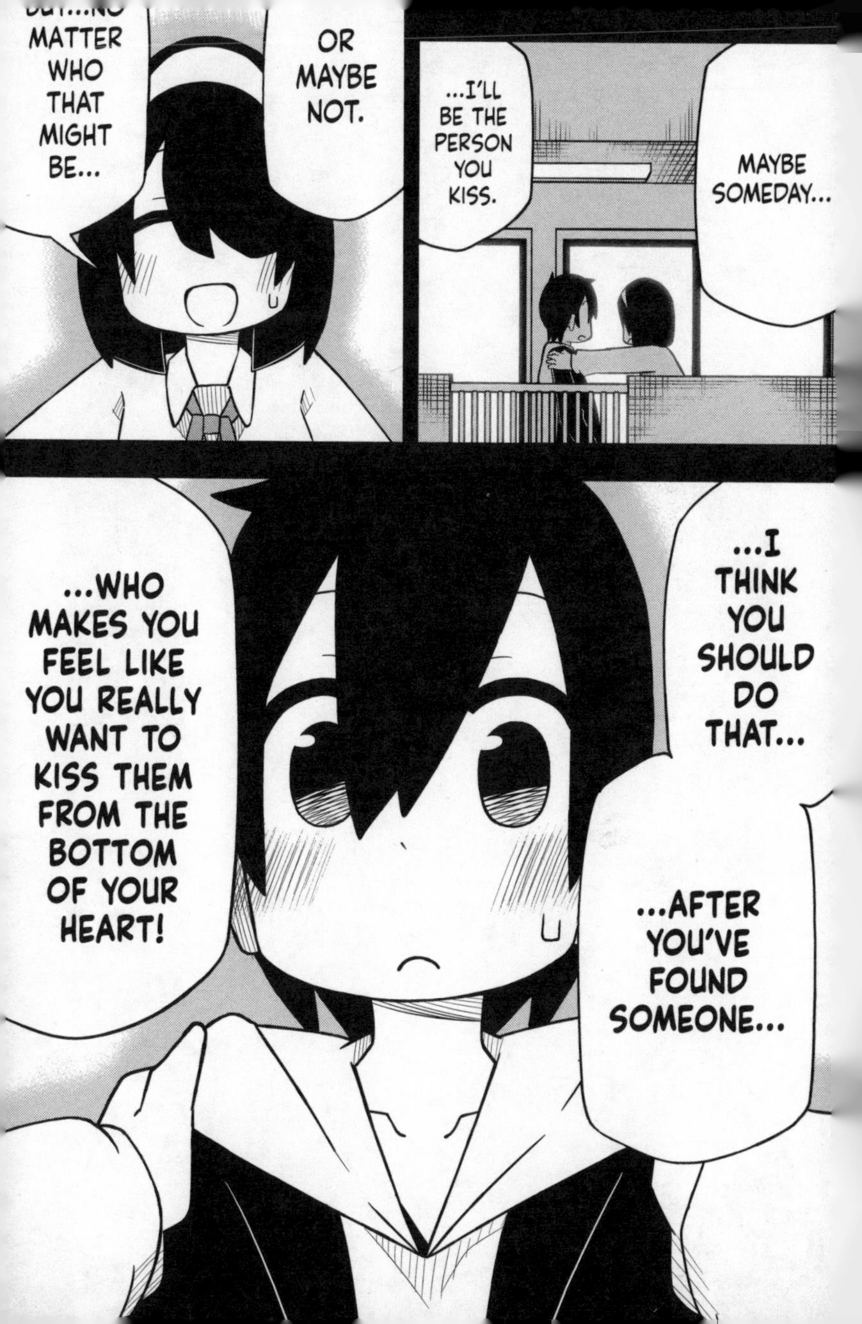
MAYBE SOMEDAY...
...I'LL BE THE PERSON YOU KISS.
OR MAYBE NOT.
MATTER WHO THAT MIGHT BE...
...I THINK YOU SHOULD DO THAT...
...AFTER YOU'VE FOUND SOMEONE...
...WHO MAKES YOU FEEL LIKE YOU REALLY WANT TO KISS THEM FROM THE BOTTOM OF YOUR HEART!

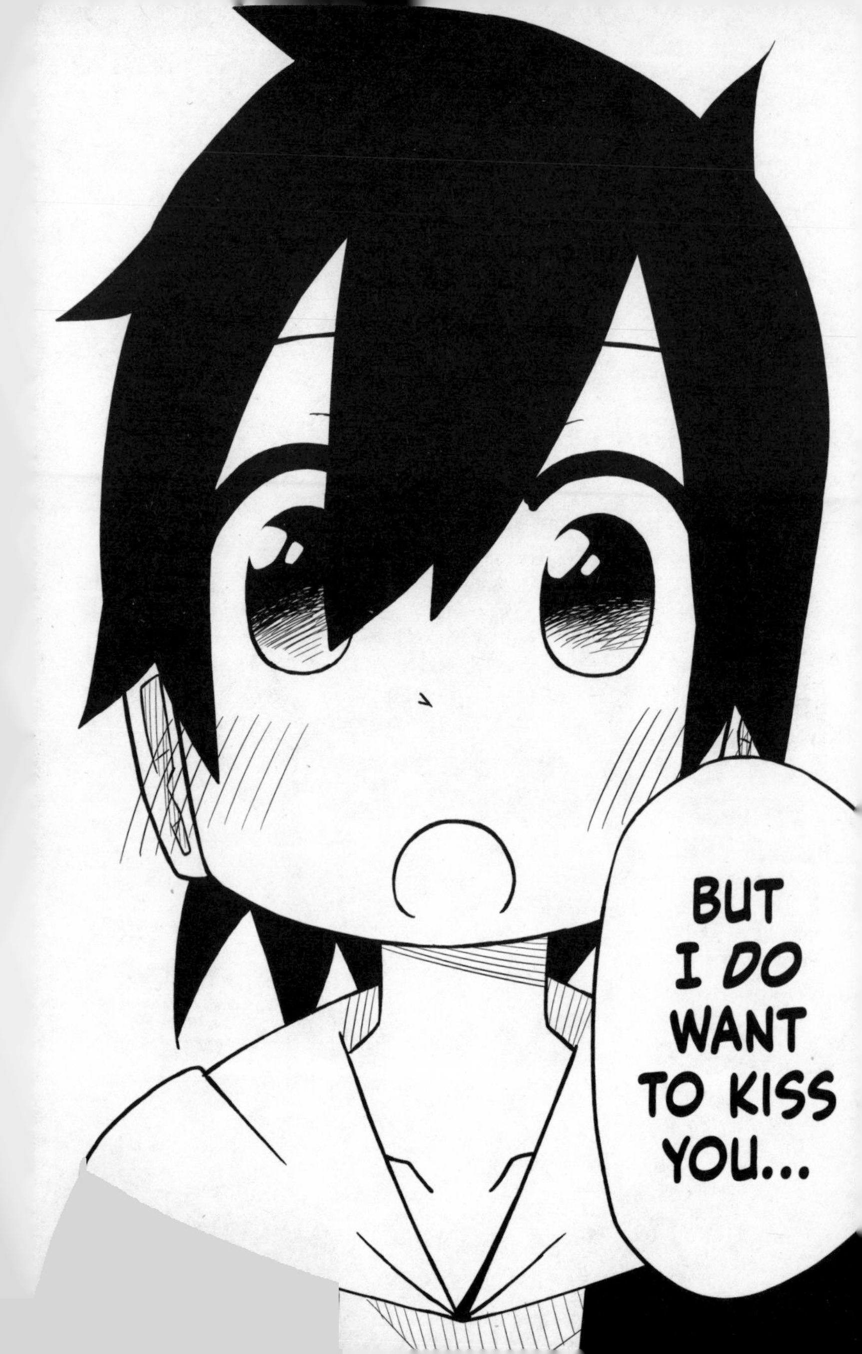
BUT I *DO* WANT TO KISS YOU...

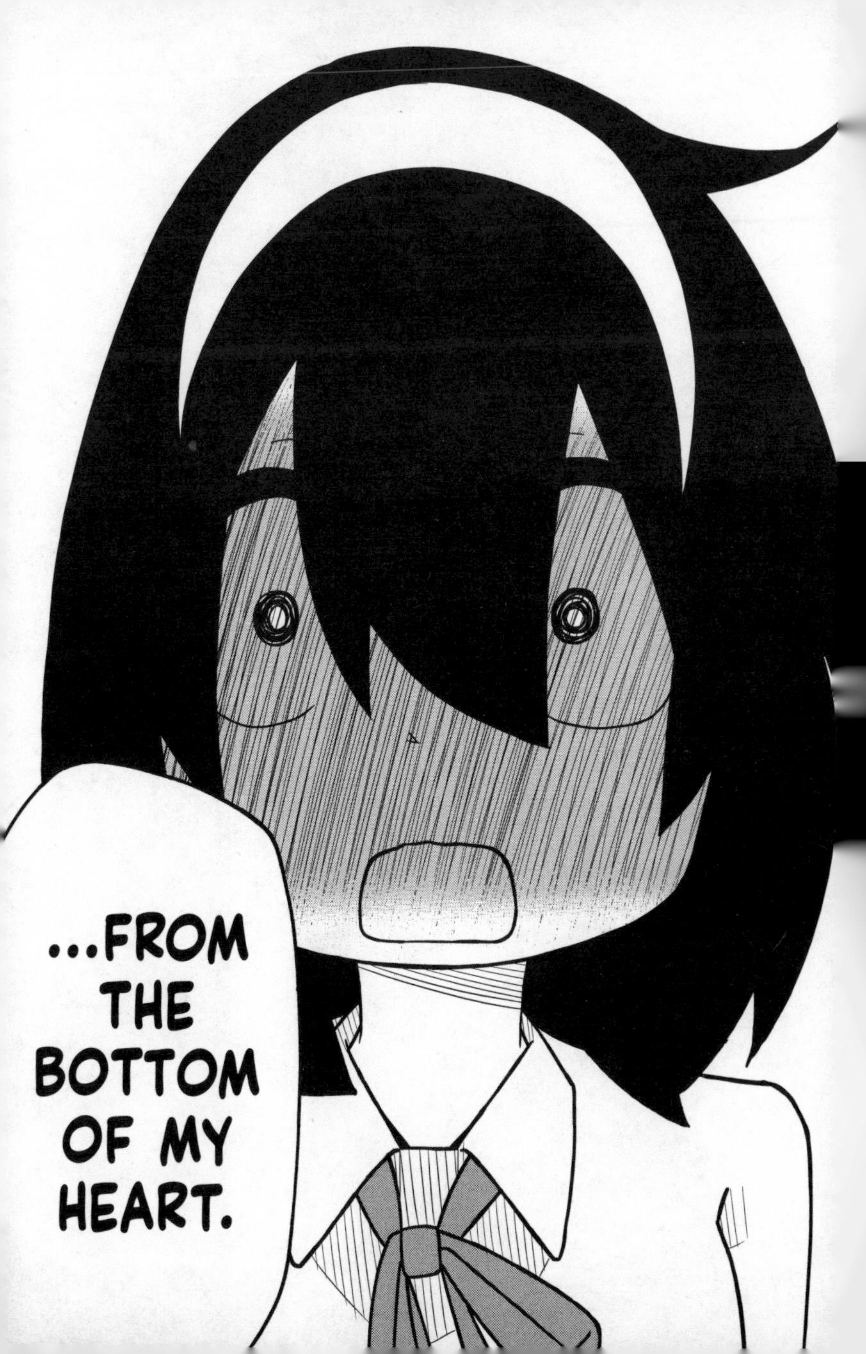
...FROM THE BOTTOM OF MY HEART.

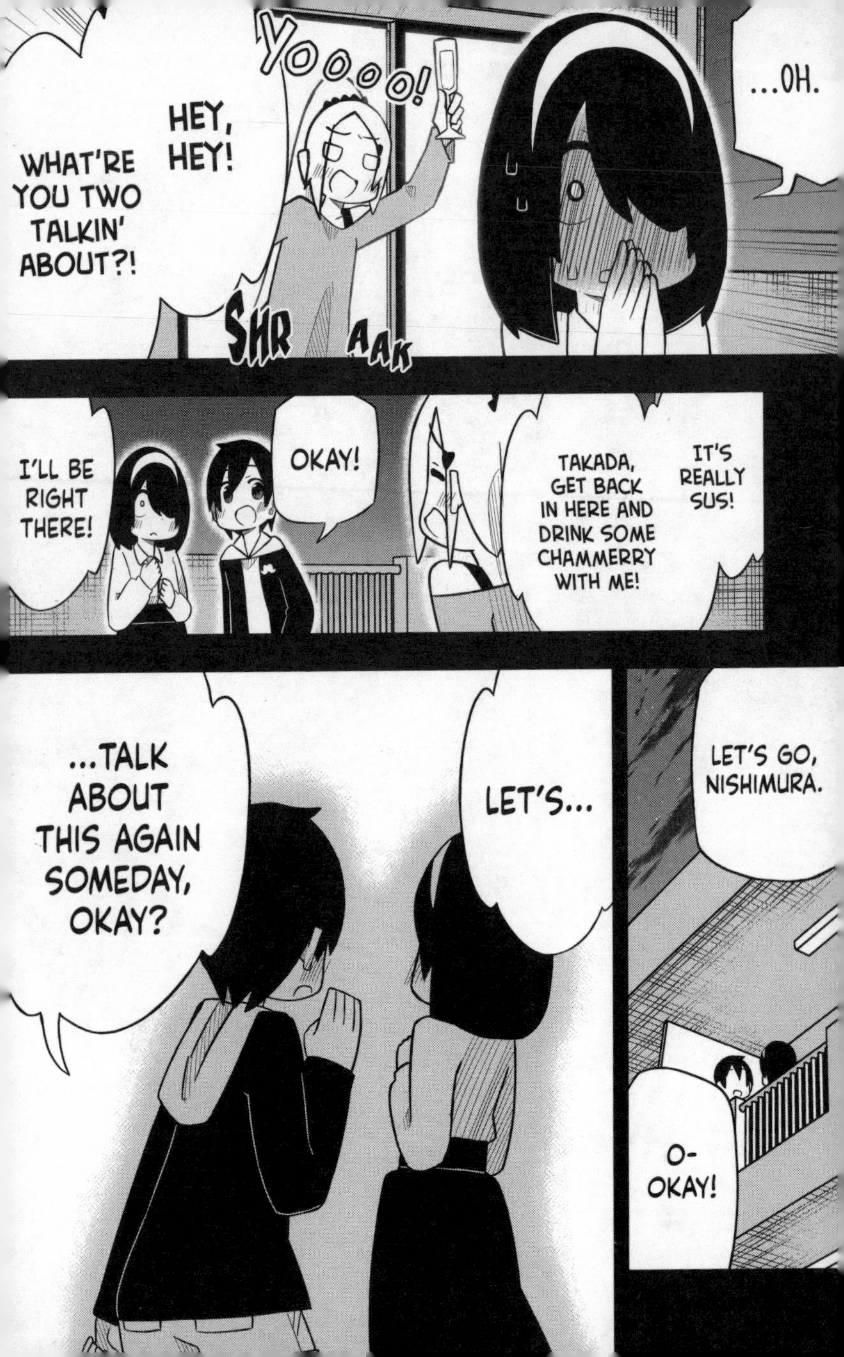
...OH.
YOOOOO!
HEY, HEY!
WHAT'RE YOU TWO TALKIN' ABOUT?!
SHRAAK
IT'S REALLY SUS!
TAKADA, GET BACK IN HERE AND DRINK SOME CHAMMERRY WITH ME!
OKAY!
I'LL BE RIGHT THERE!
LET'S GO, NISHIMURA.
O-OKAY!
LET'S...
...TALK ABOUT THIS AGAIN SOMEDAY, OKAY?

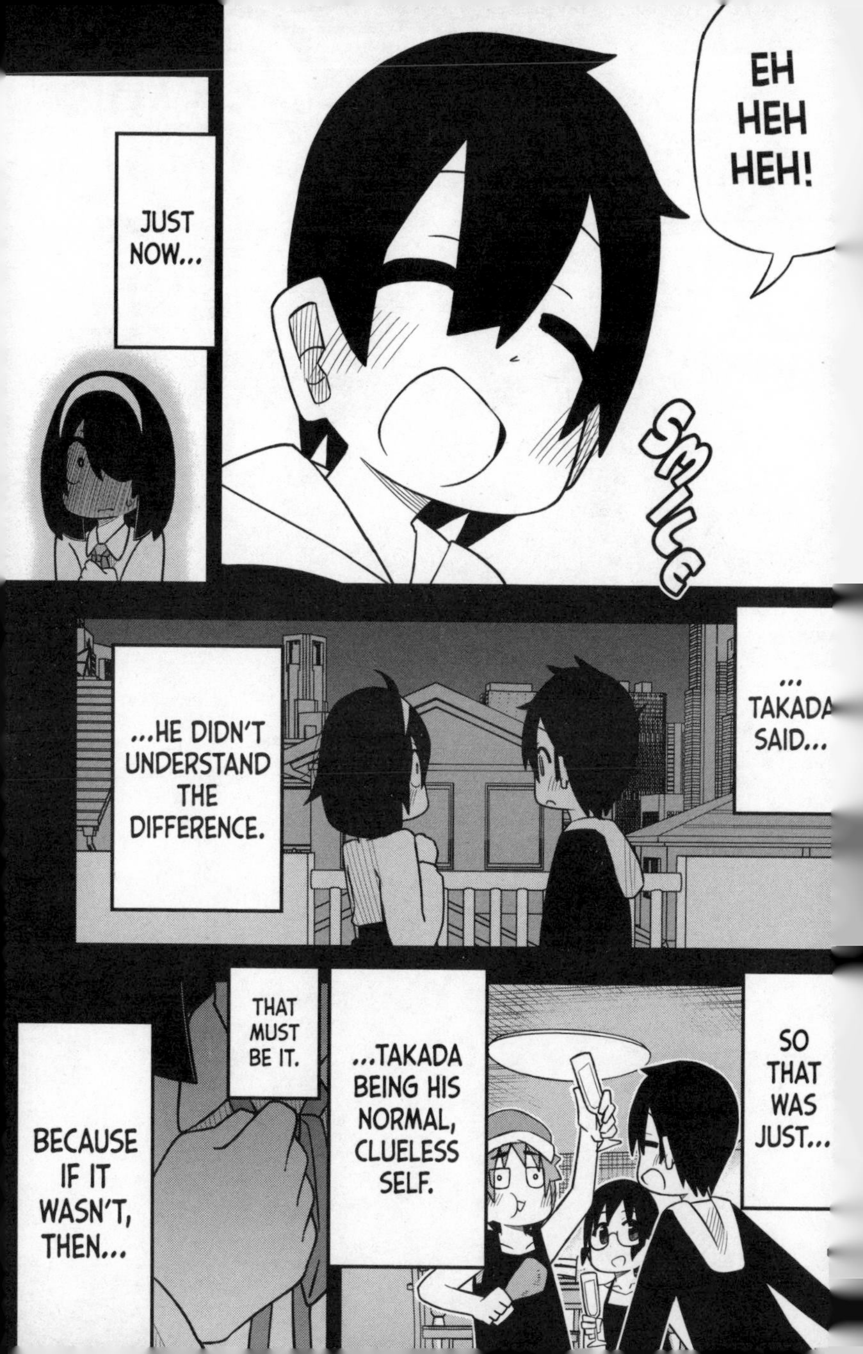
EH HEH HEH!
SMILE
JUST NOW...
...TAKADA SAID...
...HE DIDN'T UNDERSTAND THE DIFFERENCE.
SO THAT WAS JUST...
...TAKADA BEING HIS NORMAL, CLUELESS SELF.
THAT MUST BE IT.
BECAUSE IF IT WASN'T, THEN...

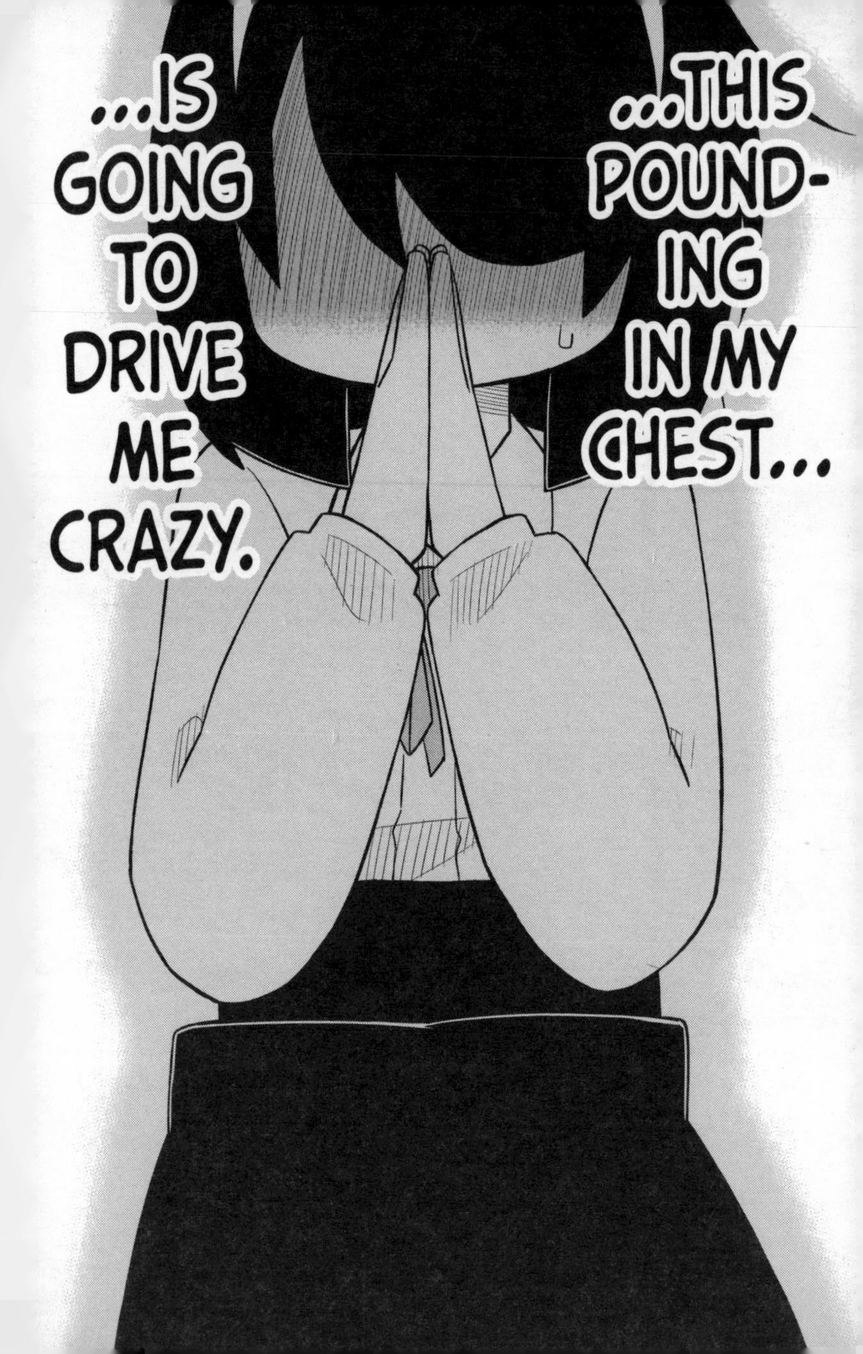

...THIS POUNDING IN MY CHEST...
...IS GOING TO DRIVE ME CRAZY.

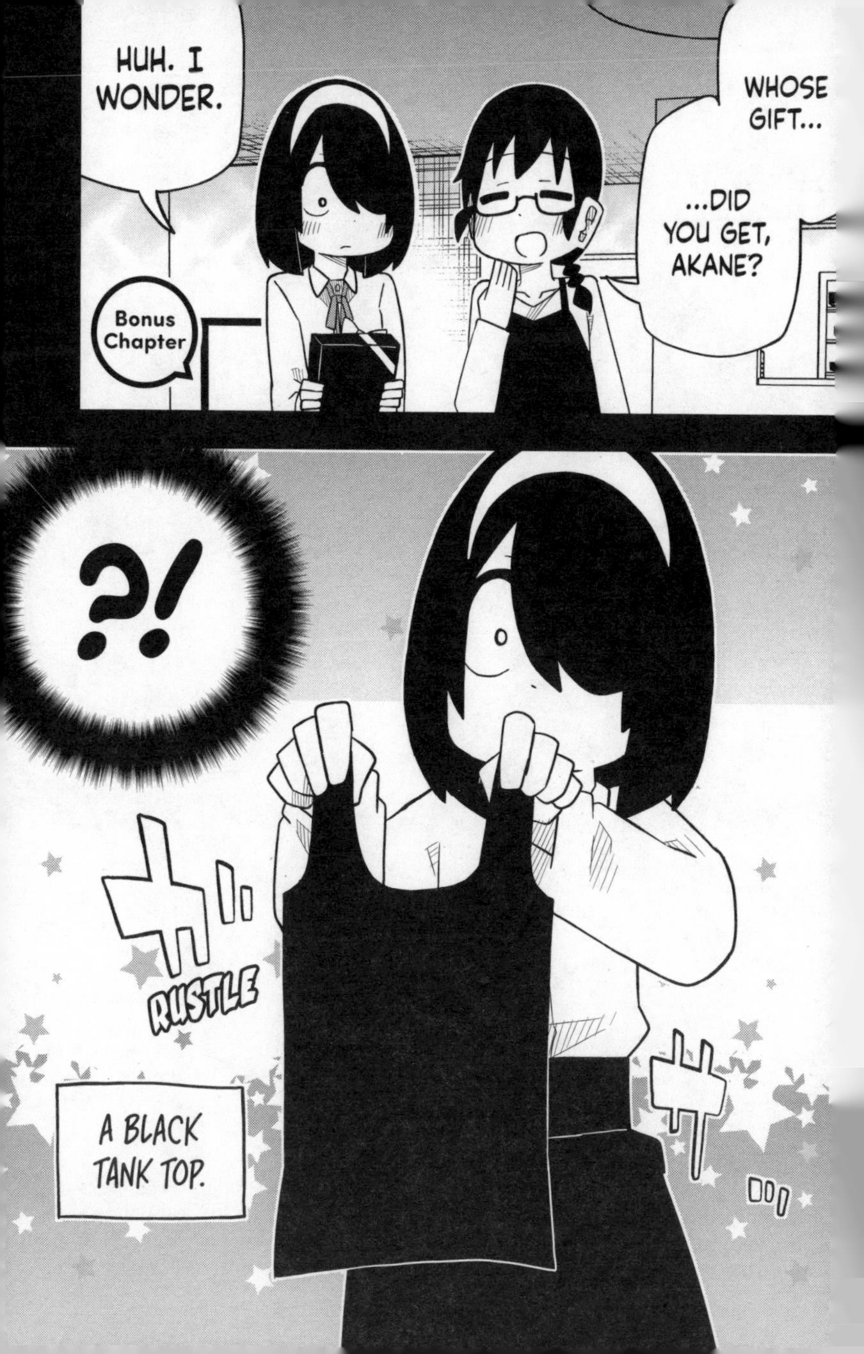
WHOSE GIFT...
...DID YOU GET, AKANE?
HUH. I WONDER.
Bonus Chapter
?!
RUSTLE
A BLACK TANK TOP.

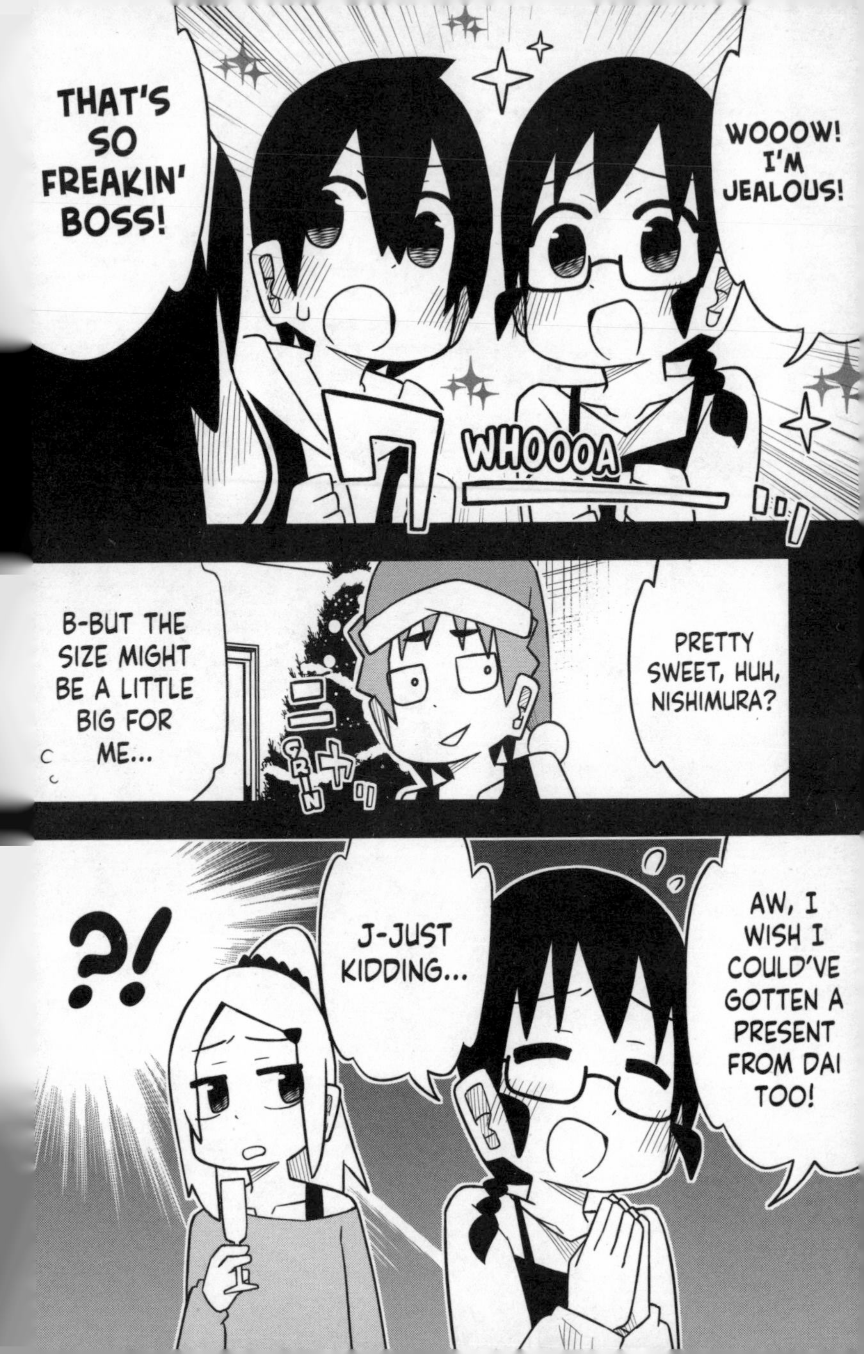
WOOOW! I'M JEALOUS!
THAT'S SO FREAKIN' BOSS!
WHOOOA
PRETTY SWEET, HUH, NISHIMURA?
GRIN
B-BUT THE SIZE MIGHT BE A LITTLE BIG FOR ME...
AW, I WISH I COULD'VE GOTTEN A PRESENT FROM DAI TOO!
J-JUST KIDDING...
?!

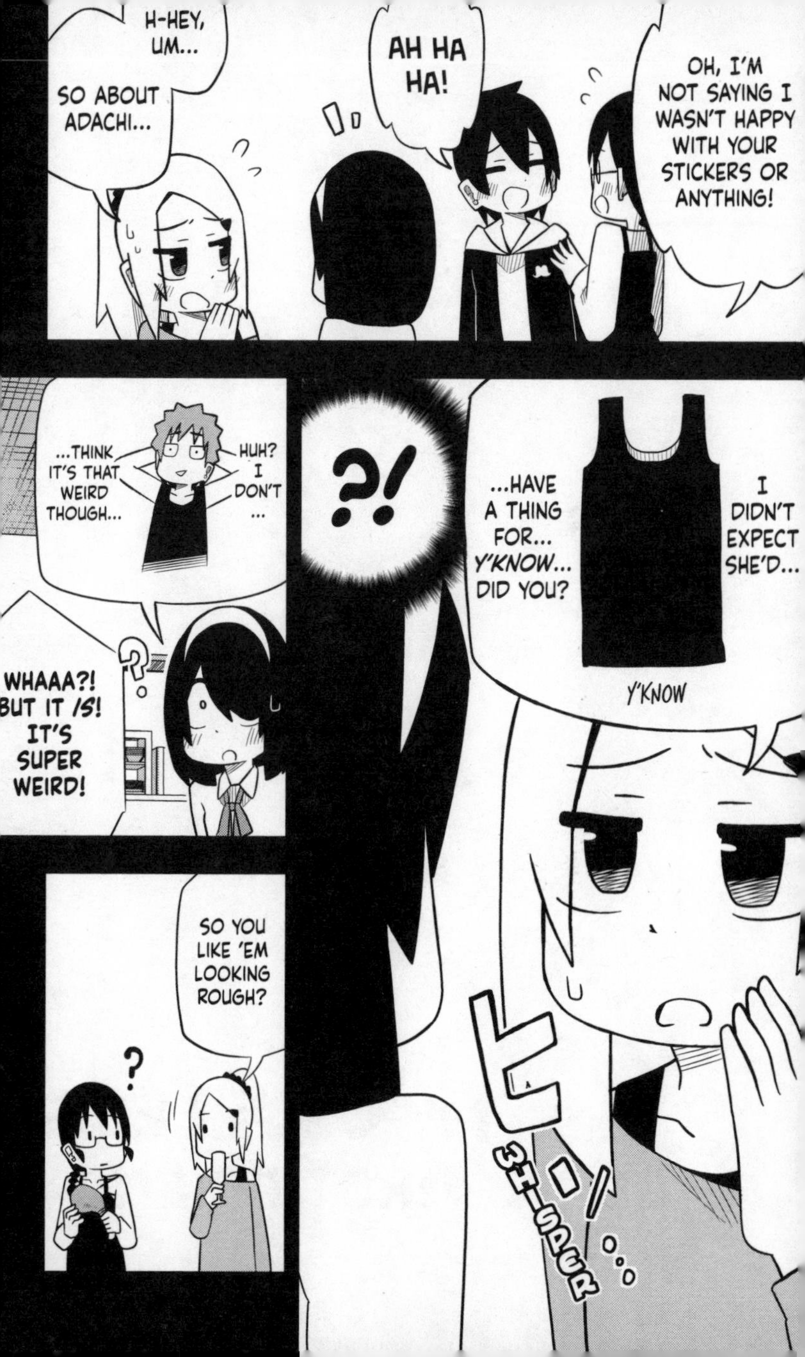
OH, I'M NOT SAYING I WASN'T HAPPY WITH YOUR STICKERS OR ANYTHING!
AH HA HA!
!
H-HEY, UM...
SO ABOUT ADACHI...
I DIDN'T EXPECT SHE'D...
...HAVE A THING FOR... Y'KNOW... DID YOU?
Y'KNOW
?!
WHISPER
HUH? I DON'T ...
...THINK IT'S THAT WEIRD THOUGH...
?
WHAAA?! BUT IT IS! IT'S SUPER WEIRD!
SO YOU LIKE 'EM LOOKING ROUGH?
?

MY CLUELESS
FIRST FRIEND

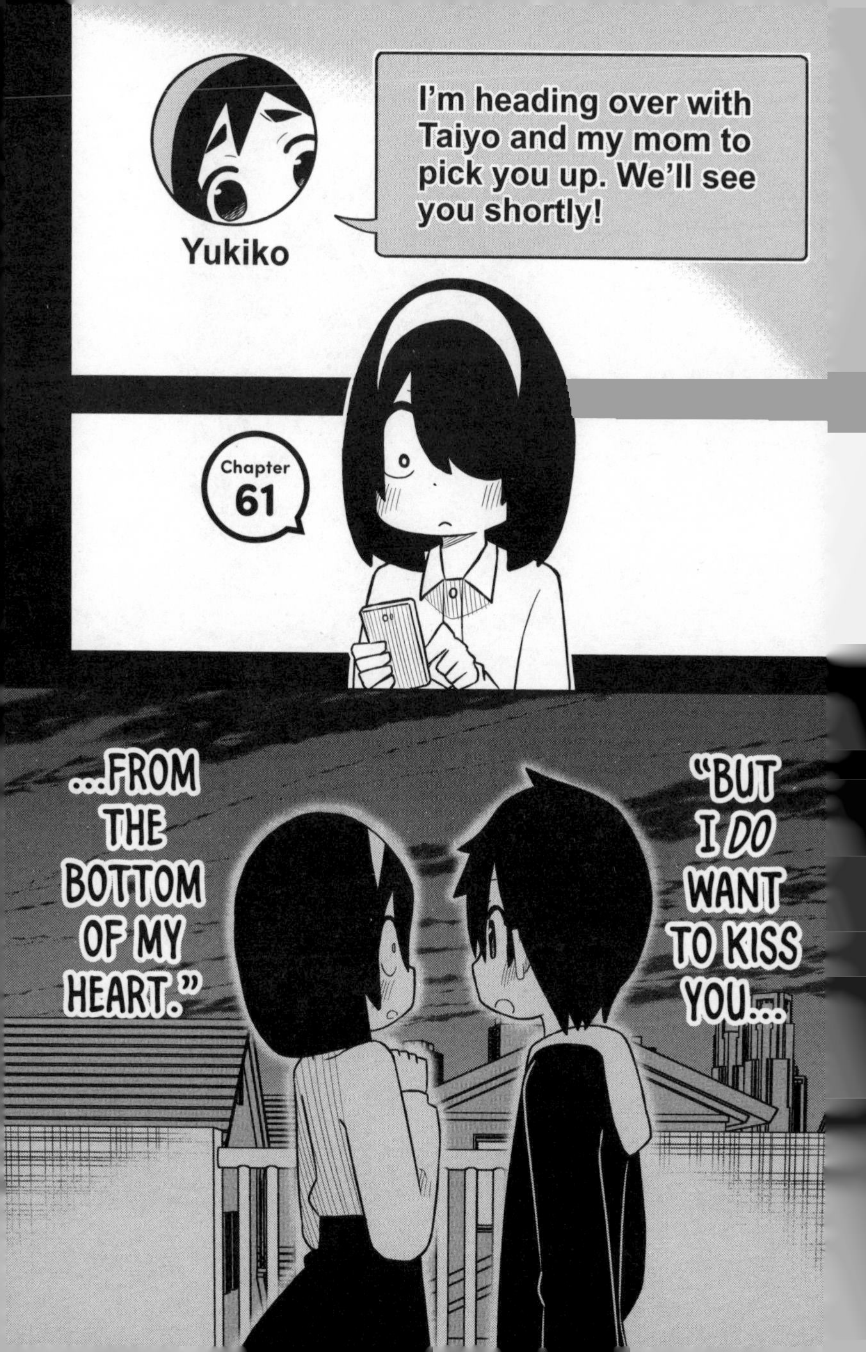
Yukiko
I'm heading over with Taiyo and my mom to pick you up. We'll see you shortly!
Chapter 61
"BUT I *DO* WANT TO KISS YOU...
...FROM THE BOTTOM OF MY HEART."

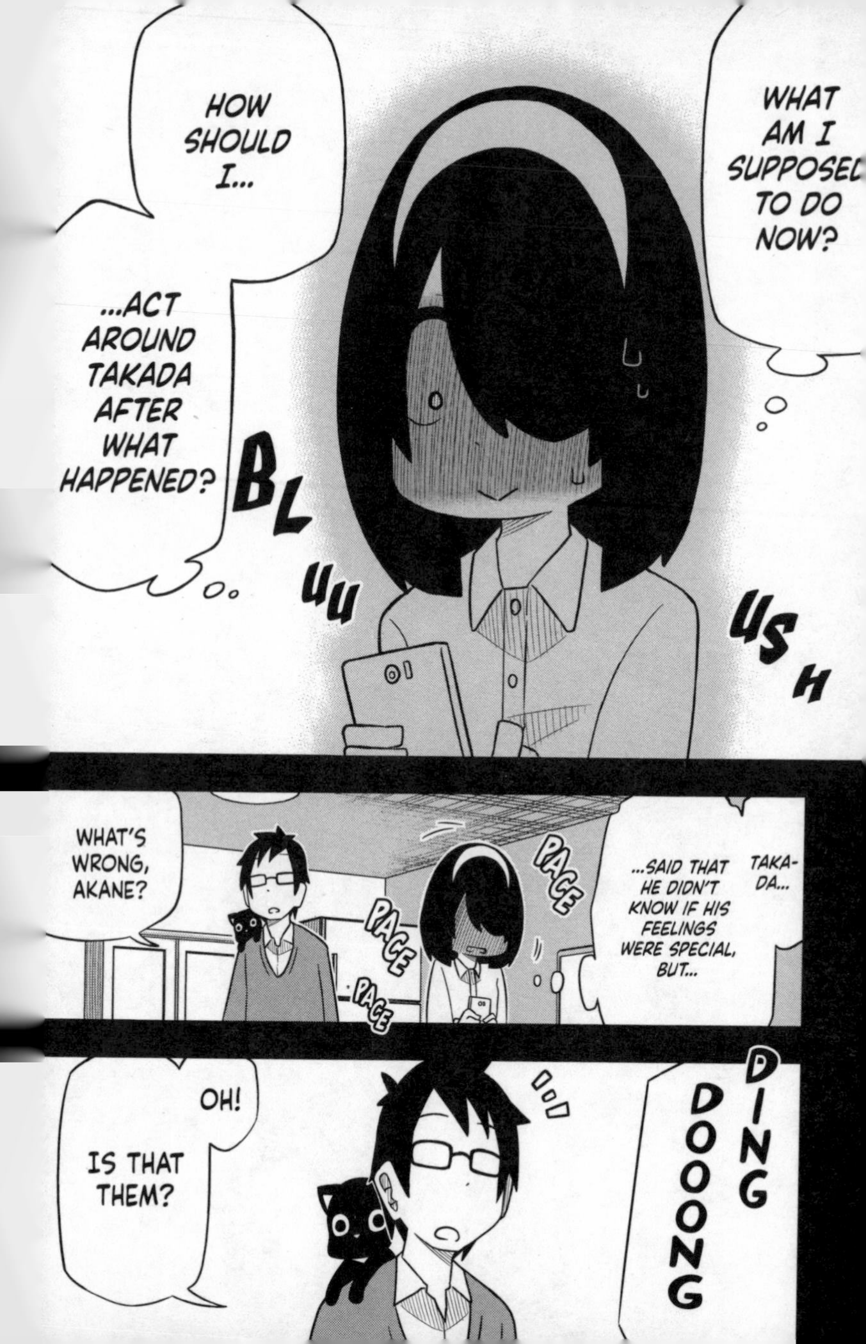
WHAT AM I SUPPOSED TO DO NOW?
HOW SHOULD I...
...ACT AROUND TAKADA AFTER WHAT HAPPENED?
BLUUUSH
TAKADA...
...SAID THAT HE DIDN'T KNOW IF HIS FEELINGS WERE SPECIAL, BUT...
PACE
PACE
PACE
WHAT'S WRONG, AKANE?
DING DOOONG
OH!
IS THAT THEM?

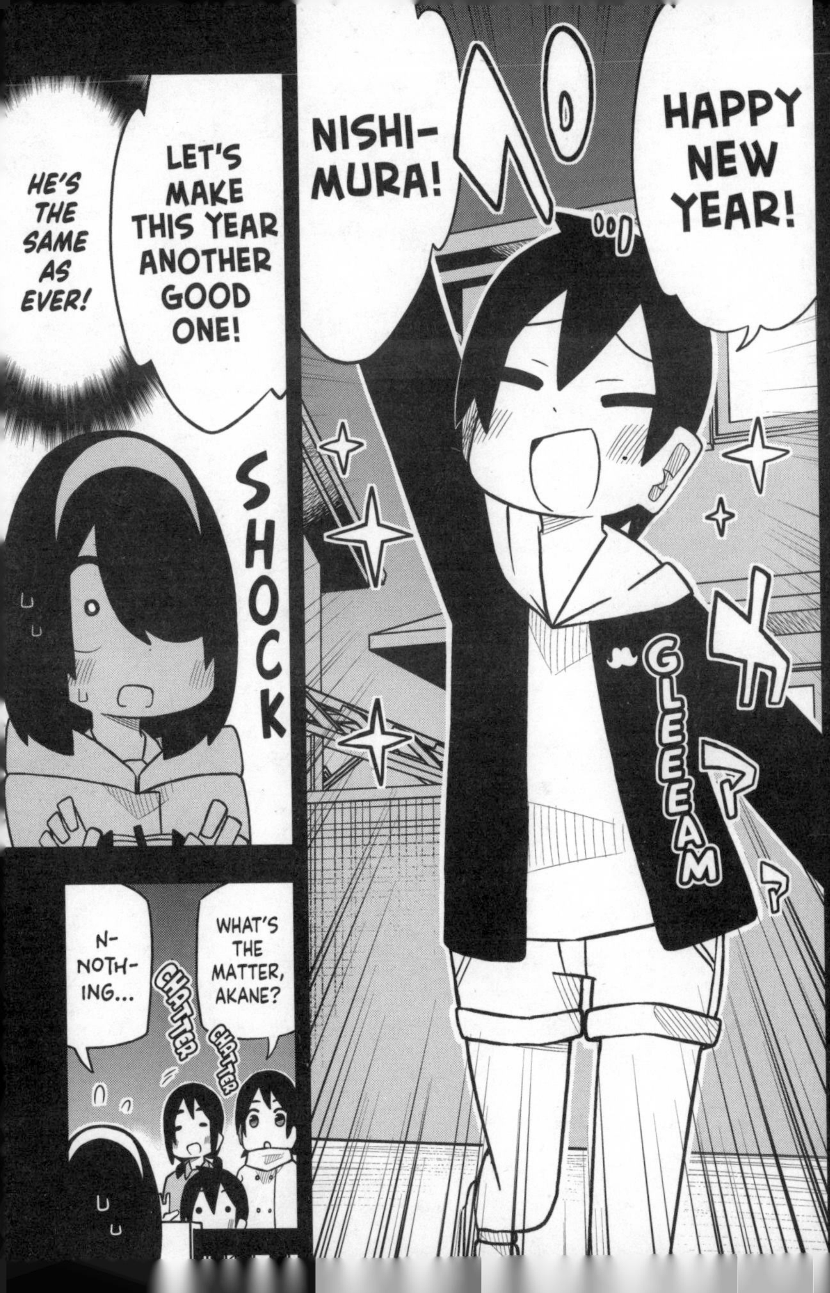
HAPPY NEW YEAR!
NISHI-MURA!
GLEEEAM
LET'S MAKE THIS YEAR ANOTHER GOOD ONE!
HE'S THE SAME AS EVER!
SHOCK
WHAT'S THE MATTER, AKANE?
N-NOTH-ING...
CHATTER
CHATTER

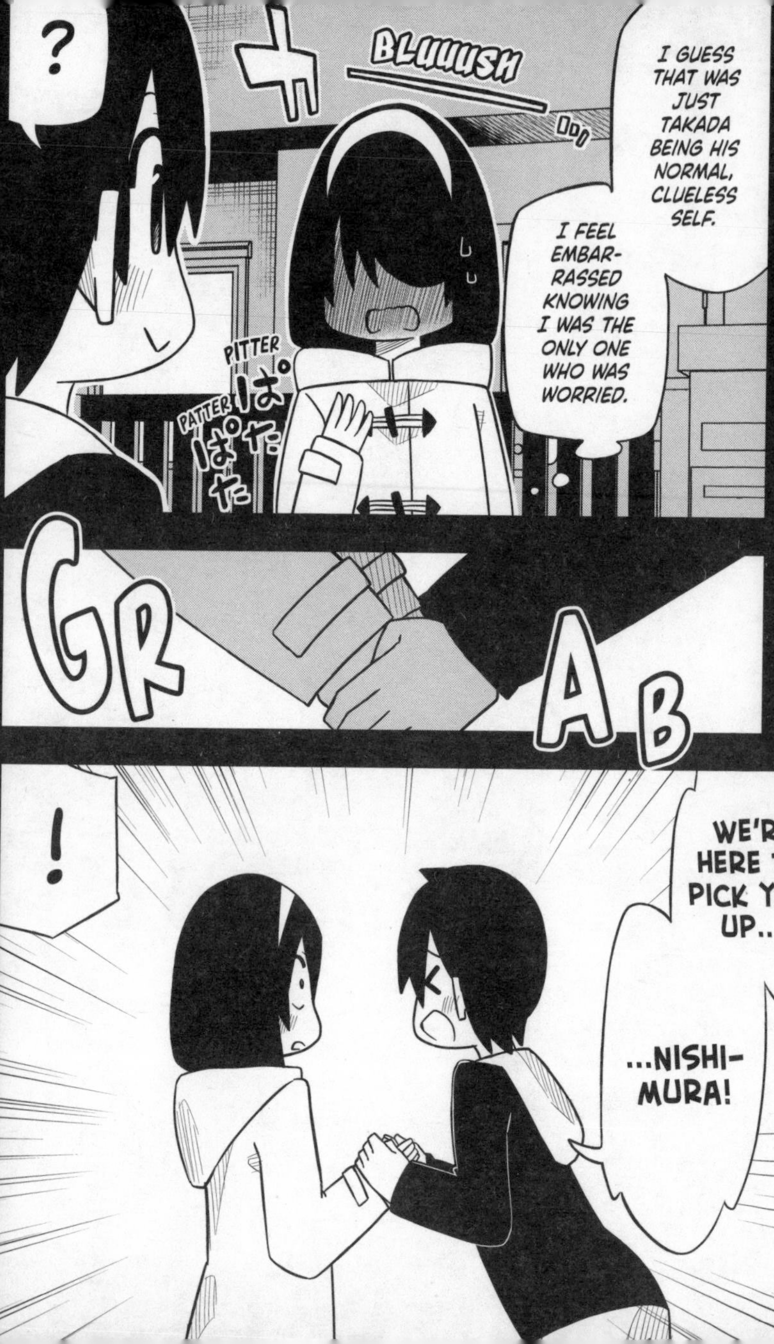
I GUESS THAT WAS JUST TAKADA BEING HIS NORMAL, CLUELESS SELF.
I FEEL EMBAR-RASSED KNOWING I WAS THE ONLY ONE WHO WAS WORRIED.
BLUUUSH
PITTER
PATTER
?
GRAB
WE'RE HERE TO PICK YOU UP...
...NISHI-MURA!
!

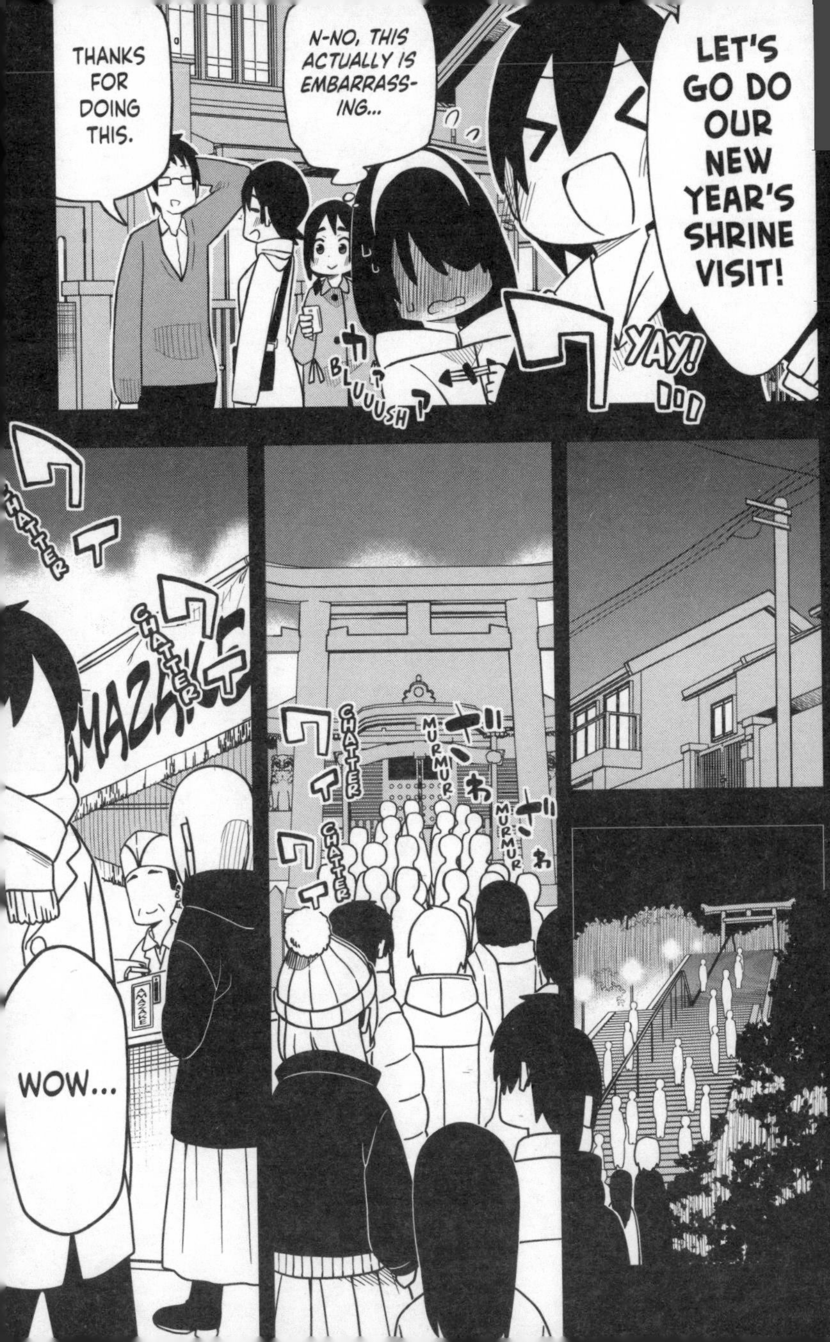
LET'S GO DO OUR NEW YEAR'S SHRINE VISIT!
N-NO, THIS ACTUALLY IS EMBARRASS-ING...
THANKS FOR DOING THIS.
YAY!
BLUUUSH
CHATTER
MURMUR
MURMUR
CHATTER
CHATTER
CHATTER
AMAZAKE
AMAZAKE
WOW...

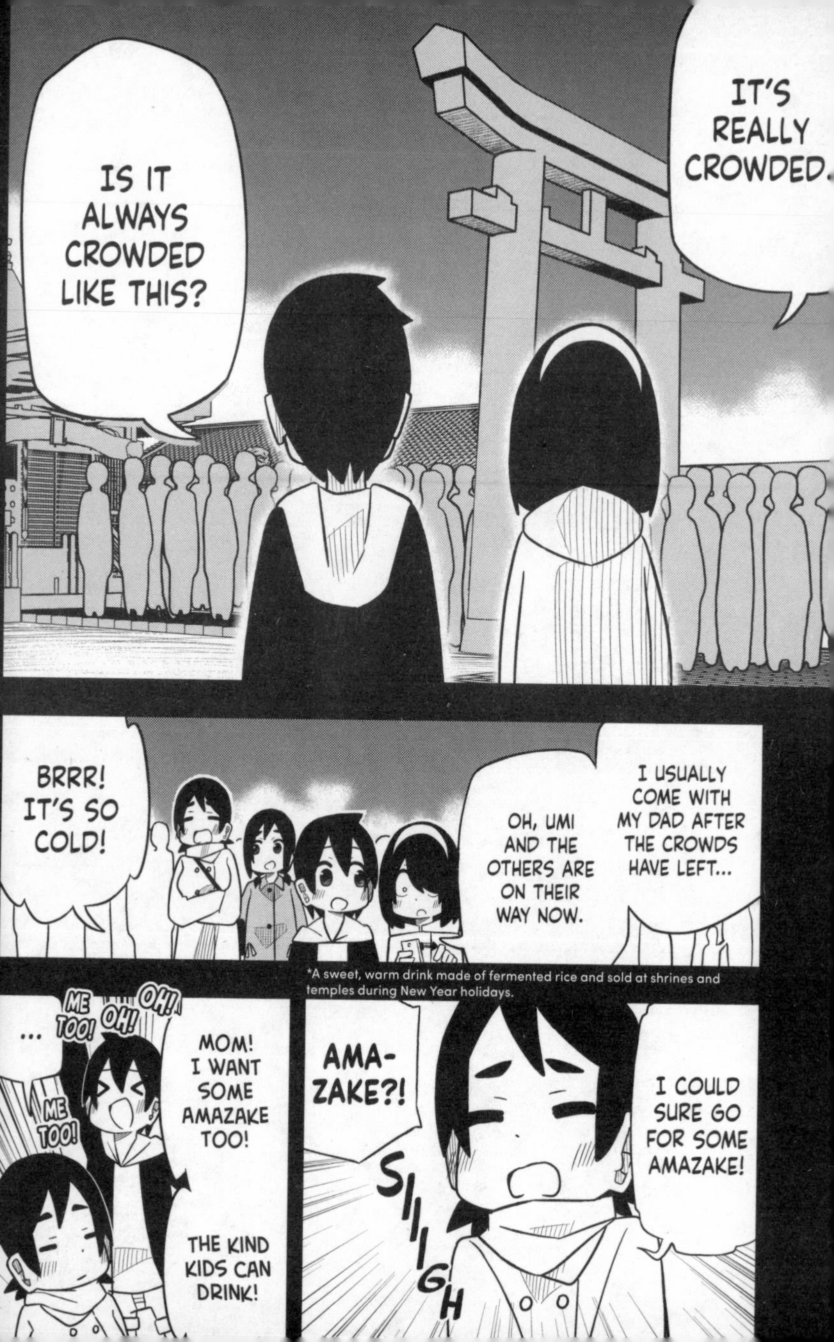
IT'S REALLY CROWDED.
IS IT ALWAYS CROWDED LIKE THIS?
I USUALLY COME WITH MY DAD AFTER THE CROWDS HAVE LEFT...
OH, UMI AND THE OTHERS ARE ON THEIR WAY NOW.
BRRR! IT'S SO COLD!
I COULD SURE GO FOR SOME AMAZAKE!
SIIIGH
AMA-ZAKE?!
MOM! I WANT SOME AMAZAKE TOO!
OH! OH!
ME TOO!
ME TOO!
...
THE KIND KIDS CAN DRINK!

*A sweet, warm drink made of fermented rice and sold at shrines and temples during New Year holidays.

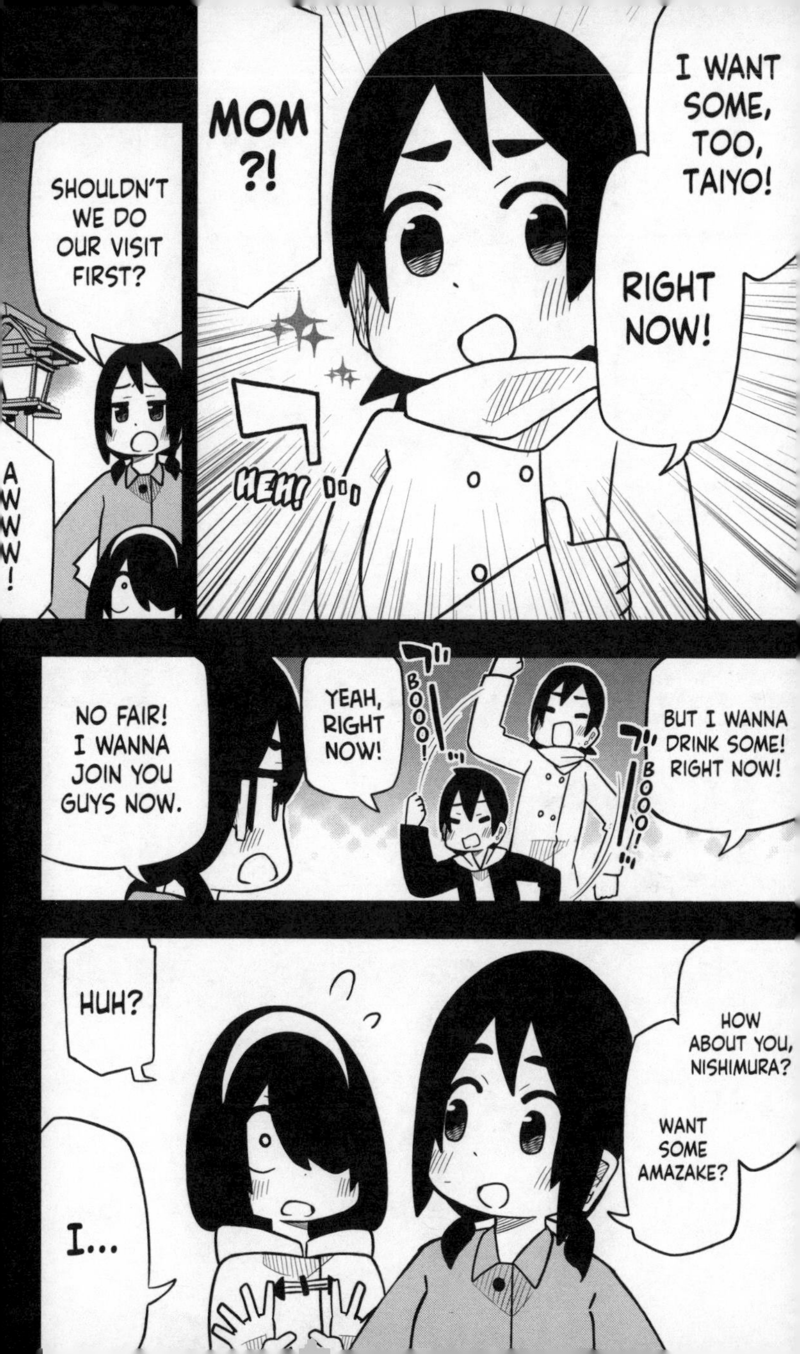
I WANT SOME, TOO, TAIYO!
RIGHT NOW!
MOM ?!
HEH! ...
SHOULDN'T WE DO OUR VISIT FIRST?
AWWWW!
BUT I WANNA DRINK SOME! RIGHT NOW!
BOOOO!
BOOOO!
YEAH, RIGHT NOW!
NO FAIR! I WANNA JOIN YOU GUYS NOW.
HOW ABOUT YOU, NISHIMURA?
WANT SOME AMAZAKE?
HUH?
I...

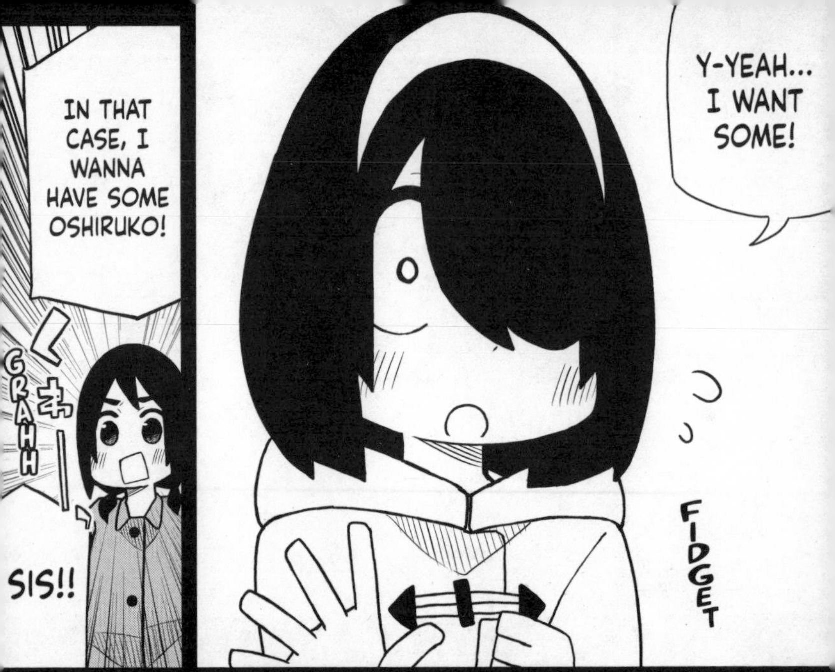
Y-YEAH... I WANT SOME!
FIDGET
IN THAT CASE, I WANNA HAVE SOME OSHIRUKO!
GRAHH
SIS!!

Red bean soup typically served during New Year holidays.

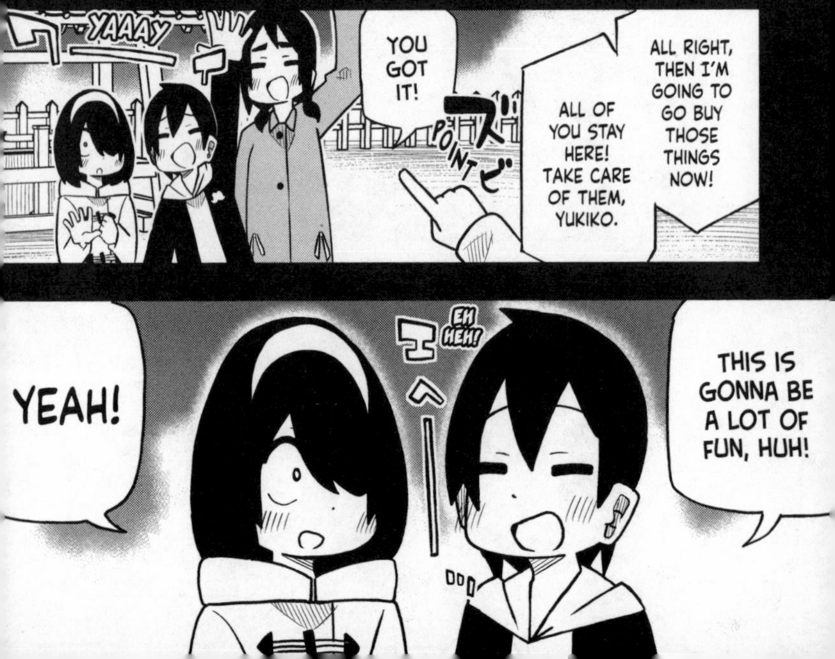
ALL RIGHT, THEN I'M GOING TO GO BUY THOSE THINGS NOW!
ALL OF YOU STAY HERE! TAKE CARE OF THEM, YUKIKO.
POINT
YOU GOT IT!
YAAAY
THIS IS GONNA BE A LOT OF FUN, HUH!
EH HEH!
YEAH!

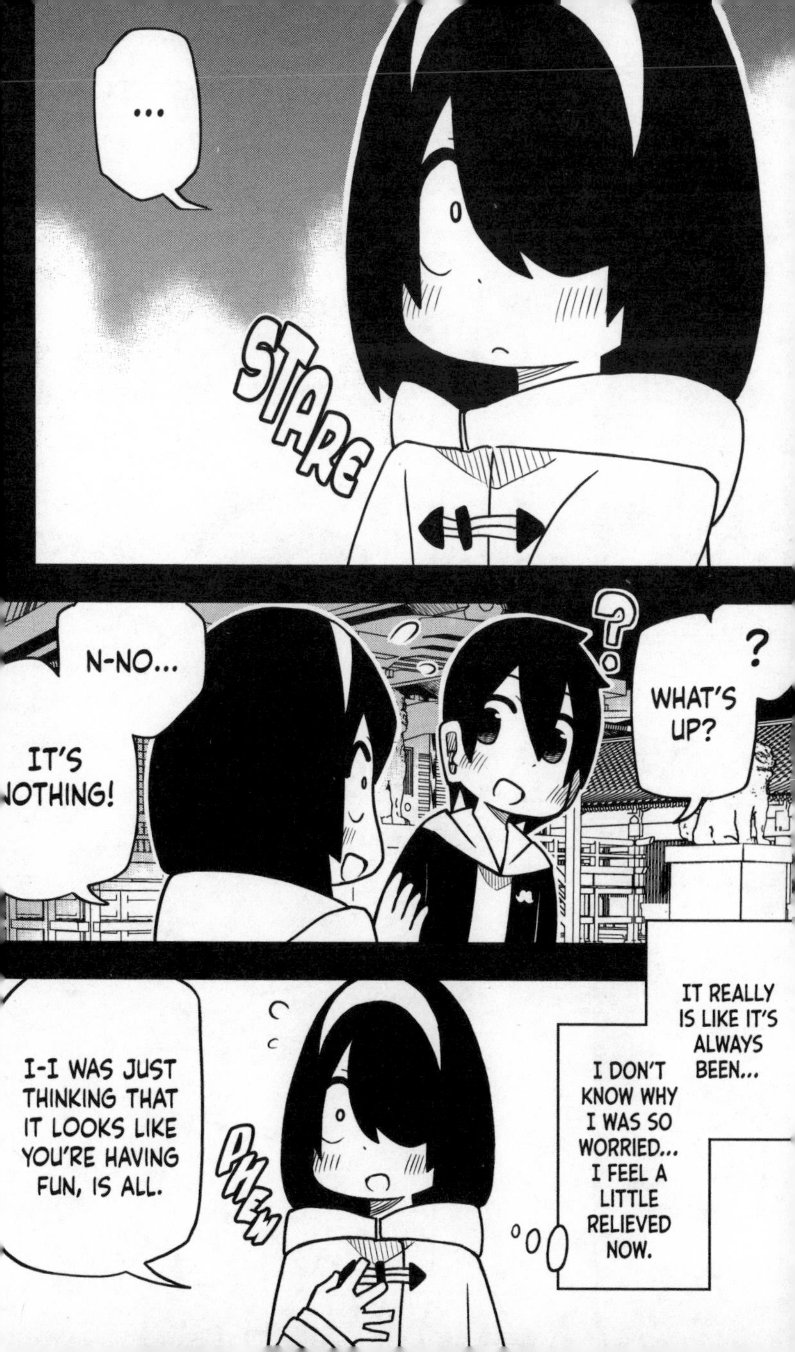
...
STARE
? WHAT'S UP?
N-NO...
IT'S NOTHING!
IT REALLY IS LIKE IT'S ALWAYS BEEN...
I DON'T KNOW WHY I WAS SO WORRIED... I FEEL A LITTLE RELIEVED NOW.
PHEW
I-I WAS JUST THINKING THAT IT LOOKS LIKE YOU'RE HAVING FUN, IS ALL.

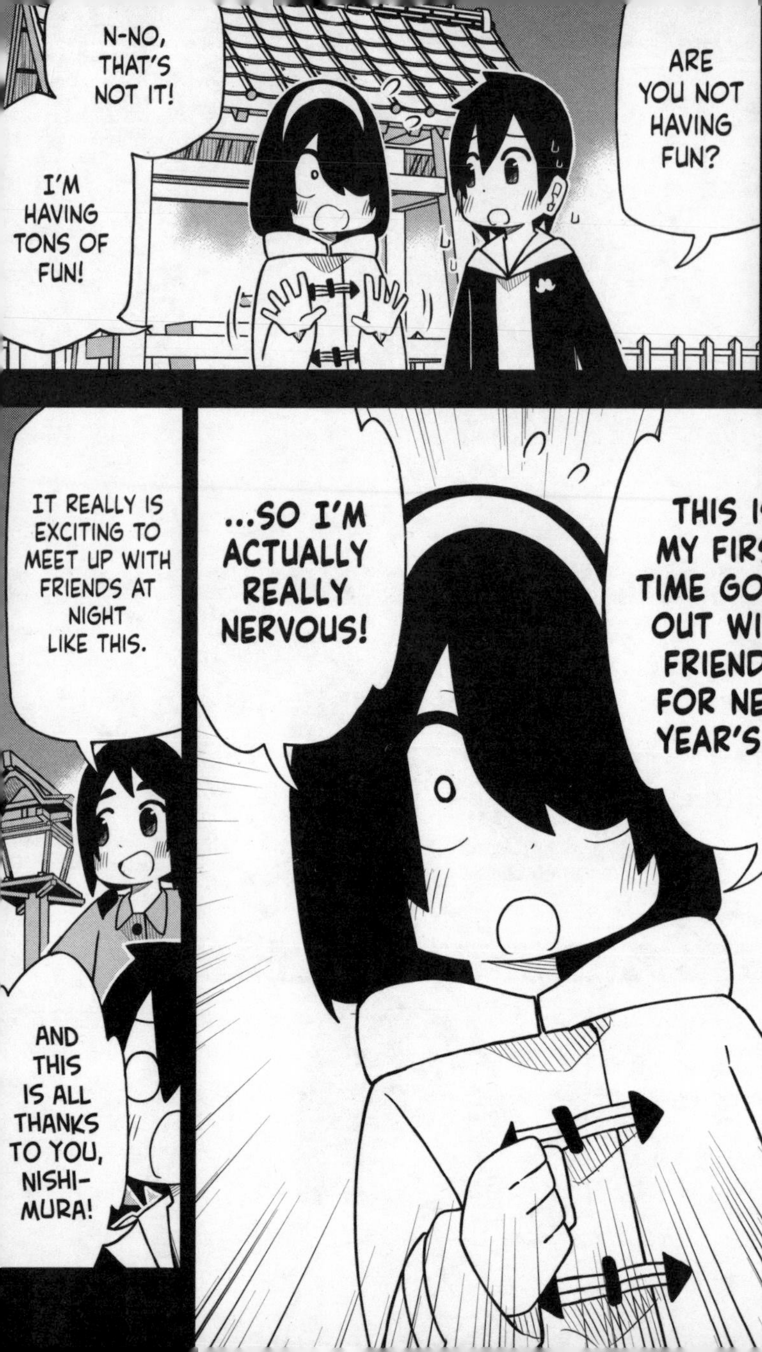
ARE YOU NOT HAVING FUN?
N-NO, THAT'S NOT IT!
I'M HAVING TONS OF FUN!
THIS IS MY FIRST TIME GOING OUT WITH FRIENDS FOR NEW YEAR'S...
...SO I'M ACTUALLY REALLY NERVOUS!
IT REALLY IS EXCITING TO MEET UP WITH FRIENDS AT NIGHT LIKE THIS.
AND THIS IS ALL THANKS TO YOU, NISHIMURA!

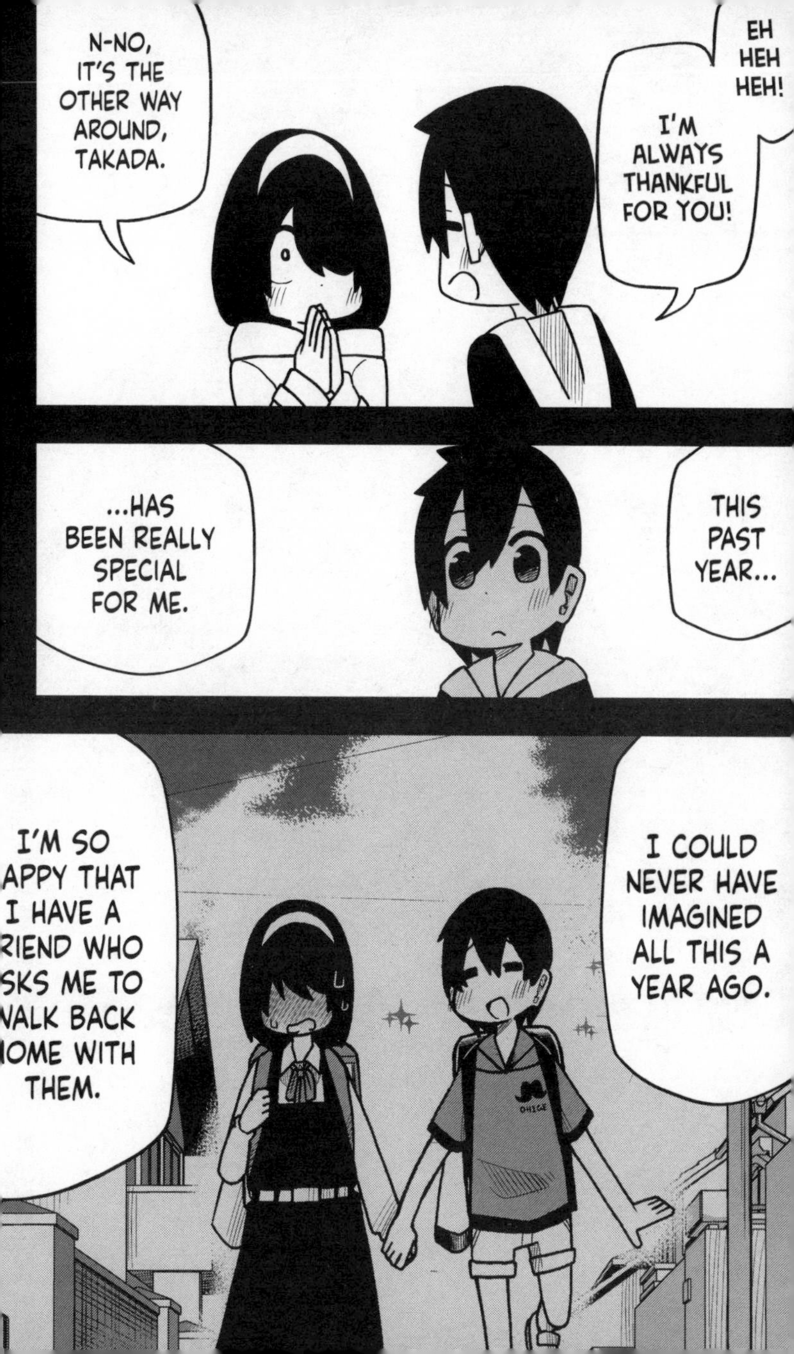
EH HEH HEH!
I'M ALWAYS THANKFUL FOR YOU!
N-NO, IT'S THE OTHER WAY AROUND, TAKADA.
THIS PAST YEAR...
...HAS BEEN REALLY SPECIAL FOR ME.
I COULD NEVER HAVE IMAGINED ALL THIS A YEAR AGO.
I'M SO APPY THAT I HAVE A RIEND WHO SKS ME TO VALK BACK IOME WITH THEM.

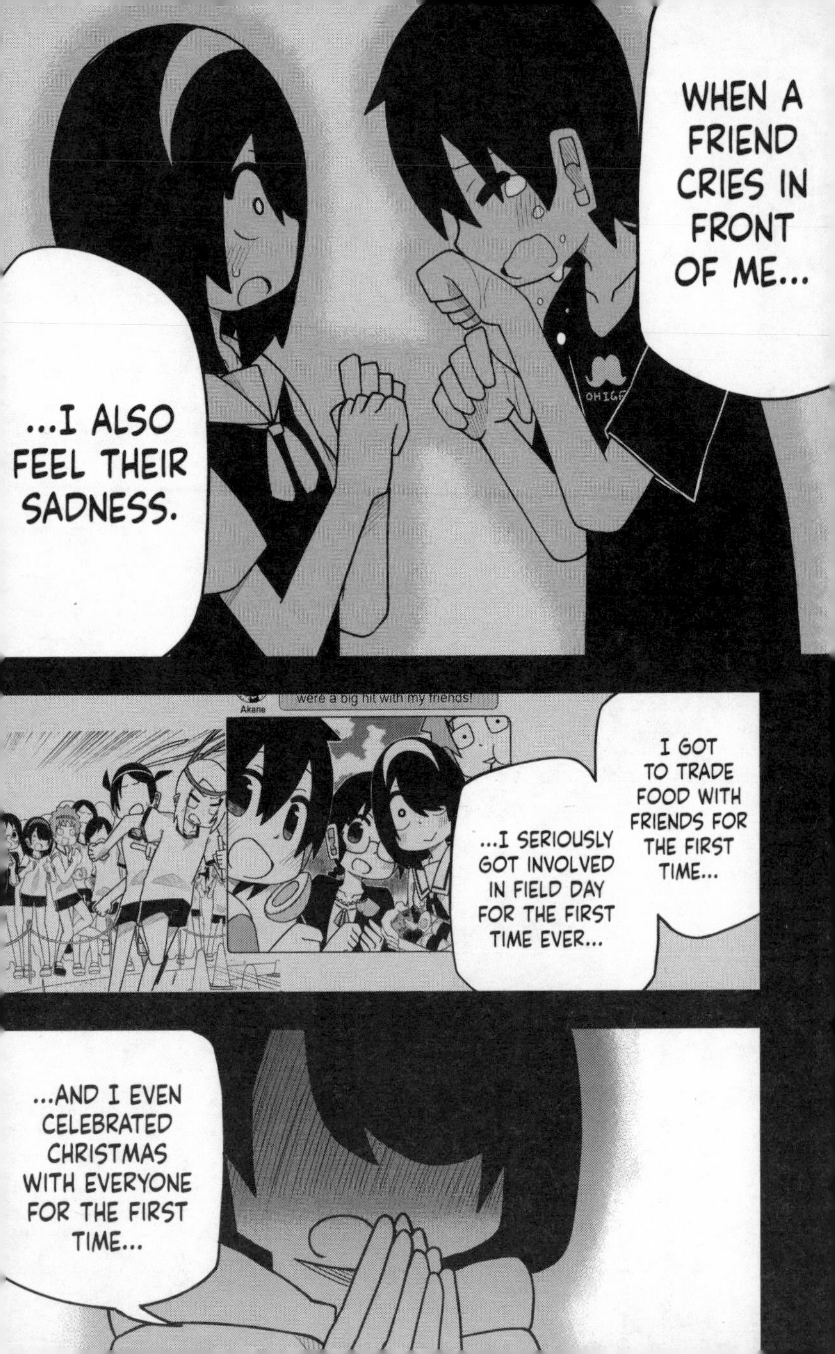
WHEN A FRIEND CRIES IN FRONT OF ME...
...I ALSO FEEL THEIR SADNESS.
Akane
were a big hit with my friends!
I GOT TO TRADE FOOD WITH FRIENDS FOR THE FIRST TIME...
...I SERIOUSLY GOT INVOLVED IN FIELD DAY FOR THE FIRST TIME EVER...
...AND I EVEN CELEBRATED CHRISTMAS WITH EVERYONE FOR THE FIRST TIME...

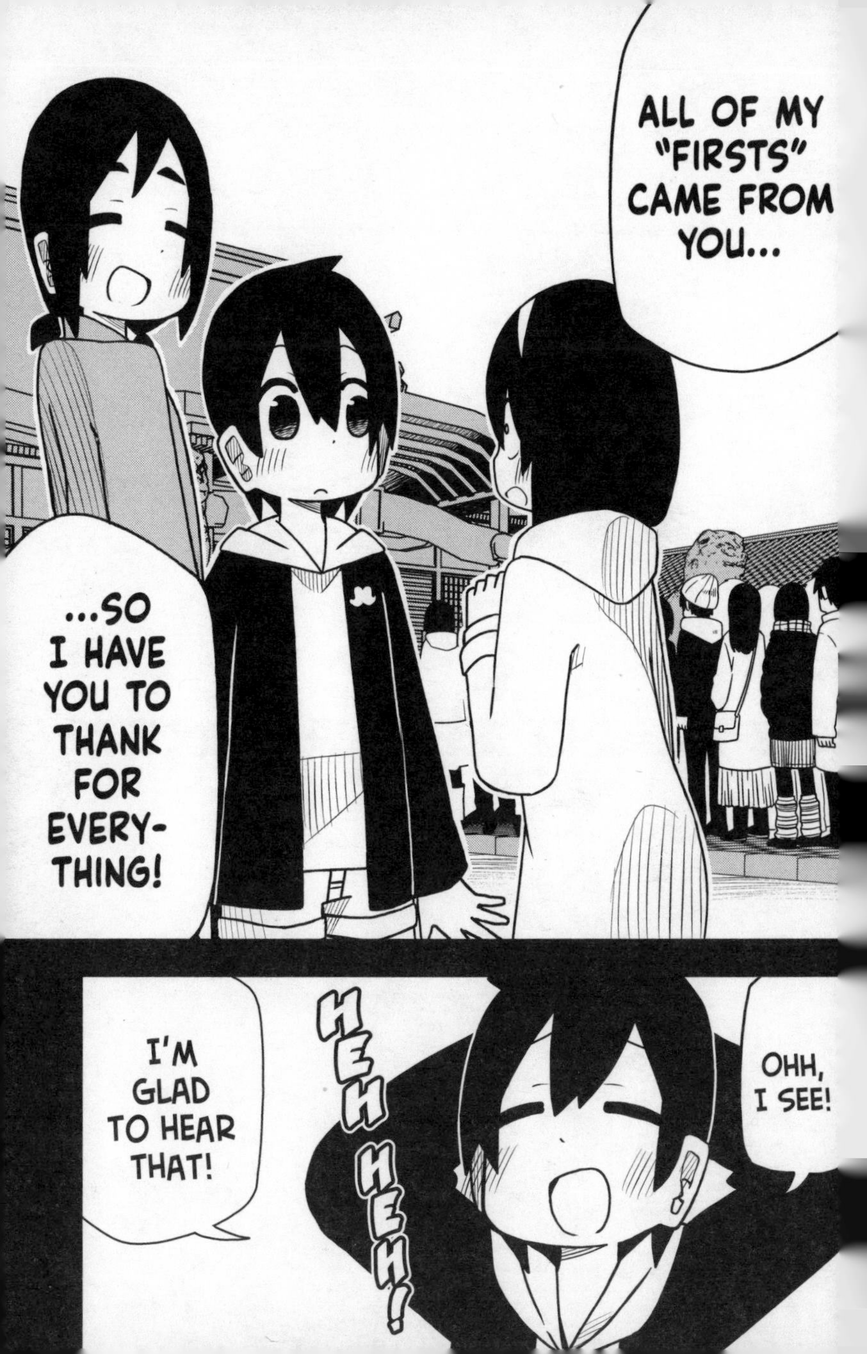
ALL OF MY "FIRSTS" CAME FROM YOU...
...SO I HAVE YOU TO THANK FOR EVERY-THING!
OHH, I SEE!
HEH HEH!
I'M GLAD TO HEAR THAT!

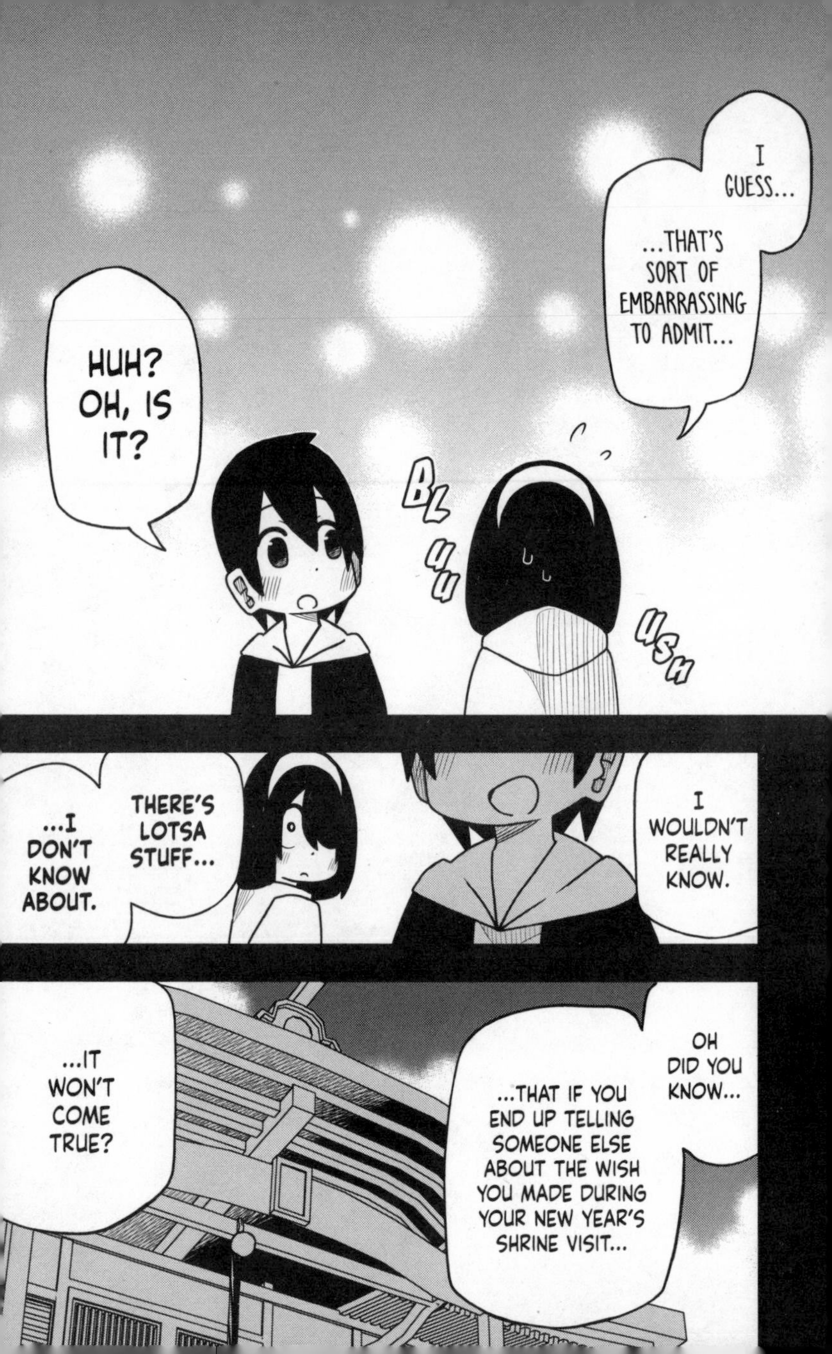
I GUESS... ...THAT'S SORT OF EMBARRASSING TO ADMIT...
BLUUUSH
HUH? OH, IS IT?
I WOULDN'T REALLY KNOW.
THERE'S LOTSA STUFF...
...I DON'T KNOW ABOUT.
OH DID YOU KNOW...
...THAT IF YOU END UP TELLING SOMEONE ELSE ABOUT THE WISH YOU MADE DURING YOUR NEW YEAR'S SHRINE VISIT...
...IT WON'T COME TRUE?

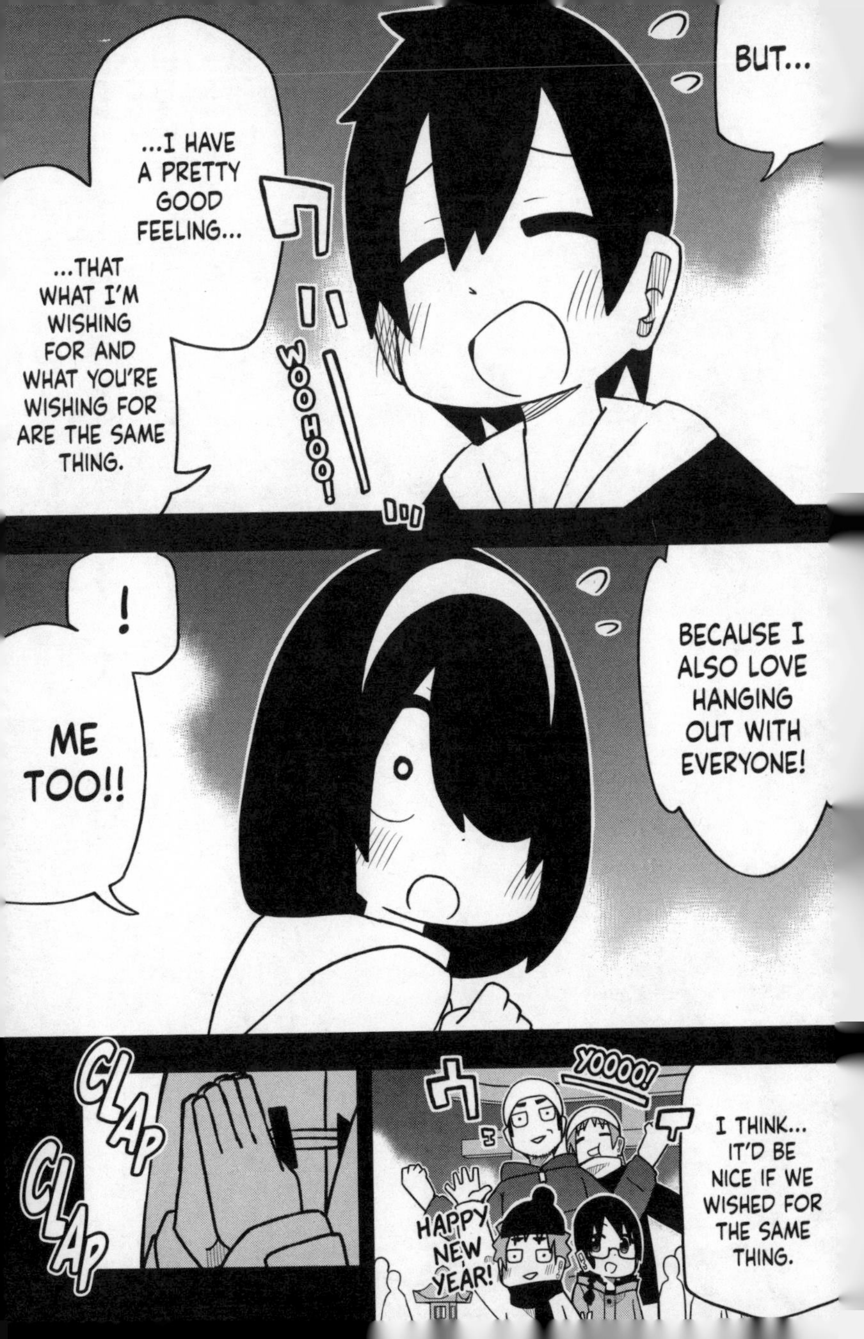
BUT...
...I HAVE A PRETTY GOOD FEELING...
...THAT WHAT I'M WISHING FOR AND WHAT YOU'RE WISHING FOR ARE THE SAME THING.
WOOHOO!
BECAUSE I ALSO LOVE HANGING OUT WITH EVERYONE!
!
ME TOO!!
I THINK... IT'D BE NICE IF WE WISHED FOR THE SAME THING.
YOOOO!
HAPPY NEW YEAR!
CLAP
CLAP

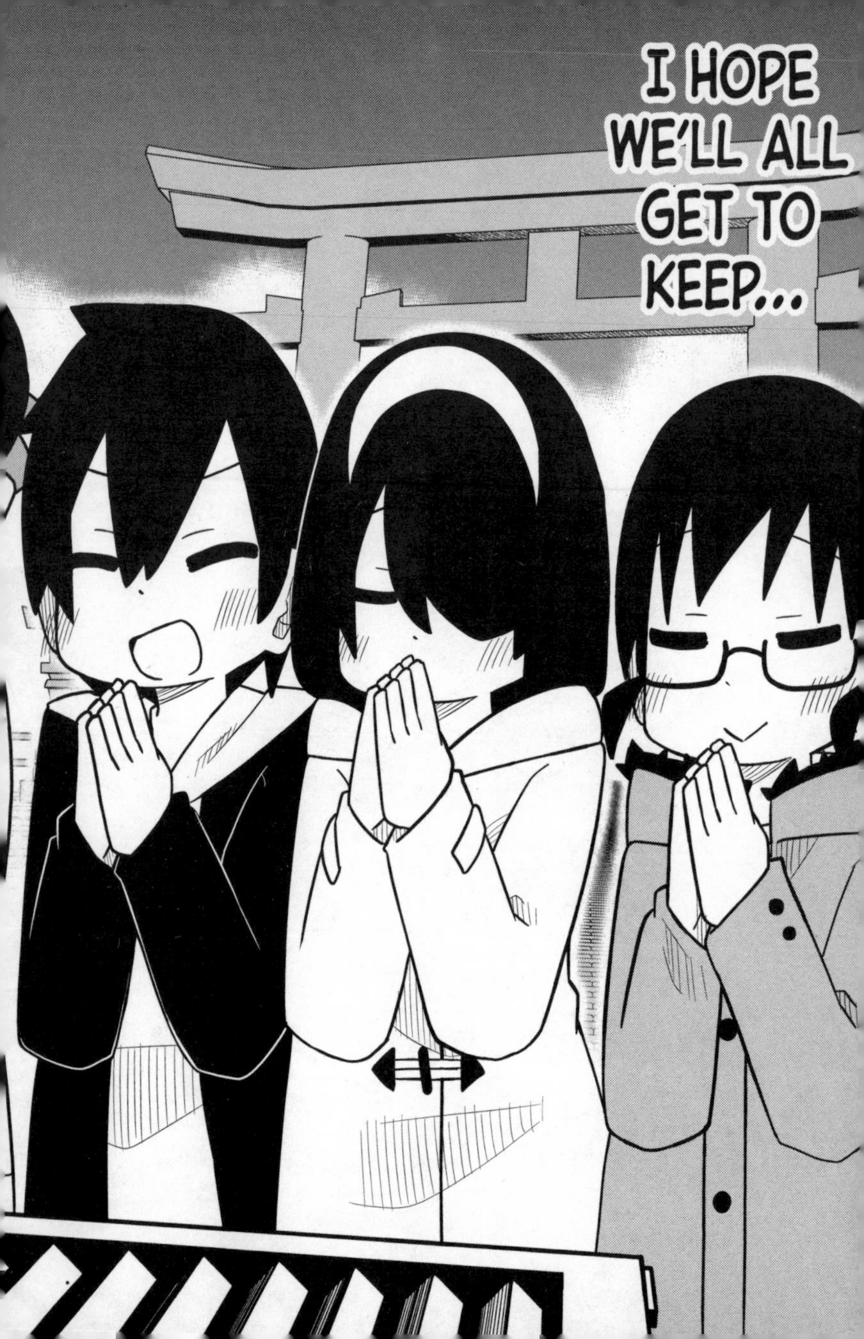
I HOPE WE'LL ALL GET TO KEEP...

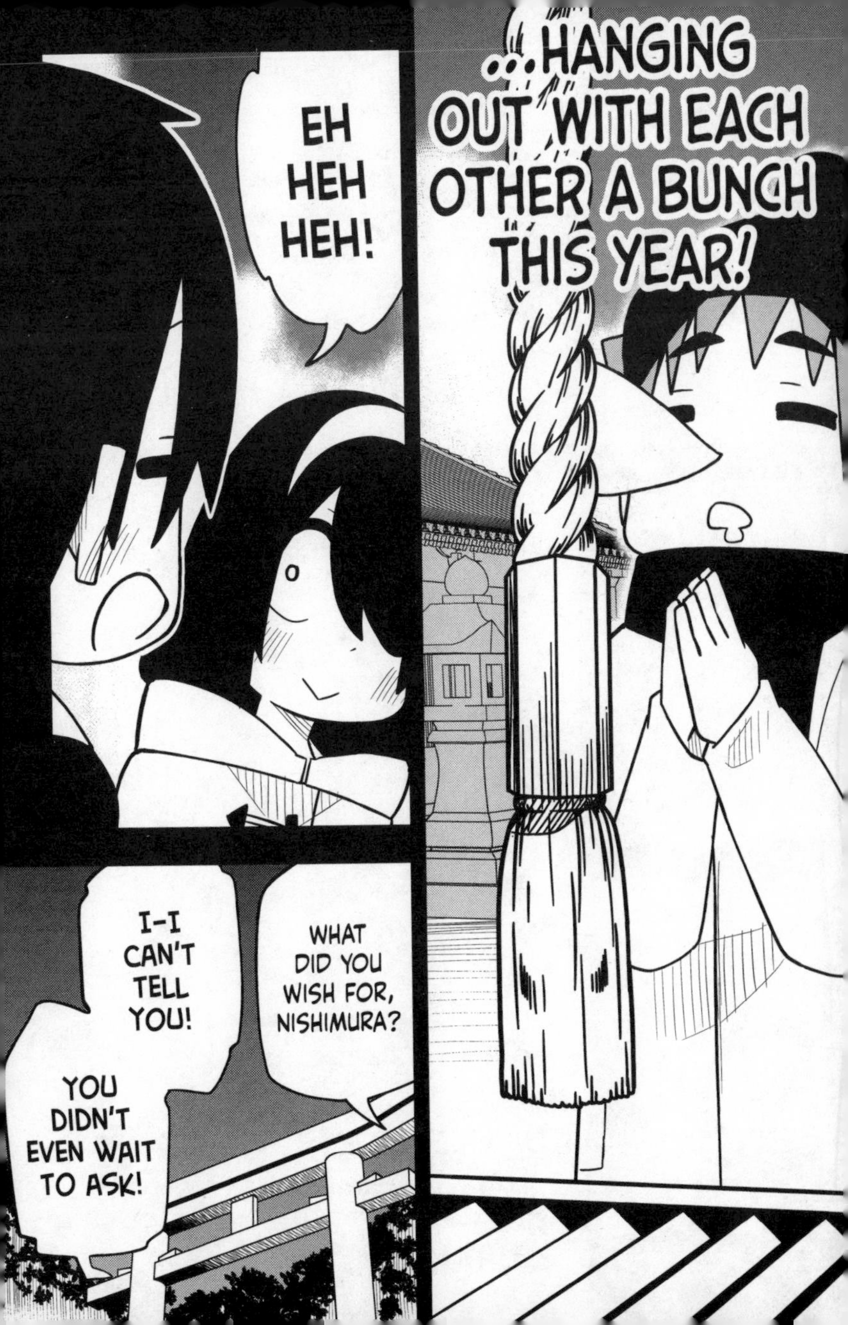
...HANGING OUT WITH EACH OTHER A BUNCH THIS YEAR!
EH HEH HEH!
WHAT DID YOU WISH FOR, NISHIMURA?
I-I CAN'T TELL YOU!
YOU DIDN'T EVEN WAIT TO ASK!

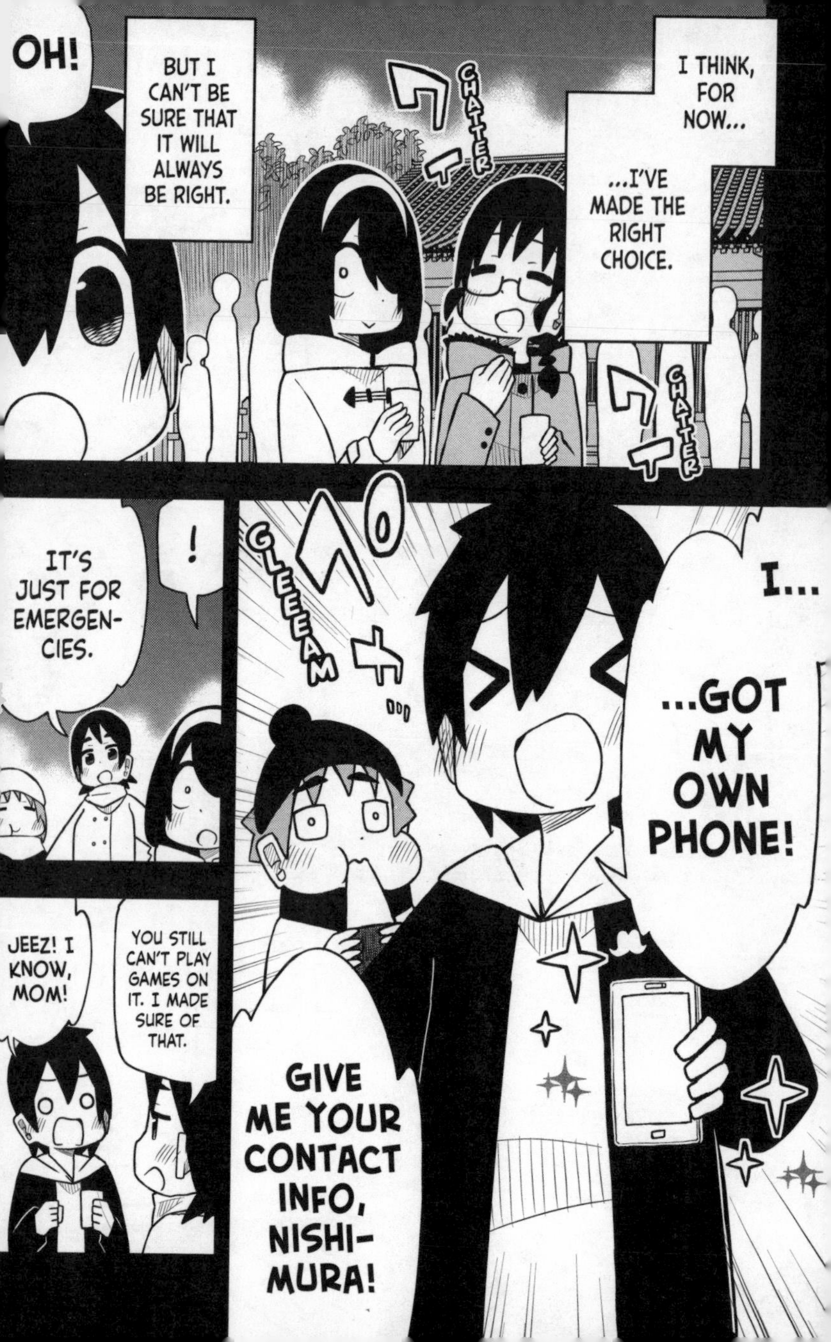
I THINK, FOR NOW...
...I'VE MADE THE RIGHT CHOICE.
CHATTER
CHATTER
BUT I CAN'T BE SURE THAT IT WILL ALWAYS BE RIGHT.
OH!
I...
...GOT MY OWN PHONE!
GLEEEAM
GIVE ME YOUR CONTACT INFO, NISHI-MURA!
!
IT'S JUST FOR EMERGEN-CIES.
YOU STILL CAN'T PLAY GAMES ON IT. I MADE SURE OF THAT.
JEEZ! I KNOW, MOM!

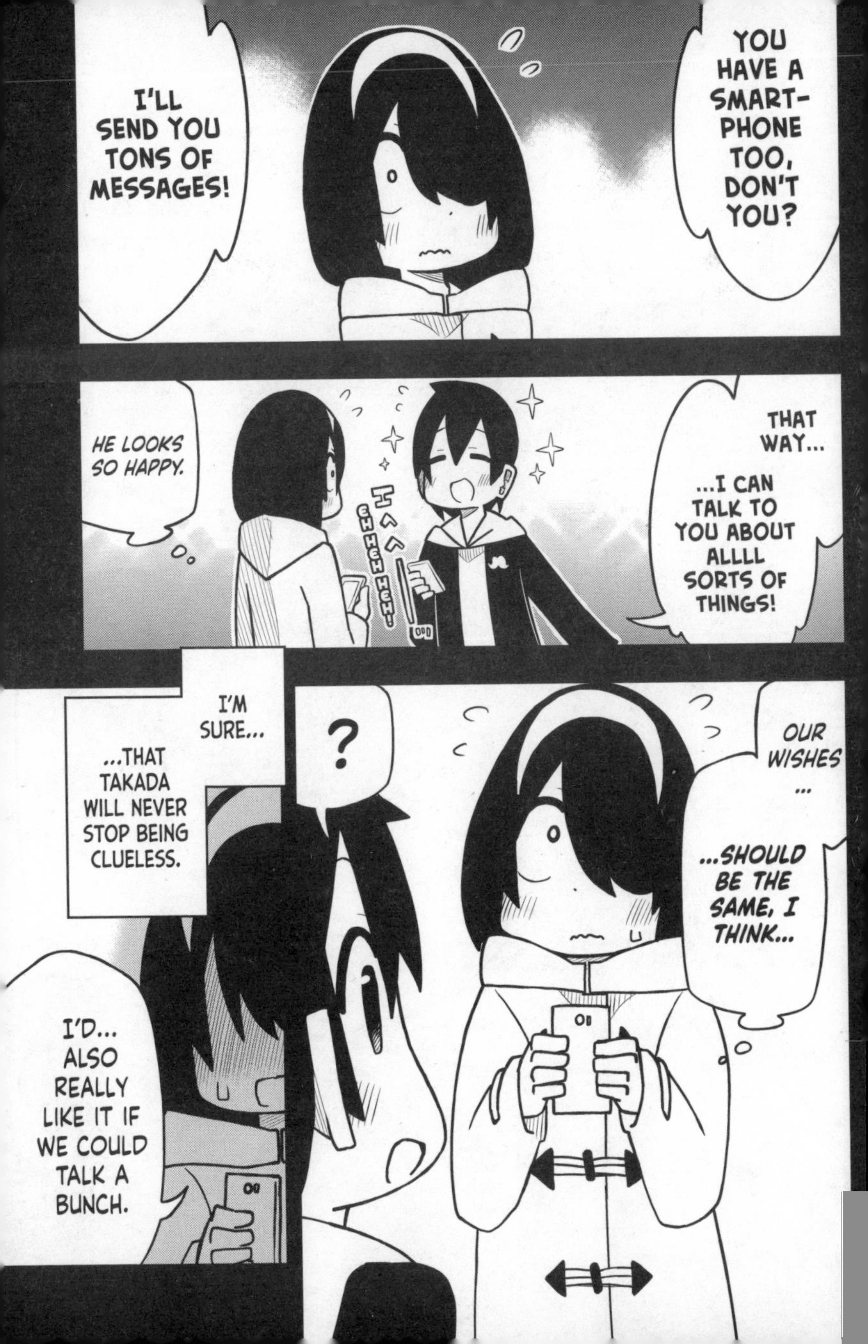
YOU HAVE A SMART-PHONE TOO, DON'T YOU?
I'LL SEND YOU TONS OF MESSAGES!
THAT WAY...
...I CAN TALK TO YOU ABOUT ALLLL SORTS OF THINGS!
EH HEH HEH!
HE LOOKS SO HAPPY.
OUR WISHES...
...SHOULD BE THE SAME, I THINK...
?
I'M SURE...
...THAT TAKADA WILL NEVER STOP BEING CLUELESS.
I'D... ALSO REALLY LIKE IT IF WE COULD TALK A BUNCH.

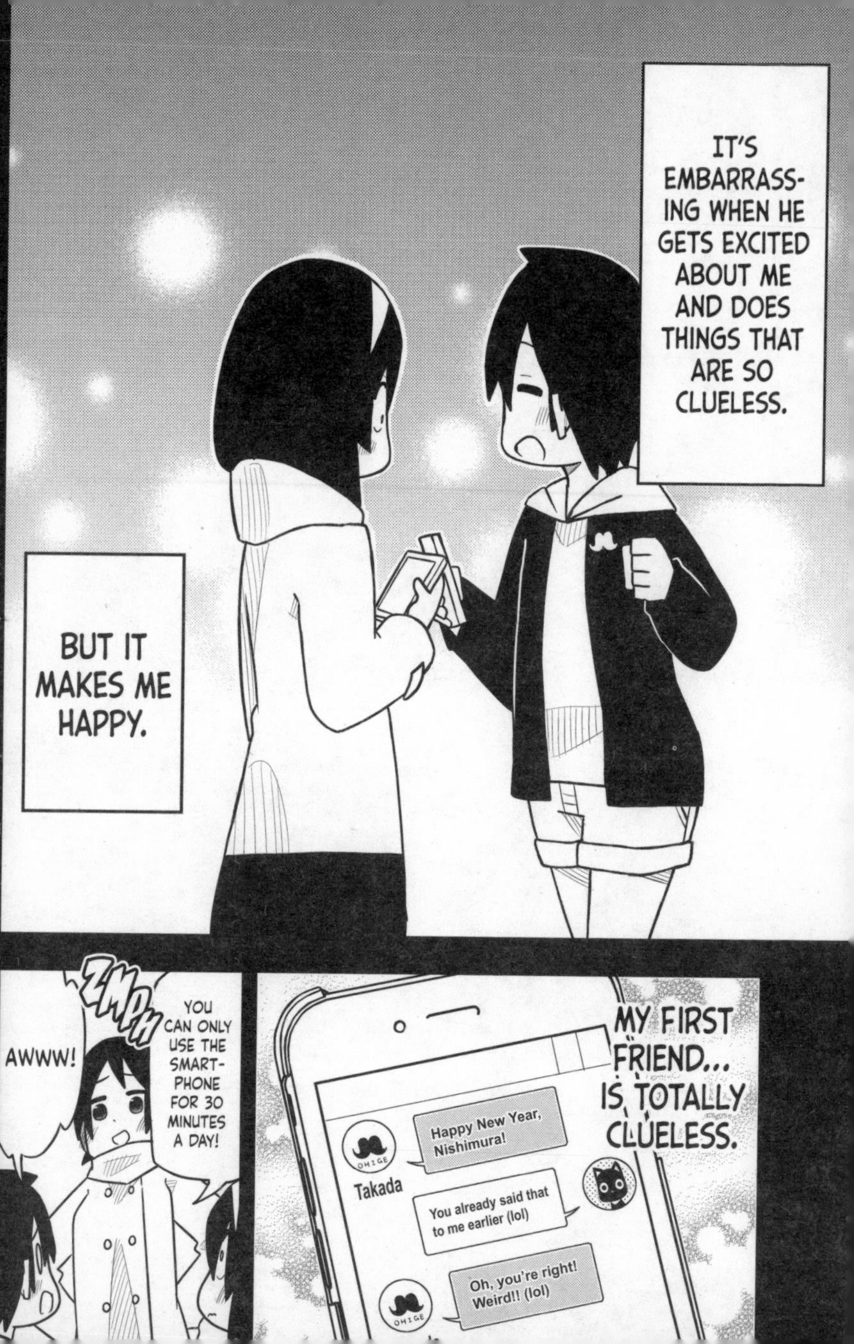
IT'S EMBARRASS-ING WHEN HE GETS EXCITED ABOUT ME AND DOES THINGS THAT ARE SO CLUELESS.
BUT IT MAKES ME HAPPY.
Happy New Year, Nishimura!
OHIGE
Takada
You already said that to me earlier (lol)
Oh, you're right! Weird!! (lol)
OHIGE
MY FIRST FRIEND... IS TOTALLY CLUELESS.
ZMPH
YOU CAN ONLY USE THE SMART-PHONE FOR 30 MINUTES A DAY!
AWWW!

MY CLUELESS FIRST FRIEND

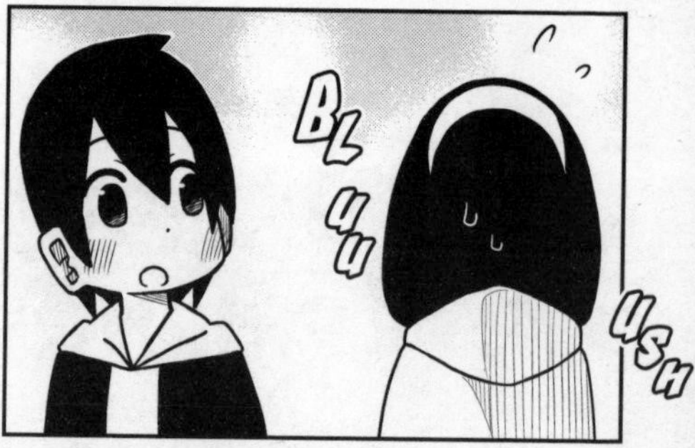
BLUUUSH

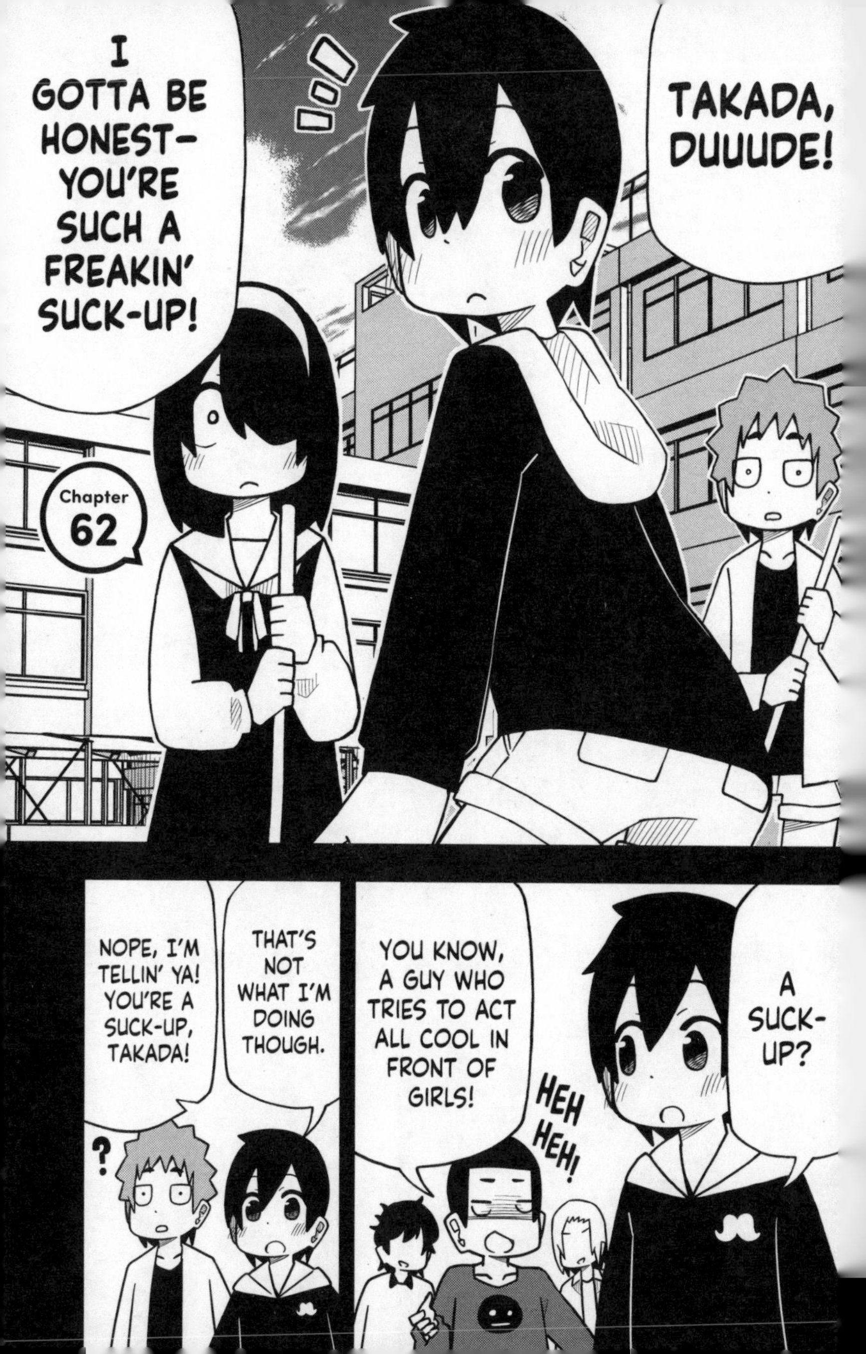
TAKADA, DUUUDE!
I GOTTA BE HONEST- YOU'RE SUCH A FREAKIN' SUCK-UP!
Chapter 62
A SUCK-UP?
YOU KNOW, A GUY WHO TRIES TO ACT ALL COOL IN FRONT OF GIRLS!
HEH HEH!
THAT'S NOT WHAT I'M DOING THOUGH.
NOPE, I'M TELLIN' YA! YOU'RE A SUCK-UP, TAKADA!
?

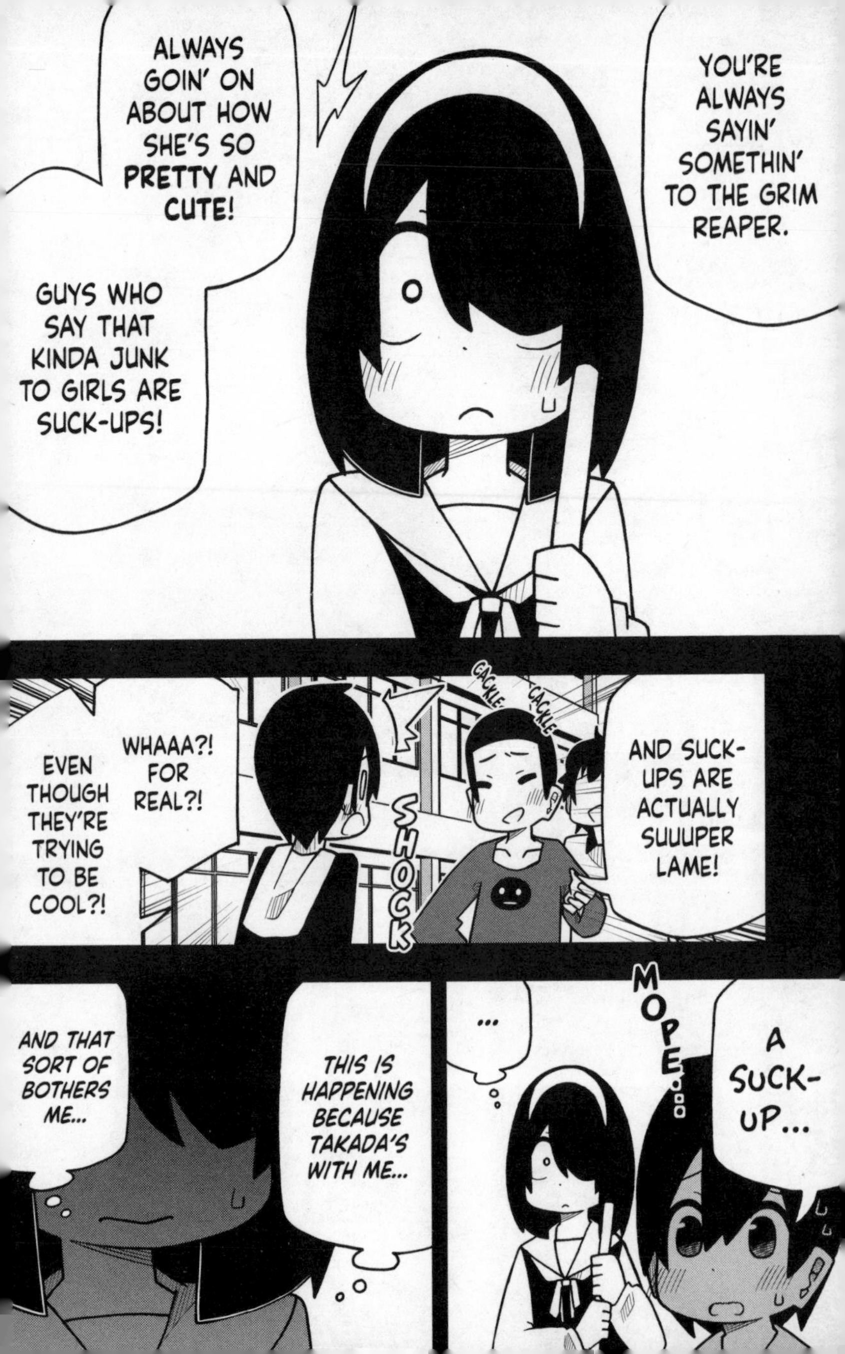
YOU'RE ALWAYS SAYIN' SOMETHIN' TO THE GRIM REAPER.
ALWAYS GOIN' ON ABOUT HOW SHE'S SO PRETTY AND CUTE!
GUYS WHO SAY THAT KINDA JUNK TO GIRLS ARE SUCK-UPS!
AND SUCK-UPS ARE ACTUALLY SUUUPER LAME!
CACKLE
CACKLE
SHOCK
WHAAA?! FOR REAL?!
EVEN THOUGH THEY'RE TRYING TO BE COOL?!
A SUCK-UP...
MOPE...
...
THIS IS HAPPENING BECAUSE TAKADA'S WITH ME...
AND THAT SORT OF BOTHERS ME...

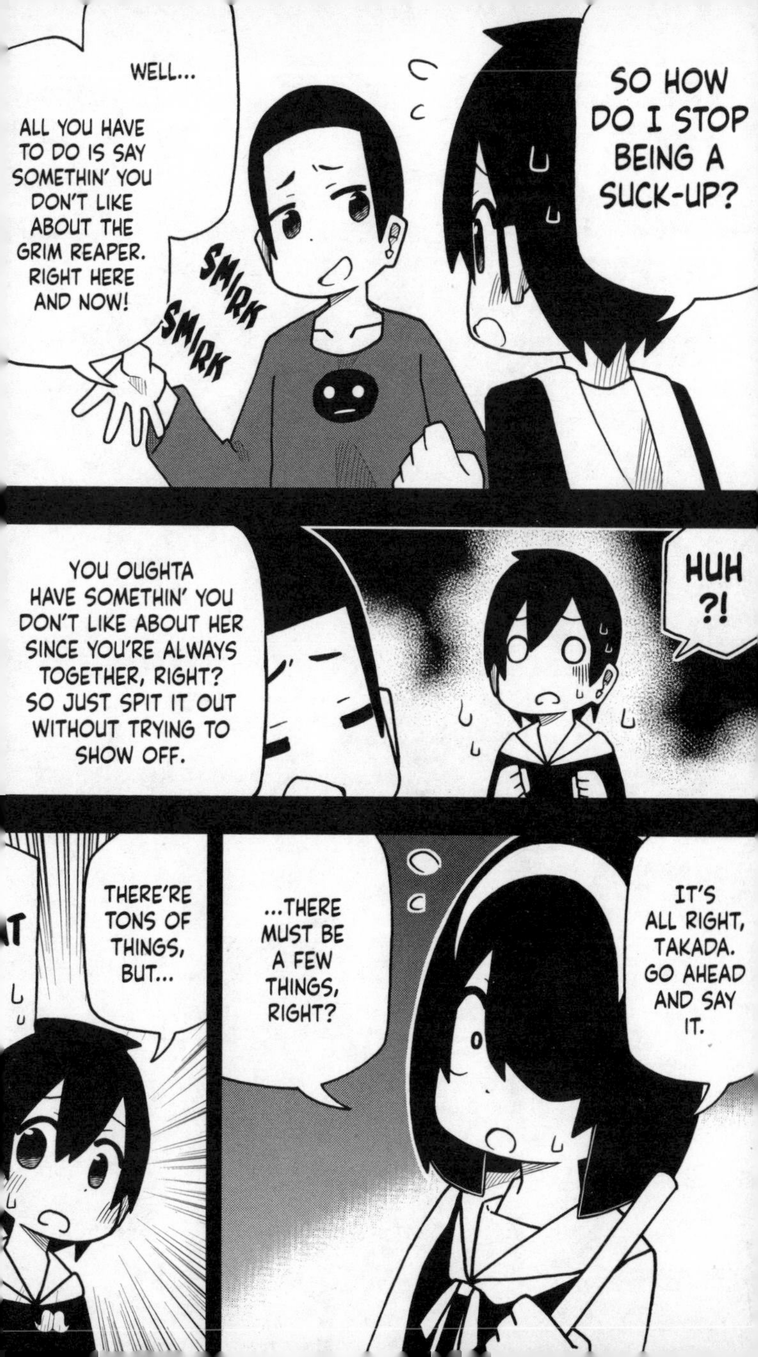
SO HOW DO I STOP BEING A SUCK-UP?
WELL...
ALL YOU HAVE TO DO IS SAY SOMETHIN' YOU DON'T LIKE ABOUT THE GRIM REAPER. RIGHT HERE AND NOW!
SMIRK SMIRK
HUH ?!
YOU OUGHTA HAVE SOMETHIN' YOU DON'T LIKE ABOUT HER SINCE YOU'RE ALWAYS TOGETHER, RIGHT? SO JUST SPIT IT OUT WITHOUT TRYING TO SHOW OFF.
IT'S ALL RIGHT, TAKADA. GO AHEAD AND SAY IT.
...THERE MUST BE A FEW THINGS, RIGHT?
THERE'RE TONS OF THINGS, BUT...

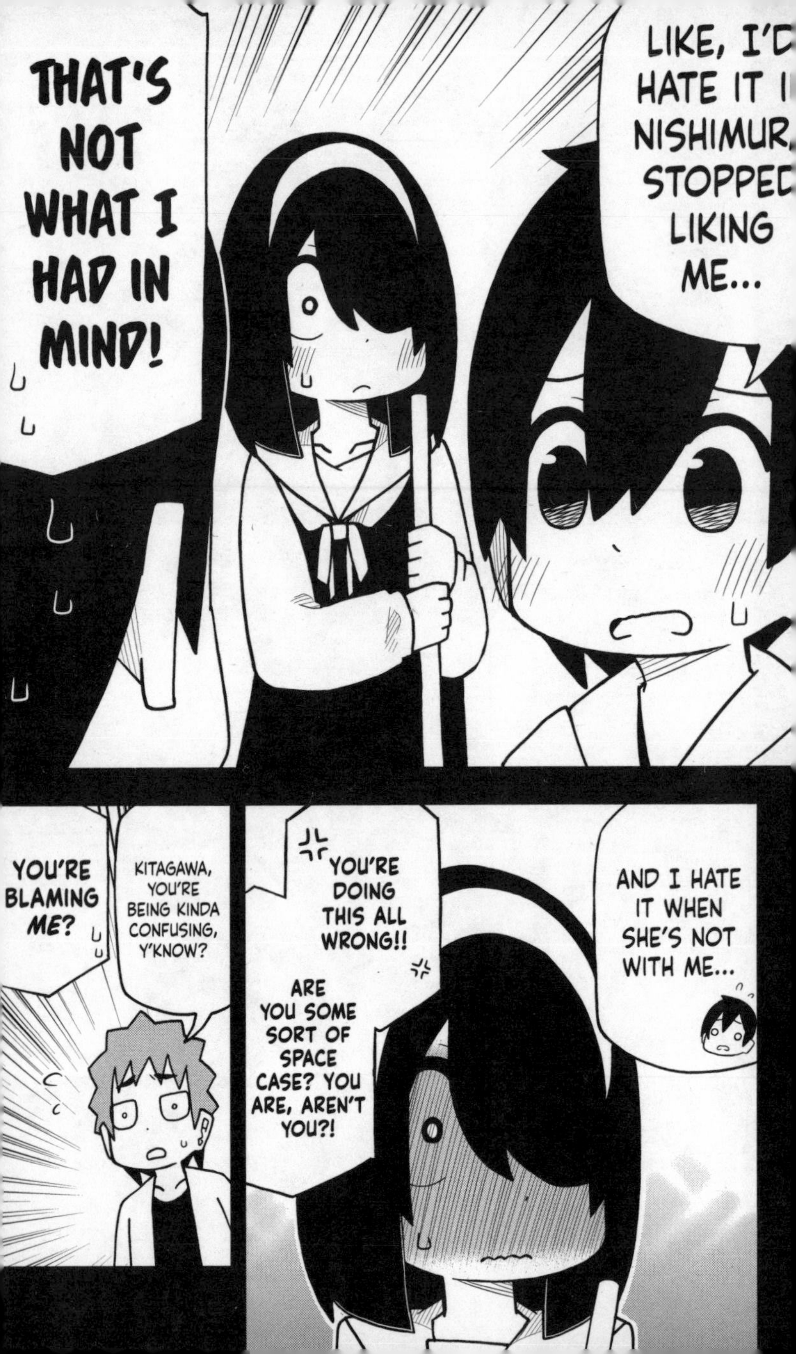
LIKE, I'D HATE IT I NISHIMURA STOPPED LIKING ME...
THAT'S NOT WHAT I HAD IN MIND!
AND I HATE IT WHEN SHE'S NOT WITH ME...
YOU'RE DOING THIS ALL WRONG!!
ARE YOU SOME SORT OF SPACE CASE? YOU ARE, AREN'T YOU?!
KITAGAWA, YOU'RE BEING KINDA CONFUSING, Y'KNOW?
YOU'RE BLAMING ME?

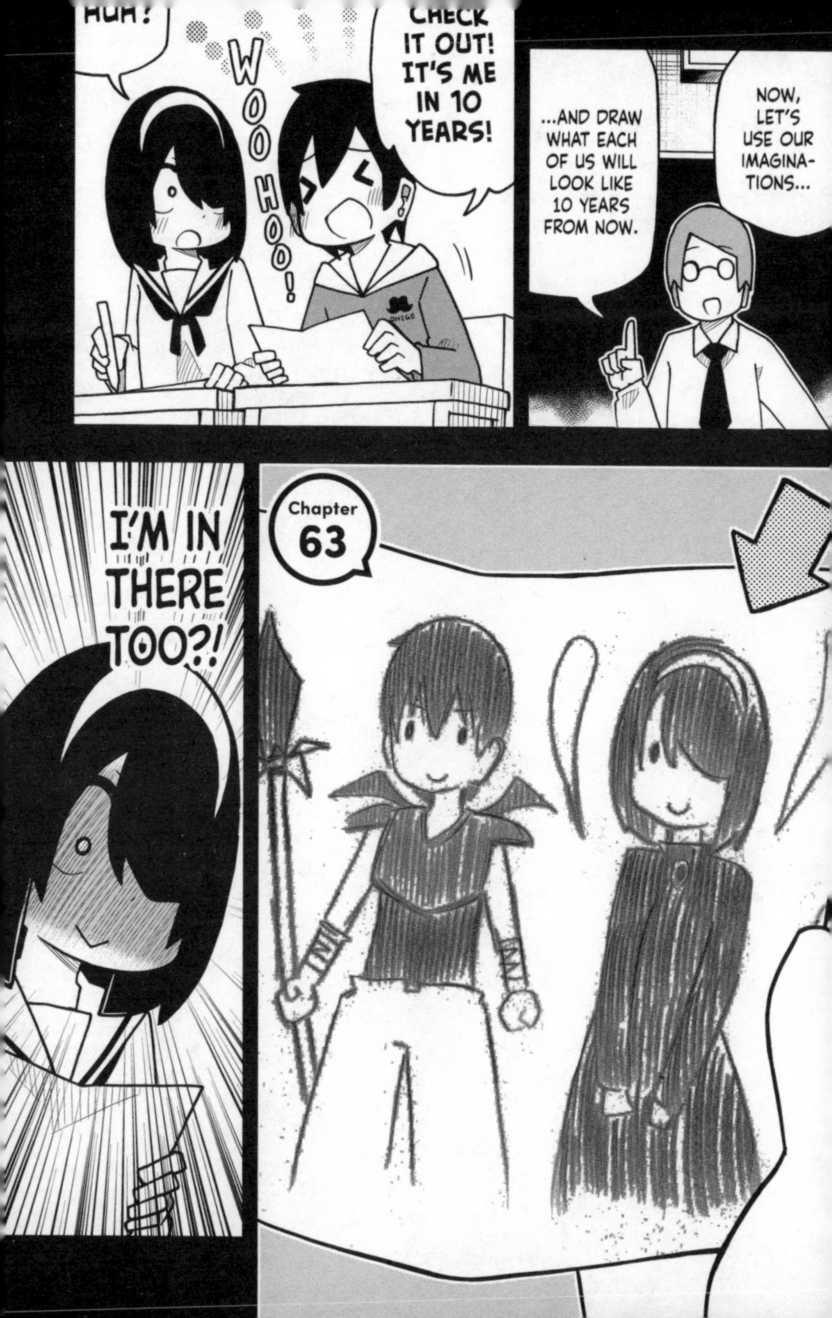
NOW, LET'S USE OUR IMAGINATIONS...
...AND DRAW WHAT EACH OF US WILL LOOK LIKE 10 YEARS FROM NOW.
CHECK IT OUT! IT'S ME IN 10 YEARS!
WOO HOO!
HUH?
Chapter 63
I'M IN THERE TOO?!

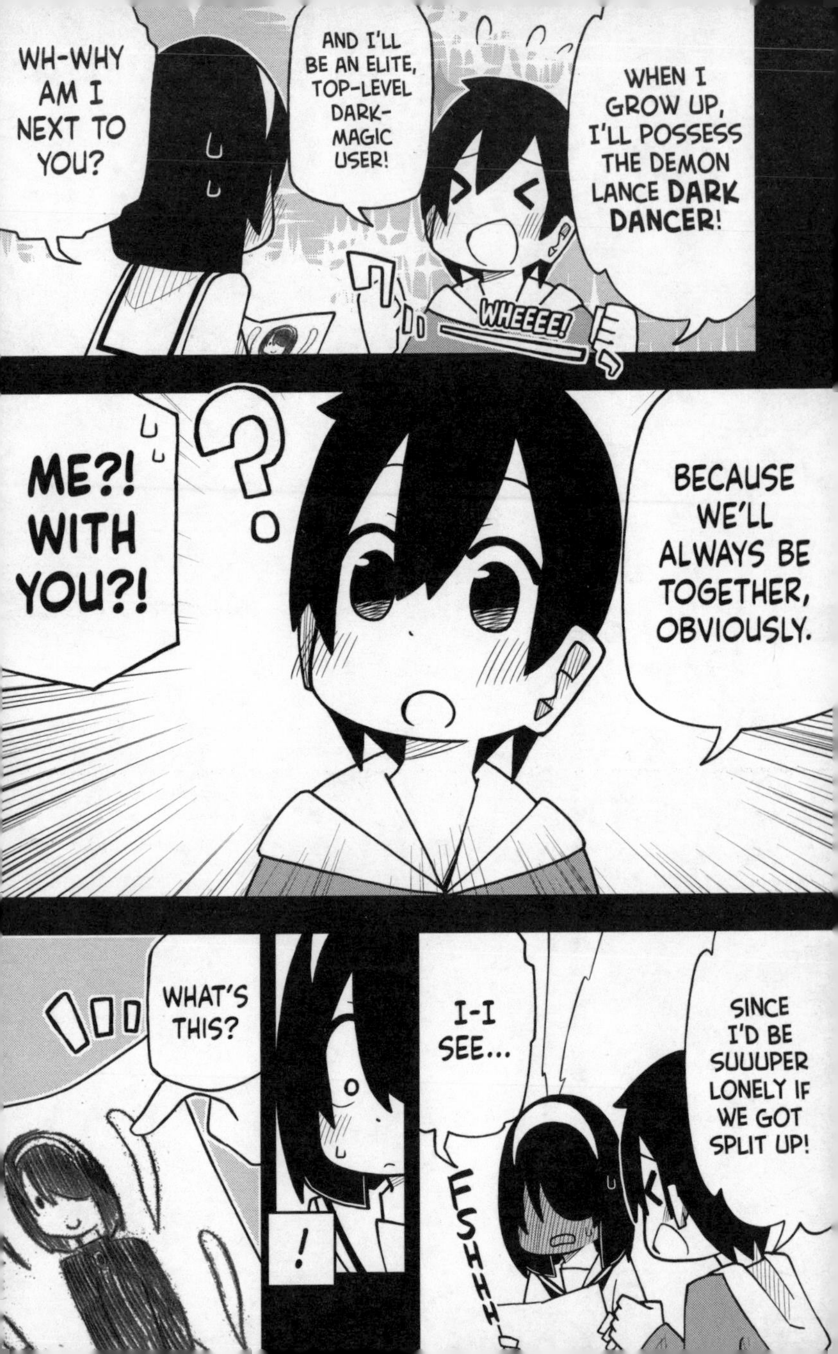
WHEN I GROW UP, I'LL POSSESS THE DEMON LANCE DARK DANCER!
WHEEEE!
AND I'LL BE AN ELITE, TOP-LEVEL DARK-MAGIC USER!
WH-WHY AM I NEXT TO YOU?
BECAUSE WE'LL ALWAYS BE TOGETHER, OBVIOUSLY.
ME?! WITH YOU?!
SINCE I'D BE SUUUPER LONELY IF WE GOT SPLIT UP!
I-I SEE...
FSHHH
!
WHAT'S THIS?
!!!

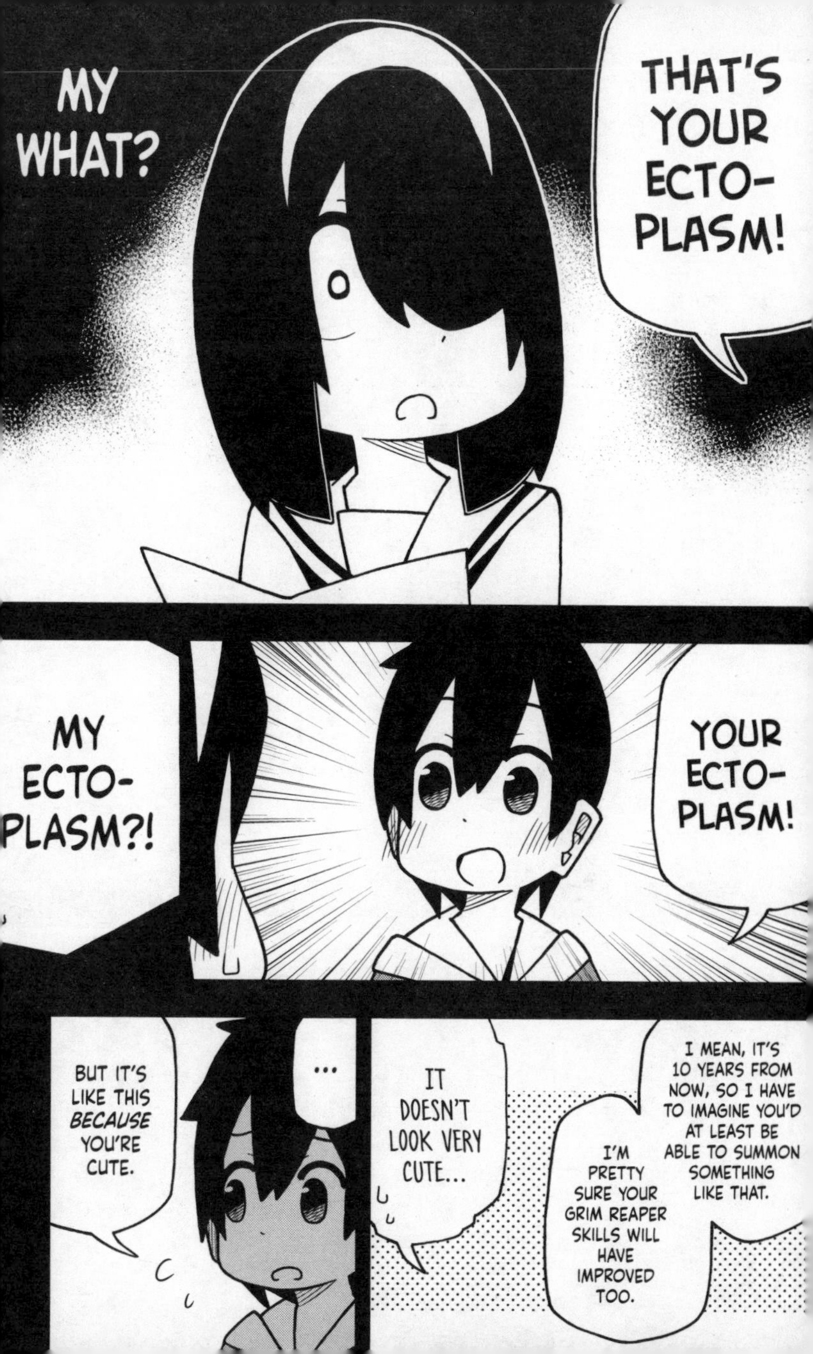
THAT'S YOUR ECTO-PLASM!
MY WHAT?
YOUR ECTO-PLASM!
MY ECTO-PLASM?!
I MEAN, IT'S 10 YEARS FROM NOW, SO I HAVE TO IMAGINE YOU'D AT LEAST BE ABLE TO SUMMON SOMETHING LIKE THAT.
I'M PRETTY SURE YOUR GRIM REAPER SKILLS WILL HAVE IMPROVED TOO.
IT DOESN'T LOOK VERY CUTE...
...
BUT IT'S LIKE THIS *BECAUSE* YOU'RE CUTE.

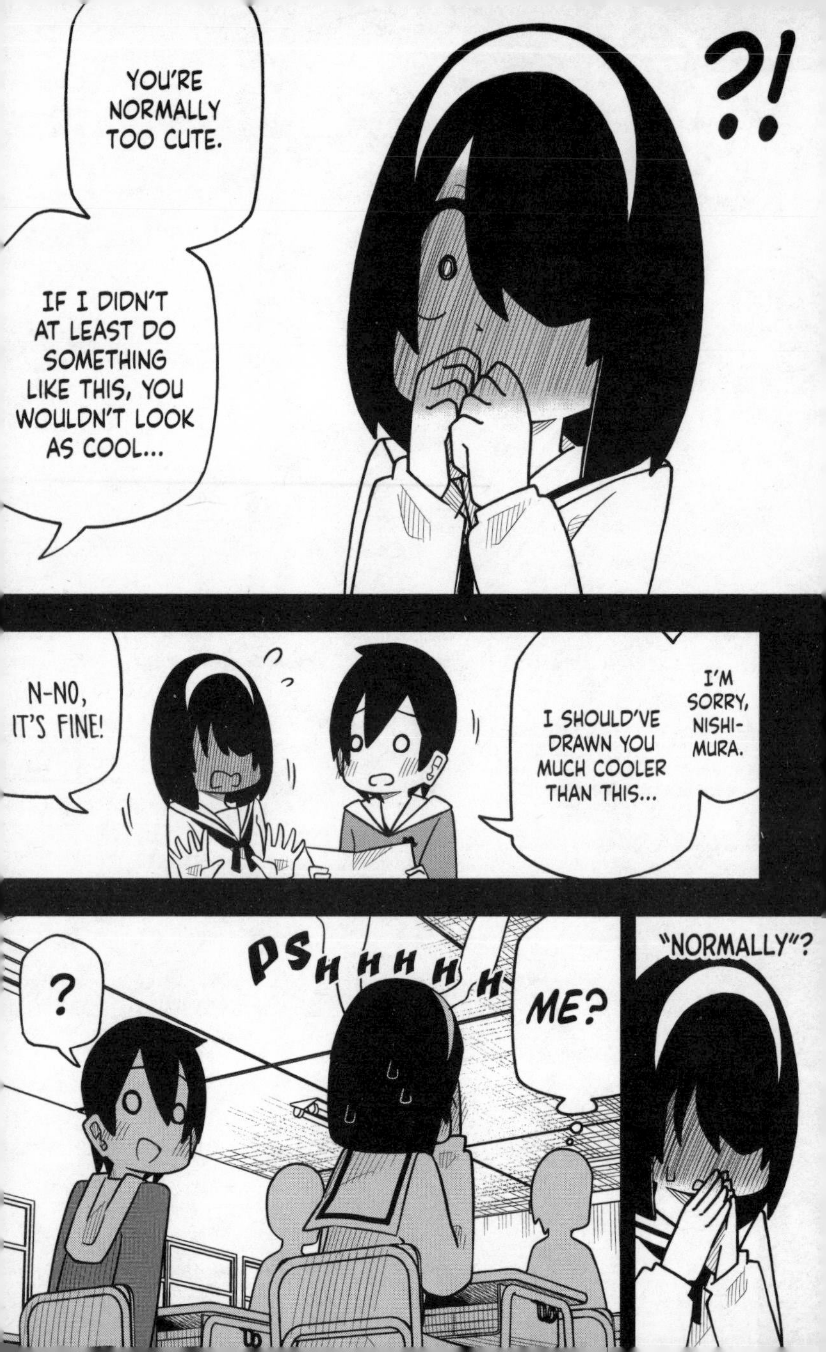
?!
YOU'RE NORMALLY TOO CUTE.
IF I DIDN'T AT LEAST DO SOMETHING LIKE THIS, YOU WOULDN'T LOOK AS COOL...
I'M SORRY, NISHIMURA.
I SHOULD'VE DRAWN YOU MUCH COOLER THAN THIS...
N-NO, IT'S FINE!
"NORMALLY"?
ME?
PSHHHHHH
?

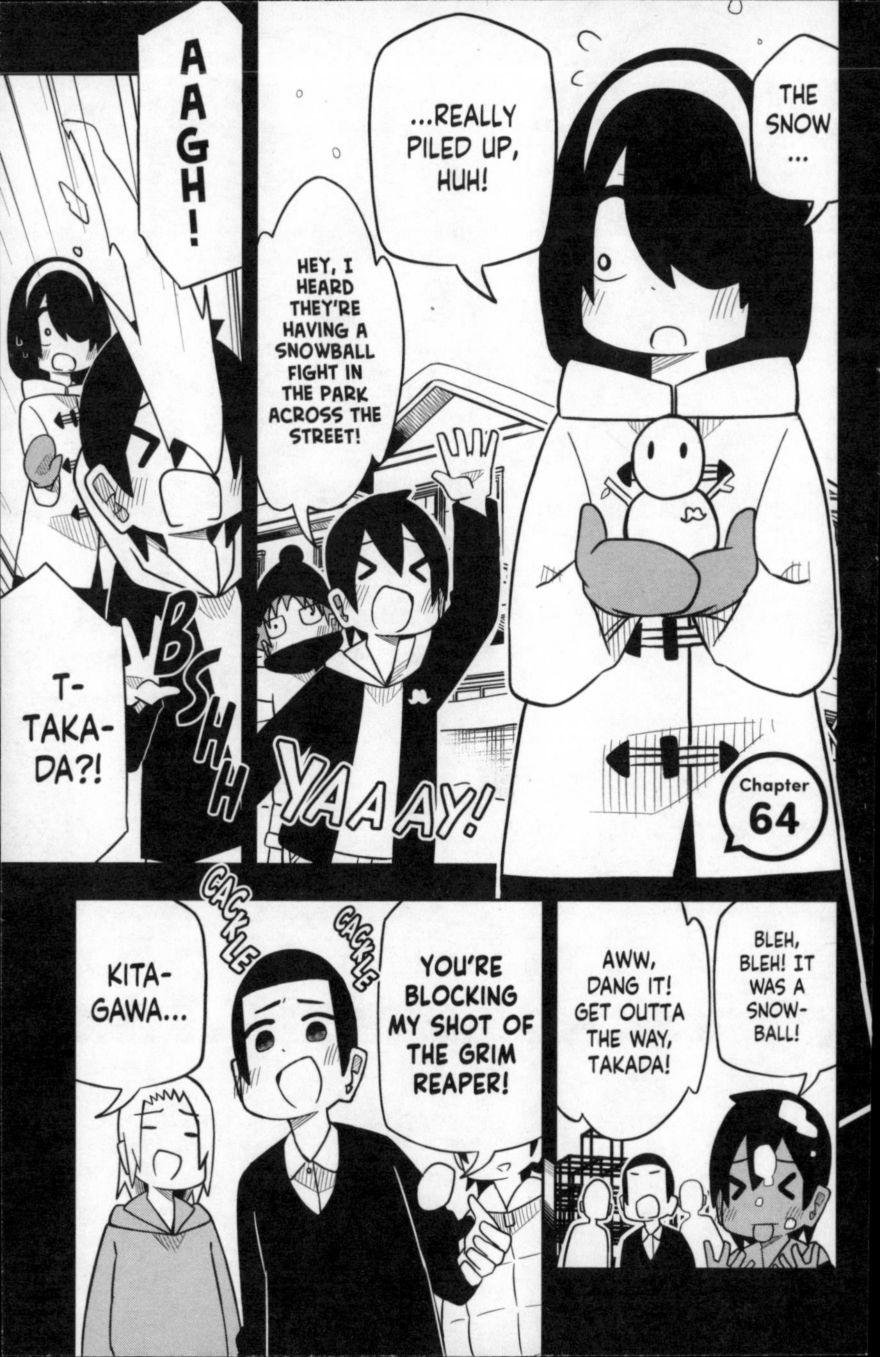
THE SNOW ...
...REALLY PILED UP, HUH!
Chapter 64
HEY, I HEARD THEY'RE HAVING A SNOWBALL FIGHT IN THE PARK ACROSS THE STREET!
YAAAY!
AAGH!
BSHHH
T-TAKADA?!
BLEH, BLEH! IT WAS A SNOWBALL!
AWW, DANG IT! GET OUTTA THE WAY, TAKADA!
CACKLE
CACKLE
YOU'RE BLOCKING MY SHOT OF THE GRIM REAPER!
KITAGAWA...

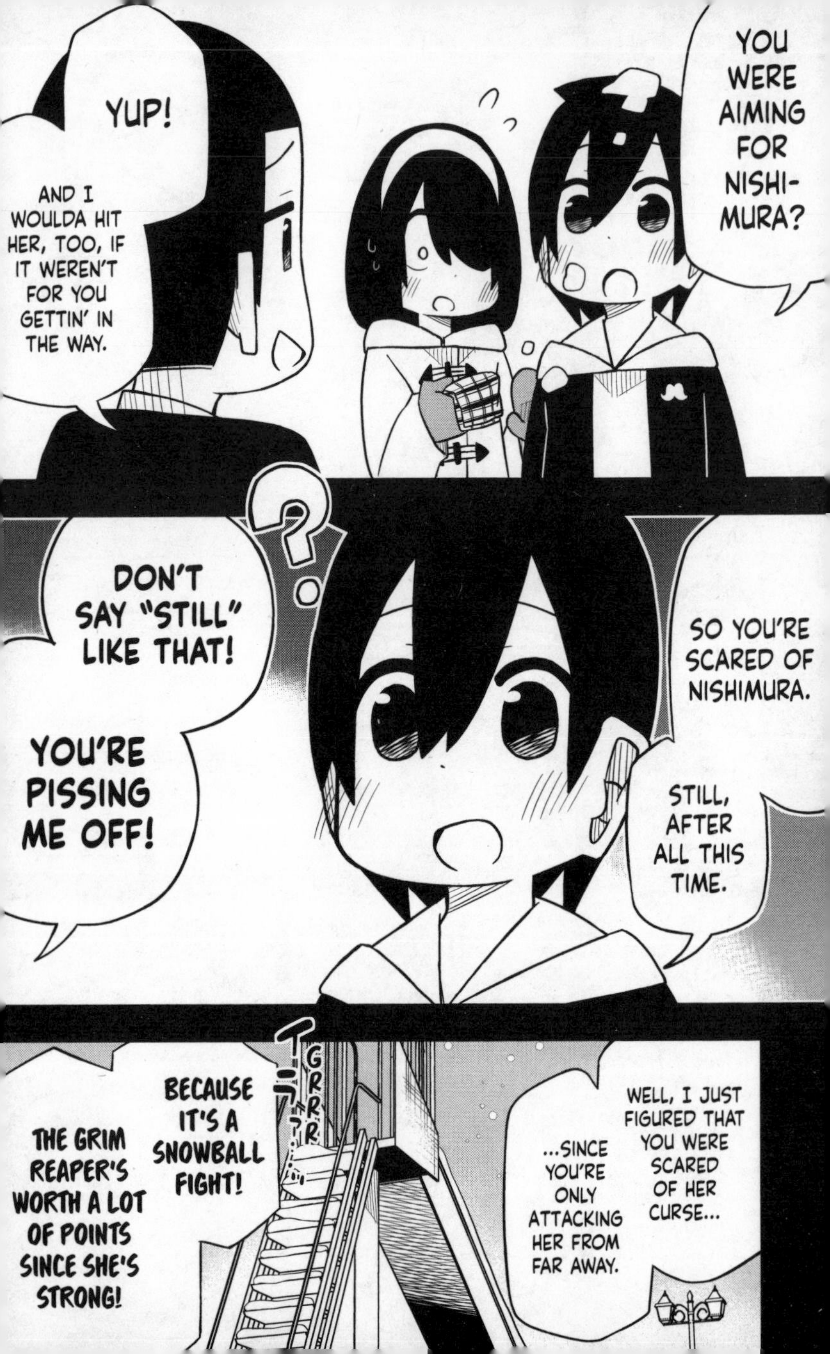
YOU WERE AIMING FOR NISHIMURA?
YUP!
AND I WOULDA HIT HER, TOO, IF IT WEREN'T FOR YOU GETTIN' IN THE WAY.
SO YOU'RE SCARED OF NISHIMURA.
STILL, AFTER ALL THIS TIME.
DON'T SAY "STILL" LIKE THAT!
YOU'RE PISSING ME OFF!
WELL, I JUST FIGURED THAT YOU WERE SCARED OF HER CURSE...
...SINCE YOU'RE ONLY ATTACKING HER FROM FAR AWAY.
GRRR
BECAUSE IT'S A SNOWBALL FIGHT!
THE GRIM REAPER'S WORTH A LOT OF POINTS SINCE SHE'S STRONG!

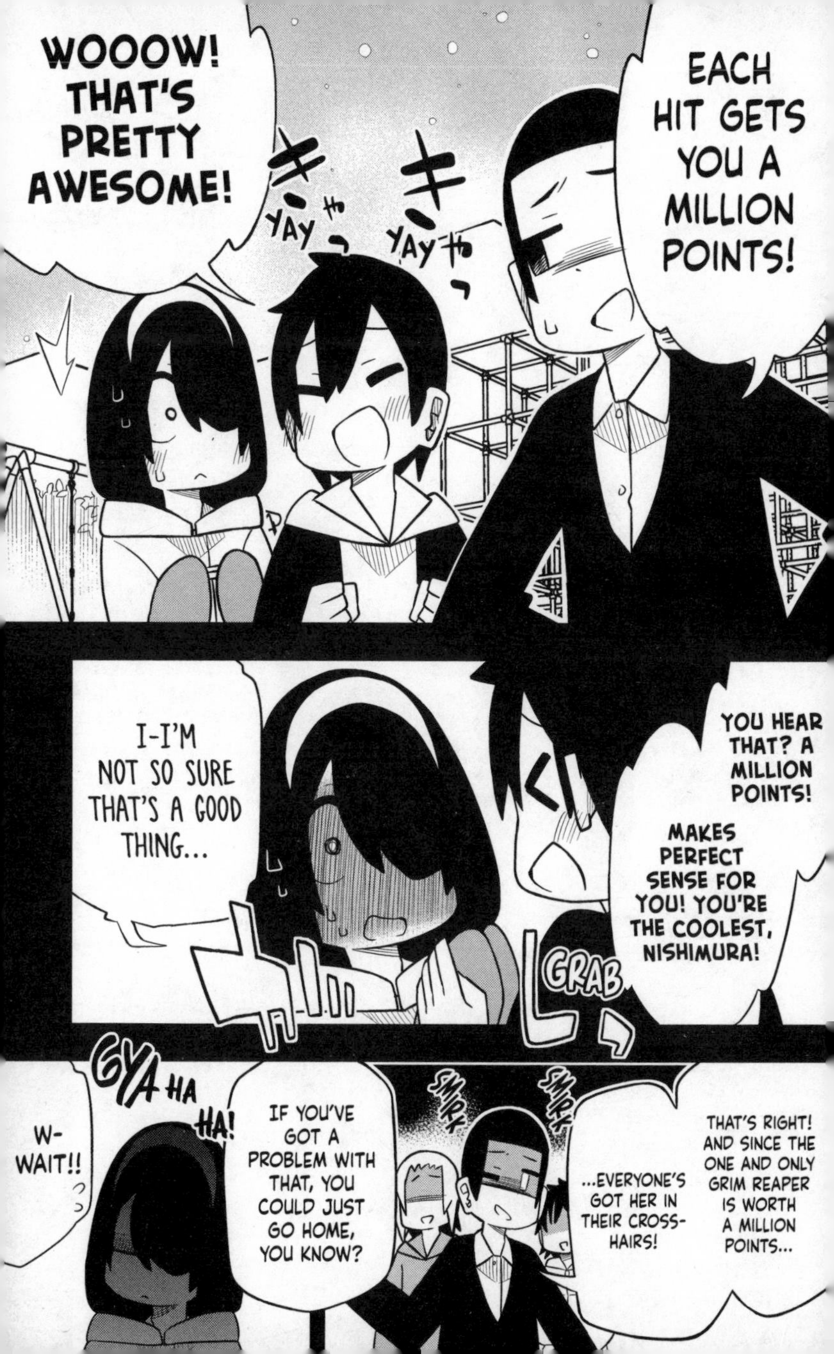
EACH HIT GETS YOU A MILLION POINTS!
YAY
YAY
WOOOW! THAT'S PRETTY AWESOME!
YOU HEAR THAT? A MILLION POINTS!
MAKES PERFECT SENSE FOR YOU! YOU'RE THE COOLEST, NISHIMURA!
GRAB
I-I'M NOT SO SURE THAT'S A GOOD THING...
THAT'S RIGHT! AND SINCE THE ONE AND ONLY GRIM REAPER IS WORTH A MILLION POINTS...
...EVERYONE'S GOT HER IN THEIR CROSS-HAIRS!
SMIRK
SMIRK
IF YOU'VE GOT A PROBLEM WITH THAT, YOU COULD JUST GO HOME, YOU KNOW?
GYA HA HA!
W-WAIT!!

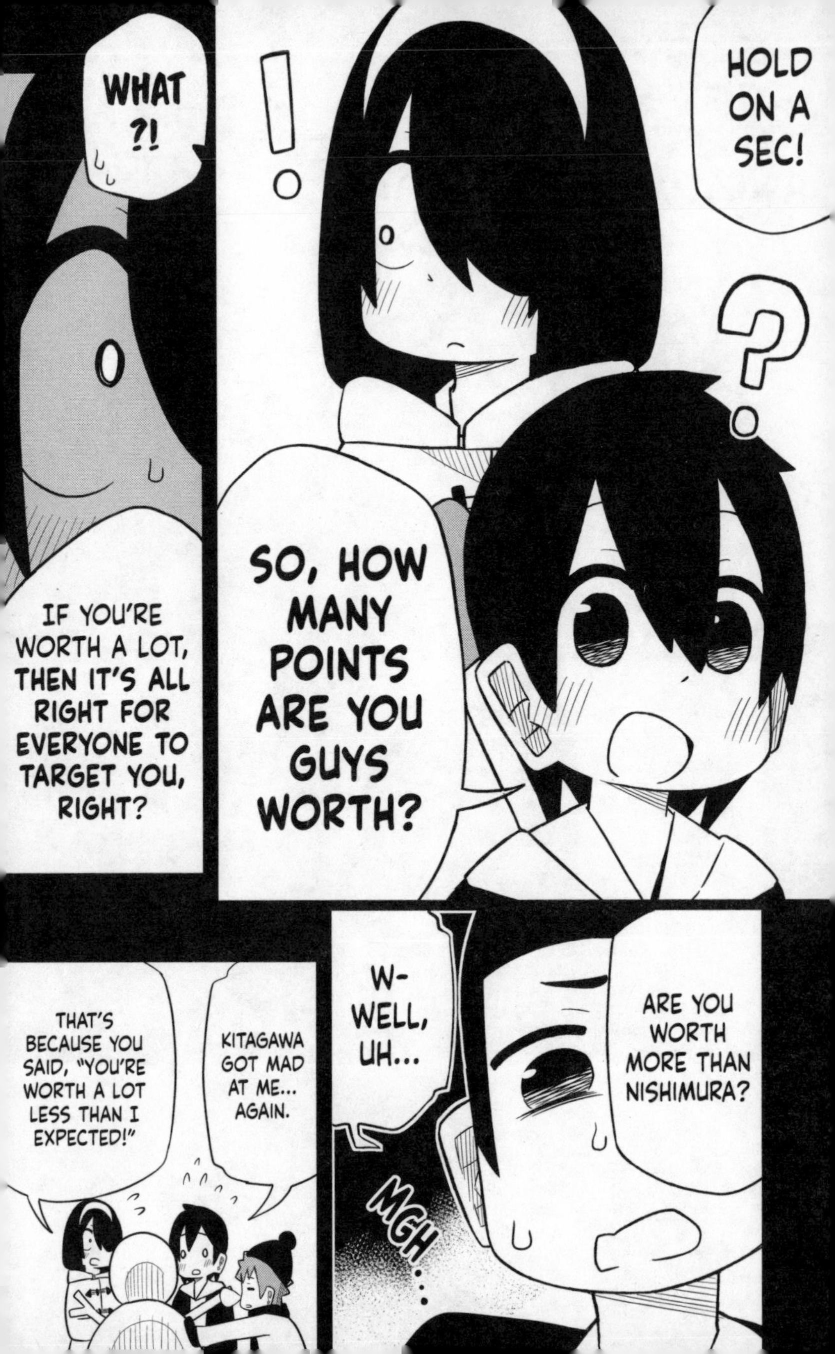
HOLD ON A SEC!
SO, HOW MANY POINTS ARE YOU GUYS WORTH?
WHAT?!
IF YOU'RE WORTH A LOT, THEN IT'S ALL RIGHT FOR EVERYONE TO TARGET YOU, RIGHT?
ARE YOU WORTH MORE THAN NISHIMURA?
W-WELL, UH...
MGH...
KITAGAWA GOT MAD AT ME... AGAIN.
THAT'S BECAUSE YOU SAID, "YOU'RE WORTH A LOT LESS THAN I EXPECTED!"

MY CLUELESS
FIRST FRIEND

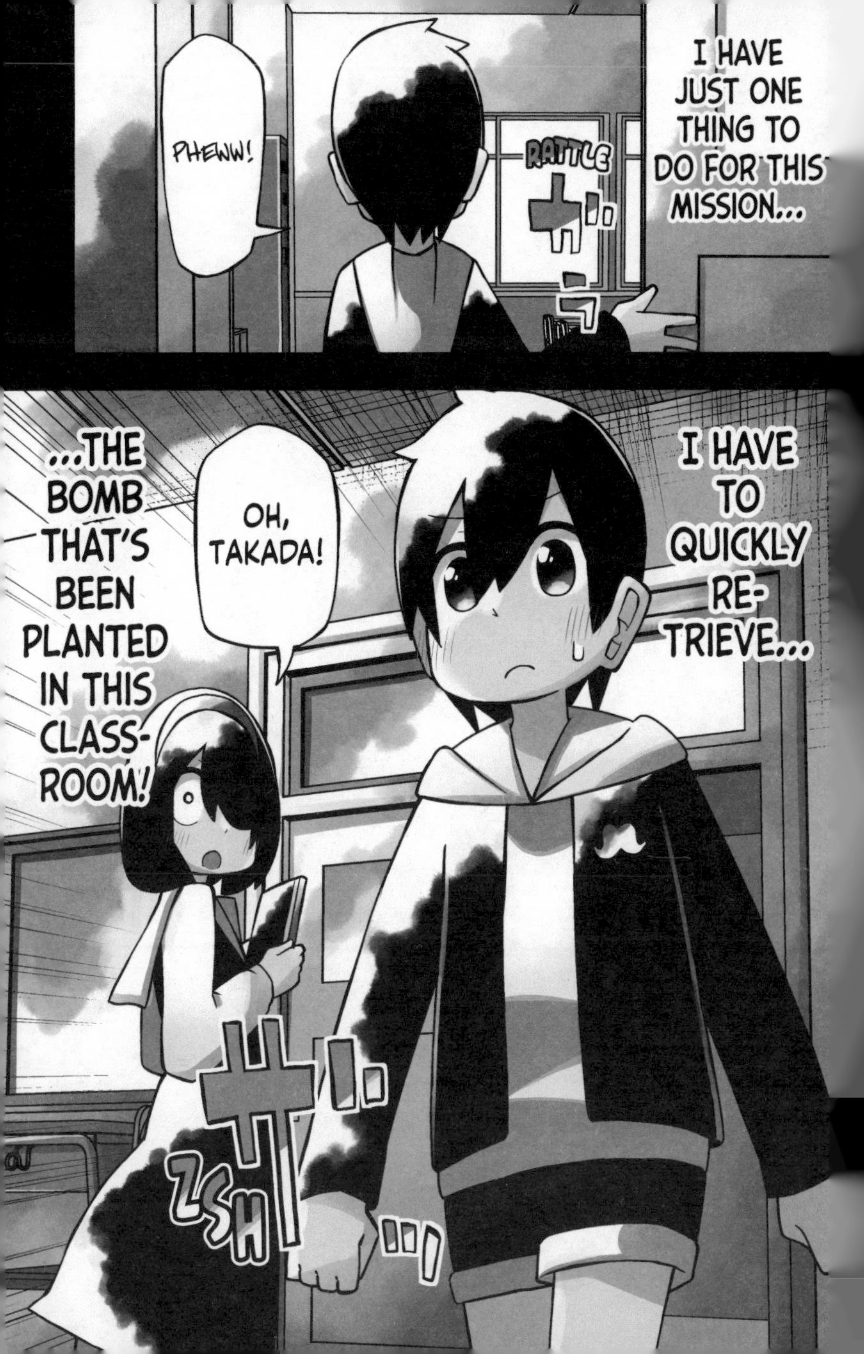
I HAVE JUST ONE THING TO DO FOR THIS MISSION...
RATTLE
PHEWW!
I HAVE TO QUICKLY RE-TRIEVE...
OH, TAKADA!
...THE BOMB THAT'S BEEN PLANTED IN THIS CLASS-ROOM!
ZSH

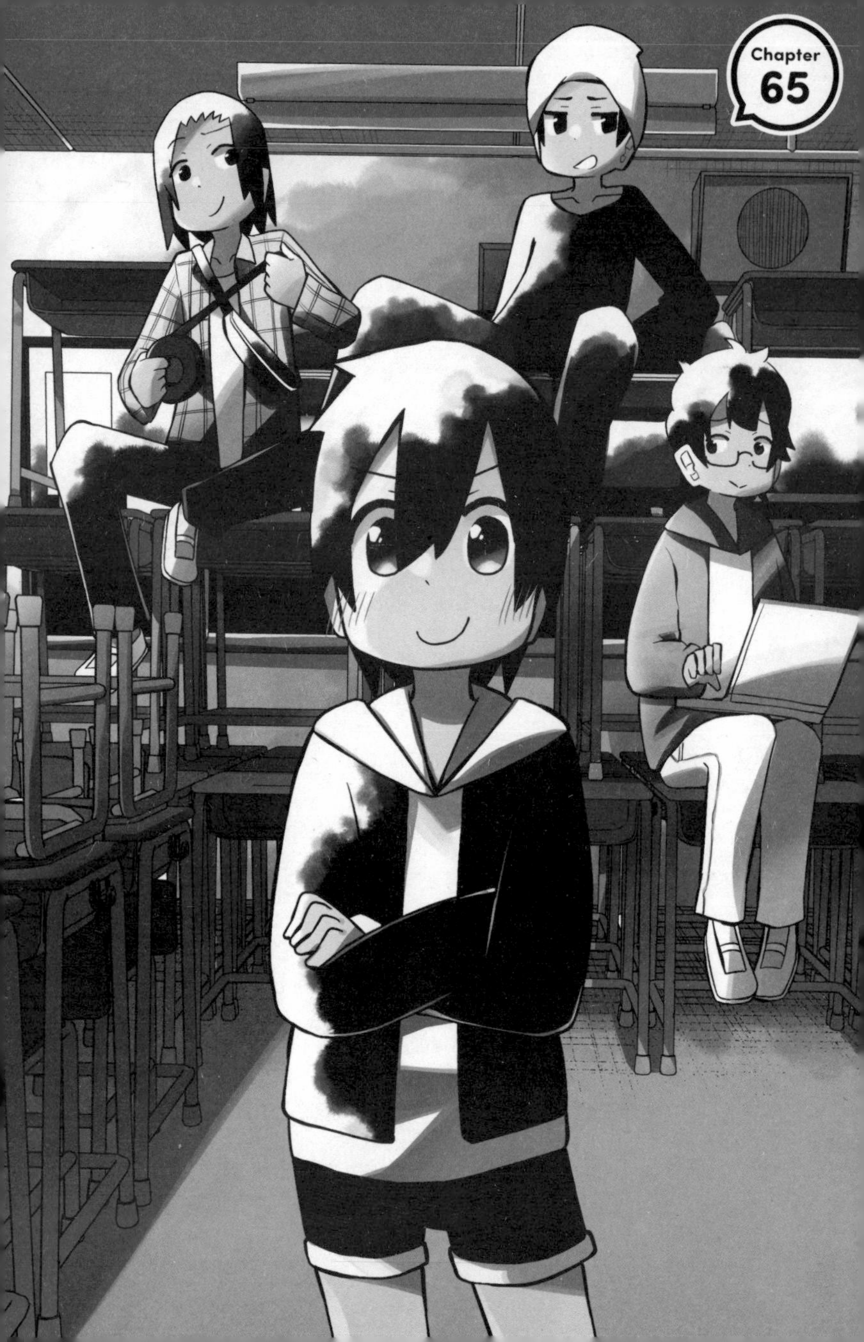
Chapter
65

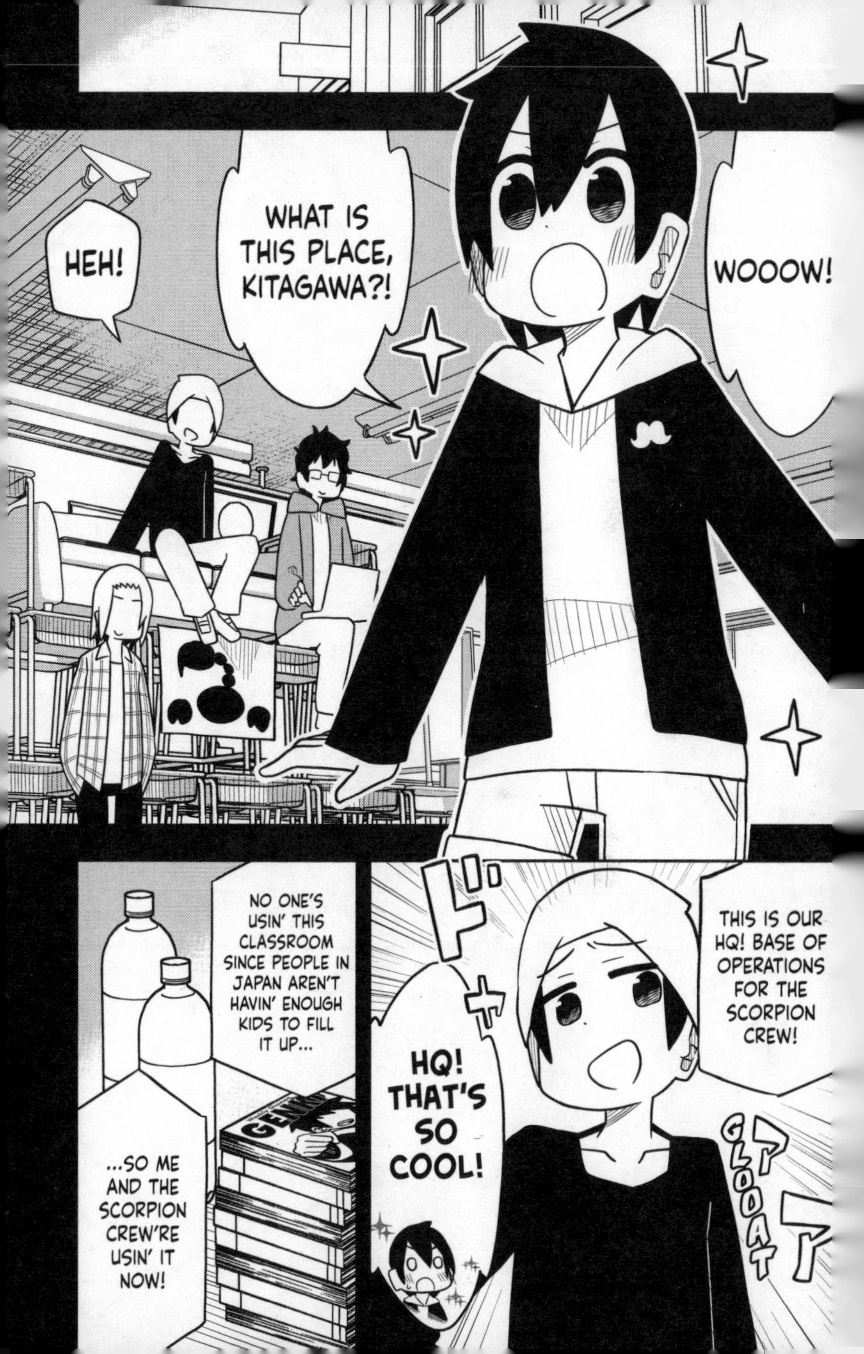
WOOOW!
WHAT IS THIS PLACE, KITAGAWA?!
HEH!
THIS IS OUR HQ! BASE OF OPERATIONS FOR THE SCORPION CREW!
HQ! THAT'S SO COOL!
GLOAT
NO ONE'S USIN' THIS CLASSROOM SINCE PEOPLE IN JAPAN AREN'T HAVIN' ENOUGH KIDS TO FILL IT UP...
...SO ME AND THE SCORPION CREW'RE USIN' IT NOW!

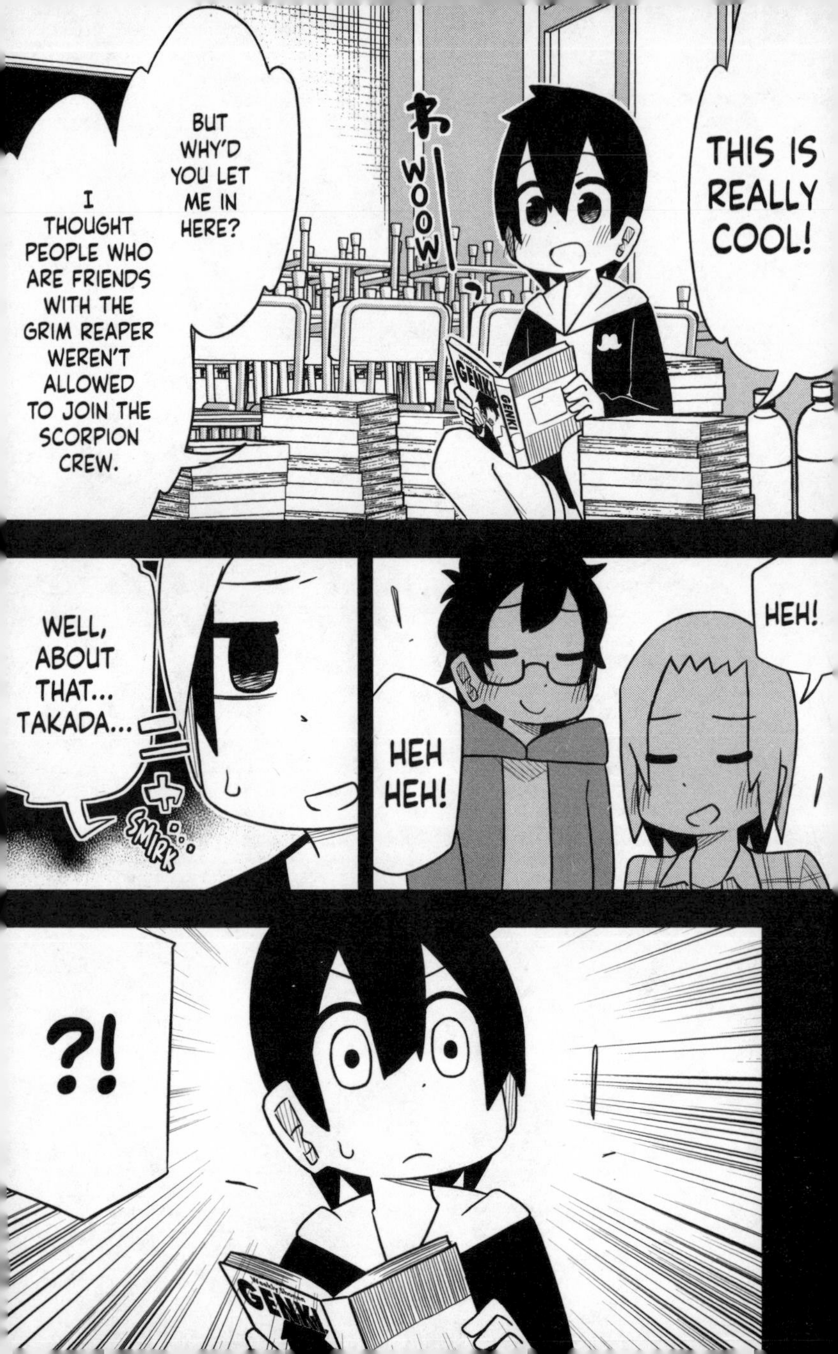
THIS IS REALLY COOL!
お
WOOOW—
BUT WHY'D YOU LET ME IN HERE?
I THOUGHT PEOPLE WHO ARE FRIENDS WITH THE GRIM REAPER WEREN'T ALLOWED TO JOIN THE SCORPION CREW.
HEH!
HEH HEH!
WELL, ABOUT THAT... TAKADA...
SMIRK
?!

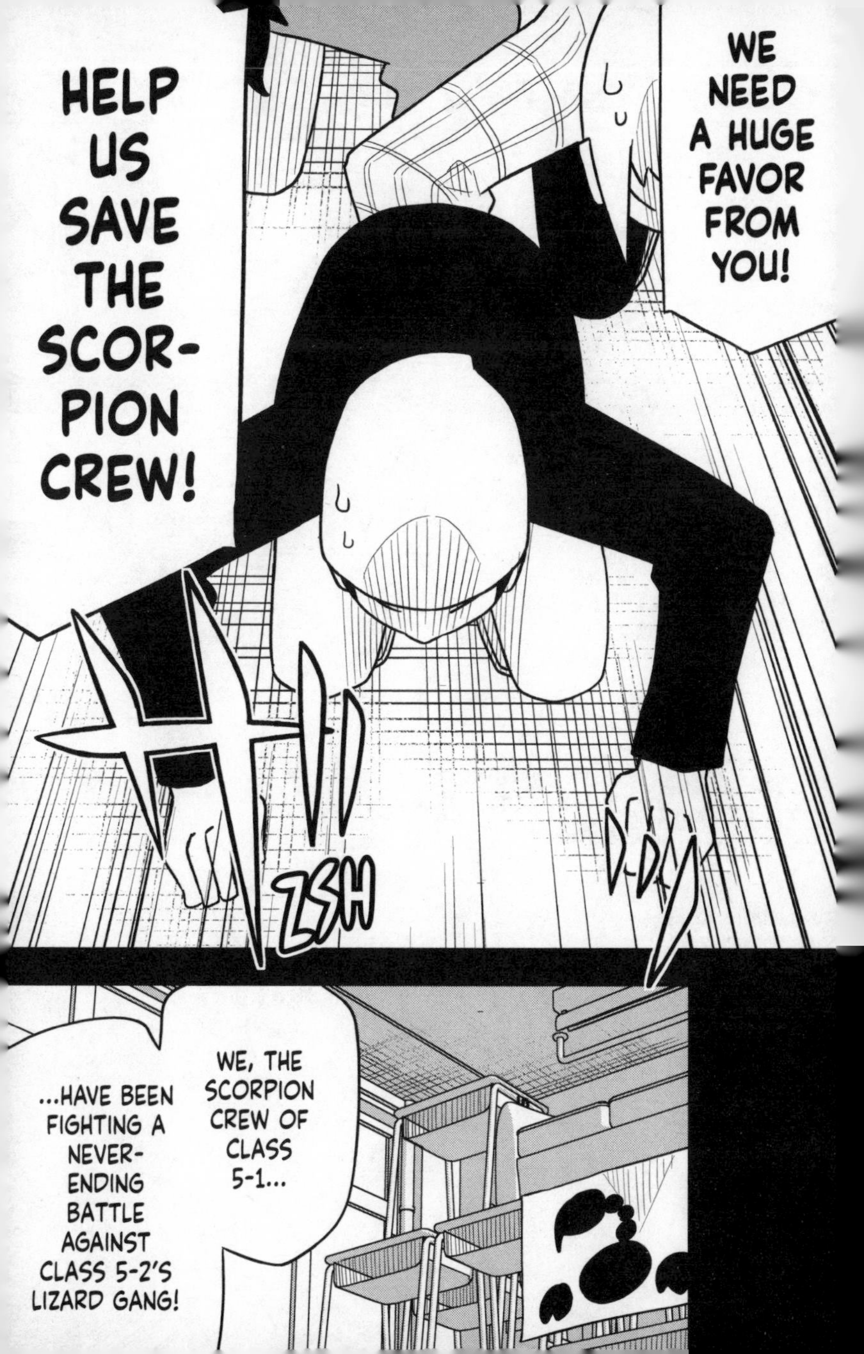
WE NEED A HUGE FAVOR FROM YOU!
HELP US SAVE THE SCOR-PION CREW!
ZSH
WE, THE SCORPION CREW OF CLASS 5-1...
...HAVE BEEN FIGHTING A NEVER-ENDING BATTLE AGAINST CLASS 5-2'S LIZARD GANG!

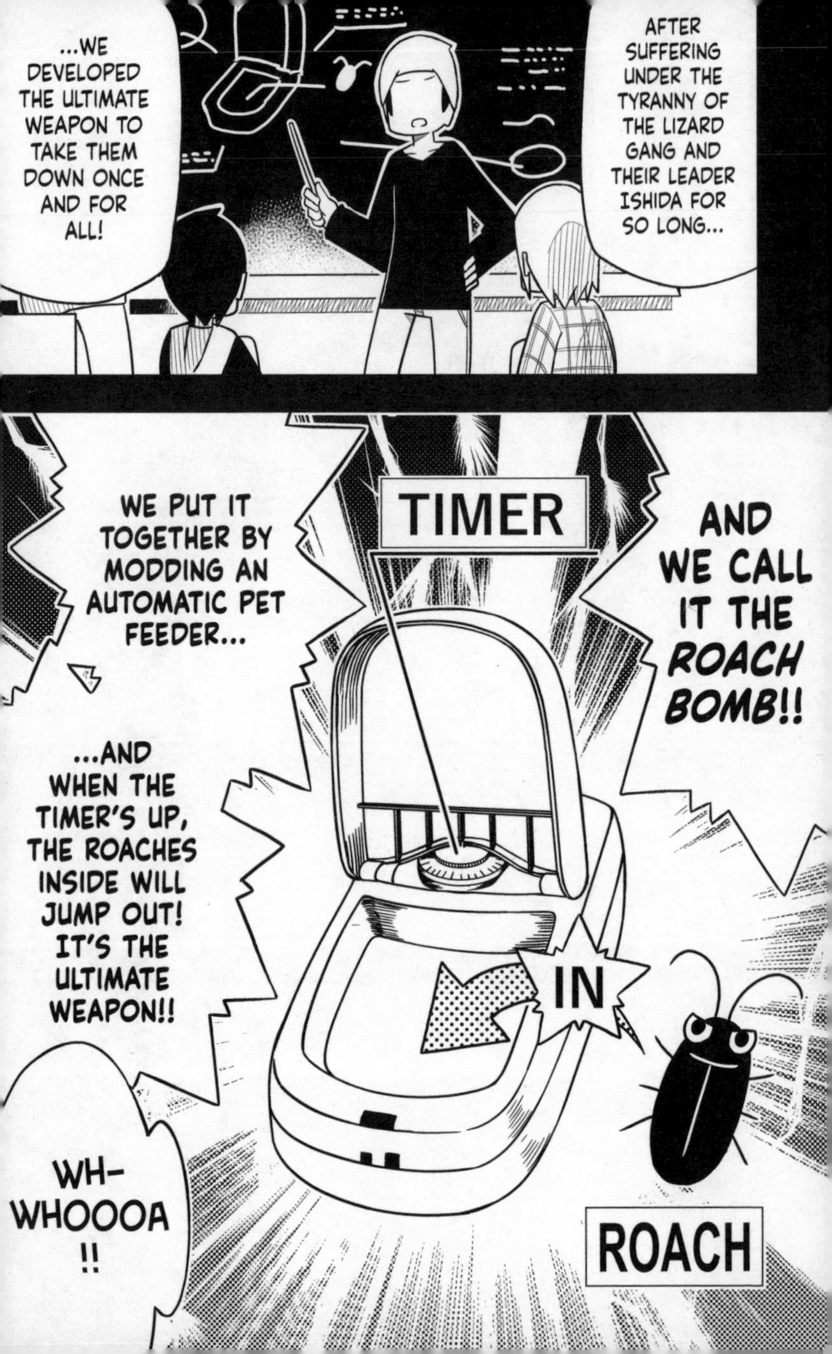
AFTER SUFFERING UNDER THE TYRANNY OF THE LIZARD GANG AND THEIR LEADER ISHIDA FOR SO LONG...
...WE DEVELOPED THE ULTIMATE WEAPON TO TAKE THEM DOWN ONCE AND FOR ALL!
AND WE CALL IT THE *ROACH BOMB*!!
TIMER
WE PUT IT TOGETHER BY MODDING AN AUTOMATIC PET FEEDER...
...AND WHEN THE TIMER'S UP, THE ROACHES INSIDE WILL JUMP OUT! IT'S THE ULTIMATE WEAPON!!
IN
ROACH
WH-WHOOOA!!

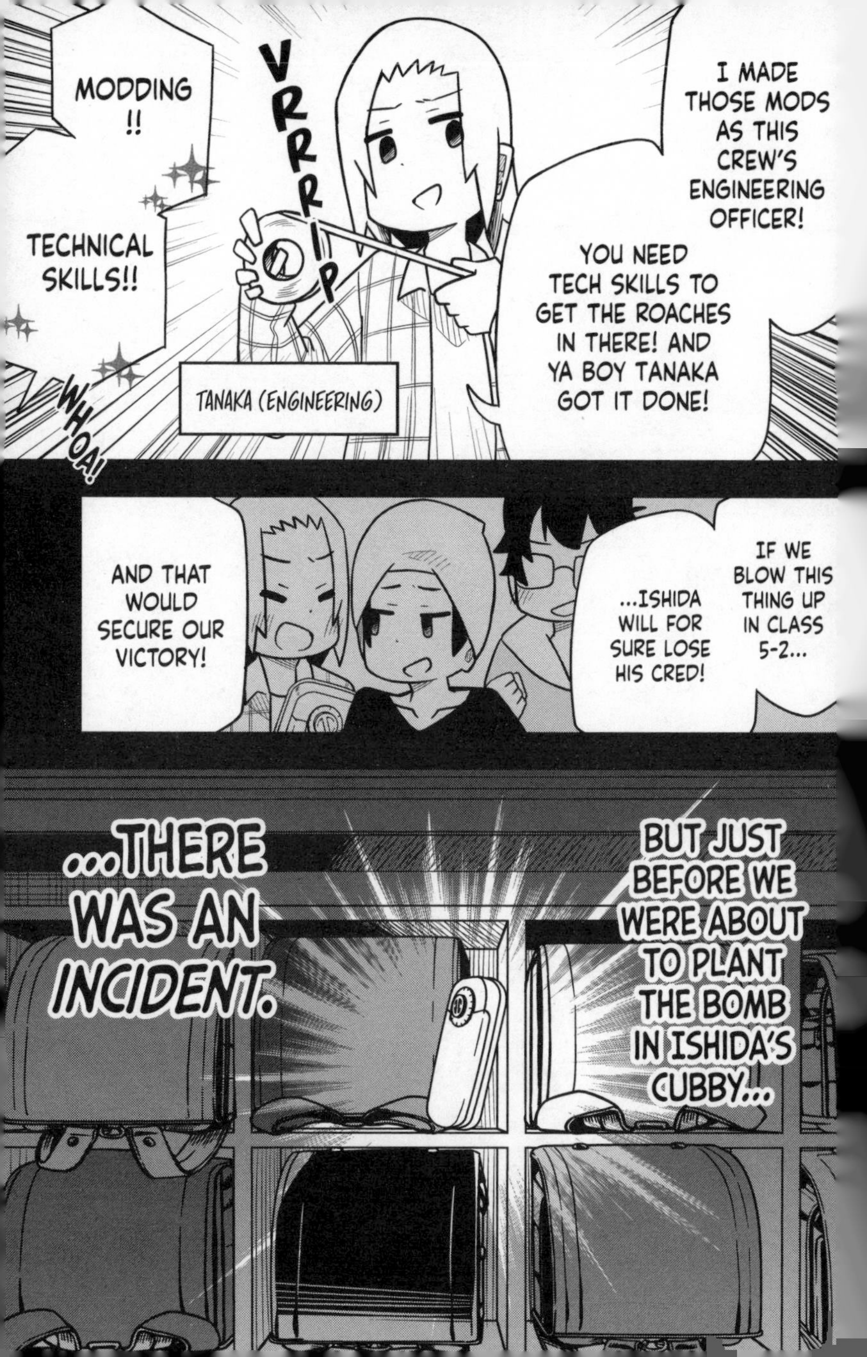
I MADE THOSE MODS AS THIS CREW'S ENGINEERING OFFICER!
YOU NEED TECH SKILLS TO GET THE ROACHES IN THERE! AND YA BOY TANAKA GOT IT DONE!
VRRRRIP
TANAKA (ENGINEERING)
MODDING!!
TECHNICAL SKILLS!!
WHOA!
IF WE BLOW THIS THING UP IN CLASS 5-2...
...ISHIDA WILL FOR SURE LOSE HIS CRED!
AND THAT WOULD SECURE OUR VICTORY!
BUT JUST BEFORE WE WERE ABOUT TO PLANT THE BOMB IN ISHIDA'S CUBBY...
...THERE WAS AN INCIDENT.

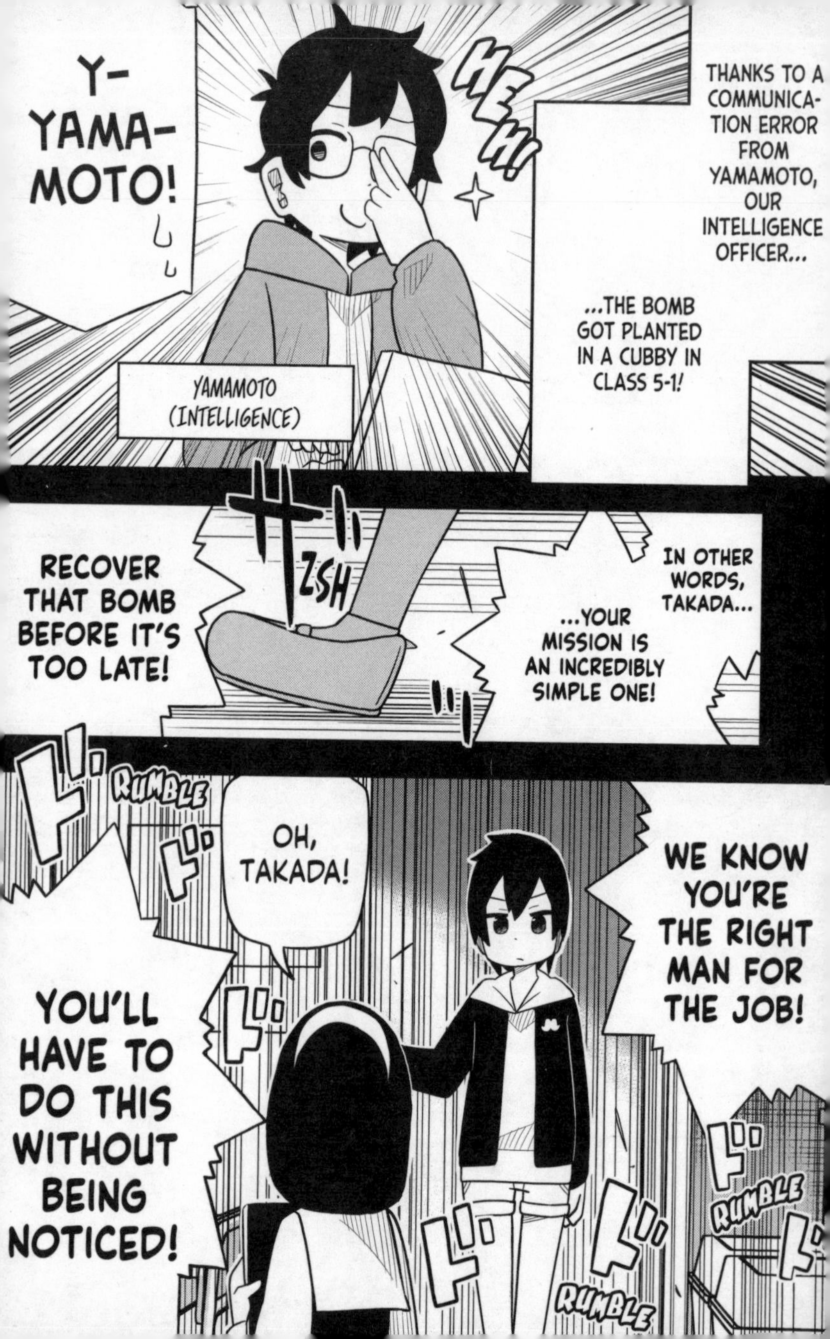
THANKS TO A COMMUNICATION ERROR FROM YAMAMOTO, OUR INTELLIGENCE OFFICER...
...THE BOMB GOT PLANTED IN A CUBBY IN CLASS 5-1!
HEH!
Y-YAMAMOTO!
YAMAMOTO (INTELLIGENCE)
IN OTHER WORDS, TAKADA...
...YOUR MISSION IS AN INCREDIBLY SIMPLE ONE!
ZSH
RECOVER THAT BOMB BEFORE IT'S TOO LATE!
RUMBLE
WE KNOW YOU'RE THE RIGHT MAN FOR THE JOB!
OH, TAKADA!
RUMBLE
YOU'LL HAVE TO DO THIS WITHOUT BEING NOTICED!
RUMBLE

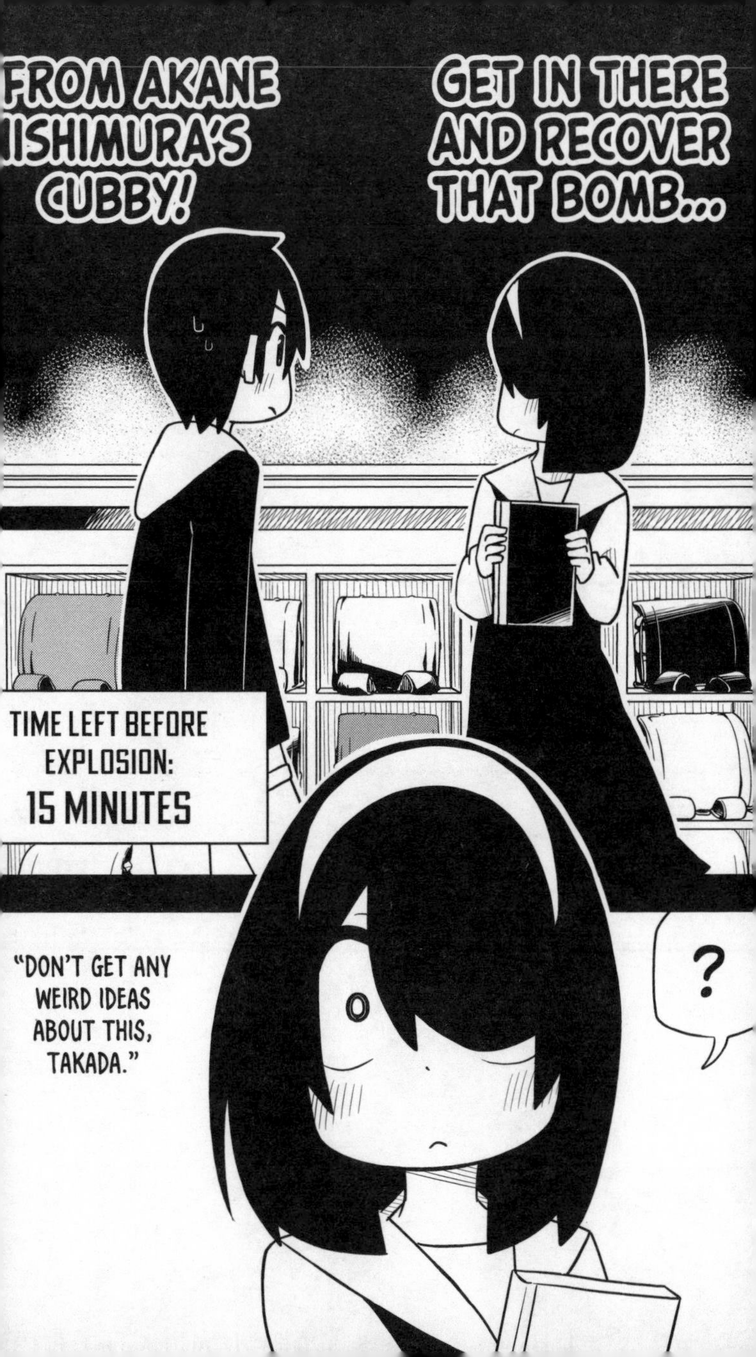
GET IN THERE AND RECOVER THAT BOMB...
FROM AKANE ISHIMURA'S CUBBY!
TIME LEFT BEFORE EXPLOSION: 15 MINUTES
?
"DON'T GET ANY WEIRD IDEAS ABOUT THIS, TAKADA."

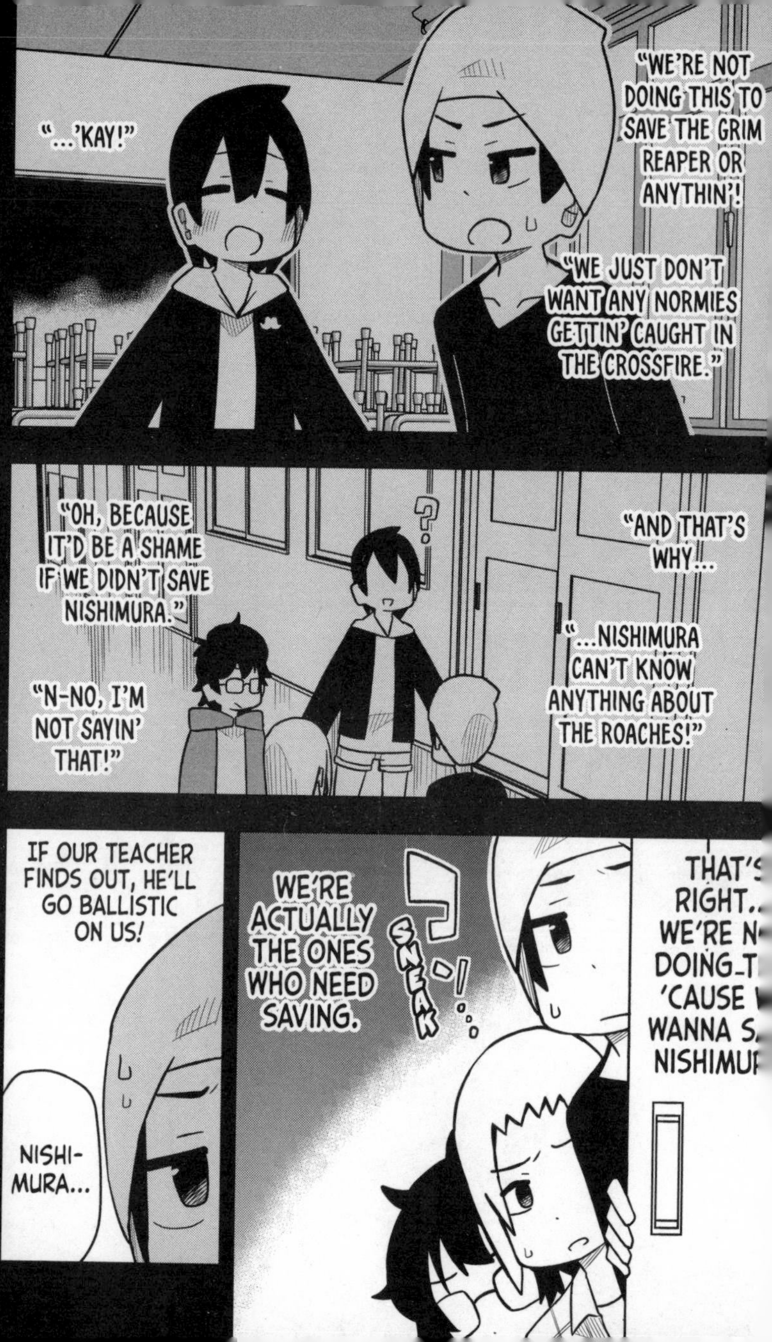
"WE'RE NOT DOING THIS TO SAVE THE GRIM REAPER OR ANYTHIN'!
"WE JUST DON'T WANT ANY NORMIES GETTIN' CAUGHT IN THE CROSSFIRE."
"...'KAY!"
"AND THAT'S WHY...
"...NISHIMURA CAN'T KNOW ANYTHING ABOUT THE ROACHES!"
?
"OH, BECAUSE IT'D BE A SHAME IF WE DIDN'T SAVE NISHIMURA."
"N-NO, I'M NOT SAYIN' THAT!"
THAT'S RIGHT.. WE'RE N DOING T 'CAUSE WANNA S NISHIMUR
SNEAK
WE'RE ACTUALLY THE ONES WHO NEED SAVING.
IF OUR TEACHER FINDS OUT, HE'LL GO BALLISTIC ON US!
NISHI-MURA...

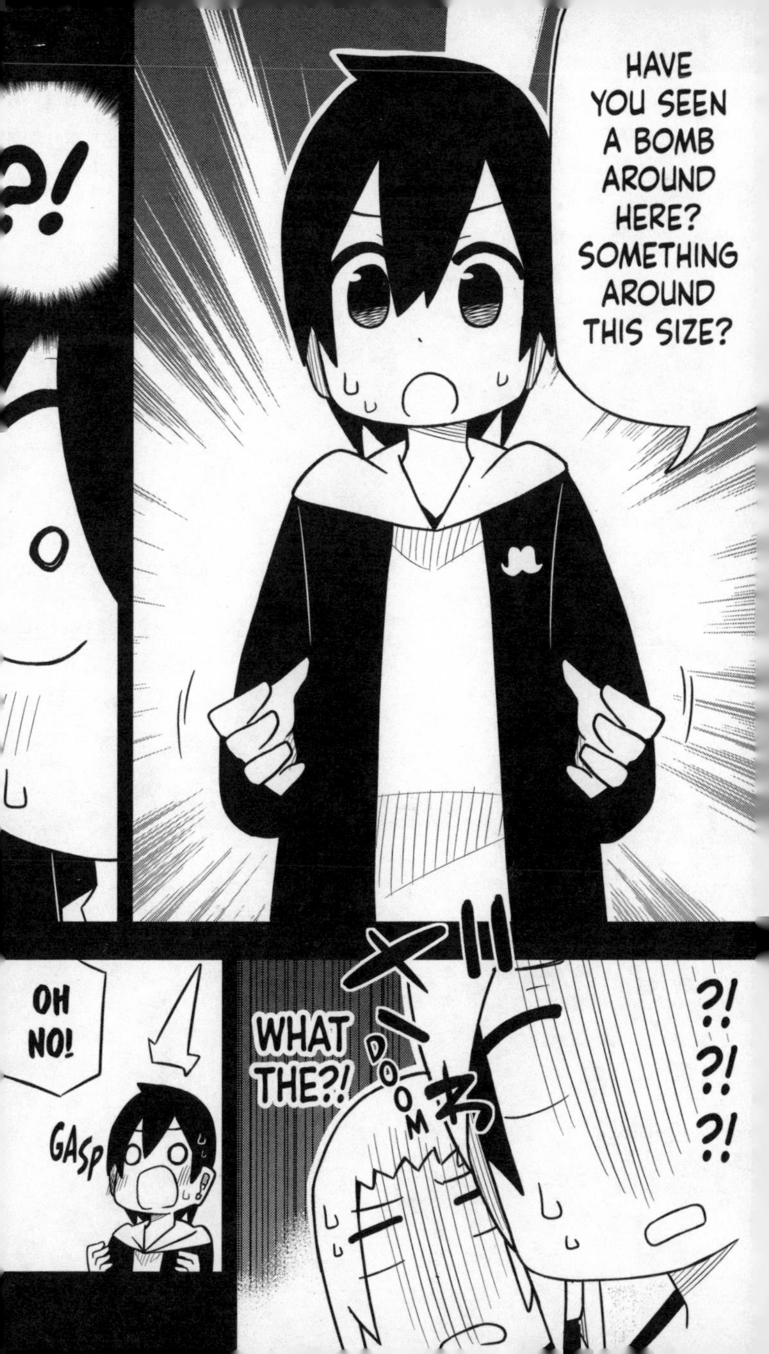
HAVE YOU SEEN A BOMB AROUND HERE? SOMETHING AROUND THIS SIZE?
?!
?! ?! ?!
WHAT THE?!
DOOM
OH NO!
GASP

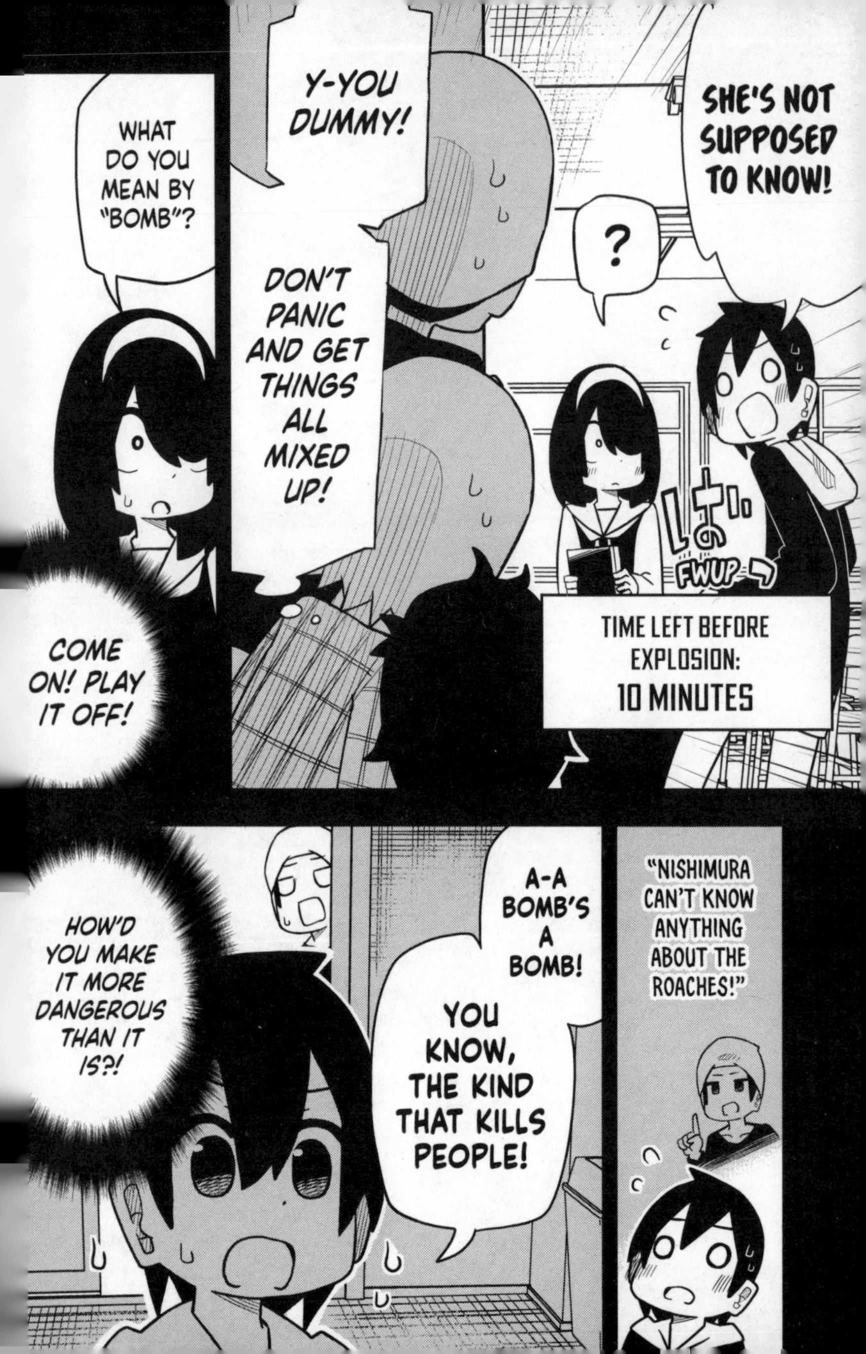
SHE'S NOT SUPPOSED TO KNOW!
?
FWUP
Y-YOU DUMMY!
DON'T PANIC AND GET THINGS ALL MIXED UP!
TIME LEFT BEFORE EXPLOSION: 10 MINUTES
WHAT DO YOU MEAN BY "BOMB"?
COME ON! PLAY IT OFF!
"NISHIMURA CAN'T KNOW ANYTHING ABOUT THE ROACHES!"
A-A BOMB'S A BOMB!
YOU KNOW, THE KIND THAT KILLS PEOPLE!
HOW'D YOU MAKE IT MORE DANGEROUS THAN IT IS?!

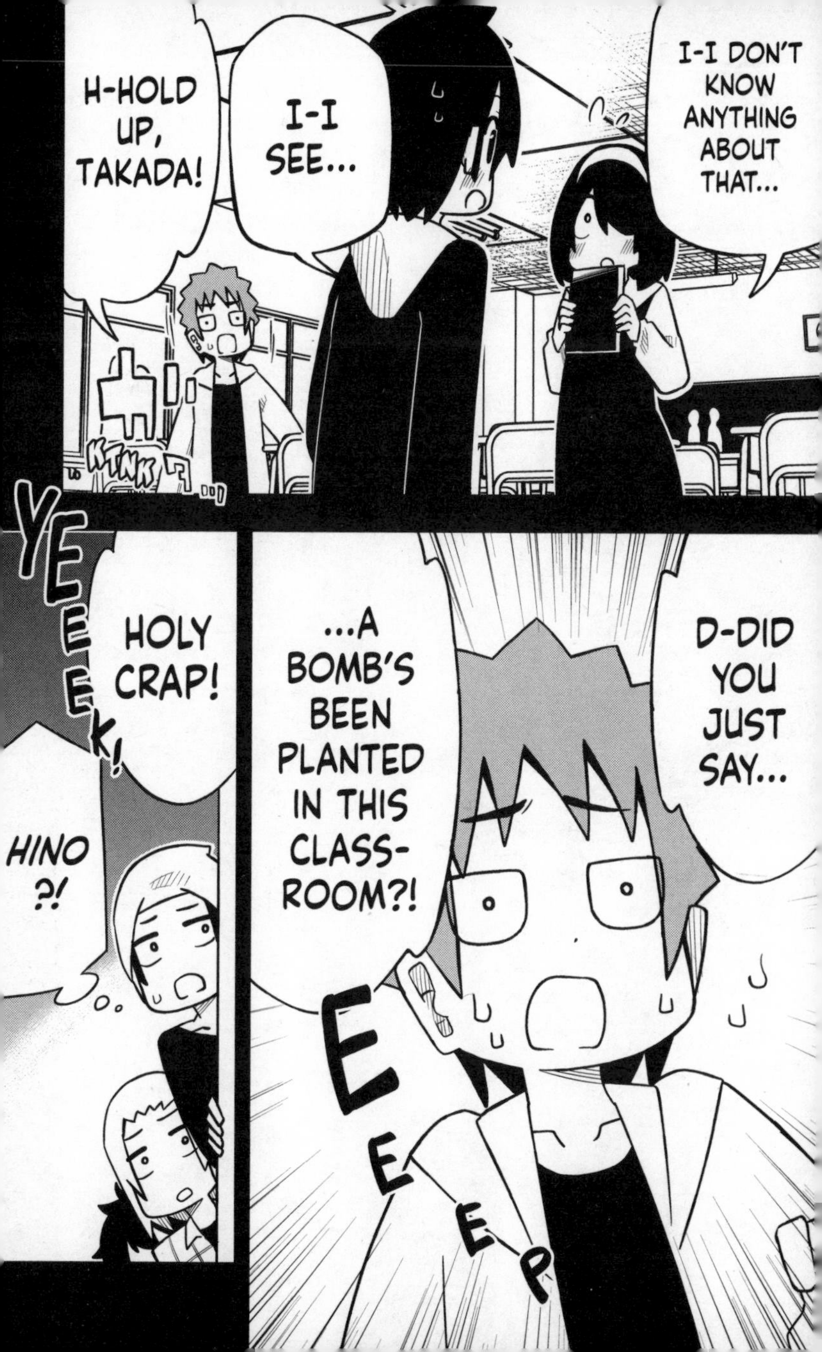
I-I DON'T KNOW ANYTHING ABOUT THAT...
I-I SEE...
H-HOLD UP, TAKADA!
KTNK
D-DID YOU JUST SAY...
...A BOMB'S BEEN PLANTED IN THIS CLASS-ROOM?!
EEEEP
YEEEEK!
HOLY CRAP!
HINO ?!

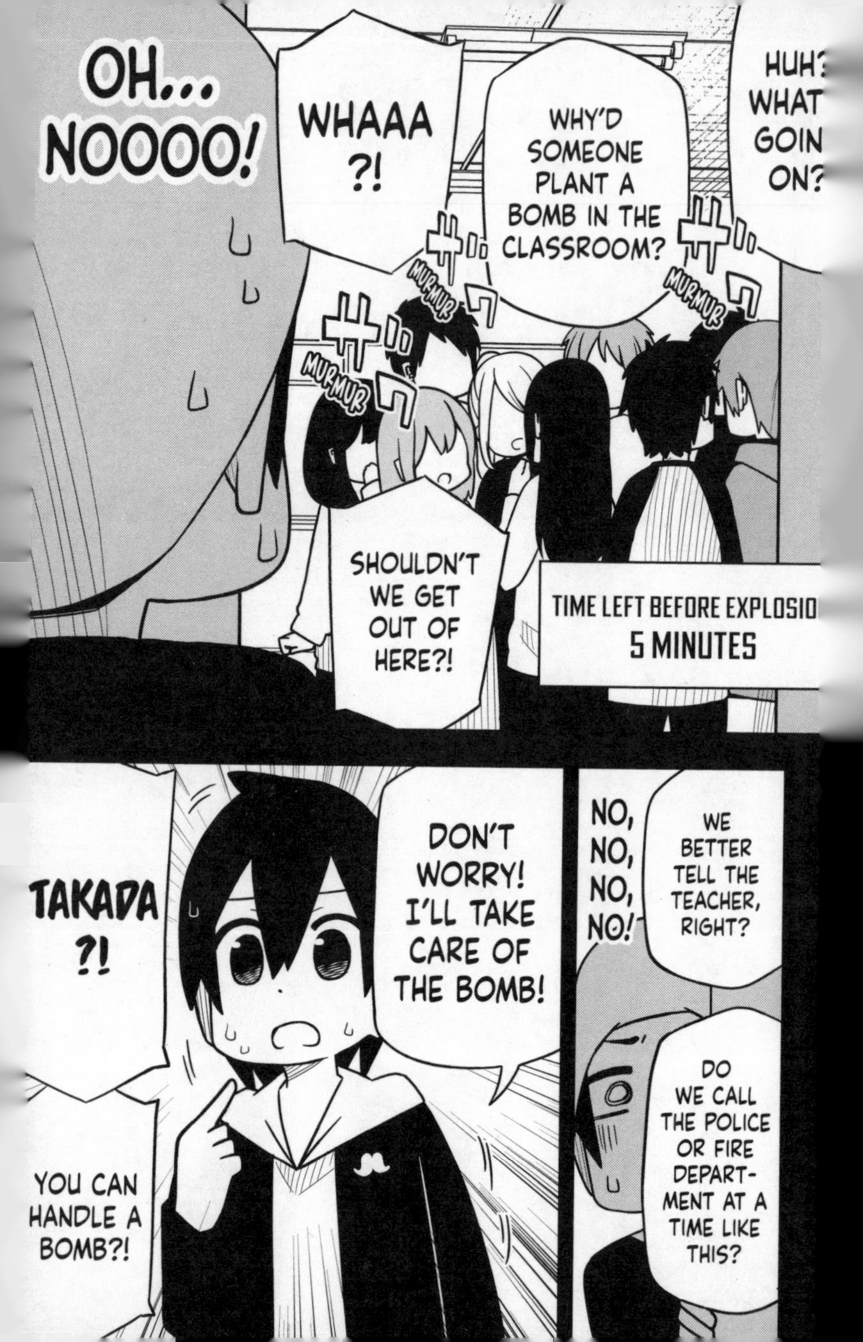
HUH? WHAT GOIN ON?
WHY'D SOMEONE PLANT A BOMB IN THE CLASSROOM?
WHAAA?!
OH... NOOOO!
MURMUR
MURMUR
MURMUR
TIME LEFT BEFORE EXPLOSIO 5 MINUTES
SHOULDN'T WE GET OUT OF HERE?!
WE BETTER TELL THE TEACHER, RIGHT?
NO, NO, NO, NO!
DO WE CALL THE POLICE OR FIRE DEPART-MENT AT A TIME LIKE THIS?
DON'T WORRY! I'LL TAKE CARE OF THE BOMB!
TAKADA?!
YOU CAN HANDLE A BOMB?!

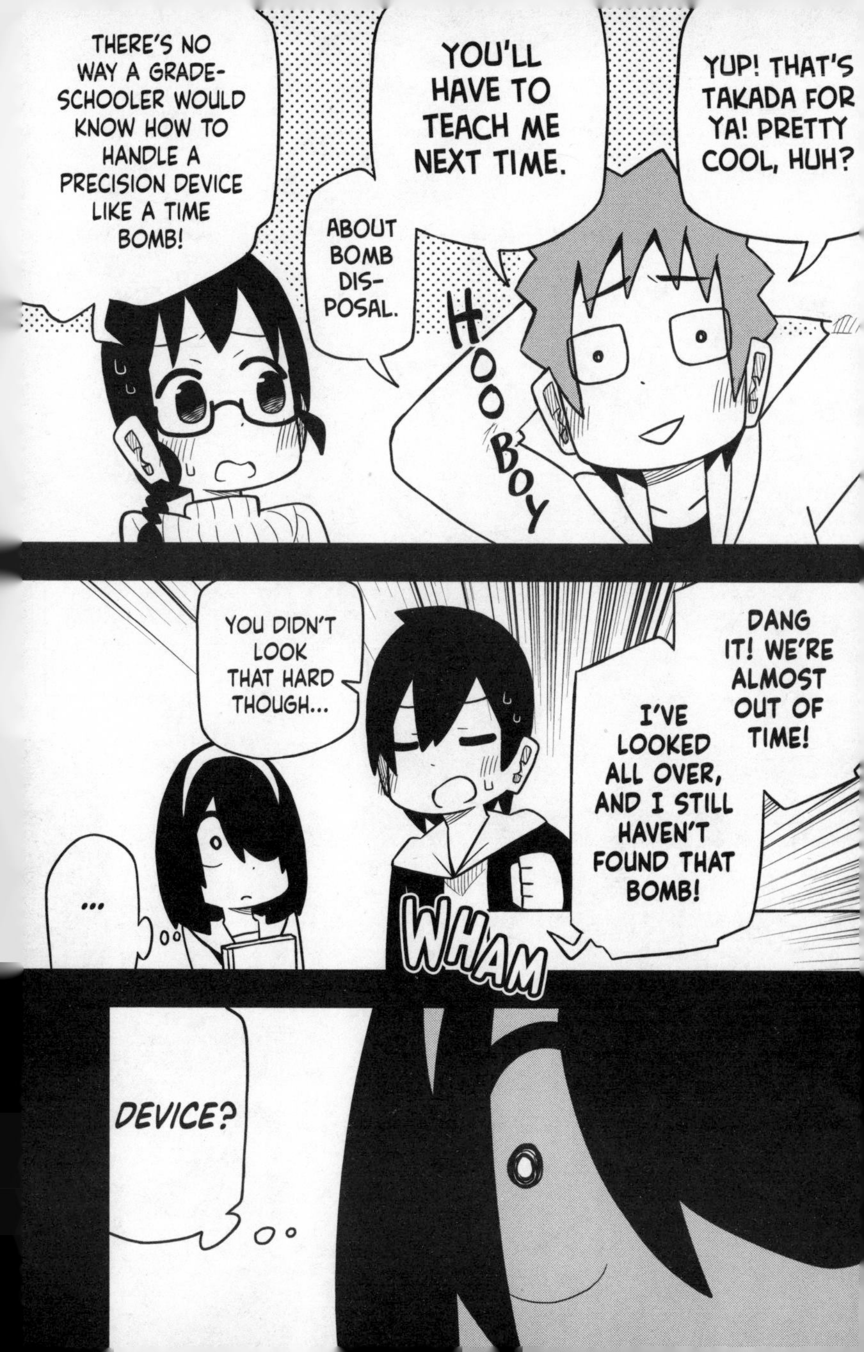
YUP! THAT'S TAKADA FOR YA! PRETTY COOL, HUH?
YOU'LL HAVE TO TEACH ME NEXT TIME.
ABOUT BOMB DISPOSAL.
HOO BOY
THERE'S NO WAY A GRADE-SCHOOLER WOULD KNOW HOW TO HANDLE A PRECISION DEVICE LIKE A TIME BOMB!
DANG IT! WE'RE ALMOST OUT OF TIME!
I'VE LOOKED ALL OVER, AND I STILL HAVEN'T FOUND THAT BOMB!
WHAM
YOU DIDN'T LOOK THAT HARD THOUGH...
...
DEVICE?

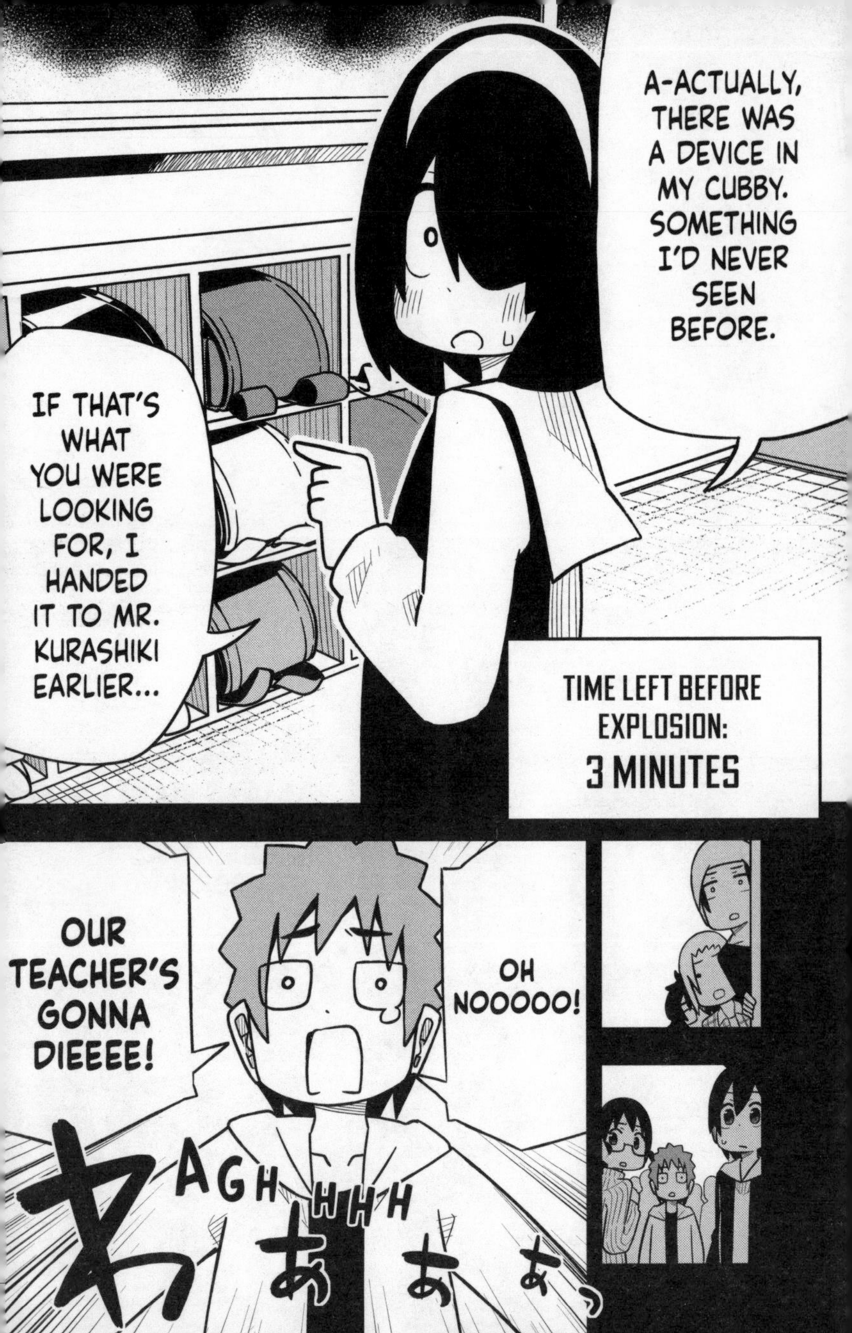
A-ACTUALLY, THERE WAS A DEVICE IN MY CUBBY. SOMETHING I'D NEVER SEEN BEFORE.
IF THAT'S WHAT YOU WERE LOOKING FOR, I HANDED IT TO MR. KURASHIKI EARLIER...
TIME LEFT BEFORE EXPLOSION:
3 MINUTES
OH NOOOOO!
OUR TEACHER'S GONNA DIEEEE!
AGHHHHH
わあああっ

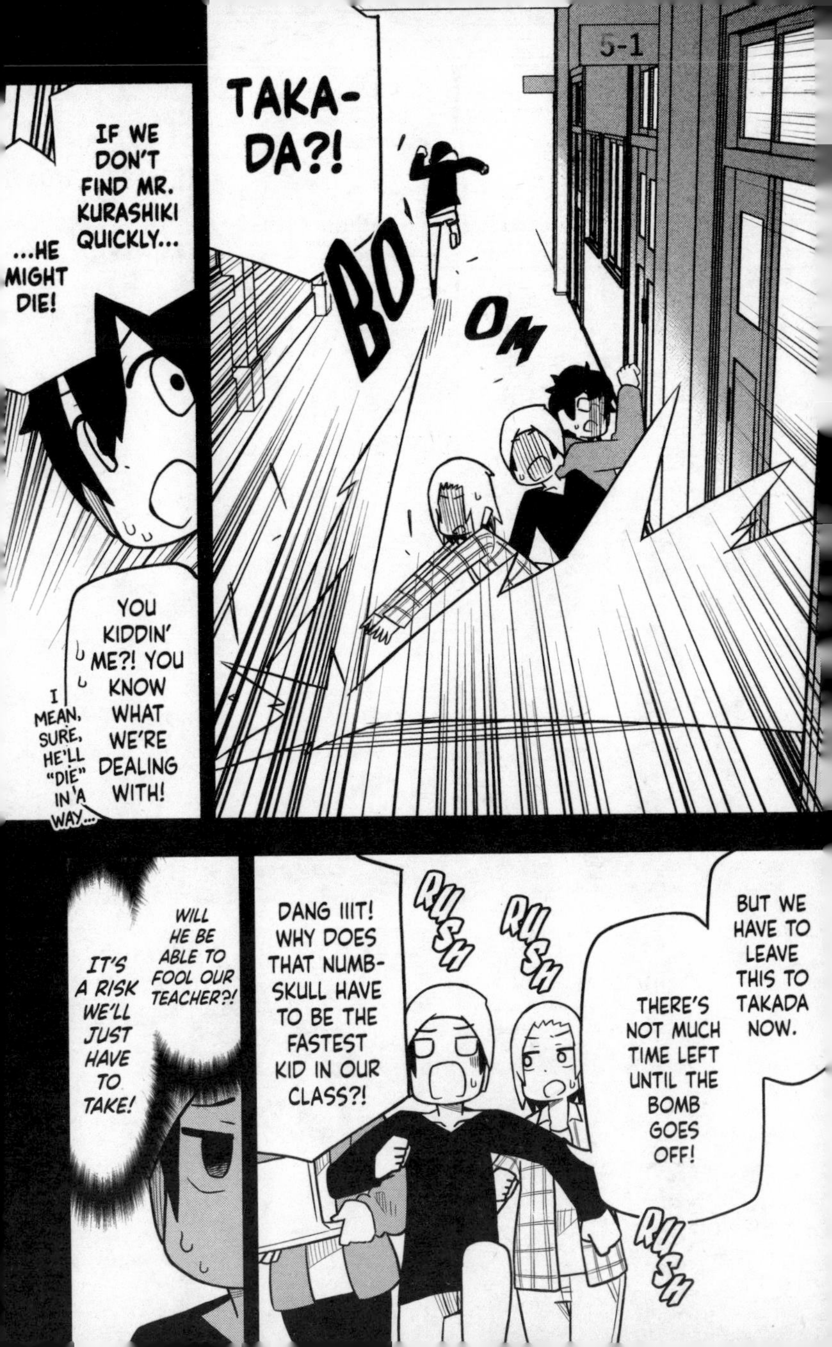
TAKA-DA?!
BOOM
IF WE DON'T FIND MR. KURASHIKI QUICKLY...
...HE MIGHT DIE!
YOU KIDDIN' ME?! YOU KNOW WHAT WE'RE DEALING WITH!
I MEAN, SURE, HE'LL "DIE" IN A WAY...
BUT WE HAVE TO LEAVE THIS TO TAKADA NOW.
THERE'S NOT MUCH TIME LEFT UNTIL THE BOMB GOES OFF!
RUSH
RUSH
DANG IIIT! WHY DOES THAT NUMB-SKULL HAVE TO BE THE FASTEST KID IN OUR CLASS?!
RUSH
WILL HE BE ABLE TO FOOL OUR TEACHER?!
IT'S A RISK WE'LL JUST HAVE TO TAKE!

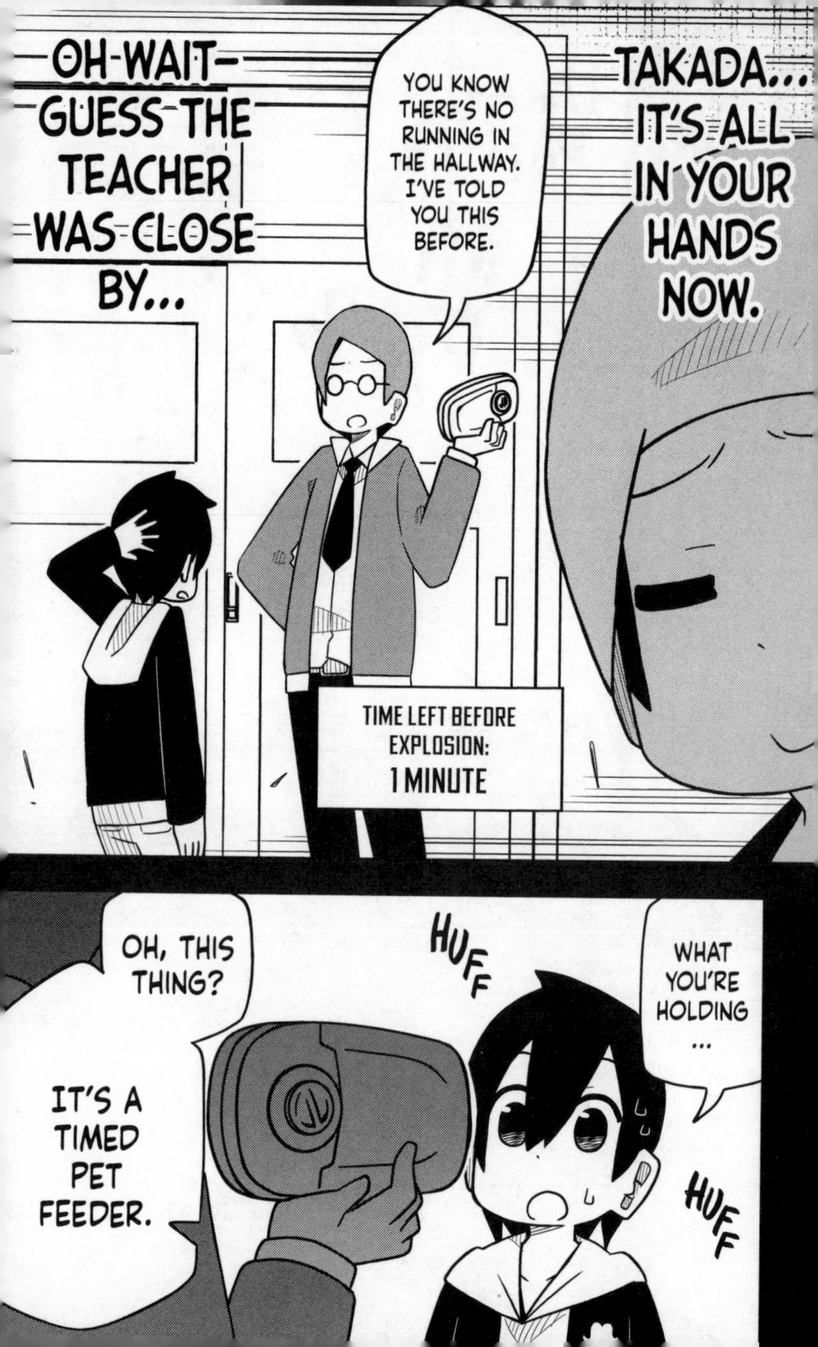
TAKADA... IT'S ALL IN YOUR HANDS NOW.
YOU KNOW THERE'S NO RUNNING IN THE HALLWAY. I'VE TOLD YOU THIS BEFORE.
OH-WAIT-GUESS THE TEACHER WAS CLOSE BY...
TIME LEFT BEFORE EXPLOSION: 1 MINUTE
WHAT YOU'RE HOLDING ...
HUFF
HUFF
OH, THIS THING?
IT'S A TIMED PET FEEDER.

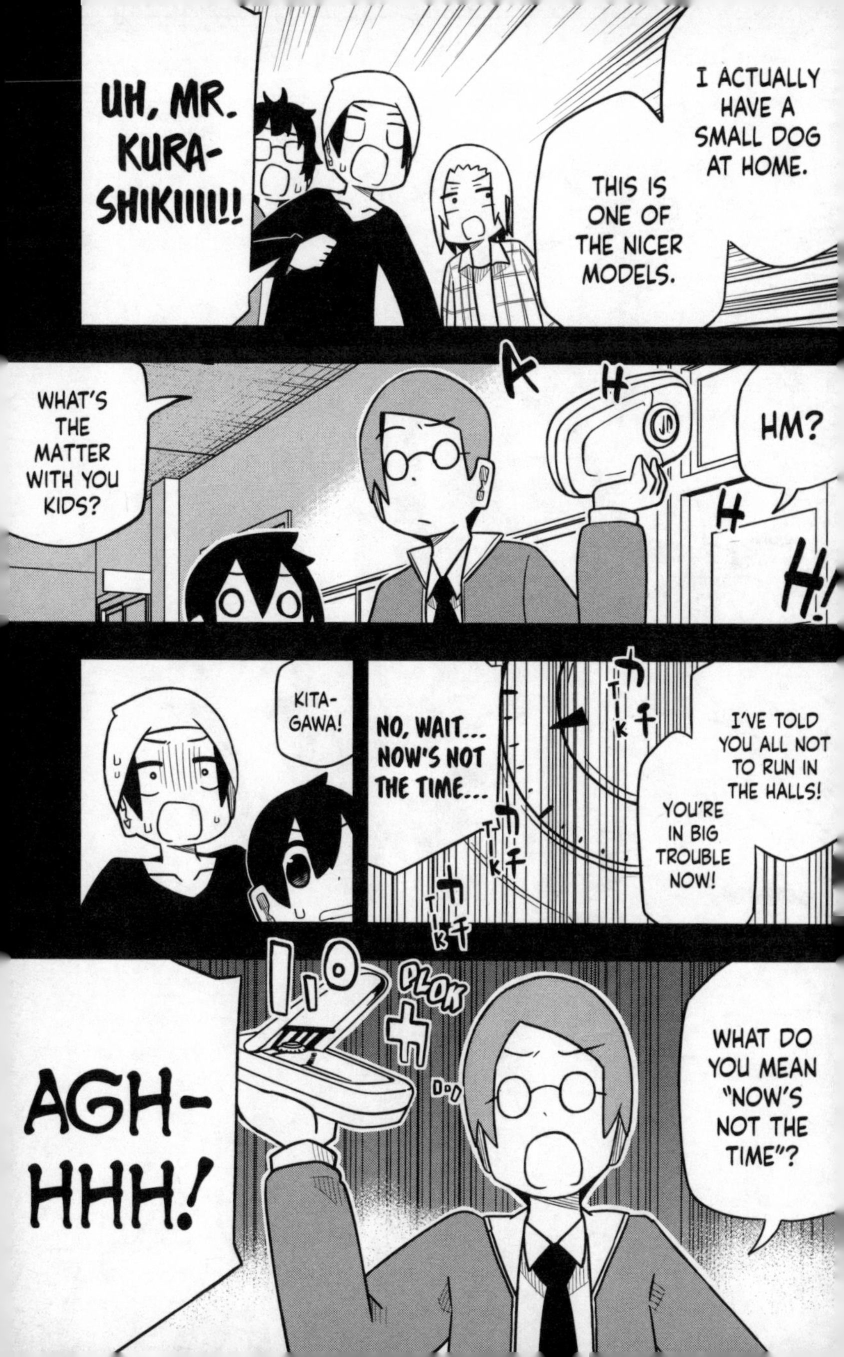
I ACTUALLY HAVE A SMALL DOG AT HOME.
THIS IS ONE OF THE NICER MODELS.
UH, MR. KURA-SHIKIIIII!!
HM?
AHHH!
WHAT'S THE MATTER WITH YOU KIDS?
I'VE TOLD YOU ALL NOT TO RUN IN THE HALLS!
YOU'RE IN BIG TROUBLE NOW!
TIK
TIK
TIK
NO, WAIT... NOW'S NOT THE TIME...
KITA-GAWA!
WHAT DO YOU MEAN "NOW'S NOT THE TIME"?
PLOK
AGH-HHH!

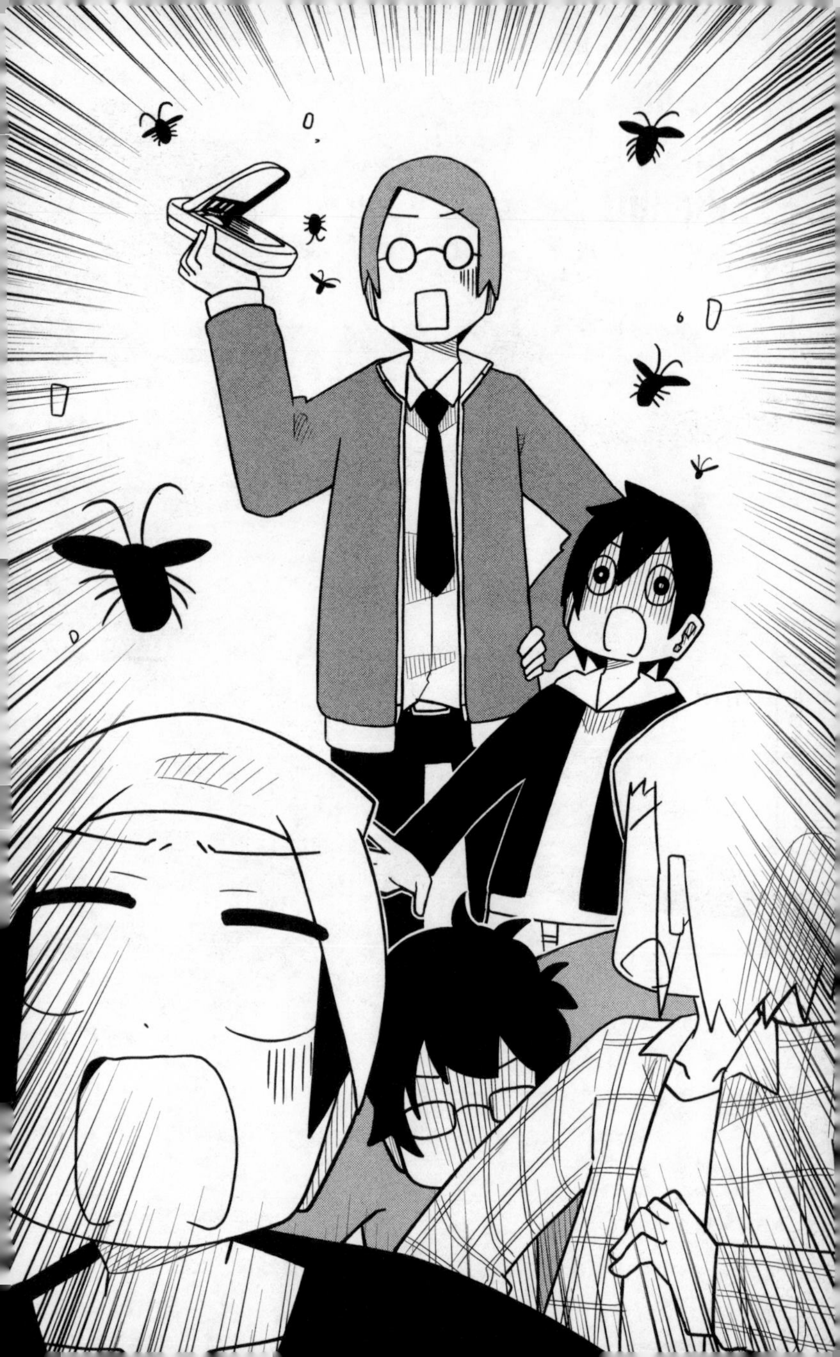

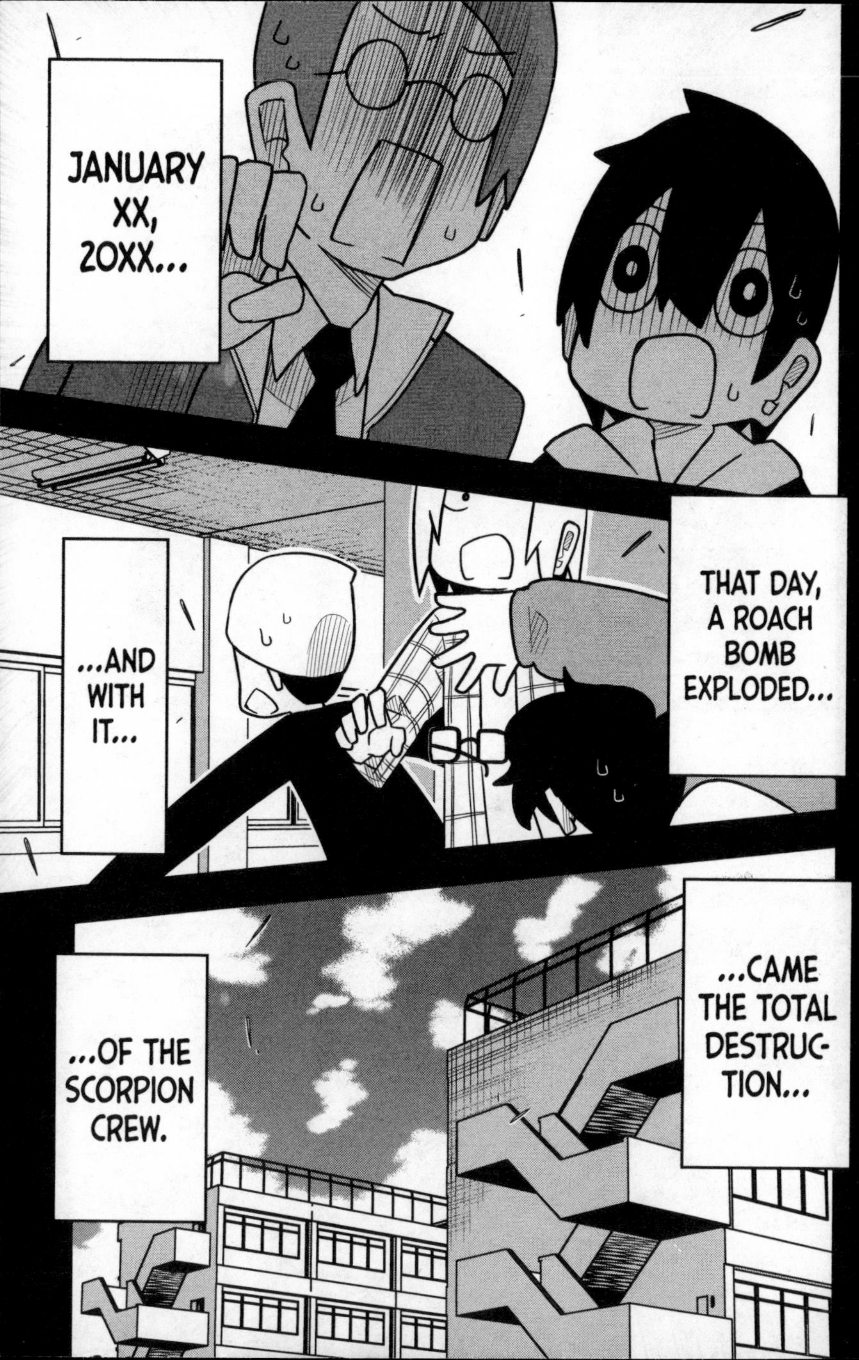
JANUARY XX, 20XX...
THAT DAY, A ROACH BOMB EXPLODED...
...AND WITH IT...
...CAME THE TOTAL DESTRUC-TION...
...OF THE SCORPION CREW.

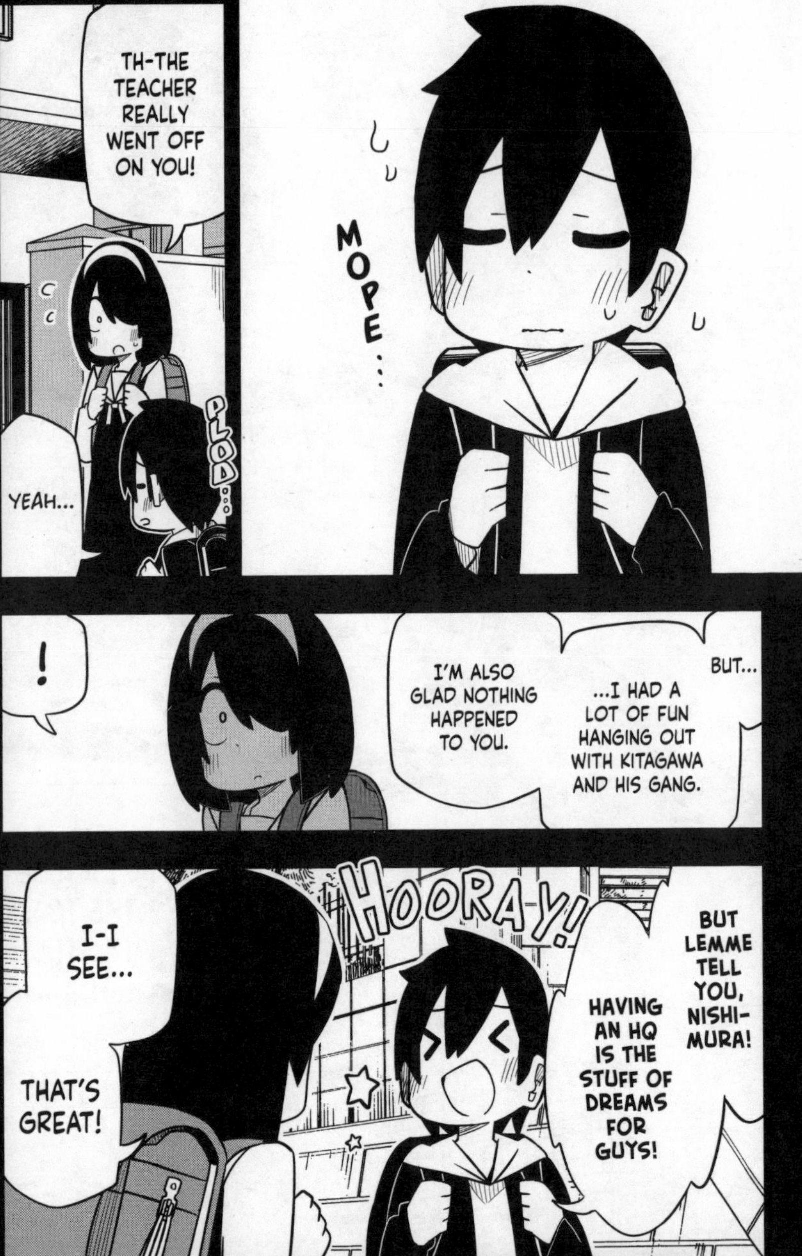
MOPE...
TH-THE TEACHER REALLY WENT OFF ON YOU!
PLOD...
YEAH...
I'M ALSO GLAD NOTHING HAPPENED TO YOU.
BUT...
...I HAD A LOT OF FUN HANGING OUT WITH KITAGAWA AND HIS GANG.
!
BUT LEMME TELL YOU, NISHIMURA!
HAVING AN HQ IS THE STUFF OF DREAMS FOR GUYS!
HOORAY!
I-I SEE...
THAT'S GREAT!

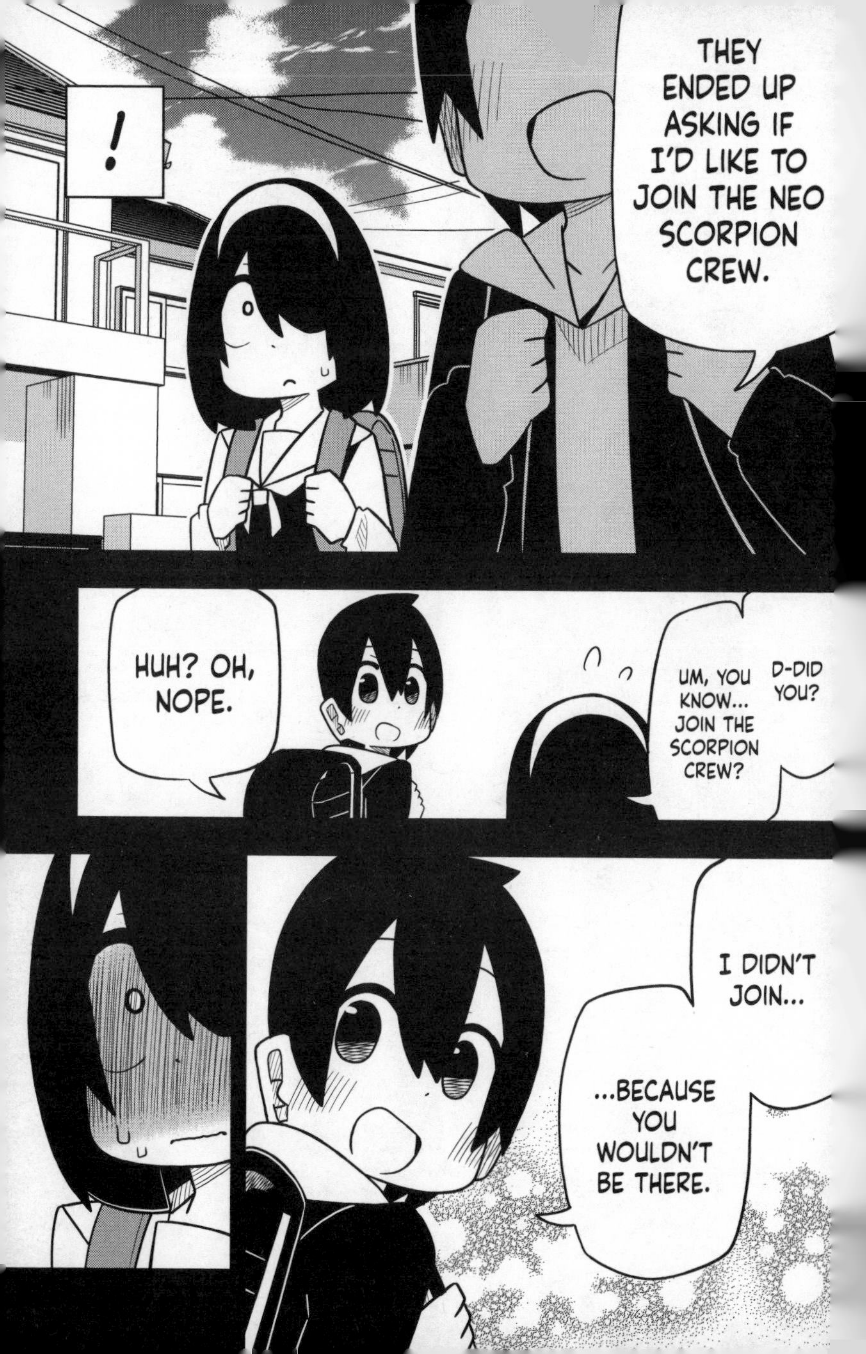
THEY ENDED UP ASKING IF I'D LIKE TO JOIN THE NEO SCORPION CREW.
!
D-DID YOU?
UM, YOU KNOW... JOIN THE SCORPION CREW?
HUH? OH, NOPE.
I DIDN'T JOIN...
...BECAUSE YOU WOULDN'T BE THERE.

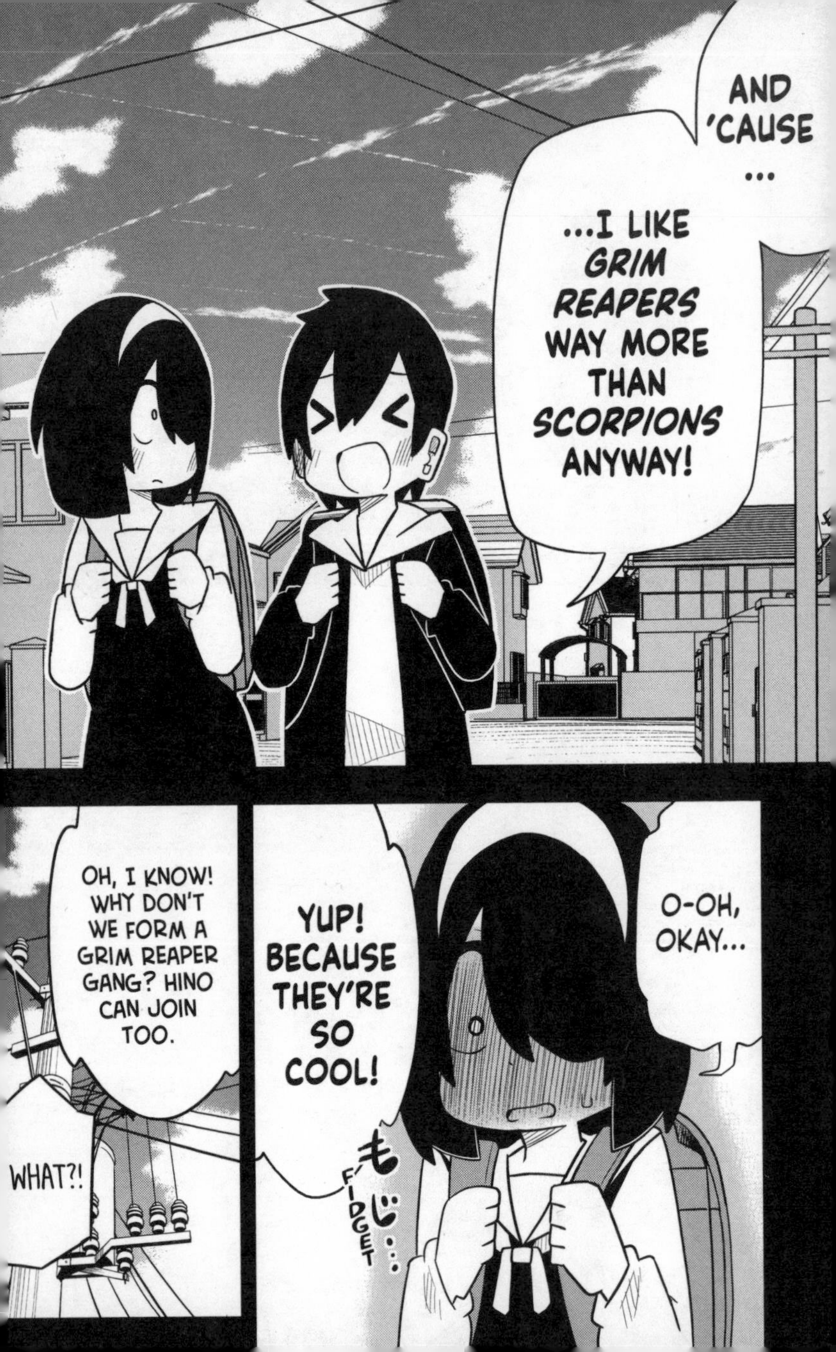
AND 'CAUSE ...
...I LIKE GRIM REAPERS WAY MORE THAN SCORPIONS ANYWAY!
O-OH, OKAY...
YUP! BECAUSE THEY'RE SO COOL!
もじ... FIDGET
OH, I KNOW! WHY DON'T WE FORM A GRIM REAPER GANG? HINO CAN JOIN TOO.
WHAT?!

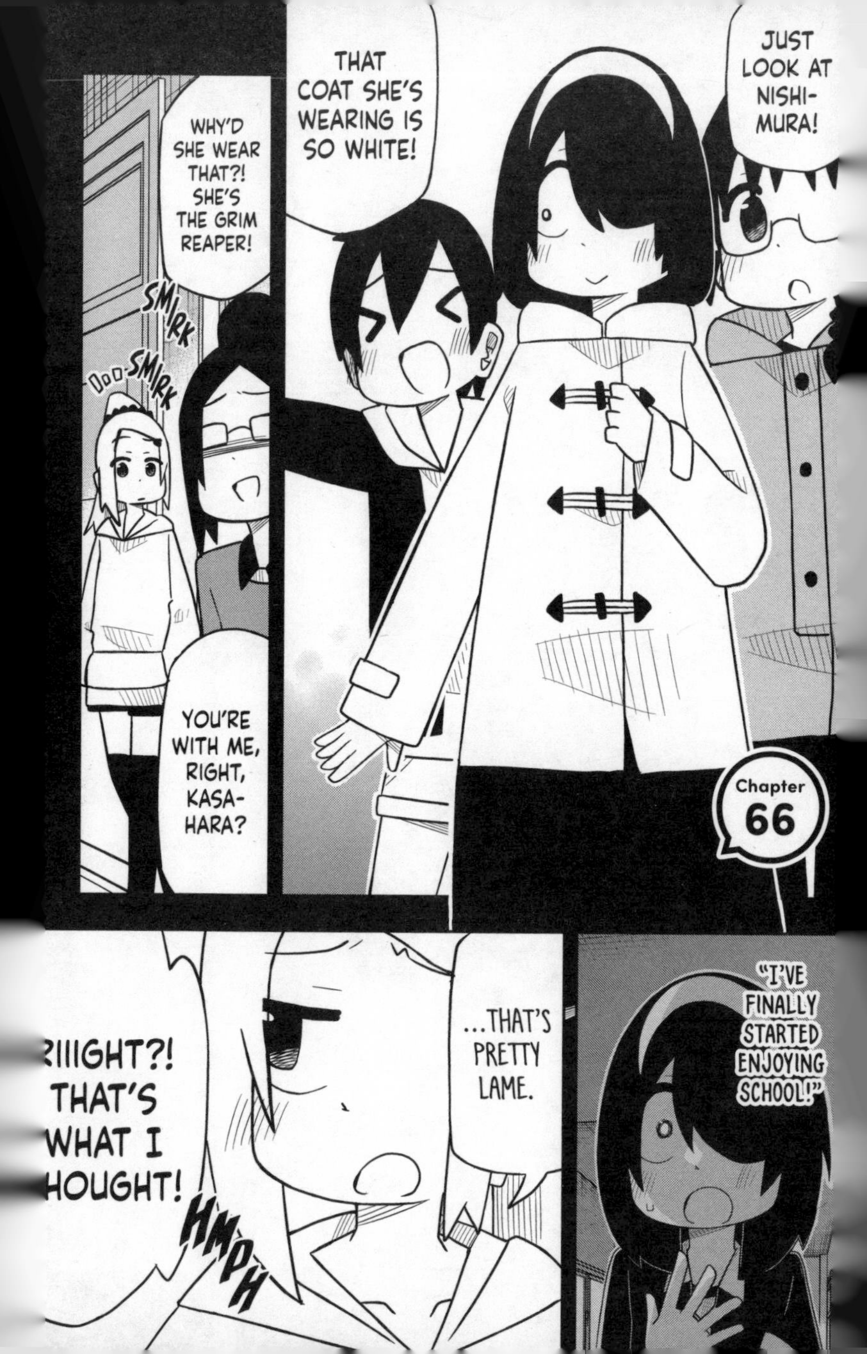
JUST LOOK AT NISHIMURA!
THAT COAT SHE'S WEARING IS SO WHITE!
WHY'D SHE WEAR THAT?! SHE'S THE GRIM REAPER!
SMIRK
SMIRK
YOU'RE WITH ME, RIGHT, KASAHARA?
Chapter 66
"I'VE FINALLY STARTED ENJOYING SCHOOL!"
...THAT'S PRETTY LAME.
IIIGHT?! THAT'S WHAT I HOUGHT!
HMPH

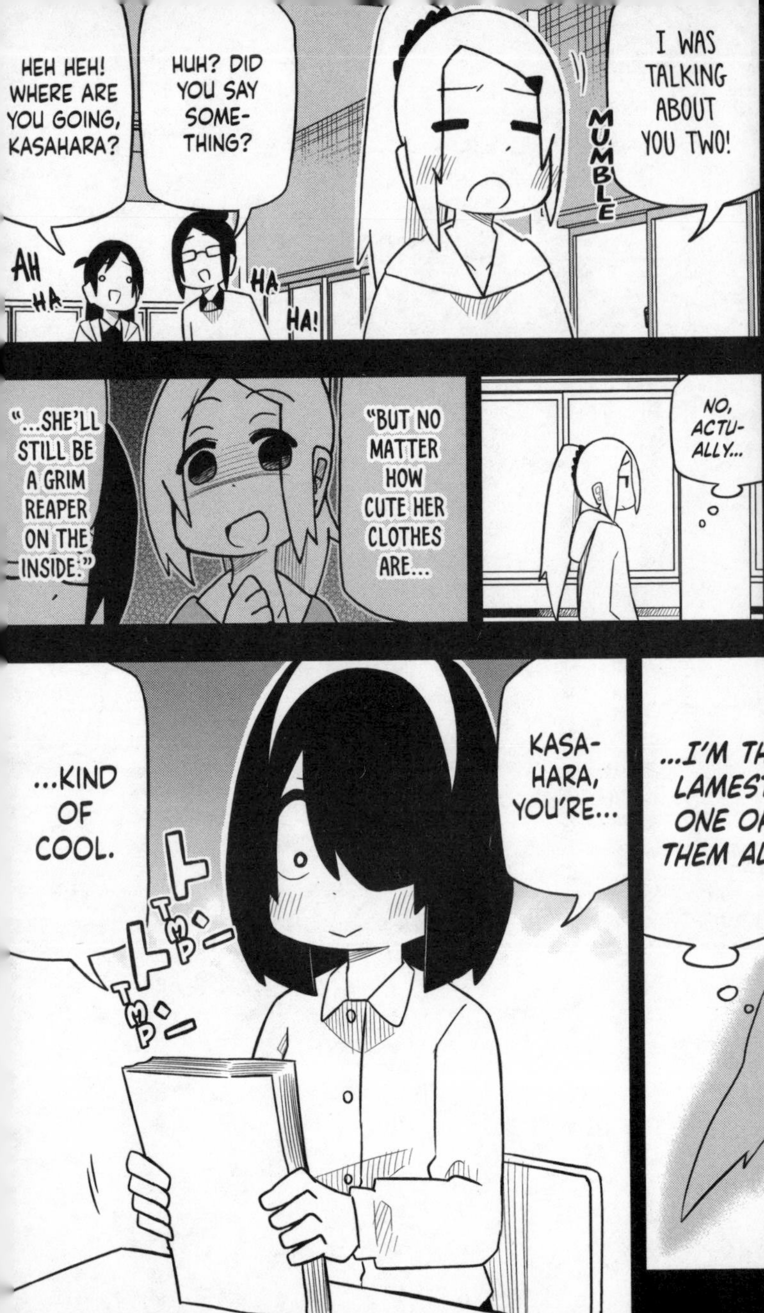
I WAS TALKING ABOUT YOU TWO!
MUMBLE
HUH? DID YOU SAY SOME-THING?
HEH HEH! WHERE ARE YOU GOING, KASAHARA?
AH HA HA HA!
NO, ACTU-ALLY...
"BUT NO MATTER HOW CUTE HER CLOTHES ARE...
"...SHE'LL STILL BE A GRIM REAPER ON THE INSIDE."
...I'M THE LAMEST ONE OF THEM ALL.
KASA-HARA, YOU'RE...
...KIND OF COOL.
TMP TMP

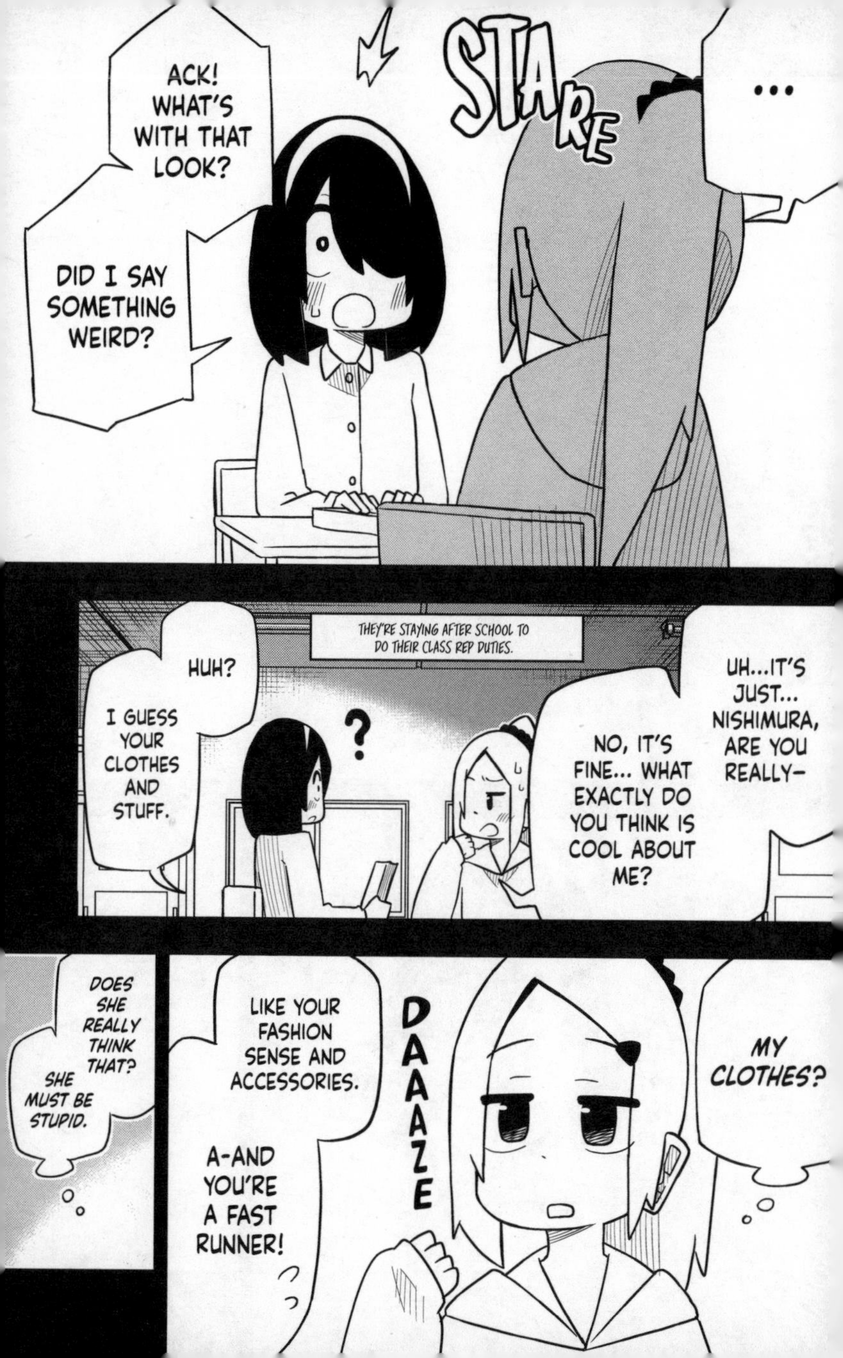
...
STARE
ACK! WHAT'S WITH THAT LOOK?
DID I SAY SOMETHING WEIRD?
THEY'RE STAYING AFTER SCHOOL TO DO THEIR CLASS REP DUTIES.
UH...IT'S JUST... NISHIMURA, ARE YOU REALLY–
NO, IT'S FINE... WHAT EXACTLY DO YOU THINK IS COOL ABOUT ME?
?
HUH?
I GUESS YOUR CLOTHES AND STUFF.
MY CLOTHES?
DAAAZE
LIKE YOUR FASHION SENSE AND ACCESSORIES.
A-AND YOU'RE A FAST RUNNER!
DOES SHE REALLY THINK THAT?
SHE MUST BE STUPID.

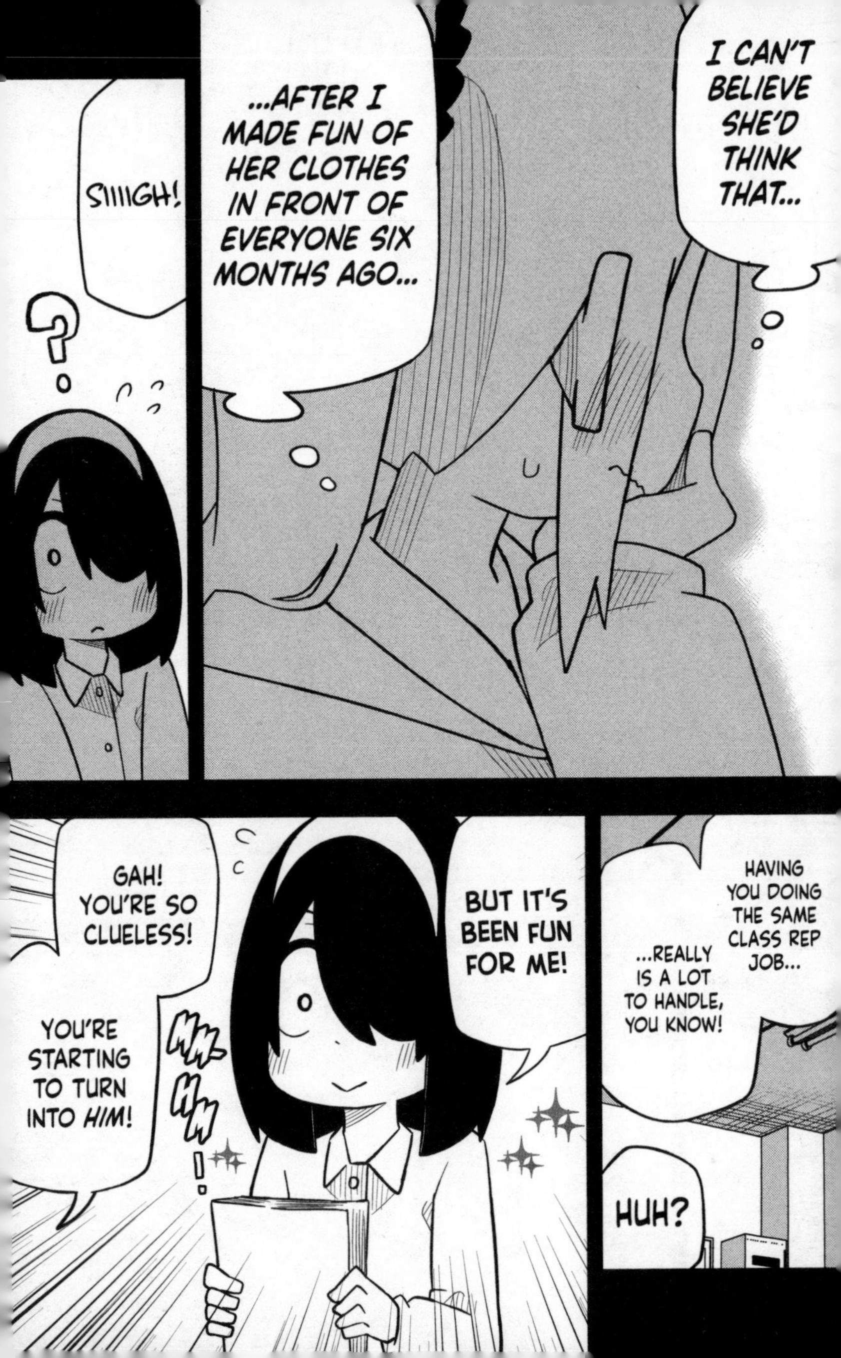
I CAN'T BELIEVE SHE'D THINK THAT...
...AFTER I MADE FUN OF HER CLOTHES IN FRONT OF EVERYONE SIX MONTHS AGO...
SIIIIGH!
?
HAVING YOU DOING THE SAME CLASS REP JOB...
...REALLY IS A LOT TO HANDLE, YOU KNOW!
HUH?
BUT IT'S BEEN FUN FOR ME!
GAH! YOU'RE SO CLUELESS!
YOU'RE STARTING TO TURN INTO *HIM*!

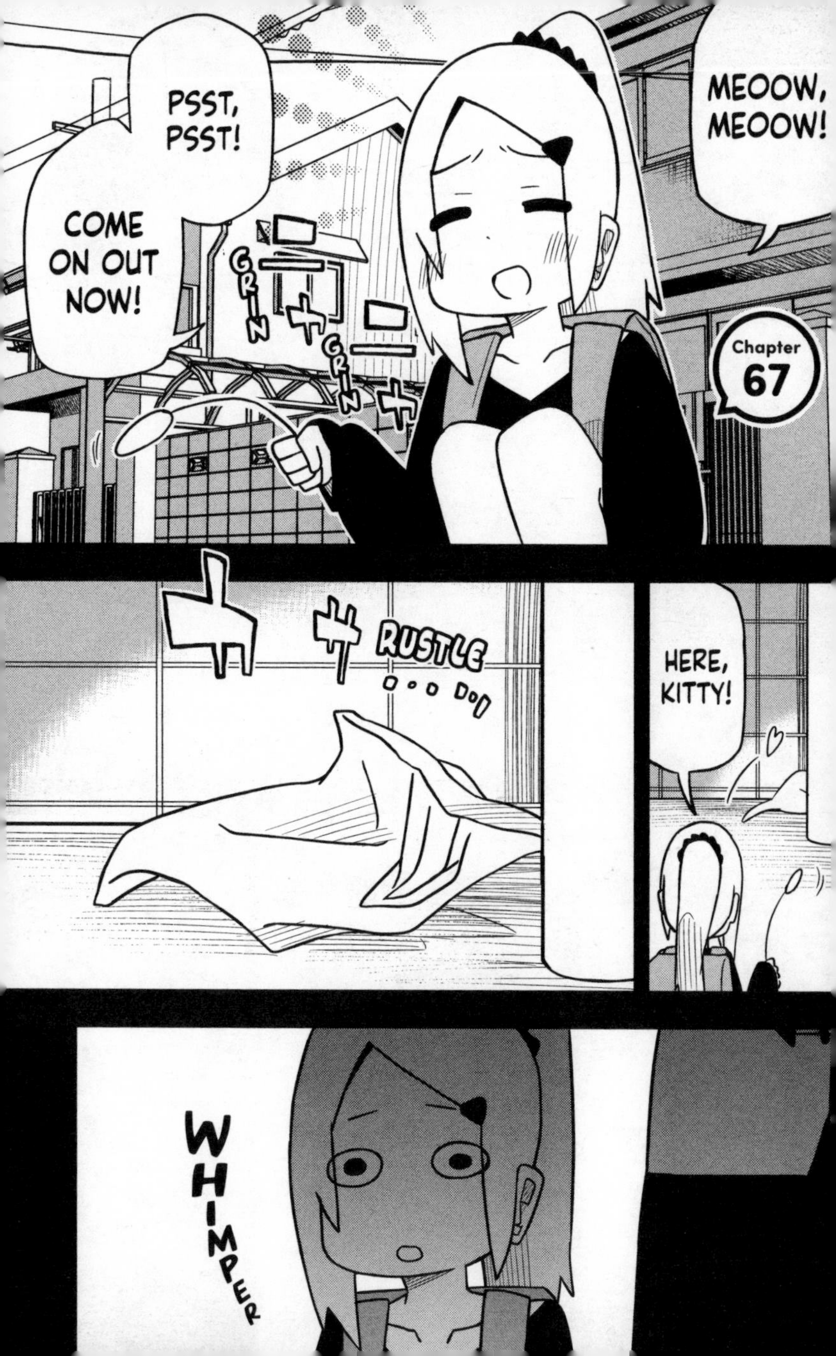

MEOOW, MEOOW!
Chapter 67
PSST, PSST!
COME ON OUT NOW!
GRIN
GRIN
HERE, KITTY!
RUSTLE
WHIMPER

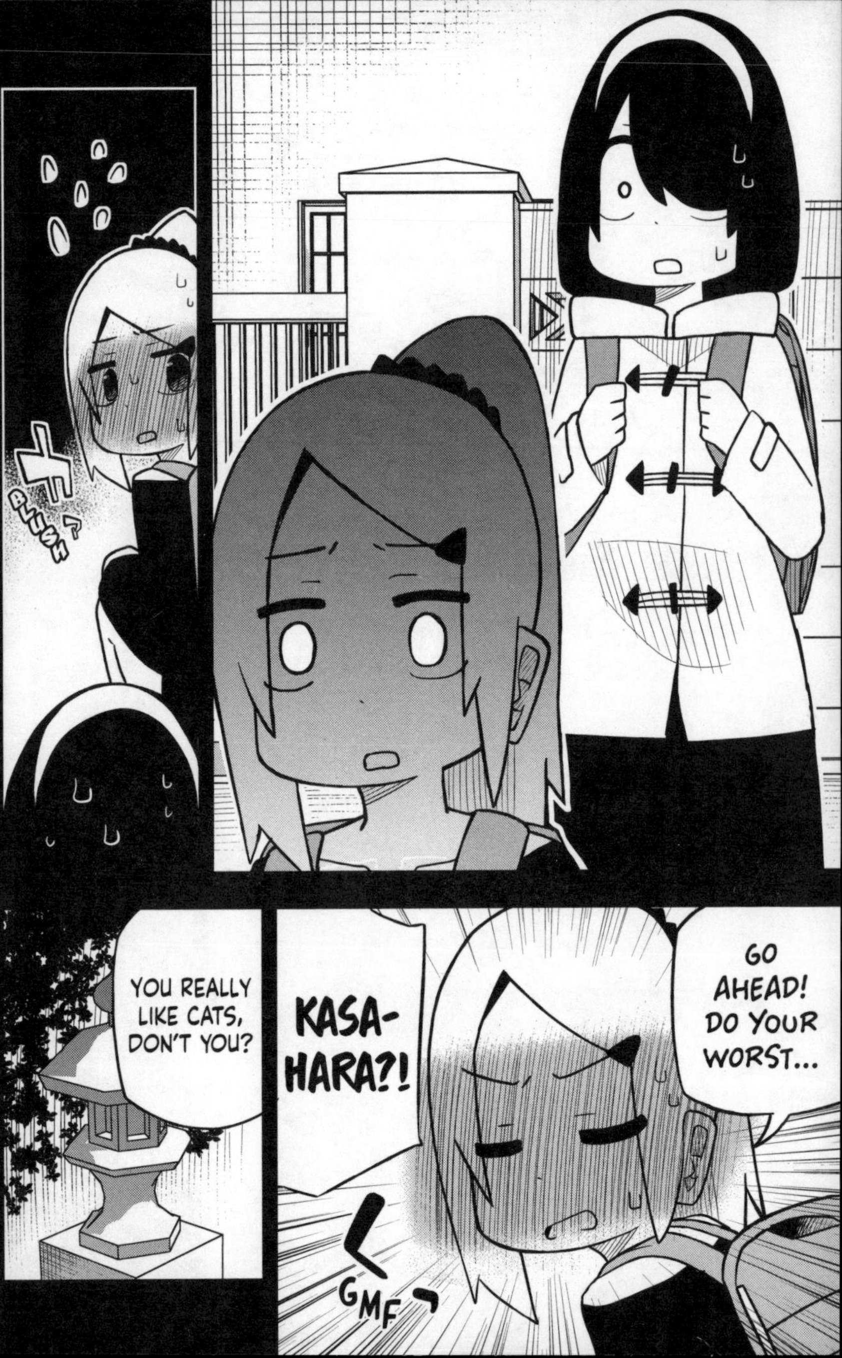
BLUSH
GO AHEAD! DO YOUR WORST...
KASA-HARA?!
GMF
YOU REALLY LIKE CATS, DON'T YOU?

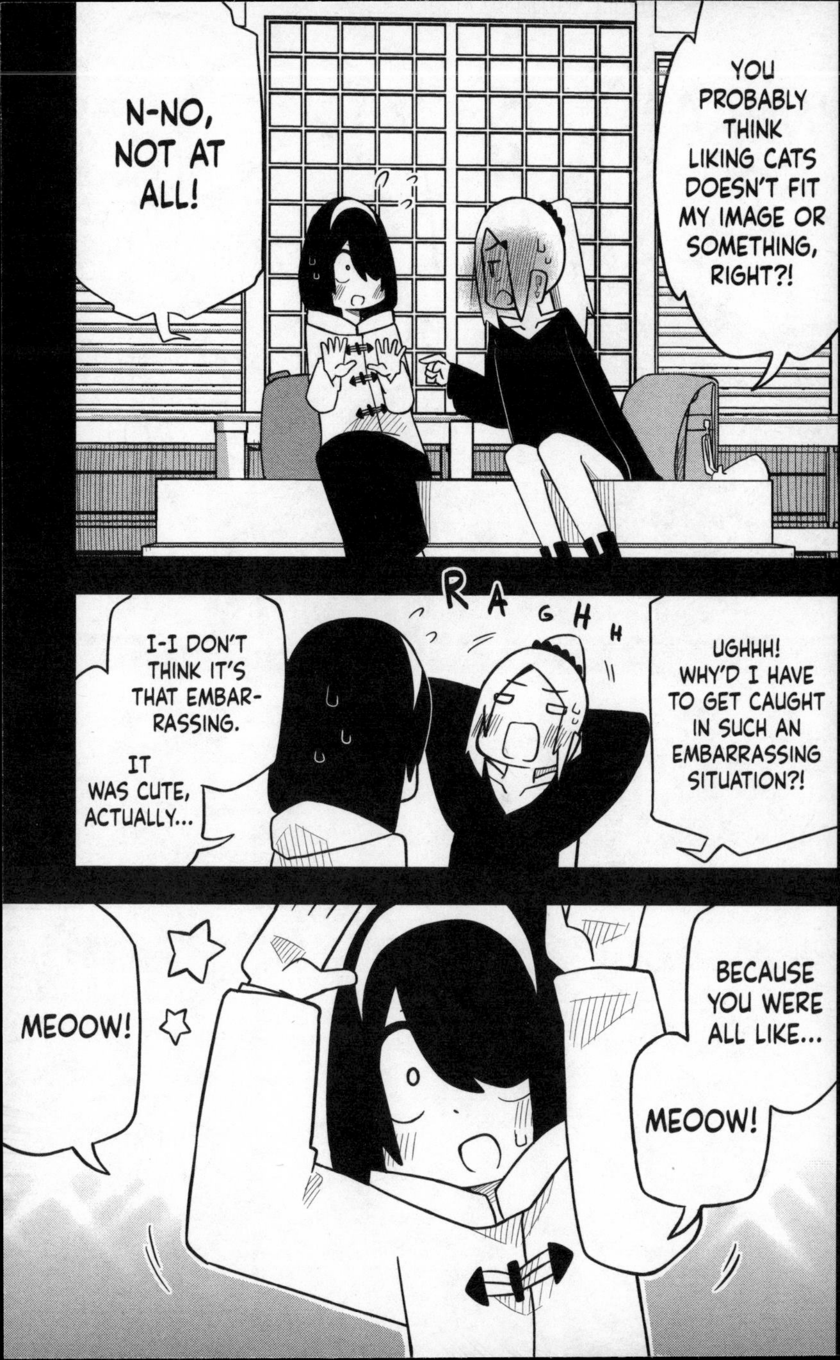
YOU PROBABLY THINK LIKING CATS DOESN'T FIT MY IMAGE OR SOMETHING, RIGHT?!
N-NO, NOT AT ALL!
UGHHH! WHY'D I HAVE TO GET CAUGHT IN SUCH AN EMBARRASSING SITUATION?!
RAGHH
I-I DON'T THINK IT'S THAT EMBARRASSING.
IT WAS CUTE, ACTUALLY...
BECAUSE YOU WERE ALL LIKE...
MEOOW!
MEOOW!

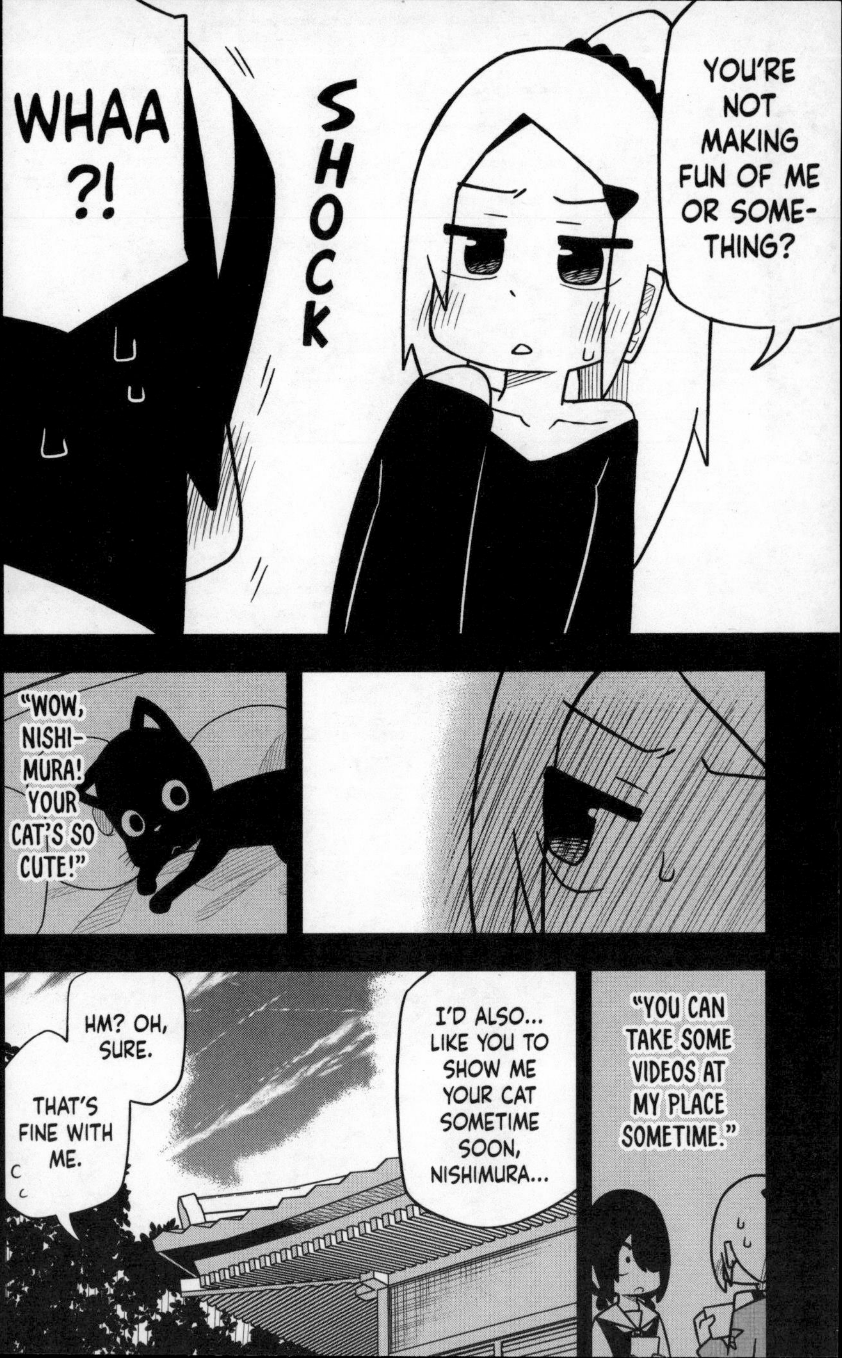
YOU'RE NOT MAKING FUN OF ME OR SOME-THING?
SHOCK
WHAA ?!
"WOW, NISHI-MURA! YOUR CAT'S SO CUTE!"
"YOU CAN TAKE SOME VIDEOS AT MY PLACE SOMETIME."
I'D ALSO... LIKE YOU TO SHOW ME YOUR CAT SOMETIME SOON, NISHIMURA...
HM? OH, SURE.
THAT'S FINE WITH ME.

MY CLUELESS FIRST FRIEND

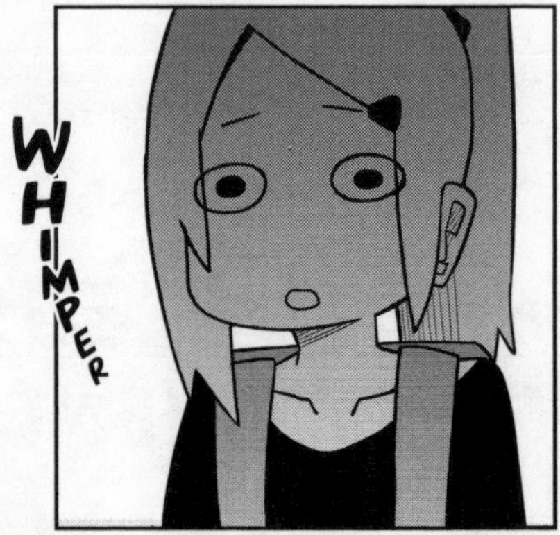
WHIMPER

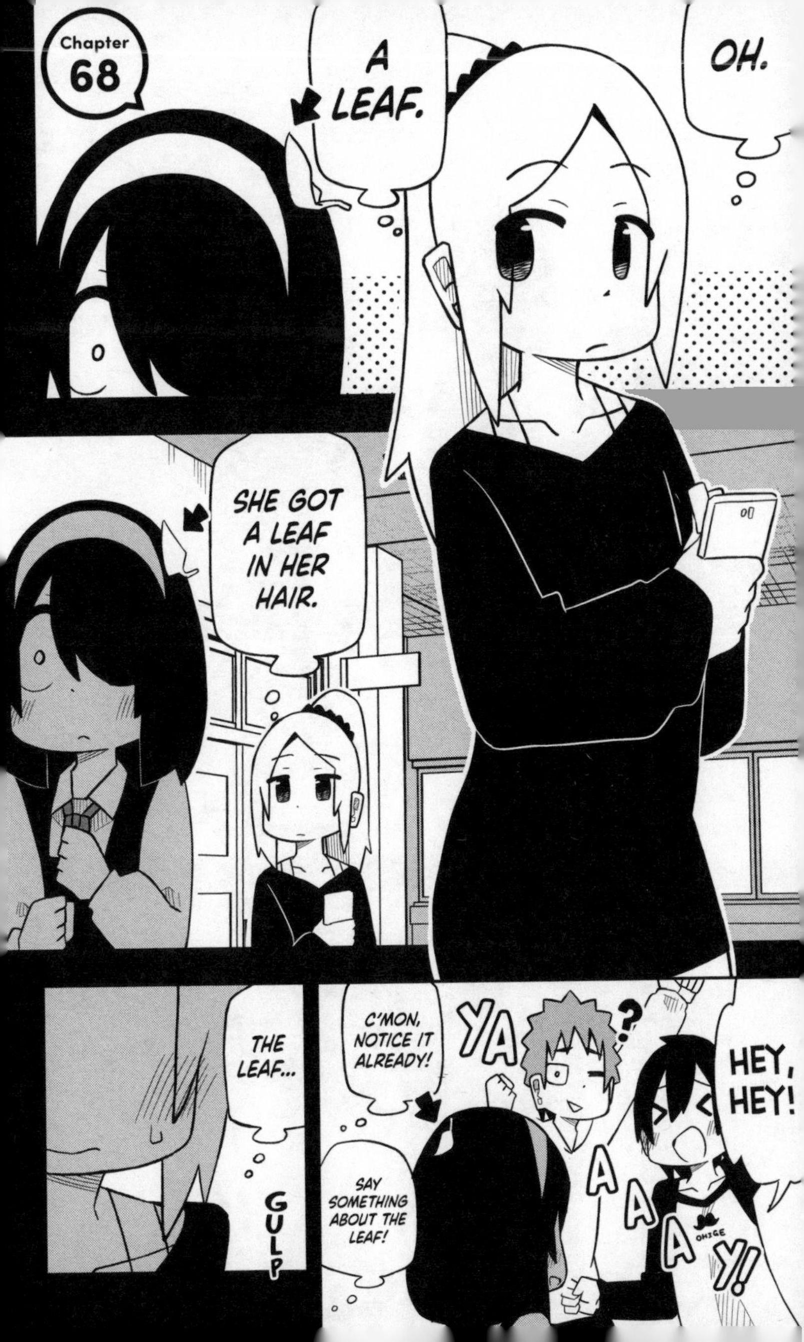
Chapter 68
OH.
A LEAF.
SHE GOT A LEAF IN HER HAIR.
HEY, HEY!
YAAAAAY!
?
OHIGE
C'MON, NOTICE IT ALREADY!
SAY SOMETHING ABOUT THE LEAF!
THE LEAF...
GULP

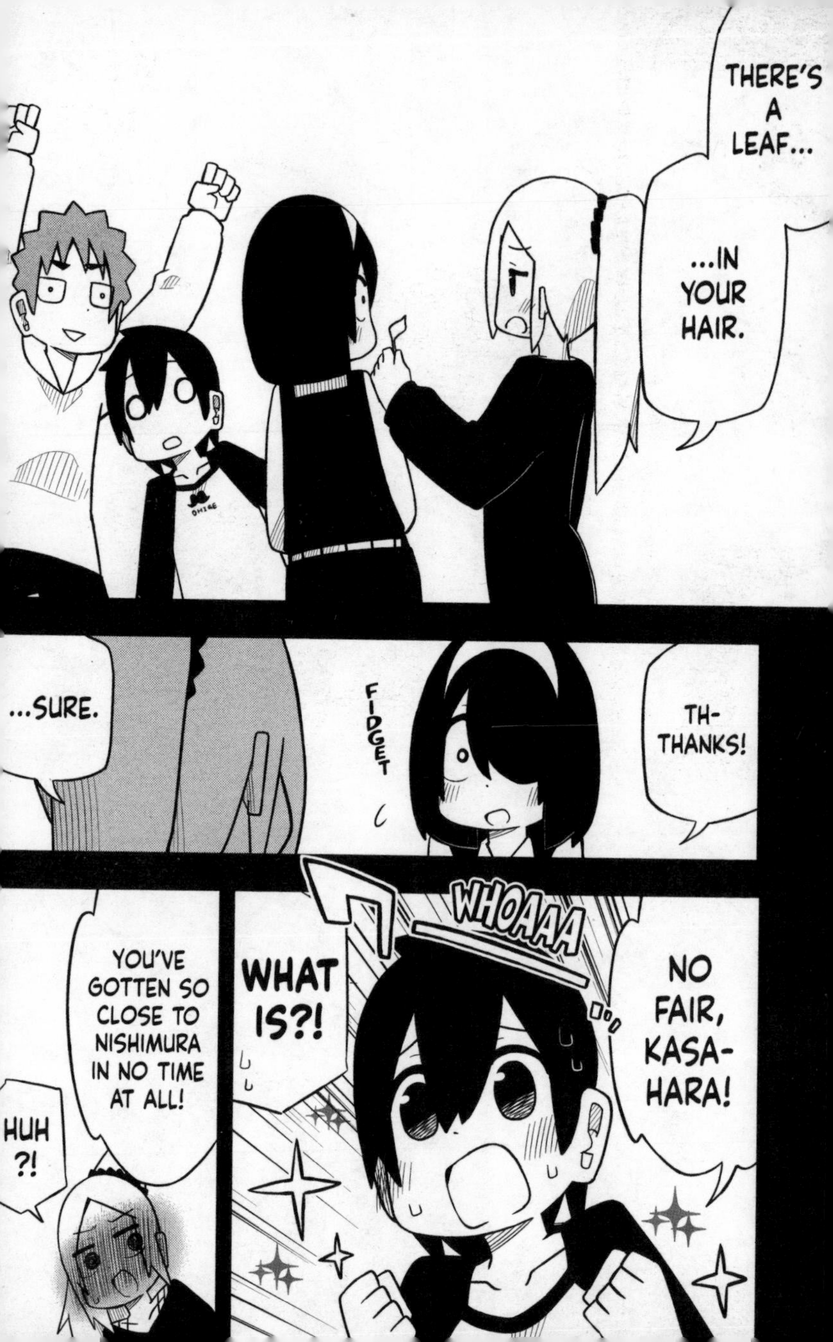
THERE'S A LEAF...
...IN YOUR HAIR.
TH- THANKS!
FIDGET
...SURE.
WHOAAA
NO FAIR, KASAHARA!
WHAT IS?!
YOU'VE GOTTEN SO CLOSE TO NISHIMURA IN NO TIME AT ALL!
HUH ?!

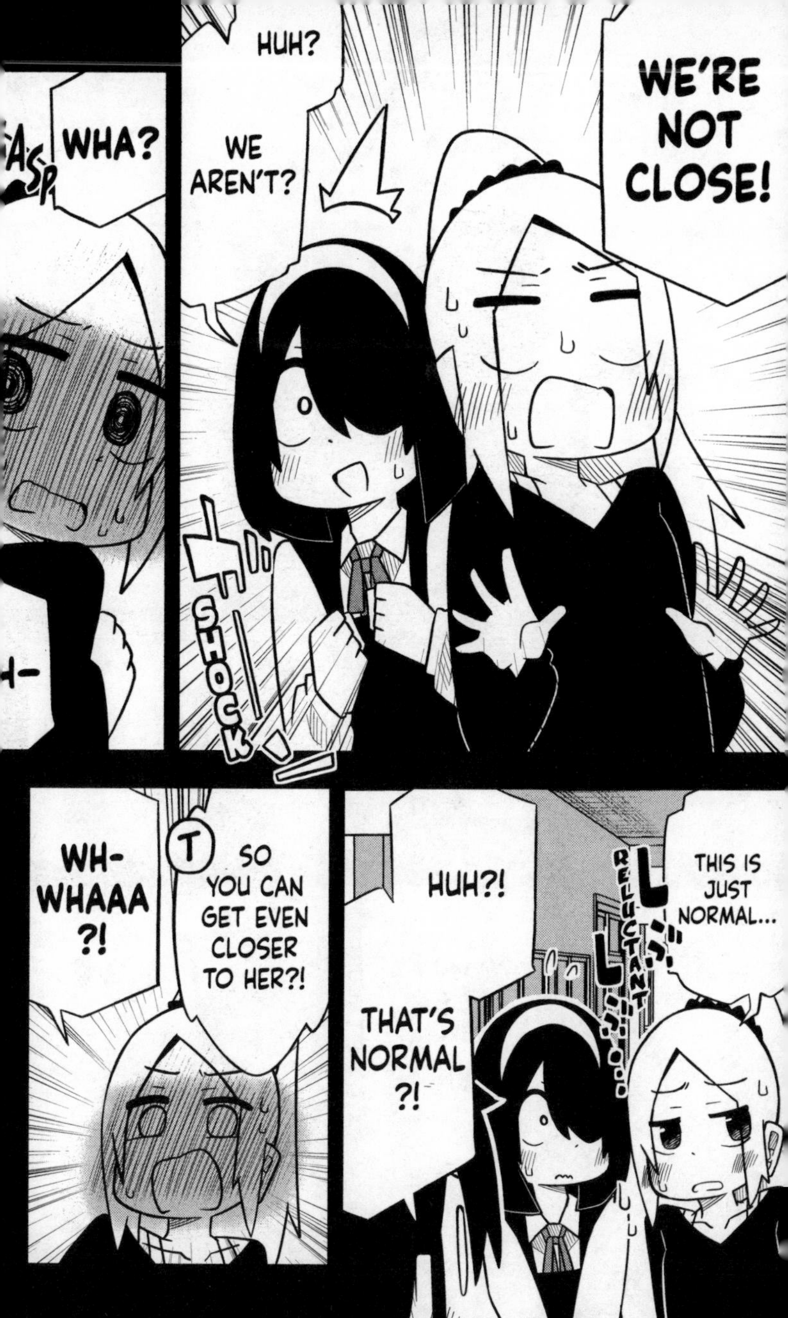
WE'RE NOT CLOSE!
HUH?
WE AREN'T?
SHOCK
WHA?
THIS IS JUST NORMAL...
RELUCTANT
HUH?!
THAT'S NORMAL?!
SO YOU CAN GET EVEN CLOSER TO HER?!
WH-WHAAA?!

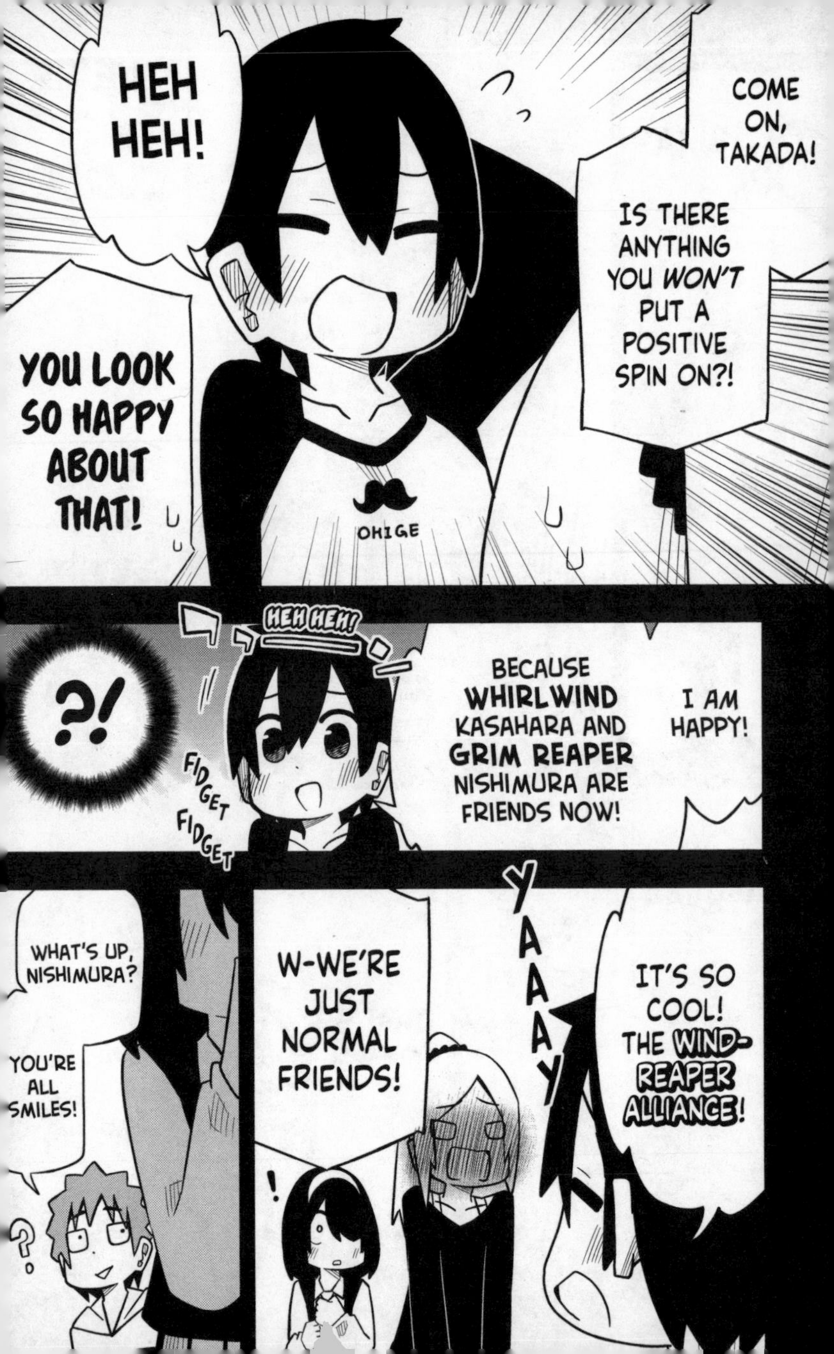
COME ON, TAKADA!
HEH HEH!
IS THERE ANYTHING YOU *WON'T* PUT A POSITIVE SPIN ON?!
YOU LOOK SO HAPPY ABOUT THAT!
OHIGE
I AM HAPPY!
BECAUSE **WHIRLWIND** KASAHARA AND **GRIM REAPER** NISHIMURA ARE FRIENDS NOW!
HEH HEH!
FIDGET FIDGET
?!
IT'S SO COOL! THE WIND-REAPER ALLIANCE!
YAAAY
W-WE'RE JUST NORMAL FRIENDS!
WHAT'S UP, NISHIMURA?
YOU'RE ALL SMILES!

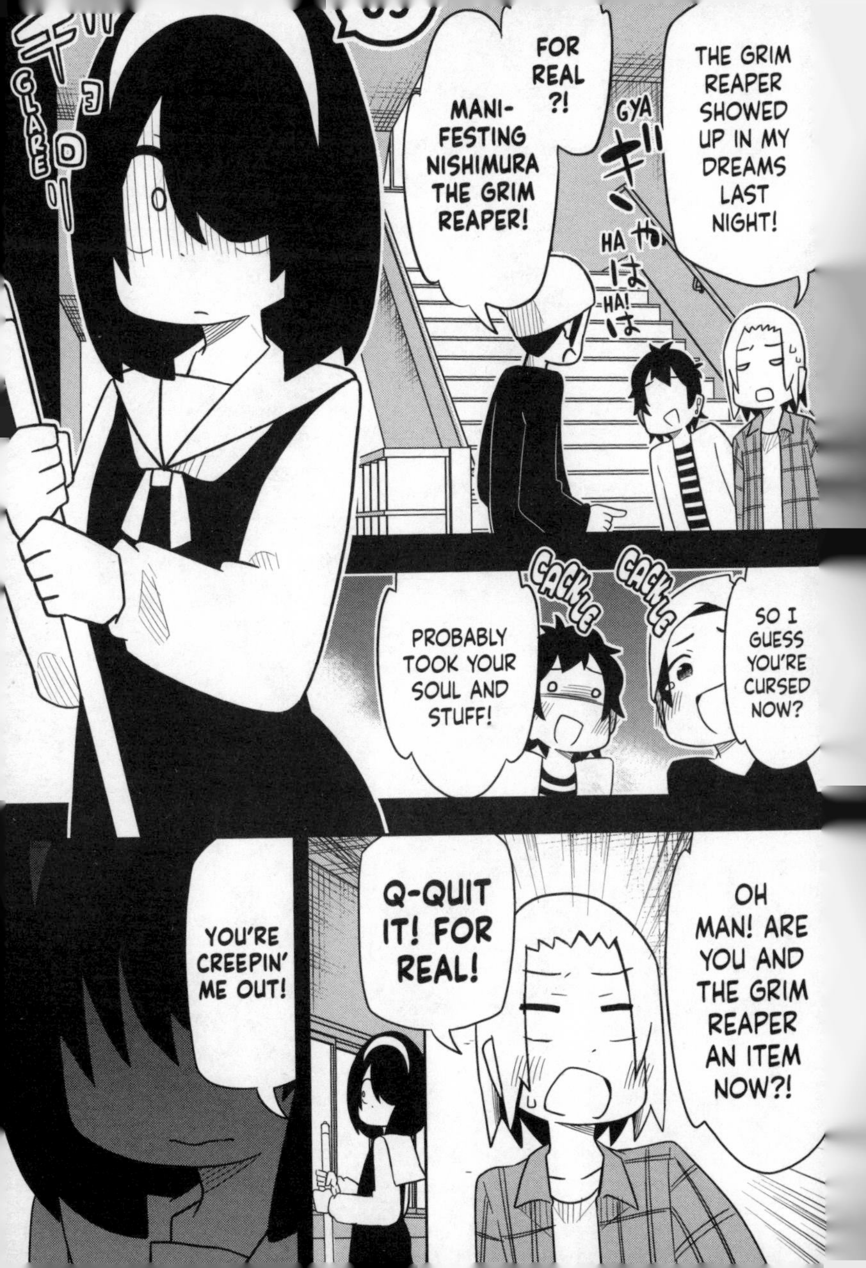
THE GRIM REAPER SHOWED UP IN MY DREAMS LAST NIGHT!
GYA
HA
HA!
FOR REAL?!
MANI-FESTING NISHIMURA THE GRIM REAPER!
CACKLE
CACKLE
SO I GUESS YOU'RE CURSED NOW?
PROBABLY TOOK YOUR SOUL AND STUFF!
GLARE
OH MAN! ARE YOU AND THE GRIM REAPER AN ITEM NOW?!
Q-QUIT IT! FOR REAL!
YOU'RE CREEPIN' ME OUT!

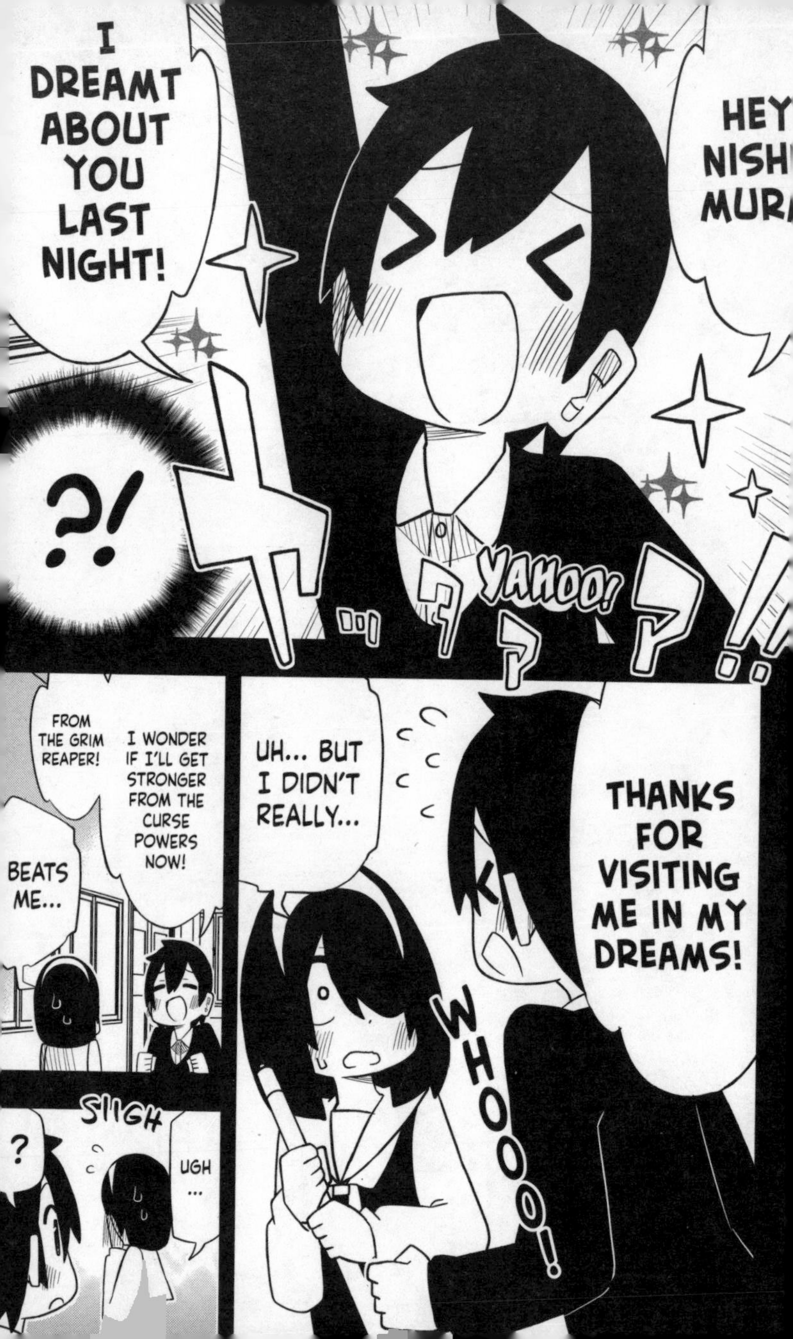
HEY NISH MUR
I DREAMT ABOUT YOU LAST NIGHT!
?!
YAHOO!
THANKS FOR VISITING ME IN MY DREAMS!
WHOOOO!
UH... BUT I DIDN'T REALLY...
I WONDER IF I'LL GET STRONGER FROM THE CURSE POWERS NOW!
FROM THE GRIM REAPER!
BEATS ME...
SIIGH
UGH ...
?

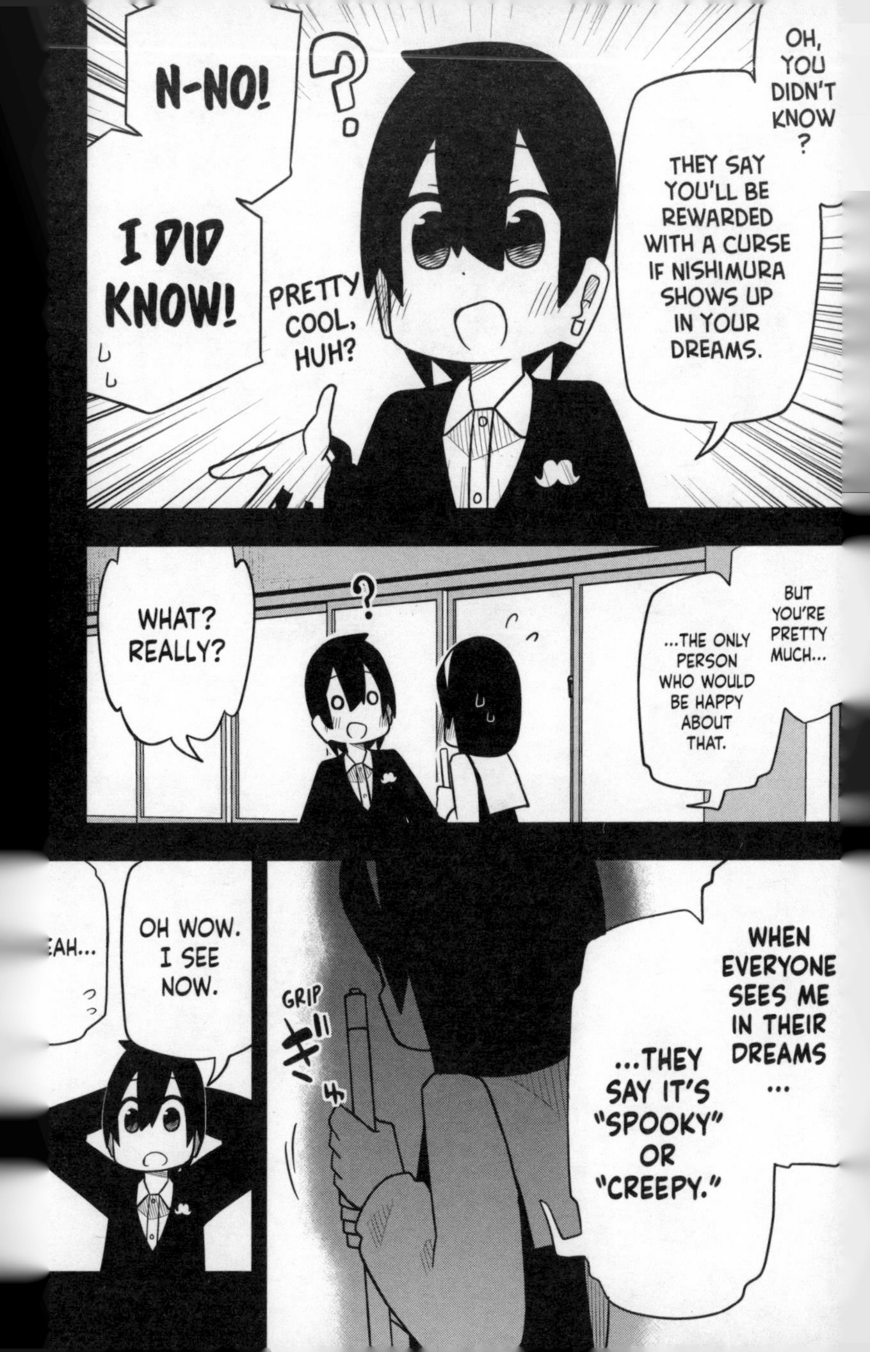
OH, YOU DIDN'T KNOW?
THEY SAY YOU'LL BE REWARDED WITH A CURSE IF NISHIMURA SHOWS UP IN YOUR DREAMS.
PRETTY COOL, HUH?
N-NO!
I DID KNOW!
BUT YOU'RE PRETTY MUCH...
...THE ONLY PERSON WHO WOULD BE HAPPY ABOUT THAT.
WHAT? REALLY?
WHEN EVERYONE SEES ME IN THEIR DREAMS...
...THEY SAY IT'S "SPOOKY" OR "CREEPY."
GRIP
OH WOW. I SEE NOW.
EAH...

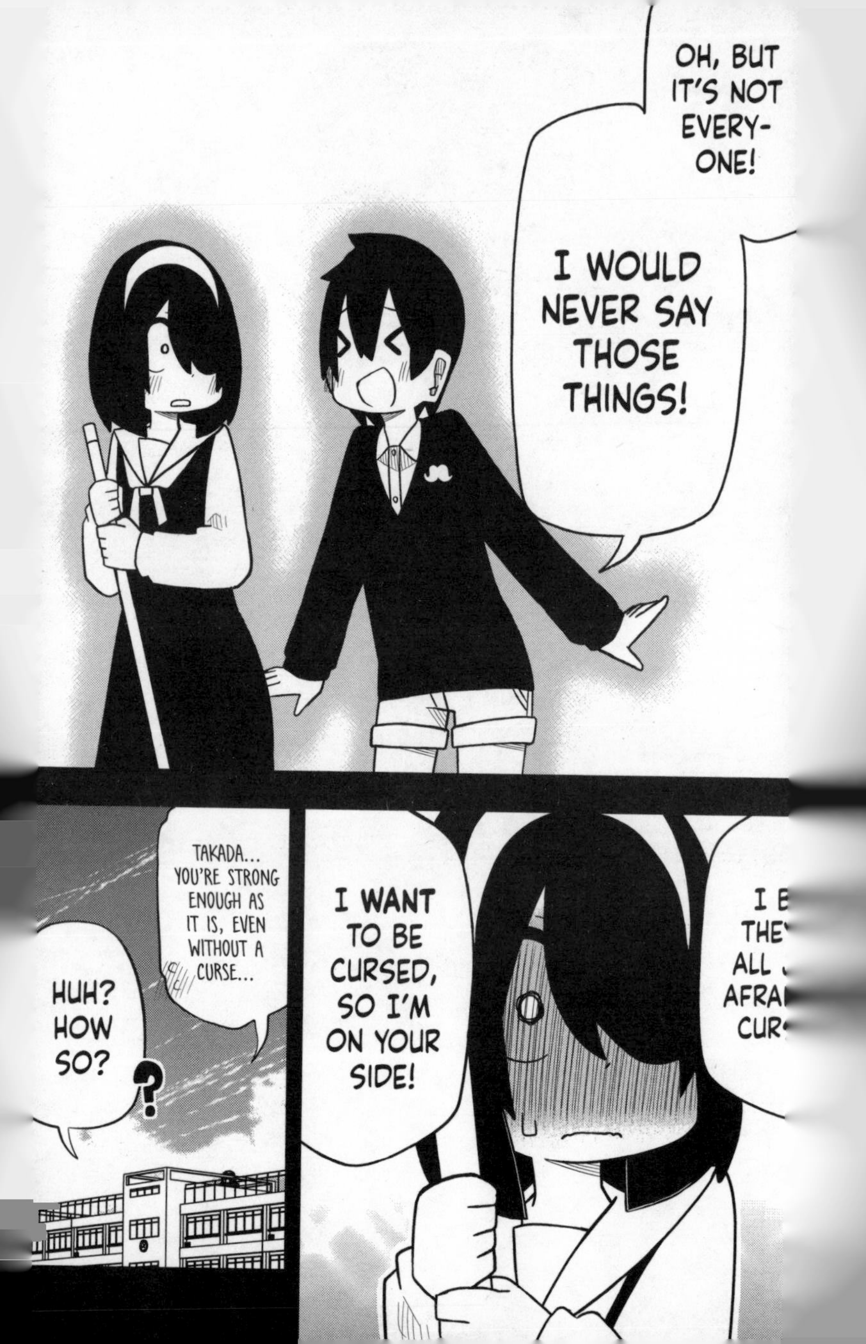
OH, BUT IT'S NOT EVERY-ONE!
I WOULD NEVER SAY THOSE THINGS!
I WANT TO BE CURSED, SO I'M ON YOUR SIDE!
TAKADA... YOU'RE STRONG ENOUGH AS IT IS, EVEN WITHOUT A CURSE...
HUH? HOW SO?
?

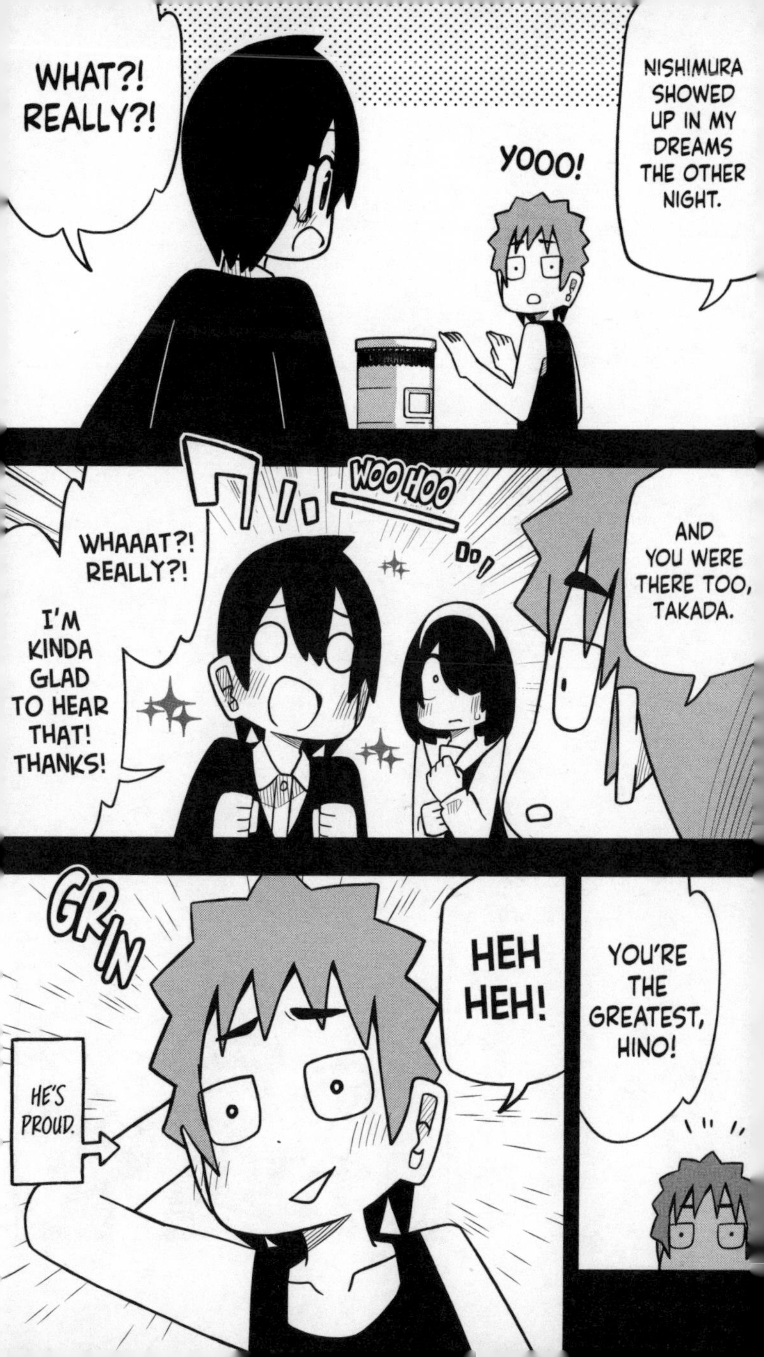
NISHIMURA SHOWED UP IN MY DREAMS THE OTHER NIGHT.
YOOO!
WHAT?! REALLY?!
AND YOU WERE THERE TOO, TAKADA.
WOO HOO
WHAAAT?! REALLY?!
I'M KINDA GLAD TO HEAR THAT! THANKS!
YOU'RE THE GREATEST, HINO!
HEH HEH!
GRIN
HE'S PROUD.

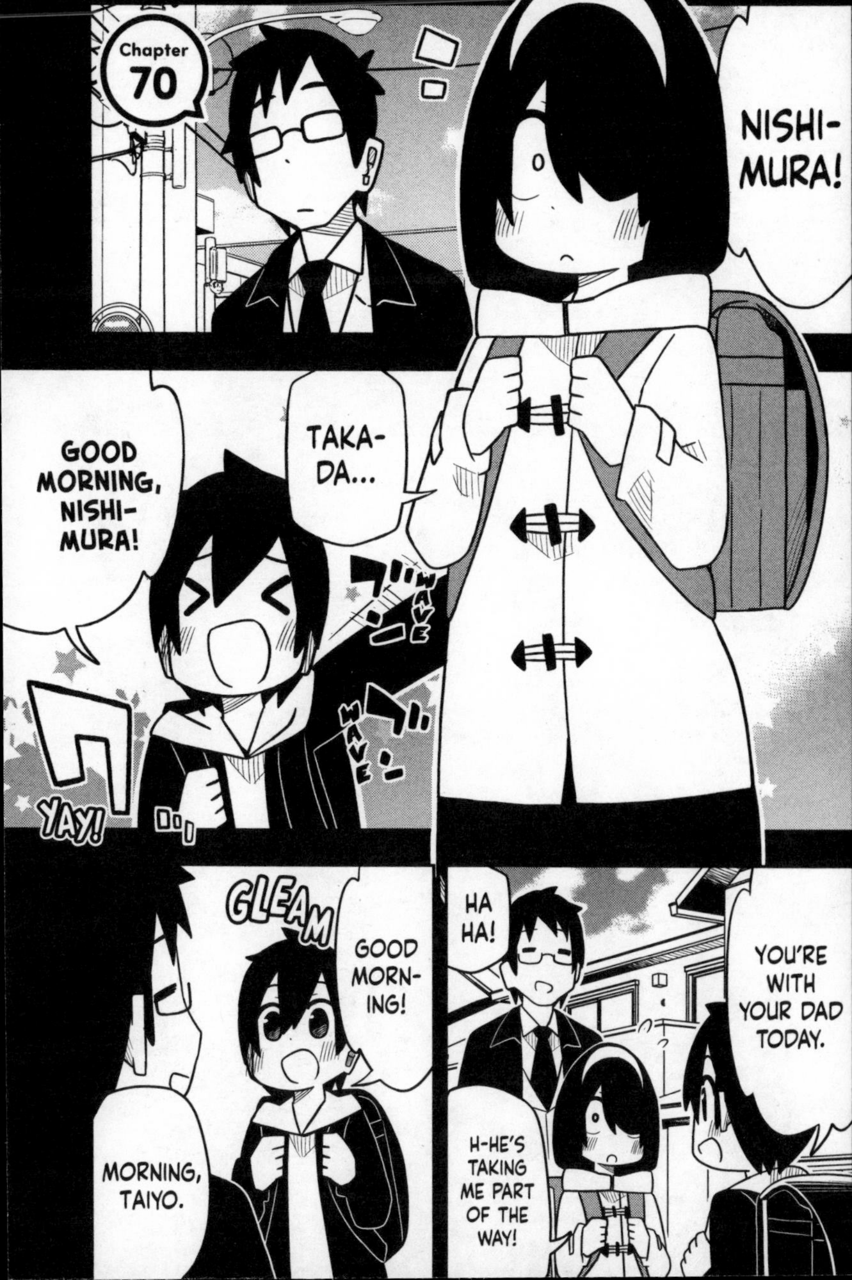
Chapter 70
NISHI-MURA!
TAKA-DA...
GOOD MORNING, NISHI-MURA!
WAVE
WAVE
YAY!
YOU'RE WITH YOUR DAD TODAY.
HA HA!
H-HE'S TAKING ME PART OF THE WAY!
GOOD MORN-ING!
GLEAM
MORNING, TAIYO.

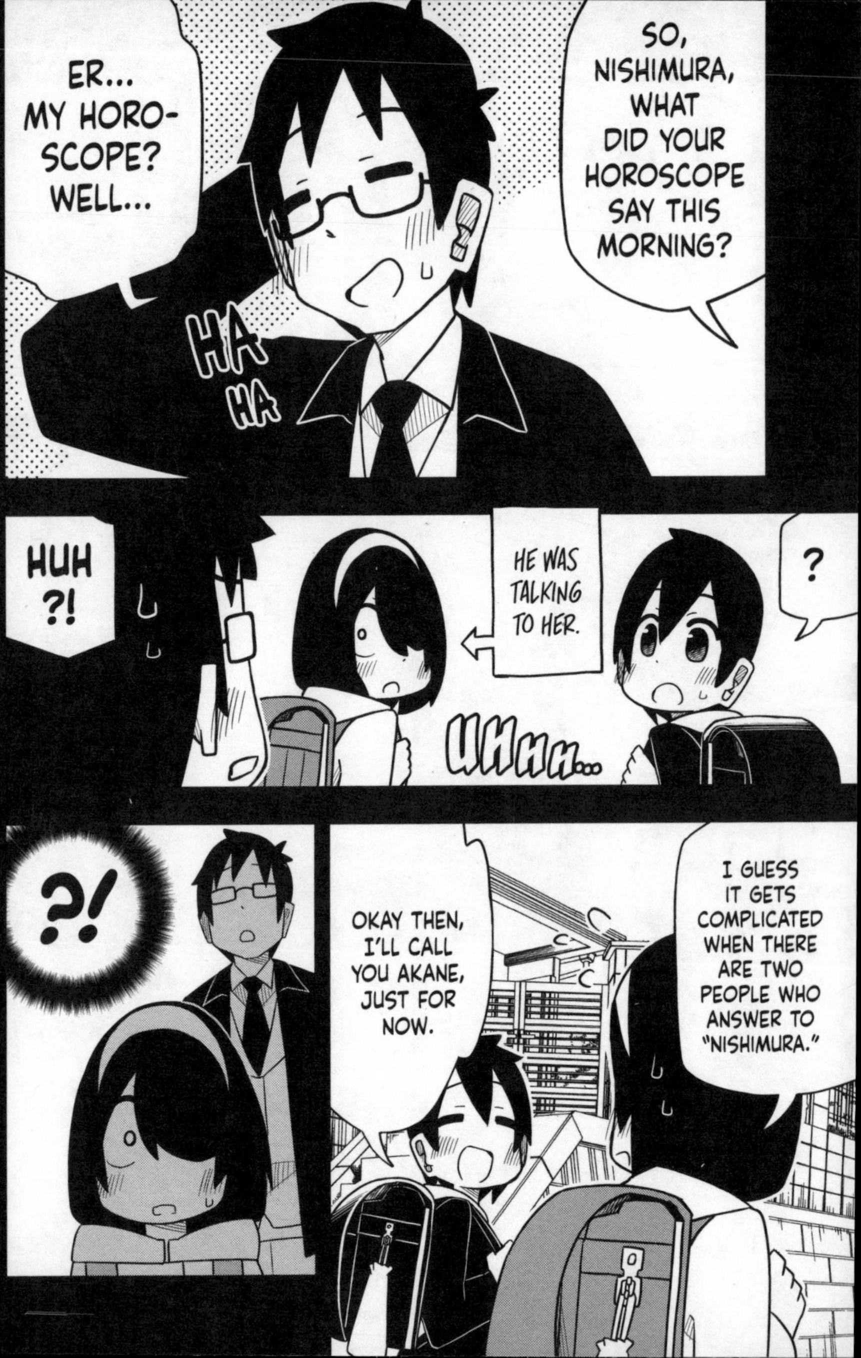
SO, NISHIMURA, WHAT DID YOUR HOROSCOPE SAY THIS MORNING?
ER... MY HORO-SCOPE? WELL...
HA HA
?
HE WAS TALKING TO HER.
UHHH...
HUH ?!
I GUESS IT GETS COMPLICATED WHEN THERE ARE TWO PEOPLE WHO ANSWER TO "NISHIMURA."
OKAY THEN, I'LL CALL YOU AKANE, JUST FOR NOW.
?!

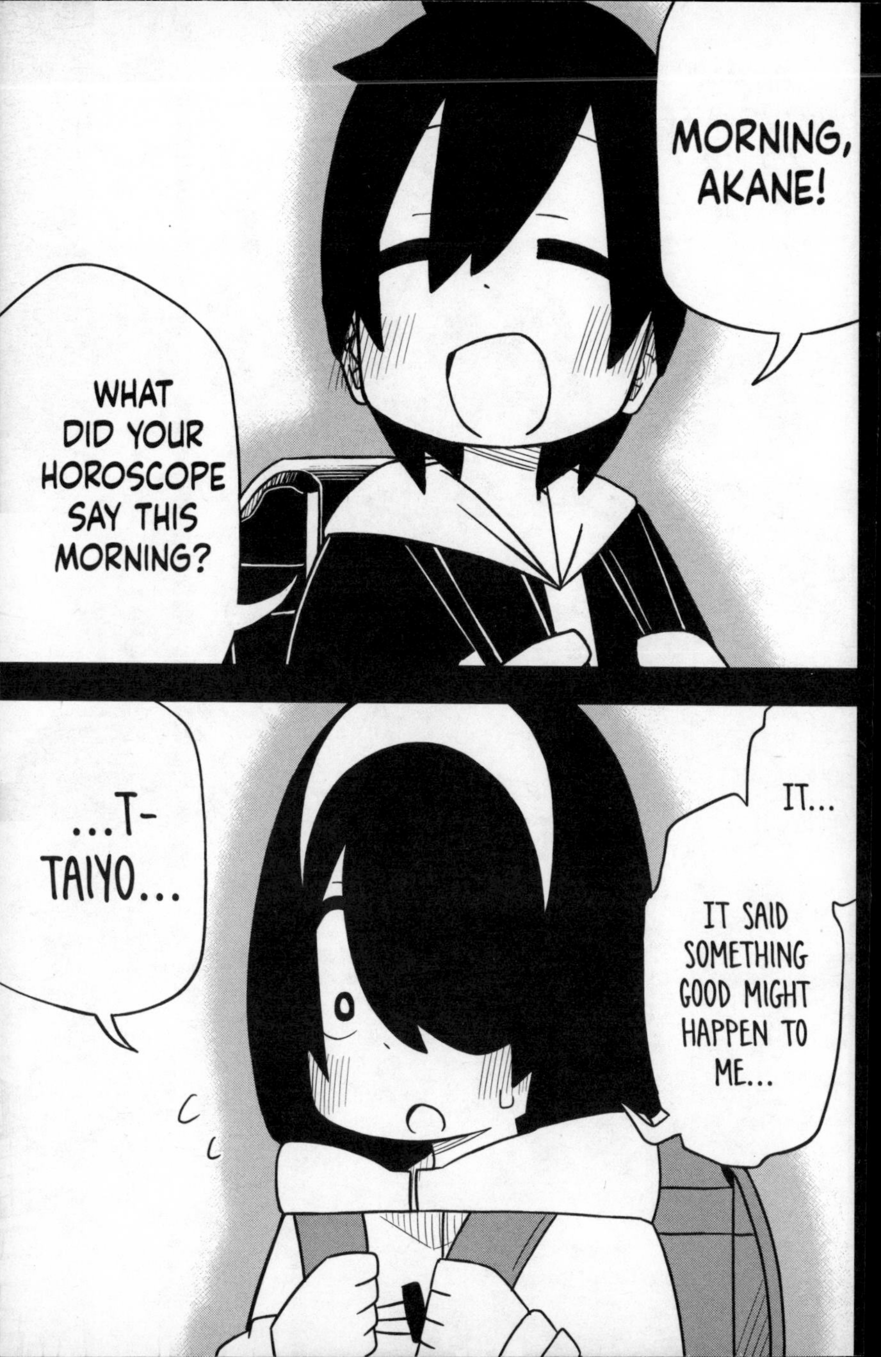
MORNING, AKANE!
WHAT DID YOUR HOROSCOPE SAY THIS MORNING?
IT...
IT SAID SOMETHING GOOD MIGHT HAPPEN TO ME...
...T-TAIYO...

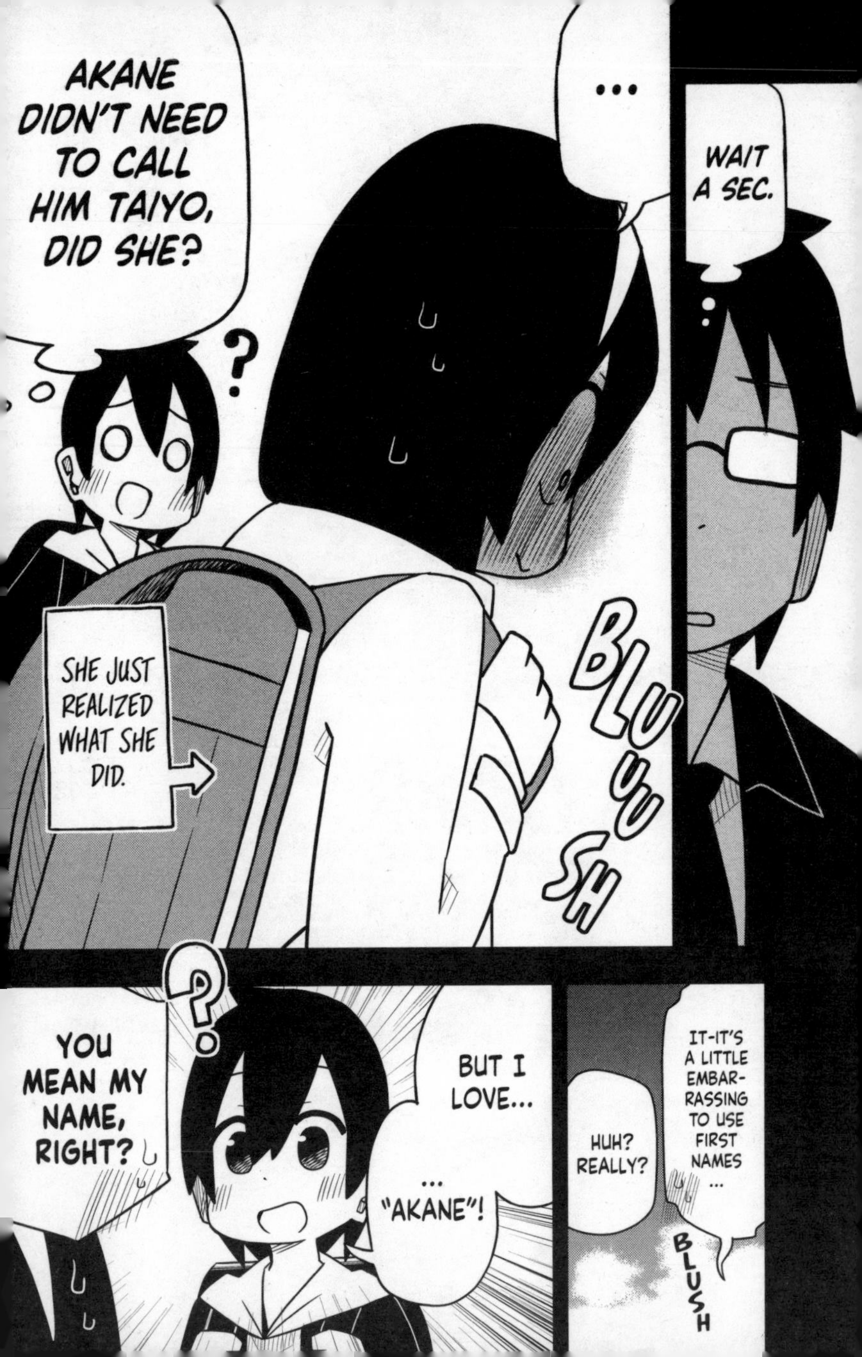
WAIT A SEC.
...
AKANE DIDN'T NEED TO CALL HIM TAIYO, DID SHE?
?
SHE JUST REALIZED WHAT SHE DID.
BLUUUSH
IT-IT'S A LITTLE EMBAR-RASSING TO USE FIRST NAMES...
HUH? REALLY?
BLUSH
BUT I LOVE...
..."AKANE"!
?
YOU MEAN MY NAME, RIGHT?

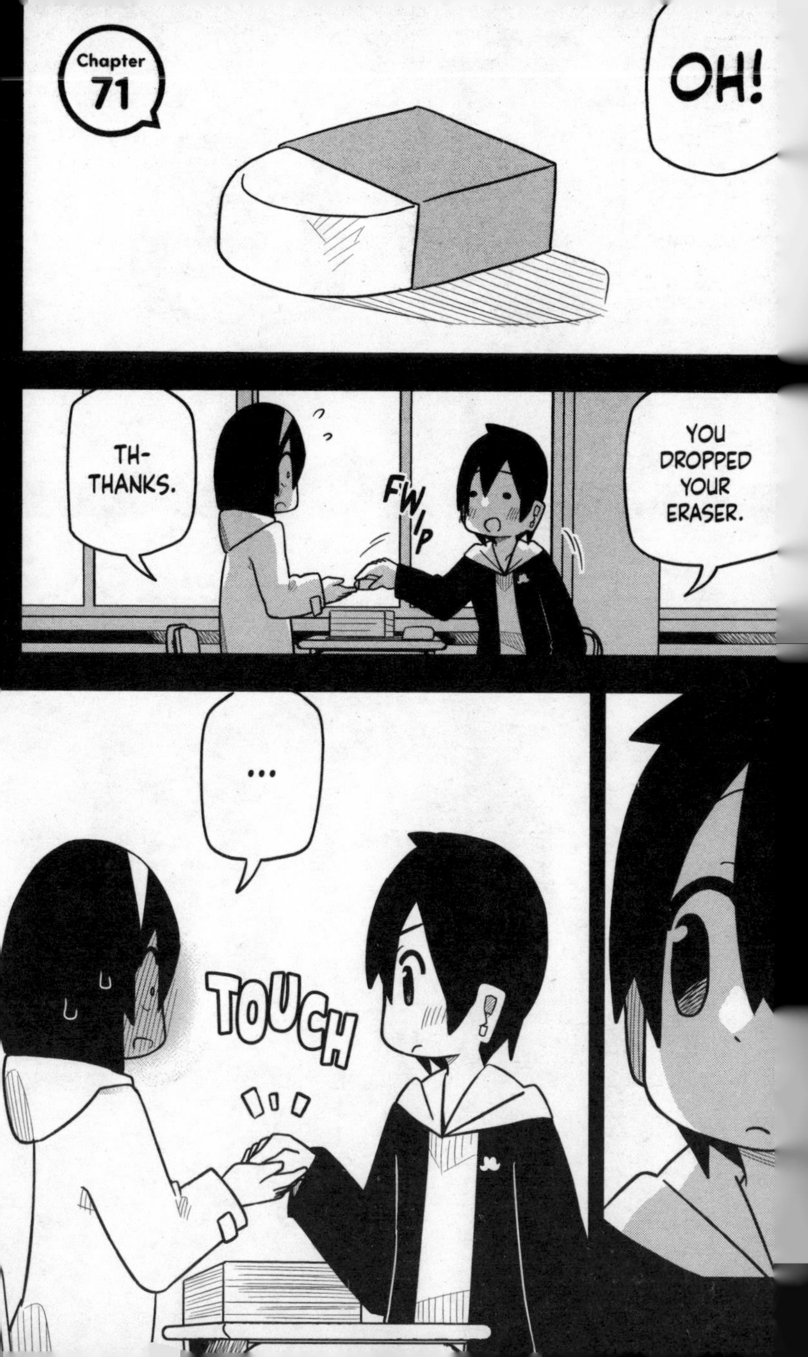
Chapter 71
OH!
YOU DROPPED YOUR ERASER.
FWIP
TH- THANKS.
TOUCH
...

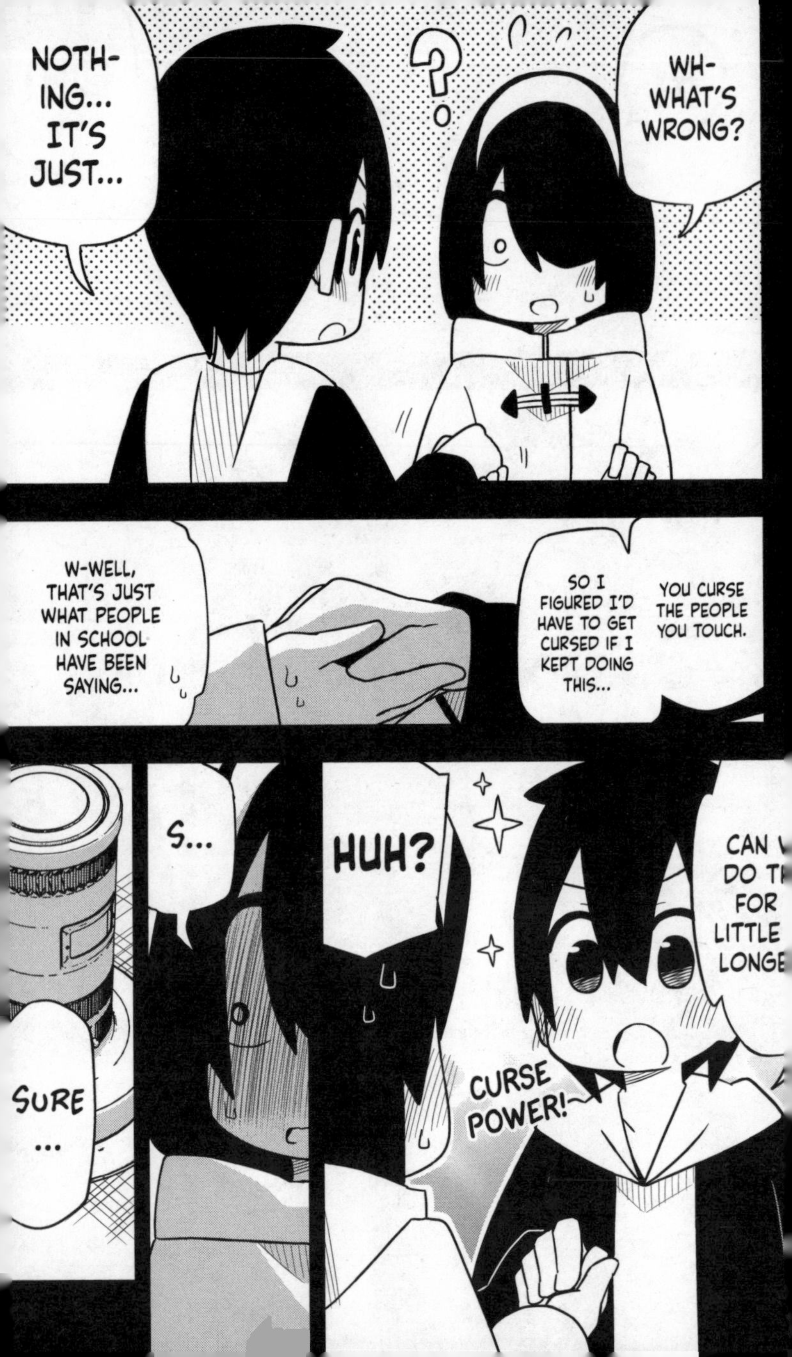
WH- WHAT'S WRONG?
NOTH- ING... IT'S JUST...
YOU CURSE THE PEOPLE YOU TOUCH.
SO I FIGURED I'D HAVE TO GET CURSED IF I KEPT DOING THIS...
W-WELL, THAT'S JUST WHAT PEOPLE IN SCHOOL HAVE BEEN SAYING...
CAN DO T FOR LITTLE LONGE
CURSE POWER!~
HUH?
S...
SURE ...

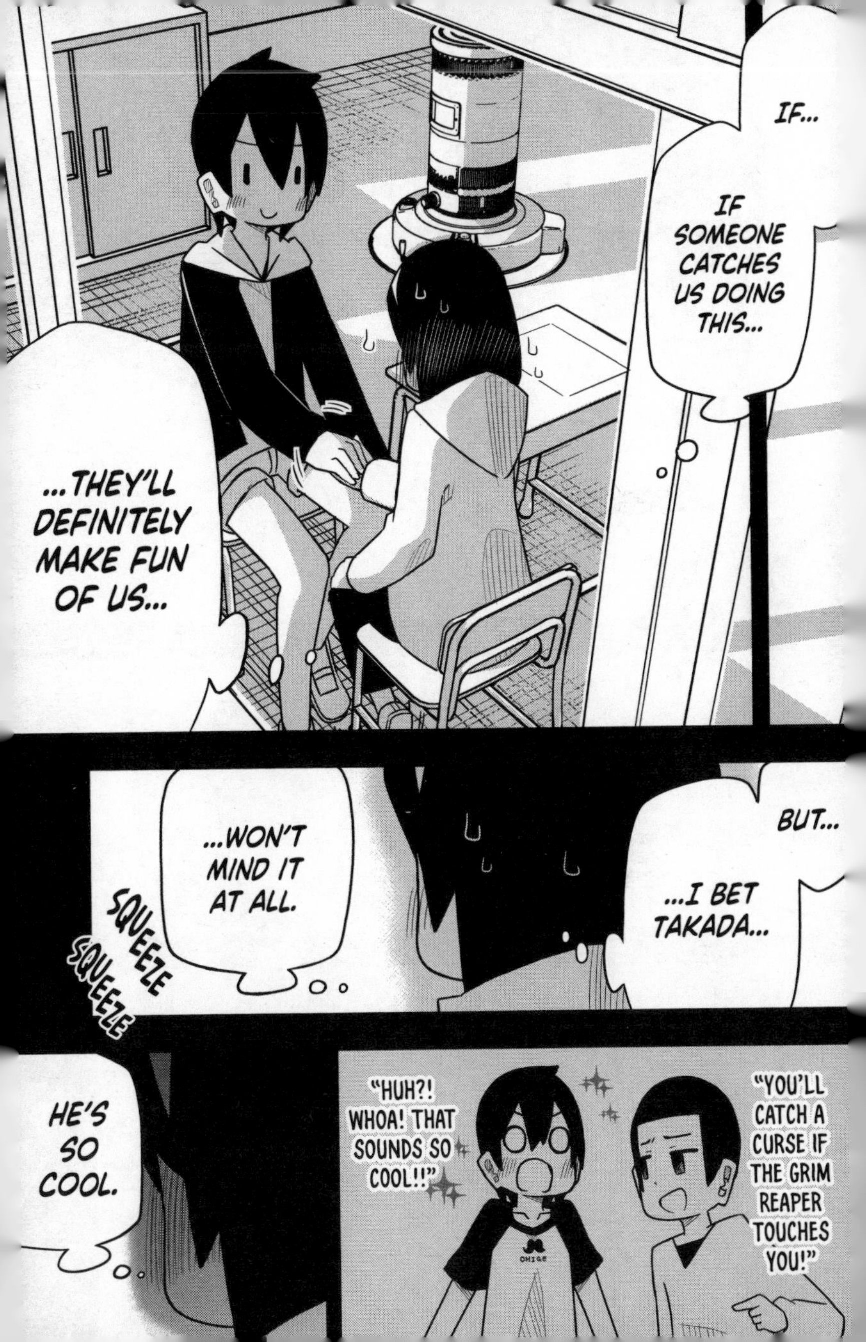
IF...
IF SOMEONE CATCHES US DOING THIS...
...THEY'LL DEFINITELY MAKE FUN OF US...
BUT...
...I BET TAKADA...
...WON'T MIND IT AT ALL.
SQUEEZE SQUEEZE
"YOU'LL CATCH A CURSE IF THE GRIM REAPER TOUCHES YOU!"
"HUH?! WHOA! THAT SOUNDS SO COOL!!"
HE'S SO COOL.

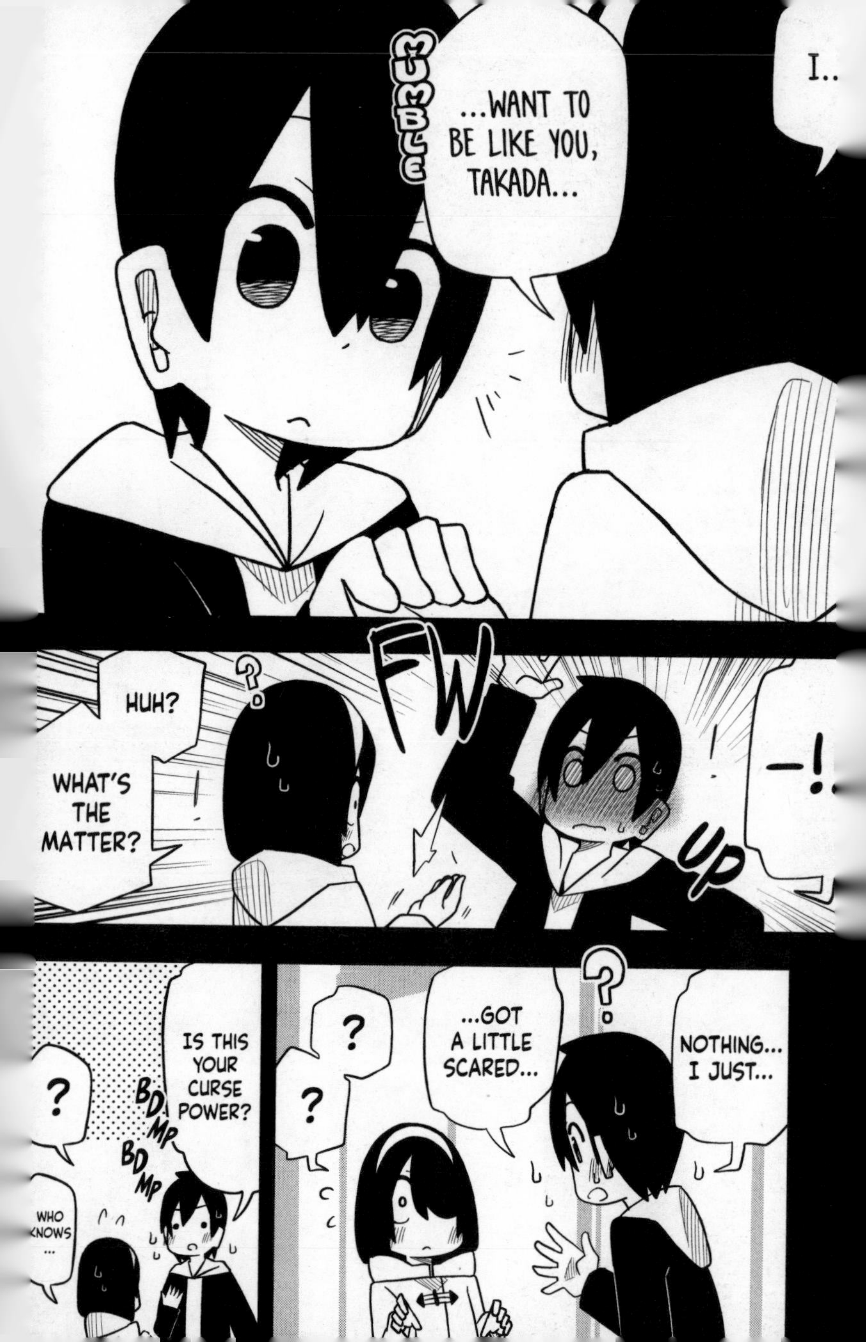
I...
MUMBLE
...WANT TO BE LIKE YOU, TAKADA...
—!
UP
FW
?
HUH?
WHAT'S THE MATTER?
NOTHING... I JUST...
?
...GOT A LITTLE SCARED...
?
?
IS THIS YOUR CURSE POWER?
BDMP
BDMP
?
WHO KNOWS...

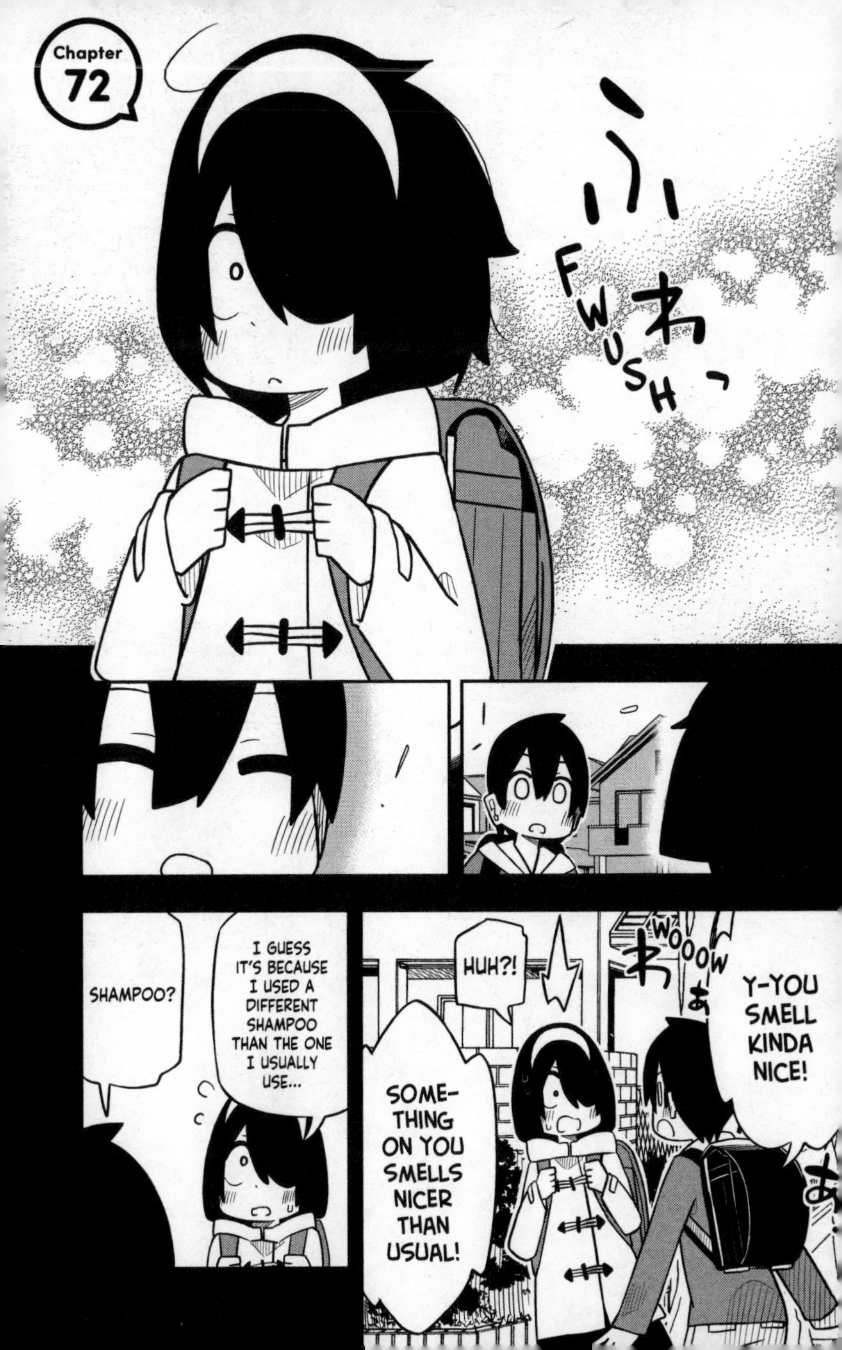
Chapter 72
ふわっ
FWUSH
WOOOW
わあ
Y-YOU SMELL KINDA NICE!
HUH?!
SOME-THING ON YOU SMELLS NICER THAN USUAL!
I GUESS IT'S BECAUSE I USED A DIFFERENT SHAMPOO THAN THE ONE I USUALLY USE...
SHAMPOO?

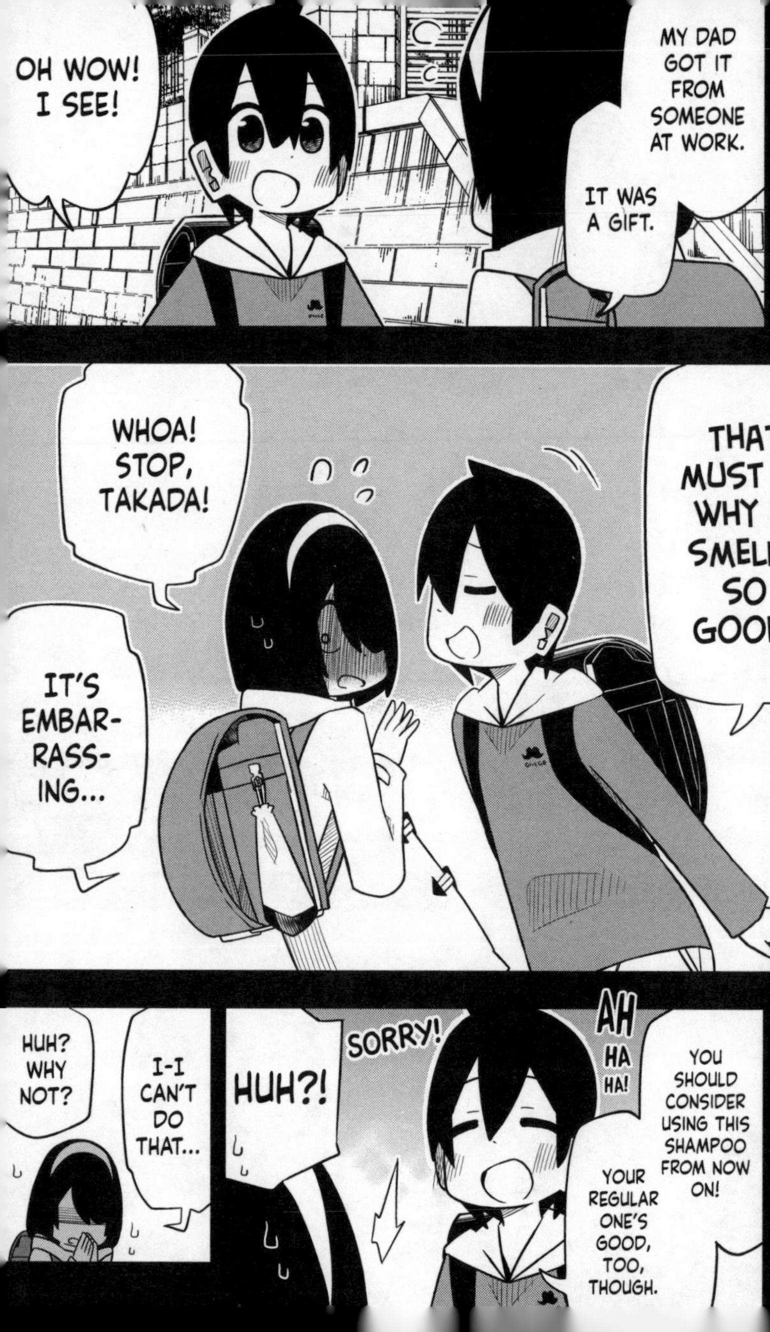
MY DAD GOT IT FROM SOMEONE AT WORK.
IT WAS A GIFT.
OH WOW! I SEE!
THAT MUST BE WHY IT SMELLS SO GOOD!
WHOA! STOP, TAKADA!
IT'S EMBARRASSING...
AH HA HA!
YOU SHOULD CONSIDER USING THIS SHAMPOO FROM NOW ON!
YOUR REGULAR ONE'S GOOD, TOO, THOUGH.
SORRY!
HUH?!
I-I CAN'T DO THAT...
HUH? WHY NOT?

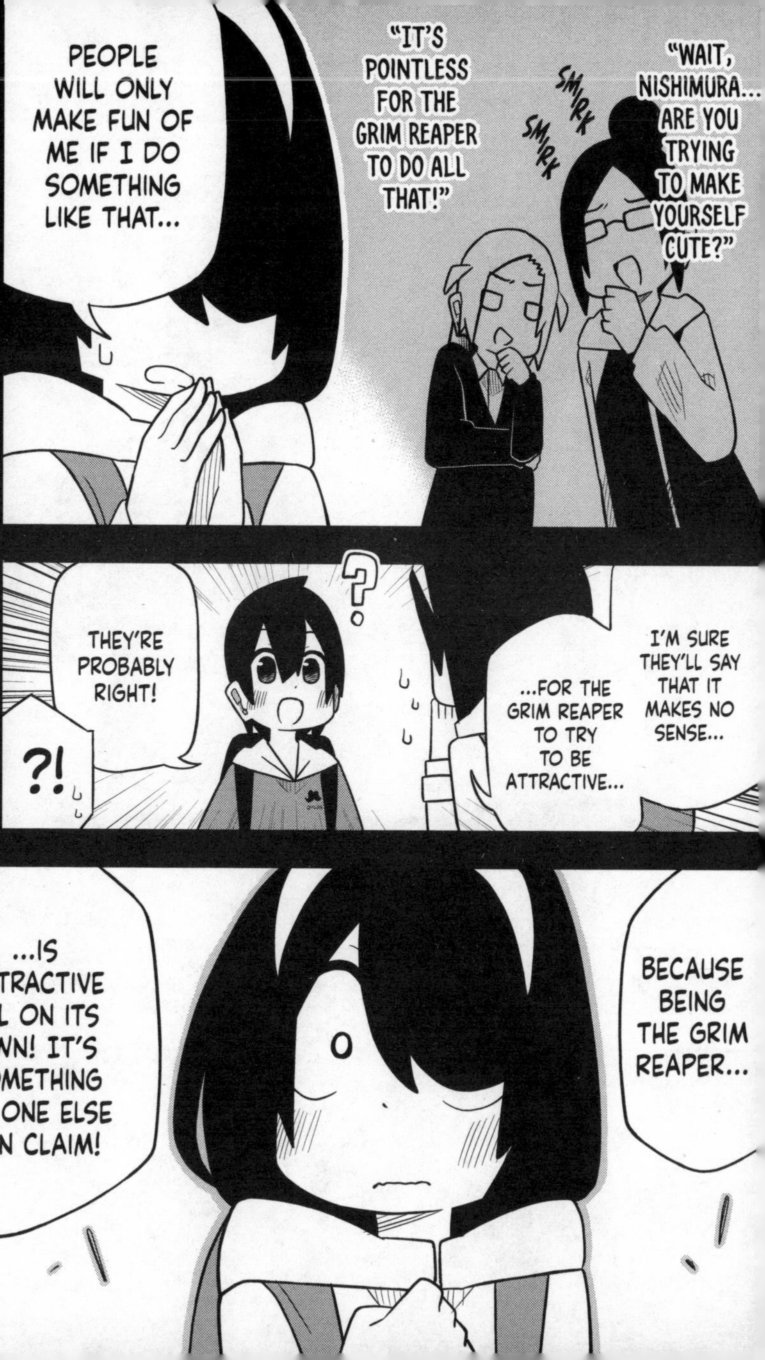
"WAIT, NISHIMURA... ARE YOU TRYING TO MAKE YOURSELF CUTE?"
SMIRK
SMIRK
"IT'S POINTLESS FOR THE GRIM REAPER TO DO ALL THAT!"
PEOPLE WILL ONLY MAKE FUN OF ME IF I DO SOMETHING LIKE THAT...
I'M SURE THEY'LL SAY THAT IT MAKES NO SENSE...
...FOR THE GRIM REAPER TO TRY TO BE ATTRACTIVE...
?
THEY'RE PROBABLY RIGHT!
?!
BECAUSE BEING THE GRIM REAPER...
...IS ATTRACTIVE ALL ON ITS OWN! IT'S SOMETHING NO ONE ELSE CAN CLAIM!

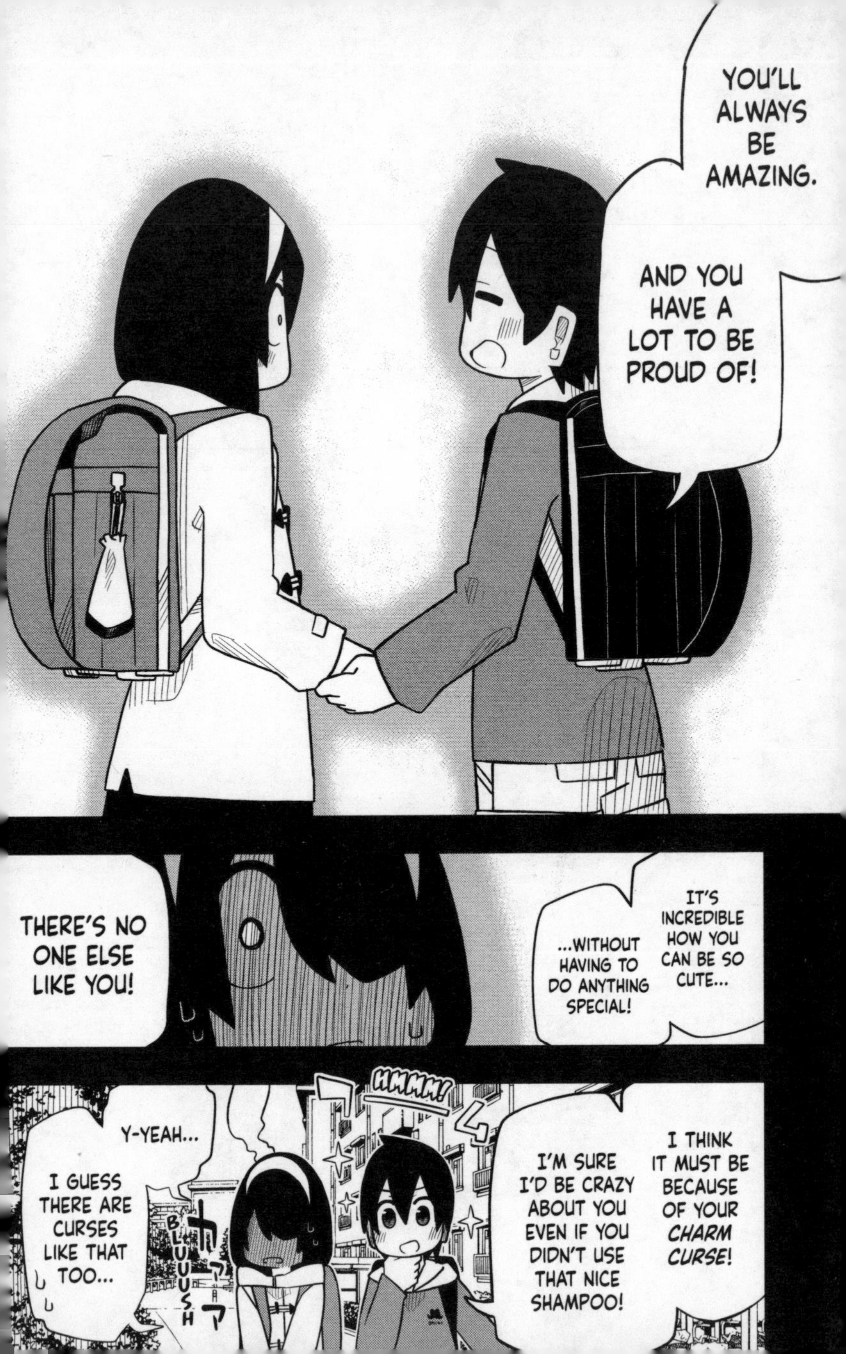
YOU'LL ALWAYS BE AMAZING.
AND YOU HAVE A LOT TO BE PROUD OF!
IT'S INCREDIBLE HOW YOU CAN BE SO CUTE...
...WITHOUT HAVING TO DO ANYTHING SPECIAL!
THERE'S NO ONE ELSE LIKE YOU!
I THINK IT MUST BE BECAUSE OF YOUR *CHARM CURSE*!
I'M SURE I'D BE CRAZY ABOUT YOU EVEN IF YOU DIDN'T USE THAT NICE SHAMPOO!
HMMM!
BLUUUSH
Y-YEAH...
I GUESS THERE ARE CURSES LIKE THAT TOO...

MY CLUELESS FIRST FRIEND

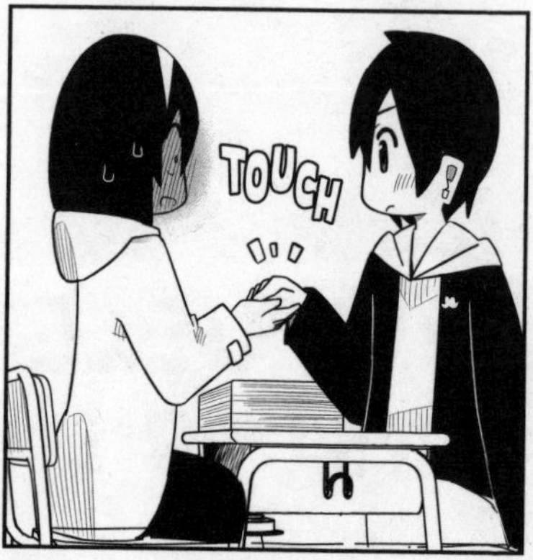
TOUCH

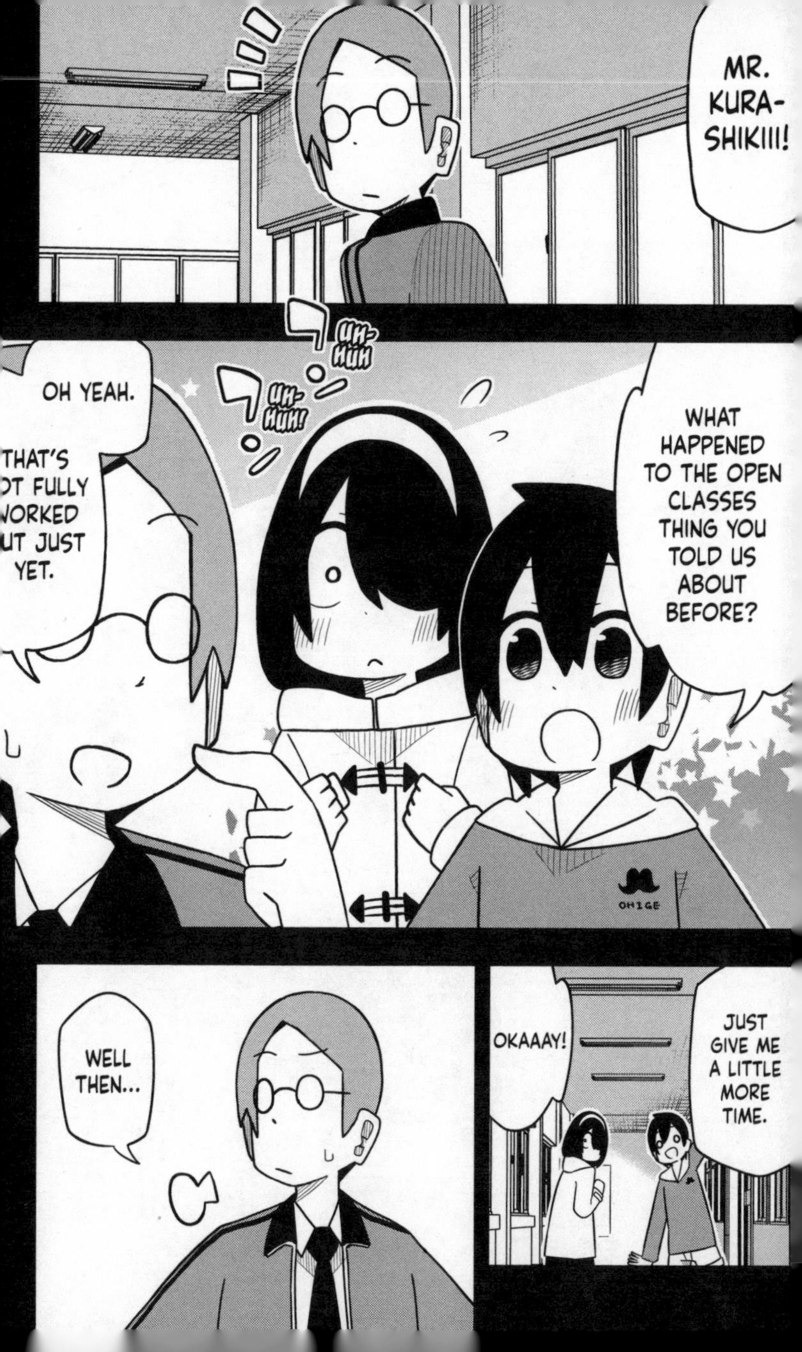
MR. KURA-SHIKIIII!
WHAT HAPPENED TO THE OPEN CLASSES THING YOU TOLD US ABOUT BEFORE?
UH-HUH
UH-HUH!
OH YEAH.
THAT'S OT FULLY ORKED UT JUST YET.
OHIGE
JUST GIVE ME A LITTLE MORE TIME.
OKAAAY!
WELL THEN...

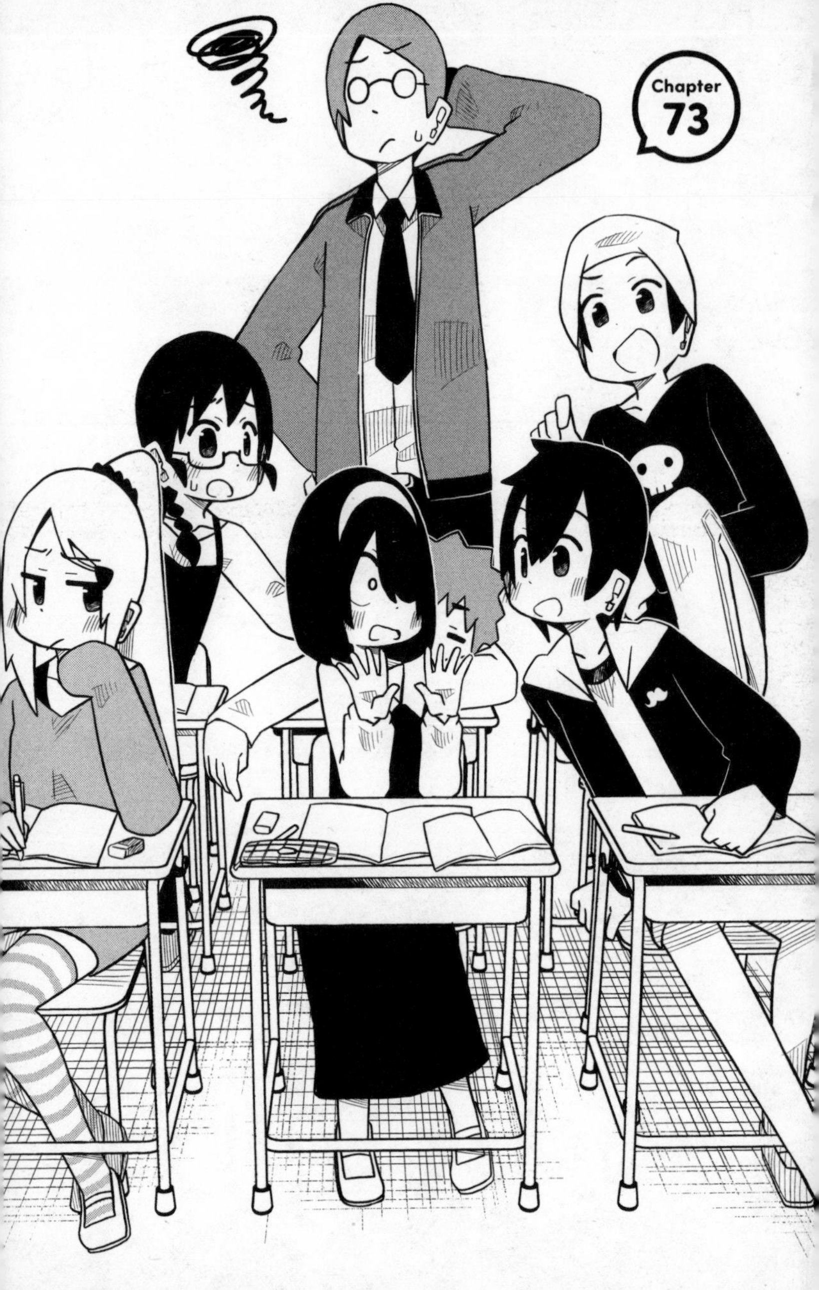
Chapter
73

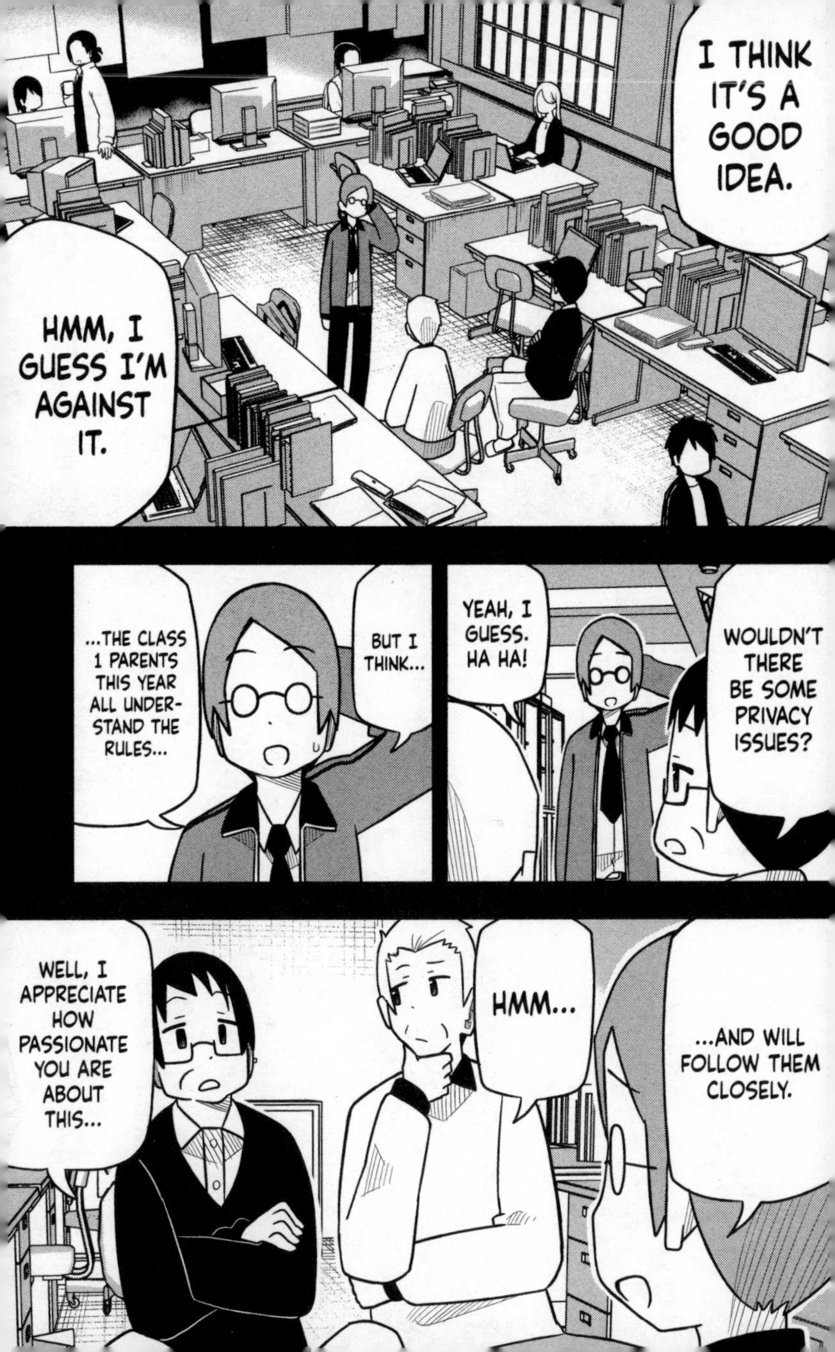
I THINK IT'S A GOOD IDEA.
HMM, I GUESS I'M AGAINST IT.
WOULDN'T THERE BE SOME PRIVACY ISSUES?
YEAH, I GUESS. HA HA!
BUT I THINK...
...THE CLASS 1 PARENTS THIS YEAR ALL UNDER-STAND THE RULES...
...AND WILL FOLLOW THEM CLOSELY.
HMM...
WELL, I APPRECIATE HOW PASSIONATE YOU ARE ABOUT THIS...

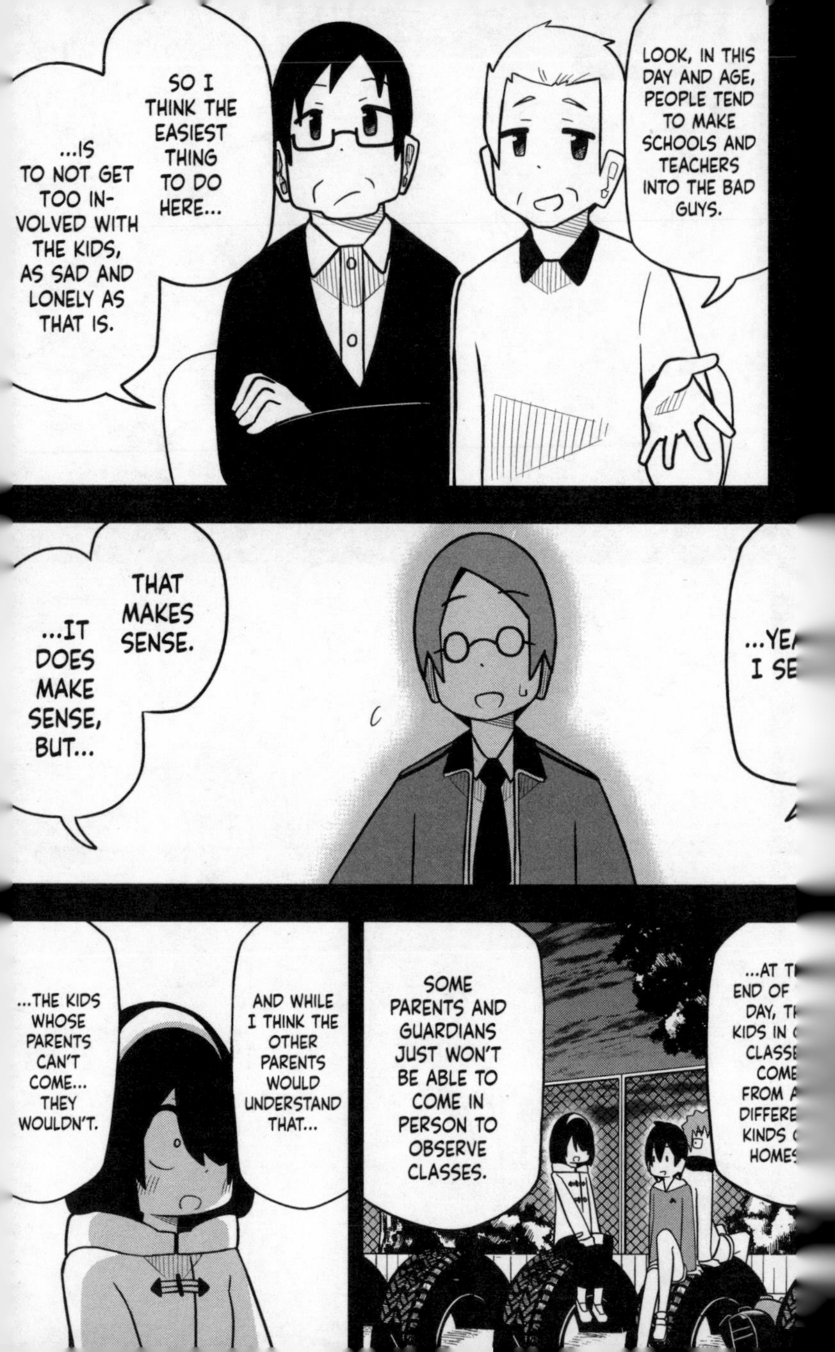
LOOK, IN THIS DAY AND AGE, PEOPLE TEND TO MAKE SCHOOLS AND TEACHERS INTO THE BAD GUYS.
SO I THINK THE EASIEST THING TO DO HERE...
...IS TO NOT GET TOO IN-VOLVED WITH THE KIDS, AS SAD AND LONELY AS THAT IS.
THAT MAKES SENSE.
...IT DOES MAKE SENSE, BUT...
SOME PARENTS AND GUARDIANS JUST WON'T BE ABLE TO COME IN PERSON TO OBSERVE CLASSES.
AND WHILE I THINK THE OTHER PARENTS WOULD UNDERSTAND THAT...
...THE KIDS WHOSE PARENTS CAN'T COME... THEY WOULDN'T.

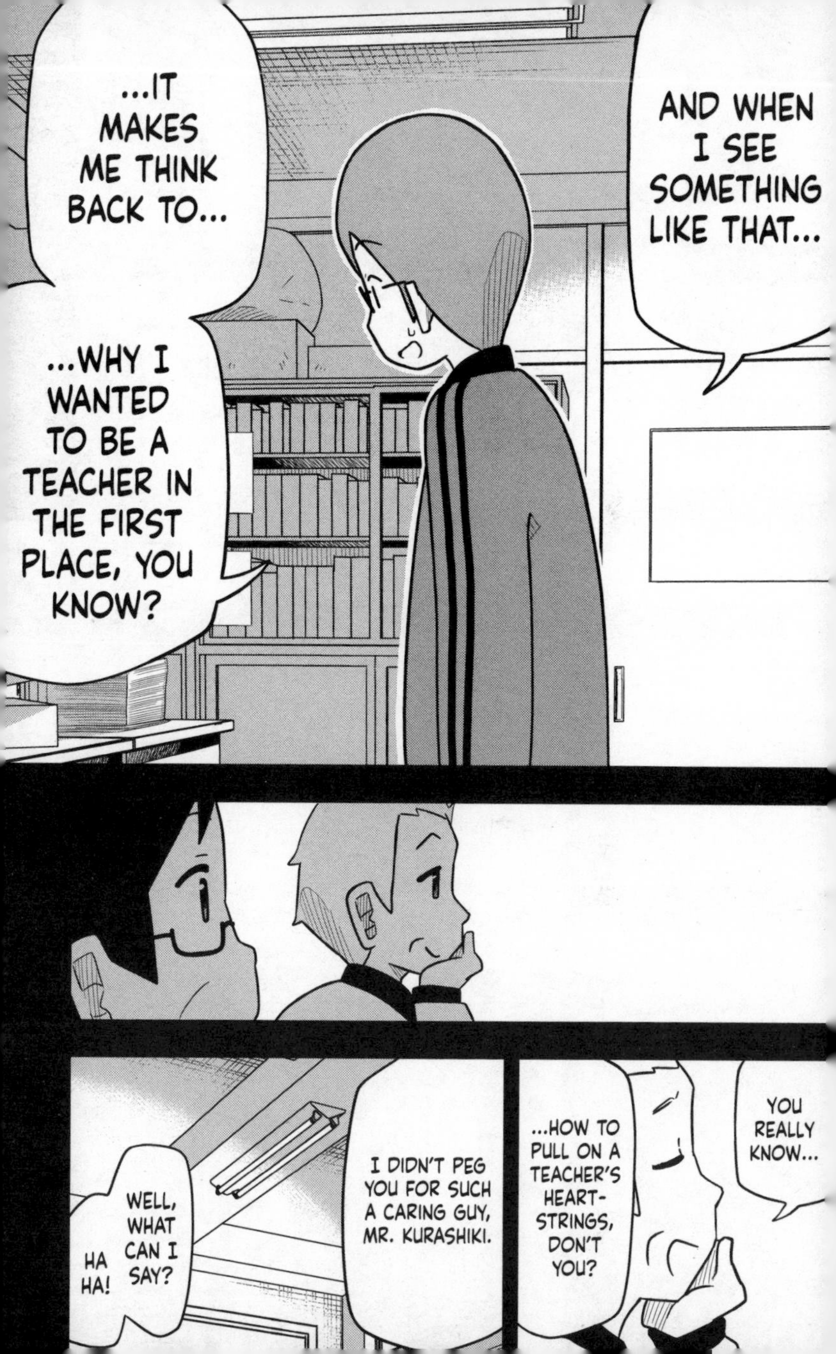
AND WHEN I SEE SOMETHING LIKE THAT...
...IT MAKES ME THINK BACK TO...
...WHY I WANTED TO BE A TEACHER IN THE FIRST PLACE, YOU KNOW?
YOU REALLY KNOW...
...HOW TO PULL ON A TEACHER'S HEART-STRINGS, DON'T YOU?
I DIDN'T PEG YOU FOR SUCH A CARING GUY, MR. KURASHIKI.
WELL, WHAT CAN I SAY?
HA HA!

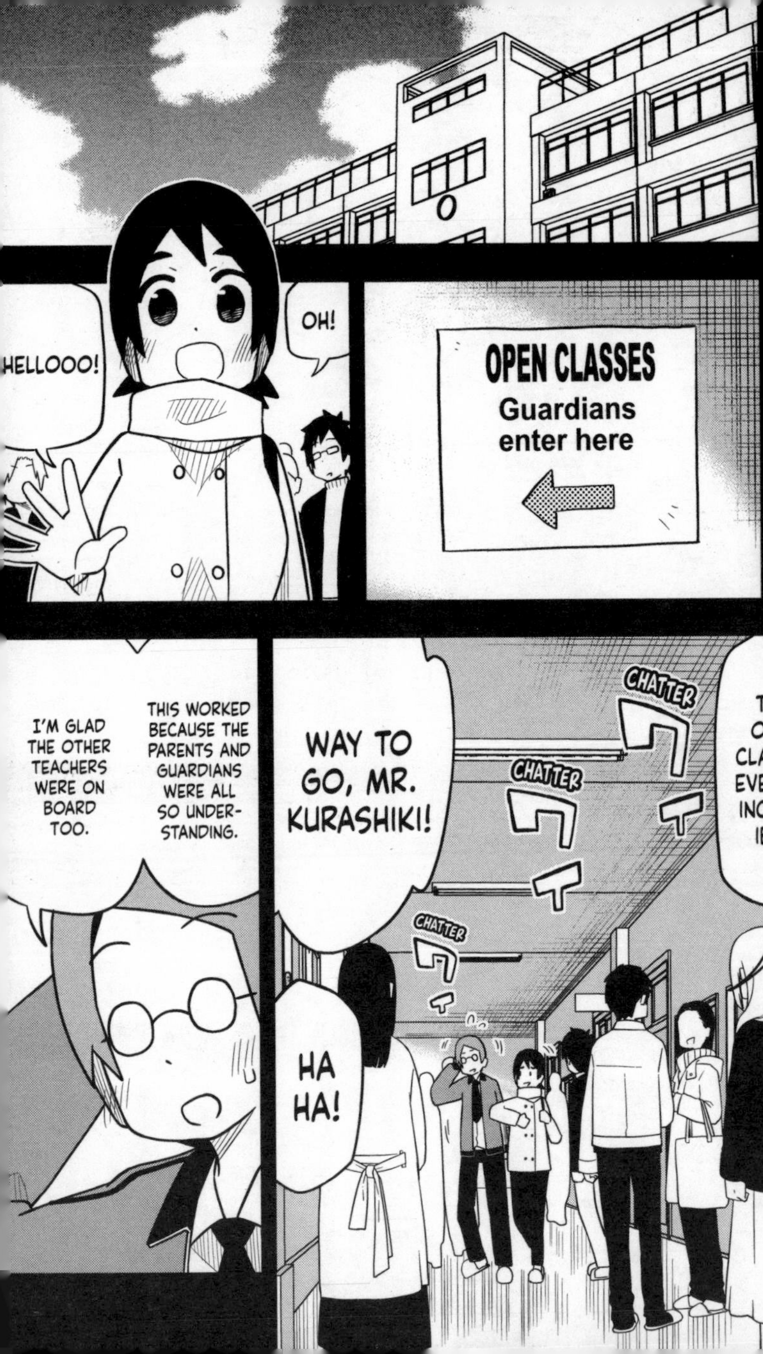
OPEN CLASSES
Guardians enter here
OH!
HELLOOO!
THIS OPEN CLASSES EVENT IS INCRED-IBLE!
CHATTER
CHATTER
CHATTER
WAY TO GO, MR. KURASHIKI!
HA HA!
THIS WORKED BECAUSE THE PARENTS AND GUARDIANS WERE ALL SO UNDER-STANDING.
I'M GLAD THE OTHER TEACHERS WERE ON BOARD TOO.

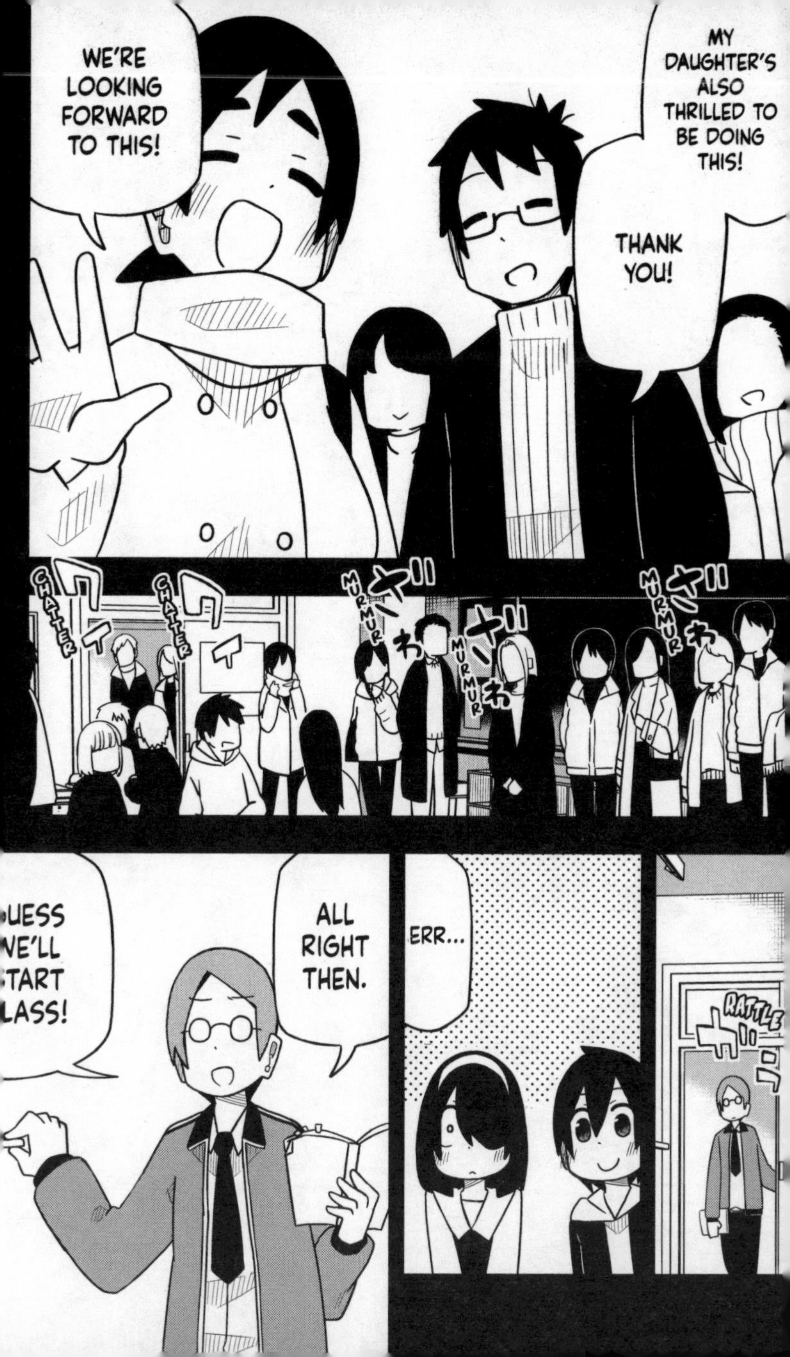
MY DAUGHTER'S ALSO THRILLED TO BE DOING THIS!
THANK YOU!
WE'RE LOOKING FORWARD TO THIS!
MURMUR
MURMUR
MURMUR
CHATTER
CHATTER
RATTLE
ERR...
ALL RIGHT THEN.
UESS E'LL TART LASS!

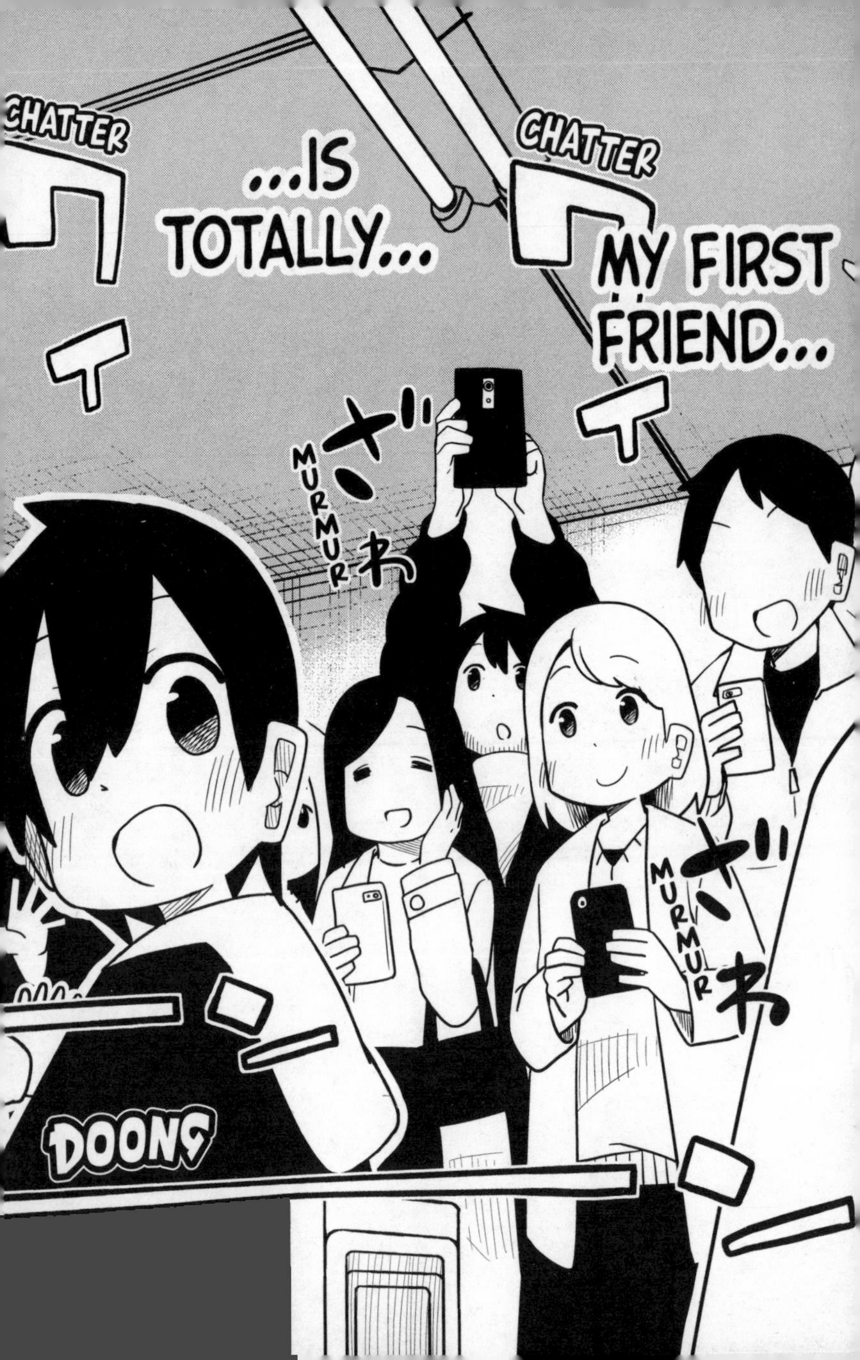
CHATTER
MY FIRST FRIEND...
...IS TOTALLY...
CHATTER
MURMUR
MURMUR
DOONG

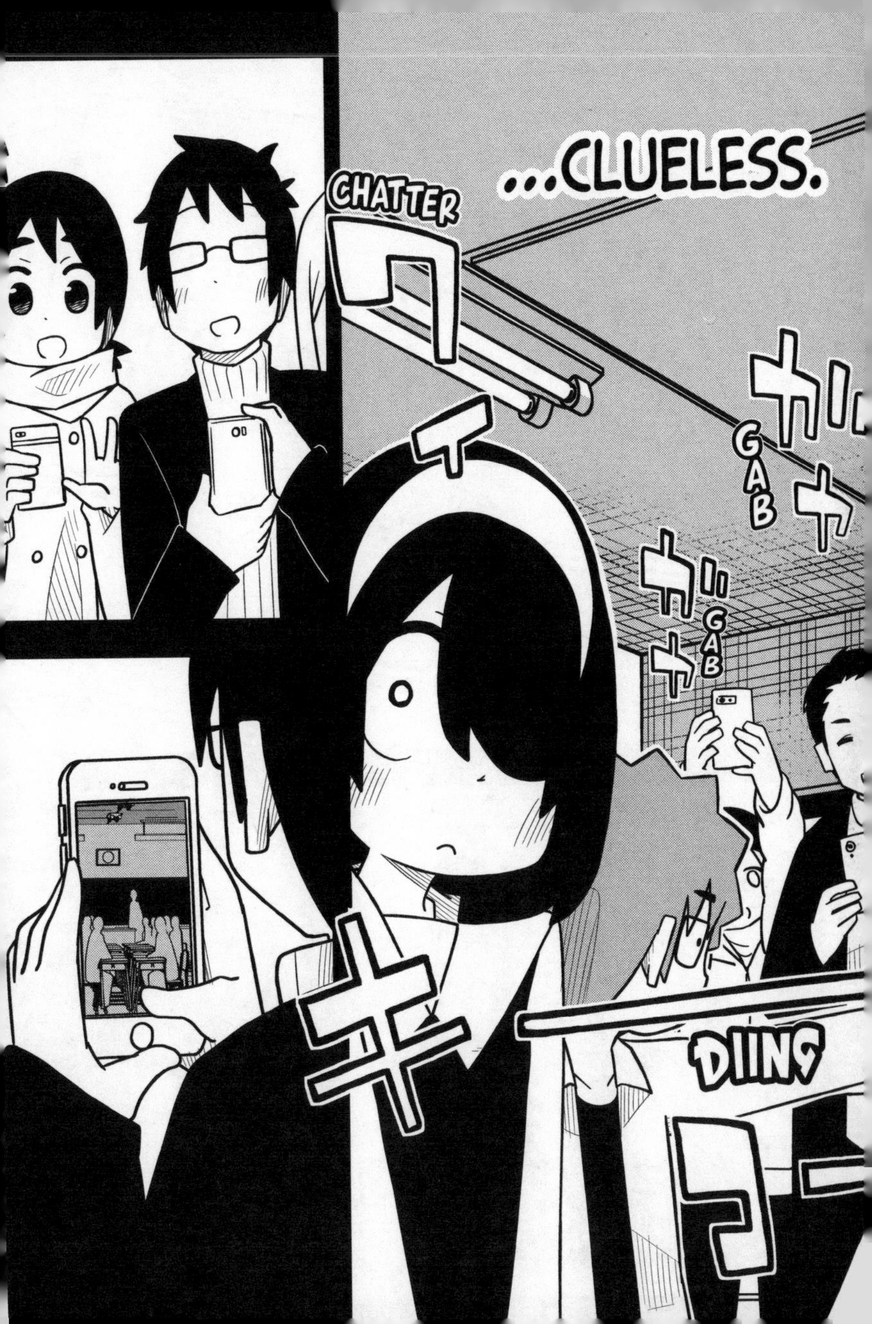
...CLUELESS.
GAB
GAB
DIING
CHATTER

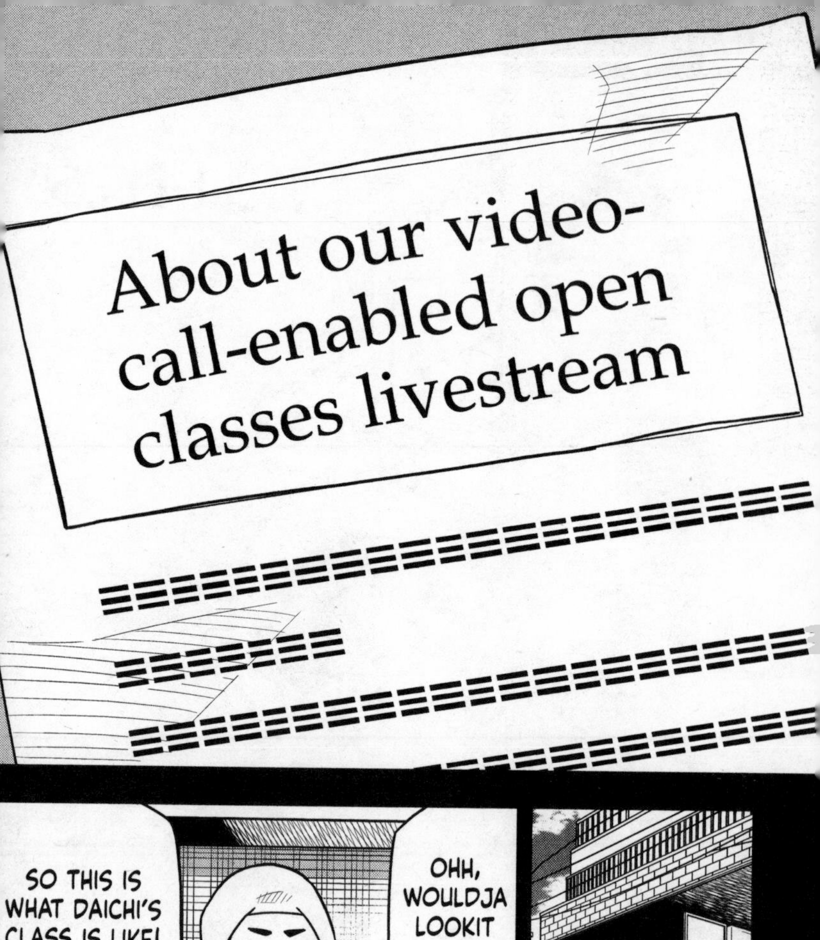
About our video-call-enabled open classes livestream
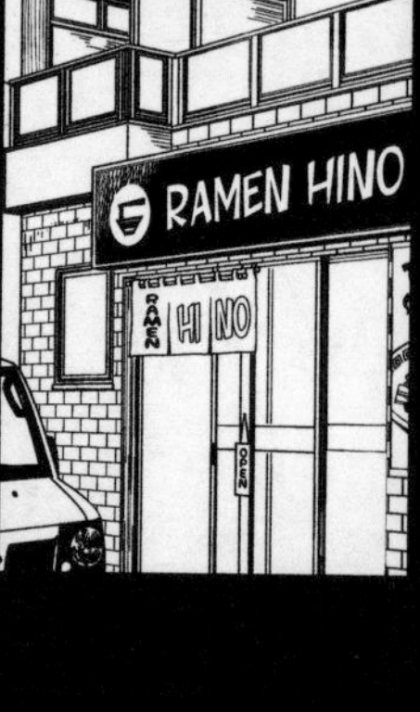
RAMEN HINO
RAMEN
HI NO
OPEN
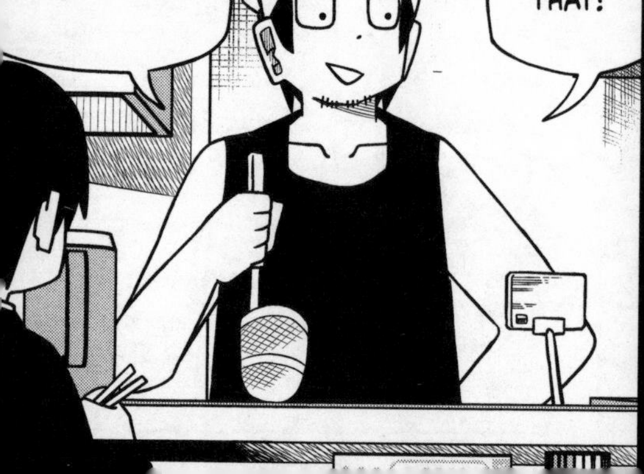
OHH, WOULDJA LOOKIT THAT!
SO THIS IS WHAT DAICHI'S CLASS IS LIKE!

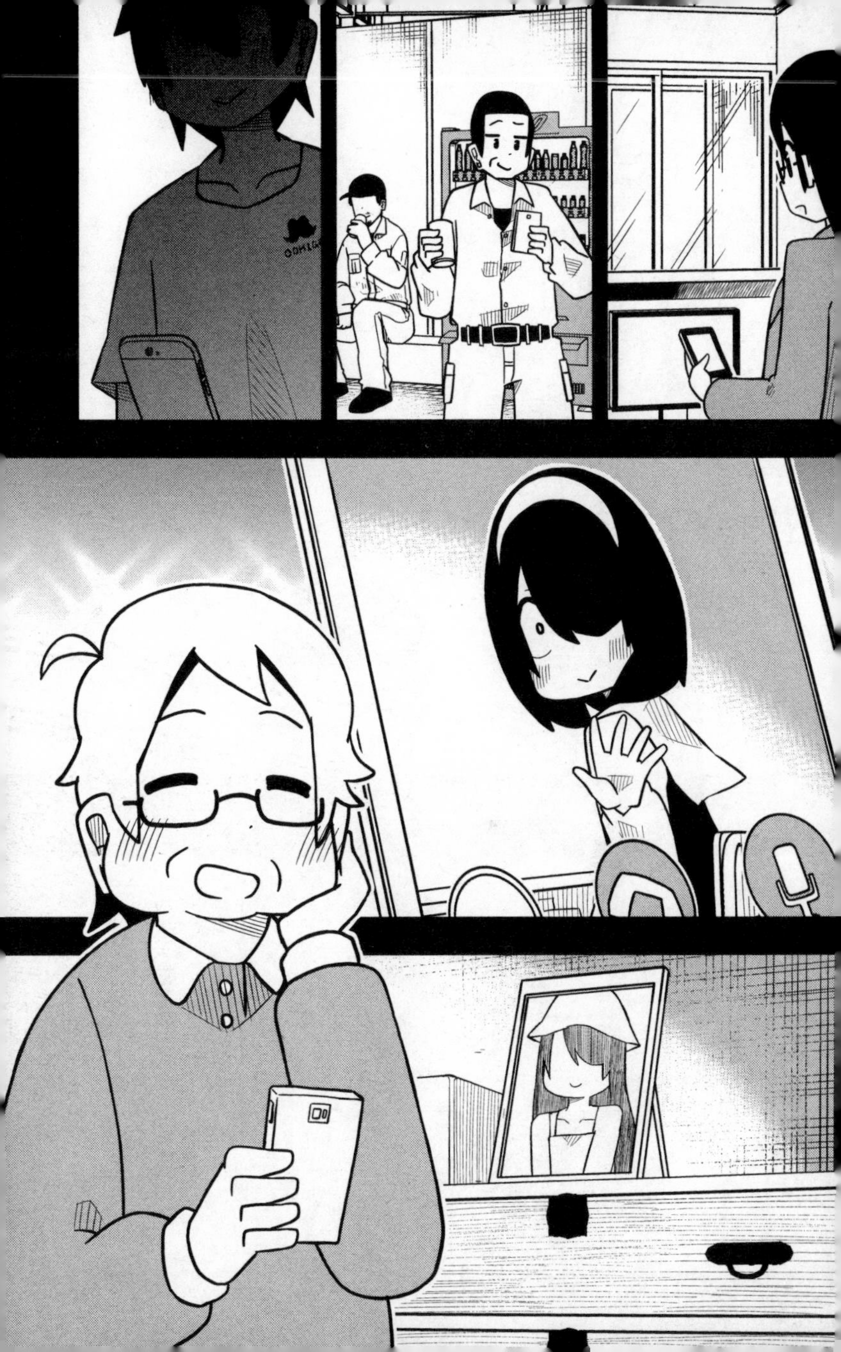

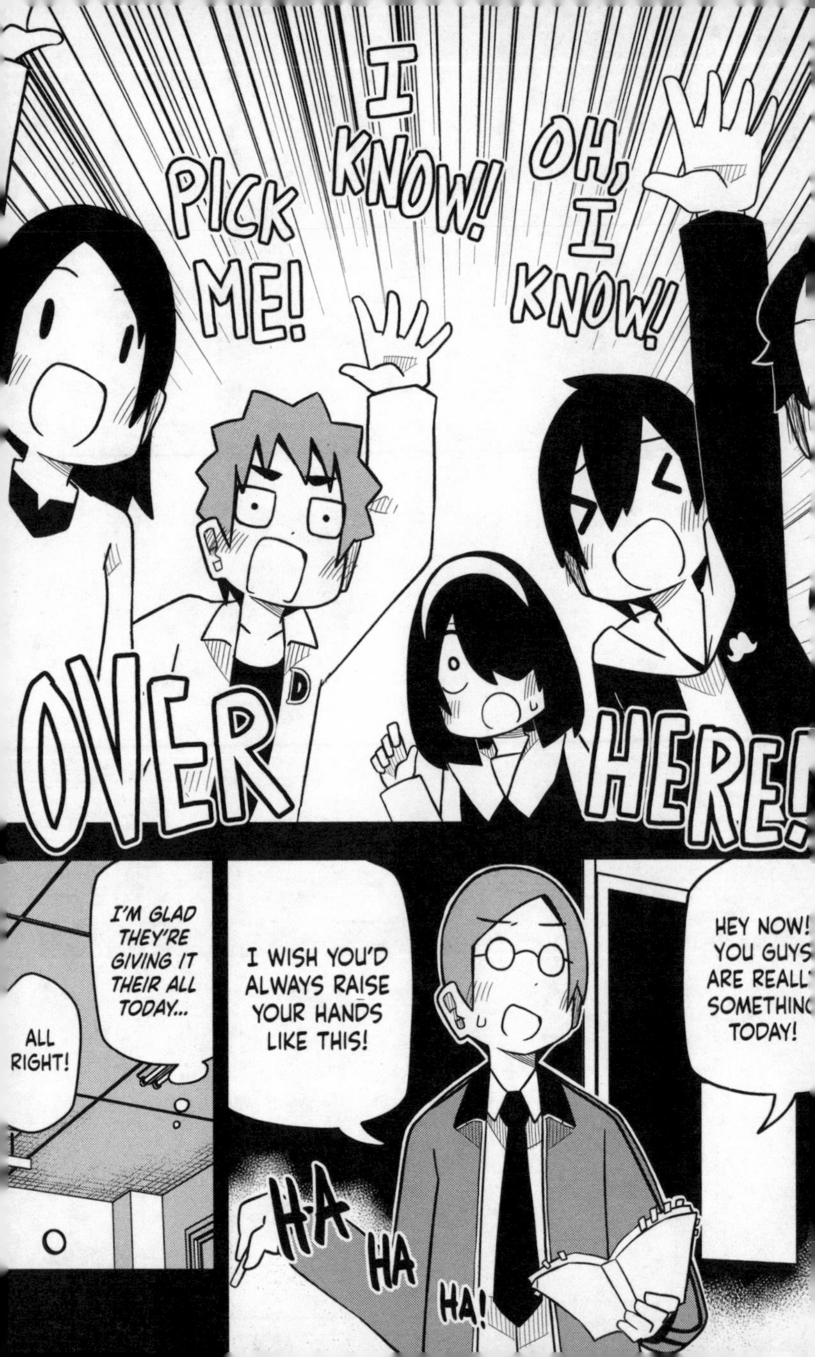
OH, I KNOW!
I KNOW!
PICK ME!
OVER HERE!
HEY NOW! YOU GUYS ARE REALLY SOMETHING TODAY!
I WISH YOU'D ALWAYS RAISE YOUR HANDS LIKE THIS!
HA HA HA!
I'M GLAD THEY'RE GIVING IT THEIR ALL TODAY...
ALL RIGHT!

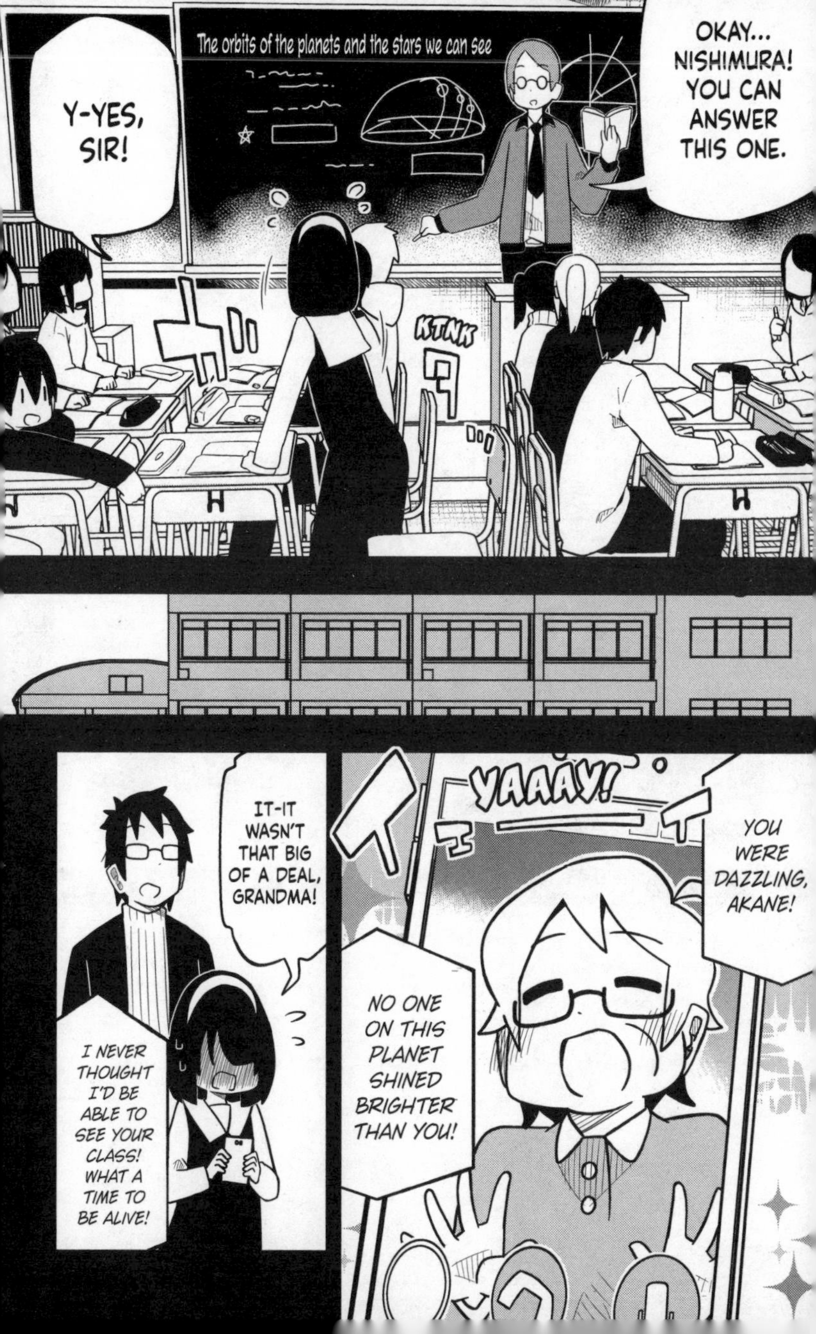
OKAY... NISHIMURA! YOU CAN ANSWER THIS ONE.
The orbits of the planets and the stars we can see
Y-YES, SIR!
KTNK
YAAAY!
YOU WERE DAZZLING, AKANE!
NO ONE ON THIS PLANET SHINED BRIGHTER THAN YOU!
IT-IT WASN'T THAT BIG OF A DEAL, GRANDMA!
I NEVER THOUGHT I'D BE ABLE TO SEE YOUR CLASS! WHAT A TIME TO BE ALIVE!

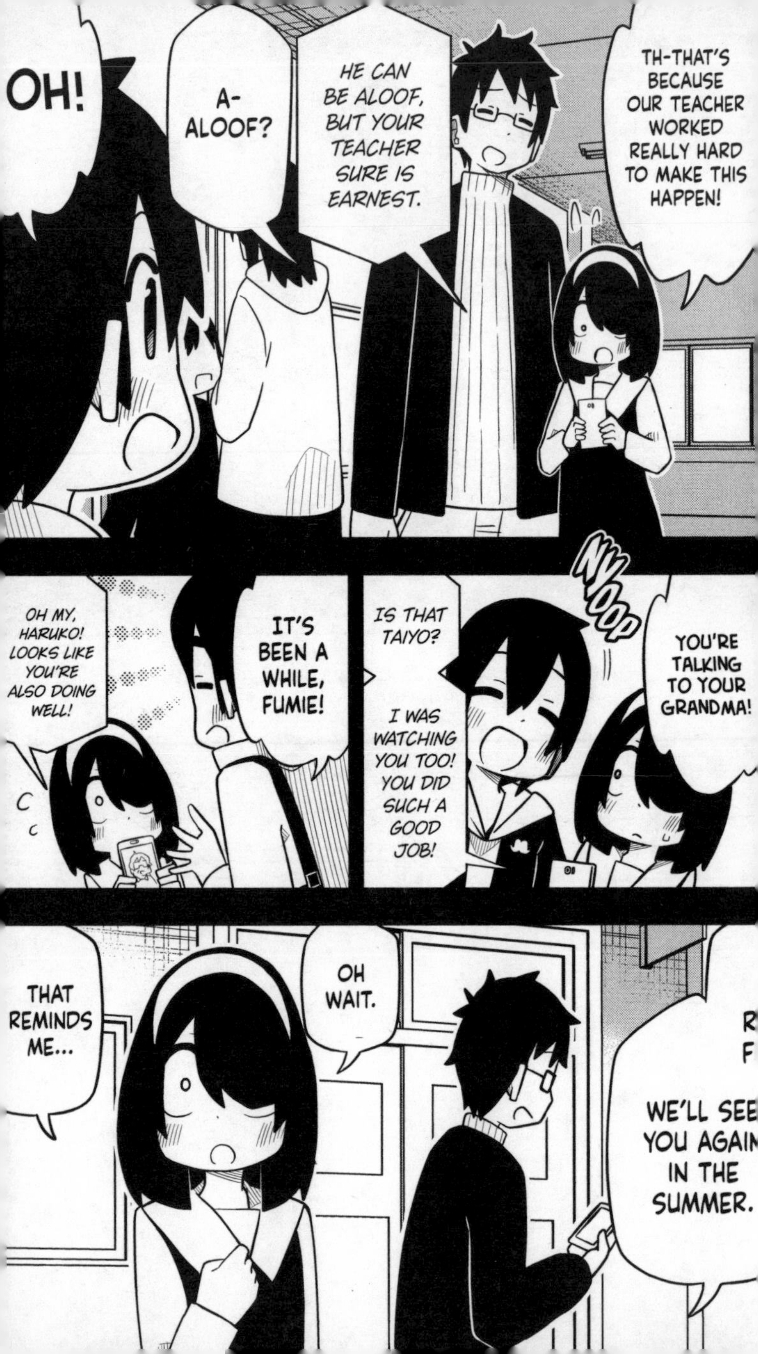
TH-THAT'S BECAUSE OUR TEACHER WORKED REALLY HARD TO MAKE THIS HAPPEN!
HE CAN BE ALOOF, BUT YOUR TEACHER SURE IS EARNEST.
A-ALOOF?
OH!
NYOOP
YOU'RE TALKING TO YOUR GRANDMA!
IS THAT TAIYO?
I WAS WATCHING YOU TOO! YOU DID SUCH A GOOD JOB!
IT'S BEEN A WHILE, FUMIE!
OH MY, HARUKO! LOOKS LIKE YOU'RE ALSO DOING WELL!
WE'LL SEE YOU AGAIN IN THE SUMMER.
OH WAIT.
THAT REMINDS ME...

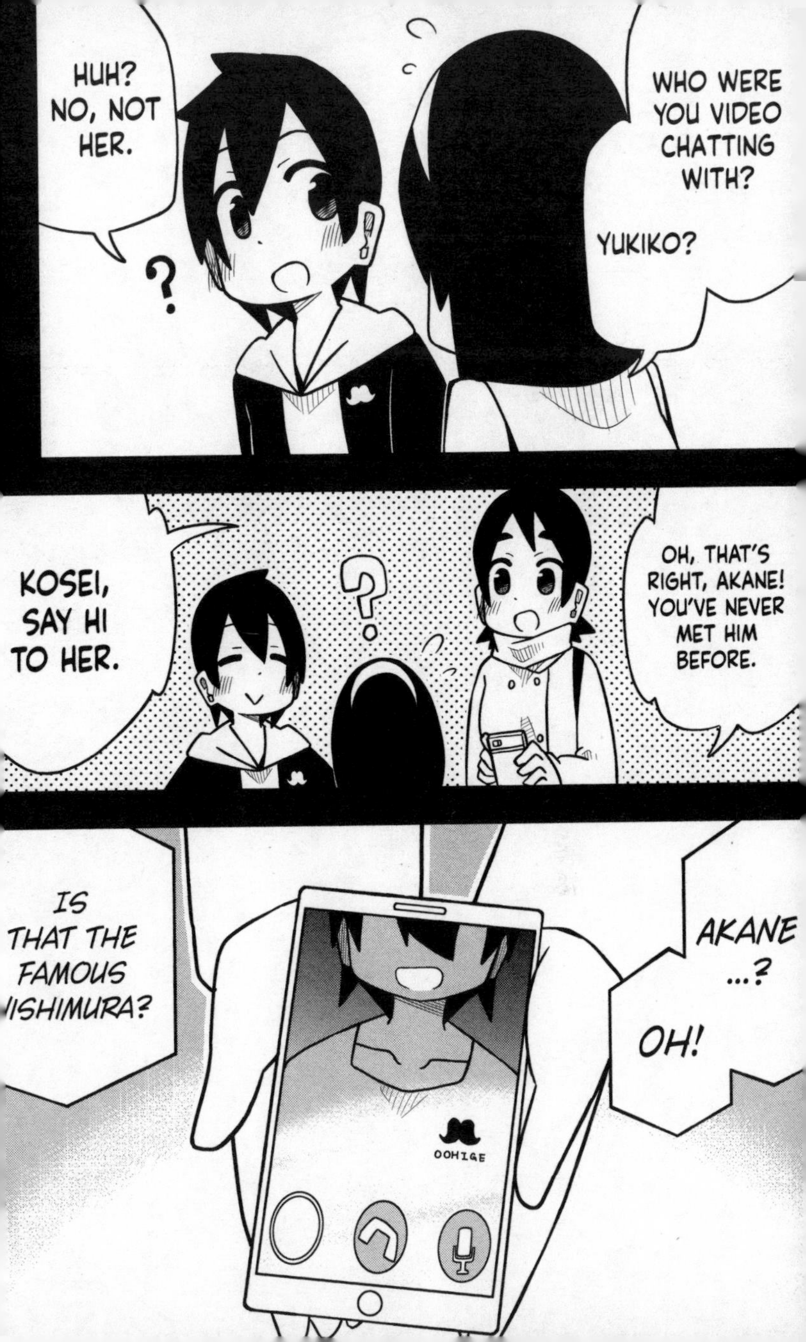
WHO WERE YOU VIDEO CHATTING WITH?
YUKIKO?
HUH? NO, NOT HER.
OH, THAT'S RIGHT, AKANE! YOU'VE NEVER MET HIM BEFORE.
KOSEI, SAY HI TO HER.
AKANE ...?
OH!
OOHIGE
IS THAT THE FAMOUS ISHIMURA?

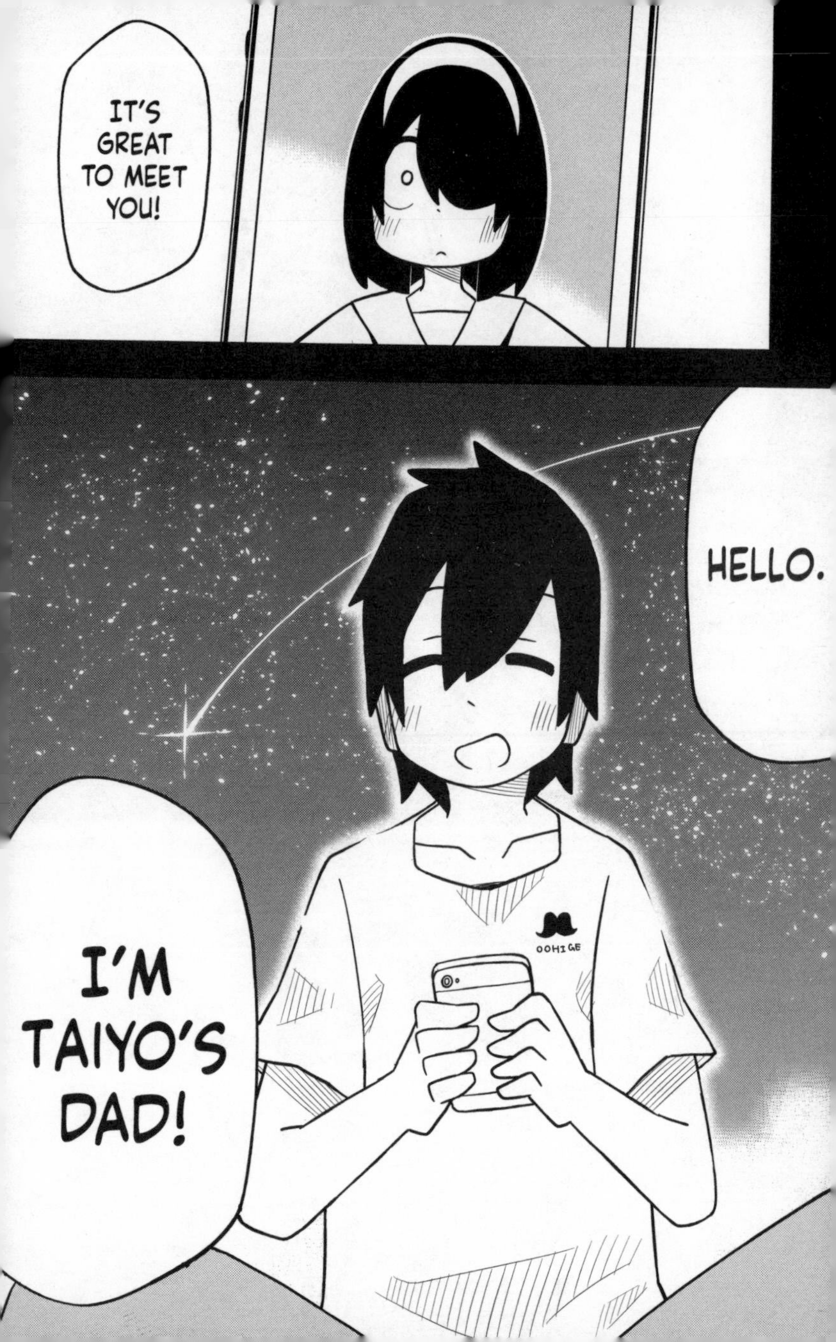
IT'S GREAT TO MEET YOU!
HELLO.
I'M TAIYO'S DAD!
OOHIGE

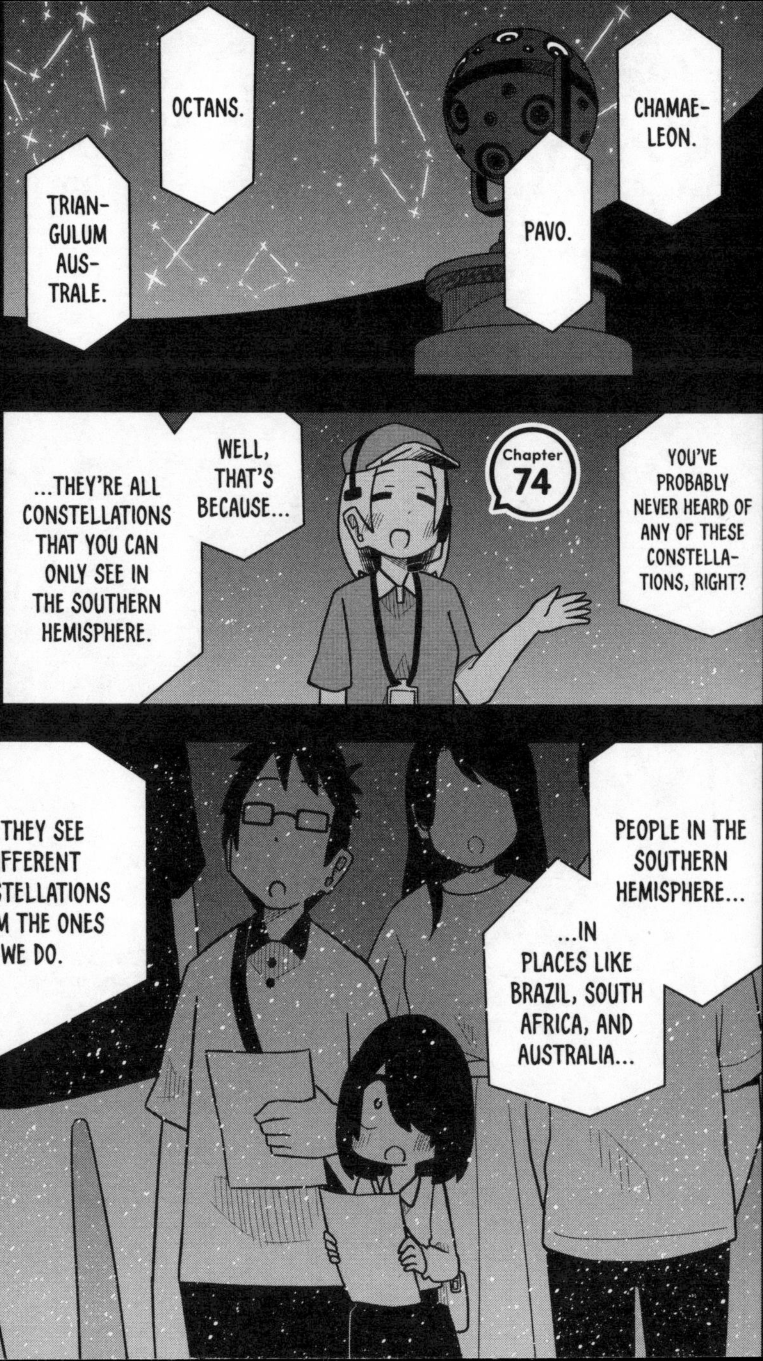

CHAMAE-LEON.
PAVO.
OCTANS.
TRIAN-GULUM AUS-TRALE.
YOU'VE PROBABLY NEVER HEARD OF ANY OF THESE CONSTELLA-TIONS, RIGHT?
Chapter 74
WELL, THAT'S BECAUSE...
...THEY'RE ALL CONSTELLATIONS THAT YOU CAN ONLY SEE IN THE SOUTHERN HEMISPHERE.
PEOPLE IN THE SOUTHERN HEMISPHERE...
...IN PLACES LIKE BRAZIL, SOUTH AFRICA, AND AUSTRALIA...
...THEY SEE DIFFERENT CONSTELLATIONS FROM THE ONES WE DO.

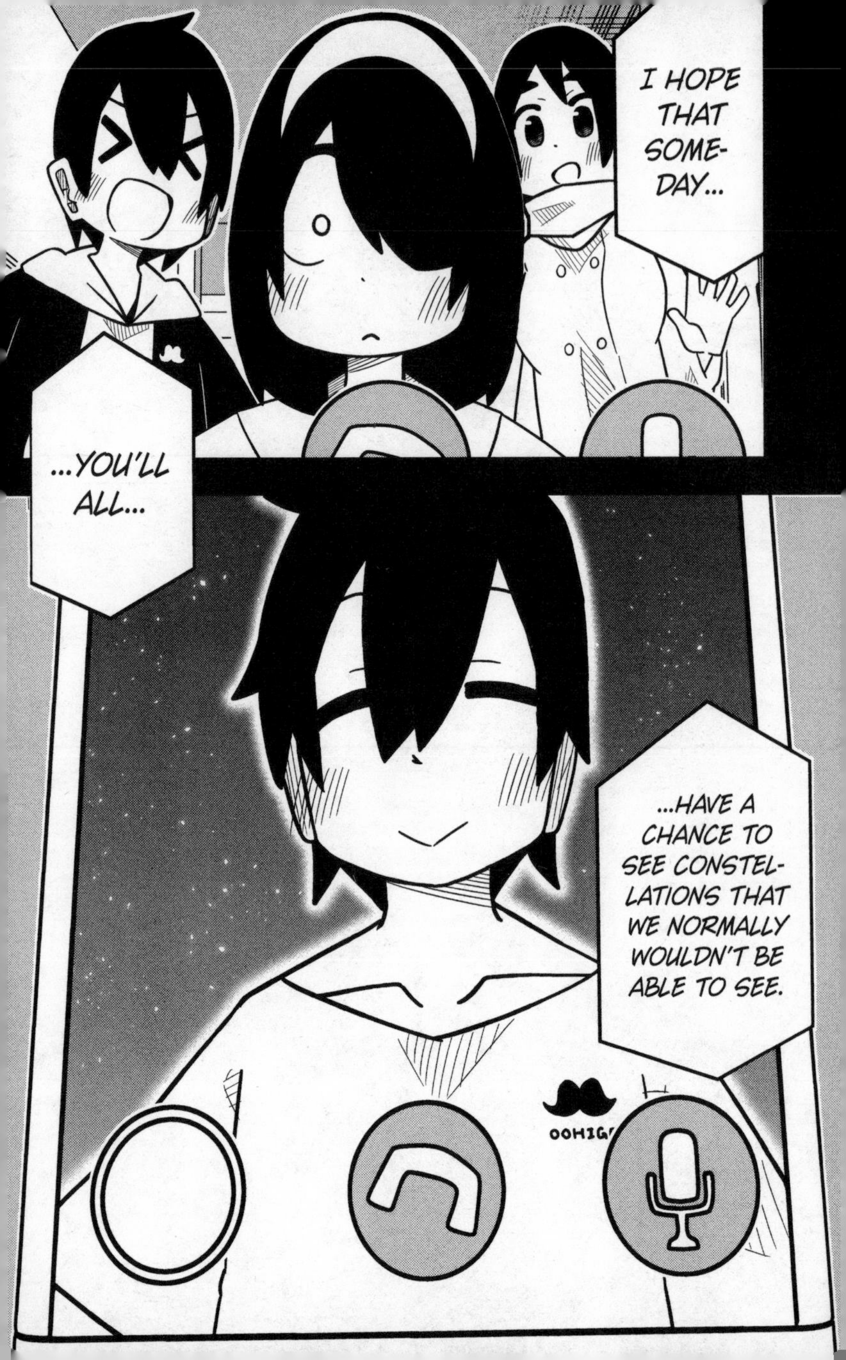
I HOPE THAT SOME-DAY...
...YOU'LL ALL...
...HAVE A CHANCE TO SEE CONSTEL-LATIONS THAT WE NORMALLY WOULDN'T BE ABLE TO SEE.

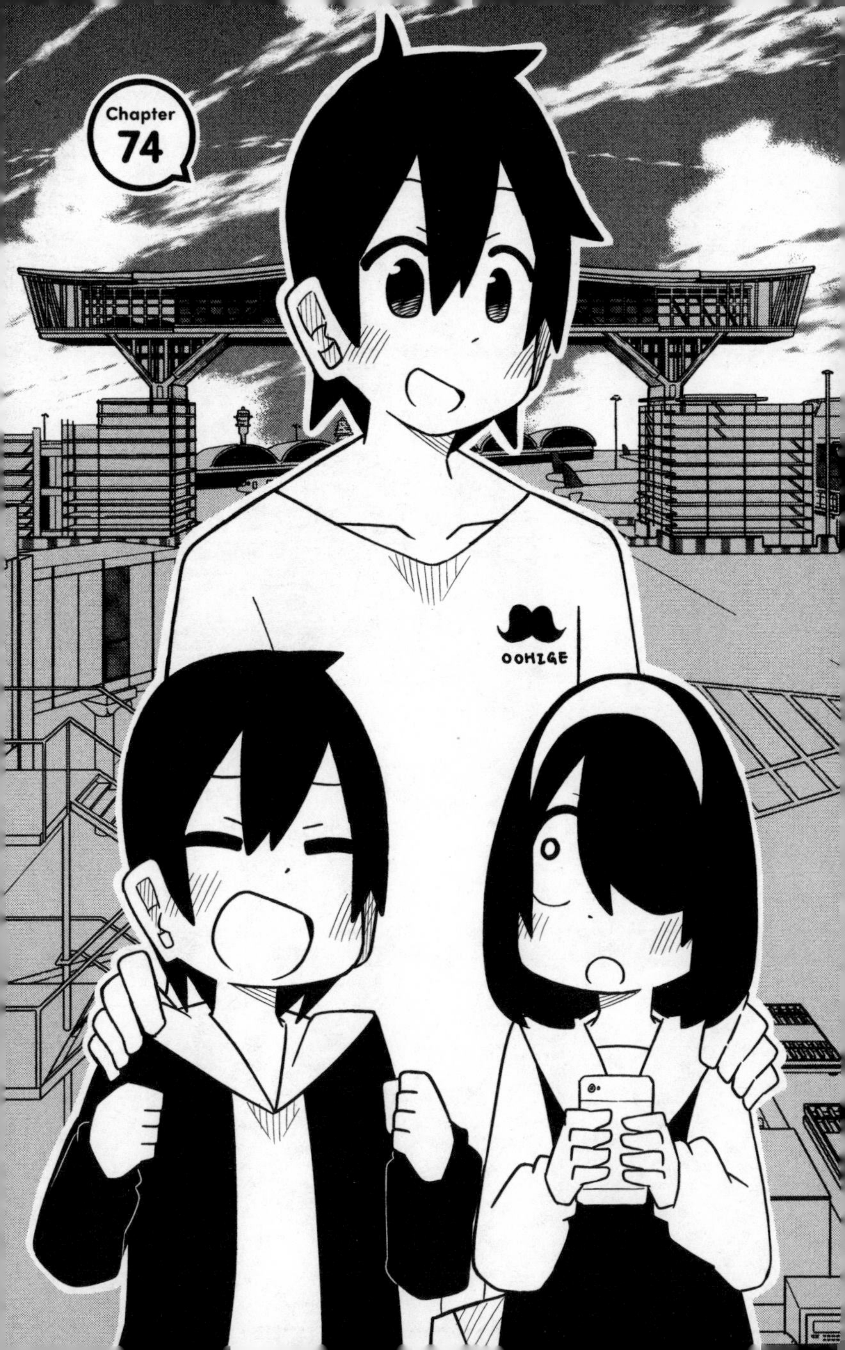
Chapter 74
OOHIGE

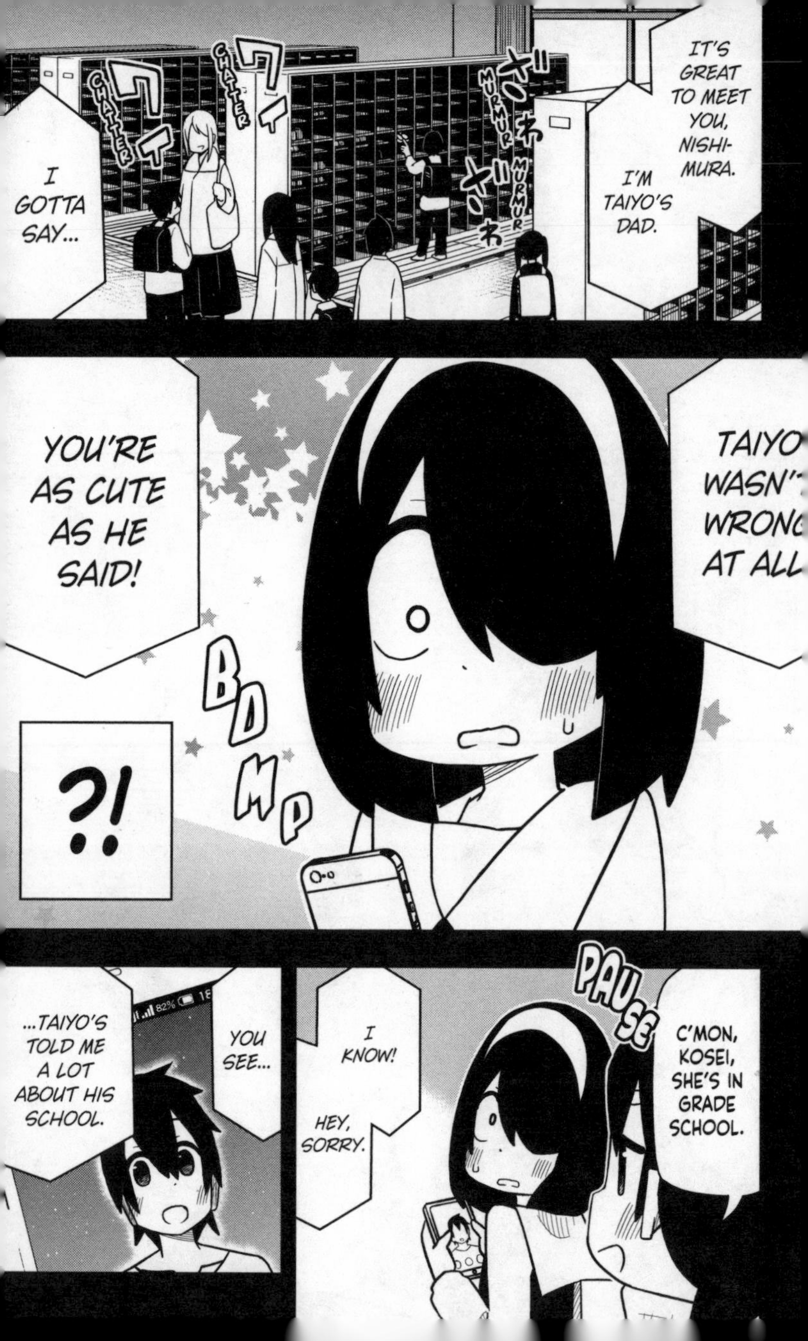
IT'S GREAT TO MEET YOU, NISHI-MURA.
I'M TAIYO'S DAD.
MURMUR
MURMUR
CHATTER
CHATTER
I GOTTA SAY...
TAIYO WASN'T WRONG AT ALL
YOU'RE AS CUTE AS HE SAID!
BDMP
?!
PAUSE
C'MON, KOSEI, SHE'S IN GRADE SCHOOL.
I KNOW!
HEY, SORRY.
YOU SEE...
...TAIYO'S TOLD ME A LOT ABOUT HIS SCHOOL.

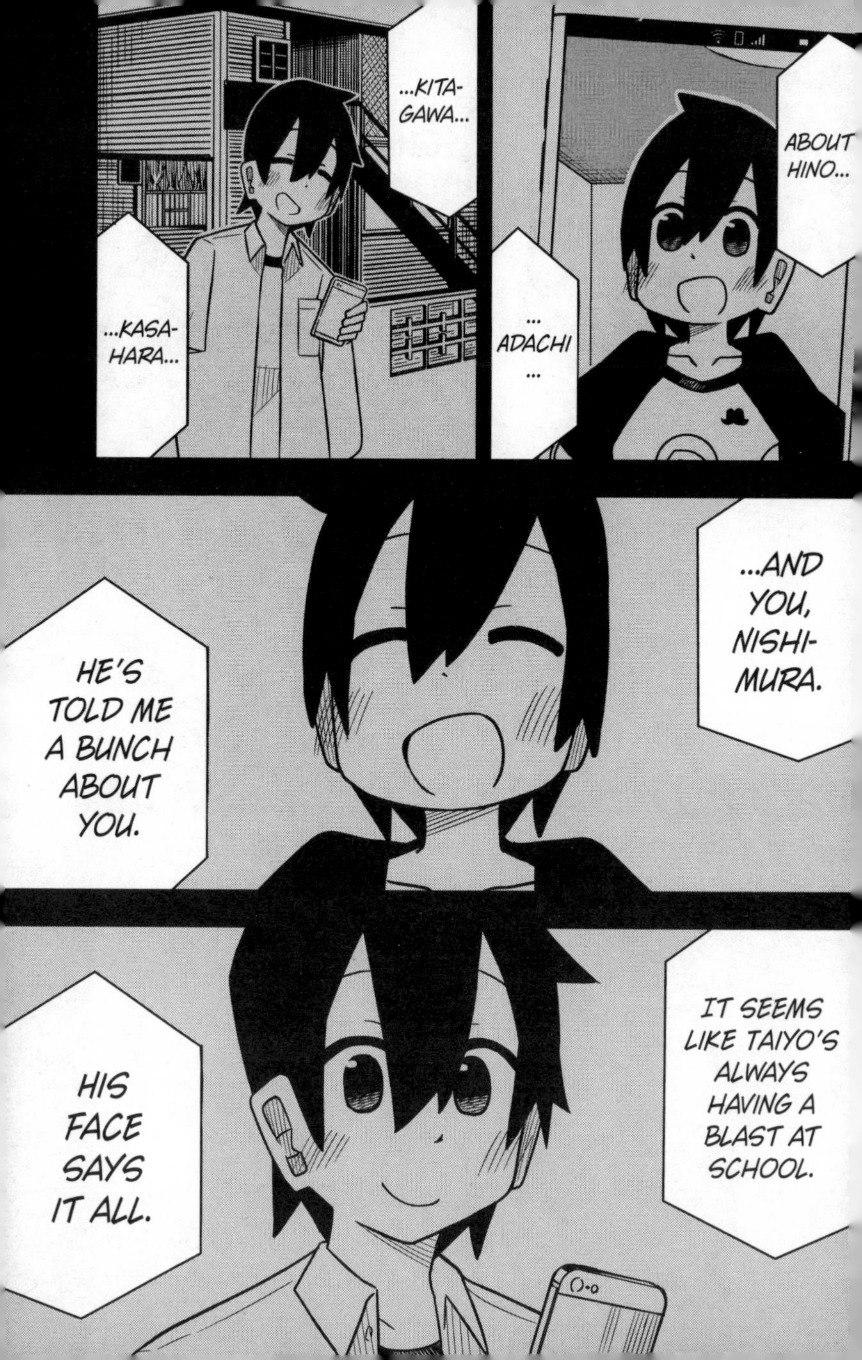
ABOUT HINO...
...ADACHI...
...KITA-GAWA...
...KASA-HARA...
...AND YOU, NISHI-MURA.
HE'S TOLD ME A BUNCH ABOUT YOU.
IT SEEMS LIKE TAIYO'S ALWAYS HAVING A BLAST AT SCHOOL.
HIS FACE SAYS IT ALL.

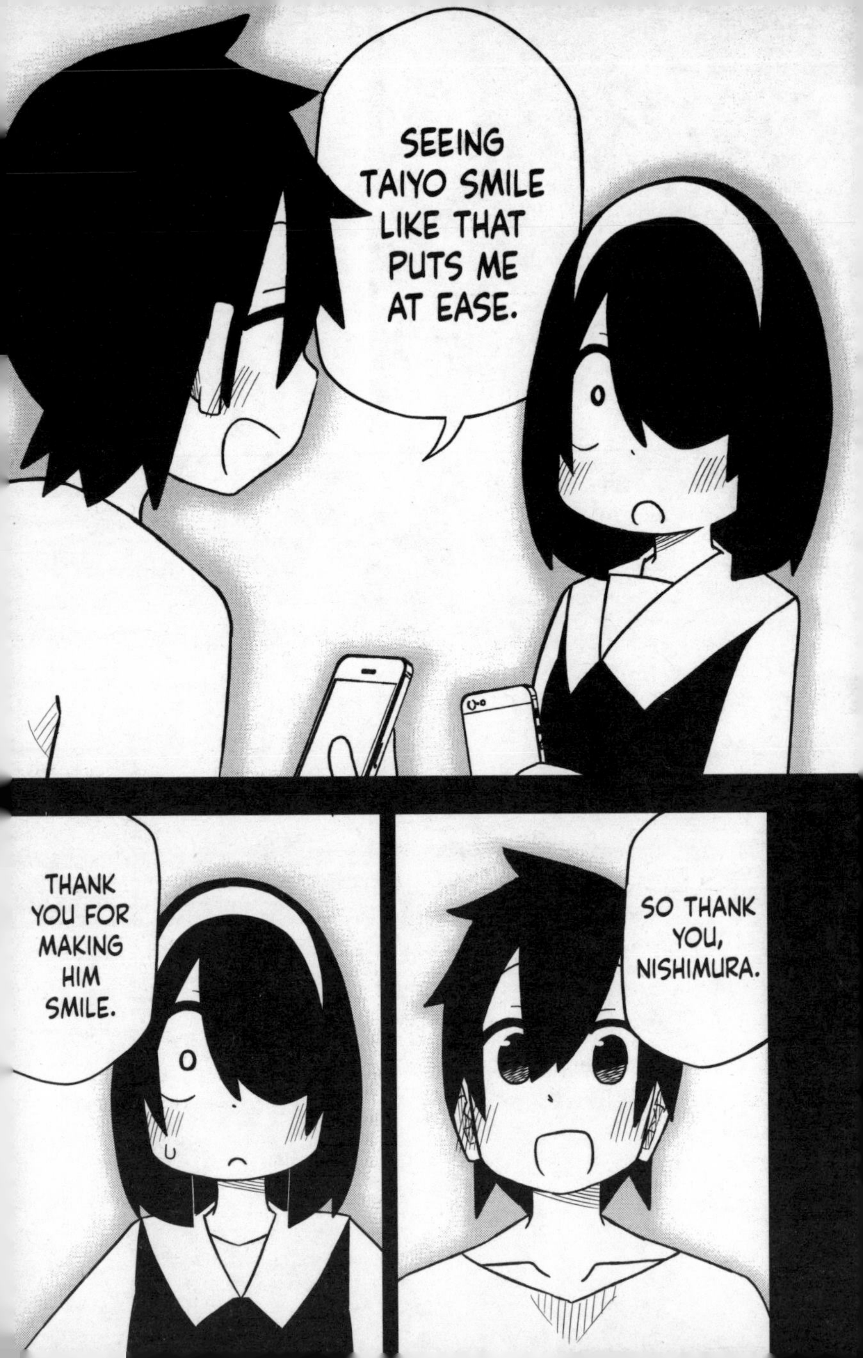
SEEING TAIYO SMILE LIKE THAT PUTS ME AT EASE.
SO THANK YOU, NISHIMURA.
THANK YOU FOR MAKING HIM SMILE.

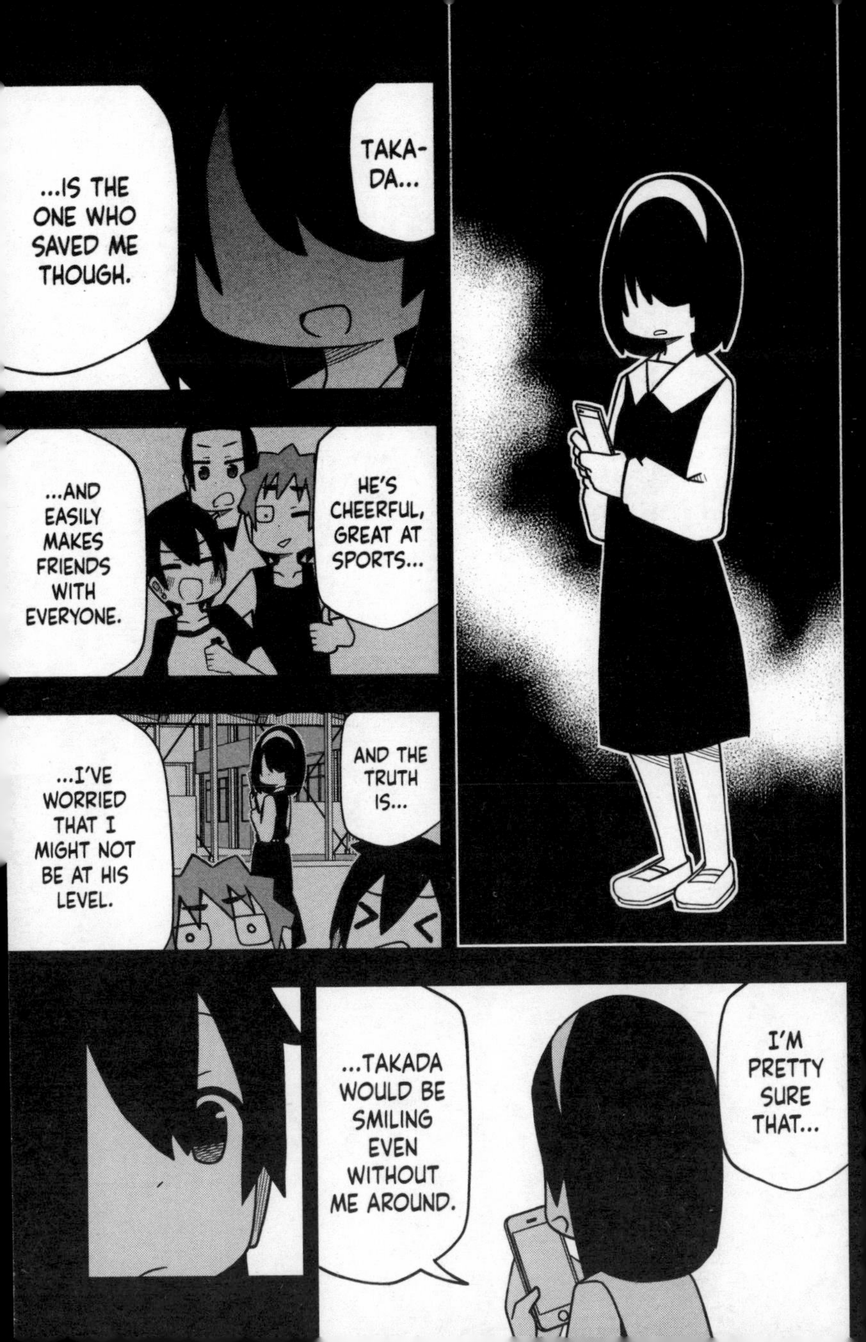
TAKA-DA...
...IS THE ONE WHO SAVED ME THOUGH.
HE'S CHEERFUL, GREAT AT SPORTS...
...AND EASILY MAKES FRIENDS WITH EVERYONE.
AND THE TRUTH IS...
...I'VE WORRIED THAT I MIGHT NOT BE AT HIS LEVEL.
I'M PRETTY SURE THAT...
...TAKADA WOULD BE SMILING EVEN WITHOUT ME AROUND.

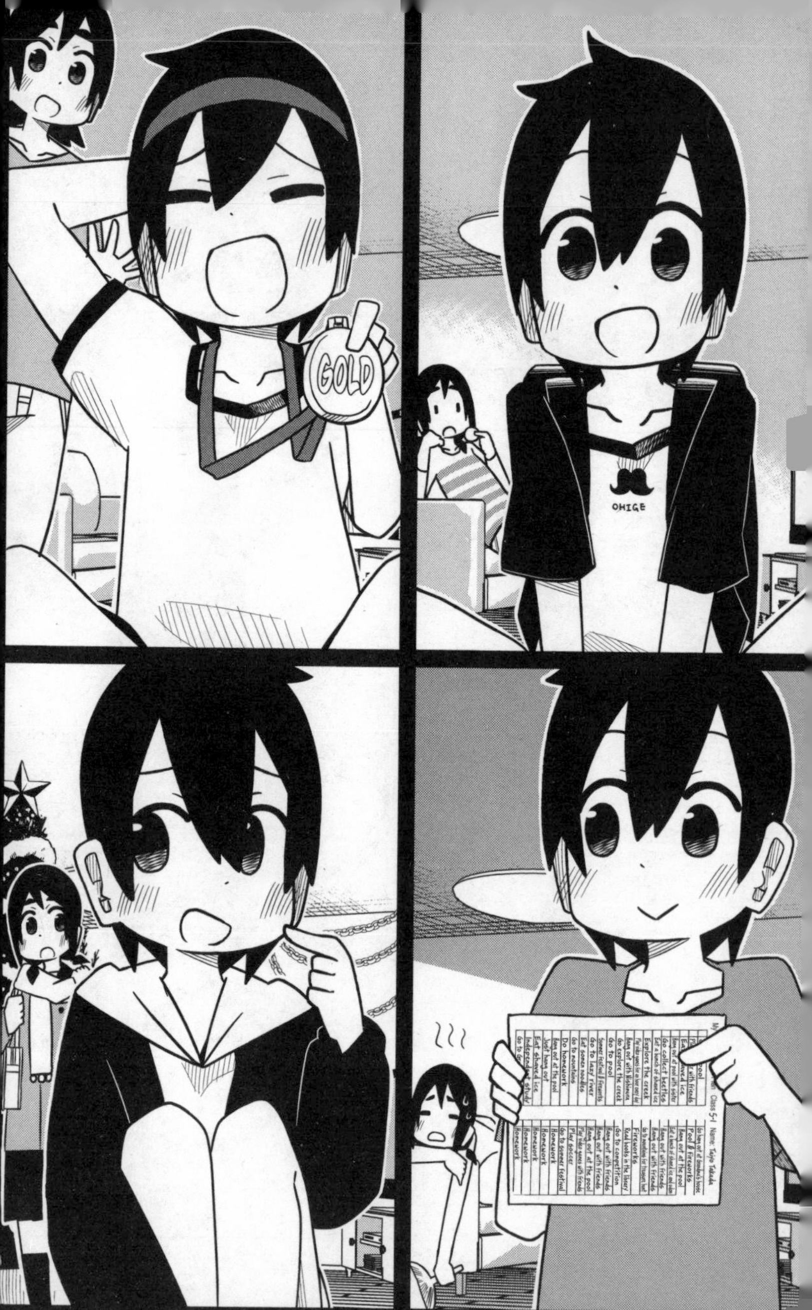
OHIGE
GOLD
Class 5-1 Name: Taiyo Takada
Hang out at pool with sister
Go collect beetles
Eat a bunch of shaved ice
Explore the creek
Hang out with Nishimura
Go explore the creek
Go to pool
Summer festival & fireworks
Go to lazy river
Eat somen noodles
Go to mountains
Do homework
Hang out at the pool
Just hang out
Eat shaved ice
Go hang out at Grandma's house
Pool & fireworks
Hang out at the pool
Hang out with friends
Hang out with friends
Fireworks
Read books in the library
Go to competition
Hang out with friends
Hang out with friends
Hang out at the pool
Play video games with friends
Play soccer
Go to summer festival
Homework
Homework
Homework
Homework
Homework

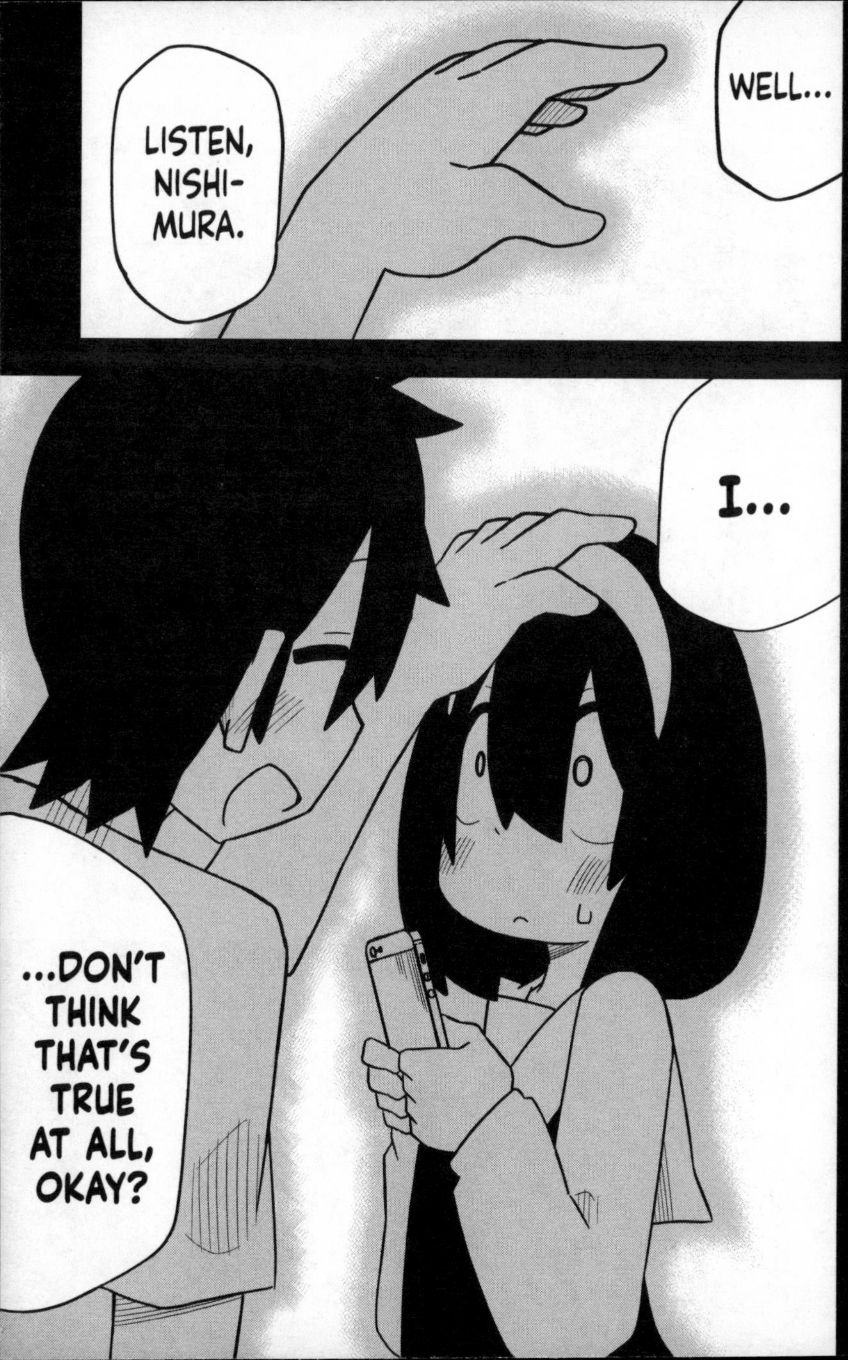
WELL...
LISTEN, NISHI-MURA.
I...
...DON'T THINK THAT'S TRUE AT ALL, OKAY?

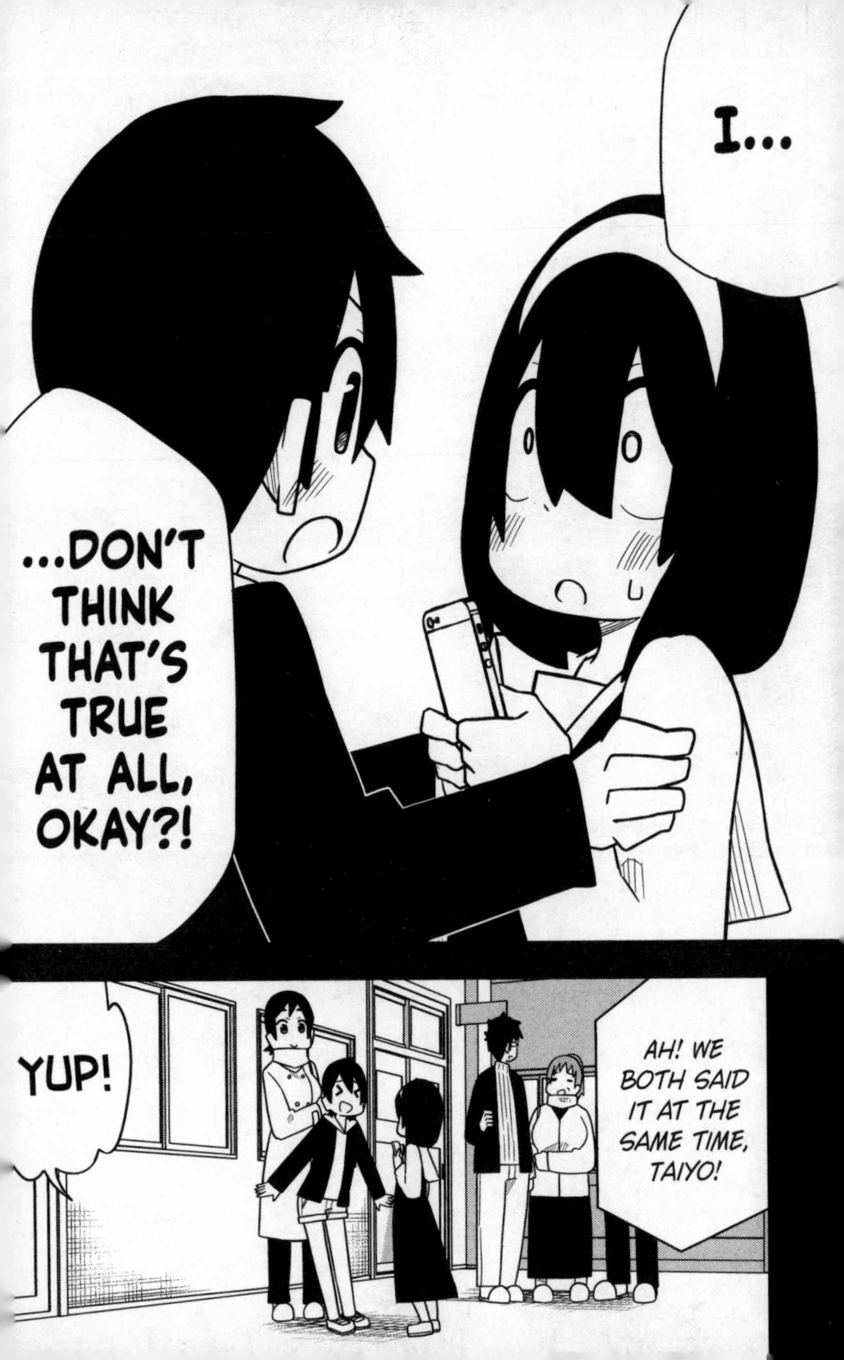
I...
...DON'T THINK THAT'S TRUE AT ALL, OKAY?!
AH! WE BOTH SAID IT AT THE SAME TIME, TAIYO!
YUP!

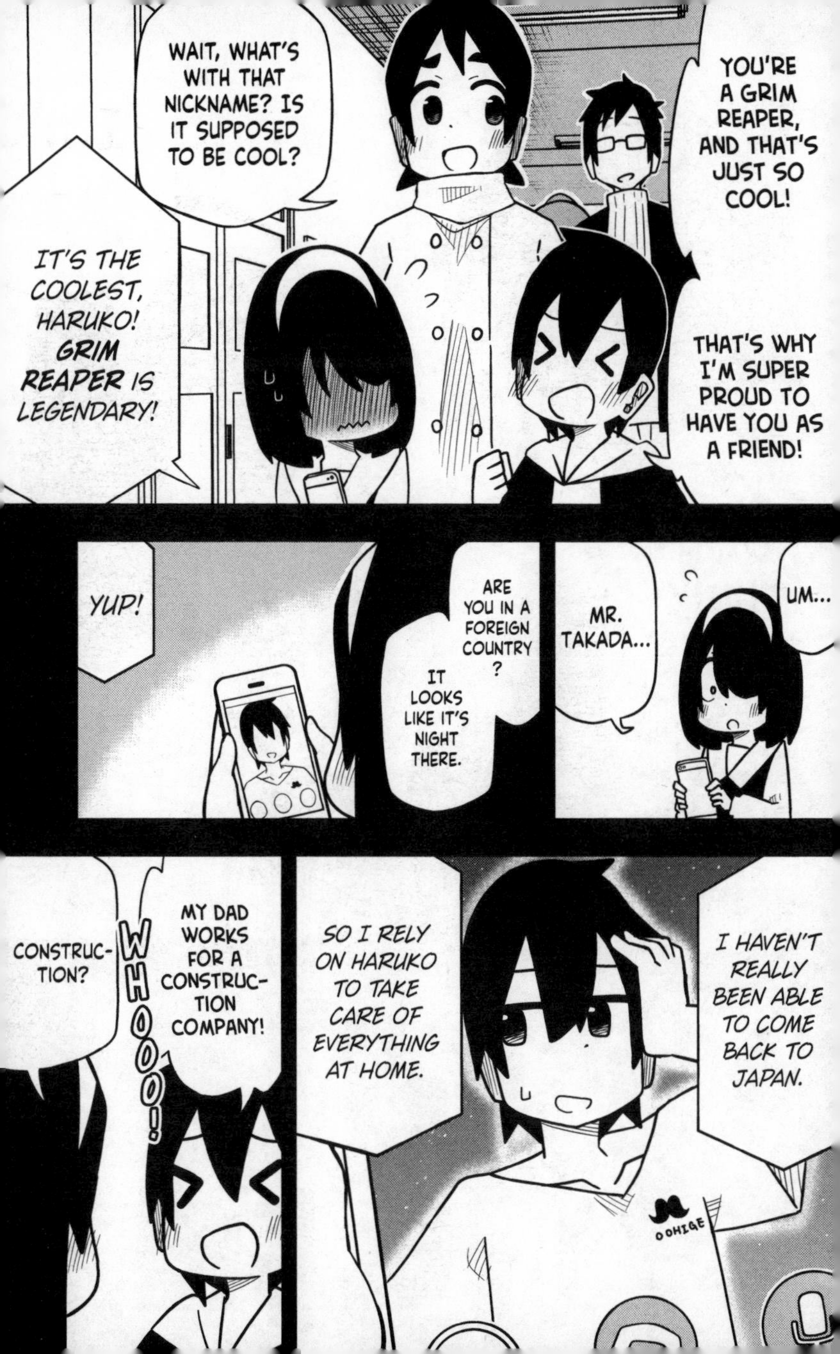
YOU'RE A GRIM REAPER, AND THAT'S JUST SO COOL!
THAT'S WHY I'M SUPER PROUD TO HAVE YOU AS A FRIEND!
WAIT, WHAT'S WITH THAT NICKNAME? IS IT SUPPOSED TO BE COOL?
IT'S THE COOLEST, HARUKO! GRIM REAPER IS LEGENDARY!
UM...
MR. TAKADA...
ARE YOU IN A FOREIGN COUNTRY?
IT LOOKS LIKE IT'S NIGHT THERE.
YUP!
I HAVEN'T REALLY BEEN ABLE TO COME BACK TO JAPAN.
SO I RELY ON HARUKO TO TAKE CARE OF EVERYTHING AT HOME.
OOHIGE
MY DAD WORKS FOR A CONSTRUCTION COMPANY!
WHOOOO!
CONSTRUCTION?

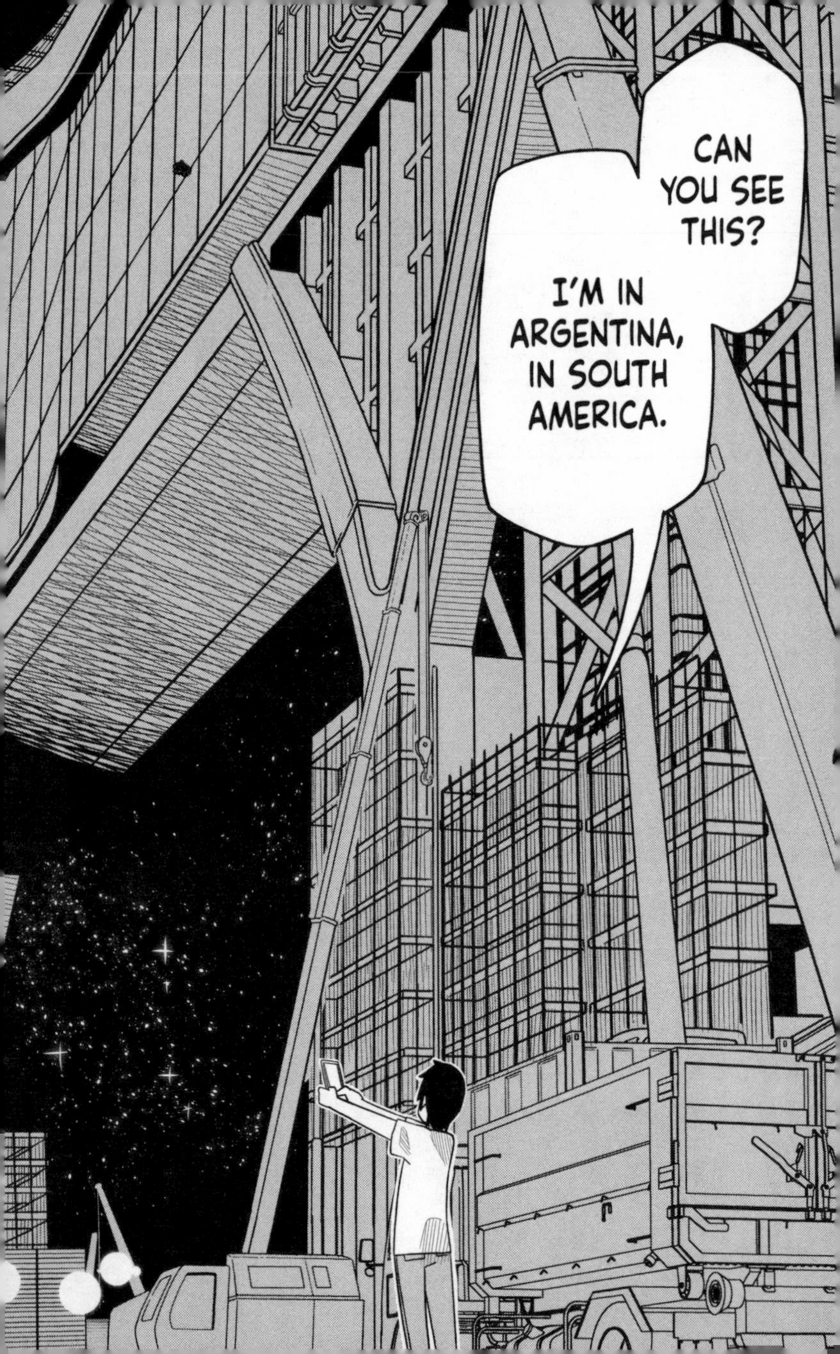
CAN YOU SEE THIS?
I'M IN ARGENTINA, IN SOUTH AMERICA.

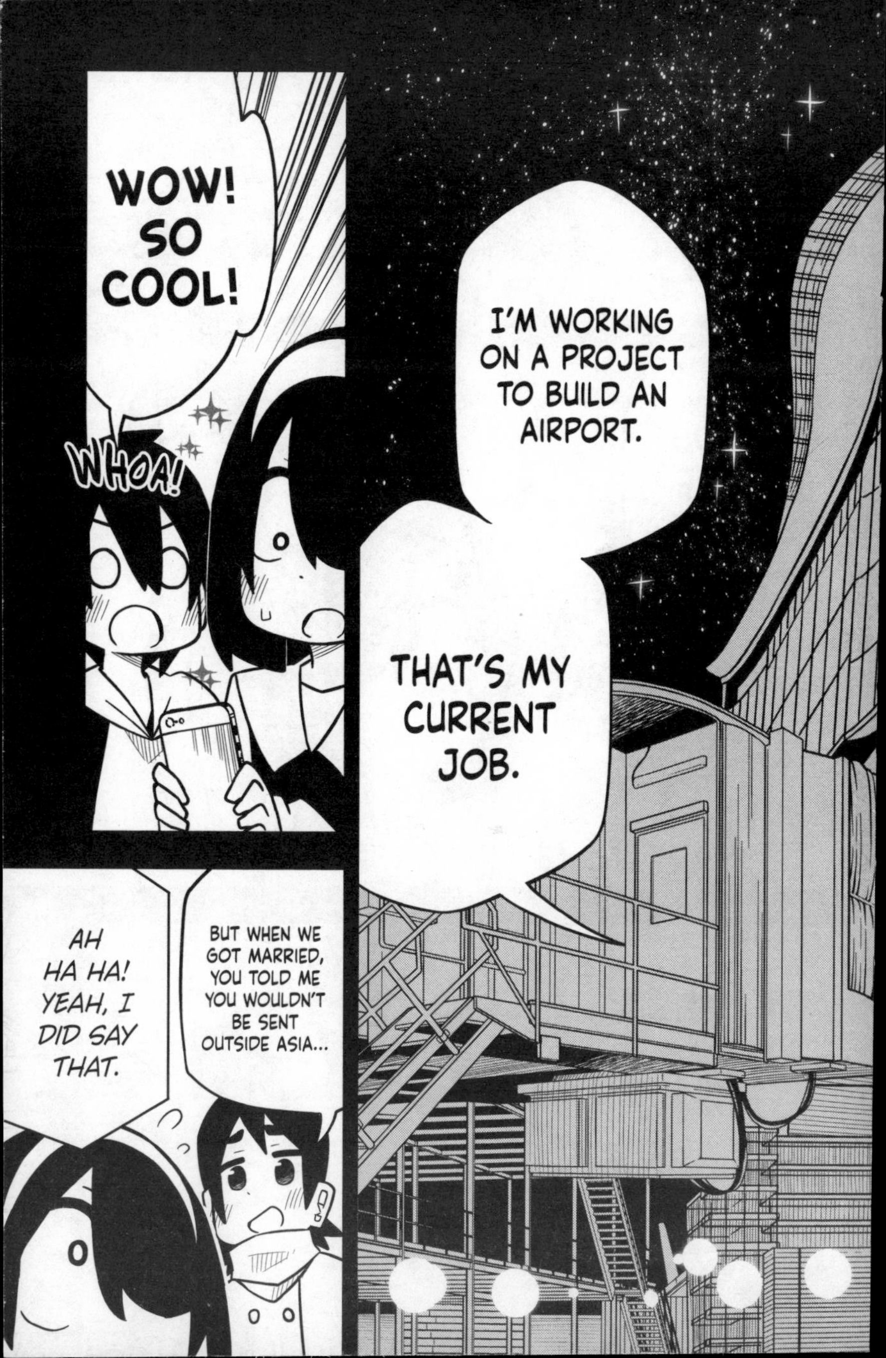

I'M WORKING ON A PROJECT TO BUILD AN AIRPORT.
THAT'S MY CURRENT JOB.
WOW! SO COOL!
WHOA!
BUT WHEN WE GOT MARRIED, YOU TOLD ME YOU WOULDN'T BE SENT OUTSIDE ASIA...
AH HA HA! YEAH, I DID SAY THAT.

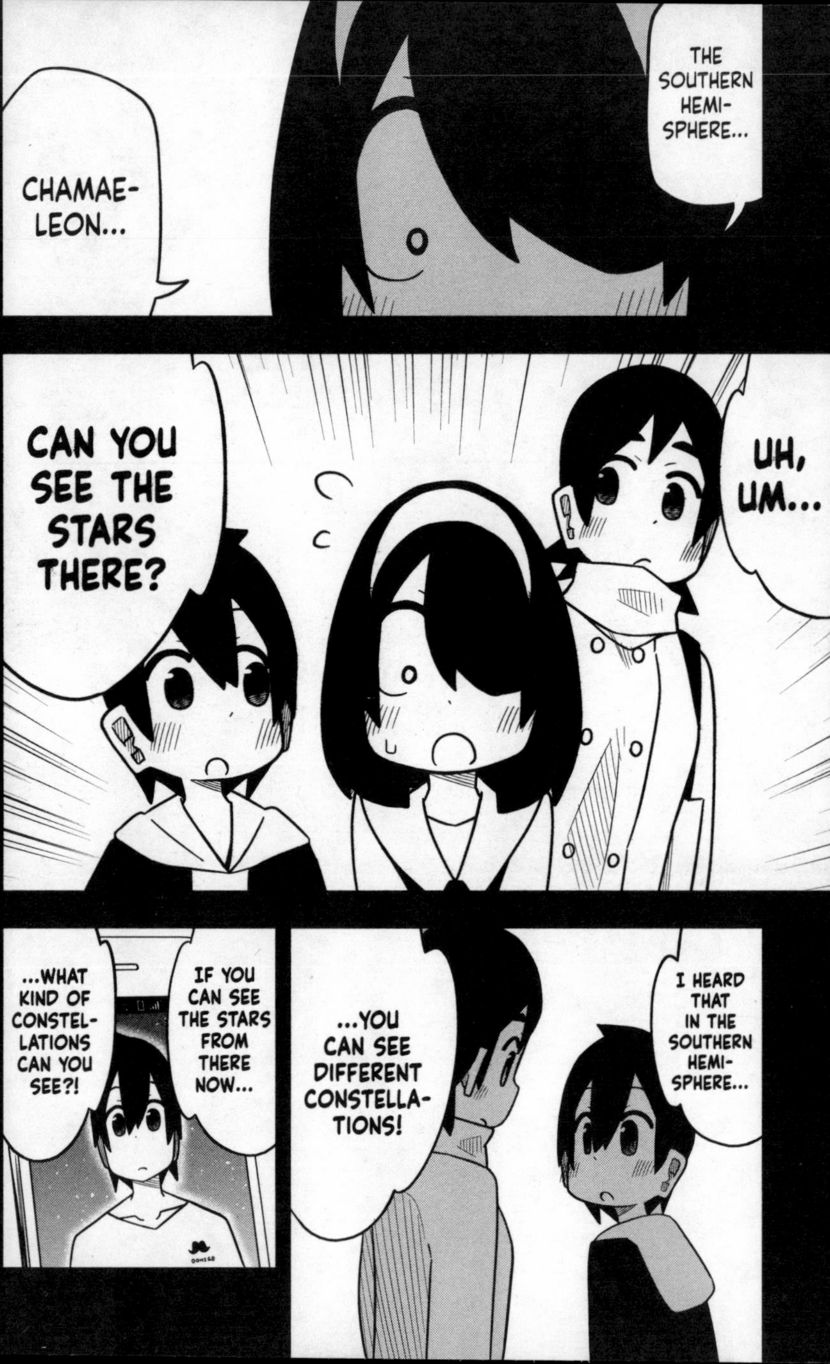
THE SOUTHERN HEMI-SPHERE...
CHAMAE-LEON...
UH, UM...
CAN YOU SEE THE STARS THERE?
I HEARD THAT IN THE SOUTHERN HEMI-SPHERE...
...YOU CAN SEE DIFFERENT CONSTELLA-TIONS!
IF YOU CAN SEE THE STARS FROM THERE NOW...
...WHAT KIND OF CONSTEL-LATIONS CAN YOU SEE?!

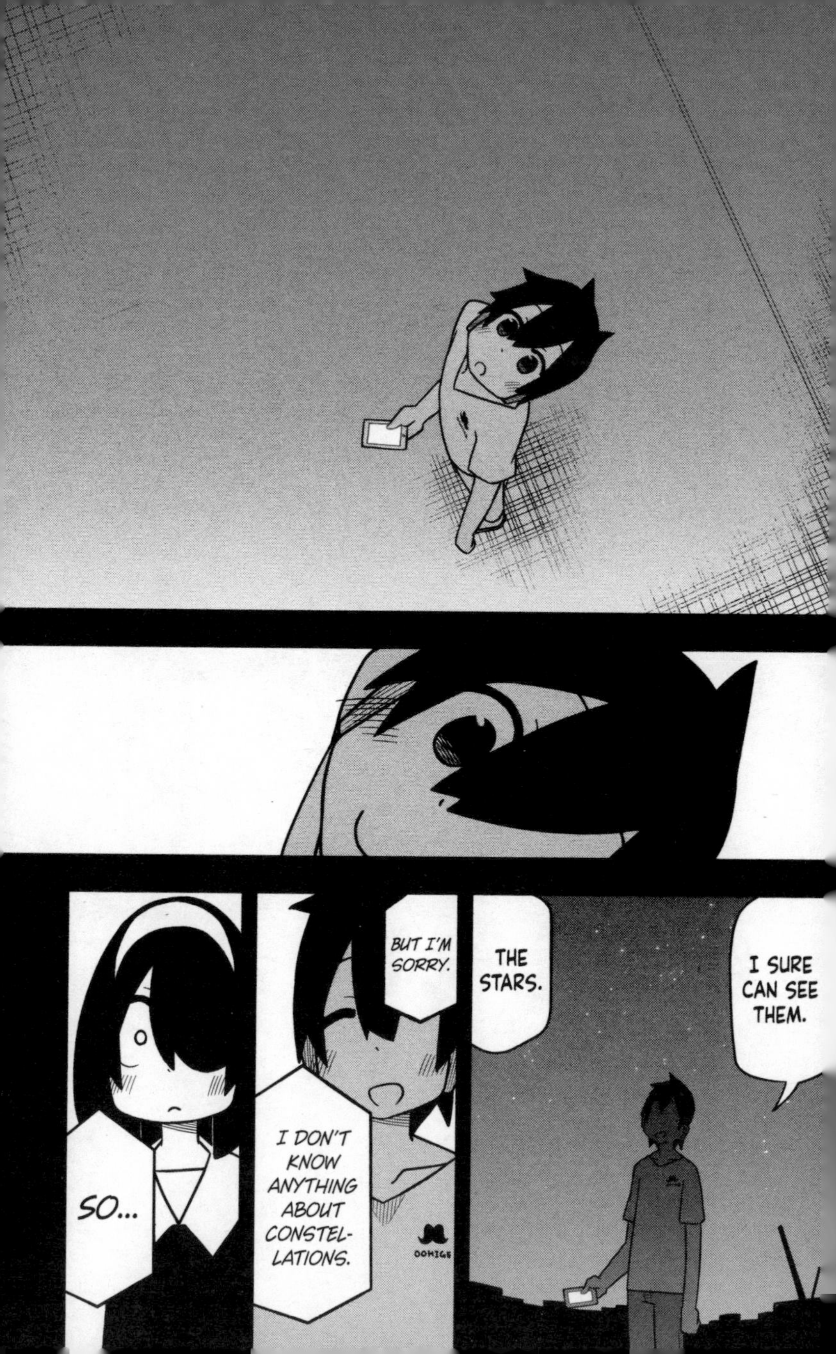
I SURE CAN SEE THEM.
THE STARS.
BUT I'M SORRY.
I DON'T KNOW ANYTHING ABOUT CONSTEL-LATIONS.
SO...

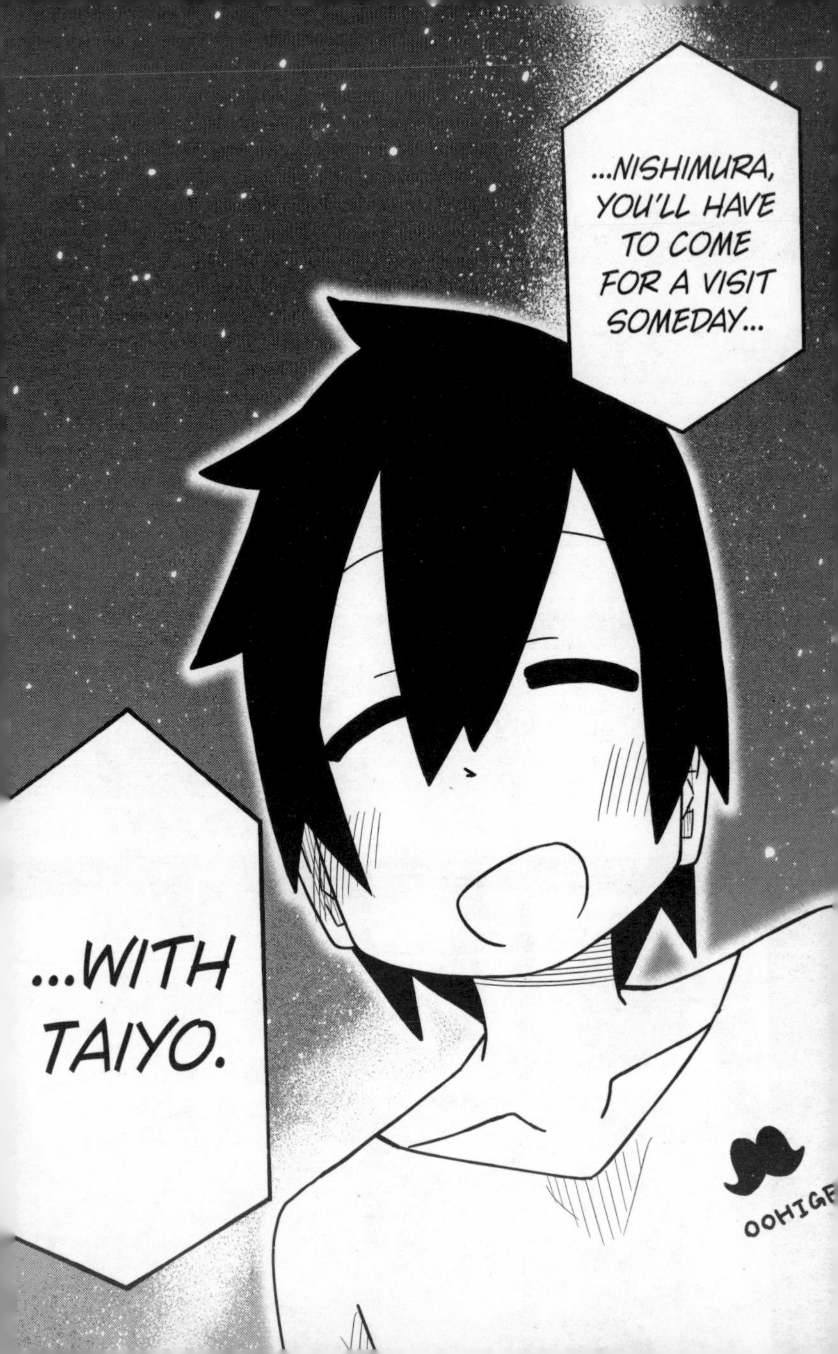
...NISHIMURA, YOU'LL HAVE TO COME FOR A VISIT SOMEDAY...
...WITH TAIYO.
OOHIGE

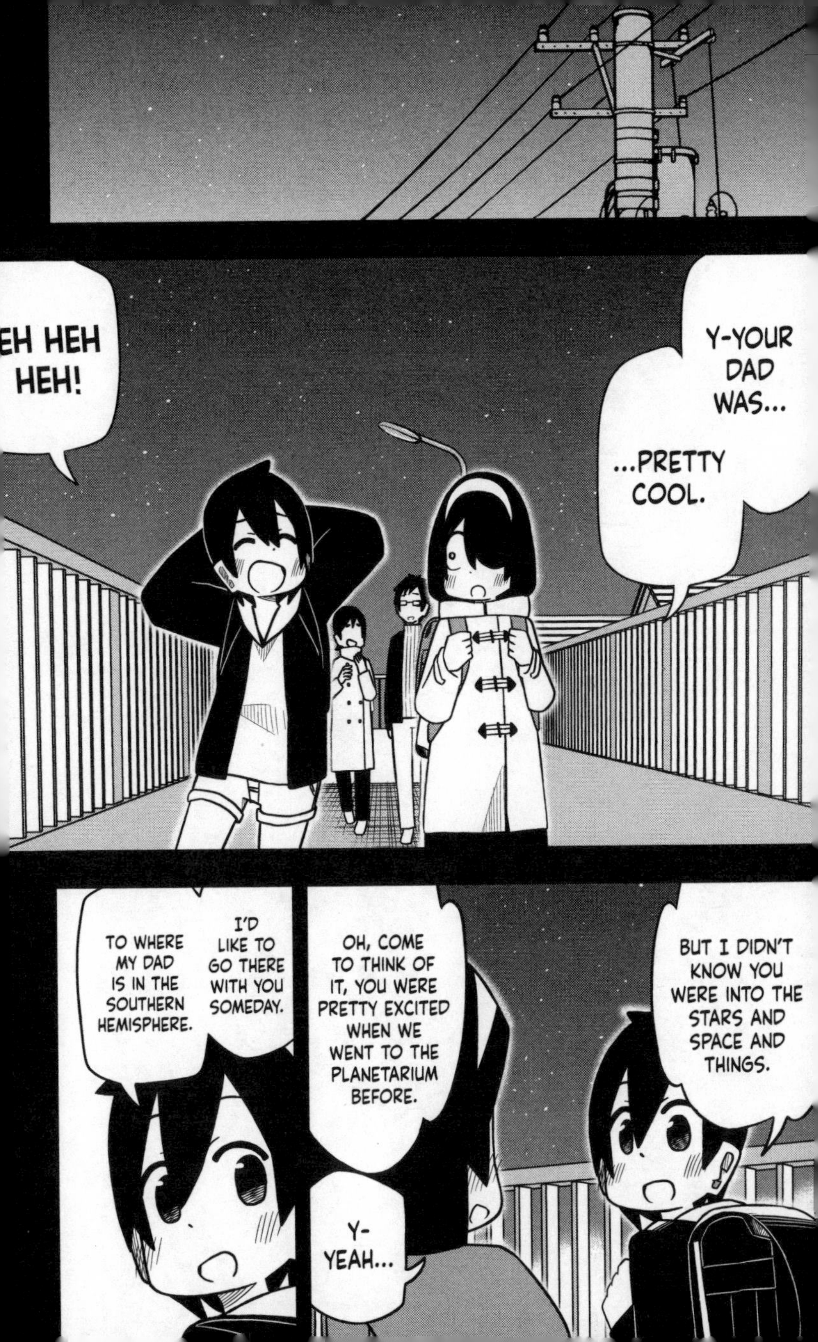
Y-YOUR DAD WAS...
...PRETTY COOL.
EH HEH HEH!
BUT I DIDN'T KNOW YOU WERE INTO THE STARS AND SPACE AND THINGS.
OH, COME TO THINK OF IT, YOU WERE PRETTY EXCITED WHEN WE WENT TO THE PLANETARIUM BEFORE.
Y- YEAH...
I'D LIKE TO GO THERE WITH YOU SOMEDAY.
TO WHERE MY DAD IS IN THE SOUTHERN HEMISPHERE.

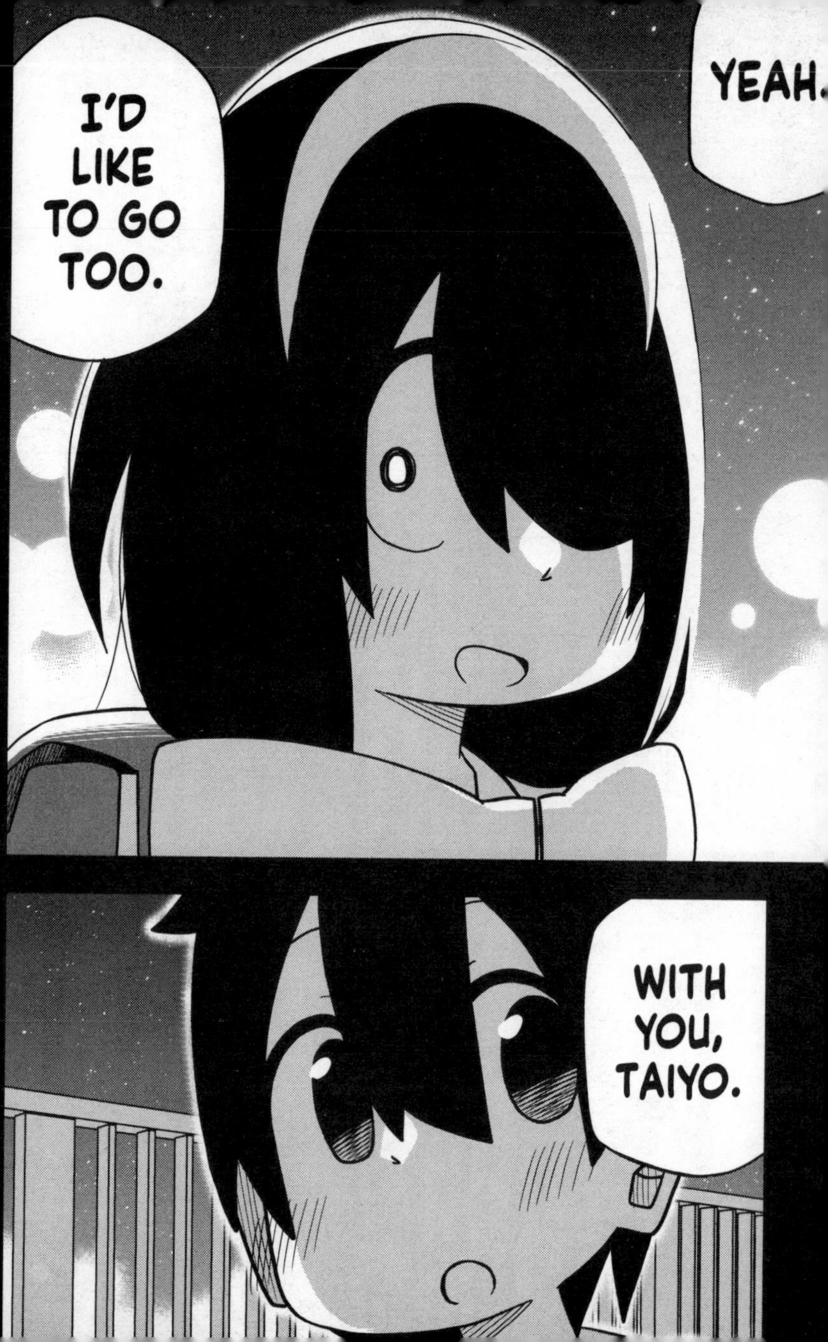
YEAH.
I'D LIKE TO GO TOO.
WITH YOU, TAIYO.

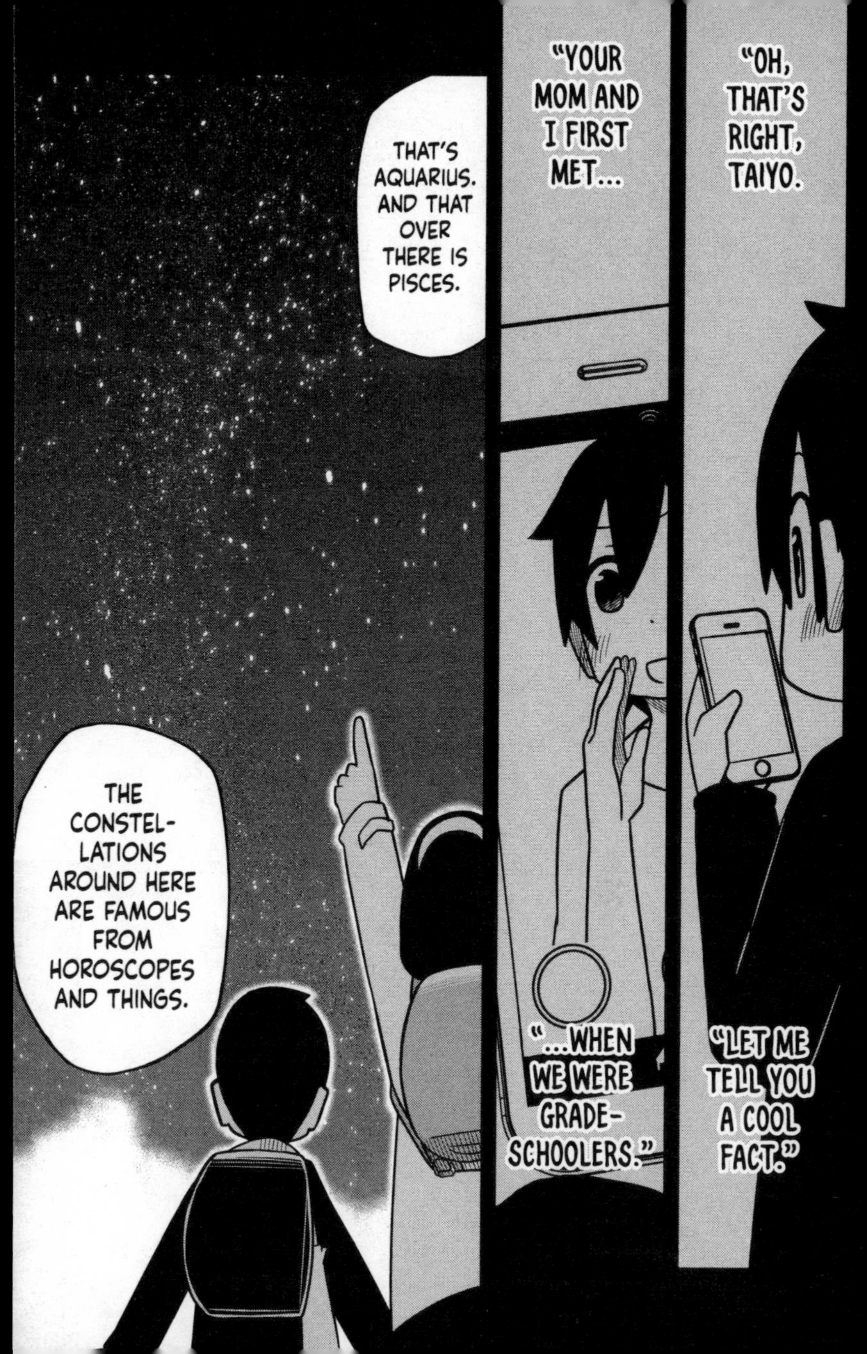
"OH, THAT'S RIGHT, TAIYO.
"LET ME TELL YOU A COOL FACT."
"YOUR MOM AND I FIRST MET...
"...WHEN WE WERE GRADE-SCHOOLERS."
THAT'S AQUARIUS. AND THAT OVER THERE IS PISCES.
THE CONSTEL-LATIONS AROUND HERE ARE FAMOUS FROM HOROSCOPES AND THINGS.

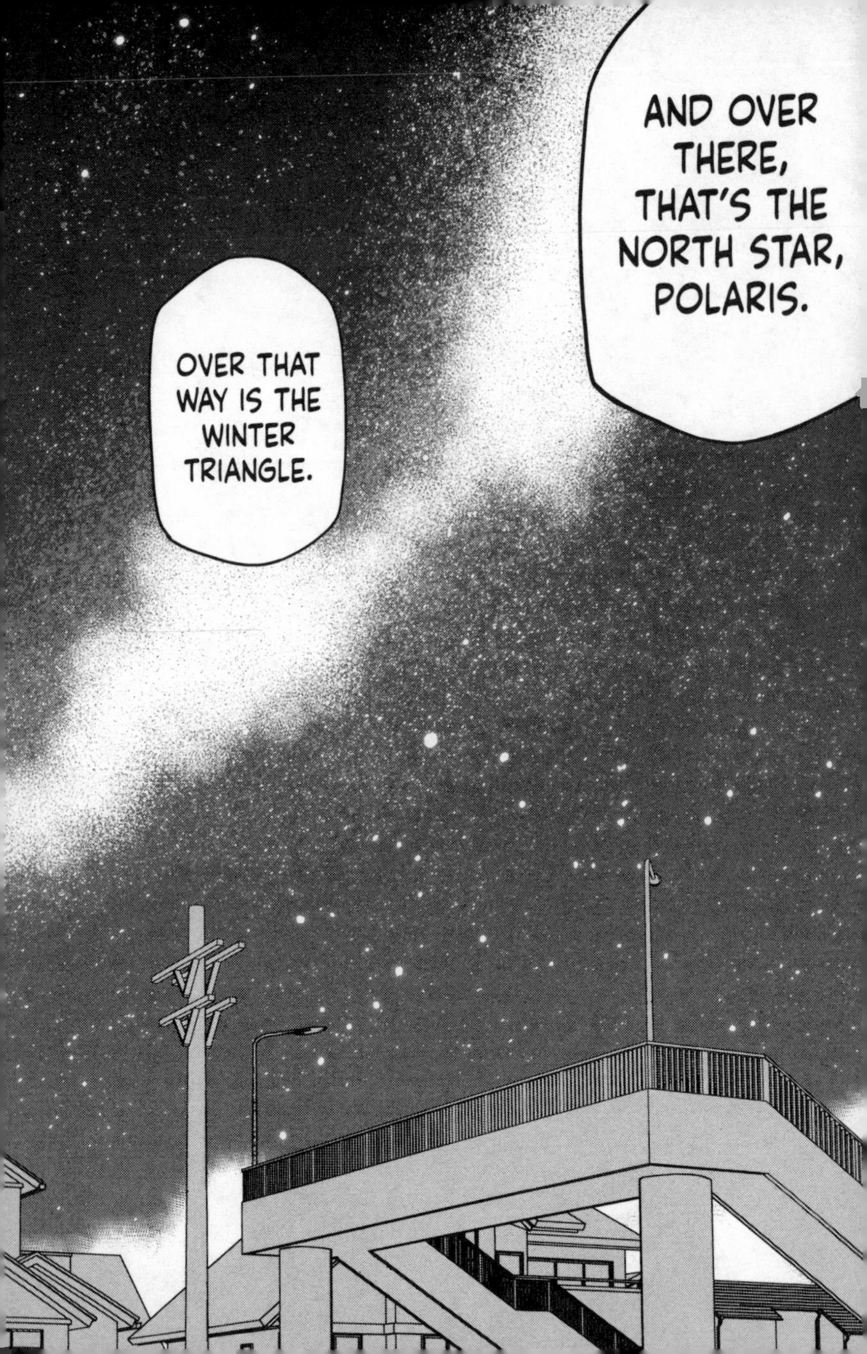
AND OVER THERE, THAT'S THE NORTH STAR, POLARIS.
OVER THAT WAY IS THE WINTER TRIANGLE.

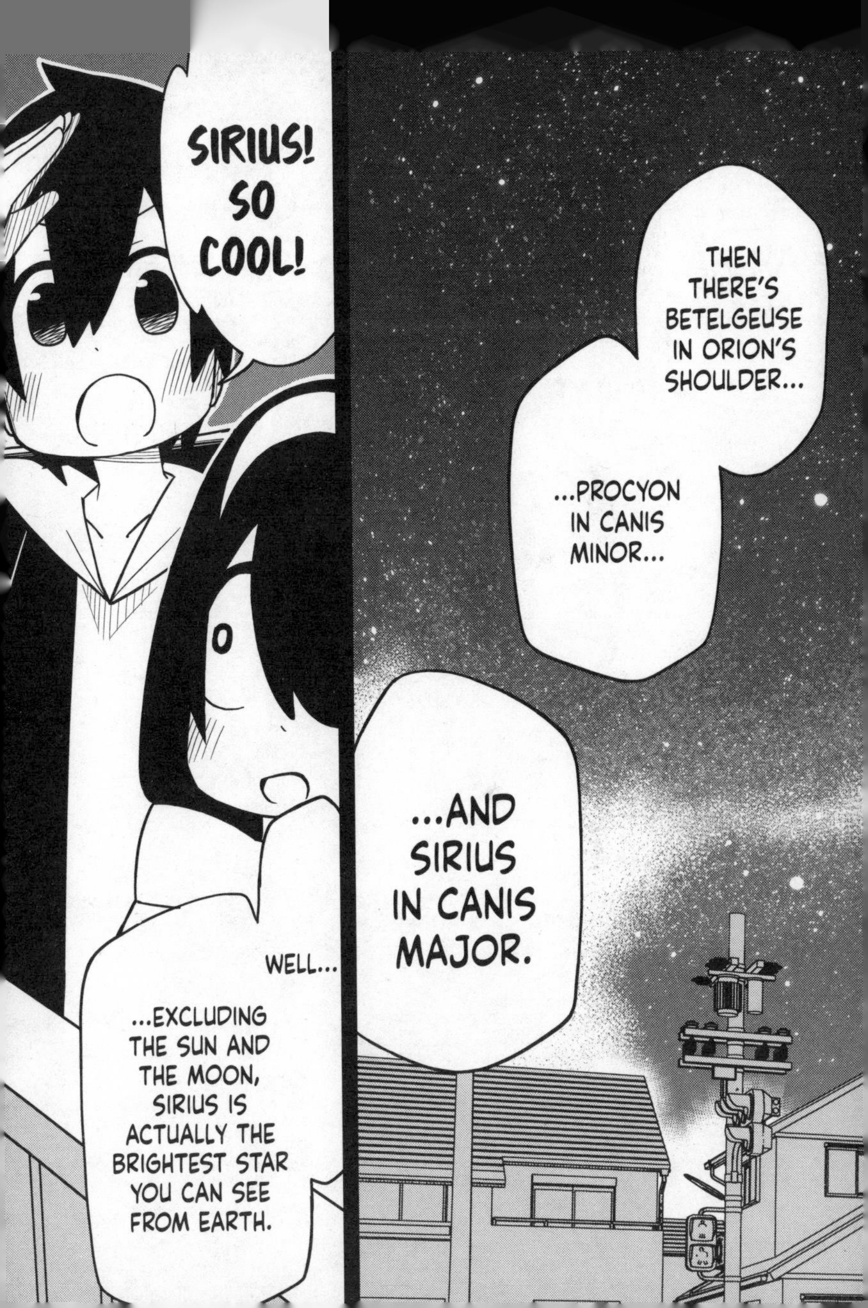
THEN THERE'S BETELGEUSE IN ORION'S SHOULDER...
...PROCYON IN CANIS MINOR...
...AND SIRIUS IN CANIS MAJOR.
SIRIUS! SO COOL!
WELL...
...EXCLUDING THE SUN AND THE MOON, SIRIUS IS ACTUALLY THE BRIGHTEST STAR YOU CAN SEE FROM EARTH.

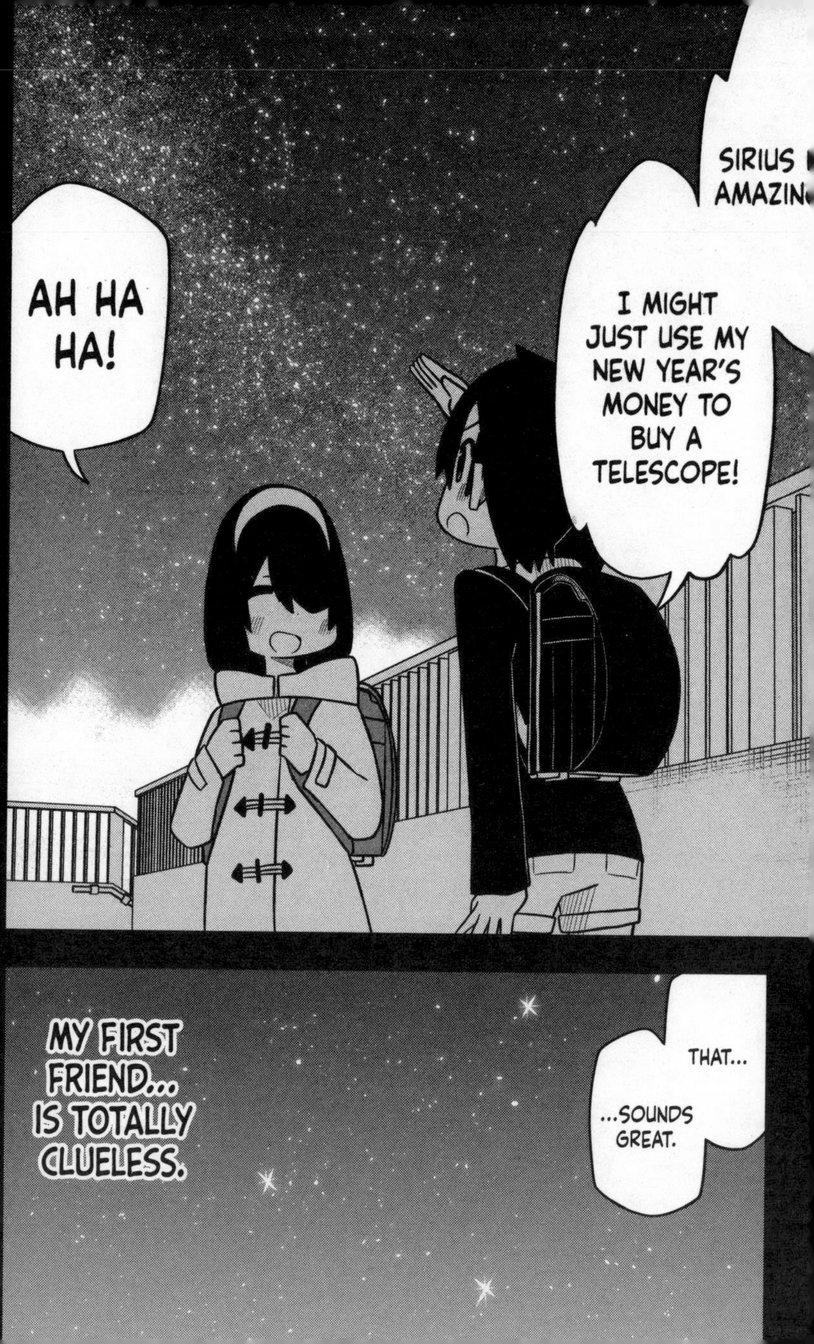
SIRIUS
AMAZIN
I MIGHT JUST USE MY NEW YEAR'S MONEY TO BUY A TELESCOPE!
AH HA HA!
THAT...
...SOUNDS GREAT.
MY FIRST FRIEND... IS TOTALLY CLUELESS.

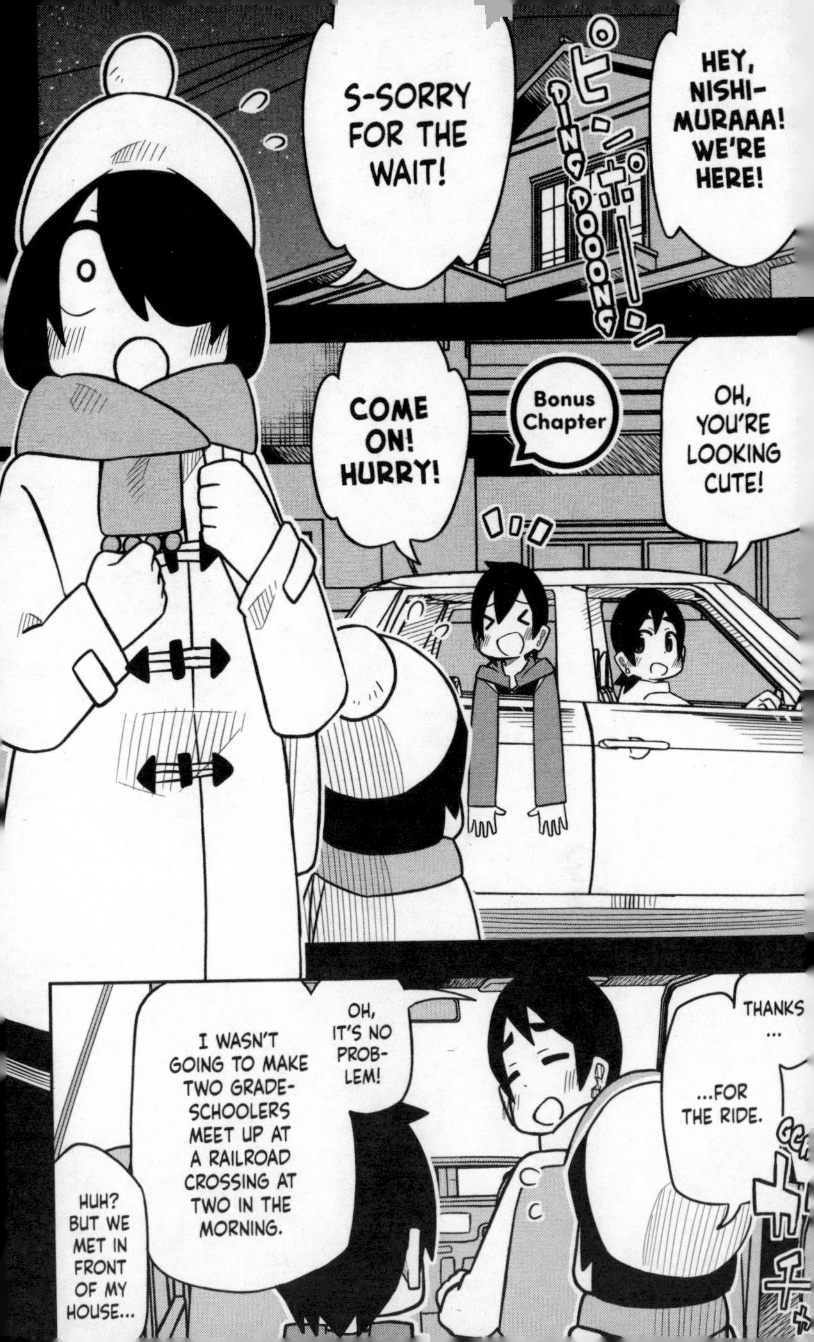
HEY, NISHI-MURAAA! WE'RE HERE!
DING DOOONG
S-SORRY FOR THE WAIT!
OH, YOU'RE LOOKING CUTE!
Bonus Chapter
COME ON! HURRY!
THANKS ...
...FOR THE RIDE.
OH, IT'S NO PROB-LEM!
I WASN'T GOING TO MAKE TWO GRADE-SCHOOLERS MEET UP AT A RAILROAD CROSSING AT TWO IN THE MORNING.
HUH? BUT WE MET IN FRONT OF MY HOUSE...

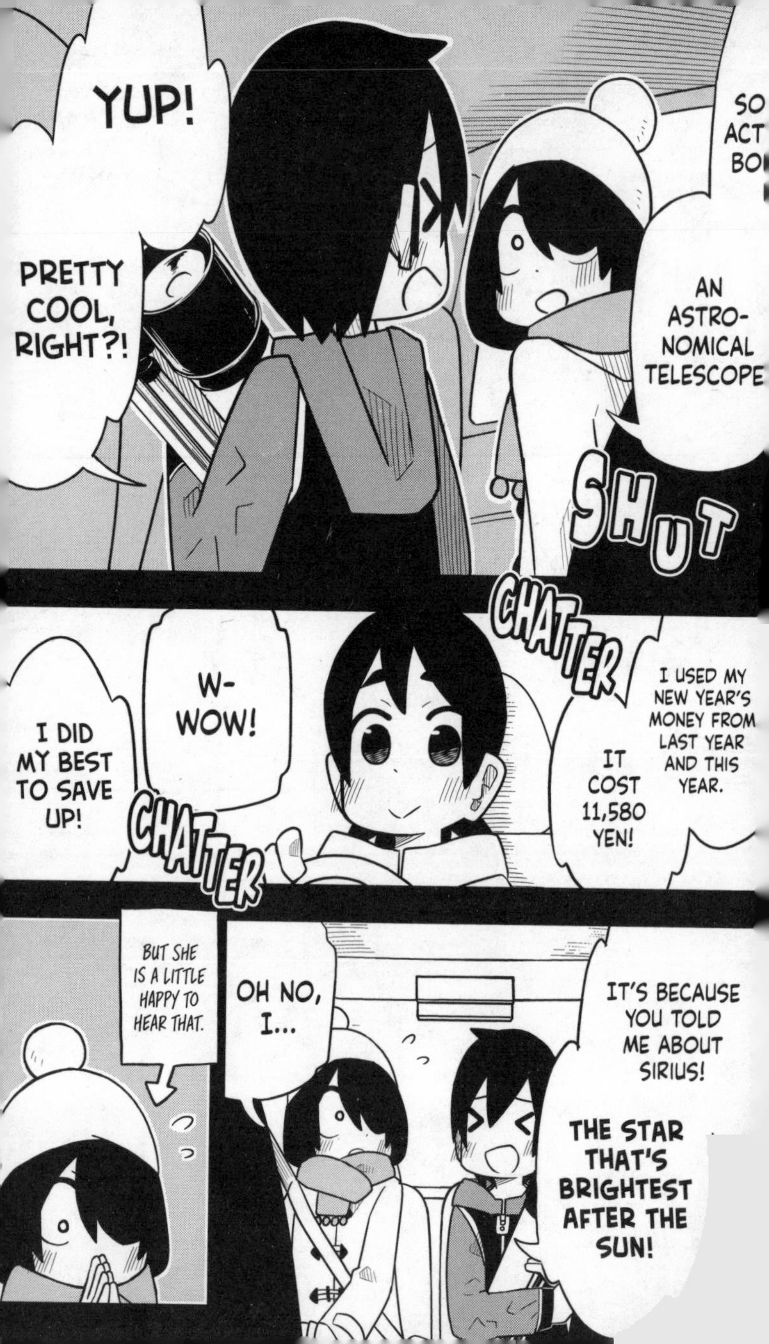
SO ACT BO
AN ASTRO-NOMICAL TELESCOPE
SHUT
YUP!
PRETTY COOL, RIGHT?!
CHATTER
I USED MY NEW YEAR'S MONEY FROM LAST YEAR AND THIS YEAR.
IT COST 11,580 YEN!
W-WOW!
I DID MY BEST TO SAVE UP!
CHATTER
IT'S BECAUSE YOU TOLD ME ABOUT SIRIUS!
THE STAR THAT'S BRIGHTEST AFTER THE SUN!
OH NO, I...
BUT SHE IS A LITTLE HAPPY TO HEAR THAT.

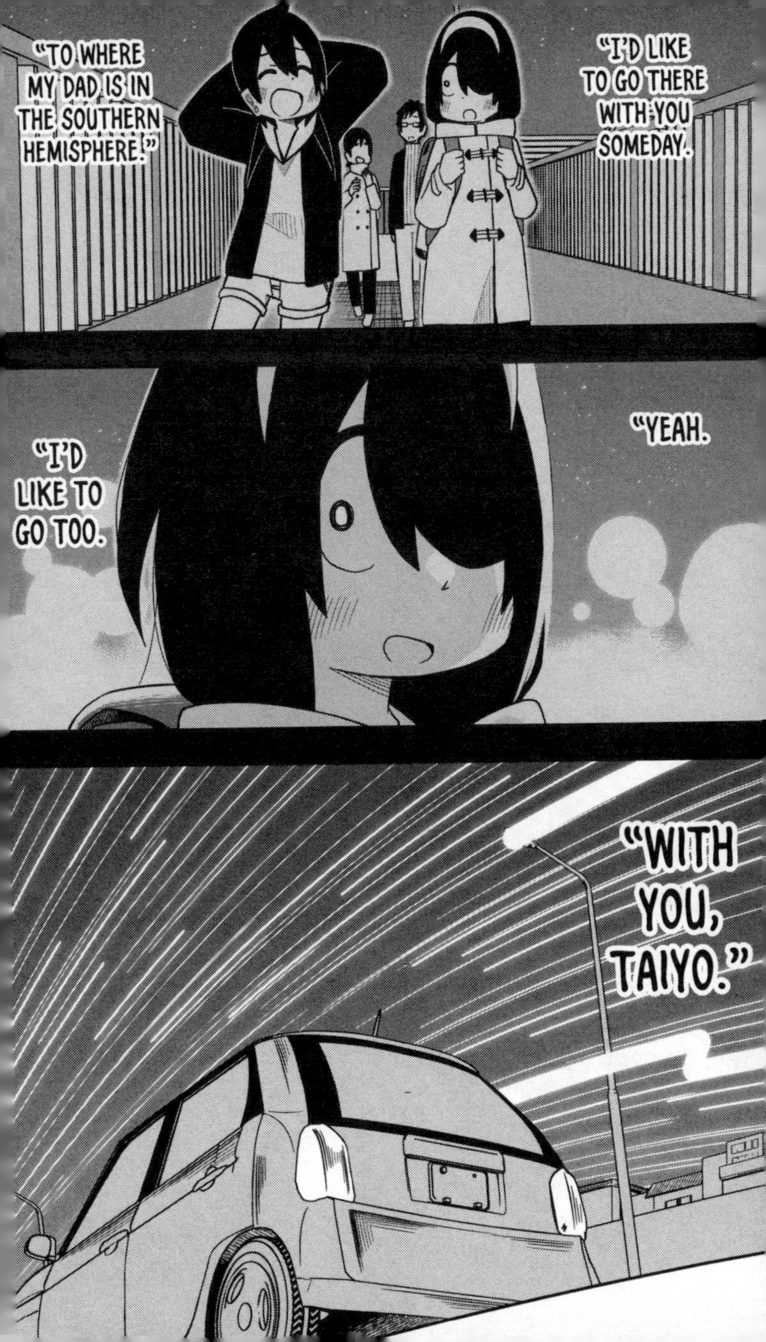
"I'D LIKE TO GO THERE WITH YOU SOMEDAY.
"TO WHERE MY DAD IS IN THE SOUTHERN HEMISPHERE."
"YEAH.
"I'D LIKE TO GO TOO.
"WITH YOU, TAIYO."

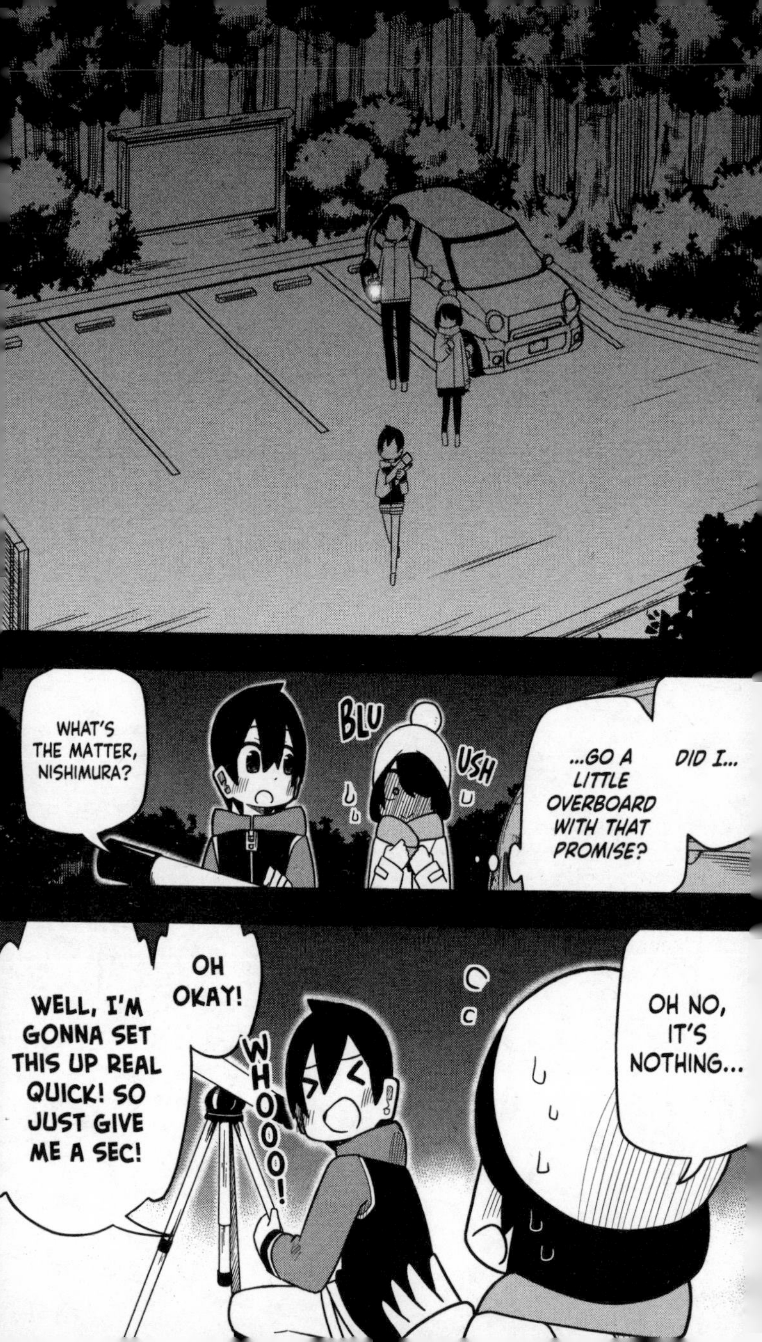
DID I...
...GO A LITTLE OVERBOARD WITH THAT PROMISE?
BLUSH
WHAT'S THE MATTER, NISHIMURA?
OH NO, IT'S NOTHING...
OH OKAY!
WHOOOO!
WELL, I'M GONNA SET THIS UP REAL QUICK! SO JUST GIVE ME A SEC!

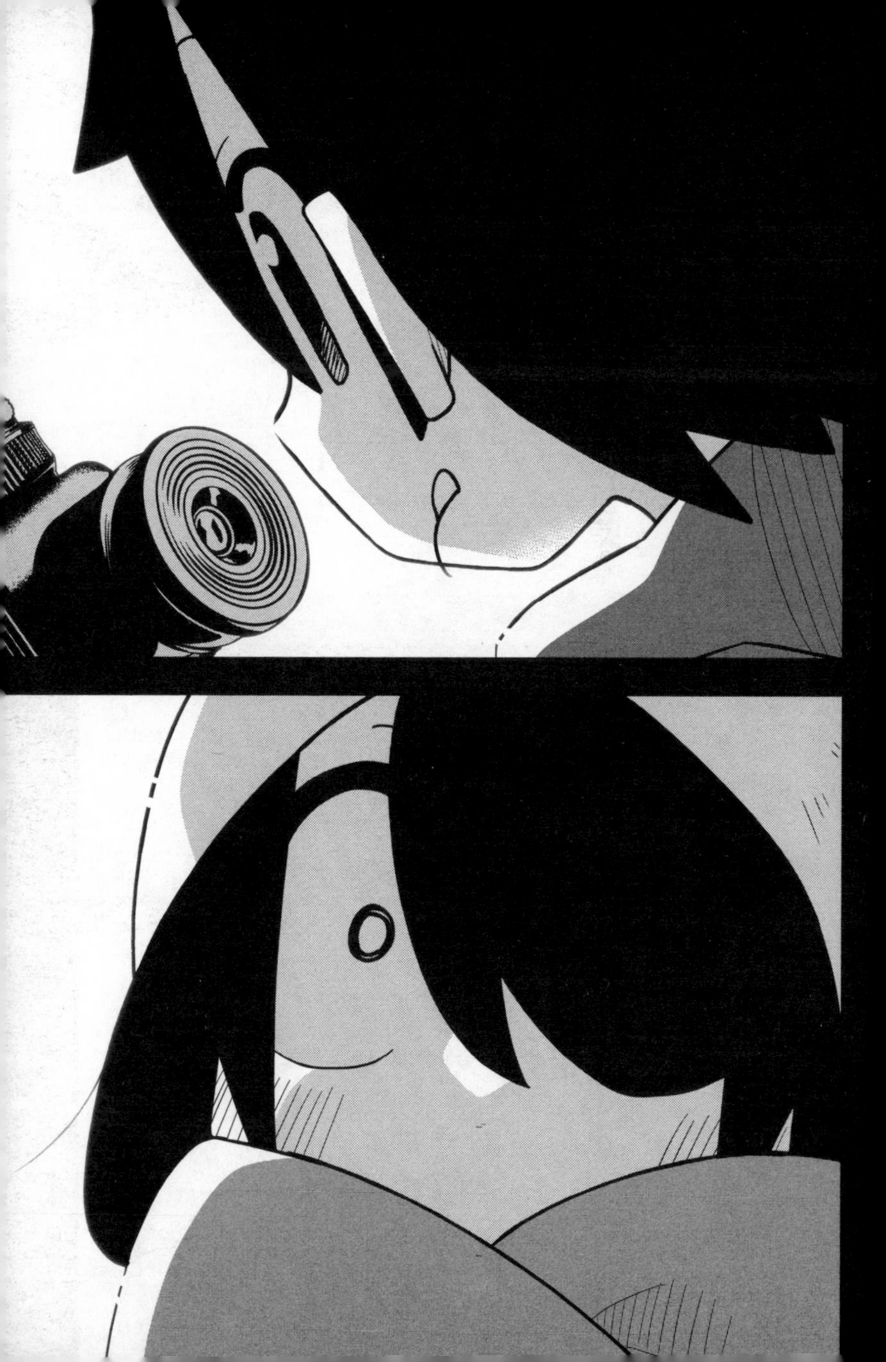

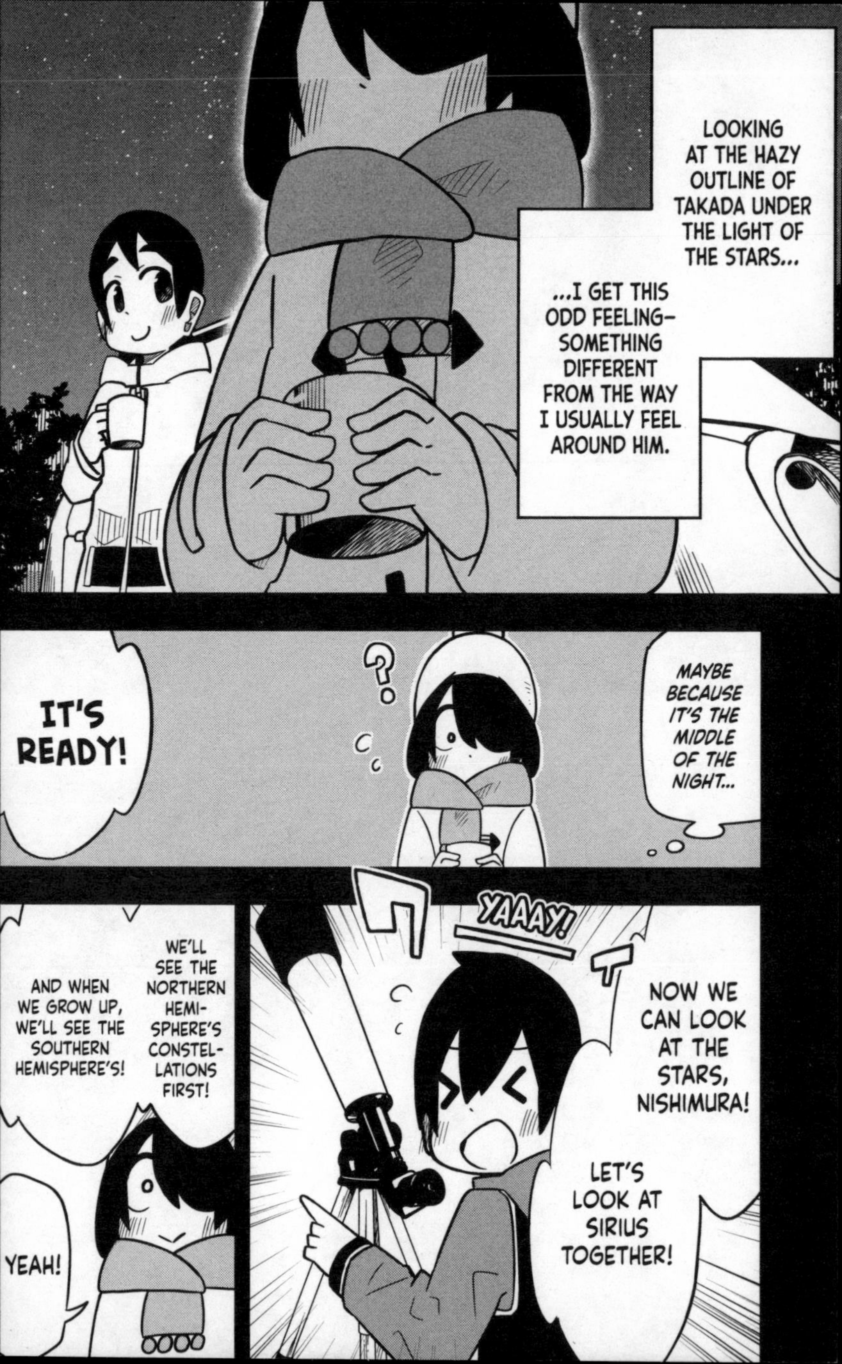

LOOKING AT THE HAZY OUTLINE OF TAKADA UNDER THE LIGHT OF THE STARS...
...I GET THIS ODD FEELING—SOMETHING DIFFERENT FROM THE WAY I USUALLY FEEL AROUND HIM.
MAYBE BECAUSE IT'S THE MIDDLE OF THE NIGHT...
?
IT'S READY!
YAAAY!
NOW WE CAN LOOK AT THE STARS, NISHIMURA!
LET'S LOOK AT SIRIUS TOGETHER!
WE'LL SEE THE NORTHERN HEMISPHERE'S CONSTELLATIONS FIRST!
AND WHEN WE GROW UP, WE'LL SEE THE SOUTHERN HEMISPHERE'S!
YEAH!

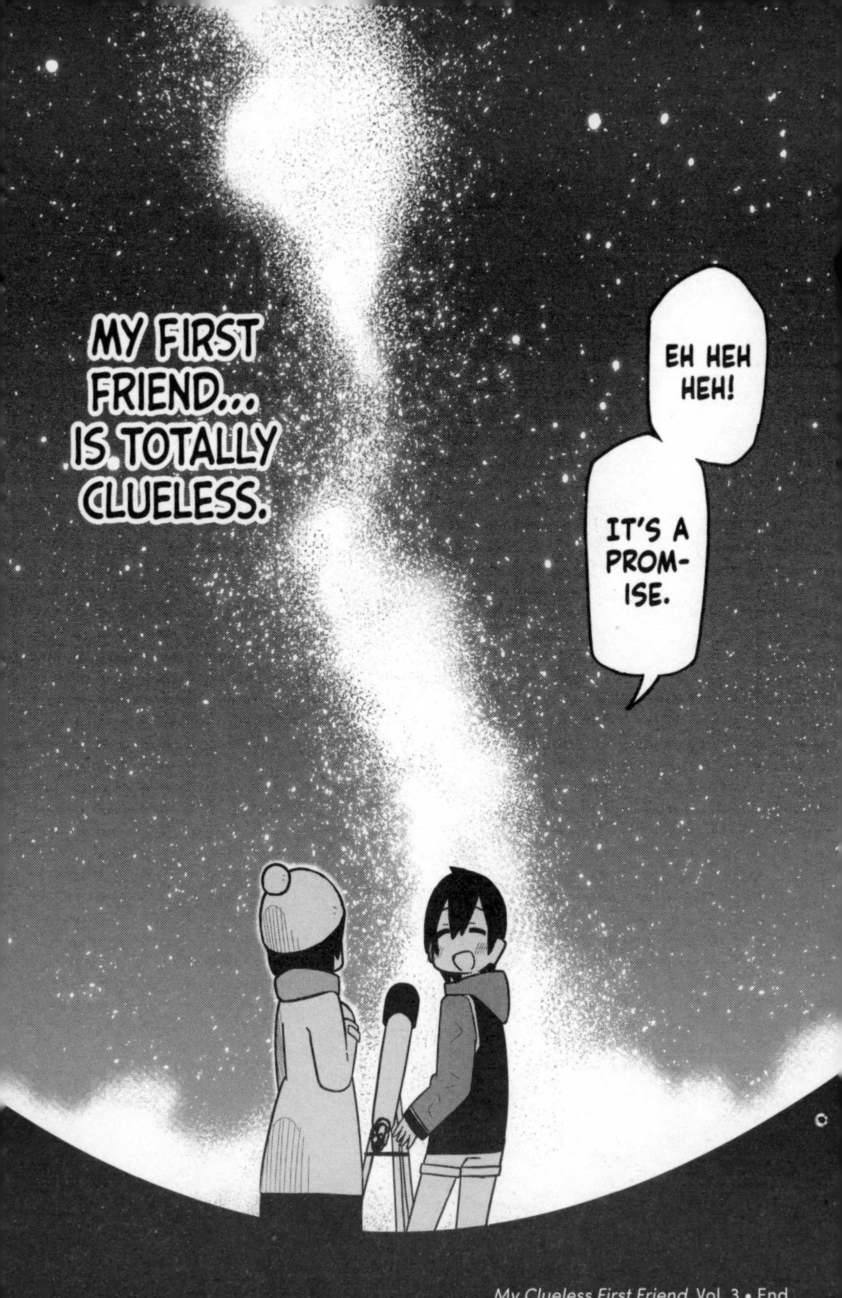
EH HEH HEH!
IT'S A PROM-ISE.
MY FIRST FRIEND... IS TOTALLY CLUELESS.

My Clueless First Friend, Vol. 3 • End

MY **CLUELESS**
FIRST FRIEND

MY **CLUELESS**
FIRST FRIEND

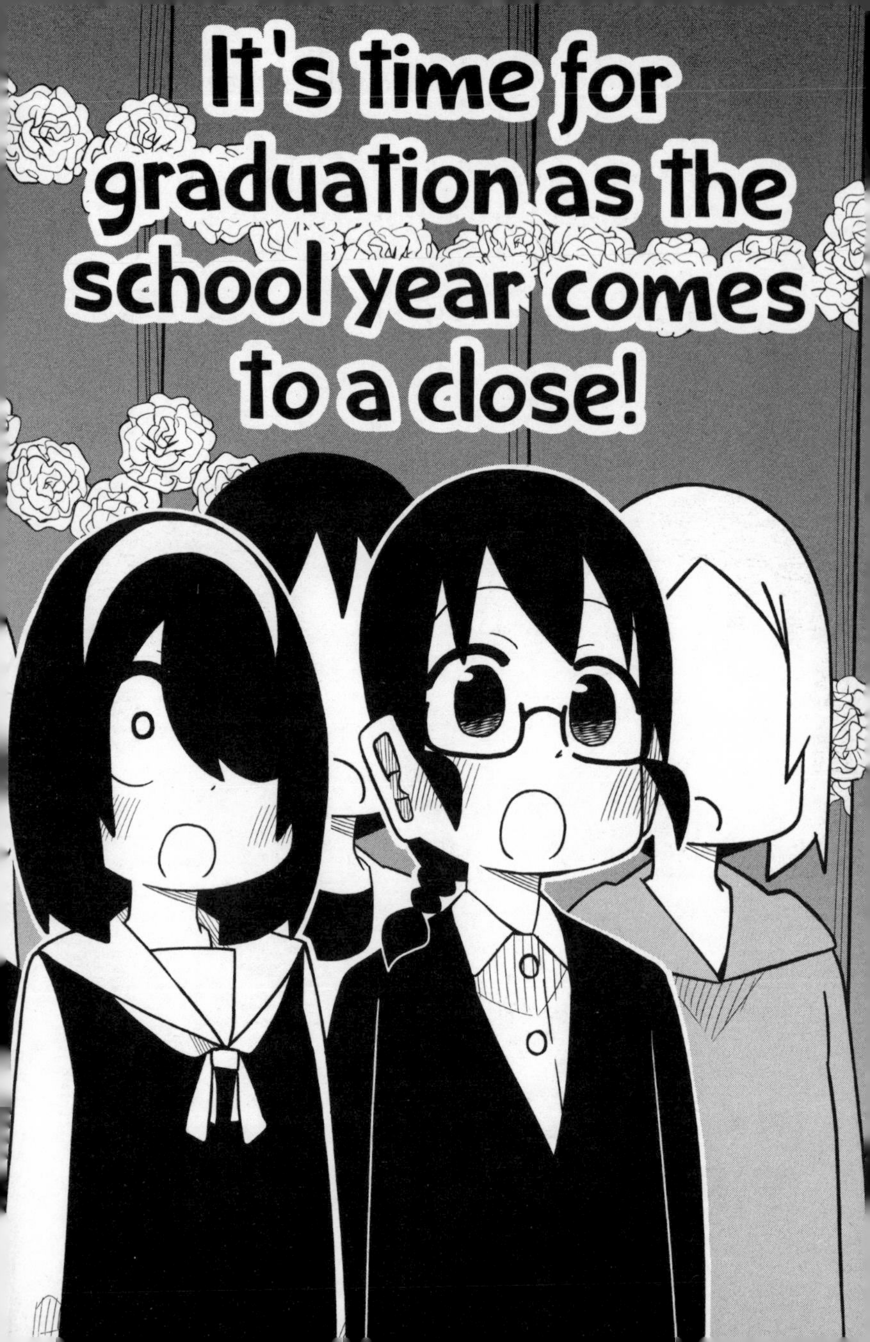
It's time for graduation as the school year comes to a close!

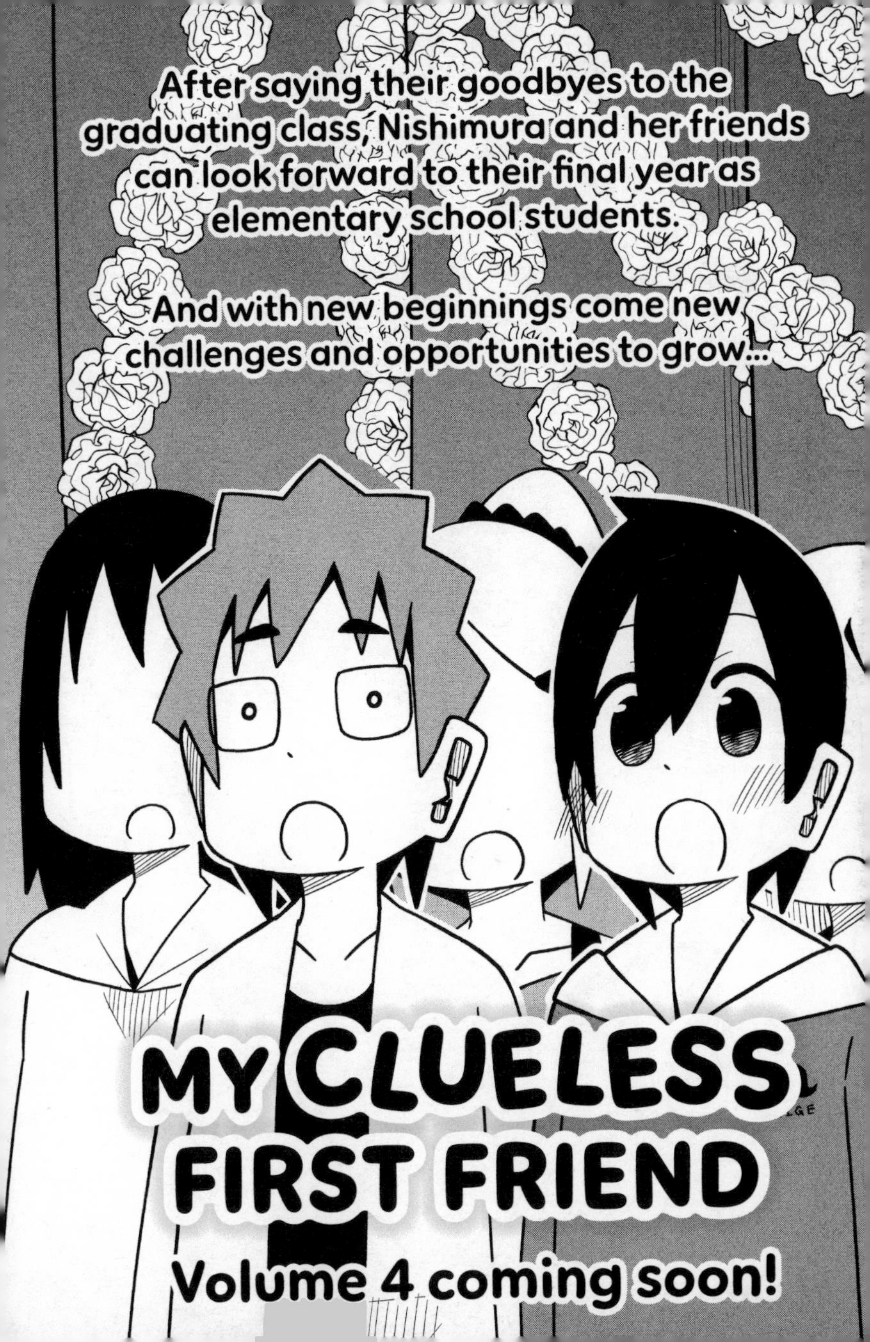
After saying their goodbyes to the graduating class, Nishimura and her friends can look forward to their final year as elementary school students.
And with new beginnings come new challenges and opportunities to grow...
MY CLUELESS FIRST FRIEND
Volume 4 coming soon!

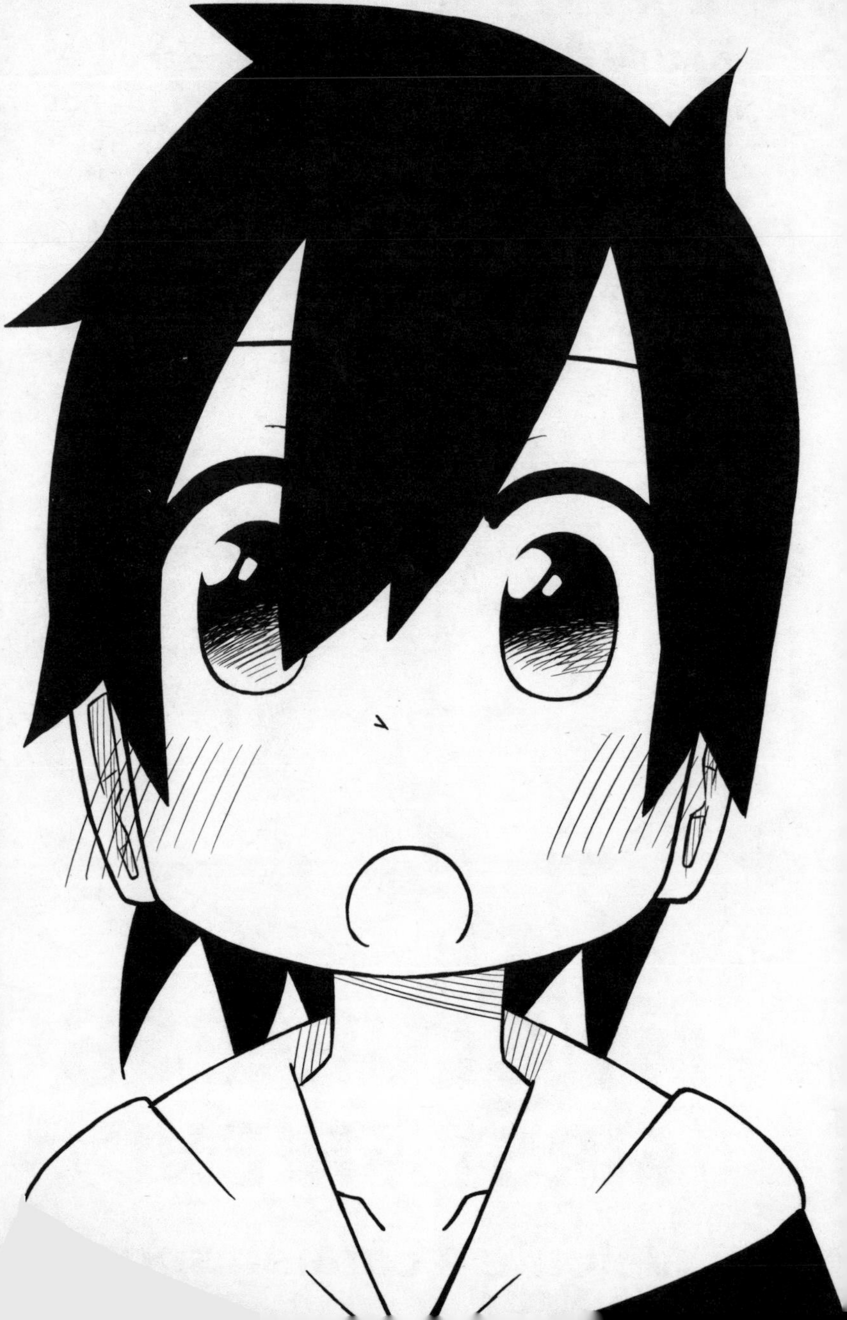

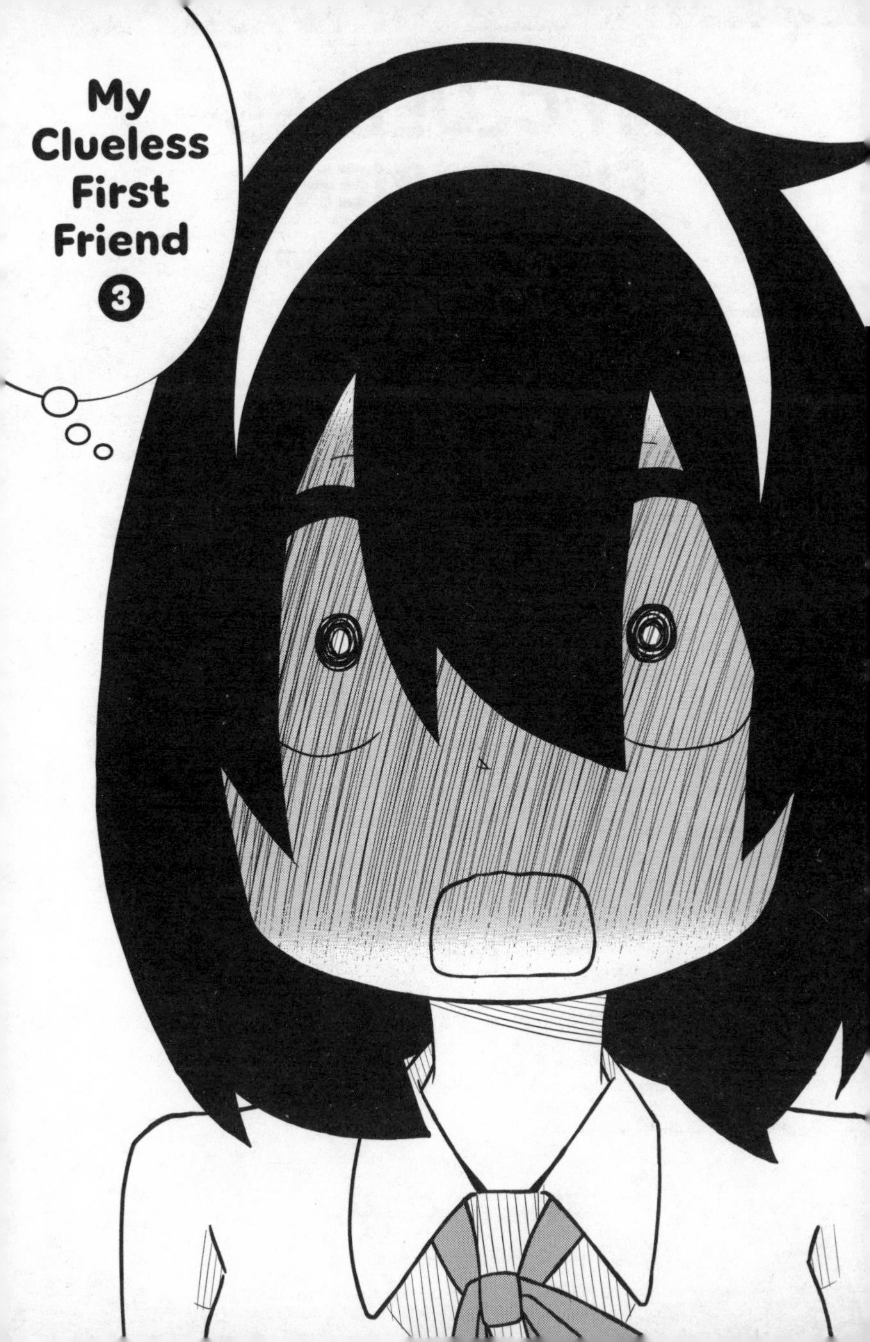
My Clueless First Friend 3

MY CLUELESS FIRST FRIEND

story and art by TAKU KAWAMURA

3

Translator: Ajani Oloye
Letterer: Vanessa Satone
Cover Designer: Stephani Stilwell
Editor: Sarah Tangney

My Clueless First Friend Volume 3
© 2020 Taku Kawamura/SQUARE ENIX CO., LTD.
All rights reserved.
First published in Japan as *Jijou o Shiranai Tenkousei
ga Guigui Kuru* in 2020 by SQUARE ENIX CO., LTD.
English translation rights arranged with
SQUARE ENIX CO., LTD. and SQUARE ENIX, INC.
English translation © 2023 by SQUARE ENIX CO., LTD.

ISBN (print): 978-1-64609-207-9
ISBN (ebook): 978-1-64609-685-5

Library of Congress Cataloging-in-Publication Data is available upon request.

Library of Congress Control Number: 2022917176

Manufactured in Canada
First Edition: September 2023
1st Printing

Published by Square Enix Manga & Books, a division of SQUARE ENIX, INC.
999 N. Pacific Coast Highway, 3rd Floor
El Segundo, CA 90245, USA

SQUARE ENIX
MANGA & BOOKS
square-enix-books.com